MONUMENTA SERICA MONOGRAPH SERIES
LXVIII/2
Editor: Zbigniew Wesołowski s.v.d.
Sankt Augustin

Rooted in Hope / In der Hoffnung verwurzelt
Festschrift in Honor of / Festschrift für
Roman Malek s.v.d.

Edited by / Herausgegeben von:
Barbara Hoster, Dirk Kuhlmann, Zbigniew Wesołowski s.v.d.

Volume 2

Monumenta Serica Monograph Series
———— LXVIII/2 ————

Rooted in Hope
China – Religion – Christianity

In der Hoffnung verwurzelt
China – Religion – Christentum

Festschrift in Honor of
Festschrift für

Roman Malek S.V.D.

on the Occasion of His 65th Birthday
zu seinem 65. Geburtstag

Volume 2

Edited by
Herausgegeben von

Barbara Hoster
Dirk Kuhlmann
Zbigniew Wesołowski S.V.D.

Institut Monumenta Serica • Sankt Augustin

Sumptibus Societatis Verbi Divini (S.V.D.)

Cover: Chinese Calligraphy: 扎根于望德中—马雷凯教授六十五寿辰纪念文集,
by Ren Dayuan 任大援

Copy Editors: BARBARA HOSTER, DIRK KUHLMANN, ZBIGNIEW WESOŁOWSKI S.V.D.

English Language Editor: DANIEL BAUER S.V.D.

Cover and Layout: JOZEF BIŠTUŤ S.V.D.

Monumenta Serica Institute
Arnold-Janssen-Str. 20
53757 Sankt Augustin, Germany
Fax: +49-2241-237-486
E-mail: institut@monumenta-serica.de
www.monumenta-serica.de

First published 2017
by Routledge
2 Park Square, Milton Park, Abingdon, Oxon OX14 4RN

and by Routledge
711 Third Avenue, New York, NY 10017

Routledge is an imprint of the Taylor & Francis Group, an informa business

© 2017 Monumenta Serica Institute

The right of Barbara Hoster, Dirk Kuhlmann and Zbigniew Wesołowski S.V.D.
to be identified as authors of the editorial material, and of the authors
for their individual chapters, has been asserted by them in accordance
with sections 77 and 78 of the Copyright, Designs and Patents Act 1988.

All rights reserved. No part of this book may be reprinted or reproduced or utilised in any
form or by any electronic, mechanical, or other means, now known or hereafter invented,
including photocopying and recording, or in any information storage or retrieval system,
without permission in writing from the publishers.

Trademark notice: Product or corporate names may be trademarks or registered trademarks,
and are used only for identification and explanation without intent to infringe.

British Library Cataloguing-in-Publication Data
A catalogue record for this book is available from the British Library.

Library of Congress Cataloging-in-Publication Data
A catalog record for this book has been requested.

ISBN: 978-1-138-71805-0 (hbk)
ISBN: 978-1-315-16392-5 (ebk)
ISBN: 978-1-138-71808-1 (Set, vols. 1 & 2)
ISSN 0179-261X

Typeset by Monumenta Serica Institute

TABLE OF CONTENTS / INHALTSVERZEICHNIS

Volume 2 / Band 2

XI-XVI   List of Abbreviations / Abkürzungsverzeichnis

Christianity in Today's China / Christentum im heutigen China

433-466   Rediscovering Christian Life in China during Crucial Years (1978–1983). In Honour of Roman Malek

Die Neuentdeckung christlichen Lebens in China in den wichtigen Jahren von 1978–1983. Zu Ehren von Roman Malek

ANGELO S. LAZZAROTTO P.I.M.E.

467-480   Updating the China Mission. Guided by Pope Benedict XVI and Pope Francis

Die Chinamission auf den neuesten Stand bringen unter Führung von Papst Benedikt XVI und Papst Franziskus

JEROOM HEYNDRICKX C.I.C.M.

481-505   Fit for Religious Services? The Requirements on Religious Personnel in Today's China. With a Special Focus on the Official Protestant Churches

Fit für religiöse Dienstleistungen? Die Anforderungen an religiöses Personal im heutigen China mit einem besonderen Fokus auf die offiziellen evangelischen Kirchen

EVELINE WARODE

Other Religions in China / Andere Religionen in China

509-526   The Textual Canonization of Guandi

Die Entstehung des Schriftenkanons zu Guandi

VINCENT GOOSSAERT

527-539   Islam and Confucianism. An Offering to Fr. Malek

Islam und Konfuzianismus. P. Malek zugeeignet

FRANÇOISE AUBIN

541-569   Der Einfluss der Urbanisierung auf die muslimischen Gemeinschaften in China im Spiegel chinesischer Fachzeitschriften

The Influence of Urbanization on Muslim Communities in China as Reflected in Chinese Academic Journals

KATHARINA WENZEL-TEUBER

571-596   Qianliyan und Shunfeng'er in *xiaoshuo* und anderen Texten der Yuan- und Ming-Zeit

Qianliyan und Shunfeng'er in *xiaoshuo* and Other Texts of the Yuan- and Ming-Period
RODERICH PTAK

597-605 Jews and Jewish Studies in China. Notes for a Bibliography
Juden und die Forschung über Judentum in China. Notizen für eine Bibliographie
PIER FRANCESCO FUMAGALLI

Chinese Language and Literature / Chinesische Sprache und Literatur

609-616 Translating King David
Die Übersetzung der Geschichte von König David
IRENE EBER

617-647 Shandong Drum Songs of the Bible
Biblische Geschichten in Trommelgesängen aus Shandong
MONIKA MOTSCH

649-664 "Omnia Consummata sunt." Xiang Peiliang's Version of the Biblical Story of Jesus between Bethany and Gethsemane
„Omnia Consummata sunt". Xiang Peiliangs Darstellung der biblischen Erzählung von Jesus auf dem Weg von Bethanien nach Gethsemane
MARIÁN GÁLIK

665-682 "A Fortunate Encounter." Su Xuelin as a Chinese Catholic Writer
„Eine glückliche Begegnung". Su Xuelin als chinesische Schriftstellerin und Katholikin
BARBARA HOSTER

683-711 „Erst jetzt wusste er, dass es keine einfache Sache war, an Gott zu glauben." Die Religion in der Gegenwartsliteratur Chinas
"Only then Did He Realize that It Is Not an Easy Thing to Believe in God." Religion in Contemporary Chinese Literature
THOMAS ZIMMER

713-726 The Competitiveness of Modern Han-Chinese
Die Wettbewerbsfähigkeit des modernen Han-Chinesisch
LEOPOLD LEEB S.V.D.

Encounter of Cultures / Begegnung der Kulturen

729-759 Buddhistische Malerei im mingzeitlichen Beijing. Begegnungen von Völkern und Kulturen im Spiegel der Kunst

Buddhist Painting in Ming-dynasty Beijing. Encounters of Peoples and Cultures as Reflected in Art
URSULA TOYKA

761-787 Communication and Exchange of Knowledge between West and East (17th and 18th c.). The Routes, Illustrated by the Case of the "Via Ostendana"
Kommunikation und Wissenstransfer zwischen West und Ost im 17. und 18. Jahrhundert. Die Routen am Beispiel der „Via Ostendana"
NOËL GOLVERS

789-809 明清之际"西学汉籍"的文化意义
Cultural Significance of the "Chinese Books on Western Learning" in Late Ming and Early Qing
Die kulturelle Bedeutung „chinesischer Bücher über westliches Wissen" am Ende der Ming- und zu Beginn der Qing-Dynastie
ZHANG XIPING 张西平 – REN DAYUAN 任大援

811-844 Die Sammlung Kowalewski. Der erste europäische Katalog mongolischer, tibetischer, manjurischer und chinesischer Bücher (1834)
The Kowalewski Collection. The First European Catalogue of Mongolian, Tibetan, Manchu, and Chinese Books (1834)
HARTMUT WALRAVENS

845-859 Die Neuvermessung einer alten Kultur. *Monumenta Serica* und die wissenschaftliche Beschäftigung mit China und seinen Nachbarn
Remapping an Ancient Culture. *Monumenta Serica* and the Academic Research on China and Her Neighbours
HELWIG SCHMIDT-GLINTZER

861-871 African Muslims and Christians and Their "Chinese Dream"
Der „chinesische Traum" von afrikanischen Muslimen und Christen
PIOTR ADAMEK S.V.D.

873-887 The Mission of Multi-faceted Christianity in a Globalized World
Die Mission eines vielfältigen Christentums in einer globalisierten Welt
FRANZ GÜNTHER GESSINGER S.V.D.

889-899 Notes on Contributors

901-907 Appendix. Colored Illustrations from Ursula Toyka, "Buddhistische Malerei im mingzeitlichen Beijing. Begegnungen von Völkern und Kulturen im Spiegel der Kunst"

List of Illustrations and Tables / Verzeichnis der Abbildungen und Tabellen

Cover Volume 2: Chinese Calligraphy: 扎根于望德中—马雷凯教授六十五寿辰纪念文集, by Ren Dayuan 任大援

481-505 Fit for Religious Services? The Requirements on Religious Personnel in Today's China. With a Special Focus on the Official Protestant Churches
EVELINE WARODE

    p. 482: Diagram 1: Clergy/laity ratios of Kaifeng and Nanyang. Source: Compare data as quoted in Duan Qi 2013, p. 254; Wenzel-Teuber 2014, p. 31

    p. 483: Diagram 2: Attendance at religious activities. Source: Compare data of CFPS 2012 as quoted in Lu Yunfeng 2014, p. 23

527-539 Islam and Confucianism. An Offering to Fr. Malek
FRANÇOISE AUBIN

    p. 534: Table: The Three Levels of the Knowledge of God

541-569 Der Einfluss der Urbanisierung auf die muslimischen Gemeinschaften in China im Spiegel chinesischer Fachzeitschriften
KATHARINA WENZEL-TEUBER

    p. 559: Tabelle: Muslimische Gebetsteilnehmer in Shanghai nach Gruppen. (Ge Zhuang 2011, S. 152, Tabelle 1. Zahlen: Islamische Vereinigung Shanghai.)

617-647 Shandong Drum Songs of the Bible
MONIKA MOTSCH

    p. 642: Fig. 1. Drum Song *The Great Flood* by Fei Jinbiao

            Fig. 2. Latin imprimatur for *The Great Flood*

    p. 643: Fig. 3. The scene "I am the Angel" in Drum Song *The Great Flood*

            Fig. 4. Advertisement of the Yanzhou Press for Fei Jinbiao

    p. 644: Fig. 5. *Fabiola* by Cardinal Wiseman (New York 1886)

            Fig. 6. Chinese Drumsong of *Fabiola* by Fei Jinbiao

    p. 645: Fig. 7. *Valeria* by de Waal (Regensburg 1884)

            Fig. 8. The Chinese *Valeria*, ed. Fr. Röser

    p. 646: Fig. 9. *The Filial Son*, ed. Fr. Stenz

            Fig. 10. *The Black Prince*, ed. Fr. Stenz

    p. 647: Fig. 11. The Nonni Fountain in Cologne

            Fig. 12. The Chinese *Iceland Boys* of Jón Svensson

713-726 The Competitiveness of Modern Han-Chinese
LEOPOLD LEEB S.V.D.

    p. 713: "Yan: Goutong" 言：沟通 (Word: Communication). Drawing by Leopold Leeb in: Lei Libo 雷立柏, *Xifangren kan Hanzi de aomiao. Han-Ying duizhao* 西方人看汉字的奥妙—漢英對照. *How a Westerner Sees the Mysteries of Chinese Characters* (Beijing: Zhongguo shuji chubanshe, 2012, p. 13)

729-759 Buddhistische Malerei im mingzeitlichen Beijing. Begegnungen von Völkern und Kulturen im Spiegel der Kunst

URSULA TOYKA

p. 901: Abb. 1: „Vajranairātmyā-Maṇḍala", datiert 1479, 151 x 99,1 cm, Gouache mit Gold auf präparierter Baumwolle, Peabody Museum, Salem, E. 61-1911. © 2009 Peabody Essex Museum. Photograph by Jeffrey R. Dykes

p. 902: Abb. 2: „Vajradhara-Maṇḍala", datiert 1479, 153 x 102 cm, Gouache mit Gold auf präparierter Baumwolle, Verbleib unbekannt

p. 903: Abb. 3: „Vajradhara-Maṇḍala", Detail: Buddha Vajradhara

Abb. 4: „Vajradhara-Maṇḍala", Detail: Bodhisattva Saḍakṣarilokeśvara

p. 904: Abb. 5: „Vajradhara-Maṇḍala", Detail: Buddha Vairocana mit *thathāgata-mudrā*

Abb. 6: „Vajradhara-Maṇḍala", Detail: Bodhisattva Ratnapaṇi

Abb. 7: „Vajradhara-Maṇḍala", Detail: Bodhisattva Vajrapaṇi

Abb. 8: „Vajradhara-Maṇḍala", Detail: Schutzgottheit Bhairava

p. 905: Abb. 9: „Vajradhara-Maṇḍala", Detail: Schutzgottheit Prañjara Mahākāla

Abb. 10: „Vajradhara-Maṇḍala", Detail: Schutzgottheit Kuro Mahākāla

Abb. 11: „Vajradhara-Maṇḍala", Detail: Segnender Bodhisattva auf der rechten Bildseite

Abb. 12: „Vajradhara-Maṇḍala", Detail: Segnender Bodhisattva auf der linken Bildseite

p. 906: Abb. 13: „Tausendarmige Guanyin", Meister des Fahai si (Wan Fuqing, Wang Shu *et al.*) zugeschrieben, Mitte 15. Jh., Farben mit Tusche und Gold auf Seide, Gesamtmaße 223 x 117 cm (87 13/16 x 46 1/16 inches), Bildmaße 139 x 81 cm (54 3/4 x 31 7/8 inches), Museum of Fine Arts, Boston, Special Chinese and Japanese Fund, Inv. No. 06.1902, Photograph © 2016 Museum of Fine Arts, Boston

p. 907: Abb. 14: „Vajradhara-Maṇḍala", Detail: 1479 datierte Stiftungsinschrift „Am 15. Tag des 4. Monats im 15. Jahr (der Ära) Chenghua der Großen Ming gestiftet"

LIST OF ABBREVIATIONS

ACMR	Archivio della Congregazione della Missione – Roma
AFH	*Archivum Franciscanum Historicum*
AHSI	*Archivum Historicum Societatis Iesu*
AIHS	*Archives Internationales d'Histoire des Sciences*
AM	*Asia Major*
Annotationes	„G.W. Leibniz, *Annotationes de cultu religioneque Sinensium*", in: *Discours sur la théologie naturelle des Chinois*, S. 265-270. See under *Discours*
AOV	*Acta Orientalia Vilnensia*
AP	*Asian Philosophy*
APF	Archivio Storico de Propaganda Fide, Rome
APF, SOCP	Archivio Storico de Propaganda Fide: Scritture originali della congregazioni particulari
ARSI	Archivum Romanum Societatis Iesu
AS/EA	*Asiatische Studien / Études Asiatiques*
BA	Bundesarchiv
BEFEO	*Bulletin de l'École française d'Extrême-Orient*
BHStA	Bayerisches Hauptstaatsarchiv (München)
BM	*Bibliotheca Missionum*, vols. 1, 4, 5, 7. Freiburg 1963, 1929–1932.
BMFEA	*Bulletin of the Museum of Far Eastern Antiquities*
BSOAS	*Bulletin of the School of Oriental and African Studies*
BUAR	KU Leuven, Universiteitsarchief: OU/G/D 126/3
BVE	Biblioteca Nazionale Centrale Vittorio Emanuele II (Rome)
CAFFC	Chinese Association for Friendship with Foreign Countries
CASS	Chinese Academy of Social Sciences
CCC	China Christian Council
CCCM	Centro Científico e Cultural de Macao
CCP	Chinese Communist Party
CCPA	Chinese Catholic Patriotic Association
Chh	*China heute*
China-Korrespondenz	G.[ottfried] W.[ilhelm] Leibniz, *Der Briefwechsel mit den Jesuiten in China (1689–1714)*, herausgegeben und mit einer Einleitung versehen von Rita Widmaier. Textherstellung und Übersetzung von Malte-Ludolf Babin. Französisch/lateinisch – deutsch (Hamburg: Felix Meiner, 2006)

Clark	*Bibliographies of Mongolian, Manchu-Tungus, and Tibetan Dictionaries*. Compiled by Larry V. Clark, John R. Krueger, Manfred Taube, Hartmut Walravens, Michael L. Walter. Orientalistik, Bibliographien und Dokumentationen 20 (Wiesbaden: Harrassowitz, 2005)
CPF	Congregationis de Propaganda Fide
CPPCC	Chinese People's Political Consultative Conference
CRep	*The Chinese Repository*
CT	*Collectanea Theologica* (Warszawa)
CWME	Commission on World Mission and Evangelism
Dehergne	Joseph Dehergne, *Répertoire des Jesuites de Chine de 1552 à 1800* (Roma *et al.*: Institutum Historicum Societatis Iesu, 1973)
Discours	G.W. Leibniz, *Discours sur la théologie naturelle des Chinois*. Mit einem Anhang: Nicolas Longobardi, *Traité sur quelques points de la religion des Chinois*, Antoine de Sainte Marie, *Traité sur quelques points importans de la Mission de la Chine*, Leibniz, *Annotationes de cultu religioneque Sinensium*, [*et al.*]. Hrsg. und mit Anmerkungen versehen von Wenchao Li und Hans Poser (Frankfurt a.M.: Vittorio Klostermann, 2002)
DZ	*Daozang* 道藏
EBA	Erfgoedbibliotheek Antwerpen
EIC	East India Company
FABC	Federation of Asian Bishops' Conferences
FR	Pasquale M. d'Elia (ed.), *Fonti Ricciane*, 3 vols. (Roma: La Libreria dello Stato, 1942-1949)
GP	Carl Immanuel Gerhardt (Hrsg.), *Die philosophischen Schriften von G.W. Leibniz*, Bde. I-VII (Berlin: Weidmann, 1875-1890; Neudruck: Hildesheim 1960-1961)
GWLB	Gottfried Wilhelm Leibniz Bibliothek
HCC 1	Nicolas Standaert (ed.), *Handbook of Christianity in China I: 635-1800*, Handbook of Oriental Studies Section 4: China, 15/1 (Leiden: Brill, 2001)
HCC 2	Rolf G. Tiedemann (ed.), *Handbook of Christianity in China. Volume Two: 1800-Present*. Handbook of Oriental Studies, Section 4: China 15/2. Handbuch der Orientalistik, Abt. 4: China, 15/2 (Leiden – Boston: Brill, 2010)
Heissig	Walther Heissig (mit Klaus Sagaster), *Mongolische Handschriften, Blockdrucke, Landkarten*; mit 16 Lichtdrucktafeln. Verzeichnis der orientalischen Handschriften in Deutschland 1 (Wiesbaden: Steiner, 1961)
HJAS	*Harvard Journal of Asiatic Studies*

HWPh	*Historisches Wörterbuch der Philosophie*, herausgegeben von Joachim Ritter, Karl Gründer *et al.*, 13 Bde. (Darmstadt: Wissenschaftliche Buchgesellschaft, 1971–2007).
ICI	Italian-Chinese Institute
Inc.	Incipit (first words of a document)
j.	*juan* 卷
JA	*Journal Asiatique*
Jachontov – Walravens	K.S. Jachontov – H. Walravens, *Katalog der mandjurischen Handschriften und Blockdrucke in den Sammlungen der Bibliothek der Orientalischen Fakultät der Sankt-Petersburger Universität. Aus dem russischen Manuskript übersetzt und herausgegeben.* Orientalistik, Bibliographien und Dokumentationen 14 (Wiesbaden: Harrassowitz, 2001)
JAH	*Journal of Asian History*
JAOS	*Journal of the American Oriental Society*
Jap. Sin.	Japonica et Sinica in ARSI
JAS	*Journal of Asian Studies*
JCP	*Journal of Chinese Philosophy*
JCR	*Journal of Chinese Religions*
Jinian liu wei guoji zhujiao	Furen daxue Tianzhujiao shi yanjiu zhongxin 輔仁大學天主教史研究中心 (ed.), *Jinian liu wei guoji zhujiao zhusheng qishi zhounian wo guo jianli shengtongzhi wushi zhounian ji Tian gong Gengxin jinsheng shuji wushi zhounian xueshu yantao huiyi* 紀念六位國籍主教祝聖七十週年我國建立聖統制五十週年暨田公耕莘晉陞樞機五十週年學術研討會議 (*Symposium in Commemoration of the 70th Anniversary of the Consecration of the First Six Native Chinese Bishops and the Elevation to the Cardinalate of Thomas Tien SVD and the 50th Anniversary of the Establishment of Roman Catholic Hierarchy in China, May 9–10, 1997*) (Taibei: Chengban, 1997)
JRAS	*Journal of the Royal Asiatic Society*
JY	*(Chongkan) Daozang jiyao* (重刊) 道藏輯要, 1906 (electronic version: http://www.kanripo.org/dzjy/texts/dzjy)
KBR	Koninklijke Bibliotheek van België (Brussels)
KPCh	Kommunistische Partei Chinas
KSB	*Kalendarz Słowa Bożego*
LAA	*Leibniz-Akademie-Ausgabe. Sämtliche Schriften und Briefe*, hrsg. von der Preußischen [später Deutschen, zuletzt: Berlin-Brandenburgischen] Akademie der Wissenschaften und der Akademie der Wissenschaften in Göttingen (Darmstadt [später: Leipzig, zuletzt: Berlin] 1923ff.)

Lebbe I,II,III Recueil des Archives Vincent Lebbe: *Pour l'église chinoise. I. La visite apostolique des missions de Chine 1919–20.* Introduction et notes par Cl[aude] Soetens, (Louvain-la-Neuve: Publications de la Faculté de Théologie, 1982). *II. Une Nonciature à Pékin en 1918?* Introduction et notes par Cl[aude] Soetens, (*ibid.* 1983). *III. L'encyclique Maximum illud.* Introduction et notes par Cl[aude] Soetens (*ibid.* 1983)

LEC M. Louis Aimé-Martin (ed.), *Lettres édifiantes et curieuses concernant l'Asie, l'Afrique et l'Amérique, avec quelques relations nouvelles des missions, et des notes géographiques et historiques* (Paris: Paul Daffis Libraire-Éditeur, 1875–1877)

Lettre *Lettre sur la philosophie chinoise à Nicolas de Rémond*, in: G.W. Leibniz, *Zwei Briefe über das binäre Zahlensystem und die chinesische Philosophie*, franz./dt., aus dem Urtext neu ediert, übersetzt und kommentiert von Renate Loosen und Franz Vonessen (Stuttgart: Belser, 1968), S. 39-132

Longobardi, *Traité*
"Nicolas Longobardi, *Traité sur quelques points de la religion des Chinois*," in: *Discours sur la théologie naturelle des Chinois*, S. 113-156. See under *Discours*

LThK *Lexikon für Theologie und Kirche*, hrsg. von Joseph Höfer und Karl Rahner, Bd. 1-10, 2. Aufl. (Freiburg i.Br.: Herder, 1957–1965). Bd. 1-11, 3. Aufl. (Freiburg i.Br.: Herder, 1993–2001)

MEP Missions Etrangères de Paris

MSMS Monumenta Serica Monograph Series

MZWX *Mazu wenxian shiliao huibian* 媽祖文獻史料彙編, hrsg. von Zheng Lihang 鄭麗航, Jiang Weitan 蔣維錟 *et al.*, several series, various places and publishers

Novissima Sinica
G.W. Leibniz, *Novissima Sinica (1697). Das Neueste von China*, herausgegeben und übersetzt von Heinz-G. Nesselrath und Herman Reinbothe (Köln 1979), aktualisierter Nachdruck von Gregor Paul und Adolf Grünert (München: Judicium Verlag, 2010)

NPC National People's Congress

NTR *Nanjing Theological Review / Jinling shenxue zhi* 金陵神学志

NZM *Neue Zeitschrift für Missionswissenschaft*

OE *Oriens Extremus*

OS Pietro Tacchi Venturi (ed.), *Opere storiche del P. M. Ricci*, 2 vols. (Macerata: Filippo Giorgetti, 1911–1913)

PAAA Politisches Archiv des Auswärtigen Amtes in Berlin

PEW *Philosophy East and West*

PIBA	Prosopographia Iesuitica Belgica Antiqua
P.I.M.E.	Pontificio Istituto Missioni Estere
PLB	Walther Heissig, *Die Pekinger lamaistischen Blockdrucke*. Göttinger Asiatische Forschungen 2 (Wiesbaden: Harrassowitz, 1954)
PRC	People's Republic of China
QTS	*Zhongguo di yi lishi dang'anguan* 中國第一歷史檔案館 (ed.), *Qing zhong qianqi Xiyang Tianzhujiao zai Hua huodong dang'an shiliao* 清中前期西洋天主教在華活動檔案史料 (Historical Materials on the Activities in China of Catholicism in the Early Qing) (Beijing: Zhonghua shuju, 2003)
Sainte Marie, *Traité*	"Antoine de Sainte Marie, *Traité sur quelques points importans de la Mission de la Chine*," in: *Discours*, S. 157-206
Sazykin	A.G. Sazykin, *Katalog mongol'skich rukopisej i ksilografov Instituta Vostokovedenija Akademii Nauk SSSR*. Tom 1 (Moskva: Nauka, 1988)
SCR	"Succincta chronologica relatio et historia Missionis Sinensis conscripta a R.P Kiliano Stumpf Missionario Sinensi et in Europam missa mense Octobri 1710. Dedicatoria ad Sanctos Angelos super remedio conservandæ Missionis Sinicæ"
SF	*Sinica Franciscana*
SWCRJ	*Sino-Western Cultural Relations Journal*
Taube	Manfred Taube: *Tibetische Handschriften und Blockdrucke*. Bd. 1-4 (Stuttgart: Steiner, 1966)
Théodicée, Discours	*Essais de Théodicée, Discours de la conformité de la foi avec la raison*, in: *GP* VI, S. 45-101.
TF	*Tianfeng* 天風 (中国基督教杂志) / *Tianfeng: The Magazine of the Protestant Churches in China*
TP	*T'oung Pao*
TSPM	Three-Self Patriotic Movement
Uspensky	*Catalogue of Mongolian Manuscripts and Xylographs in the St. Petersburg State University Library*. Compiled by Vladimir Uspensky, with assistance from Osamu Inoue. Edited and foreword by Tatsuo Nakami (Tokyo: Institute for the Study of Languages and Cultures of Asia and Africa, 1999)
Visschers	Pieter Jozef Visschers, *Onuitgegeven brieven van eenige paters der Sociëteit van Jesus* [sic]*, Missionarissen in China, van de 17e en 18e eeuw, met aanteekeningen* [sic] (Arnhem: Witz, 1857)
VOC	Vereenigde Oostindische Compagnie
VR	Volksrepublik

WCC	World Council of Churches
YTS	Zhongguo di yi lishi dang'anguan 中國第一歷史檔案館 (ed.), *Yongzheng chao Hanwen zhupi zouzhe huibian* 雍正朝漢文朱批奏摺彙編 (A Compilation of Chinese Language Vermillion Rescripted Memorials from the Court of the Yongzheng Emperor) (Nanjing: Jiangsu guji chubanshe, 1989).
YXYX	*Yuzhi Xiaojing yanyi xu* 御製孝經衍義序 (Imperial Preface to "Expanded Explications of the *Classic of Filial Piety*") in: Ye Fang'ai 葉方藹 – Zhang Ying 張英 (eds.), *Siku quanshu. Zi bu rujia lei* 四庫全書—子部儒家類
YZM	Zhongguo di yi lishi dang'anguan 中国第一历史档案馆 (ed.), *Yongzheng chao Manwen zhupi zouzhe quan yi* 雍正朝满文朱批奏折全译 (A Complete Translation of the Manchu Language Secret Memorials with Vermilion Endorsement of the Yongzheng Period) (Hefei: Huangshan shushe, 1998)
ZDMG	*Zeitschrift der Deutschen Morgenländischen Gesellschaft*
ZMATK	*Zeszyty Misjologiczne ATK (Warszawa)*
ZMR	*Zeitschrift für Missionswissenschaft und Religionswissenschaft*

Christianity in Today's China
Christentum im heutigen China

今日中國基督宗教

REDISCOVERING CHRISTIAN LIFE IN CHINA DURING CRUCIAL YEARS (1978–1983)

IN HONOUR OF ROMAN MALEK*

Angelo S. Lazzarotto

I feel it my duty to honour Roman Malek. On the occasion of my 85th birthday, the Festschrift Light a Candle – Encounters and Friendship with China, *edited by Roman Malek and Gianni Criveller, proved a sign of shared friendship and a gift beyond any expectation.*

Sadly, on that 14 May 2010, Father Roman could not join the family gathering held at the P.I.M.E. Cultural Centre in Milan. He had to hurry home, to Poland, because the health of his mother was deteriorating. And for several months thereafter, he kept travelling back and forth between his home town and Sankt Augustin, anxious to keep up with his duties at the Monumenta Serica Institute.

The stress proved beyond his generous determination. The Risen Christ, in His mysterious ways, was asking Father Roman to continue his missionary endeavour for China while carrying a heavy cross.

May the solidarity of so many friends and their prayers give him strength, confirming that he is always present among us with his example and enthusiasm.

In this spirit, I am happy and honoured to have the opportunity to add my little voice to the choir of appreciation, on the 65th birthday of Father Roman.

A.S.L.

1. A New Chance for the Chinese people

I visited Mainland China for the first time in May 1978, a year of transition, heavy with untold sufferings and unexpressed hopes. The political scene was difficult to assess. Soon after the death of Mao Zedong (September 1976), China was shocked by the arrest of the "Gang of Four" headed by Mao's powerful wife Jiang Qing. The following public trial allowed the world to know something of the atrocities perpetrated during the Great Cultural Revolution (1966–1976), which had been acclaimed as a triumph of Mao Zedong's leadership. The Eleventh Congress of the Chinese Communist Party (CCP) held in mid-1977 chose Hua Guofeng as leader, confirming that a new day was dawning for the People's Republic of China (PRC), but nobody dared to guess how the country would develop. Deng Xiaoping, recalled once more to join the leading group, was made head of the Chinese People's Political Consultative Conference (CPPCC) in Feb-

---

* N.B.: The following notes should not be expected to give full cover to the slow re-emerging and development of the Chinese Church after the tragedy of the Cultural Revolution. They simply represent a personal impression and commentary to the official history.

ruary 1978, originally created by the Party's United Front to co-opt non-communist sectors of Chinese society to fight Japanese invasion. Such a Consultative Conference, disregarded for thirteen years as a useless infrastructure, was convened to support the legislators at the Fifth National Assembly of the People. The international press stressed the unexpected participation, among the 1,989 delegates of the resurrected CPPCC, of 16 representatives of "religious circles."[1] It was such marginal news item that prompted me to look around for a way to enter the PRC, curious to understand what was really happening there in regard with religions.[2] What could be expected, after the protracted radical efforts to destroy all "superstitious beliefs" among the people? As a matter of fact, the fate of Chinese Christianity was discussed in recent years at some ecumenical meetings in Europe, jointly sponsored by the Lutheran Federation and the Catholic "Pro Mundi Vita" Centre. In the specific group "Catholics in Europe concerned with China" (formed in Bruges in autumn 1976), we were anxious to know more about the new opening.

The meaning of the event was far from clear.[3] On 5 March, the Fifth National People's Congress (NPC) approved a new Constitution of the Country. Many abnormities imposed by the Cultural Revolution were amended, but the sentence touching on religion was repeated as before: "Citizens enjoy freedom to believe in religion and freedom not to believe in religion and to propagate atheism"; only it was made into a separate article (No. 46). Yet things were changing: the *Renmin ribao* (12 and 13 March 1978) revealed that since the downfall of the "Gang of Four" over ten thousand citizens and leaders had been rehabilitated in Shanghai (but no religious people were mentioned). An encouraging sign seemed to be also the re-organization of the Chinese Academy of Social Sciences (CASS), with one of its ten research institutes studying world religions (Daoism, Buddhism, Islam, and Christianity). But at a seminar held in Beijing in April Ren Jiyu, in charge of an institute interested in religions, stressed "the need to resolutely safeguard the atheistic theory of Marxism." Obviously, our attention centred mostly on the two Catholic prelates attending the CPPCC, Archbishop Pi Shushi of Mukden in Manchuria[4] and Bishop Zhang Jiashu of Shanghai.[5]

---

[1] In Paris, *Le Monde* (beginning of March 1978) carried a column on "La Chine et les religions." In Italy, most papers, like the lay weekly *Panorama* (14 March) amply commented the fact; even the communist daily *L'Unità* carried a detailed article (9 March), hinting at possible new developments between Beijing and the Vatican. The Catholic daily *Avvenire*, besides the specific news, dedicated a full page (on 24 March) to explain the difficult situation of the Church in China.

[2] The religious leaders mentioned by *Renmin ribao* included Daoists, Muslims, and Buddhists (the Panchem Lama and lay leader Zhao Puzhu); also two Catholics were mentioned, and among the Protestants the well known bishop Ding Guangxun (K.H. Ting) from Nanjing.

[3] Curiously, the French edition of the semi-official magazine *Peking Information* (of March 1978) mentioned the expression "liberté de pratiquer la religion" (instead of "de croire"), with regard to the religious situation in China.

[4] Ignatius Pi Shushi, appointed in mid-1949 by Pope Pius XII, for some years was given as dead by the *Annuario Pontificio*. In the summer of 1957, summoned to attend the Confer-

Aware of the ambivalence of many signs coming from the PRC, I perceived the opportunity of entering the country thanks to Italian Senator Vittorino Colombo, a politician of the Christian Democratic Party. As a member of the Italian government, he worked for an early diplomatic *entente* of Italy with China, and was known for his endeavour to open dialogue with the Communist regime. Colombo was inspired by Giorgio La Pira, the charismatic Mayor of Florence, who did not hesitate to dialogue with leaders of the Soviet Block, when "cold war" seemed to be the only correct line for the free world. In early 1971, Senator Colombo established in Milano the "Italian-Chinese Institute for Economic and Cultural Relations" (ICI), and in November of that year, visiting China for the first time, he had the privilege of a long personal meeting with premier Zhou Enlai.[6] And on the following Sunday morning, as well known, he could attend Mass at the Southern church (Nantang), which remained since then the only venue accessible for worship (at least to foreigners) in the whole country. Senator Colombo made other journeys to China, always adding to his official duties a discreet but close attention to the cause of religious freedom. When I learned that in May 1978 Vittorino Colombo (then minister of Transportation and of Mercantile Marine) was to lead a new delegation to China, I wrote to him sharing my thoughts about the new situation emerging in Chinese society,[7] and he did not hesitate to add my name as a member of his staff, introducing me as his "religious adviser." To my surprise, this rather strange designation was accepted by China and I was granted my first visa to the Mainland.

2. 1978: Mixed Feelings at the First Impact

Our official delegation and the accompanying groups of businessmen and technicians approached China via Hong Kong, reaching Guangzhou by train, and then boarding a plane for Shanghai in the afternoon of May 15, 1978. Unfortunately, Senator Colombo was not with us. He had to postpone his departure from Rome in order to attend the funeral service of Aldo Moro, the great Italian statesman killed by the Red Brigades just a few days earlier; he would reach the delegation in Beijing. The inviting Chinese Association for Friendship with Foreign Countries (CAFFC) offered us special attention, with several interpreters and escorts helping us; most of them had taken language courses also in Italy. The rich pro-

---

ence of Catholic Representatives, he was elected the president of the newly formed Catholic Patriotic Association. In such capacity, between 1958 and 1962 Pi Shushi presided over the illicit ordination of several new bishops imposed by the official government structures.

[5] The legitimate bishop of Shanghai Ignatius Gong Pinmei was arrested in September 1955 and condemned to life imprisonment in March 1960. Soon after, Jesuit priest Louis Zhang Jiashu was chosen by official religious structures to replace him. As Zhang's episcopal ordination was considered illegal, his name did not appear in the *Annuario Pontificio*.

[6] Though well aware that all religious structures had disappeared due to the Cultural Revolution, Colombo expressed the desire, as a Christian, of attending Mass on Sunday.

[7] I had just written a short commentary ("Is the Church Re-emerging in China?") in *Mondo e Missione* No. 9 (May 1978), pp. 334-336.

gramme offered to us included one day in the beautiful city of Suzhou, a visit to the Shanghai Communication University (Jiaotong daxue), to the model commune of Machao and to some factories. At the official receptions to greet the "Italian friends," the "Gang of Four" was often referred to with contempt, while Mao Zedong's leadership was openly upheld; but it was difficult to perceive the real feelings of the common people. If some of us happened to touch on religious topics, the usual answer of our escorts was that now people in China felt no need for religion ... At the request of Antonio Marzotto (also a member of the Italian Parliament), who was the acting chairman of the delegation, some of us were offered the opportunity to visit the Jade Buddha Temple, then still officially closed. We met there some old men who presented themselves as retired monks, performing daily prayers and burning incense for foreign visitors; we were told that the temple had not been damaged by the Red Guards and were shown the treasure of the monastery library: some 7,000 ancient Buddhist volumes.

A certain Mr. Gao, who was introduced to me as representing Catholic circles, kept significantly silent. Yu Quanxi, an interpreter of the Foreign Office who had been assigned to assist Senator Colombo, followed me with some interest in Shanghai: while professing to be an atheist, he was curious perhaps at my qualification as "religious advisor." He had spent some years in Rome at the Commercial Office before the opening of the Beijing Embassy and spoke very good Italian. One day, while travelling together on a car we had a long discussion on religious freedom. As I happened to carry with me a printed copy of the Constitution approved two months earlier, I pointed to the unfair treatment reserved to believers, as article 46 stated: "freedom to believe in religion and freedom not to believe in religion *and to propagate atheism*": "What about freedom to propagate religion?" I asked. He had no answer to the question.

Antonio Marzotto, recalling that Senator Colombo would have liked to meet the Shanghai Catholic bishop who had attended the CPPCC in Beijing, made the same request. The answer was uncommitted till the last day, when just a few of us were told to wait before dinner in our rooms, at the Jinjiang Tower. We were taken then to a reserved hall where two tables had been arranged; soon after, an elderly man in ordinary dress was introduced as the Catholic bishop Zhang Jiashu. Being seated next to him, I tried to put him at ease by adding some Latin sentence, but was told by the interpreter to use the Italian language that he would translate. The conversation went on without addressing any delicate topic. Bishop Zhang said that, considering his old age, he was allowed to stay with relatives, and that he had been taken by car to our hotel; he was glad to meet Italian friends coming to China, etc. We were also "allowed" to take some photos. At the end, Antonio Marzotto mentioned that we had some small presents to give to Bishop Zhang on behalf of Senator Colombo, and the three of us were taken to a separate room. While I reached out to collect the gifts, Marzotto recalled that among his sons he had also a priest presently working in Rome and asked bishop Zhang whether he had ordained any new priests in Shanghai; the answer was no; asked about other bishops in China, Zhang said he did not know how many there were ...

When I joined them, the bishop's escort was surprised to see that in fact our gifts were some Chinese books: the Vatican Council documents, the Mass liturgy and a copy of the Bible in Chinese. Mentioning that the Second Vatican Council was held over 20 years earlier in Rome, I explained that all the Council documents were available also in Chinese and that Catholics around the world could now celebrate Mass in the local languages. Bishop Zhang, who appeared in good health and alert, did not hide his surprise. When I added that I was taking to him the special greetings from the Jesuit Superior General in Rome, Bishop Zhang said that in his youth years the General (Ledochowski) was a Pole; then, while studying in Paris, he had a chance to meet with J.B. Janssens, the Belgian provincial who at the end of the war was elected General (and died in 1964). He had not heard of the present General, Pedro Arrupe and was glad to know that he had been a missionary in Japan. Mentioning that in Beijing we expected to attend Mass, I expressed the hope that soon also in Shanghai some churches could be reopened; he smiled, but gave no answer. While leaving the room, I was able to tell him: "*Etiam Summus Pontifex cogitat de vobis et orat pro vobis*" (The Pope also thinks of you and prays for you); he understood well and answered very clearly: "*Gratias, gratias ago!*" (Many thanks!). As we tried to accompany the bishop down, his "guardian" told us to remain behind; he then took the bag, saying that he would have a look at the books.

We were supposed to depart for Beijing in the early afternoon of 18 May, but our plane left with seven hours delay; transportation was obviously an aspect needing attention in the modernization of China. While sitting at the airport, I had a long chat with Mr. Gao, our "Catholic representative." When I happened to mention Bishop Gong Pinmei, at first he seemed not to understand; but then he burst out: "This man is a criminal!" I recalled that he was arrested with many of his priests and lay faithful in 1955 and then sentenced to life imprisonment in 1960: "But now, I added, also on account of his old age, his position might hopefully be re-considered: when in 1970 American bishop James Walsh was freed on humanitarian reasons, the world appreciated the gesture." He kept silent for a moment; then: "It is better you keep away from these matters! ..." And after a while, he added: "For us it is very uncomfortable to talk about such topics." I could only say: "Sorry!"

The next morning in Beijing, we were given a glimpse of the Temple of Heaven and the White Mongol Pagoda, as originally planned; in the afternoon a very competent and elegantly dressed Mrs. Wang introduced us to the treasures of the "Forbidden City." The dinner was offered to the Italian delegation by the Chinese Ministry of Postal Services. Back at the hotel, a few of us met in the room of Senator Colombo who had just reached the capital to assess the situation. He had been informed of the "privilege" granted to us in Shanghai of having dinner with Bishop Zhang Jiashu, "and even of having photos taken with him." Informed that Bishop Pi Shushi had just passed away, Colombo insisted to have a talk with a representative of the Beijing Church.

On Saturday 20 May, I accompanied Carlo M. Butti, director of the ICI, on a visit to the Foreign Languages Centre *Guoji shudian*, where new fields of cooperation were discussed. In the afternoon, Senator Colombo was entertained with a small delegation at the headquarter of the Chinese Association for Friendship. In the long and friendly conversation with the association's president, Wang Pingnan, Colombo explained that it was not easy to promote a positive perception of China in Italy, given the tendency of the so called "Eurocommunism" to privilege friendship with Russia rather than China. In mentioning the main areas of activity of the ICI, Colombo highlighted the cultural field, with the quarterly magazine *Mondo Cinese* started in 1973 and a positive presence in the academic world, particularly through Professor Piero Corradini and Professor Franco Demarchi.[8] The ICI was running courses of Chinese language and talks to explain specific aspects of life in China, sponsoring tourism to China with attention to prepare the participants to the impact of the ancient civilization. Thanks to a convention with the ministry of Postal services, the ICI could make Chinese stamps available in Italy. In cooperation with Italian firms, special courses were offered to visiting Chinese technicians, and Chinese artistic events were facilitated.

In thanking "our great Italian friend Vittorino Colombo," President Wang Pingnan underlined the philosophy of his CAFFC: "Pave the way to officiality through non-official work," adding that his Friendship Association entertained contacts with 64 countries. Though the ICI took inspiration from different ideological roots, it proved to be a sincere and steady friend of Communist China. This was remarkable, President Wang added, when we consider the other Italian friendship network, the Associazione Italia-Cina: they claim to have a socialist basis, but as a matter of fact have embraced the radical positions of the "Gang of Four" and are now in great difficulties ... In mentioning religious freedom, Wang Pingnan minimized the constitutional clause allowing "to propagate atheism": he saw in it a pragmatic recognition of the feelings of common people, who in the past suffered a lot without getting support from religion.

On Sunday morning, an ICI delegation went to the recently opened mausoleum of Mao Zedong, to lay a wreath on behalf of the Italian government. Then, after attending Mass at the Nantang church, Senator Colombo was led with a few of us to the clergy house next to the church, for a meeting with Bishop Yang Gaojian, who introduced himself as the bishop of Changde diocese (Hunan province) and vice secretary general of the Chinese Catholic Patriotic Association (CCPA). He mentioned that the previous day he had gone to the Babaoshan Revolutionary Cemetery to pay homage to the deceased bishop Pi Shushi, and noticed the presence also of members of the official government structures. The conversation, lasting over an hour in a friendly atmosphere, was translated by the interpreter Yu; some photos were taken. Pressed by Senator Colombo's specific questions, Yang Gaojian confessed that he had little information on the concrete

---

[8] Piero Corradini was teaching at the Macerata University, while Franco Demarchi, a priest, taught sociology at Trento University. Demarchi, who accompanied Senator Colombo in his first trip to China (1971), was asked to take the editorial responsibility of the new magazine *Mondo Cinese*. He also initiated a familiar association called *Ianua Coeli* (Gate of Heaven), to foster a "crusade of prayers" for China.

situation of the Chinese Church, on the number of bishops, priests etc. His own diocese, where the Augustinians from Spain first preached the Gospel, had some 5,000 Catholics and only five priests. As he stressed the principle of mutual independence of all bishops, he was questioned about the common faith in the leadership of the bishop of Rome as successor of St. Peter. From the point of view of China – Yang replied – the Chinese side was concerned with the role of the Pope as head of the Vatican State, with which Beijing had no diplomatic relations. This was an old problem in need of clarification, as they did not want outside people to interfere with their internal affairs. Senator Colombo mentioned that he had recently the opportunity to meet with Paul VI and was asked by the Pope to convey his love and prayers for all Chinese clergy and lay faithful. Thanking, Bishop Yang insisted on the need to add concrete political facts to the nice words. Colombo then asked: "How could past misunderstandings be overcome? Could the CCPA develop to offer a contribution to this end?" Bishop Yang did not have an answer. Asked finally whether he would accept an invitation by the ICI to go to Italy for a visit, he politely said "no," due to poor health condition. But he accepted the books presented to him in the simple exchange of gifts.

A meeting with "a high personality of the State and the Party" was announced for Monday 22 May. That morning, in fact, the official delegation could meet with Deng Xiaoping in the Great Hall of the People, who shook hands with each of us,[9] and then had a private meeting with Senator Colombo and just six ICI officials. The main topics discussed were obviously of a political and economic nature, with the two sides agreeing on the need to foster cooperation between Europe and China to contrast Soviet hegemonic aims. And Senator Colombo remarked that Italy with her Christian heritage was a consistent promotor of peace, as this was "a battle for civilization and progress on which the whole of mankind can progress."[10]

3. Probing the Wind of Change

On leaving China, I was fully aware of having caught just a glimpse of a complex reality. Yet, convinced of the importance of strengthening friendship, once back in Italy I suggested to the ICI directorate to act promptly on a few opportunities: finding teachers ready to go to Beijing to help young officials with the Italian language, as requested; fostering the exchange of technicians and scholars in different fields, including that of religious studies; providing some useful collections for the library of the Beijing Institute of World Religions, etc.

As a growing number of people, thanks to Deng Xiaoping's new policies, were finding their way to Mainland China, it was somehow easy to glean new information from their experiences. An exceptional visit to China was made at

---

[9] The official photo of this encounter appeared the next day on the *Renmin ribao* with a *Xinhua* note.

[10] Cf. *Gli editoriali di Vittorino Colombo per le riviste "Italia Cina," "Cina Notizie" e "Mondo Cinese" 1971–1995*, ed. Franco Cajani (Monza: Quaderni Brianza, 2006), pp. 63-64.

the end of 1978 (6 November – 27 December) by Peter Zhao Yunkun (Tchao Yun-koen), a priest living in Rome with whom I was quite familiar.[11] Holding an Italian passport, in September 1977 he applied to visit his family in China's northeastern provinces, after such a long absence. Permission was granted one year later, and an embassy official assured him that, since the "Gang of Four" had been overthrown also in Manchuria, he could go there safely and could meet freely with priests and bishops. Unexpected favours and facilities were offered to Peter Zhao's family in view of their reunion; besides informing all the relatives of his arrival, the authorities provided transportation for them to the Changchun airport, where a welcoming party was offered. The next day Fr. Zhao was given the opportunity to go some 10 km from the city to pray on the tomb (*saomu*) of his parents who had died in the 1960s; he was surprised to see that the original Catholic cemetery had not been converted to agricultural use as in other provinces; several tomb stones carried recently painted red crosses. His brothers and sisters working at a local car manufacture were granted fully paid holidays for the 21 days he spent at home, and their families were provided with chosen and abundant food: an exceptional privilege, Zhao underlined. He recalled also two very special attentions. His elder brother Zhao Yunhui, then 68 years old, who after graduating at the Shanghai Fudan Catholic University taught for years in the diocesan seminary, was imprisoned three times and deprived of his civil rights for 30 years. A few days before Fr. Peter's arrival, he was summoned by a Party cadre; as he was down with flu, a car was sent to take him to the office. To his great surprise, he found that many people had gathered there waiting for him, and a "rehabilitation process" was initiated. Investigation – it was stated – proved that his father, though a land-owner, did not exploit the workers and was always ready to help those in need; as for Yunhui, though a religious person, he was no longer considered a parasite, on the contrary he proved a very good worker. The leader's conclusion was: As of today, this man is a full-right citizen; he should not be called "the one carrying the hat" (i.e., one who is regarded as a "bad element"), nor one who was "freed from the hat": he was simply a comrade.[12] Also Fr. Zhao's elder sister, who had spent over three months in prison during the Cultural Revolution for corresponding with him, was reinstated to her original rank before his arrival, with her wage refunded; and his brother-in-law, a Catholic who kept away from the Party, was promoted office-head just in those days.

In meetings with Party officials, Fr. Zhao was often asked questions on the Vatican and the Church organization. He was told that, rejecting the religious

---

[11] Zhao Yunkun was born in the diocese of Siping (Jilin) in 1925; from 1947 he studied in Rome where he was ordained a priest in 1953. He then became a professor at the Pontifical Urbaniana University and a contributor to the Chinese programme of Vatican Radio. His untimely death in 1981 proved a great loss.

[12] There were also practical benefits, as he could enjoy a normal pension, besides a monetary indemnity for the years he had been deprived of the right wage. Fr. Zhao was sure that such decision had been taken at a high level.

policy of the "Gang of Four," religion should not be a cause for social discrimination; temples and churches that had been destroyed, damaged or put to different use would be gradually restored. As a matter of fact, in his home city Changchun, the convent of the Sisters of Charity had been turned into a factory, where ten elderly priests and some sisters were kept doing manual work; the Manchuria Regional seminary had become a hospital for traditional medicine. The cathedral church, which had the cross at the top of the belfry torn down by the Red Guards using a tractor, was occupied by the army with the attached residence. For lack of alternative premises, the military did not move out, even after three orders from Beijing.

Fr. Zhao chose to celebrate Mass privately at home, even though in the city there were still about a hundred Catholic families. He intended to meet with Bishop Mathew Wang Weimin who lived in Changchun, but the local faithful stopped him, saying that "he was a traitor who had caused great harm."[13] Fr. Zhao mentioned that in neighbouring dioceses priests and other believers freed after up to 25 years in labour camps were still under police supervision. While appreciating Deng Xiaoping's new freedom and modernizations, people kept a prudential waiting attitude, as public expression of faith was still at one's own risk.[14] In the Catholic village of Xiaobajiacun, some 25 km from Changchun, where the magnificent old church had been completely destroyed and the bricks used to build the agricultural commune, religious life was still heavily controlled. Up to March 1978 people were forbidden to use prayer books publicly, even hand copied; and after lifting such interdiction, cadres insisted that religious scripts should not be distributed. An elderly priest, Chen Jisheng, returning home in poor health condition after years in labour camp, was still "bearing the hat"; some ten old sisters lived privately by their regular work.[15]

While spending a few days in Beijing, Fr. Zhao visited the Nantang church. He was told that some 20 Beijing priests were kept at a factory in Ya'er hutong, No. 50, doing cardboard boxes and receiving some pay; but no visitors were admitted. He heard that a Beijing priest held in high esteem, Peter Wang Jizhi (at that time about 70), past vice-rector in the diocesan minor seminary, was confined to home and allowed to go out only once a week. The Beijing "Eastern Church," the Dongtang in Wangfujing road, was used as an elementary school, while the huge compound of the "Northern Church," the Beitang, housed the

---

[13] Mathew Wang Weimin (1915–1996) became a priest in 1943 and was illegally ordained as bishop of Jilin in 1959 by Pi Shushi; he was known to live a married life.

[14] Typical was the case of Mrs. Yan, a generous catechist of Changchun, who had been arrested several times; the last time in April 1978 for distributing a prayer composed for the "Holy Year 1975." When Fr. Zhao arrived, she was out of prison but confined to home, and he had no opportunity to meet her.

[15] Fr. Zhao learned that the Sujiawobang Catholic community (also of Jilin diocese) had been kept united and faithful thanks to the heroic witness of two priests, John Baptist Xia Guiyi and Francis Ding Shiting who were buried alive on some unknown day between the years 1957-1960; they had publicly pardoned their executioners: cf. G. Politi, *Martiri in Cina* (Bologna: EMI, 1998), p. 161.

39th Beijing middle school. In Shanghai, where Fr. Zhao met Bishop Zhang Jiashu, he learned that not far from the cathedral, some 30 priests (10 of them Jesuits) and 20 sisters lived in a convent turned into a factory, with no opportunity of doing pastoral activities. Also in Wuhan, he was told, a group of priests were kept working in a factory with some Buddhist bonzes.[16]

4. 1979: Returning to Hong Kong, with Eyes and Heart to China

With the conclusion of the 8th P.I.M.E. General Assembly (January 1978), my long service as an assistant to the superior in Rome had come to an end. Later that year I was happily re-assigned to my original mission, Hong Kong, with a special mandate: trying to follow and encourage the timidly re-emerging Christian communities in Mainland China.[17] After the May trip with his delegation, Senator Colombo had made me a consultant of the ICI, thus facilitating contacts also with cultural sectors of Chinese society.

In the meantime, Yu Quanxi had been sent to the Press Office of the Chinese embassy in Rome, where his main job was analysing political affairs. He and the cultural attaché, Chen Suizhi, were eager to understand the Church events that marked 1978 summer months: after Paul VI passed away (6 August), there was the brief service of John Paul I, and then the great surprise of the election of a Polish Pope. The Chinese observers kept wondering about the impact John Paul II might have on the general strategy of the Church. One of the first questions addressed to me was: could he be considered "anti-Russian"? The two Chinese officials were also asking what the Vatican meant for Catholics around the world and for the States entertaining diplomatic relations with it. Mr. Chen, who did not know Italian, was glad to get an English translation of the programmatic speech of the new Pope. The assurance given (in mid-December 1978) by John Paul II to the visiting Foreign Minister of Bulgaria was received favorably: the Holy See would not expect any privilege from the various states; simply freedom to contribute, according to its nature, to the good of mankind. And well appreciated was the evidence given by *L'Osservatore Romano* to the news that China was about to establish diplomatic relations with the USA, and to Hua Guofeng's declaration about it (17–19 December 1978).

That offered me the opportunity to remark that, before opening negotiations with the USA, the Beijing authorities had not imposed as a pre-condition the breaking of relations with Taiwan. For the Church, the active presence in Rome

---

[16] Fr. Zhao was kind enough to give me copy of the 21 page confidential report he wrote upon his return. Mentioning the special treatment given him in many cities he visited, he wrote (on page 4): "Was this a courtesy for me or for the Vatican?"

[17] The option that I might not be available for pastoral activities in Hong Kong was discussed by the Superior with Bishop John Baptist Wu Cheng-Chung. On 22 December 1978 the P.I.M.E. vicar general specified: "We would like him to devote his time and energy to study the problems connected with the situation of religion and Christianity in China," adding: "We are encouraged by the interest that the Sacred Congregation for the Evangelization of Peoples is showing for this important issue."

of an "Embassy of China" (Taiwan) appeared in fact a formidable block to dialogue with Beijing, as recognized in an early June interview given by the Vatican Foreign Minister archbishop Agostino Casaroli. But Casaroli assured also that the Holy See was ready to look for an acceptable solution to that obstacle (born out of historical developments). Yet, I was reminded, Vice Premier Deng Xiaoping had recently clearly repeated during a conversation with visiting Italian Minister Rinaldo Ossola: "Vatican must break ties with Taiwan before any dialogue could be considered by China." Beijing expected a credible sign of good will and accountability of the Holy See; having sent a simple *Chargé d'Affairs* to the Taipei Nunciature *in lieu* of the archbishop was not enough. I tried to explain that the Vatican was conditioned by expectations of world Catholic believers, who did not trust the Beijing attitude to religion. In such a complex situation, we agreed, a constructive approach was offered by the words often repeated by President Wang Pingnan (CAFFC): "By using non-diplomatic channels, we prepare the way to diplomatic relations." I was informed that Mr. Wang would come on an official visit to Italy during Spring, at the invitation of the ICI. Mr. Yu called my attention to the "Message to Taiwan compatriots" issued by the permanent committee of the National People's Congress (1 January 1979): the Taiwanese population could continue living with their specific social features. Vice Premier Deng, preparing to visit the USA, had also mentioned his hope that the "Taiwan problem" could be solved peacefully within one year. More important appeared the document approved by the 3rd Session of the XI Party Congress (22 December 1979) endorsing Deng Xiaoping's modernisation programme.

When in early February I could return to Hong Kong with a working permit requested by the diocesan chancery, I was happy to discover a more sympathetic attention to the social development and religious life "inside." The local press had given evidence (on 22 January 1979) to a meeting of 800 "patriotic personages" in Shanghai earlier in the month, in which "the city angrily exposed and criticised political extremists in the past for undermining the Party's policy on religions and ruthlessly persecuting religious believers." It was stated that the Shanghai municipality had decided to restore the Bureau of Religious Affairs and to introduce constitutional provisions to help "religious patriotic organisations to develop normal activities."[18] In Hong Kong I had the opportunity of contacts with people dealing for different reasons with Chinese affairs.[19] I was glad to discover also the serious work done by various groups on the Protestant side: Chinese Church Research Centre directed by Jonathan Chao, Hong Kong Bible Society,

---

[18] That seemed to encourage also new hopes for the presence of Christian witnesses. After a new visit to China made on behalf of the ICI in January 1979, Franco Demarchi wrote: "I would encourage religious congregations to prepare one third of their future missionaries towards China. Right from now."

[19] Australian priest Douglas Conlan, who knew a member of the Chinese Foreign Affairs office, was trying to negotiate a visit to China of Mons. Pietro Rossano (of the Roman Secretariat of non-Christians).

Tao Fong Shan Centre, and China Study Project connected with Missionary Societies in Great Britain and Ireland.

5. Sharing Experiences with Other Friends of China

There were numerous accounts of Catholics visiting relatives in the Mainland, with situations differing quite a lot from place to place. Rich in practical suggestions was a report on the Church in China written in March 1979 by Michael Chu, S.J., out of his personal experiences.

In June 1979, having returned to Europe, I attended a useful Colloquium organized in Hofheim, Germany, by the group "Catholics in Europe Concerned with China." During the same month, when the official delegation of the CAFFC came to Italy, I had the opportunity to accompany them on behalf of the ICI. Then, at the end of September, I gladly joined an Italian group visiting China, with three other priests, including a Chinese one.

Entering with the group by train from Hong Kong, I could carry also two parcels of books offered by the ICI, which proved very useful in the following months. In Guangzhou, besides visiting factories, communes and monuments according to programme, I had a special task from retired Hong Kong bishop Lawrence Bianchi, with whom I had enjoyed my first missionary experience two decades before. He had resigned and left Hong Kong in 1969 after 46 years of missionary activity. But obviously he kept a loving memory of the long years spent announcing the Gospel on Chinese soil, particularly in the Haifeng costal area, beyond the boundary of the Hong Kong colony. In 1962, he had been saddened to learn of the episcopal ordination imposed on one of his good priests, Joseph Ye Yinyun (in Cantonese Yip Yam-wan), who was made the head of a new "official" diocese, Huizhou. The project of the new diocese was de facto cancelled soon after, due to the Cultural Revolution's dramatic developments. In recent times, news that Bishop Ye was still alive and hiding somewhere in Guangzhou had reached Lawrence Bianchi; so he decided to send him a note of encouragement.

When reaching Guangzhou, we learned that Bishop Dominic Deng Yiming (in Cantonese Tang Yee-ming) was still in prison and were told that the Seksat (Shengxin, "Sacred Heart") cathedral was still closed, so we celebrated Mass in a hotel hall. As for Bishop Ye, I had a rather vague note stating that he lived at no. 30 of a lane at a junction not far from the cathedral. The last evening of our stay, reaching Seksat cathedral by taxi and taking time to walk around, I had no difficulty to find the lane; entering at the given number and climbing a wooden, dark staircase, I heard people talking; I then asked in Cantonese for "Mr. Yip." A young man explained that he was out and would be back rather late. As I mentioned that I was passing by Guangzhou and would like to bring him just the greetings of an old friend, he said that I could meet him early next morning and kindly promised to inform him. So when I returned the following morning at about 6.30 a.m., the same young man called out at the top of the stair: "*Ah suk*" (uncle); soon from the last room in the corridor, a short man appeared, thin and looking uneasy but in good health. As I tried to kiss his ring, Bishop Ye took me into his poor, little room. When I mentioned Bishop Lawrence Bianchi, he was obviously moved and we embraced. After he went through Bishop Bianchi's letter, he accepted with pleasure also the books I brought (Council documents and New Testament in Chinese, liturgy books and Special Faculties granted by Propaganda Fide). Speaking with caution and in a low voice, he said that presently they experienced a little more freedom; the Seksat cathedral was due to open by mid-October. "Is it possible," I asked, "to do some pastoral work? Do you have contacts with the local priests?" – "A little," he answered, "a lot of patience is needed, and prudence also." – "And who will be given charge of this diocese?" – "That will depend on the 'will of the people'," he added with a timid smile. Touching on the usual accusations to the Vatican, I mentioned the friendly expressions towards China used by Pope John Paul II in a recent speech (19 August); he had not heard of it. I promised to bring his greetings to Bishop Bianchi, but he did not offer to write anything. Preparing for a photo, he wore a white shirt. As I was moving out, he inquired if somebody had noticed my coming to this place, because – he said – he was still under control and followed in his movements. Luckily I could assure him that nobody was around as I entered. He then accompanied me down, looking out to make sure that the lane was deserted.

Our group, moving on to Guangxi province, had a taste of the unique beauty of Guilin and of the minorities' cultural richness in Nanning. Then we reached Kunming, the capital of Yunnan province, with its splendid views and important monuments. When I asked to see Bishop Paul Kong Lingzhong, who had been ordained in 1962, our national guide after inquiries answered that the provincial office looking after religions was not functioning yet. One hour flight on a four-engined old plane took us to Chengdu, capital of the large Sichuan province. Among the numerous tourist attractions, we visited an ancient Buddhist temple, where it was possible to talk to some monks. We had the opportunity of meeting also with the 70 years old Bishop Paul Li Xiting, who was accompanied by a lay man named Xiu Shi. He explained that the large cathedral church, built at the beginning of the century, along with the bishop's house, had been ravaged during the Cultural Revolution. Now the large structure was under repair: "You are invited to return next year and to take part in our liturgy," he said. Speaking good Latin, he told us that the diocese had about thirty thousand faithful (two to three thousand in the city); he could count on some ten priests altogether, four of whom were in the city. After a simple exchange of gifts, Bishop Li started singing the "Our Father" in Latin and offered his blessing to the group. As we moved around we met two middle aged men who said they were seminarians; they had to interrupt their studies two decades before, when the seminaries were disbanded. Surprised, I looked at the bishop, who answered simply: "*Magister docet et discipuli apprehendent ...*" (meaning that he was their teacher and tutor); obviously, some philosophical and theological texts in Latin would prove very useful to him, he added.

Another moving experience marked the time we spent in Chengdu. The family of Father Frank Yang, the Chinese priest travelling with us (presently working in

Florence), had undertaken a two-day journey to come to Chengdu from the Wanxian area in the eastern part of Sichuan (which was later merged with Chongqing), waiting for his arrival. Among the eight relatives who came, some nephews had been baptized by Fr. Yang's elder sister, acting as catechist in the village. At the Mass presided by father Yang in a hall of the hotel, a nephew and a nice received their first communion, surrounded in great joy by our whole group.

The final stage of our journey was Beijing; the 2,400 km flight on a Iliusin 18 took almost three hours. We were put up at the Qianmen Hotel in the central area, and Little Wu, our local Beijing guide, proved a good friend having accompanied various Italian groups. He was glad to tell us that for the first time the national TV programme had showed Pope John Paul II in his visit to Ireland. The following day, while the group went to the Great Wall, a few of us had a meeting at Nantang church. The exchange between Frs. Yang and Lawrence Shi Yukun was quite vivacious but friendly, with accusation of past missionary mistakes and admission of present limits in religious activity. When the following day, Sunday, the group went to attend a morning Mass at the Nantang church, I was surprised to find a more numerous attendance than the previous year, with about 300 persons present; together with some foreign personnel, there were many local people both old and young. After Mass several went to talk with the celebrant, Father Sun, a Lazarist: later he told me that he was busy translating some religious texts from French.

6. Looking for Christian Life in Beijing

As the Italian group left a couple of days later, I was able to remain behind and moved to the Beijing Hotel. Armando Martinazzoli, a friend who was the Italian Embassy's scientific attaché, besides obtaining a fresh 10-day visa, was seeking for me a further extension of stay, to help me getting to know the great country a bit better. As mentioned, my main concern was about the re-emerging religious life. Walking east from Wangfujing road in the Dongdan Beidajie area, I reached a Protestant church. Being a week day it was closed. A lady who could speak English told me that three pastors were living there, one of Presbyterian origin, one Anglican and one Methodist. She recalled that since the 1950s the various Christian denominations had been merged into a sort of Union Church; now, on Sundays an inter-denominational communion service was held. There was no choir yet, but the whole congregation, mostly elderly persons, joined in singing and praying. The church, rather small, had been closed but was not damaged by the Cultural Revolution, and many Bibles and Hymn books could be saved. At a certain point, Pastor Kan, the Presbyterian, joined our conversation (with the lady translating for him): since September he was giving a course on "Bible classics" at the Institute for World Religions for a group of 20 young university graduates who had passed an examination to enter that new institution. Are they any believers? I asked. He did not know, because so far he had no contact with them. Not far from that church a mosque had also been reopened; during the dark years its minaret had been toppled over.

In order to discuss possible cooperation opportunities, I visited the Friendship Association on behalf of the ICI, the publications department Guoji shudian, the international tourist office Lüxingshe and the CASS. Here, meeting with the Vice Director of the Institute for the Study of World Religions, Zhao Fushan, proved particularly interesting. Of Anglican formation and well acquainted with religious developments in the West, he asked many questions about the Vatican's new Secretariats. He was glad to receive a copy of the Catholic Bible (translated by Father Allegra's Biblical Institute) and of the documents of Vatican Council II which he did not know. Talking of the Institute's depleted library (presently he was using the Philosophy section's library of the CASS), mention was made also of the Monumenta Serica Monograph Series and the journal *Monumenta Serica*: I promised to verify with the Divine Word fathers in Germany the possibility to receive the missing publications, if he let me know when their collection was stopped. Commenting on the Catholic situation, Professor Zhao said that for the government the official level comes first; and this inevitably affects the contacts of the Chinese Church with the Bishop of Rome (conditioned by the Vatican diplomatic relations with Taiwan).

While in Beijing, I had a long interview also with the newly elected bishop Michael Fu Tieshan, at the Nantang residence next to the church; with him were two priests (Lawrence Shi and Anthony Liu) and a certain John Tian representing the Patriotic Association. I excused myself for not having been able to take along an interpreter, and Michael went on speaking English, slowly but clearly, and translated our whole conversation for the other persons. He gladly accepted the books I offered him on behalf of Senator Colombo (Chinese missal, New Testament and Vatican documents), and expressed appreciation for the efforts made by the ICI to strengthen friendship with China. At a certain point, Lawrence Shi handed me an envelope, saying that a Hong Kong visiting priest had given him – among other religious articles – also some photos with the blessing of the new pope John Paul II: "We cannot keep them, he added, because the Pope does not show respect for the Chinese Church ..."

As Bishop Michael Fu asked many questions about the liturgical reform and Church life in Italy and in Hong Kong, the conversation went on for about two and a half hours, in a simple and friendly atmosphere, even when touching on controversial points of Church history and the present situation, in which also the two priests and John Tian joined the discussion.[20] While repeating that the Chinese Church is part of the "*una, sancta, catholica, apostolica ecclesia ...,*" they would not accept that the Vatican could not approve its independent management. The recent criticism expressed by Rome over Michael Fu's "democratic election"

---

[20] As the whole conversation was carried out in the two languages, I was able to write down practically all that was said. Today, 35 years later, those pages appear a sad confirmation that none of the old problems and obstacles facing the Church in China has been removed yet ...

was proof of such "Vatican hostility," I recalled the Canon Law rules valid for the universal Church, and also the ancient Chinese tradition, which asked the children in a family to be the first to express their respect for the father. The answer was that the real head of the Church is Jesus, who is above Peter (who even betrayed Jesus ...). As we went on with a long series of contentions, I took the liberty to insist that Bishop Michael Fu should write to the pope, asking for his approval and blessing, adding that my secret hope was that the pope himself, who was planning to visit Asia and the Philippines, might perform his ordination. As a matter of fact, Fu told me that three bishops had already been invited to perform the ceremony. In his Chinese translation he kept referring to me simply as "Liang shenfu" (Father Liang, my Chinese name), and the friendly contact built on that encounter continued also later: every time I passed through Beijing, even accompanying a group, Bishop Michael Fu would make himself available.

As I spent a few more days in Beijing preparing for my new trip, I could visit with some friends the old Guangqi Buddhist temple and monastery, northwest of the imperial city. Closed during the Cultural Revolution, it still had a dozen old monks living there, and now three days a month people were allowed in to pray and burn incense. At the Beijing Hotel I also happened to meet and exchange views with two other foreign guests: Karl Moser, auxiliary bishop of Vienna and Prelate Eberhard Mühlbacher, who were expecting to meet Bishop Michael Fu and the director of the Religious Affairs Office Xiao Xianfa. They told me that a few months later Franz Cardinal König of Vienna would also be visiting China.

7. A Precious Opportunity to Know More about Country and Church

On 3 November 1979, I left Beijing by train on a hard sleeper coach to Zhengzhou (Henan). The programme arranged with the Lüxingshe included travel and hotel bookings, with local guides available in the various cities. At the new Zhengzhou city station, the guide waiting for me had arranged for an art and craft factory and an exhibition on the Yellow River. When I mentioned that, being Sunday, as a Christian I would like to go to a church, I received this answer: "There is no Christian church here. But you will see a Catholic church tomorrow in Kaifeng." He explained that his family lived there and he had learned English at the Kaifeng Normal College. I was also interested to see that city, till recently capital of Henan province, where my confreres (of P.I.M.E., the Milan Foreign Missions Society) had been working for several decades. Among the Kaifeng ancient monuments I was shown the "Iron Pagoda" with a huge Buddha statue nearby. Then I spent some time walking around, and it was not difficult to discover the western style Catholic church with its bell tower; the compound taken over by a government school was full of children. But when I enquired about the old bishop He Chongming, the local guide confessed that he had never heard his name. But, confidentially, he then added: "Here in Kaifeng Christians have no priests and cannot hold their religious services in the church: so on Sundays they gather to pray in private houses ..." I asked how he knew that: "A friend of mine who is a believer told me ... He even invited me to join with them, but I said no.

I am not a believer, I am a Marxist." My comment was that people were right to do so, since freedom to believe was now publicly acknowledged. As a token of friendship, I offered him a small size Gospel, explaining what it was about ...

The next leg of my journey took me to Wuhan (Hubei), where I spent the first day walking around the old commercial city of Hankou. People appeared curious and yet quite friendly to the few foreigners that could be seen on the streets. Reaching Shanghai street where I knew that the cathedral church was located, at the gate I asked in Chinese for Dong Guangqing. I was in fact looking for one of the very first two bishops ordained in China (in 1958), Bernardinus Dong, a Franciscan friar. The doorkeeper replied that he was out, but that he could be seen the next day in the early hours. As I returned the following morning before 7 a.m., finding the gate open I proceeded to the old residential building in the church compound. I repeated my enquiry to a man whom I met there, and he kindly took me upstairs and into a dark corridor. But the door he showed me was locked: he then went to inquire and told me that "Mr. Dong" would be back soon. The bishop arrived dressed as a worker, but we were quick to familiarise as we exchanged a couple of sentences in Latin. The room to which Bishop Bernardinus took me was marked by a plate "Patriotic Association." He explained that he had returned to Hankou not long before, when the authorities decided that the cathedral should be repaired and reopened; in fact, he himself was busy working there. He added that the whole mission house, taken over by the government, was presently used as a special school of young artists, who were noisily moving around. Bernardinus was interested in the circumstances of my visit to China, in connection with Senator Colombo's ICI at the invitation of Wang Pingnan. He mentioned some Italian Franciscan missionaries who had worked in Hunan and whom I also knew, and was glad to accept the religious articles and liturgy books I could offer. In Wuhan, he added, 40 to 50 sisters were kept working in the hospitals taken over by the government; though not dressed as sisters, everybody knew and appreciated their dedication. There are now some ten priests in the diocese, but there is no contact with the catholic community yet. The cathedral church, now under repair, could be opened in a few months time. He hopes that future groups visiting China with the ICI may include his city in their itinerary and ask to visit the cathedral. Before leaving, I also visited the huge Guiyuan Buddhist monastery and temple in the Hanyang district, where the merciful Guanyin is particularly honoured.

The following day a flight brought me to Nanjing, where I had some Italian contacts: a young man studying Chinese literature, and three engineers with family, working at a petrochemical plant. With the local guide (Miss Yang) I visited some historical spots, and while climbing to the Sun Yat-sen Mausoleum we had a long open conversation. She recalled the years lost during the Cultural Revolution, mentioning with scorn the slogan "Better red than expert." She was glad to hear of Sun Yat-sen political vision and was surprised to discover that he was a Christian believer. She knew that his widow, very old now, was elected Vice President of the China Congress, and that her younger sister was married to Chiang Kaishek. She did not know of any active Christian presence in Nanjing. I then went for short visits to Wuxi and Suzhou, where the guide, a French speaking middle aged man, while showing some of the famous gardens and ancient pagodas of this "Venice in the Orient," could not hide his frustration for having been unable to complete his studies (in 1966, he had been sent to do manual work for four years). Later, while accompanying a medical mission in Cameroun, he could appreciate the service of Catholic sisters working in a poor village there. He had no information of Catholic activity in Suzhou, where the Bureau of Religious Affairs was being organized and the Buddhist association had already reconvened. He kept a good memory of his mother, a fervent Buddhist, but he added that her reaction to adversity was perhaps too passive, as she was ready to accept anything from Buddha ... Religion in China, he commented, is easily tarnished by superstition; besides, foreign capitalist powers in the past often exploited religion, stirring the reaction of Chinese intellectuals and patriots.

From Nanjing, a forty-five minutes journey by train brought me to Shanghai. Having booked at the classic Heping Hotel on the Bund, it was easy to move around the old city. The following day, a Sunday, I reached a Protestant church whose address I had been given in Beijing. When I asked an old passerby, he whispered in English that all churches were closed, and pointed to a brick building, at the junction of Xizang – Hankou Road, with a damaged tower and the stained-glass windows broken. In fact it appeared locked up, but following the many people entering a side gate I reached the main hall that was already crowded. An attendant took me to an upper side wing, where also a few other foreigners were sitting. The service was simple; from a reading-desk on the stage an elderly pastor in civilian cloth commented on a page of the New Testament; people were invited to join the choir in singing; but no communion service was held. As I learned later, the building was under repair, but Sunday services had started already two months earlier. In Shanghai two other churches were functioning, all belonging to the Three-Self Movement.

I then reached Xujiahui district, hoping to see Bishop Zhang Jiashu; the well-positioned church appeared locked and not accessible. After several enquiries I was shown an old house of the sisters on the opposite side of the big square, where some 40 priests were also kept doing manual work. The old lady at the entrance said that Bishop Zhang was too busy, too tired ... Finally, as I insisted, she suggested that I return early the next morning. When arriving, before 7 a.m., I was met by Berchmans Shen Baozhi, who spoke some French; at first rather reserved, he gradually opened up and we had a long conversation. He accepted the photos and some books I had taken for the bishop; but as I touched on Bishop Gong Pinmei and expressed my hope of a mercy gesture in his favour, Berchmans repeated that Gong had caused great harm to country and religion ... When I mentioned the three Protestant churches already functioning, he said that the Catholic church, dedicated to Mary Mother of God, was still used as a fruit market warehouse, but would be soon restored. Since the previous month, Mass was celebrated daily in a chapel behind the church; he accepted to take me there, and as we walked by the impressive red brick cathedral our comments went to the huge damages it suffered, from the broken bell towers to the rose windows hit by slink. It was expected, Berchmans added, that also the old clergy residence may be returned soon to Church use.

During a brief visit to Hangzhou, I was told that no Christian church was available. Miss Liu, who took me to the nine-centuries old Lingyin Buddhist temple on the hills outside the city, was well-informed on its history and devotions. Many people were burning incense in front of the huge Sakyamuni statue, and I was told that some 40 monks could remain there even during the Cultural Revolution, as the temple was protected by a wall. Impressive also the ancient religious images sculpted on the hill rock.

Then, reaching Guangzhou by night train, I did not miss the opportunity to visit Seksat cathedral, where I knew that some priests had returned. Asking in Cantonese a worker nearby, I was told that I could enter from the back of the church. In fact, pushing a gate I found myself in a simple residence where, called by a lady, a priest named Aloysius Ye (Yip in Cantonese) came to meet me. He mentioned that six priests (some quite old) had been freed from labour camps, where he himself had spent eleven years. He gladly accepted some religious books, showing them to a "lady guardian" watching us. I was then taken inside the Gothic cathedral, where all the altars, statues, liturgical vestments and other religious signs had been destroyed.

Two Mass services – I was told – were held on Sundays on a wooden altar recently arranged; I noticed that the cross was still without crucifix; a wooden banister and a confessional had also been added. Father Ye mentioned that they were looking for art models to give to the craftsmen so that they could reconstruct the religious statues and paintings. The lady offered to let us exit from the main gate, and as she went to get the key I handed Father Ye an envelope with some pictures of the Holy Father, the Special Faculties and Eucharistic prayers in Chinese, which he put into his pocket. "Any news about Bishop Dominic Deng?" I asked later; they knew that he was alive, but were ignorant about whether he would be freed. In front of the cathedral, after a photo, mentioning that in my hotel room I had some artistic religious pictures, I suggested that Father Ye could go with me to get them. Before answering, he turned to his "guardian," who stressed that there was too much work to do, and I had to leave alone.[21] Before my extended visa (seven weeks) expired, on 15 November a comfortable Hovercraft took me back to Hong Kong.

8. China's Religious Structures and Policies Renewed

Settling back there, I was heartened to perceive a growing attention to the Chinese religious situation, with shared information also on the Protestant side. I was especially glad to discover how deeply committed to the Church in Mainland

---

[21] I was not surprised to read some time later (12 September 1980) a *UCANews* note entitled "Cathedral Amazon," recalling a letter sent to the *Hong Kong Standard* on August 27 by an "enraged woman" who had visited the Canton Cathedral: "I wanted to talk to one of the priests," wrote Mrs. Reikhoupt, when "a fierce woman demanded of me who I was, where I came from and what I wanted to see the priest about."

China Bishop John Baptist Wu was:[22] he encouraged the diocesan clergy and the religious congregations present in Hong Kong to reflect on their common responsibility and on ways to help overcome the exceptional difficulties of their brothers and sisters living beyond the boundary. To this effect, he appointed diocesan priest John Tong Hon[23] as a coordinator of possible initiatives regarding Christianity in contemporary China. By late November, interested representatives of religious and missionary groups started gathering to share and compare experiences after visiting China. This became known as the "Ricci Study Team" sponsored by the diocese.[24] In the following months, besides this rather loose frame, the diocese established in Aberdeen, next to the Holy Spirit Seminary, a Study Centre on Chinese Christianity, directed by John Tong and concerned with planning and executing specific research projects.

Soon after, "private visits" by French cardinal Roger Etchegaray, Archbishop of Marseille (27 February – 14 March 1980), and by the Austrian Cardinal Franz König, Archbishop of Vienna (10–20 March), were seen by the international press as signs of possible initiatives to open a dialogue between Beijing and Rome. Would future developments confirm such hope? About the same time, the Chinese Religious Affairs Bureau was taking steps to reconvene the "patriotic" structures of the five recognized religions: an important step to revive the CCP's United Front policies in a sensitive sector of society, but also a public recognition for all religious believers. The Islamic Association held its conference in April 1980, followed closely by the Taoist one, while the Protestant Three-Self Movement and the Buddhist Association convened their leadership in the last quarter of the year. The members of the CCPA were called to Beijing on 22 May for a week of discussion; to the 198 representatives (including 30 bishops) nine other people were added, possibly government officials; Xiao Xianfa, director of the Religious Affairs Bureau addressed the delegates. It was commonly agreed that the Association is "not a church, ... but simply a social grouping of Catholics for dealing with the wide society and with the government."[25] Right after the works of the Association were concluded, a "Conference of Chinese Catholic Represen-

---

[22] John Baptist Wu Cheng Chung (1925–2002) was born in a village of Guangdong province; after joining the seminary in his diocese of Kaying (Meizhou), he studied and was ordained a priest in Hong Kong and then worked as a parish priest in the county of Miaoli (Diocese of Hsinchu since 1961), Taiwan. He was made Bishop of Hong Kong in 1974 and Cardinal in 1988. Invited twice to mainland China, in 1986, he was able to visit his family and embrace his old mother.

[23] John Tong Hon, born in Hong Kong in 1939, was ordained priest in 1966. He received episcopal ordination in 1996 and became Bishop of Hong Kong in 2009; in 2012, he was elevated to Cardinal.

[24] Right from the first encounter (21 November 1979), John Tong was supported by a few volunteers, namely Peter Barry and Elmer Wurth of the Maryknoll Society and by myself. Naturally, to formulate goals and objectives, people with particular experience (like László Ladány [1914–1990], S.J., and Norberto Pieraccini, O.F.M.) were also consulted.

[25] Such was a statement given by Bishop Michael Fu Tieshan in an interview to the *UCANews* on 8 October 1980.

tatives" (for the third time in two decades) was also formally convened from 31 May to 2 June. Its main task was to establish a "Chinese Catholic Bishops College" and a "Chinese Catholic Church Affairs Committee." Sadly, this Conference of Catholic Representatives was practically composed of the same persons as the Patriotic Association, giving a political overtone to most speeches and setting the "love for the country" as prerequisite for all religious decisions. The Holy See was easily made the target of criticism for many mistakes of the colonial times, and a letter addressed to all Catholics in the country rejected any "interference" of the Vatican: China was determined to safeguard its independence in religious affairs no less than in other areas.[26] A positive news emerging from such double Beijing meeting was a call to prepare for the opening of a Catholic Philosophy and Theology School.

During Summer 1980, I could join a Hong Kong ecumenical group on a visit to some cities, thus gaining a closer look especially at the situation of re-emerging Protestant communities. In Hangzhou we had a long evening conversation in the hotel with a pastor and his wife: in the Christian Church, two thousand members enrolled since it opened nine months earlier, and 3,000 worshippers participated in the Sundays services. On the Catholic side, he said, the local church built in the 17th century is still occupied by families and the old bishop Wu was forced to return to his village. In Ningbo some Protestant churches were already functioning, while the Catholic bishop was sick and no church was open yet. In Shanghai we could establish more contacts with both Catholics and Protestants. On Sunday 29 June, some of us attended one of the Masses celebrated (in Latin, ancient style) in chapels next to the Xujiahui church, which was still under repair. Returning there in the evening, we were told by the parish priest Etienne Li and the bishop's secretary Berchmans Shen that some 3,000 faithful participated in the Easter and Pentecost celebrations, and that new people were asking for instruction. Some new churches were to be opened soon, and possibly also the Sheshan Marian Shrine.

Visiting the headquarters of the Three-Self Movement, we discussed several topics with the Acting Chairman, Pastor Shen Deyong, and some of his colleagues. Present was also Dr. Jiang Wenhan, happy to meet with Bishop Gilbert Baker[27] (a member of our group) who had been his fellow student from 1946 to 1949 in New York. Dr. Jiang, recalling a booklet he had written against Marxist ideology upon returning to China and his double experience of hard labour, explained his present attitude: rather than discussing philosophical and theological principles, it is important to be identified as Christians while working concretely

---

[26] Addresses by bishops Zong Huaide of Jinan (Shandong), Zhang Jiashu of Shanghai, Yang Gaojian of Changde (Hunan) and Tu Shihua of Hanyang (Hubei) appeared particularly critical. The voice of Bishop Duan Yinming of Wanxian (Sichuan), defending the role assigned by Jesus to Peter (and to the Bishop of Rome), remained a solitary one in the conference contest.

[27] John H. Gilbert Baker (1910–1986) was Bishop of the Anglican Diocese of Hong Kong and Macau from 1966 to 1980.

for the modernization of the country. He added that the Shanghai Academy of Social Sciences had invited him to be a fellow researcher and continue a work he had recently undertaken on the history of Christianity in China.

From Shanghai by train we reached Nanjing where we spent three days. After visiting the Sun Yat-sen Memorial, we were received by an officer of the Nanjing University, who explained the origin of the institution (from a Protestant initiative) and its present problems and prospects. Then we had a long meeting in our hotel with bishop Ding Guangxun[28] and some colleagues who teach at the Institute for World Religions of Nanjing University. Bishop Ding said that thirty years experience taught him that fighting religion is not a priority for Communists. Since the 1950s the Three-Self Movement, helping Christians to love their country and gain a common identity, was well accepted by intellectuals. Though many contradictory measures along the years have betrayed Mao's United Front policy, the active presence of Christians at Nanjing University proved encouraging. Later, I went looking for the Nanjing Catholic church, which – I knew – had been turned into a workshop; reaching the location with a friend, we were allowed to have a look inside: it was full with machinery, but we were told that it would soon be vacated. Then we could meet with Father Wang Hao, responsible for the re-emerging Catholic community, who had been given a desk space in the compound of a nearby mosque, presently under repair. From Nanjing we flew to Beijing, and a meeting was arranged at Nantang with Bishop Michael Fu, who answered questions previously prepared and gave an ample account of the recent double meetings held in the capital. In a private meeting afterwards, I offered him a four volume edition of the *Missale Romanum* and suggested to send him, once a month, wrapped up in an envelope, the Hong Kong Catholic weekly newspapers.

On the way back it was possible to spend two more days in Guangzhou. Having learned from the local newspapers that Bishop Dominic Deng had been released from prison, a few of us went to the temporary priests residence, behind the "Stone house" cathedral. Two priests received us and helped us to meet the bishop. His health appeared not so good, but he was glad to see us; he showed us his Rosary and the Cross that were given back to him after 22 years; he did not say Mass yet, while getting acquainted with the new liturgy; he was happy to hear of the Jesuit General Father Arrupe and of his new assistant Father Michael Chu. Early the next morning I went to see, at his side lane room, Bishop Joseph Ye Yinyun, who gladly received greetings and the gift of a fountain pen from "his" Bishop Lawrence Bianchi. He had been invited to meet Cardinal Etchegaray, who gave him a rosary as a souvenir. Bishop Ye had also been in Beijing (representing Huiyang Church), with Father Ye Shang who was the Guangzhou delegate. According to Bishop Ye, to make it possible for the Chinese Church to

---

[28] Better known abroad as K.H. Ting, Bishop Ding Guangxun (1915–2012) was born in Shanghai; in 1946, he went with his wife to study in Canada and USA; returning to China in 1951, he was made an Anglican bishop in 1955. After the Cultural Revolution, he became the principal of the Nanjing Union Theological Seminary.

dialogue directly with the Pope, the political (and diplomatic) problem between Beijing and the "Vatican" needs to be addressed wisely. Chinese public opinion should be helped to perceive the official attitude of the "Vatican" as one of sincere respect for the Chinese people, its traditions and its institutions, rejecting any neo-colonialist attitude.[29]

9. Contributions of Missionaries from the Past

Back in Hong Kong, a few months later I was invited to join a delegation from the city and university of Trento passing through Hong Kong. We entered China by train and flew from Guangzhou to Shanghai where, besides the usual visit to monuments, communes and factories, an agreement to exchange scholarships was signed at the Foreign Languages Institute. There, I was able to visit again father Vincent Zhu, leaving some books with him and learning more about his Jesuit confrères still partially limited in their freedom. More important was our visit to Hangzhou, the city where Martino Martini, S.J. (great missionary scholar from Trento) had lived and worked four centuries before: a friendship agreement was signed between the cities of Hangzhou and Trento. Then in Nanjing the delegation visited the local university and the Academia Sinica, where a photostat copy of Martini's *Novus Atlas Sinensis* was offered to the Urban Land Institute. I was able to spend some time also with a Lasalle Brother from Peru who was there teaching Spanish, and to visit the local church again: the renovation work was progressing and five elderly Sisters were busy repairing religious articles and vestments dispersed by the Red Guards.

When we reached Beijing, the CAFFC organized an important joint conference of Academia Sinica with the Academies of Natural Sciences and of Social Sciences on Martino Martini. Stressing mutual cooperation, a formal invitation was extended to Chinese researchers to contribute preparing an international Conference on that great scholar that would be held in Trento. I had a separate meeting with Professor Zhao Fusan of the CASS, glad to receive the three volumes of Pasquale d'Elia's *Fonti Ricciane*, plus a copy of the Bible translated by the Franciscans and some journals from Rome. He was grateful for some volumes of *Monumenta Serica* received from Germany, and inquired about an English translation of the *Summa Theologica* of Saint Thomas and other Scholastic literature. Zhao explained that, among 30 young men preparing to enter the Academy, seven were studying Christianity, adding that to one of them, Ren Yanli, he had suggested to make a research on the Vatican Council II. When I met Ren Yanli, he had just passed the exam to enter the Beijing Academy's World Religions section, and I got a good impression of him. So, back in Milan, I presented his case to the Catholic University of the Sacred Heart, where in 1982 he was ac-

---

[29] As an example, he mentioned the "democratic" election of Fu Tieshan to become Bishop of Beijing. When a Vatican spokesman simply rejected the choice as contrary to the Canon Law, the Chinese press interpreted it as a sign that the Pope does not appreciate China, recalling the old story of a petition sent to Rome and rejected in 1958.

cepted as a post-graduate researcher in the department of Religious Sciences, while the ICI offered to help him cover the living expenses. But he had to overcome bureaucratic difficulties before he could reach Milan, where he was able to study from 1985 to 1987 and prepare a dissertation on the Vatican Council II.[30]

From Beijing the group headed back to Italy, while I returned to Hong Kong, where plenty of information was also available, thanks to the sharing opportuneities of the "Ricci Study Team" and a collection of press reports being initiated there. I learned that during that summer Australian University Economics Professor Audry Donnithorne, born in Sichuan, had made an extended visit to China. On 19 June, she had an interview in Beijing with Xiao Xianfa, head of the Religious Affairs Bureau, to whom she suggested that the legitimate Catholic bishops in China should be allowed to go to Rome for discussions. Mr. Xiao replied that they would be permitted to go if they wished, and that the Chinese government would not stop them, "but they do not wish to go."[31] International press offered wide attention also to a short address given by Pope John Paul II (7 September 1980) in Castelgandolfo in which, congratulating Bishop Dominic Deng on his 50th anniversary of religious life, he expressed "deep joy, emotion, gratitude and due appreciation" at the news of his release.[32] Later, on 6 November it was reported that Bishop Deng was allowed to go to Hong Kong for medical treatment.

In the same month of November 1980, upon the request to accompany another team of Italians, I spent 20 more days visiting the usual northeastern tourist attractions. In Beijing, at the Nantang church we had a friendly conversation with some priests; but not without criticism of past "imperialistic" policies and of

---

[30] Ren Yanli was born in 1944 in Yan'an (Shaanxi), into a family appreciated for its revolutionary spirit. After secondary school, Ren Yanli was sent to the countryside; in 1963 he started to study Italian and in 1968 graduated at the Beijing Foreign Languages Institute. He had then to work for two years in a rural commune and spent 8 more years teaching mathematics in a middle school in the Shandong province, before he could apply for the Academy of Social Sciences. In recent years, as a Chinese expert on the Catholic Church in China he was often invited to academic events. Among others: on 24 October 2001 he gave a talk at the Gregorian University in Rome ("Dalla controversia dei *riti* cinesi alla *via cinese moderna* attraverso il Vaticano II"), printed in the monthly *Asia News* (May 2002), pp. 23-28. A talk he gave in Milan at the Accademia Ambrosiana (Classe di Studi sull'Estremo Oriente) on "La questione della Chiesa cattolica in Cina," was printed by Bulzoni in *Asiatica Ambrosiana* No. 1 (March 2009), pp. 65-73. See also his contribution "The innovations of the Second Vatican Council," in *Catholic Church and China in the 20th century*, ed. Elisa Giunipero (Macerata: Edizioni Università Macerata 2010), pp. 169-180.

[31] Professor Donnithorne later wrote to Mr. Xiao stating that she had been able to ascertain, from good sources, that the bishops concerned would in fact like to go to Rome. She then published an open letter, with an appeal to the Chinese Government to give these bishops exit visas and any other facilities necessary to leave China for Rome.

[32] The Pope then added: "The Lord ... is surely close, in a particular way, to those sons and daughters of the Church in China; while keeping the Catholic faith in the Gospel, they show at the same time love to their country and they work with greater good will to its prosperity": *Papal Documents Related to China, 1937-2005*, researched by Elmer Wurth, M.M., ed. Betty Ann Maheu, M.M. (Hong Kong 2006), p. 323.

"negative attitudes" of the Vatican. At the Chinese Academy of Social Sciences, during a long conversation with Vice President Gao Wangzhi, I could present him with some books requested for the library. In Hangzhou the Catholic church was not yet open, but we had a joyful surprise: the Protestant pastor, who had been told of our visit, kindly invited the Catholic priest Joannes Zhu (just returned to the city two months earlier) to meet us in his own place. On my way back to Hong Kong, passing by the Seksat church in Guangzhou, I learned that Bishop Ye Yinyun had joined the community of local priests.[33]

10. The Party Reconsiders Its Role in Leading the Country

Preparing to celebrate the 60th anniversary of the Communist Party's foundation, members of the Central Committee held protracted discussions on the need to reconsider Mao Zedong's leadership. At the end of June 1981, when the Sixth Plenum of the Party's Central Committee convened, a statement was issued in which the Cultural Revolution was drastically described as "the most severe setback and the fiercest losses suffered by the Party, the State and the people since the founding of the PRC." Without nuances it was also stated that such disaster "was initiated and guided by comrade Mao Zedong." This was, no doubt, a victory for the pragmatic leadership of Deng Xiaoping and his modernization drive. He was then promoted to preside over the powerful commission of military affairs, while Hua Guofeng was replaced as Party chairman by Hu Yaobang. But an overall positive assessment of Mao's role was confirmed: Mao Zedong's Thought is still to be considered the "great and valuable spiritual asset of our Party." And Hu Yaobang in his official speech specified: "Our Party has reiterated that it is necessary to uphold the four fundamental principles of the socialist road, the people's democratic leadership (i.e., the dictatorship of the proletariat), the Communist Party leadership; and Marxism-Leninism and Mao Zedong's Thought" (*Beijing Review*, 13 June 1981). While a new constitution of the CCP was prepared along these lines, a "socialist spiritual civilization" was promoted to rekindle the revolutionary enthusiasm, and intellectuals were offered new "guided freedom," following Deng's principle of searching truth from facts.[34]

It was in such context that, at the beginning of March 1981, the CCP official magazine *Hongqi* (Red Flag) published an article entitled: "Why must China practise freedom of religious belief?" The author, Lei Zhenchang, started off by confirming that the ideology guiding the Party and the country is Marxism, which "is thorough going materialism. Not only is it in disagreement with the religious idealist world outlook, but it also attempts to gradually emancipate those who believe in religion from the fetters of religion." He consequently found nothing

---

[33] Spending a Sunday in Guangzhou, I was happy to be invited to celebrate Mass in the cathedral, at a side altar dedicated to Our Lady. Obviously, the missal available was the Latin one with the old liturgy. I was impressed by the several people attending in devout prayer.

[34] Cf. Angelo S. Lazzarotto, *The Catholic Church in Post-Mao China* (Hong Kong 1982), pp. 94-96. I am taking the liberty to use the documentation and comments collected for that book extensively in this chapter, published by the Hong Kong Holy Spirit Study Centre.

amiss with article 46 of the current Constitution: "A clergyman enjoys freedom to preach theism in a house of worship, and an atheist enjoys freedom to propagate atheism." The same interpretation of the "freedom of religious belief" was proposed to the general public (*Guangming Ribao*, *China Reconstructs*, etc.), while feudal superstitious activities were condemned, along with witchcraft and sorcery. The nature of superstition, however, was not explained, simply repeating that "religion is a kind of superstition, but feudal superstitious activity is not religious activity."

For the Church in China, the year 1981 developed along somehow contradictory lines, alternating hope and disappointment. Pope John Paul II's visit to the Philippines in February proved a major event also for the Christians of Overseas Chinese Communities. On 18 February, the Pope, meeting with their representatives at the Manila Apostolic Nunciature, extended a specific rich message also to "the dear brothers and sisters in China," expressing his "esteem for the great country." He mentioned how the Jesuit Matteo Ricci "understood and appreciated Chinese culture fully from the beginning," regretting that his example was not always followed. He recalled that "a genuine and faithful Christian is also a genuine and good citizen," and stressed that "a good Chinese Catholic works loyally for the progress of the nation, observes the obligations of filial piety towards parents, family and country." Hinting at his desire to open a constructive dialogue with the Chinese authorities, Pope John Paul II repeated that "the Church has no other aim than to be faithful to the mission entrusted to her ... She desires no privileges, but only that all those who follow Christ may be able to express their faith freely and publicly and to live according to their consciences." News of the papal visit was practically ignored by the Chinese press, and comments of the official Catholic structures were along the usual lines: Rome, besides repeating conciliatory words, should prove its respect for the Church in China by acting on the two main bones of contention, the Taiwan issue and the Chinese Church's right to manage its affairs.

As Pope John Paul II continued his pilgrimage in Japan, he asked Cardinal Agostino Casaroli to go and meet Bishop Dominic Deng, then aged 72, who was recovering in Hong Kong from an operation for intestinal cancer. The content of their talks was not revealed, but obviously Deng was seen as a sign of hope by the Vatican. Observers mentioned that the Chinese Church officials surely had sufficient confidence in him as they "reappointed" him Bishop of Guangzhou, and the government was apparently also sure enough of his loyalty to allow him to go to Hong Kong. (In any case, the Cantonese Jesuit was officially reported to have repented his crimes before being released.) Meanwhile the international magazine *Newsweek* (9 March 1981) quoted Bishop Michael Fu recalling that "before liberation in 1949 the Chinese Catholic Church was a 'colonial' religion. And now, after 30 years, we see the need for the church to be independent and autonomous." He then went on mentioning underground activities ("acts of sabotage") against China by people from abroad, hinting that the Vatican might be behind them. Bishop Fu was echoing an alarming message just published as the opening statement in the second issue of the new magazine jointly signed by the

Catholic Patriotic Association and the Church Affairs Commission, entirely written in Chinese but carrying also an English title "The Catholic Church in China."

11. An Unfortunate Blunder

Bishop Dominic Deng, once his health improved to allow him to travel, left Hong Kong for Manila and Italy on 28 April, accompanied by Franco Belfiori, S.J., and two days later he was received privately by Pope John Paul II. His arrival had probably passed unnoticed. A week later in fact, Vatican observer Desmond O'Grady, mentioning Casaroli's invitation to Bishop Deng to go on a visit to the Pope, commented that "Deng would probably need a tacit approval by the Beijing authorities for such trip," and concluded: "It will therefore be important to know when Deng will reach Rome" (cf. *Il Mondo*, 8 May 1981). It was later revealed that in early May Bishop Deng made a courtesy visit to the Chinese embassy in Rome, where he was politely received by the officer in charge, in the absence of the ambassador, but there had been no discussion of specific issues. Deng met John Paul II again a few days before the assassination attempt on the Pope (on 13 May) that polarized world attention. In the weeks that followed, the bishop visited some old friends and schoolmates, besides going as a pilgrim to Lourdes and Fatima. At the beginning of June he was back in Rome, attending the centenary celebrations of the Councils of Constantinople and Ephesus at Pentecost.

Things changed dramatically on Saturday 6 June, the eve of Pentecost, when *L'Osservatore Romano* carried among routine Vatican news the following statement: "The Holy Father has promoted Mons. Dominic Tang (Deng), S.J., to the metropolitan See of Canton, of which he had till then been the apostolic administrator as titular bishop of Elathea" (translation taken from the weekly English edition of 15 June). Technically speaking, Deng's "promotion" was but the recognition of a title due to him already in 1950, when Pope Pius XII made him responsible of the Canton archdiocese; at that time, to succeed the old French archbishop Fourquet, Dominic Tang (Deng) had in fact been appointed only as apostolic administrator.

But how to judge the sudden decision taken by the Vatican authorities? The way Bishop Deng, being present in Rome, let things develop shows that perhaps, after two decades in prison and in isolation, "his political awareness was insufficient," as somebody wrote afterwards. But the way the Roman Curia bureaucrats have handled the case betrays a total lack of consideration for the delicate situation of the Church and for national feelings in New China. The decision taken with the so-called "promotion" should have been explained first to the Chinese side and a satisfactory account offered to the press and to public opinion.

Over the weekend, the *Osservatore*'s casual news item was generally picked up by the international press as a sign of improved relations between Vatican and Beijing, while no word was coming from China. The situation exploded on 11 June with a violent statement of, Bishop Yang Gaojian on behalf of the official Chinese Church. His accusation was repeated the same day by the official Xinhua agency and widely echoed throughout the whole country. Within days, Deng's elevation was bitterly denounced by various officials of the CCPA and by individual bishops, accusing the Vatican of "rudely interfering in the sovereign affairs of the Chinese Church." On 22 June, the Guangzhou Catholic Patriotic Association declared Deng a "running dog of the Roman Curia" and a traitor of the Chinese people, and voted to dismiss him as bishop. A month later (18 July), a long "Letter to all the clergy and faithful throughout China" signed by the three Church executive committees was circulated among the Catholic communities in the country. Besides accusing the Vatican of spreading rumours and secretly distributing booklets of a reactionary nature, the letter tried to prove the right of the local clergy and faithful to choose their bishops ("this is the apostolic tradition"). Soon after, the Xinhua agency reported the solemn consecration in Beijing of five new bishops, "democratically" elected by their respective congregations (for the diocese of Shenyang, Tianshui, Dali, Nanjing and Suzhou); the entire ceremony was filmed by the State television, as "a counter-blow to the Vatican."

The incident had shattered hopes of rapprochement between Holy See and China with Archbishop Deng playing a leading role. It was aptly described as a "blunder on both sides."[35] The failure was bitterly felt in Hong Kong, where Deng was well appreciated. The Director of the Holy Spirit Study Centre, Father John Tong, wrote an accurate account of the event for the Chinese diocesan weekly and for the magazine *Tripod/Ding*.[36] He offered also some useful suggestions to help break the impasse caused by lack of communication and understanding between China and the Vatican. The first issue of *Tripod/Ding*, the new bilingual publication of the Holy Spirit Study Centre, had come out rather timidly in January 1981. Today, over three decades later, it is rightly appreciated as a major link and support of the Hong Kong Church to the sister Churches in the Mainland. Counting on a committed research and editorial staff, *Tripod* is happily reaching out to its 35th volume.

At the beginning of October 1981, the China-Canada Programme organized in Montréal an international conference on "China and the Churches: A New Beginning." Among the 150 delegates personally invited (in majority Protestants), eleven were from China, with four Catholics. I found the gathering quite informative. In the concrete context, the position of the official Chinese Catholic leadership was proposed as could be expected; but bishops Michael Fu Tieshan and Anthony Tu Shihua did not try to impose their presence at the Eucharist celebrated by the participating Catholic priests.

---

[35] R. Pascoe (Reuter), "Bishop Tang (Deng) affair was blunder on both sides," *H.K. Standard* (3 July 1981).

[36] *Kung Kao Po* (17 July 1981); *Tripod/Ding* No. 4 (1981), pp. 29-31: "The Vatican approach and the feeling of the Chinese."

12. The Priority of Promoting Friendship

In the same month of October 1981, an international gathering to celebrate the Jesuit Martino Martini (1614–1661) was held in Trento (Italy).[37] The participation of some scholars from the Beijing Academy of Social Sciences and Academia Sinica, which had been negotiated during previous ICI's visits, highlighted the importance of Martino Martini as a missionary and a recognized scientist.

A new official delegation of the ICI went to China in December 1981, at the invitation of Mr. Wang Pingnan's CAFFC. As I was asked by Senator Vittorino Colombo to join in, it was for me a fresh chance to meet with State officials and get acquainted with new expressions of Chinese society and its modernization efforts. Besides Beijing, the programme included Hangzhou, Shanghai and Guangzhou. In the capital, of particular interest proved the meeting we had at the People's Assembly Hall with Vice Premier Bo Yibo, who spoke of the Chinese priorities to reform the economy and bureaucratic structure. Also interesting was a visit to the Beijing University, where the rector Professor Zhang Longxiang told us that he had recently signed a cooperation protocol with Rome University. Senator Colombo was then invited to give a talk to a selection of students and answer their questions. At a dinner offered at the Italian embassy for the Chinese officers, Wang Pingnan recalled the meeting Senator Colombo had just the previous day with Deng Xiaoping. With reference to the Vatican question, the Chinese leader was quoted as saying that, if the Holy See breaks diplomatic relation with Taiwan, Beijing is ready to discuss positively the various standing problems. But on the same day (13 December 1981) Xinhua published a denunciation by Zhang Zhiyi, deputy head of the CCP's United Front, of "increasing infiltration by reactionary foreign religious forces," following the wishes of the *Curia Romana* ... While in the capital, we paid a short visit also to the restored tomb of Matteo Ricci, which stands out in the ancient small cemetery between those of Adam Schall and Ferdinand Verbiest. An archaeologist of the ministry of Cultural Treasures explained that the bilingual main stone of Ricci's tomb had been knocked down by the Red Guards but not broken, nor the body been touched.

On a Sunday afternoon I had an unexpected encounter. That morning, while standing at the gate of the (still closed) Dongtang church along Wangfujing road, I was approached by a man who, speaking French, expressed the wish to talk about Church problems, and we agreed to meet again that afternoon. As he saw me arriving, he just started walking casually at my side for a while; then he mentioned that his name was Jacques and that he would be glad if I could visit his home. Wouldn't that be dangerous for him, I asked. No, he assured, as he lives outside the urban area; besides, he had taken precautions. We boarded a couple of buses and then walked five minutes towards a railway yard, to a building where he lived with other co-workers. On the way he told me that his family had

---

[37] The Acts of such Symposium were published (in Italian and English) under the title: *Martino Martini. Geografo – Cartografo – Storico – Teologo. Atti del Convegno Internazionale* (Trento 1983).

converted to Christianity some 300 years before and had known martyrdom. He, after studying theology with the Lazarist Fathers, had taken the vows in 1957, but the religious communities were soon disbanded and he asked and obtained dispensation and married; yet, soon he and his wife were sent to labour camps. He knows all the priests at Nantang church, but he feels that they do not like to see him. Now he works on the trains and his wife is a nurse at a railway clinic: today, being Sunday, she is having rest. At a certain point he asks whether I am a priest. I answer vaguely: "What do you think?" and he looks at me smiling ... As we entered his home, he did not hesitate to introduce me: "He is a priest!" With his wife and a ten year old boy (a teenage girl, they mentioned, was out), there was also an elderly lady. They all knelt down asking to be blessed. Mentioning Rome, they then asked if I had seen the Pope: they knew he had been wounded. The old lady, Aloysia by name, explained that she had been in the same labour camp as Jacques's wife; she was a religious sister of the Servants of the Holy Spirit and still remembers German and speaks some French. She had prepared a letter for her congregation, and when I assured that I could take it to Europe, she happily gave it to me, simply wrapped with packing paper. They asked me to bless some water and to sprinkle the house and some holy pictures with it. As they wanted to send their greetings to Pope John Paul II, Jacques sat down to write a short message in Latin, which they all signed. They were happy to receive some rosaries and medals, with a prayer book, that I had with me.

The year ended with the sad news that several Jesuits and some diocesan priests, who had already spent years in labour camps, had been arrested again, including the well-known Zhu Hongshen, in Shanghai and other provinces. This decision was connected perhaps with a general crackdown on Chinese dissidents having contacts with foreigners.

13. New Chinese Constitutional Law and Religious Policy

During 1982, numerous accounts coming from China confirmed the growing presence and vitality of Catholic communities, and at the same time political overtones and accusations often hitting the Vatican. An occasion of fresh misunderstanding was a Letter sent by Pope John Paul II on Lunar New Year to the world bishops asking them to pray for the Church in China; even more provoking appeared his special celebration held for the same purpose on 21 March in Saint Peter Basilica. Though the Pope made no explicit mention of persecution, Bishop Yang Gaojian declared it a "vicious slander" simply implying that Chinese Catholics were being persecuted.

In the first half of April 1982, I was invited to accompany a new group of Italian friends, who had chosen to come first to Hong Kong, entering China via Canton, to Hangzhou, Shanghai, Chengdu, Xi'an and Beijing. I only mention here a few details from my travel notes. In Hangzhou it was possible to meet with a local history professor, Xu Mingde, who helped the local authorities to appreciate the contribution to dialogue and cultural exchange with the West offered in the 17th century by Father Martino Martini; as a consequence, both Martini's tomb and the church erected by him were now being restored. In Shanghai, visiting the history faculty at Fudan University, I had the opportunity to explain the Macerata project to celebrate the 4th centenary of Matteo Ricci's entering China. In Chengdu, visiting the restored cathedral church, though it was not possible to meet Bishop Li Xiting, I could present some sets of church vestments (also for Bishop Duan of Wanxian) offered by Professor Demarchi. We reached Xi'an on Easter Sunday, and could admire the cathedral crowded by devout faithful. Returning there in the evening, I noticed how the church property occupied by the authorities had been used for industrial projects, with a candy factory erected just in front of the cathedral. After the solemn Mass, I had a friendly conversation with Bishop Johannes Ji Huairang. The following day, visiting the ancient Mosque, we had the opportunity to meet and talk also with the local Imam.

The new Constitution of the Country adopted by the People's National Assembly on 4 December, in which article 36 guarantees freedom of religious belief, proved a positive page in China's political life. While a draft of this new Constitution was publicly discussed,[38] the CCP was preparing for its 12th Congress, due in September. In such context, reconsidering the Party's policy on religion was of crucial importance. In June 1982, *Hongqi*, the ideological organ of the Party's Central Committee, came out with a lengthy editorial entitled: "The fundamental policy of our Party on religious questions during the Socialist period." On reading it, I became convinced of its enduring importance, and studied it carefully; commentaries I wrote about such comprehensive view of religion were published in Chicago and Rome.[39] As a matter of fact, more than 30 years later, religious questions are treated in China still according to that "fundamental policy."

A welcoming good news for Catholics was the opening in Shanghai, on 11 October 1982, of the first seminary, with 36 students coming also from neighbouring dioceses. The simple ceremony held at Sheshan hill was presided over by the Jesuit father Aloysius Jin Luxian, the rector, at the presence of Shanghai bishop Zhang Jiashu and other bishops from Jiangsu, Zhejiang and Anhui. In the same month, an International Study Conference on the fourth centenary of the coming of Matteo Ricci to China was held in Macerata and Rome. Pope John Paul II chose to attend the concluding session at the Gregoriana University on 25

---

[38] Published in *Renmin ribao* on 28 April, the following day an official "Explanation" also appeared, suggesting that comments to the draft would be welcome. An Editorial in *Tripod/Ding* No. 9 (June 1982), pp. 71-72, praised the progress made, when compared with the previous Constitutions of the Country. It offered also a double comment: the meaning of "normal" religious activities entitled to receive state protection should be clarified. As for the question of excluding "any foreign domination" in religious affairs: "It is not clear whether the article also includes the unity between the local (Catholic) Church and the universal Church."

[39] "The Chinese Communist Party and Religion," *Missiology. An International Review* XI (July 1983) 3, pp. 267-290; "La politica della Cina Comunista nei confronti della Religione," *Nuova Umanità* No. 34/35 (July/October 1984), pp. 59-99.

October '82. The address he delivered was a significant recognition of Ricci's contribution to mediate between East and West and an authoritative declaration of openness towards New China's realities.[40]

14. Rediscovering Giulio Aleni, the "Scholar from the West"

Just about that time, I was struck by a study on "Giulio Aleni, conveyor of medieval Western learning," which appeared in the bilingual magazine of the Hong Kong Holy Spirit Study Centre.[41] The research by Bernard Hung-kay Luk of the local Chinese University had been inspired by a happy coincidence: The Jesuit Giulio Aleni (1582–1649) was born just as Matteo Ricci was beginning his outstanding experience in China. Having followed Ricci in China, Aleni (Ai Rulüe in Chinese) became one of the most outstanding exemplar of Ricci's methods. After residing in Hangzhou, he spent several years as a trusted and privileged friend of many Chinese scholars in Fuzhou, where he was buried with honour.[42]

Such portrait induced me to learn more about Aleni, in the hope that his memory might open new ways of cooperation and intercultural exchange. In Spring 1983, I was able to spend a week in Fujian province. In the capital Fuzhou, travelling alone I was particularly impressed by the popular support enjoyed by a couple of Protestant churches. Then, on reaching the Cangshan district, south of the river Min, I had a taste of Catholic life right in the compound of the Cathedral of the Holy Rosary. Besides greeting the parish priest, I was introduced to father Joseph Huang Ziyu, who was happy to tell me that he had studied theology in Rome. He explained that his diocese was Xiamen (Amoy), whose former Spanish bishop, J.B. Velasco, O.P., appointed him as vicar capitular in 1948, upon leaving the country. According to him, the great majority of believers, priests and bishops in China (even those officially bound to the patriotic structures), are loyal to our common faith, though they cannot express their heart. In our long conversation he said and insisted that the Holy See should pay more attention to the real needs of the Chinese Church and to the sensitive social situation. Huang considered unacceptable, for instance, that the exiled foreign bishops, almost three decades after their forced departure, still retained the former canonical titles (and authority). He was coming often from Xiamen to Fuzhou to teach some local young people wishing to enter the seminary; he ap-

---

[40] Father Matteo Ricci, the Pope said, "succeeded in establishing between the Church and Chinese culture a bridge, which still appears solid and safe, despite the misunderstandings, which have taken place in the past and are still renewed." He also stressed that "what the Chinese people particularly admire in Father Ricci's scientific work in China is his humble, honest and disinterested attitude, not inspired by ulterior motives and free from links with any foreign economic or military power." See *Papal Documents Related to China, 1937–2005*, p. 310.

[41] *Tripod/Ding* No. 11 (1982), pp. 45-50.

[42] His tomb, on a hill outside the city, had become with time the cemetery of the Catholic community. It was destroyed, unfortunately, during the Cultural Revolution, and the site was taken over by the military.

preciated some books I had with me and the promise to send him more. He mentioned that many members of the Fuzhou community avoid attending services at the cathedral, in whose compound official bishop Lin Quan (ordained in 1958) was still living, as most people believed him to have married. When I paid a visit to Bishop Lin Quan, he also stressed that he felt rather isolated. I then reminded him that the Holy See was ready to reconsider the position of priests and bishops who found themselves in a wrong position, if they expressed the wish to be reconciled. He did not react.

Before returning to Hong Kong I visited briefly also Quanzhou and Xiamen. But my main concern was to know more about Giulio Aleni. Having expressed my interest on Christianity in Fujian to Professor Ma Yong, a Beijing historian who had taken part in the Trento Conference on Martino Martini, he suggested that I should try to meet Professor Lin Jinshui, of the Fuzhou Teachers Training Institute, who had done a doctoral research on Matteo Ricci's writings. So I contacted Lin Jinshui, inviting him to my hotel, and we could spend about one hour together. He knew little about Aleni, and was glad to receive copy of Bernard Luk's article on *Tripod/Ding,* plus one issue on Ricci, and a Chinese translation of Dunne's *Generation of Giants*. He was somehow intrigued to hear of my contacts with Zhao Fushan and Li Fuhua at the Beijing Academy of Social Sciences. Hearing of the books I had sent for the Library of the Institute of World Religions and the copies of Fang Hao's historical research on Christianity in China provided also to the Hangzhou University, he felt encouraged to remain in contact and to continue studying Aleni's figure.

Upon returning to Italy, I sadly realized that the great figure of Aleni was practically forgotten even in his native city of Brescia.[43] Luckily, his outstanding stature was fully understood by Monsignor Anthony Fappani who, soon after establishing the "Fondazione Civiltà Bresciana" (1984), expressed his determination to make Giulio Aleni fully appreciated by the Church community as well as by Brescia city. We cooperated to this end with various initiatives. In 1992, during a new visit to Fuzhou, I could meet the new bishop Joseph Zheng Changcheng, an outstanding Church figure.[44] He remembered well how Aleni's tomb was, on the hillside, before being destroyed. At the request of Professor Lin Jinshui, Bishop Zheng agreed to take us on his car up to the military limit; proceeding then on foot, we reached the place, but no trace of the original tomb was

---

[43] A portrait of Giulio Aleni presented in 1950 by Mario Santambrogio in a scholarly series ("Memorie storiche della diocesi di Brescia") had passed practically unnoticed by the community. It was only in 1988 that Fausto Balestrini included in a popular book (*Uomini di Brescia*) also "Padre Giulio Alenis, missionario gesuita in Cina – 1582-1649."

[44] Bishop Joseph Zheng Changcheng (1990-2006) had been made diocesan administrator of Fuzhou in 1951 by exiled Bishop T. Labrador, O.P.; he then spent over 20 years in prison. When, at the end of the 1980s, the authorities insisted that he accepted the episcopal ordination, he was able to impose his own conditions. Most local Catholics showed him great respect.

visible.[45] In October 1994, the Fondazione Civiltà Bresciana organized an International Symposium on Giulio Aleni (the "Scholar from the West"), joyfully participated by the entire city of Brescia.[46] Among the numerous sinologists who participated from different countries, most appreciated was the presence of Professor Lin Jinshui with a delegation from Fuzhou city.

I am particularly happy to recall how the Monumenta Serica Institute of Sankt Augustin actively participated in the international Brescia Symposium on Giulio Aleni. As a matter of fact, it was such close cooperation that offered me the opportunity to know and appreciate Professor Roman Malek, S.V.D. who committed himself deeply in the event and assured a splendid edition of the Symposium Acts.[47] The success of the symposium proved a stimulus for the Fondazione Civiltà Bresciana to look for new initiatives aiming to make Aleni better known and loved:[48] most challenging, the project (still under way) of translating into Italian all of his works, originally published in Chinese.

---

[45] Insisting in his research, Professor Lin was finally able to unearth Aleni's tomb stone, as he wrote me enthusiastically on 8 March 1996: See *Quaderni del Centro Giulio Aleni* No. 4 (2014), pp.19-21.

[46] A colourful exhibition attracted many visitors, and a comprehensive biography produced by Eugenio Menegon helped to make known the ancient missionary: *Un Solo Cielo. Giulio Aleni S.J. (1582–1649). Geografia, Arte, Scienza, Religione dall'Europa alla Cina* (Brescia 1994).

[47] Tiziana Lippiello – Roman Malek (eds.), *"Scholar from the West." Giulio Aleni S.J., (1582–1649) and the Dialogue between Christianity and China,* jointly published by Fondazione Civiltà Bresciana, Brescia, and Monumenta Serica, Sankt Augustin (Nettetal 1997).

[48] For an idea of the growing interest on Aleni, see a brief note of mine ("Alla riscoperta di padre Giulio Aleni"), in: *Padre Giulio Aleni, S.J. il Confucio di Occidente,* Atti del convegno nazionale di studi, 12 settembre 2007 (Brescia 2009), pp. 43-54.

UPDATING THE CHINA MISSION
GUIDED BY POPE BENEDICT XVI AND POPE FRANCIS

JEROOM HEYNDRICKX

Introduction

Church renewal – which started after Vatican II – means: the Church, in faithfulness to the Gospel and in line with the Vatican II documents tries to respond better to the needs of the times. For China missionaries, it implies that also the way of doing mission to China must be revised. By his letter to the Church in China Pope Benedict XVI showed us the way to do that. It is our task to define more concretely what this updated China Mission implies. Reinventing China Mission is an historical task for the Church in China, for the Universal Church and for all missionary congregations involved in evangelization in China. To be able to do that we must first reflect on questions as: why did the pope write a letter to the Church in China? How did it come about? What was the genesis of that letter? Understanding the answer to these questions will help us in updating the content of China Mission. Following are some reflections and suggestions in answer to these questions. They are based on conversations and encounters during 35 years (since 1980) of visiting China.

Vatican II Prompts Us to Reinvent the China Mission

Already for 50 years – ever since 1965 – the Universal Church is engaged in church renewal. Communities of the People of God (*Lumen Gentium*) celebrate their unity in the Lord inspired by the Word of God (*Dei Verbum*). Bishops are confirmed as the guiding shepherds of their flock in each autonomous Local Church (*Christus Dominus*) closely united with their brothers in the priesthood (*Optatum Totius*) and preparing lay faithful to take upon them the pastoral ministry to which they are called (*Apostolicam Actuositatem*). The Church looks for ways to bring "Joy and Hope" (*Gaudium et Spes*) to society in spite of the violence and injustice which prevail. She strives to enter into dialogue with different ideologies and religions (*Nostra Aetate*) and revises her ways of mission (*Ad Gentes*) to different cultures and societies. To implement all those documents is a huge undertaking that justifies saying: indeed the Church has to reinvent itself. This represents probably the biggest effort ever of the Church to update itself. We should not be surprised therefore that after 50 years we seem to have achieved so little. Much more time is needed to make the beautiful Vatican II dream come true. We should rather admit that much was achieved already but more and even bigger challenges lie in front of us.

This applies also to the Church in China and to the mission of evangelization to Chinese people. There is a need to reinvent the China Mission in faithfulness to the Gospel and to Vatican II and that is also a huge task; all the more because both the Church and China have changed so much. The Catholic Church of Vatican II is no more the Catholic Church of the time when Mao Zedong came to power. China after the Open Door Policy of Deng Xiaoping (starting in 1978) is very different from the China at the time of Mao. The Church in China today tries to implement the ideal of Vatican II while at the same acculturating itself to the People's Republic of China. She has to overcome century-old obstacles and prejudices before she can achieve that. Here too we should not be surprised that it takes so long before there is a breakthrough. During the last 40 years the Church of China met with opposing views between authorities of China and of the Universal Church. Attempts by the Church to overcome these difficulties were repeatedly blocked, sometimes by the opposite party, sometimes by people from its own camp.

Missionaries from outside China offer help and seek to cooperate with the Church in China. But one often wonders whether they are fully aware that their role in the China Mission has changed considerably. The concrete implementation of Mission in China is in the hands of Chinese bishops, no more in the hands of religious missionary congregations as it used to be.

Such a delicate and crucial revision can only happen in a serene atmosphere that allows dialogue inside China, dialogue between the Church in China and civil authorities as well as between authorities of the Universal Church and China. Confrontation can only produce more confusion. In the encyclical *Ecclesiam Suam* (Paul VI) the Church has officially accepted dialogue as a guiding principle. Pope Francis has from the beginning shown that he follows the line of dialogue to make the Church into the "Church of Mercy." China has also, since the beginning of its Open Door Policy, officially expressed that it wishes to dialogue with different ideologies. Both Beijing and the Vatican have taken initiatives towards dialogue and achieved some results. That is the big change. But we all observe that both Beijing and the Vatican are learning through experience, trial and error. Not everybody in the Church or in China backs the line of dialogue. Even though there are no signs of a breakthrough, the very fact that dialogue between the Vatican and Beijing is carried on at all means progress. It proves that leaders in both China and the Vatican decided not to follow the advice of those in their own camp who promote confrontation. Another reason for hope is the fact that the predecessor of Pope Francis had already drawn up a road map for dialogue with China, namely the letter of Pope Benedict XVI to the Church in China. This letter is so fundamental to our subject that we should first reflect on some questions related to it: What is its history, its genesis? Why did the pope write this letter? How does it help us to revise the China Mission?

The Letter of Pope Benedict XVI:
The Compass that Guides Us in Updating the China Mission

The pastoral letter written by Pope Benedict XVI to the Church in China in 2007 is one of the most important documents in the history of the Church in China. Its importance is often underestimated. When it was promulgated it was generally applauded as a call from the Vatican to the Church in China to restore unity. Some, however, requested that parts of it needed to be "clarified" – in fact to be revised – and that weakened the effect of the letter. Without this questioning the initiatives towards restoring unity in China in answer to the letter would have been more generally spread and more efficient. In spite of that, the letter continues to serve till today as the compass that guides the Universal Church, the Church in China and also the China missionaries in their efforts to revise the China Mission. The fact that we have at our disposal such a compass is in itself an enormous achievement but it came about only as the fruit of a painful struggle.

The letter should not and cannot be separated from certain events that prompted its writing. Without these events no pope could have written such a letter. I refer here to the doubts, the struggle and disagreements that preceded the writing of the letter. These grew out of the concrete situation of the Church in China after the Cultural Revolution (1966–1976). The Church faced its own painful internal division. Confronting this, justifying or explaining it caused misunderstandings and pain within the Christian community. The Vatican, bishops and priests in China as well as missionaries engaged in a difficult search to find the correct answer. We see these disagreements and misunderstandings inside the church community of believers and the answers they came up with as efforts of believers who, true to their own faith, tried to overcome divisions and misunderstandings. I refer here to the documents "13 Points" and the "8 Points" which were the object of controversy for so long. We see them as efforts not to create further division but to build unity. Only these apparent causes of division could make the writing of the letter of the pope possible and necessary.

I share here below what I remember from my own experience and personal notes during the 25 years preceding the publication of the letter. Recalling facts that happened during these years will help us to appreciate the progress that in fact has been made. It will hopefully help and motivate us to look ahead with hope also today.

Lack of Factual Information:
The Problem of the Vatican during the 1980s and 1990s

On December 6, 1980, I met (quite unexpectedly) with Pope John Paul II in Rome for the first time. The Pope said: "If you can go to China please go and try to understand whether there is a schismatic church or not; because we do not know." These words reflected the true situation in Rome. At that time the Vatican received much information from the "unofficial church community" (often called the "underground"). Quite understandably this information reported on the suffering which the Chinese faithful had gone through. The reports caused much sympathy in the Vatican for the fate of the unofficial church community. But the "official church community" (often called "patriotic") sent practically no reports because they were unable to communicate with Rome. Whatever Rome understood about the official church community was therefore based only on the critical and aggressive articles against the Vatican published in Catholic periodicals in

China: *Zhongguo Tianzhujiao* 中国天主教 (Catholic Church in China). They caused of course no sympathy at all from Rome. On the opposite, they created the impression that an independent (i.e., schismatic) Catholic Church was growing in China. But were these publications reliable? It was generally believed that, in many cases, the name of the authors who signed the aggressive articles against the Vatican did not represent the real author. The unofficial community succeeded in communicating quite a bit with Rome, the official community did not. This made it difficult for the Vatican to obtain an objective view of the situation. There was a need for personal testimony of the faithful, priests or bishops of the official community inside China.

Starting from my first visit to China, I always made it a point to meet with bishops, priests, and the faithful of both the official and the unofficial communities. In the early years that was quite possible. I listened to their dramatic stories without making any comments out of respect, for it was clear to me that the two church communities were both going through painful experiences. I reported objectively to the Holy Father about what I learned: the isolation, persecution, and suffering of the unofficial community. Official bishops were ordained illegally, some of the clergy were married. Yet there was also the big good news which I could share with the Holy Father, namely that there was no schism. In spite of all what was written or said, in spite of internal disagreements, all prayed the same *Credo* as the Universal Church does and all wished to remain united with the Pope and the Universal Church.

But I knew very well that the Holy Father, while he was happy to hear my report, would probably the day after my visit hear or read another report from another China visitor stating that there really was a schism – the opposite of what I reported. What could Rome do? The situation was similar to the time of the historical Rite Controversy of the Jesuits, when the popes heard missionaries from one side reporting "white" and missionaries from the other side reporting "black." It took patience, time and much charity to evaluate correctly the reliability of the various reports.

Events of the 1980s and 1990s Leading to the Letter of Pope Benedict XVI

In 1985 Bishop Fan Xueyan (1907–1992, Baoding) officially declared in a letter to his faithful that the official church community was schismatic and that the faithful attending their Mass committed mortal sin and would go to hell. His letter became later known as the "Thirteen Points" document. It was signed by Bishop Fan Xueyan but faithful in Hebei repeated that a layman was the real author. The letter spread the "mortal sin rule" among the whole unofficial community forbidding the faithful to attend the Eucharist in any official church community. Some unofficial bishops disagreed with Bishop Fan. Several China visitors who had contact with both church communities also disagreed. Still the document caused confusion and more division inside the Church of China. Christians of two communities started from then on to celebrate the Eucharist in separate communities while confessing their unity with Rome and the Universal Church. This division inside China was also reflected in the Universal Church outside China. Pope John Paul II was concerned about this situation.

At that time Archbishop Ryan (former archbishop of Dublin) was appointed as the new Prefect of the Propaganda Fide (SCEP), succeeding Cardinal Agnello Rossi. He confessed to be totally ignorant of the situation in China and anxiously asked left and right for clarification and advice from China visitors. He learned how confusing the situation was and thought that something should be done. He considered calling a meeting of experts from around the world in the Vatican to exchange views and ask for their advice to the Holy See. Unfortunately, he died suddenly after only six months in Rome and was unable to organize and preside that planned China meeting.

Still the three-day meeting took place in early March 1986. I consider it as one of the best – if not the best – meeting I ever attended in Rome. The Vatican had meant it to be confidential, even secret. But on the second day of the meeting the list of all participants was published in a newspaper in Hong Kong, causing Vatican authorities to be quite upset. Among the (about 15) participants were cardinals, bishops and experts in charge of dicasteries of the Holy See and also experts representing the churches of Hong Kong and Taiwan as well as missionary congregations. They each reflected whole range of existing viewpoints on the situation of the Church in China: some were more open, others less open or even closed and very conservative. But this precisely allowed for a frank and open sharing of information and opinions – without confrontation – putting the complexity of the issue clearly on the table. That is exactly what was needed and what made the meeting successful.

At the very end of the meeting came a request of the Holy Father: a document should be written expressing the view of the Holy See on the situation of the Church in China, addressed to the Chinese faithful of both communities. It should also serve as a guideline for visitors from abroad to China informing them on how to behave in their contacts with the two church communities. Two participants of the meeting – one Chinese and one non-Chinese – were asked to write a first draft. We later learned that this draft was submitted in September 1986, but it was not approved by the Holy See. In the course of 1987, other drafts were written by different authors but, apparently, those were also not approved. Finally, in October 1988 Rome promulgated a document which became known as the "Eight Points." This document did not repeat verbally the accusation "schismatic church" as expressed in the "Thirteen Points" document but it confirmed in fact the controversial rule that attending Mass at the official community was mortal sin. The document provoked reactions mainly from those who visited China more regularly and who had contact with both communities. To the disappointment of Rome, Manila openly disagreed and called the document obsolete and not reflecting objectively the situation in the Church of China.

Nevertheless the "Eight Points" document – including the "mortal sin" pastoral rule – remained the guiding line for the unofficial church community all through the 1990s. It confirmed the internal division instead of alleviating it and this disappointed many inside and outside of China. Bishops in China as well as missionaries continuously expressed the hope that authorities in Rome should clarify this situation as soon as possible. But then the events of Tiananmen (1989), the aggressive White Paper on Religion (1997) and even more the illegal ordinations that happened in Beijing on Epiphany 2000 caused new commotion and controversy. In this situation Rome apparently did not find it opporune to come up with any new document for fear of creating even more confusion. In the course of the 1990s the opinion grew among pastors in China that the "mortal sin rule" would disappear and die out by itself. But inside the pastoral situation of the Chinese flock, the need was continuously expressed that a way should be found to break the continuous harm done to the faithful by repeating the "mortal sin rule."

In 2003 one unofficial bishop even wrote a letter to the official bishops of the dioceses in his neighborhood – who were in fact his good friends – inviting them to publicly concelebrate and openly state that they were all united with the Pope and the Universal Church. That was a daring step which honestly reflected his personal opinion. It would openly make clear to his Christians and those of other dioceses that there was no reason for the "mortal sin rule." The concelebration which he proposed never took place but the testimony of his letter remained.

That same year (2003), the Verbiest Foundation organized the European Colloquium on China in Leuven (Belgium), with 100 participants among them 50 Chinese priests and religious studying in Europe. With the agreement of one Vatican official and of the unofficial Chinese bishop who had called for a concelebration with official bishops, we published his letter in Leuven during the colloquium. Cardinal Danneels, with the silent approval of the same Vatican official and referring to the letter of that unofficial bishop expressed the view that time had come to pass beyond the "Eight Points" document and to encourage Christians in China to all join in one Eucharistic celebration. The participants applauded. It sounded almost as if this cleared up the controversy.

But only four months later – in early 2004 – as I visited the church in Xi'an, Bishop Li Du'an showed me a letter in Chinese that was signed by the same Vatican official and sent to all unofficial bishops in China stating "the 'Eight Points' document is still to be followed." That was in contradiction with what only months earlier had been stated to us by the same person. When questioned about it the official admitted that he made a mistake sending out that letter. Also some higher authorities in Rome were upset about this. But the harm had been done. All unofficial authorities had received it and sent it around in hundreds of copies. Priests of the unofficial communities started once again openly forbidding their faithful to participate in the Eucharist of the official communities scaring them "that this was mortal sin and they would go to hell." That message was again promulgated in parishes through loudspeakers every Sunday after the Eucharist.

It became clear that in this situation a higher Church authority in Rome should, for the sake of unity in the Church in China, prepare an official declaration to finally clear up the confusion that had lasted for too long and was now even aggravating. Later that same year (2004) it was said that a small group in the Vatican would draft a statement under direct supervision of higher Church authorities. Whether such a group existed remains a question. No names were ever revealed but it became known that a document was being drafted. The illness of Pope John Paul II followed by his death in 2005 postponed the publication of any document. But those concerned with promoting unity in the internally divided Chinese Catholic community waited anxiously for a statement to be promulgated. Confusion in the pastoral situation in China called for it.

Less than a year after he had become the new pope, Pope Benedict XVI convened a China meeting in the Vatican on January 19-20, 2007. This happened only months after three bishops had been ordained illegally in China provoking a furious reaction and commotion in the media. The same media – mainly in Hong Kong – predicted that the January 2007 meeting called by Pope Benedict XVI would undoubtedly come up with a sharp reaction and perhaps even decide on some excommunications. But to the surprise of everybody the final statement of that China meeting did not include any condemnations or criticism at all. On the opposite, it expressed the hope to engage in a constructive dialogue with Chinese civil authorities so as to overcome the existing misunderstandings. Moreover, the statement announced officially that soon a letter of the Holy Father would be sent to the Church in China. This meant that the pope took upon himself the final drafting of the promised "statement" which had been awaited for so long. The "statement" finally became the historic "Letter of the Holy Father Pope Benedict XVI to the Bishops, Priests and Lay Faithful of the Catholic Church in the People's Republic of China." It was signed by the pope on May 27, 2007.

The meaning and importance of this letter is obviously better understood when one reads it against the background of events that happened in China in the 1980s and 1990s but even also the events of the 1950s. That evolution makes clear that the letter of the pope is the peak and the fruit of a long history.

Documents of the 1980s and 1990s that Contributed to the Letter of Pope Benedict XVI

The first attack of the Communists against the internal unity of the Church happened when the Chinese Catholic Patriotic Association was established in 1957. The situation aggravated when in 1958 two bishops were appointed and consecrated in China without appointment of the pope. These events and the continuation of that policy during the following years tried to impose on Chinese Catholics the independence from Rome of the Catholic Church in China. The faithful did not want that. Some rejected it outright. Others worried about the good of the Church community in the future and chose to "accommodate" to the illegal bishops and the Patriotic Association while remaining faithful in their hearts.

From then on signs of internal division in the Church appeared. The question was raised – in China as well as in Rome – whether there was indeed a "schismatic Church." The "confidential" meeting of bishops and experts in Rome, in March 1986, mentioned above, was called out of concern for this apparent internal division. This also was a first time that the need for "a statement" from Rome was expressed and the first attempt was made to write a statement to create clarity for Catholics in and outside China in order to protect unity. But, apparently – as we have shown above – the time was not yet ripe for publishing such a document. The "Thirteen Points" as well as the "Eight Points" found their roots in the concrete pastoral situation of division inside the Church. They were written by bishops and Christians who cared for the unity of the Church and they represented an important group of Christians in China. In spite of their critical tone – and even though many disagreed with their content – we understand these documents as positive stepping stones and written out of genuine pastoral concern. But the fact remains that they caused internal disagreements. Much time was needed to grow over these disagreements and allow the situation to mature. Only then could Pope Benedict XVI write his important, official statement.

The most important message of the letter is that after the doubts and suspicions of preceding years on the question whether there is a schismatic church community in China or not, the pope – for the first time – formally stated that in the understanding of Rome there was no schismatic Church in China. There was only one Church which, unfortunately, was divided in two communities taking each a different attitude towards the situation they face. No mention is made of any "mortal sin rule." The letter uses a vocabulary that reflects understanding, deep respect and Christian charity for Chinese Christians of both the official and unofficial communities. As it discusses the very complex situation it shows both flexibility and firmness. It points to situations in China which are unacceptable to the Catholic Church; yet it encourages bishops and Church leaders to enter into open dialogue with civil authorities in order to clear up these existing abnormal situations. All this makes the letter an exceptional, historical document, a compass with a message that indicates dialogue as the way to go for the Church in China. It implies that dialogue is also the guiding line of any revision of the China Mission.

Defining More Concretely the Content of the China Mission Today

Our question remains: how to describe more clearly the content of the China Mission today after Vatican II, after the Open Door Policy of China and in the light of the letter of Pope Benedict XVI? This is first of all the task of the Church in China but also China missionaries should do their part in the reflection. The letter of the pope is the compass showing the direction in which the pope wishes the Universal Church as well as the Church in China to search in order to overcome the existing disagreements both internally and with the State of China. But what does that imply concretely? Below is an attempt to define some principles which are in line with the letter of the pope. The suggestions are also based upon impressions which I gathered through conversations in China over the past 35 years. I consider them as basic principles of the China Mission today, a must for anybody who wishes to engage in cooperation with the Church in China.

1 Since There Is Only One Catholic Church in China We Visit All Catholics in China and Do Away with Existing Prejudices

One immediate consequence of the statement that there is only one Church in China is that anybody who engages in the China Mission is expected to deal with both church communities in China on an equal basis avoiding all prejudices for or against anyone of the two. The Universal Church, dealing with persons and situations in the Church of China – in public statements or applying Church law – must avoid using double standards favoring one side and disfavoring the other. Whoever visits the Church in China or plans to cooperate with it, is expected to visit both communities and be open to cooperation with both. If we adopt this attitude, we spread a message fostering unity. If we fail to do so, we foster division whether we do so on purpose or not. Christians of all levels of the Universal Church should reflect on this and check whether we are applying this. Nobody is exempt from this discernment: Christians of the two church communities in China and Christians of the Universal Church as well; Christians on all levels. If all do that, much will change for the good of unity in the Church. This may very well be the most important aspect of updating the China Mission today.

2 We Trust That Chinese Catholics Themselves Will Remake Their Internal Unity

The Holy Father repeatedly invited Chinese Catholics to make an effort at reconciliation. To unite all the Chinese Catholics in one flock is a pilgrimage in faith and healing that will need time. It is a slow process of building up trust among the church communities and their leaders; trust also between the Universal Church and the Church in China. The Universal Catholic Church has an historical duty to fulfill to the Chinese bishops, priests and Catholics, namely: to trust that they themselves will be able to obtain the recognition of the Chinese Catholic hierarchy by their government. The Chinese will be able to achieve these goals by themselves. But they live in a country where people have recently learned to rather distrust other persons, making the situation even more difficult. One cannot program Church unity. It must grow. It is the work of the Spirit in the hearts of priests and Catholics and He works wherever Catholics pray and celebrate Eucharist together. Unity will be achieved only by the Spirit and by Chinese Catholics who respond to the Spirit. The Universal Church rejoices whenever Chinese Catholics of both communities – official and unofficial – celebrate the Eucharist together.

The China Mission can and must contribute to this process not so much by repeating only what the law prescribes but first of all by human friendship, understanding eventually by "fraternal correction" but not without encouraging words of confirmation in faith and prayer. This is in line with what Pope Francis preaches as the "Church of mercy." Fostering Church unity is a meaningful part of the China Mission. We are confident that the grace of the Spirit will win over the forces that try to harm the Church by prolonging its internal division.

3 The China Mission is Guided and Directed by the Chinese Bishops

China missionaries are partners in dialogue and cooperation with bishops and priests in China mutually accepting each other and cooperating on a basis of equality and mutual respect. Even though belonging to different Local Churches they feel united in brotherly communion: "koinonia." Both sides do away with all possible existing prejudices because an honest and open dialogue can only grow from unprejudiced mutual understanding. If a bishop is in an illegal situation, missionaries will, as brothers and sisters in faith, search together with him for ways to normalize his situation. Limiting oneself to continuously reminding bishops of their "illegal situation" (which the bishops themselves know well enough and are anxious about but not yet able to change) is not constructive and not conducive to fruitful cooperation.

Pope Benedict XVI, after observing that there are irregular situations in the Church in China that need to be clarified, states clearly that an independent Church cannot be a true Catholic Church. But he then expresses full trust in the intentions and abilities of the local Chinese bishops and in their judgment to decide on how to deal with local situations: "... the Holy See ... leaves the decision to the individual bishop who, after having consulted his presbyterate, is better able to know the local situation ... ."[1] This is a message for the faithful and priests in China as well as for those who wish to engage in evangelization in China.

Moreover, the pope then repeats what was stated in *Christus Dominus* (the Vatican II Decree on the Pastoral Office of Bishops) as well as in other documents[2] that the bishops of the Local Church in China are the ones guiding and directing the establishment of the Local Church. They must of course follow the guidelines expressed in documents of the Universal Church, but they are the ones to define the pastoral priorities in their diocese. China missionaries will keep in mind that no mission activity can be undertaken in any diocese by missionaries from abroad without the approval of the local bishop.[3]

There is no doubt that contributions by various religious missionary congregations are crucial. By their own respective charisms and expertise they all can contribute to various aspects needed in building a mature Local Church: methods of evangelization, spirituality, social ethics etc. Indeed, many of them participate in this task. However, whereas in the past missionary congregations had a great influence in deciding policies of the China Mission, the stress is now on the service of building the local church. To satisfy the needs of one's own congregation is in itself not a sufficient reason to go to China. A missionary congregation

---

[1] Letter of the Holy Father Pope Benedict XVI to the Church in China, section 7 ("Ecclesial Communities and State Agencies: Relationships to be Lived in Truth and Charity"), see http://w2.vatican.va/content/benedict-xvi/en/letters/2007/documents/hf_ben-xvi_let_20070527_china.html

[2] See also the Vatican document *Lumen Gentium* and also document *Mutuae Relationes* (published in 1978).

[3] *Ibid.*

should first of all agree with the local bishop in which way it can contribute to establising the Local Church community.

4 Mutuality Between Local Churches Is an Important Part of the China Mission

In this time of secularization many Local Churches in the Universal Church and also the Church in China need the confirmation of their faith by Christians from other Churches. Exchange between Local Churches is an important aspect in the practice of Mission today. The faith of Christians in China confirms Christians outside China in their own faith. Rom 1:8-13 inspires our China Mission.

We apply the words of St Paul to the Church in China:

> First, I thank my God through Jesus Christ for all of you, because the whole world is hearing about your faith. God is my witness that what I say is true – the God whom I serve with all my heart by preaching the Good News about his Son. God knows that I remember you every time I pray. I ask that God in his good will may at last make it possible for me to visit you now. For I want very much to see you, in order to share a spiritual blessing with you to make you strong. What I mean is that both you and I will be helped at the same time, you by my faith and I by yours. You must remember, my brothers, that many times I have planned to visit you but something has always kept me from doing so.

In the past, China missionaries from outside China were living in China, actively preaching the Word and building up communities of faith. These have now become Chinese communities guided by their own shepherds who autonomously guide their Church. When and where needed they do invite China missionaries for occasional and temporary cooperation and also for visits. They also like to visit church communities abroad and receive visits from Christians and their shepherds from other Local Churches. The China Mission is so not limited to China missionaries. It is an exchange between local church communities. This kind of exchange has become a new meaningful part of the China Mission.

5 The Ministry of Reconciliation Is an Important Part of the China Mission

Unity inside the Christian community was the main concern of the Lord Jesus. Fostering reconciliation is a ministry needed by every Christian community. In the particular situation of the Church in China overcoming division is a priority task and part of the China Mission. Missionaries are automatically confronted with existing situations of internal division in China. A spirituality of reconciliation gives them the courage to speak words of peace and unity when meeting with Christians trying to overcome differences. After the explicit calls of the Holy Father towards unity, fostering reconciliation has become a priority pastoral concern. Years ago joint Eucharistic celebrations of the two communities were discouraged, even severely forbidden. They are now to be encouraged because the Eucharist is the channel through which the Holy Spirit inspires unity in faith. In any pastoral program the promotion of joint Eucharistic celebrations of the two communities deserves priority attention.

6 The China Mission Should Contribute to Dialogue between Church and Society in China

At the time of Matteo Ricci, Adam Schall von Bell, Ferdinand Verbiest and their Jesuit confreres, dialogue of the Church with the Chinese society was an important and successful part of their China Mission. The situation degenerated after the Opium War and all through the 19th and a great part of the 20th centuries. After the Communist takeover there was even confrontation which caused considerable harm to the Church and caused its internal division. The letter of the pope and its call for dialogue is an historical attempt to end this confrontation. The Church in China as well as China missionaries are thereby called upon to take initiatives that develop cooperation between Church and society in China. Many missionaries have been doing this. More can and should be done.

One of the privileged channels of cooperation with institutes in China are the universities and institutes of higher learning. Scholars engaged in historical research deal precisely with events that caused the prejudices and loss of trust between East and West. They study the documents in which China and the West explain the historical events, each giving its own ideologically prejudiced version. China missionaries who actively participate in this research using strictly academic scientific norms to "seek truth from facts" contribute to the improvement of the relation of the Church in China with its society and also to the relation between China and the Universal Church. *Veritas liberabit* (The truth shall make you free).[4]

All through history the Church in China has been involved in social development, education and health care. Today, more than ever before, cooperation with the Church in China in these fields in an attitude of service that contributes directly to building up friendship and trust. It helps the Local Church to become an active part of its own society and overcomes prejudices of Chinese citizens and authorities against foreign missionaries.

The Church in China is confronted with a great challenge for which it needs encouragement and trust, namely: to dialogue with its own government in order to obtain official recognition of the Chinese Catholic hierarchy. Catholic bishops are not just administrators but pastors of their diocese and members of the Universal College of Bishops presided by the pope. To complete this difficult dialogue is the Chinese Local Church's historical challenge and duty. We respect the guidelines of the letter of Pope Benedict XVI who encourages the Local Church in China to dialogue with civil authorities in China honoring the principle of the gospel: "Give to Caesar what belongs to Caesar and to God what belongs to God" (Mt 22:21).[5]

---

[4] Jn 8:32.

[5] Letter of the Holy Father Pope Benedict XVI to the Church in China, section 7.

7 Learning to Be "Servus Inutilis" (Useless Servant)

After the China missionary has done all this he remembers what the Lord Jesus said: "And after you have done all what you have been commanded, say 'we are useless servants; we have done only what we were obliged to do'" (Luke 17:10). This summarizes yet another part of the spirituality that inspires the China missionary. Without this he will not be able to live meaningfully such a demanding China Mission. Learning this spirituality of service is an important aspect of the formation of a China missionary today. To be a China missionary today requires not only knowledge but first of all the spirituality of a servant.

8 Searching with Pope Francis for "True Unity in the Richness of Diversity"

On July 27, 2013 Pope Francis said, "What is needed now is not unanimity, but true unity in the richness of diversity."[6] Although the pope said this to South American bishops it applies to what the Church in China needs today. The pope also spoke of church ministers "capable of walking with people in the night, of dialoguing with their hopes and disappointments, of mending their brokenness." The whole Church needs that; the Church in China too. Pope Francis is the shepherd who can inspire the China Mission. And it is with this pope – and his delegates – that the Communists are now in dialogue searching to overcome some obstacles towards creating a normal pastoral situation of the church. The whole Church of China and all China missionaries look and pray with great hope towards a positive outcome of these efforts: not necessarily unanimity but unity in the richness of diversity.

Conclusion

Soon after Mao Zedong came to power (1949), it was clear that the China Mission had to be revised significantly in the future. Later Vatican II (1965) introduced even bigger changes inside the Church and in its mission of evangelization; and after Mao had died, the Open Door Policy of Deng Xiaoping (1978) changed China once again fundamentally. The Church went through a crisis learning how to deal with critical events in China: the establishment of the Chinese Patriotic Association (1957), the ordination of the first illegal bishops (1958) and the Cultural Revolution (1966-1976). Then suddenly the Open Door Policy brought peace and new hope; but the internal division of the Church became also evident and clear. When Bishop Fan Xueyan promulgated the "Thirteen Points" document (1985) calling the official church community schismatic, precisely at that same time some bishops of the official ("patriotic") community (among others Bishop Dong Guangqing of Wuhan) were taking big risks by secretly – without permission of civil authorities – applying to the Holy See to be legally appointed by the pope.

---

[6] Pope Francis speaking to South American bishops on July 27, 2013.

All these facts, including the writing of the "Eight Points" document, represent stepping stones of the pilgrimage of the Church which matured and culminated in the letter by Benedict XVI: a prophetic document of grace offered to the Church today as a compass to find its way, through dialogue, to a better future passing beyond the confusion of the past.

The content of an updated China Mission as described here is not new. This article may be an opportunity for readers in- and outside China to ask themselves the following questions: in our approach to the Church in China, are we as unprejudiced to the two church communities as Pope Benedict XVI in his letter? Are we free from using double standards in our judgments and decisions? Are we open and able to follow the advice of Pope Francis and "dialogue with the hopes and disappointments and able to mend the brokenness of brothers and sisters in both communities of the church in China?" Our honest positive answer to these questions would be a sign that we are involved in a well-updated China Mission.

FIT FOR RELIGIOUS SERVICES?
THE REQUIREMENTS FOR RELIGIOUS PERSONNEL IN TODAY'S CHINA WITH A SPECIAL FOCUS ON THE OFFICIAL PROTESTANT CHURCHES

EVELINE WARODE

1. The Situation of Religious Personnel in China Today

An ongoing increase of religious activities in China has occurred since the re-opening of churches and temples in 1979 and the reform of relevant policies in the Peoples Republic of China (PRC).[1] For that reason, all of the five officially recognized religions in China – Daoism, Buddhism, Islam, Catholicism, and Protestantism – have had to cope more or less with an increased demand in what we may delicately term "religious market."[2] In the author's opinion, one of the central factors for the performance of a religion in the market is the religious personnel who clearly play an important role because of the various services they provide for their respective churches and society at large. This article aims therefore to offer some initial insights into a few of the key aspects which are related to the situation of religious personnel in the PRC today. We will first view the situation of religious personnel in the religious market. Obviously, as we will see, an under-supply of ministry-linked personnel has created a high demand for religious personnel as such. We will then consider a variety of aspects related to the effects which governmental regulations have had in the past, and continue to have at present on the situation of religious personnel, in particular in the official Protestant Churches. Finally, we will focus on questions related to what we may term the social security of religious personnel in today's PRC.

1.1 The Religious Market

It is not easy to grasp the situation distinctive to the religious market in the PRC because there is no general tradition of formal membership in religious institutions.[3] Some people do not want to give information about their religious activities.[4] Some are affiliated with a certain religious community, but others simply occasionally attend religious activities of one or more institutional religions, or

---

Translations of German and Chinese quotations are by the author, unless otherwise stated.

[1] Yang Fenggang 2005, p. 429; Madsen 2010, pp. 162-164; Liu Chengyou 2012, p. 231; and Duan Qi 2013, p. 273.
[2] Madsen 2010, pp. 163-164.
[3] Yang 1961, pp. 327-328.
[4] Wenzel-Teuber 2012, p. 31.

perhaps of one or the other folk belief.[5] Therefore statistics on the number of believers are often incomplete. As a result, we must handle statistical data carefully.

In 2005, the sociologist Yang Fenggang stated that nearly all of the government-sanctioned Protestant churches which were reopened after 1979 in urban areas were regularly overcrowded, because their limited number is not able to meet the demand. Furthermore, there has always been a chronic shortage of clergy in these churches. Thus, according to Yang Fenggang, "the clergy/laity ratio was 1:508 in 1982 and 1:556 in 1995."[6]

From 10–26 May 2012 a field study was conducted by a research group from the Institute of World Religions of the Chinese Academy of Social Sciences (Zhongguo shehui kexueyuan 中国社会科学院) concerning the present situation of religions in the prefecture-level cities Kaifeng and Nanyang, Henan province (including also the counties and county-level cities under their administration).[7] If we take the data of the corresponding official statistics into account, in 2011 there were the following clergy/laity ratios for Kaifeng and Nanyang:

Diagram 1: Clergy/laity ratios of Kaifeng and Nanyang

	Kaifeng	Nanyang
Buddhism	1:216	1:539
Daoism	1:188	1:504
Islam	1:1,259	1:1,188
Catholicism	1:250	1:544
Protestantism	1:168	1:272

Source: Compare data as quoted in Duan Qi 2013, p. 254; Wenzel-Teuber 2014, p. 31.

In 2014 Luo Yingfu, Deputy Director and Secretary General of the Protestant China Christian Council (CCC) / Three-Self Patriotic Movement (TSPM) of Guizhou province, states in the official Protestant magazine *Tianfeng* 天风 that in Guizhou province, there are only 56 pastors, 20 teachers and 316 elders who care for about 400,000 believers.[8] This means that the clergy/laity ratio in Guizhou province is about 1:1,020. In addition, Luo Yingfu demands that the size and the allocation of churches should be adapted to the changes of population distribution according to the flow of migrant workers, tourists, students, and so on, who move about in the course of economic development.[9]

As seen from this data selection, the clergy/laity ratios differ from place to place and from religion to religion, and can lie between 1:168 and 1:1,259. What

---

[5] Wenzel-Teuber 2012, pp. 29-32; Lu Yunfeng 2014, pp. 13-15; and Zhu Haibin 2011, pp. 46-50.
[6] Yang Fenggang 2005, p. 429.
[7] Duan Qi 2013, pp. 252-253; for an English overview see Wenzel-Teuber 2014, pp. 31-37.
[8] Luo Yingfu 2014, p. 10.
[9] *Ibid.*

makes the situation more complex is the fact that these ratios are not stable, but change constantly with the flow of migrants, a phenomenon caused by urbanization and economic development. Clergy/laity ratios are not the only clue for an estimation of the situation of the religious market. Another question is: how often do lay people attend religious services?

Lu Yunfeng, Associate Professor of the Department of Sociology at Beijing University, in his analysis of the "Zhongguo jiating zhuizong diaocha" 中国家庭追踪调查 (China Family Panel Studies, CFPS) of 2012, which was carried out in three stages between 2010 and 2012, observes among other things the frequency of religious activities of Chinese believers.[10] According to this CFPS survey, a high percentage of believers of the traditional Chinese religions (Daoism and Buddhism) does not attend religious activities at all (Daoism 60.7% and Buddhism 40.2 %), whereas only 24.7% of the Catholics, 21.9% of the Muslims, and 16.7% of the Protestants abstain from religious activities.[11] And if we look at the aggregated attendance numbers per year, month and week, the attendance of Buddhists and Daoists decreased from 44.8% respectively 29.5% to less than 2%, whereas 54.3% of the Protestants, 30.2% of the Muslims and 23.6% of the Catholics attended religious services from one to several times a week.[12] Because of the very low total number of the sample (see Diagram 2), these attendance numbers are surely not accurate with regard to the overall Chinese population, but, in the author's opinion, at least show a certain tendency.

Diagram 2: Attendance at religious activities

	Not at all	One to several times per year	One to several times per month	One to several times per week	Total number of sample
Buddhism	40.2%	44.8%	13.4%	1.6%	1,412
Daoism	60.7%	29.5%	8.9%	0.9%	112
Islam	21.9%	45.9%	2.0%	30.2%	96
Protestantism	16.7%	19.5%	9.6%	54.3%	396
Catholicism	24.7%	38.9%	12.9%	23.5%	85
Other	79.5%	10.8%	3.6%	6.0%	83

Source: Compare data of CFPS 2012 as quoted in Lu Yunfeng 2014, p. 23.

Therefore, we can conclude that the offer of weekly services for Protestants, Muslims and Catholics in general might be higher than that for Daoists and Bud-

---

[10] Lu Yunfeng 2014, p. 11. In the explanation of the random sample, which included all persons living in 16,000 households of 25 provinces, cities and autonomous regions, Lu Yunfeng refers readers to http://www.isss.edu.cn/cfps/ for further information. Among other places, Xinjiang, Tibet, Qinghai, Inner Mongolia, Ningxia, and Hainan are all excluded from the random sample. This leads to an underestimate of the proportion of Buddhism and Islam adherents (Lu Yunfeng 2014, pp. 11-12).

[11] Ibid., p. 23.

[12] Ibid.

dhists, whose participation in temple activities may amount to merely one or, at best, several times a year or month. This obviously suggests that the workload for the religious personnel of Protestantism, Islam, and Catholicism presumably may be higher than that of the religious personnel for traditional Chinese religions.

1.2 The Impact of Laws and Regulations

In China, there has been a long tradition of regulating the growth of institutional religions by the limitation of the number of clergy and sites for religious activities.[13] Today on the basis of the "Regulations on Religious Affairs" (Zongjiao shiwu tiaoli 宗教事务条例) of the State Council of the PRC, which stipulate a duty of registration for religious personnel,[14] there are several more concrete "Measures" (banfa 办法) of the State Administration for Religious Affairs (SARA) which must be followed, concerning, for example, such topics as the reporting of religious personnel and chief posts for the record or the approval of qualification certificates, assessment of professional titles and appointment of teachers at institutes for religious education.[15]

According to the "Measures for Reporting Religious Personnel for the Record," on one hand all religious organizations are required to report the names of religious personnel for registration in official files, and on the other hand, the relevant state authorities must check to be certain that the person concerned is acknowledged according to the relevant "Measures" of the national religious organization of that particular religion.[16] Therefore, a person without affiliation to a particular religious organization, e.g., the CCC and the TSPM in the case of the Protestant Churches, is unable to be confirmed as official religious personnel.

For the approval of religious personnel by religious organizations, the "Measures for Licensing Chinese Protestant Clergy" first of all require a certain qualification according to the various positions of the respective religious personnel.[17] For example, at the minimum, pastors/ministers (mushi 牧师) have to prove they have earned a degree as a result of four years of regular study in theology (shenxue benke 神学本科), plus two years of experience in pastoral work, or a degree of two-years or three-years specialist study in theology (shenxue zhuanke 神学专科), or in Bible school (Shengjing xuexiao 圣经学校), plus three years of experience in pastoral work.[18] Elders (zhanglao 长老) must have a high school degree, five years of experience in pastoral work, and have completed a one-year training course in theology recognized by the CCC/TSPM on the provincial lev-

---

[13] Yang 1961, p. 213.

[14] Document 2005b; for a German translation see Document 2005a.

[15] For an overview of PRC's state regulations concerning religion see Wenzel-Teuber 2013.

[16] Document 2008c, p. 47; for a German translation see Document 2007, p. 31.

[17] Document 2006, pp. 18-19; Document 2007, pp. 25-27.

[18] Document 2006, p. 18; Document 2007, pp. 25-26.

el.[19] Furthermore, before they can take up a post as a member of the clergy, prospective bishops, pastors/ministers, teachers, and elders are required to have received holy orders (*shengzhi* 圣职) which require a public ceremonial act at a Protestant church.[20] This requirement is in accord with the "Church Order of Protestant Churches in China" of January 8, 2008, which stipulates that only properly ordained personnel are allowed to perform the two sacraments of Baptism and Eucharist.[21]

For the appointment of positions of chief of personnel at religious sites, for example, the posts of leading pastors (*zhuren mushi* 主任牧师) or full-time elders (*zhuanzhi zhanglao* 专职长老), the "Measures for Reporting for the Record the Holding of Chief Posts at Sites for Religious Activities" not only require the approval of the local religious organizations, but also a democratic consultation of the administrative body of the site for religious activities. An official evidence of resignation is needed, and a financial inspection on the occasion of resignation from his/her former post must have also occurred.[22] Furthermore, this regulation states that usually religious personnel are permitted to hold a chief post at one religious site alone.[23]

In consideration of all these regulations, we can identify the following three possible obstacles for the expansion of the number of religious personnel:

1. State authorities can limit the number of religious personnel and the number of religious sites.
2. In the event that some Protestant Churches do not want to cooperate with the CCC/TSPM and, loosely speaking, simply do not become CCC/TSPM Churches, religious personnel may not be approved and registered.[24]
3. The prospective religious personnel thus may lack required qualifications.

1.3 The Socio-economic Situation of Religious Personnel

The socio-economic situation of religious personnel of Protestant Churches is not easy to determine. The situation differs according to family background, work unit (*danwei* 单位), for example, religious institutions / religious training places / religious assembly places, household registration (urban/rural *hukou* 户口), and kind of employment (fulltime/part-time work).

---

[19] Document 2006, p. 18; Document 2007, p. 26.

[20] Document 2006, p. 19; Document 2007, p. 26.

[21] Document 2008a, pp. 5-6; also at http://www.ccctspm.org/quanguolianghui/jiaohuiguizhang.html (accessed on August 16, 2016); for a German translation see "Revidierte Kirchenordnung der Chinesischen Evangelischen Kirche," *Chh* XXVII (2008) 6, pp. 209-215, here pp. 211-213.

[22] Document 2008b, pp. 47-48; Document 2007, pp. 32-33.

[23] Document 2008b, p. 48; Document 2007, p. 33.

[24] For further insights in reservations towards CCC/TSPM policies see Duan Qi 2013, pp. 264-268.

In China, the family is traditionally regarded as the basic unit for consumption.[25] Therefore the household income *per capita* is used as an indicator of the economic situation of a family.[26] The author of this article did not find a reliable large scale investigation concerning the salary of religious personnel. The case study of Jin Ke, Central China Normal University, School of Management (Huazhong shifan daxue 华中师范大学, Guanli xueyuan 管理学院) concerning the situation of religious personnel, gives some hints for a first estimation. In interviews conducted in 2009, Jin Ke was told that the salaries of religious personnel in the investigated area were relatively low, in urban areas about 2,000 *yuan* RMB per month, and in rural localities about 1,000 *yuan* RMB.[27] Guan Xinping, Department of Social Work and Social Policy, Nankai University, Tianjin, in a study of poverty and anti-poverty measures of 2011, gives the following figures: poor families income *per capita* after receiving Minimal Living Guarantee benefits was 437.1 *yuan* RMB per month in urban areas and 272.8 *yuan* RMB per month in rural areas. In that particular year, the average income of the population in urban areas was 1,817.5 *yuan* RMB per month, and in rural areas 581.4 *yuan* RMB per month.[28] Compared with these figures, the above cited salaries of religious personnel in 2009 are a bit higher than the average income of the population in 2011, but if 1,000 *yuan* RMB were the only income for a family of three persons in rural areas, the figure would be only slightly above the Minimal Living Guarantee of state projects. According to Jin Ke, religious personnel can improve their situation by going out to preach in other places for a subsidy. In addition, religious personnel sometimes do receive goods from believers, contributions which as a rule are not usually recorded in statistics.[29]

Another important point for an estimation of the socio-economic situation of religious personnel is their social security. In 2010, the publication "Opinions on Appropriately Solving the Social Security Problem of Religious Personnel" was released by the SARA and four other departments, giving details about what we might term "social insurance" for religious personnel. According to their work unit, registered religious personnel are permitted to voluntarily take part in the local insurance systems for health, pension, unemployment, work related accidents, and motherhood.[30] These systems are not yet unified for the whole country, and apart from local disparities, the systems for rural and urban areas are very different.[31]

---

[25] Guan Xinping 2014, p. 273.
[26] *Ibid.*
[27] Jin Ke 2010, pp. 13, 16, and 19. For further details of this study see section 3.1.
[28] Guan Xinping 2014, pp. 270 and 277.
[29] Jin Ke 2010, p. 16.
[30] Document 2010b, pp. 11-12; for a German translation see Document 2010a, pp. 158-160.
[31] Document 2010b, pp. 11-12; Document 2010a, pp. 158-160. For more details about the social insurance policy in rural and urban China see Darimont 2014.

Therefore, Li Mo, Heilongjiang University, Administration Management Research Center (Heilongjiang daxue 黑龙江大学, Xingzheng guanli yanjiu zhongxin 行政管理研究中心) has stated in *Zhongguo zongjiao*, the official journal of SARA, that the following problems must be solved:

First, the basic pension of rural areas is rather low (merely some ten *yuan* RMB per month), and insufficient for supporting oneself in old age. In cases in which religious personnel in urban areas participate in various pension insurance plans, income of the religious personnel must be reported for contribution assessment. The actual income of religious personnel is often not easy to determine. The self-governance and self-supply of Protestant Churches make it particularly difficult for these Churches to pay stable salaries to their religious personnel. Under these circumstances, some Churches report a high annual income for their religious personnel, three times the average income in society for the previous year. In cases such as this, the continuity of the insurance contributions on such a high level is not ensured.[32]

Second, various religions hold different views about voluntary decisions to participate in an insurance or pension system. Buddhist religious personnel, for example, prefer not to care so much about plans for pension or insurance because of their custom of spending the latter part of their lives in monasteries. Muslim and Protestant religious personnel, on the other hand, must care for elderly family members and raise children. They tend therefore to be much more interested in pension and insurance plans. Furthermore, important local differences exert an influence. In well-off areas, religious personnel with relatively high incomes are able to care for themselves. Religious personnel in less developed areas are keen on financial assistance from society or the government, due to their low incomes.[33]

Third, because of the diversity in systems of pension and insurance in rural and urban areas, problems may arise if someone wants to move from one system to another. Thus, in cases in which the place of household registration and the work unit are not the same, there are differences in the amount of contributions and pensions. When moving to another place, religious personnel are required to give up their original pension entitlement. Women may well be compelled to accept in the end a higher pensionable age line in a different system.[34]

Incomes and social security systems differ widely in rural or urban areas, and also according to respective local situations of economic development. Such a description typifies the socio-economic condition of religious personnel in Protestant Churches. In summary, great disparities therefore exist for religious personnel on the whole in the PRC.

---

[32] Li Mo 2013, p. 58.
[33] *Ibid.*, pp. 58-59.
[34] *Ibid.*, pp. 59-60.

2. The Role and Function of Religious Personnel

As already mentioned, because of the varieties of religious practice, the role and the function of religious personnel for different religions are not the same. In regard to Christian Churches, the role of the ordained religious personnel's contribution is an interesting illustration. As Ian Smith, Senior Lecturer in the School of Economics and Finance at the University of St. Andrew[35] states, "[...] the contribution of clergy is widely considered to be central to the performance of churches. Whether outcomes are measured in terms of numerical growth, member satisfaction, congregational giving, the size of the Sunday school or missionary support, it is the choices, personalities, and leadership qualities of the clergy that are often perceived to matter most."[36] In the following we cast a more detailed look on the function and areas of responsibilities of religious personnel in the perspectives of the official Protestant Churches and the religious personnel themselves. Then we will examine the demands in regard to the quality and performance of religious personnel.

2.1 The Perspective of the Official Protestant Churches

The "Church Order of Protestant Churches in China" which was adopted at the Joint (National) Conference of the Seventh Standing Committee of the Chinese Christian Three-Self Movement Committee of the Protestant Churches in China and the Fifth Standing Committee of the CCC in 2008, describes the function of Protestant clergy as follows:

- Bishops are responsible for the interpretation of the Christian doctrine and the promotion of theological reconstruction. They have no special administrative authority, but they direct the work of ministry, and give guidance and care for the pastoral needs of religious personnel and the faithful;
- Pastors are responsible for the management of the Church and its associated meeting points, Church ministry, and the administration of the sacraments, as well as for the guidance and pastoral care of the faithful;
- Teachers assist pastors in their duties, and may also administer the sacraments;
- Elders assist the pastors and teachers in the management of the Church and its associated meeting points, but their duties are limited to their own church and its associated meeting points. They provide pastoral care, and give guidance for the faithful, but they are only allowed to administer the sacraments at the request of the pastor.[37]

---

[35] Oslington 2014, p. xi.
[36] Smith 2014, p. 472.
[37] Document 2008a, p. 6, Article 21; also at http://www.ccctspm.org/quanguolianghui/jiao huiguizhang.html (accessed on August 16, 2016); for a German translation see "Revidierte Kirchenordnung der Chinesischen Evangelischen Kirche," *Chh* XXVII (2008) 6, pp. 209-215, here p. 213.

2.2 The Perspective of Religious Personnel Themselves

According to Pastor Li Yanfeng, director of the office of the Protestant CCC/TSPM in Guangxi, in addition to passing on the teachings of the Bible, religious personnel have to manage pastoral work in order to help new believers find their place in the church system, and to let them grow personally.[38] In order to achieve the goal of developing "a sense of commitment" (*weishengan* 委身感), religious personnel must evidence a high level of sensitivity as to the care they offer believers.[39] They do this by employing two methods: They must first personally visit the believers so that if problems arise, close and trusting relations may make it possible for religious personnel to advise and comfort. Second, organize small-sized groups which are guided by religious personnel, in which the believers can share experiences and come in touch with like-minded people to develop a sense of Church identity.[40]

Pastor Luo Yingfu states that the attraction of a Church depends on the abilities of the pastor in the pulpit.[41] To improve the range of pastoral supply, the Church can organize meetings for special interest groups as businessmen, migrant workers, students, single youths, and so forth.[42] During holidays the Church can hold meetings with special content as spiritual training, exchange of experiences, witnessing, preaching, and the like.[43]

Li Hua, pastor of the Chongwenmen Church (Chongwenmen tang 崇文门堂) in Beijing, also confirms that the needs of the faithful in urban Churches are increasingly pluralistic, because these include migrant workers, businessmen, students, but also ill people who come to large urban centers for better clinics and medical treatments, and tourist-related interests.[44] With the development of urban areas, the living conditions are changing and therefore religious personnel should be familiar with solving problems of daily life such as occupation, dwelling, marriage, illness or set-backs.[45] Li Hua believes that for these reasons the Churches need well educated religious personnel who sincerely care for the faithful and really participate in their lives.[46]

2.3 The Quality and Performance of Religious Personnel

From the above-mentioned it follows that the quality (*suzhi* 素质) of the Church is connected with the quality of the clergy who are responsible for the quality of

---

[38] Li Yanfeng 2014, pp. 6-7.
[39] *Ibid.*, p. 7; see also Zhang Zhongcheng 2014, p. 14.
[40] Li Yanfeng 2014, p. 7; see also Zhang Zhongcheng 2014, p. 14.
[41] Luo Yingfu 2014, p. 11.
[42] *Ibid.*, p. 11.
[43] *Ibid.*
[44] Li Hua 2014, p. 11.
[45] *Ibid.*, p. 11-12.
[46] *Ibid.*, p. 12.

faith of the Christians.[47] Andrew Kipnis, a specialist in sociocultural anthropology, stresses that *suzhi* – a keyword in education for quality (*suzhi jiaoyu* 素质教育) since the late 1980s – represents on the one side the overall quality of a people and, on the other, specific qualities of a person (e.g., "bodily *suzhi*, thought and moral *suzhi*, and educational *suzhi*").[48] With the great need for *suzhi* among Protestant clergy in mind, Guo Sanshun of Wuzhi county (Wuzhi xian 武陟县), Henan province, demands "a neat and solemn appearance, good work and reputation, a loving heart, serious spiritual pursuit, and cultural knowledge."[49]

Scrutiny of the actual quality of the Protestant clergy in China, however, reveals no uniform picture. The quality of the clergy in the Protestant Churches differs from place to place and from Church to Church. On the one end, there are Church leaders who belong to the well-educated middle class of prosperous young boss Christians with high *suzhi* as far as their social, political, and economic influence is concerned.[50] On the other end, there are old-fashioned elderly Church leaders who live pious lives, and who suffered persecution during the Cultural Revolution.[51] These believers therefore have spiritual *suzhi*, but are not ready to introduce changes in Church work.[52]

All religious personnel must cope with the different tasks of Church work. They are involved in "pastoral care, conflict resolution, evangelism, prayer, preparation for worship services, [...], general administration and planning, leading church meetings, organizing church staff and volunteers, and participation in fundraising and local community activities."[53] Therefore, qualifications for religious personnel appear to be clear:

> One has to be able to give advice and to accompany people in life crises. One must show skill at controlling and management, be able to lead personnel, hold together the community, integrate learned theological wisdom into practice, with sacramental catechesis be sensitive to the interests of participants, promote relationships, [and] develop abilities which truly absorb the whole person. [...] As representative of the Church one lives between excessive appreciation and constant criticism. Again and again, one must concern oneself with basic conflicts such as failure, suffering, reconciliation, [and] has to commit oneself to [questions of] faith and relationship with God of [other] people.[54]

Therefore religious personnel not only need theological and professional knowledge and practical experience, but also "people skills."[55]

---

[47] Cf. Cao Nanlai 2009, p. 57.
[48] Kipnis 2006, pp. 295, 297-298, 301, and 303-304; citation from p. 304.
[49] Guo Sanshun 1997, pp. 37-38; quotation according to Cao Nanlai 2009, p. 57.
[50] Cao Nanlai 2009, p. 60.
[51] *Ibid.*, pp. 60-61.
[52] *Ibid.*
[53] Smith 2014, p. 474.
[54] Abel 1995, p. 44.
[55] Schall 1993, pp. 36-37.

3. Occupational Problems and Their Impact

The problems resulting from these various demands on religious personnel are multi-layered and complex. Some stem from the situation in the religious market and distribution issues. Some find their origin in the social-economic situation of religious personnel themselves. The problems pertain to questions of holy orders, overly heavy workloads, and problems with health and interpersonal relations.

3.1 General Problems of Religious Personnel: Results of a Case Study of 2009

The results of a case study of June 2009 which were published in the journal *Dangdai zongjiao yanjiu* 当代宗教研究 (Contemporary Religious Studies) of the Institute of Religious Studies (Zongjiao yanjiusuo 宗教研究所) of Shanghai Academy of Social Sciences (Shanghai shehui kexueyuan 上海社会科学院) offer some hints about practical problems that religious personnel face. For this case study, 49 pastors, 53 teachers, 172 elders, and 105 full-time preachers (*chuandaoyuan* 传道员) were questioned.[56] The registration statistics concerning these 379 persons revealed the following problems:

a) In 2009, the average age of the pastors was 59 years, of the elders 66 years, of the teachers 43 years, and of the preachers 38 years.[57]

b) Disparities of gender: only one third of the religious personnel are females. This proportion will change in the course of time, however, because the proportion of females among the young religious personnel is higher than the proportion of males.[58]

c) Uneven spatial distribution of religious personnel: if we take the pastors as an example, 60% of the 49 pastors are serving in urban areas (14 pastors in large cities and 16 pastors in chief district towns), whereas in one of the other areas there is only one aged pastor caring for eight churches, with more than 5,000 faithful.[59]

d) In general the educational level and theological quality of the religious personnel is low: 48.5% have up to secondary school level. A mere 8 persons out of these 379 have a university background in the first education course, all of them young people. Most of the elders have not completed a one-year training course in theology; they have completed a training course that lasted only three months.[60] Therefore, Jin Ke suggests, among other efforts, self-study and correspondence courses. Such teaching of self projects should help to improve the all-around educational level of religious personnel.[61]

---

[56] Jin Ke 2010, p. 13.
[57] *Ibid.*, p. 14.
[58] *Ibid.*
[59] *Ibid.*, pp. 14-15.
[60] *Ibid.*, p. 15.
[61] *Ibid.*, p. 18.

120 persons of the religious personnel received a questionnaire, but only 84 filled in the answers by themselves and returned their questionnaires; as a result, the sample covers only 22.2% of the above mentioned 379 persons:[62]

a) One interesting point as regards the occupational origins of the religious personnel is its diversity. Among the original occupations of religious personnel are the work of peasants and workers, students, small proprietors and entrepreneurs; still other occupations are common.[63]

b) The income of 51.2% of the religious personnel was below 20,000 *yuan* RMB per year; some 7.1% received 20,000–30,000 *yuan* RMB/year, and 5.9% 30,000–50,000 *yuan* RMB/year, and 7.1% had an income of above 50,000 *yuan* RMB/year.[64] As Jin Ke learned in some of the interviews, the average Church salary of religious personnel in the investigated area is about 1,000 *yuan* RMB/month in rural space and about 2,000 *yuan* RMB/month in urban space, but could be increased by holding sermons in other places and by receiving natural produce – which was not taken into account in the questionnaire.[65]

3.2 Special Problems: Holy Orders – Health – Human Relations

The official Protestant journal *Tianfeng* has published a series of articles (as monthly topics) about actual problems that religious personnel confront.

In 2011 holy orders (*shengzhi* 圣职) was such a topic.[66] First Wang Aiming, vice president of the Nanjing Union Theological Seminary, on the basis of the Bible explained in his article the necessity for division of labour in the growing Churches and the systems of Protestant Church administration.[67] Zhang Xiaofa, senior pastor of the Hangzhou Sicheng Church (Hangzhou Sicheng tang 杭州思澄堂), complained that especially in rural areas because of misunderstandings of the true meaning of holy orders – an oath of sacrifice, a holy contract, the grace of God – there are several cases in which preachers are ordained without possessing the above-mentioned requirements for religious personnel: sometimes it is just for getting a higher rank, sometimes for rewarding an obedient person, sometimes because of good relations to someone (*guanxi* 关系), etc.[68] Furthermore, a dilemma arises for graduates coming straight from theological seminaries relating to the fact that some Churches prefer ordained personnel: not being ordained, on the one hand is regarded as shameful and humiliating there; yet on the other hand, the above mentioned regulations for religious personnel demand a

---

[62] Jin Ke 2010, p. 15.
[63] *Ibid.*, p. 16.
[64] *Ibid.*
[65] *Ibid.*
[66] *Tianfeng* 2011/8, pp. 38-48.
[67] Wang Aiming 2011, pp. 39-41.
[68] Zhang Xiaofa 2011, pp. 42-43 and 45.

few years of pastoral work before ordination.⁶⁹ In the view of Zhang Xiaofa, ordination by the laying on of hands signifies being placed in apostolic succession. The laying on of hands in the ordination rite means a person is officially approved by the Church. Such a public (and spiritual) confirmation provides the minister with strength and resistance when confronted in the future with problems, exhaustion, or crises.⁷⁰ With regard to the right motivation for ordination Jing Jianmei, pastor of the Shanghai Jingling Church (Shanghai Jingling tang 上海景灵堂), quotes two reasons according to Calvin: "[...] pastors on one side are called by the inner vocation of Jesus Christ and simultaneously they are called by the outer vocation of the Holy Spirit mediated through the Church."⁷¹

Another topic in 2011 was the health of pastoral personnel.⁷² Lin Xueyuan, who serves the Protestant CCC/TSPM in Guangdong, lists the following problems which lead to physical and psychological distress: 1. the high burden of work which includes preparation of sermons, the leading of small and large meetings, personal bible studies, visits of the faithful, and so on; 2. the fact that religious personnel may not be able to enjoy regular meals three times a day, because they are often in a hurry, and/or meals are interrupted by visitors or phone calls, or the pastoral personnel are working out of an office; these conditions over time lead to stomach complaints, which are an "occupational disease"; 3. insufficient time for sleep, because pastoral personnel often choose the quiet nights that enter their schedule for preparations and studies, since during day time they must care not only for the spiritual needs of the faithful, but also assist with problems of life, work, and family; 4. the fact that the people around them, and they themselves may often consider that pastoral personnel are "holy and perfect," humanly strong and without needs. In this case they receive no consolation and comfort, and no encouragement for their work. When confronted with a problem, religious personnel are often thrown back on themselves. This isolated position leads to feelings of loneliness, depression, and helplessness.⁷³

In 2014 another topic discussed in *Tianfeng* was the question of relations between the personnel involved in the managing of the Churches, and other religious personnel. One article referred to the following situations: 1. Tensions occur, on the one side, between religious personnel who have managed the Church for many years, and whose long years of service have won great respect and, on the other, the newly arrived, young preachers who are more familiar with the contemporary needs of growing Churches. In some cases, new preachers are only allowed to participate in subordinate work, because long-serving Church managers regard them as a threat and are afraid of losing their leading positions if the "newer type" is allowed to exercise their talents and develop innovative

---

⁶⁹ Zhang Xiaofa 2011, p. 42.
⁷⁰ *Ibid.*, pp. 44-45.
⁷¹ Jing Jianmei 2011, p. 48.
⁷² *Tianfeng* 2011/3, pp. 36-44.
⁷³ Lin Xueyuan 2014, pp. 37-39.

measures. 2. A related but second point of controversy that has arisen involves cases in which Church managers bring the new personnel into disrepute for fear of being overtaken by them. This problem appears to be worse than the first.[74] One reaction of the new religious personnel to these situations is to quit service.[75] In that way, however, the Churches lose valuable human capital for their own precious growth because of jealousy, envy and quarrels.[76]

Sun Hongzhong, pastor of the Protestant Church of Xigu district (Xigu qu 西古区) of Lanzhou city, Gansu province, mentions in a 2014 article that one reason believers may leave Protestant Churches is the discomfort felt when disagreement and quarrels arise among some preachers. Often one of the parties involved leaves the Church to establish a new one.[77] Furthermore, in rural Churches it happens that the preachers' general level of education poses a problem because it is insufficient. The preachers lack regular training courses, whereas in urban Churches the preachers lack the time for spiritual exercises and personal Bible study which leads to insufficient preparation of services and causes dissatisfaction with the services among some of the faithful.[78]

3.3 Impact of the Problems

Confronted with this complexity of interrelated problems the religious personnel eventually feel as if put on a spot:

1. Religious market and workload: the serious undersupply of religious personnel in the religious market in some places causes forms of duplications of service. Yang Fenggang says, "[s]ome creative pastors have successfully gained government approval for holding multiple worship services each week."[79] But then the problem is that "increased worship services put greater demand on ministers for preaching and preparation," and people without official certificates are not allowed to become ministers.[80] Yang Fenggang further states: "Most of the TSPM ministers I talked with expressed feelings of exhaustion in carrying out the routine tasks of preaching, counseling, and rituals, as well as in dealing with the usual harassments of the state control apparatus."[81]
2. Salaries and holy orders: according to Qin Xiaolin, senior pastor of Shanghai Zhabei Church (Shanghai Zhabei tang 上海闸北堂), a number of Protestant Churches still give salaries to the religious personnel which are below the state fixed minimum wage. These arrangements for employment do not pro-

---

[74] Mai Zi 2014, pp. 24-25.
[75] *Ibid.*, p. 24.
[76] *Ibid.*
[77] Sun Hongzhong 2014, p. 8.
[78] *Ibid.*, pp. 8-9.
[79] Yang Fenggang 2005, p. 429.
[80] *Ibid.*
[81] *Ibid.*, p. 430.

vide for health, pension, and unemployment insurance for the pastoral personnel. Furthermore, some Churches let graduates of the theological seminaries work for the Church for up to seven or eight years, and delay the granting of holy orders.[82]

3. Salaries and health: Zhang Lili, who serves for the Protestant CCC/TSPM Shanghai, explains, "especially in areas which are rather lagging behind, many Churches have not yet established a basic health insurance system for their pastoral personnel" and "do not have regular examinations on their state of health."[83] These factors, in combination with low salaries, lead to the situation that most of the religious personnel in case of illness do not receive medical treatment in time.[84]

4. Salaries and family formation: according to the anthropologist Cao Nanlai another point of complaint is that full-time preachers often have difficulties in finding a spouse because their salaries are too low.[85]

5. Interpersonal relations: coping with unhappy believers who criticize the Church or its religious personnel because of dissatisfaction with various demands is also a problem.[86] Another problem is rivalry between some preachers who simply fight against one another in stubborn insistence that their point of view is the will of God; this may occur when the disgruntled are not able to achieve their individual aims.[87]

In such an environment it is not surprising that pastor Qin Xiaolin, when looking back at about 20 years of Church experience, describes religious personnel in rather gloomy terms. "Some become seriously ill, some die prematurely, others in turn develop mental disorders and commit suicide, some as well leave the Church because of all sorts of reasons."[88] The next section of this article deals with more details on how situations depicted above may trigger important negative consequences.

3.4 Exhaustion, Burnout, and Resignations from Positions

Religious personnel must carry out myriad daily tasks: some are the demands of the Church (for example, performing pastoral and administrative work), some are the demands of the believers (giving advice in daily life situations, especially in times of setback), and other tasks involve the demands of the religious personnel themselves (the necessity of on-going training, bible studies, and launching new initiatives). Furthermore, religious personnel must strive to build and maintain

---

[82] Qin Xiaolin 2011, pp. 41-42.
[83] Zhang Lili 2011, p. 42, see also p. 44.
[84] Ibid., p. 42.
[85] Cao Nanlai 2009, p. 61, footnotes 43 and 44.
[86] Sun Hongzhong 2014, p. 9.
[87] Ibid., p. 8.
[88] Qin Xiaolin 2011, p. 40.

good interpersonal relations with area colleges, believers, and members of their own family. Owing to a lack of time, all these demands often cannot be fulfilled, no matter how hard religious personnel work. Their hours frequently include both day and night responsibilities. Also, contradictory expectations cannot be met and additionally interpersonal conflicts arise. In such situations, physical and unmediated psychological distress can lead to burnout, a phenomenon also well-known in the West.[89]

Burnout is a phenomenon widely common in the helping professions, but can also be found in other, seemingly unrelated professions.[90] The phenomenon is not a new one among religious personnel, as pastoral psychologist Traugott Ulrich Schall states. In the past, pastors would speak of "Elias-Müdigkeit" ("Elias fatigue"),[91] an allusion to the prophet Elias in the Old Testament, whose story Schall uses in his book[92] to explain a few of the characteristics of the burnout syndrome in the perspective of Christian faith. Schall quotes the following factors which may be responsible for occupational exhaustion:
1. High personal and occupational engagement as well as high expectations of the helpers;
2. experience of limited competence in situations which overtax the personnel objectively or subjectively;
3. experience of failure despite huge efforts;
4. social isolation and socio-economic influences;
5. misjudgment of the will and command as well as of the words of encouragement of God.[93]

For religious personnel the latter is also an important point, because an occupational crisis can become a crisis of faith, too.[94] Agreeing with American researchers, training manager Peter Abel, expert for pastoral theology and pastoral psychology, stresses that

> the circumstances which cause burn out are that overtaxing burdens from outside come upon disposed personalities and that the relationship of person and environment get into an imbalance. Therefore, burn out cannot be attributed to the fault of an individual person, but to the social and structural conditions of work. Burnout is caused by burdensome social relations at work.[95]

Another hint to understand the problem is given by the researchers Mary E. Guy, Meredith A. Newman, and Sharon H. Mastracci, who investigated what we might term "emotional labor" in public service, and examined literature on this

---

[89] Schall 1993, pp. 54-56; Burisch 2010, pp. 153-154.
[90] Schall 1993, p. 9; Burisch 2010, pp. 21-24.
[91] Schall 1993, pp. 10-12; Burisch 2010, p. 4.
[92] Schall 1993.
[93] Ibid., pp. 19-20.
[94] Ibid., p. 12.
[95] Abel 1995, p. 36; cf. also Burisch 2010, pp. 100-101.

subject as well as on job satisfaction, burnout and human resources management: "Burnout is an issue of primary concern in occupations that involve lots of face-to-face contact – in other words, those with heavy emotional labor demands."[96]

> Emotional labor is that work which requires the engagement, suppression, and/or evocation of the worker's emotions in order to get the job done. [...] The performance encompasses a range of personal and interpersonal skills, including the ability to evoke and display emotions one does not actually feel, to sense the affect of the other and alter one's own affect accordingly, and to elicit the desired emotional response from the other.[97]

Emotional labor may result in outcomes in two directions: if successfully fulfilled, it leads to commitment and higher job satisfaction, but if not, it leads to emotional exhaustion and burnout.[98]

The psychologist Matthias Burisch, with the help of his diverse findings in research literature, describes the burnout symptom complex as follows: 1. In the initial phase the persons first show warning symptoms such as an exaggerated input of energy on the one side, and exhaustion on the other; 2. then follows a phase of reduced commitment for clients (disillusionment, dehumanization, etc.), for other people in general (cynicism, etc.), and for work, combined with higher demands; 3. the third phase is characterized by emotional reactions – depression in case of feelings of guilt (feelings of helplessness, thoughts of suicide, etc.) or aggression in case of recrimination toward others; 4. then follows a phase of the breaking down of cognitive capability, motivation, creativity and of dedifferentiation; 5. during the fifth phase the emotional, social, and mental life flatten; 6. in the sixth phase psychosomatic reactions occur; 7. in the end, despair prevails (hopelessness, intention of suicide, etc.).[99] Not all of these phases must necessarily occur, and also their order can change depending on individual factors and personal environment.[100]

Now the question is, how to prevent religious personnel from being caught in this process? What measures can be taken if burnout occurs? How to change the situation?

4. Getting out of the Dilemma

In this section we consider suggestions on how to diminish physical and psychological distress among religious personnel, and help them to become more mentally and physically fit for the challenges of serving their religious communities. To resolve problems of assignments in which persons may appear inappropriate or "ill-fitting," religious personnel themselves are able to take some initiatives. In other cases, the Churches can implement certain measures as well. In addition,

---

[96] Guy – Newman – Mastracci 2008, p. 104.
[97] *Ibid.*, p. 97.
[98] *Ibid.*, pp. 104-107 and 114-116.
[99] Burisch 2010, pp. 25-26.
[100] *Ibid.*, p. 27.

the State can improve various aspects in the prevailing legal and social framework.

4.1 Religious Personnel Take the Initiative

The magazine *Tianfeng* offers several suggestions in the way of counter-measures against physical and psychological distress. Religious personnel themselves can take the initiative in many important ways to help themselves cope more successfully with the problems they confront:

a) Physical Training
Because religious personnel have no regular working hours, as for example industrial workers do, they can do individual training with fitness machines, such as rowing exercises and other similar physically exerting activity that involves the legs, hips, shoulders, back, and so forth.[101] Many local governments provide appropriate public facilities for their citizens to enjoy the benefits of physical exercise, where they can also do some *qigong*, gymnastics or *taijiquan*.[102] Religious personnel can also increase their stamina by exercises like walking, swimming or jogging, all of which have advantageous effects on the cardiovascular system and metabolism, as well on the maintenance of healthy body weight.[103] Regular physical training is beneficial for the strengthening of the musculoskeletal system, improves the quality of sleep, and also provides time to think; it is therefore important for the regeneration of physical strength and mental powers.[104] In general, physical exercise is useful for stress reduction.[105]

b) Diet
For the health of religious personnel, it is also important to have regular meals with fixed quantity – at least three times a day – and a balanced and healthy diet.[106] Poor eating habits or actual malnutrition are the causes of chronic illnesses such as hypertension, obesity, arteriosclerosis, diabetes, and so on.[107] Furthermore, religious personnel should avoid excessive consumption of alcohol and tobacco products.[108]

c) Sufficient Time to Sleep
Religious personnel should also not work through the night or surf the internet unrestrainedly all night long.[109]

---

[101] Lin Xueyuan 2011, p. 38.
[102] *Ibid.*; and Qin Xiaolin 2011, p. 40.
[103] Lin Xueyuan 2011, p. 38; and Qin Xiaolin 2011, p. 40.
[104] Lin Xueyuan 2011, p. 38.
[105] *Ibid.*
[106] *Ibid.*, p. 39.
[107] *Ibid.*
[108] Qin Xiaolin 2011, p. 41.
[109] *Ibid.*

d) Alternation of Work and Relaxation

In general, it is very important to alternate between work and relaxation to avoid exhaustion.[110] Religious personnel are particularly prone to feelings of guilt, if they are not devoting themselves "all the time," and sacrificing themselves for their work.[111]

e) Health Care

When religious personnel visit sick persons or attend funerals, they should observe measures for good hygiene; in addition, they must undergo regular medical examinations, and seek timely treatment for medical assistance they may require.[112]

f) Psychological Relief by the Social Network

There are several possibilities in the challenge of escaping the role of a lone fighter and solitariness. Those possibilities lie in the wise use of a social network.[113] Of course not every problem can be discussed in public, but, depending on various circumstances, religious personnel can talk about a variety of problems with trustworthy and experienced brothers and sisters, and can pray with them together in a search for solutions.[114] In other matters religious personnel can share in dialogue with each other in weekly group meetings with colleagues or marriage partner.[115] In this way, they are no longer in an isolated position and can ease their burden and receive some support.[116] An exchange with an experienced mentor could also be of great help in regulating emotional states, especially for newcomers, young pastors coming from theological seminaries.[117] In general, unburdening themselves in appropriate ways makes problematic situations easier to cope with and can help religious personnel maintain positive attitudes and joyous hearts.[118] Learning to share joy and sorrow with others is not only a help for themselves, but for the people and the Churches they serve as well.[119]

g) Delegation of Work

Due to conditions of high workload, religious personnel themselves simply cannot carry out every task; the delegation of some items should also be considered.[120]

---

[110] Lin Xueyuan 2011, pp. 38-39.

[111] Ibid.

[112] Qin Xiaolin 2011, p. 41.

[113] See also Abel 1995, pp. 82-83.

[114] Lin Xueyuan 2011, p. 39.

[115] Ibid.

[116] Ibid.

[117] Qin Xiaolin 2011, p. 41; and Liu Shaokang 2014, p. 25.

[118] Lin Xueyuan 2011, p. 39; Qin Xiaolin 2011, pp. 41-42; and Zhang Lili 2011, p. 44.

[119] Lin Xueyuan 2011, p. 39; Qin Xiaolin 2011, p. 42; and Zhang Lili 2011, p. 44.

[120] Li Hua 2014 p. 12.

4.2 Measures of the Churches

The Protestant Churches in their role as employer bear responsibility for their employees. In the author's opinion, the relevant question here is not only the question of appropriate salaries and care for sufficient benefits, including insurance. In addition, it seems to me that persons in high levels of leadership for the Protestant Churches also have to think about their ways of managing human resources. They must show a high regard for a good working environment and, when problems arise, offer adequate help. In cases of depression or burnout, the persons concerned may need medical treatment, as for example psychotherapy.[121] And to prevent religious personnel from developing psychological ailments, the Protestant Churches simply must consider how to remedy the vital problem discussed above, that of misplaced or unsuitable persons in certain assignments. This so called situation of "misfits" is a definite challenge to be faced.

In the journal *Tianfeng*, retired pastor Liu Shaokang from Hong Kong suggests the establishment of a team of Church advisers, if possible from inside the Churches but, if not, also from outside, which might include certain specialists with very specific background and skills for practical problems as, for example, social workers, lawyers, doctors, professional instructors, pastors, and specialists for administration and management. These experts could provide relevant insights and counsel, and possibly even answer questions, if required. After all, it is impossible for religious personnel to be completely informed about every topic in modern society.[122]

Human resource management is of course of utmost importance. Truly adequate training programs for the Churches, especially for young and inexperienced religious personnel, could also prepare religious personnel for job-related challenges in work that particularly demands maturity and personal strength in dealing with human emotions.[123] Furthermore, an alternation between work projects with the faithful that are especially emotionally demanding with work that might in some cases be lighter, e.g., administrative tasks, could also be helpful in an effort to relieve the general pressure of emotional demands on religious personnel.[124]

Another point is the reduction of the workload. This could be achieved by involving lay people in Church work. As for Wenzhou Churches, Cao Nanlai states that the institutionalized lay training system of Nanjing Union Theological Seminary and Wenzhou Lay Training Centre, which was introduced in 1995, "has greatly facilitated pastoral work in Wenzhou."[125]

---

[121] Burisch 2010, p. 268.
[122] Liu Shaokang 2014, pp. 24-25.
[123] Guy – Newman – Mastracci 2008, p. 108.
[124] *Ibid.*, pp. 116-117.
[125] Cao Nanlai 2009, p. 62.

4.3 Laws and Regulations

The PRC government regulates the religious life of the official Churches by the "Regulations on Religious Affairs" and further measures seen above. The state wants to utilize the religions in some social sectors, where the means of the state are exhausted, for supporting social stability in China, as well as achieving a harmonious society.[126] In the author's opinion, such a venture can only be successful if the government is able to meet the needs of the people by its policies on religion in society.

One problem is the low number of religious personnel in the face of great workload that exists at present. As seen above, the five officially recognized religions are required to meet various demands for religious services. According to the statistics, the Protestants especially cherish the custom of attending religious activities several times a week. Therefore, the regulation of the number of religious personnel by the state, a tradition that goes back to imperial times when Buddhism and Daoism were the prevailing religions,[127] may in consideration of increased population and other factors, need adjustment in the current, modern context. If the Churches are furthermore expected to provide social services which the state is not ready to provide, the Churches need even more religious personnel, because in this case they not only provide religious services, but are also requested to offer guidance and help for the needy – poor people, sick people, unemployed people – as well as to develop special programs for those of all ages. A need also exists to establish working conditions that will effectively encourage religious personnel to shoulder these difficult tasks. One of the desiderata is the already mentioned need to adjust the widely different systems of social security, including pension and insurance packages.

To sum up, individual counter-measures to prevent burnout should not be one-sided as far as body, mind, or spirituality are concerned. Measures to alleviate the adverse conditions we have pointed to should be all-embracing and holistic, and should therefore help to build up a well-balanced personality. The Protestant Churches can promote their aims of evangelizing the people and administrating the Churches best by building up a pleasant work environment for all religious personnel. The state administration can provide a suitable legal and social framework in which religions can develop. And if these three levels – individual, Churches, and state – complement each other, the preconditions for successful religious work are set, and a first step for future improvement is taken.

---

[126] Malek 2011, p. 5. For further details of this utilization, for example, in the sectors of education, charity work, and civil society, see *ibid.*, pp. 5-7.

[127] Yang 1961, pp. 187-189.

5. Bibliography

5.1 Documents and Their Translations

Document 2005a, "Neue Vorschriften für religiöse Angelegenheiten in der Volksrepublik China," *Chh* XXIV (2005) 1-2, pp. 22-31.

Document 2005b, "Zongjiao shiwu tiaoli" 宗教事务条例 (Regulations on Religious Affairs), *Zhonghua renmin gongheguo guowuyuan gongbao* 中华人民共和国国务院公报 (Gazette of the State Council of the People's Republic of China), 2005/4, pp. 11-16.

Dokument 2006, "Zhongguo jidujiao jiaozhi renyuan rending banfa" 中国基督教教职人员认定办法, *Tianfeng* 天风 (The Magazine of the Protestant Churches in China), 2006/12, Part 1, pp. 18-19.

Document 2007, "Neue Bestimmungen für religiöse Amtsträger und die Besetzung religiöser Ämter," *Chh* XXVI (2007) 1-2, pp. 23-33.

Document 2008a, "Zhongguo jidujiao guizhang" 中国基督教教会规章, *Tianfeng* 2008/2, Part 2, pp. 4-7.

Document 2008b, "Zongjiao huodong changsuo zhuyao jiaozhi renzhi bei'an banfa" 宗教活动场所主要教职任职备案办法 (Measures for Reporting for the Record the Holding of Chief Posts at Sites for Religious Activities), *Zhonghua renmin gongheguo guowuyuan gongbao* 2008/1, pp. 47-48.

Document 2008c, "Zongjiao jiaozhi renyuan bei'an banfa" 宗教教职人员备案办法 (Measures for Reporting Religious Personnel for the Record), *Zhonghua renmin gongheguo guowuyuan gongbao* 2008/1, pp. 46-47.

Document 2010a, "Neue Richtlinien für die Aufnahme religiöser Amtsträger in die staatlichen Sozialversicherungssysteme," *Chh* XXIX (2010) 3, pp. 158-160.

Document 2010b, "Guanyu tuoshan jiejue zongjiao jiaozhi renyuan shehui baozhang wenti de yijian" 关于妥善解决宗教教职人员社会保障问题的意见 (Opinions on Appropriately Solving the Social Security Problem of Religious Personnel), *Zhongguo zongjiao* 中国宗教 (China Religion) 2010/3, pp. 11-12.

5.2 Secondary Sources

Abel, Peter. 1995. *Burnout in der Seelsorge*, Mainz: Matthias-Grünewald-Verlag.

Burisch, Matthias. 2010. *Das Burnout-Syndrom. Theorie der inneren Erschöpfung*, 4., aktualisierte Auflage, Berlin – Heidelberg – New York: Springer-Verlag.

Cao Nanlai. 2009. "Raising the Quality of Belief. *Suzhi* and the Production of an Elite Protestantism," *China Perspectives* 2009/4, pp. 54-65.

Darimont, Barbara. 2014. "Social Security in the P.R. China Exemplified by Urban and Rural Health Insurance," *Religions & Christianity in Today's China* IV (2014) 4, pp. 24-32.

Duan Qi 段琦. 2013. "Henan Kaifeng he Nanyang de zongjiao geju ji chengyin baogao" 河南开封和南阳的宗教格局及成因报告 (Field Study Report on the

Present State and Pattern of Religions in Kaifeng and Nanyang, Henan Province), in: Jin Ze – Qiu Yonghui 2013, pp. 252-280.

Guan Xinping. 2014. "Poverty and Anti-poverty Measures in China," *China Journal of Social Work* 7 (2014) 3, pp. 270-287.

Guo Sanshun 郭三顺. 1997. "Jiangdao renyuan suzhi tan" 讲道人员素质谈 [On the Quality of Preachers], *Tianfeng* 1997/1, pp. 37-38.

Guy, Mary E. – Meredith A. Newman – Sharon H. Mastracci. 2008. *Emotional Labor. Putting the Service in Public Service*, Armonk, New York – London: M.E. Sharpe.

Jin Ke 金珂. 2010. "Jidujiao jiaozhi renyuan xianzhuang fenxi yu yanjiu. Ji yu Z sheng N shi de diaocha" 基督教教职人员现状分析与研究—基于 Z 省 N 市的调查 [Analysis and Research on the Present-day State of Protestant Religious Personnel. Survey Based on the Data from N City in Z Province], *Dangdai zongjiao yanjiu* 当代宗教研究 2010/2, pp. 13-19.

Jin Ze 金泽 – Qiu Yonghui 邱永辉 (eds.). 2012. *Zhongguo zongjiao baogao (2012)* 中国宗教报告 (2012). *Annual Report on Religions in China (2012)*, Zongjiao lanpishu 宗教蓝皮书. Blue Book of Religions, Beijing: Shehui kexue wenxian chubanshe.

—. 2013. *Zhongguo zongjiao baogao (2013)* 中国宗教报告 (2013). *Annual Report on Religions in China (2013)*, Zongjiao lanpishu 宗教蓝皮书. Blue Book of Religions, Beijing: Shehui kexue wenxian chubanshe.

Jing Jianmei 景健美. 2011. "Xintu jie jisi, hai xuyao anli shengzhi ma?" 信徒皆祭司，还需要按立圣职吗？[The Faithful Are All Priests or Is There Still a Need for Holy Orders?]," *Tianfeng* 2011/8, pp. 46-48.

Kipnis, Andrew. 2006. "*Suzhi*: A Keyword Approach," *The China Quarterly*, No. 186 (June 2006), pp. 295-313.

Li Hua 李华. 2014. "Chengshi jiaohui xintu liushi yinfa de sikao" 城市教会信徒流失引发的思考 [Reflections on Reasons for the Exodus of Faithful in Urban Churches], *Tianfeng* 2014/2, pp. 11-12.

Li Mo 李沫. 2013. "Zongjiao jiaozhi renyuan shehui yanglao baoxian de ji ge wenti" 宗教教职人员社会养老保险的几个问题 (Several Questions in Social Endowment Insurance for Religious Clergy), *Zhongguo zongjiao* 2013/10, pp. 58-60.

Li Yanfeng 李燕峰. 2014. "Qian tan chengshi jiaohui muyang de tiaozhan" 浅谈城市教会牧羊的挑战 [Briefly on Challenges of Shepherding in Urban Churches], *Tianfeng* 2014/2, pp. 6-7.

Lin Xueyuan 林雪媛. 2011. "Jiaomu renyuan ruhe baochi yi ge jiankang de shenti" 教牧人员如何保持一个健康的身体 [How Can the Religious Personnel Preserve a Healthy Body], *Tianfeng* 2011/3, pp. 37-39.

Liu Chengyou 刘成有. 2012. "Dangdai Zhongguo shehui zhuanxing zhong zongiao 'huoxing'. Yi Gansu wei ge'an de kaocha" 当代中国社会转型中宗教'活性'—以甘肃为个案的考察 (Vitality of Religion in Contemporary China during Transformation. A Case Study on Gansu), in: Jin Ze – Qiu Yonghui 2012, pp. 228-244.

Liu Shaokang 刘少康. 2014. "Jiaomu xuyao zhinangtuan" 教牧需要智囊团 [Pastors Need Brain Trusts], *Tianfeng* 2014/12, pp. 24-25.

Lu Yunfeng 卢云峰. 2014. "Dangdai Zhongguo zongjiao zhuangkuang baogao. Ji yu CFPS (2012) diaocha shuju" 当代中国宗教状况报告—基于 CFPS (2012) 调查数据 (Report on Contemporary Chinese Religions Based on Data of CFPS [2012]), *Shijie zongjiao wenhua* 世界宗教文化 (The World Religious Cultures) 2014/1, pp. 11-25.

Luo Yingfu 罗应富. 2014. "Jiaqiang zishen jianshe shi fangzhi xintu liushi de guanjian" 加强自身建设是防止信徒流失的关键 [Strengthening Self-construction Is the Key to Stopping the Exodus of Faithful], *Tianfeng* 2014/2, pp. 10-11.

Madsen, Richard. (2010). "Vormoderne Religionspolitik im postsäkularen China," *Chh* XXIX (2010) 3, pp. 161-169.

Mai Zi 麦子. 2014. "Jiaohui fuziren yu qita zhuanzhi tonggong zhi jian de guanxi" 教会负责人与其他专职同工之间的关系 [The Relationship between the Persons Responsible in the Church and Other Full-Time Professionals], *Tianfeng* 2014/6, pp. 24-25.

Malek, Roman. 2011. "Zur Funktion der Religionen in China. Zwischen Autonomie und Assimilation," *Religionen unterwegs* 17 (2011) 1, pp. 4-8

Oslington, Paul (ed.). 2014. *The Oxford Handbook of Christianity and Economics*, Oxford – New York – Auckland *et al.*: Oxford University Press.

Qin Xiaolin 秦小林. 2011. "Tantan chuandaoren de shenxin jiankang" 谈谈传道人的身心健康 [On the Physical and Psychological Health of Preachers], *Tianfeng* 2011/3, pp. 40-42.

Schall, Traugott Ulrich. 1993. *Erschöpft – müde – ausgebrannt. Überforderung und Resignation: vermeiden – vermindern – heilen*, Perspektiven für die Seelsorge, vol. 8, Würzburg: Echter Verlag.

Smith, Ian. 2014. "Religious Labour Markets," in: Oslington 2014, pp. 472-488.

Sun Hongzhong 孙红忠. 2014. "Jiaohui xintu liushi, shei zhi guo?" 教会信徒流失，谁之过? [On the Exodus of Faithful: Whose Fault?], *Tianfeng* 2014/2, pp. 8-9.

Wang Aiming 王艾明. 2011. "Shengzhi zhifen yu Zhongguo jiaohui qian yi" 圣职职分与中国教会浅议" [Preliminary Opinion on the Division of Responsibilities of the Ministry and the Church in China], *Tianfeng* 2011/8, pp. 39-41.

Wenzel-Teuber, Katharina. 2012. "People's Republic of China: Religions and Churches, Statistical Overview 2011," *Religions & Christianity in Today's China* II (2012) 3, pp. 29-54.

—. (comp.). 2013. "Die staatlichen Rechtsvorschriften für die Religionen in der VR China – ein Überblick," *Chh* XXXII (2013) 3, pp. 154-159.

—. 2014. "2013 Statistical Update on Religions and Churches in the People's Republic of China," *Religions & Christianity in Today's China* IV (2014) 2, pp. 17-39.

Yang, C.K. 1961. *Religion in Chinese Society. A Study of Contemporary Social Functions of Religion and Some of Their Historical Factors*, Berkeley – Los Angeles: University of California Press.

Yang Fenggang. 2005. "Lost in the Market, Saved at McDonald's: Conversion to Christianity in Urban China," *Journal for the Scientific Study of Religion* 44 (2005) 4, pp. 423-441.

Zhang Lili 张丽丽. 2011. "Muzhe jiankang, qunyang you liang" 牧者健康, 群羊有粮 [If Pastors Are Healthy, the Faithful Are Nourished], *Tianfeng* 2011/3, pp. 42-44.

Zhang Xiaofa 张效法. 2011. "Dui shengzhi anli de shenxue sikao" 对圣职按立的神学思考 [Theological Reflections on Holy Orders], *Tianfeng* 2011/8, pp. 42-45.

Zhang Zhongcheng 张忠成. 2014. "Dui dangjin jiaohui xintu liushi de sikao" 对当今教会信徒流失的思考 [Reflections on the Exodus of Faithful in the Church Today], *Tianfeng* 2014/2, pp. 13-14.

Zhu Haibin. 2011. "Chinas wichtigste religiöse Tradition: der Volksglaube," *minima sinica* 23 (2011) 1, pp. 25-51.

Other Religions in China
Andere Religionen in China

其他宗教在中國

THE TEXTUAL CANONIZATION OF GUANDI*

Vincent Goossaert

If many of the gods of Chinese religion have an unclear past, or have been outright invented, Guan Yu 關羽 (?–220) is without doubt a historical figure, who has moved on to a second (longer, and more successful) career as a god, eventually reaching the rank of emperor, *di* 帝, as Xietian huguo zhongyi dadi 協天護國忠義大帝 in 1590, and then Sanjie fumo dadi 三界伏魔大帝 in 1614. The story of the Guandi cult is the topic of a forthcoming book by Barend ter Haar[1] which is sure to become authoritative. I am only providing here the briefest possible outline, so as to focus on its spirit-writing aspect. Guandi's cult likely began shortly after his tragic death, executed by his enemies; it long remained rather inconspicuous before rising to national visibility during the Song period, when it was actively promoted both by Buddhists, who accommodated him as a monastic guardian deity, and Daoists who turned him into one of their most prominent exorcistic martial deities.[2] He was subsequently adopted in the canon of state sacrifices, rising continually to reach the rank of di, emperor, in 1614; and being elevated to the same level as Confucius in 1853 – in the context of the Taiping Civil War (1850–1864), when he became the most prominent supernatural force fighting on the loyalist side.

My focus in this contribution is but one aspect of the Guandi cult, that appeared late but eventually became prominent: the gradual process of his revealing a canon of scriptures (*jing* 經) and other texts through spirit-writing (*fuji* 扶乩, *fuluan* 扶鸞, *jiangbi* 降筆, *feiluan* 飛鸞) between the Ming and the nineteenth century. By the mid-nineteenth century, Guandi had become together with Lord Wenchang (Wenchang Dijun 文昌帝君) and Patriarch Lü (Lüzu 呂祖) one of the three dominant gods of the innumerable spirit-writing shrines that propagated elite values and worldviews throughout the Chinese world. In a separate article, I explore how these three gods, during the eighteenth and early nineteenth centuries, went through a process of canonization – both of themselves, as divine officials, and of their revealed texts anthologized in numerous and ever-larger "complete books" (*quanshu* 全書).[3] These *quanshu* canons are important for the sheer

---

* I am extremely grateful to Hu Jiechen, a Ph.D. student at Chinese University of Hong Kong working on the Wenchang spirit-writing cults, for his generous sharing of material with me. I have also greatly benefited from discussions with Wang Chien-ch'uan and Yau Chi-on.

[1] Provisionaly titled *From Monastic Protector to Moral Paragon. The Posthumous Career of Guan Yu.*

[2] Ter Haar, "The Rise of the Guan Yu Cult."

[3] Goossaert, "Spirit-writing, Canonization and the Rise of Divine Saviors."

amount of their contents, but also for their delineation of an elite religious orthodoxy.

I contend that the canonization processes of these three gods were not only strongly similar, but also deeply intertwined. Yet, they were not simultaneous; Wenchang clearly opened the way, with an exalted divine status and a coherent set of spirit-written scriptures as early as the Song period, followed by Patriarch Lü, and still later by Guandi. The first *quanshu* canons of Wenchang and Lüzu (*Wendi quanshu* 文帝全書 and *Lüzu quanshu* 呂祖全書) were published almost simultaneously and by the same people in 1743–1744. As we will see, it took several generations after that to have a full-fledged Guandi canon. Leaving aside for now the comparison between these deities (and others, who were also engaged in canonization processes), I would like here to offer a more descriptive account of the textual canonization process of Guandi. Much of the groundwork for the history of Guandi scriptures has been laid out by Yau Chi-on and Wang Chien-ch'uan;[4] I am here expanding on their research, using rare material and a different general framework. While the bulk of this contribution is devoted to a chronological account of the revelation and canonization of Guandi's texts, I shall conclude with reflections on the coherence of a corpus of texts revealed by different mediums in different parts of China over several centuries. I hasten to add that this reconstruction of the history of Guandi scriptures is highly tentative: the amount of relevant sources is staggering, and while some of them are available in recent reprints, others still lay on the shelves of rare books sections of numerous libraries. After being able to obtain full access to some, I have so far only seen the prefatory material and table of contents of others, and nothing of yet others.

1. Early Scriptures

The massive popularity of the Guandi cult throughout Qing society, in its many guises (from the elite worship of the paragon of loyalty, to Guandi as a wealth god honored by merchants, to the rebellious cults to the martial god) explains that a great many hagiographical collections were devoted to him. Classicist scholars such as Zhou Guangye 周廣業 (1730–1798) and Cui Yingliu 崔應榴, in their *Guandi shiji zhengxinbian* 關帝事蹟徵信編, a typical *kaozheng* extensive study of the historical sources pertaining to the god, list fifty-five anthologies that they could consult in the late Qianlong period, four of which were called *quanshu*.[5] But, most of these early Guandi *quanshu* were apparently not collections of revealed scriptures. Zhou and Cui themselves were not much interested in these scriptures, which they do not include in their work. After the fifty-five anthologies, they also list some editions and commentaries of scriptures (*Jueshi*

---

[4] Yau Chi-on, "Fuhua yunei," "Ming zhongye yilai de Guandi xinyang"; Wang Chien-ch'uan, "Spirit-writing groups in Modern China"; and the articles in Wang Chien-ch'uan *et al.* (eds.), *Jindai de Guandi xinyang yu shengdian*.

[5] "Shulüe" 書略, *Guandi shiji zhengxinbian*, j. 30.

zhenjing 覺世真經, *Zhongyijing* 忠義經, *Jieshi wen* 戒士文), as well as a manuscript collection of poems and short instructions.

The rich and continuous tradition of anthologies devoted to Guandi since the Ming, documented by Zhou and Cui, mostly focused on the historical accounts of his life, his official and popular cult, and his miracles. Within this tradition of texts, scriptures revealed by Guandi through spirit-writing seem to appear with the *Guansheng dijun shengji tuzhi* 關聖帝君聖蹟圖誌 (compiled around 1692 by Lu Zhan 盧湛). This deeply influential anthology focused on hagiography and historical material (texts in his honor written through the ages, inscriptions and documents related to his temples, liturgy for the official sacrifices) but also included one revealed scripture, the *Zhongyijing*.[6] Another short scripture, a morality book, *Guansheng dijun jueshi zhenjing* 關聖帝君覺世真經, was also circulating by the turn of the 18th century. Let us now look briefly at these two scriptures.[7]

Zhongyijing

Probably the earliest scripture revealed by Guandi, the *Zhongyijing* has a particularly complex textual history and circulates in two versions, one with 18 and another with 19 chapters; from the Kangxi period on, it had a commentary by Yu Shixie 郁世燮 (*juren* 1705).[8] Most editions have a preface by Yang Bo 楊博 (?-1564). Yang was a high military official of the Ming period, and signs his preface as Minister of War (a post he assumed in 1555). The authenticity of the preface written by Yang Bo is not certain, but the fact that Guandi is referred to by the title of Marquis (*hou* 侯) speaks in favor of an early date of writing. Yang explains that this scripture has been in circulation for a long period of time – he mentions the Song period Sun Shi 孫奭 (962–1033) as the first editor. Being from southern Shanxi (like Guandi) and a devotee, he was happy to be given a copy by a fellow official in 1556, and to have it printed and distributed. Yang makes no allusion to spirit-writing whatsoever. However, later generations seem to have taken for granted that the *Zhongyijing* was spirit-written.[9]

The scripture is entirely written in verses of four characters (usually not rhyming). The nineteen sections (in the longer version) are: 1. "explaining my

---

[6] The best study on this text is Li Shiwei, "Chuangxin shengzhe." On p. 73, Li mentions that it contained a *Jueshi baoxun* 覺世寶訓 (maybe the *Jueshi zhenjing*?); however, the various editions of the *Guansheng dijun shengji tuzhi* I have been able to access do not include such a text, only the *Zhongyijing* does.

[7] Let us note that a very short scripture devoted to Guandi and included in the 1607 supplement to the *Daozang*, DZ 1446: *Taishang dasheng langling shangjiang huoguo miaojing* 太上大聖郎靈上將護國妙經, seems to have been largely forgotten afterwards and is not included in the collections discussed here.

[8] For details on the *Zhongyijing* (which went by numerous alternative titles), see my entry on JY 260 for the *Daozang jiyao* project (work in progress).

[9] Zhou Guangye and Cui Yingliu say as much: "Shulüe," *Guandi shiji zhengxinbian*, j. 30.

ambition" (*shuzhi* 述志), where Guandi tells about his own life; 2. "chaos" (*hongmeng* 鴻濛), about cosmology and moral retribution; 3. "amounts of vital energy" (*qishu* 氣數), about differing destinies given at birth; 4. "the ways of the world" (*shidao* 世道), about present-day moral decadence; 5. "places for living" (*juchu* 居處), about social harmony; 6. "marriage and education" (*peiyu* 配育), about family values; 7. "building" (*xiujian* 修建), about taboos when doing construction work; 8. "being successful in the examination" (*gongming* 功名); 9. "traveling" (*youxing* 游行), about the dangers of military life; 10. "trials" (*fusong* 符訟), about the dangers of being caught in judicial proceedings, 11. "diseases" (*jibing* 疾病), where illnesses are ascribed to gods and otherworldly trials; 12. "destinies" (*mingyun* 命運), about how different humans are endowed with different destinies; 13. "cultivating life" (*shesheng* 攝生), about physical self-cultivation; 14. "epidemics" (*wenzhai* 瘟瘵); 15. "great simplicity" (*taipu* 太樸), about moral decadence in human history; 16. "the realm of desires" (*yujie* 慾界), about the lack of morality among present-day humans; 17. "rain and sunshine" (*yuyang* 雨暘), about natural disasters; 18. "being born as a human" (*shengren* 生人), about the various gods who manage human life; 19. "retribution" (*yebao* 業報), about divine surveillance of humans and the retribution of good and bad deeds. All these sections share a common structure: after describing the hardships of human life, Guandi addresses his devotees and promise protection and blessings if they can recite his scripture and put its teachings in practice.

All in all, the *Zhongyijing* is a morality book focusing on the law of retribution and moral decadence. Guandi himself is not represented as playing a central role in the working of the divine bureaucracy managing retribution. In the text, as well as in the *Jueshi zhenjing* discussed below, Guandi assumes a soteriological role as he instructs his devotees to care for their karma, but this, again in contrast to contemporary (early 18th century) Lüzu and Wenchang texts, is not deployed in an eschatological context.[10]

Jueshi zhenjing

Until the turn of the 19th century, the *Jueshi zhenjing* was the most prestigious, and oft-quoted, annotated and republished text attributed to Guandi.[11] This short text (around 650 characters) is very close in style, themes and inspiration to the Song-period *Taishang ganyingpian* 太上感應篇 and the mid-17th-century *Wenchang dijun yinzhiwen* 文昌帝君陰騭文, and even lifts entire sentences from these two illustrious morality books. Some themes found in the *Jueshi zhenjing* would characterize the whole later corpus of Guandi texts: a focus (albeit not exclusive) on patriarchal family values, and a martial identity that pushes him to

---

[10] Goossaert, "Modern Daoist eschatology."

[11] For a discussion and translation in French, see Goossaert, *Livres de morale révélés par les dieux*, pp. 25-31. For a German translation, see Diesinger, *Vom General zum Gott*.

threaten sinners with violent execution: "If you ignore my instructions, you will taste of my sword!"[12]

The revelation of the *Jueshi zhenjing* seems to date from the early Kangxi reign, around 1660–1680; some editions carry a claim that the revelation took place in 1668.[13] The earliest reliably dated preface was written in 1691, and the earliest known edition was published during the 1720s. Like the *Yinzhiwen*, which likely served as a template, the *Jueshi zhenjing* starts with parallel prose, then quickly adopts a rigid structure of 3- and then 4-character sentences that do not rhyme. This suggests it was aimed for reading and recitation, but not chanting. The text's narrative structure follows its changes in prosody: it starts with a praise of the gentleman whose moral conscience is always vigilant, then evokes the heavenly system of moral monitoring that punishes any wrongdoing. This is followed by a long list of good actions to be performed and bad actions to be shunned. As a conclusion, Guandi promises his blessings to those who will follow the path of virtue.

In the long run, of these two earliest Guandi scriptures, it is the *Jueshi zhenjing* that would prove most successful: it would continually elicit new commentaries and independent editions through the 18th and 19th centuries, whereas the *Zhongyijing*, while always included in Guandi canons, would not (as far as I know) have new commentaries after the one written by Yu Shixie in the Kangxi period, and have far fewer stand-alone editions.

2. The First Scriptural Canon: *Wudi huibian*

For the whole 18th century, the two above texts (*Zhongyijing* and *Jueshi zhenjing*) remained the two main Guandi scriptures, but shorter texts started to accumulate, prompting the urge for the compilation of an authoritative collection. No less a literati than Peng Shaosheng 彭紹升 (1740–1796) compiled his own Guandi canon, the *Guansheng dijun quanshu* 關聖帝君全書, prefaced in 1772 by his eminent father, the minister Peng Qifeng 彭啟豐 (1701–1784). The preface and the *fanli* 凡例 of this work show that it was largely based on Lu Zhan's *Guansheng dijun shengji tuzhi* (with numerous additions and corrections); it thus carried over the *Zhongyijing* (which Peng Shaosheng explicitly qualifies as a spirit-written morality book), and adds shorter spirit-written "sermons" (*fayu* 法語) which he describes as mostly concerned with Buddhist and Daoist self-cultivation. I have not yet seen this part of the *Guansheng dijun quanshu*, but I assume that these sermons are reprints of the revelations by Guandi at altars in Suzhou over a period of one century, which Peng Shaosheng edited under the title *Yuquan* 玉詮 (*JY* 243).[14] We have here one instance of an extremely common

---

[12] 若負吾教, 請試吾刀: Goossaert, *Livres de morale révélés par les dieux*, p. 28.

[13] On dating the *Jueshi zhenjing*, see Sakai Tadao, *Zōho Chūgoku zenshu*, vol. 2, pp. 184–185 and Yau Chi-on, "Fuhua yunei," pp. 222–225.

[14] The *Yuquan* contains revelations by a large number of deities, among whom Guandi features rather prominently. On spirit-writing activities and publications of the Peng family,

process; a scholar reprints a divine canon while adding new revelations that he or his immediate circle has produced through spirit-writing.

The idea of a purely scriptural (rather than historical/hagiographical) Guandi canon emerged shortly after Peng Shaosheng's own collection: it was called *Wudi huibian* 武帝彙編. Yau Chi-on ascribes the original compilation of this canon to Liu Qiao 劉樵, the same person who supervised the first Wenchang and Lüzu respective *quanshu* canons in 1743–1744.[15] I have, however, consulted an edition that seems identical to that used by Yau, and cannot find any mention of Liu Qiao in it. Indeed neither *Wudi huibian* nor Guandi are mentioned in the *Lüzu quanshu* and *Wendi quanshu*. There does not seem to exist any surviving copy of the original edition, but a much later edition (1876)[16] is likely to be a rather faithful reprint of the original without too many additions (as it does not include the many, better known, Guandi texts that were revealed after 1800, and consists of only four *juan*).[17] Beside hagiographical material and oracles (*lingqian* 靈籤), it contains the two scriptures mentioned above (*Jueshi zhenjing* and *Zhongyijing*) and short instructions. This edition has very little in the way of paratexts. A short preface by a certain Wu Hui 吳惠 (*zi* Liuqing 柳卿) explains that he tried to compile a Guandi canon on the model of the *Wendi quanshu* that his family had already reprinted (because the two, civil and martial emperors should be treated with equal devotion). Yet, Wu could find only few texts, and thus put together what he had found under the more modest title of *Wudi huibian*. One should note, then, that Wu was apparently not involved in producing new revelations. This preface is just dated of the *xinhai* 辛亥 year: the first such year after the publication of the *Wendi quanshu* is 1791, and this definitely seems to be the right dating for this text.

This Guandi canon thus contains much fewer scriptures than the Lüzu and Wenchang canons (which both ran to 32 *juan* in their first edition and were further expanded), even though Wu Hui had wished to put it on the same level. This situation is well reflected in the major Daoist canon of that period, the *Daozang jiyao* 道藏輯要, compiled around 1806 by Jiang Yupu 蔣予蒲 (*zi* Yuanting 元庭,

---

see the Ph.D. dissertation by Daniel Burton-Rose ("Terrestrial Reward as Divine Recompense: The Self-fashioned Piety of the Peng Lineage of Suzhou, 1650s–1870s"), to whom I am very grateful for sharing many materials and ideas.

[15] Yau Chi-on, "Fuhua yunei," pp. 220, 247. In his *Quanhua jinzhen* (p. 258), Yau quoted a Republican period work on morality books (*Gujin shanshu dacidian* 古今善書大辭典) that claims that Wu Liuqing republished Liu's *Wendi quanshu* and also compiled the *Wudi huibian*, which seems to me much more likely than any involvement by Liu Qiao. Yau Chi-on reads this passage in a different way that makes Liu Qiao the compiler (email exchanges, September 9, 2014). Whatever the right reading, I am extremely grateful to Yau Chi-on for discussing these issues with me.

[16] I am extremely grateful to Paul R. Katz and Wu Cheng-che 吳政哲 for obtaining a partial copy of this work for me.

[17] It does, however, feature one text revealed in 1855, the *Jiujiepian* 救劫篇, discussed below.

1755–1819) and his fellow spirit-writing adepts in Beijing. In this canon, about 200 texts are carried over from the Ming Daoist canon, and 100 are new texts of the late Ming, and, especially, the 18th century, representing the accelerating production of elite spirit-writing groups devoted to the cult of savior deities. Many of these "new" texts were revealed by savior deities who are represented by their scriptures, litanies, and hagiography: Lüzu is the central figure with a very significant collection of texts and scriptures; Wenchang comes second. Guandi is present, but is represented only by one hagiography and one scripture;[18] the *Zhongyijing*, or more precisely, *JY 260 Sanjie fumo Guansheng dijun zhongxiao zhongyi zhenjing* 三界伏魔關聖帝君忠孝忠義眞經. This text is actually composite, adding to the well-known *Zhongyijing*, a shorter and much rarer scripture (of strong exorcistic inspiration), the *Sanjie fumo Guandi zhongxiao huguo yiyun zhenjing* 三界伏魔關帝忠孝護國翊運眞經 (*JY* 260, 90a-92b), along with short litanies (*chan* 懺) and invocations (*baohao* 寶號).

3. The *Taoyuan mingshengjing*

Guandi's spectacular rise to prominence as the universal savior of end times would only come in the following decades, with the revelation (undated but likely 1805 or shortly before) of the *Taoyuan mingshengjing* 桃園明聖經.[19] We have no clue as to the precise context of its appearance, but it clearly was an instant success, and was eventually put in first place as the highest-ranking among the Guandi texts in some later canons; it was also later republished in countless editions throughout the 19th and 20th centuries. The scripture presents itself as having been originally revealed in dream to a Buddhist monk of the Yuquansi 玉泉寺 (the temple in Hubei province at the spot where Guandi was executed and where he was supposedly first worshipped), and later re-transmitted (for a larger dissemination) through spirit-writing; but this story is clearly a myth and not an actual account of the scripture's production. The text is much longer than earlier Guandi scriptures. It is mostly in parallel sentences, with some rhymed passages, and with brusque shifts of subject matter, in a style very common among spirit-written texts, and indeed in an 1840 revealed preface to a commentary (see below) Guandi acknowledged that it is indeed poor literature, but nonetheless provides very frank and clear admonitions.

In the *Taoyuan mingshengjing*, Guandi recounts his life story, taking it as an example of the virtues he preaches. He then discusses how the Jade Emperor promoted him to ever higher celestial positions, until he reached the supreme

---

[18] See, however, a short text, *Guansheng dijun qiongli jinxing zhiming shangpin shuo* 關聖帝君窮理盡性至命上品說, included in *JY* 102 *Guanyin dashi lianchuanjing* 觀音大士蓮船經, 2.1a-3b, and a litany (關帝忠武寶懺) in *JY* 246 *Chanfa daguan* 懺法大觀, 5.48a-61b.

[19] The most detailed study of this text's origins is Wang Chien-ch'uan, "*Jindai Guandi, Yuhuang jingjuan yu Xuanmen zhengzong wenxian daoyan.*" This text, like so many revealed scriptures, also went by several alternative titles, including *Yingyan (mingsheng) jing* 應驗(明聖)經.

position below the Jade Emperor, in charge of the retribution of humans. In one fascinating passage, he mentions how he took under his command the immortal Zhang (Zhang *xian* 張仙) who was without a proper position: this clearly refers to Wenchang, and thus represents an attempt to co-opt and subsume the Wenchang cult, even though the latter clearly served as a model for the Guandi spirit-writing cult. Guandi goes on to explain that he came down to earth repeatedly through history, each time the world was on the brink of chaos, in order to restore order (a theme likely borrowed from Wenchang lore).

Some elements in the *Mingshengjing* are very classical of Daoist scriptures composed for various deities: it promises this-worldly blessings of all kinds to those who will copy and recite the scripture; and, in direct continuation with earlier texts such as the *Jueshi zhenjing*, it discusses the heavenly bureaucracy at work monitoring humans and noting every single good or bad action, and accordingly granting rewards or punishments. Other elements appear as innovations. First, Guandi's divine status has been raised as he presents himself as the overall supervisor of rewards and punishments to humans. In listing virtues that humans need to cultivate, Guandi subsumes them under eight categories: *xiao* 孝, *ti* 悌, *zhong* 忠, *xin* 信, *yi* 義, *li* 禮, *lian* 廉, and *chi* 恥. This is probably one of the earliest mentions of the "eight virtues" (*bade* 八德) that would during the course of the 19th century become a major, well-identified discourse on morality, in subsequent texts revealed by both Guandi himself and other deities (including Wenchang).[20] Much of the scripture is devoted to describing the current moral decadence of humanity, beginning with, and putting much emphasis on officials – this focus also characterizes many later shorter Guandi tracts. The end of the text mentions twenty four calamities (*ershisi jie* 二十四劫) that will come, but overall (and similarly to the earlier *Zhongyijing* and *Jueshi zhenjing*), the eschatological element is not prominent in the scripture as a whole.

4. The 1828 *Guandi quanshu*

The next *Guandi quanshu*, as far as we know, was published in 1828 by Gan Yushi 甘雨施 (*zi* Daiyun 岱雲), a scholar from Rongchang 榮昌 county (near Chongqing). This appears as a rather "conservative" canon; it does not include the *Jueshi zhenjing* nor the already circulating *Taoyuan mingshengjing*. As far as revealed scriptures are concerned, and very much like the earlier canon by Peng Shaosheng, it features one scripture (the *Zhongyijing*) and a limited set of shorter tracts, in this case twenty-one, including the *Jieshizi wen* 戒士子文, that was already circulating in the 18th century. One important feature of this canon is that it was compiled in the same effort, and published together with a *Wenchang dijun quanshu*, and several prefaces closely relate the two deities. The Gan family in eastern Sichuan was actually well known for propagating the Wenchang cult.[21]

---

[20] On the "eight virtues," see Wang Chien-ch'uan, "Spirit-writing Groups in Modern China"; Fan Chunwu, "Bade."

[21] Hu Jiechen is currently working on this family.

A slightly earlier collection of Guandi texts, the *Qiankun zhengqilu* 乾坤正氣錄 (which is mentioned as a recent source by Gan Yushi), was somewhat more inclusive – if we can judge by a 1880 edition that has later additions.[22] It features the *Zhongyijing*, plus, in a separate section in the last chapter (suggesting that these revelations were still considered less important that the *Zhongyijing*), the *Taoyuan mingshengjing*, the *Jueshi zhenjing* and a set of shorter tracts, none of which (except one revealed in 1859 and added in the 1880 edition) has a strong eschatological element.

A still later, but yet rather "conservative" collection is the *Guandi jingchan* 關帝經懺, compiled and published in 1857 by the major Guandi temple in Quanzhou (Fujian). This rather short book, clearly geared toward liturgical use, includes *Zhongyijing* and *Jueshi zhenjing* (but not the *Taoyuan mingshengjing*), along with two very short *jing* (actually, tracts), and a long litany (different from those included in the 1858 canon). It is unclear why these collections did not include all existing texts (such as the Gan Yushi canon and the *Guandi jingchan* not including the *Taoyuan mingshengjing*): it is possible (but quite unlikely) that the compilers were not aware of the text's existence; it seems more likely that they chose to exclude it, because either of their doubts of its authenticity or because they did not approve its contents.

5. The Longnüsi Revelations

Another major turn in the development of the Guandi scriptural tradition takes places in 1840 in a temple called Longnüsi 龍女寺, located in a township within the county of Dingyuan 定遠 (now renamed Wusheng 武勝), not far north of Chongqing in Sichuan province (and not far from Rongchang where Gan Yushi compiled his Guandi canon). The Longnüsi revelations seem to have been widely distributed and had a major impact, for they are frequently mentioned in later texts (sometimes with explicit reference to the Longnüsi, more often just by referring to the *gengzi* 庚子 year, i.e., 1840).[23] They are also mentioned in the local gazetteer of that county – a rather remarkable fact, given that local gazetteers rarely discuss spirit-writing groups and scriptures.[24]

Takeuchi Fusaji had first called attention to the Longnüsi revelations in an article that focused on one scripture of that corpus of revelations, the *Zhilu baofa* 指路寶筏, for which he used a 1907 edition.[25] Wang Chien-ch'uan in his article "Taiwan 'Guandi dang Yuhuang' chuanshuo de youlai" 台灣「關帝當玉皇」傳說的由來 says that this is a text based on original Longnüsi elements but much

---

[22] The 1880 edition has one text explicitly revealed in 1859.

[23] Wang Chien-ch'uan, "Spirit-writing Groups in Modern China," discussing late 19th century texts.

[24] (*Minguo*) *Wushengxian xinzhi* (民國)武勝縣新志, *j.* 1, also discussed in Wang, "Spirit-writing Groups in Modern China."

[25] Takeuchi, "Shinmatsu Shisen no shūkyō undo."

rewritten by Xiantiandao 先天道 adepts in the Guangxu period, and therefore not reliable. Wang argues that there was no Xiantiandao element at Longnüsi and that it is only later that Xiantiandao adepts appropriated the Longnüsi ideas. This is important: the Xiantiandao is one of the most important devotional (or, as many scholars describe them, "sectarian") late imperial traditions, which served as a matrix for many of the 20th century new religions and redemptive societies. It would seem that Xiantiandao adopted spirit-writing and converged with the elite spirit-writing groups from the mid-nineteenth century onward.

Following on Takeuchi, with a wider range of source material, Wang Chien-ch'uan has shown that there is one extant, reliable Longnüsi text: the *Mingshengjing zhujie* 明聖經註解. This important edition and commentary of the *Taoyuan mingshengjing* only exists in later, post-Taiping editions – this is actually a very common problem: many of the spirit-written texts originally published before or during the Taiping Civil War now exist mostly in post-1864 editions, some of which are substantially modified. Our *Mingshengjing zhujie* seems to reliably reflect the 1840 text, however, and comes with rich paratext. I have used two editions, which have different sets of prefaces and postfaces, notably prefaces revealed by Guandi (dated 1840) and other gods, and written by the actual compilers of the text, as well as an account of miracles by Zhao Shi'an 趙世安, also dated 1840.[26]

Taken together, these accounts tell the following story: in 1838, Zhao Shi'an and his brothers who had long been Guandi devotees and recited the *Mingshengjing* each day morning and evening, complained that there existed no commentary on their favorite scripture. The elder brother, Zhao Zhengzhi 趙正治, wanted to have a commentary and asked a local scholar, Hu Yintian 胡印田 to write it, but then Zhao died before he could publish it. In 1840, during an intense series of daily revelations, Gao Shouren 高守仁, a god at Guandi's service, canonized as *tianjun* 天君 by the Jade Emperor,[27] told the Zhao brothers that their brother was now City God of Xiangtan 湘潭 county (Hunan province – which as we will see was another major center of the Guandi spirit-writing cult). He explained that during a tour of local gods, Guandi had met Zhao Zhengzhi, and that Zhao had asked Guandi to order his family to publish the commentary. In a preface, the brothers also mention that their elder brother communicated directly with them in dream about this. Guandi acquiesced, and entrusted Gao *tianjun* with the task. The commentary was corrected and approved by Gao, who also wrote a

---

[26] "Yuanxu" 原序, "Xianyingji" 顯應記, *Mingshengjing zhujie* (1873), pp. 3-10, 133-136; prefaces in *Mingshengjing zhujie* (Gaoxiong edition), pp. 113-114. The prefaces call the book *Mingshengjing zhushi* 明聖經註釋, which was probably the original title, but the extant editions are titled *Mingshengjing zhujie*.

[27] Gao *tianjun* does not seem to be known outside of the Guandi corpus, but had already revealed texts before the 1780s: he is mentioned as the divine author of a litany, *Bao'enchan* 報恩懺, in a late Qianlong period list of Guandi texts: *Guandi shiji zhengxinbian*, p. 558.

preface. Zhao Shi'an also tells of his spirit-writing exchanges with Lüzu and other deities, both at his home and at the Longnüsi temple, showing once again that the Guandi cult is not independent of the other spirit-writing saviors. He also recounts stories of exorcism performed by Guandi, and promotions of local deities in the divine bureaucracy. In this fascinating story, the themes of the spirit-writing adepts' own divinization (in this case, in the classical way as promotion among local territorial gods) and the production of scriptures are intimately related.

When talking about the Longnüsi, we should distinguish two different sets of texts and ideas: those that can actually be shown to originate from the Longnüsi 1840 group (such as the *Mingshengjing zhujie*); and those that later refer to them. The first is not strongly eschatological, even though it does emphasize Guandi's brutal role in meting out punishment to sinners. The second, by contrast, is devoted to a significant extent to a turn in cosmic events that is (later) described as having taken place in that very year of 1840. According to that story, the Jade Emperor having checked the records of humans' good and bad actions, and realized that they had become irredeemably vicious, had decided to annihilate humanity and unleash hordes of demons who would usher in the final apocalypse. Pleading with him for one last chance, Guandi, assisted by other deities (notably Lüzu, Wenchang and Guanyin) obtains one last reprieve (said in some accounts to last thirty years in order to save as many humans as possible by preaching a message of moral reform through spirit-writing.

As I have shown elsewhere,[28] this story is actually a new formulation of an old theme that has existed since the first documented spirit-written revelations (by Wenchang) during the 12th century. Wang Chien-ch'uan has studied this theme as it developed during the 19th century, and shown that it exists in a number of variations:[29] other texts (notably short tracts included in the 1858 *Guandi quanshu, j.* 22-24, but themselves impossible to date precisely) tell a very similar story, but with 1816 as the date of the averted apocalypse. Wang comments that maybe these texts do not date from 1816 but from subsequent decades: the story explains the flurry of revelations after the purportedly postponed apocalypse, rather than anything that took place on that precise moment. I suggest that the same may be said of the 1840 apocalypse story. I should note that I have not found one instance of the 1840 apocalyptic theme in the 1858 *Guandi quanshu* (discussed below – which, however, features similar stories with the initial apocalypse set in 1816 or 1847). To the best of my current knowledge, the earliest text that clearly refers to the story of the 1840 apocalypse is the *Jiushengchuan* 救生船 (that collects revelations from many different gods, including Guandi), which was published during the Taiping Civil War (the four *juan* have prefaces ranging from 1860 to 1863).[30] As Wang Chien-ch'uan has shown, the

---

[28] Goossaert, "Modern Daoist eschatology."

[29] Wang Chien-ch'uan, "Spirit-writing groups in Modern China."

[30] *Jiushengchuan*, 2.1a-b (Guandi preface, 1861), 2.57b, 3.23b, 4.1a-b (undated preface by Lüzu), 4.8a-9b.

altar in Sichuan that produced the *Jiushengchuan* was created and run by some of the original Longnüsi people.³¹ There are several editions of this text, albeit I have not yet located any original edition dating from the Taiping Civil War period. It is quite possible that the Longnüsi apocalypse story was still current only in Sichuan, and not adopted by the Hunan people who compiled the 1858 *Guandi quanshu*.

In brief, the Longnüsi group was maybe the first Guandi spirit-writing group well documented in terms of their social context. But, we still do not know clearly how the theme of Guandi as the main actor of the story, whereby apocalypse is called off, first appeared, and how it was associated with the Longnüsi group; very possibly, it was created in the context of the Taiping Civil War by former Longnüsi adepts, some twenty year after the original Longnüsi revelations. In any case, by 1860 Guandi had become the main actor in a cosmic drama. This was also the case, in a contemporary but independent source: the first full-fledged Guandi canon, produced in the context of the war.

6. The 1858 *Guandi quanshu*

The textual canonization process reached full maturity with the 1858 *Guandi quanshu* 關帝全書, a massive canon of 40 *juan*. The 1858 Guandi canon is both a major resource, and a frustrating one: by contrast to other spirit-writing canons that tend to provide rich paratext and information on their compilers, the *Guandi quanshu* comes as a bare collection of Guandi texts. Its compiler, Huang Qishu 黃啟曙, is not otherwise known, and he is only listed as being from Xiangtan, central Hunan.³² I have not been able to locate an original 1858 edition, but the available 1889 reprint seems to be faithful to the original 1858 edition, as I have not found in it any post-1858 addition other than colophons.

We thus lack details on the context of the compilation of this canon, and can only infer the Taiping Civil War context, with both actual impact of Taiping armies in the Hunan province during 1851–1858, and the massive engagement in the war of the Hunan local elites and ordinary people through the Hunan army (*Xiangjun* 湘軍).³³ Most of the short tracts (*j.* 22-24, see below) that are located are from this same central Hunan area; some of them hint clearly at the war context.³⁴ The text that discusses the Taiping Civil War in the clearest terms is the *Jiujiepian* 救劫篇 (also called *Jiujie baoxun* 救劫寶訓),³⁵ revealed by Guandi at Jingzhou 荊州 (southernmost Hubei, just north of Hunan) in 1855. In this text,

---

[31] Wang Chien-ch'uan, "Spirit-writing groups in Modern China."

[32] Liu Wenxing, "Guandi *Jueshi zhenjing* zhushiben chutan," also shows that the commentaries on the *Jueshi zhenjing* in the canon comes from the same Xiangtan area.

[33] I discuss the connection of sprit-writing texts, eschatology and the Taiping Civil War, with special attention to the Hunan context (where a very large number of texts were revealed, probably some in connection to the Hunan army) in my "Guerre, violence et eschatologie."

[34] *Guandi quanshu*, *j.* 24, pp. 662, 672, 696.

[35] Ibid., pp. 662-665, also in *Wudi huibian*, 3.43a-45a, and *Jiujie yuwen huike*.

Guandi describes the mountains of corpses left by the war and explains that this is a result of the apocalypse ordered by the Jade Emperor, after the failure of Guandi's attempts (through spirit-writing) to bring back humanity to virtue. After two hundred years of peace and prosperity, says Guandi, Qing officials have fallen into utter corruption. He then compares these disasters with other wars in Chinese history, from the Yellow Turbans of the late Han to the Zhang Xianzhong 張獻忠 (1607–1647) rebellion in Sichuan, and adds that these earlier disasters were minor when compared with the current situation – in this as well as other revealed texts of that period I have seen, the Taiping are never actually mentioned explicitly. Heaven thus sent down on earth Demon Kings (*mowang* 魔王) to wage war and terror, and destroy temples. In spite of all this, Guandi promises that those who repent and engage in good actions in earnest will be saved. This short text was included in the *Jiujie yuwen huike* 救劫諭文彙刻 (Anthology of [Divine] Edicts to Save Humanity from the Apocalypse)[36] – a rather short collection of texts revealed by various gods between 1855 and 1860 (mostly in the Hunan-Hubei region), and published in early 1861.

Another important element in this canon is the last *juan*, which is a record of miracles performed by Guandi and his two generals in the framework of a spirit-writing cult in that same Xiangtan area in 1849–1851, just before the war. Barend ter Haar, who analyzed this document, suggests it might actually have been compiled by Huang Qishu himself.[37] All in all, the 1858 canon seems to be the result of a well-established Guandi spirit-writing cult in central Hunan that was given increased vibrancy by the war.

The 1858 *Guandi quanshu* identified the *Taoyuan mingshengjing* (with its 1840 commentary) as its most prominent scripture.[38] Following the *Taoyuan mingshengjing*, the *Zhongyijing* and the *Jueshi zhenjing*, other new scriptures are included (*j.* 8-11, 13-14, 19-21), none of which are known in earlier Guandi canons. Even though some of these scriptures have prefaces by other gods, notably Wenchang and Lüzu who are very consistently associated with Guandi throughout this canon, they do not come with any information as to the date and context of their production. Some may have been produced in the Hunan milieu of the 1850s; others, maybe most, may date from earlier decades.

Another important new element in the 1858 canon is the liturgical one. In all the scriptural canons of spirit-writing deities, we see that morality books appear first, then longer scriptures, and finally litanies of confession (*chan* 懺). Guandi is no exception. Guandi litanies actually existed as early as the 18th century: a *Bao'enchan* 報恩懺 was listed in the late Qianlong bibliography within the *Guandi shiji zhengxinbian*. By 1806, when Guandi was included in the *Daozang jiyao*, a very short litany of penitence, *Guandi baochan* 關帝寶懺 (99a-101a),

---

[36] The *Jiujie yuwen huike* contains eight distinct revealed texts and a postface; all are not as strongly eschatological as the first two texts, revealed by Guandi.

[37] Ter Haar, "Divine violence to uphold moral values."

[38] This canon also features a different scripture, called *Mingshengjing*.

invoking Guandi under various divine titles, along with various little known Heavenly Worthies and divine emperors, was added to the *Zhongyijing*. No independent litany was included in other Guandi canons, however (neither the Peng Shaosheng, nor the Liu Hui or the Gan Yushi canons included one), before the 1857 *Guandi jingchan*, and the 1858 canon that included two long, full-fledged litanies.

Besides scriptures and litanies, the Guandi cult in the first decades of the 19th century produced a remarkable number of shorter tracts (*xunwen* 訓文); for the 1850s milieu in Hunan, this seems to have become the most important medium for producing a Guandi discourse. We have seen that earlier canons often included one or two dozen of such texts. The 1840 preface of the *Mingshengjing zhujie* mentions a *Guandi baoxunji* 關帝寶訓集 (now lost). The 1858 *Guandi quanshu* feature a widely expanded corpus where they are collected in *j.* 22-24, with 144 texts covering some 400 pages of the modern reprint. As we have them, these tracts are very difficult to date and place; a few allude to actual people and locations (mostly in Hunan and Sichuan). Many share similar styles and vocabulary. It is very possible, even likely, that many of them were produced in central Hunan shortly before 1858.

Many of these short tracts (like the *Jiujiepian* discussed above) are devoted to developing the eschatological themes that thus became prominent in the Guandi texts during that period. I am strongly tempted to consider that this prominence results from the Taiping Civil War. At the same time, they also clearly refer to the earlier history of Guandi revelations, showing how a spirit-writing tradition could be acutely conscious of its history. Interestingly, while these 1850s Guandi revelations often refer to the *Jueshi zhenjing*, they do not mention the *Zhongyijing* or the *Taoyuan mingshengjing*. Two of them discuss the history of spirit-writing, and also denounce the "vegetarian sects" (with explicit mentions of the 1796–1804 White Lotus Rebellion) that delude people and reject spirit-writing.[39] They thus provide a vision of how these Guandi spirit-writing groups saw their place in the larger religious landscape.

7. Conclusion: The Doctrinal Coherence of a Complex Corpus

The production of Guandi texts and their canonization continued beyond 1858, and actually continues to this day.[40] I would like, however, to stop the chronological narrative at this point, and take a larger view of the texts we have surveyed so far. The corpus of Guandi revelations places special emphasis on family virtues, and elevates the twin virtues of filial piety (*xiao* 孝) and loyalty (*zhong* 忠), to the pinnacle of its moral system. However, this is a question of emphasis ra-

---

[39] *Chu yiduan wen* 黜異端文, *Guandi quanshu* (1858), *j.* 22, pp. 402-405; *Bianduan wuji wen* 辨端誣乩文; *Guandi quanshu* (1858), *j.* 23, pp. 546-550. Guandi texts often reject vegetarianism and vegetarian "sects," yet they consistently argue against killing animals, and strongly promote the beef and dog taboos.

[40] Wang Chien-ch'uan *et al.* (ed.), *Jindai de Guandi Xinyang yu shengdian*.

ther than exclusion: in all his major scriptures, from the earliest ones down to the mid-19th century, we do find the other major themes of the morality book tradition: honesty in business and commerce (Guandi is, after all, a patron saint of merchants and shopkeepers, and numerous texts in the 1858 canon are devoted to business ethics), respect for animal life, respect for social order and hierarchies, and charity for the poor. In the larger world of spirit-written texts and *shanshu* 善書, our Guandi corpus is not dissonant at all, yet it is often distinctive in tone.

In his survey of late Qing spirit-writing, Wang Chien-ch'uan talks of various systems (*xi* 系) linked to one deity, exploring more specifically the Guandi, Lüzu, and Jigong 濟公 systems.[41] Wang focuses on the social networks that developed these various cults. I would like to suggest that we can also see a theological element of coherence within these three systems: what Guandi revealed through the successive stages discussed above – from the Kangxi (if not earlier) period down to the Taiping Civil War, and from his being a relatively minor god in the world of spirit-writing to the Taiping war period apotheosis – displays a certain coherence. Divine *personae* (and this obviously does not entail any claim about their actual existence) are actants (in the sense of Bruno Latour) that have their own built-in logic, personality, and constraints. Any revelation that would appear as in contradiction with this persona would presumably be rejected as false (and indeed the canonization process of spirit-writing gods also entails a good deal of selection and rejection of "unreliable" revelations,[42] even though I have not yet seen examples in the case of Guandi. The fact that we have focused on canons (i.e., the products of selection and removal of texts not considered as orthodox) certainly helps us identify doctrinal coherence, since other texts that were certainly produced in the name of Guandi but did not fit in are absent from the picture. So the development of the corpus of Guandi revelations from the Ming to the Taiping period (and this also applies to later periods down to the present) starts from a received idea of what Guandi says; the corpus develops, aggregates new themes, grows markedly more apocalyptic from the 1840s onwards (following in the footsteps of other gods), but maintains a certain doctrinal coherence.

This core Guandi doctrine includes the sacralization of hierarchies, first in family, and then in society; the valuation of this-worldly renunciation and asceticism (saving and giving as opposed to consuming, reducing sexuality, good food, and other pleasures); the constant repetition of Guandi's own example as a role model to emulate, and the presence of violence,[43] first in the way Guandi threatens (or actually metes out) punishment for sinners, and then in the grand apocalyptic scenarios from the 1850s onwards. Several authors have characterized the early Qing phase of the Guandi cult as a process of Confucianization (*rujiahua* 儒家化); and the 19th century as the emergence of a new type of revealed texts,

---

[41] Wang Chien-ch'uan, "Spirit-writing groups in Modern China."

[42] Goossaert, "Spirit-writing, canonization and the rise of divine saviors."

[43] Barend ter Haar, "Divine violence to uphold moral values" has focused on the question of violence.

more popular, sectarian, and apocalyptic.[44] While these arguments have value, they should not obscure the continuous development of the corpus of Guandi revealed texts, and their very intimate connection to other corpuses (notably by Wenchang and Lüzu), where Buddhist and Daoist elements always remain very important.[45]

Bibliography

Primary Sources

Guandi jingchan 關帝經懺. 1857 edition from the Quanzhou Guanhuai temple, in: Wang Chien-ch'uan (ed.), *Ming Qing minjian zongjiao jingjuan wenxian* 明清民間宗教經卷文獻, vol. 10.

Guandi quanshu 關帝全書, Gan Yushi 甘雨施 (comp.), 1828, original edition at Guojia tushuguan.

Guandi quanshu 關帝全書, Huang Qishu 黃啟曙 (comp.), 1858, 1889 edition in: *Guandi wenxian huibian* 關帝文獻匯編. Beijing: Guoji wenhua chuban gongsi, 1995.

Guandi shiji zhengxinbian 關帝事蹟徵信編, Zhou Guangye 周廣業 and Cui Yingliu 崔應榴 (comps.), 1882 edition in: *Guandi wenxian huibian* 關帝文獻匯編. Beijing: Guoji wenhua, 1995.

Guansheng dijun quanshu 關聖帝君全書, Peng Shaosheng 彭紹升 (comp.), 1772 edition at Guojia tushuguan.

Guansheng dijun shengji tuzhi quanji 關聖帝君聖跡圖誌全集, Lu Zhan 盧湛 (comp.), 1849 edition, in: *Zhongguo daoguan zhi congkan xubian* 中國道觀志叢刊續編. Yangzhou: Guangling chubanshe, 2004, vols. 1-2.

Jiujie yuwen huike 救劫論文彙刻, 1861 edition at Institut des hautes études chinoises library, Collège de France.

Jiushengchuan 救生船, 1905 edition in: Wang Chien-ch'uan (ed.), *Ming Qing minjian zongjiao jingjuan wenxian xubian* 明清民間宗教經卷文獻續編, vol. 9 (see also the 1876 edition from the Beijing Yangyuzhai 北京養玉齋 in *Sandong shiyi* 三洞拾遺, vol. 6).

Mingshengjing zhujie 明聖經註解. 1873 edition in: Wang Chien-ch'uan (ed.), *Jindai Guandi, Yuhuang jingjuan yu Xuanmen zhenzong wenxian* 近代關帝、玉皇經卷與玄門真宗文獻. Taibei: Boyang, 2012, 6 vols., vol. 1.

Mingshengjing zhujie 明聖經註解, undated edition from the Yongxingtang 永興堂 (Gaoxiong), in Wang Chien-ch'uan (ed.), *Ming Qing minjian zongjiao jingjuan wenxian* 明清民間宗教經卷文獻, vol. 10.

---

[44] Yau Chi-on, "Fuhua yunei," "Ming zhongye yilai de Guandi xinyang," drawing on the work of earlier scholars, notably Sakai Tadao.

[45] I will devote a separate piece to the question of Daoism in this corpus.

Qiankun zhengqilu 乾坤正氣錄, 1880 edition in *Sandong shiyi*, vol. 4.

Wudi huibian 武帝彙編, 1876 reprint at Taiwan National Library.

Wushengxian xinzhi 武勝縣新志, Republican period.

Yuquan 玉詮, in (*Chongkan*) *Daozang jiyao*.

Secondary Sources

Burton-Rose, Daniel. "Terrestrial Reward as Divine Recompense: The Self-fashioned Piety of the Peng Lineage of Suzhou, 1650s–1870s," Ph.D. diss., Princeton University, 2016.

Diesinger, Gunter. *Vom General zum Gott. Kuan Yü (gest. 220 n.Chr.) und seine "posthume Karriere."* Frankfurt am Main: Haag und Herchen, 1984.

Fan Chunwu 范純武. "Bade. Jindai Zhongguo jiushi tuanti de daode leimu yu shijian" 八德—近代中國救世團體的道德類目與實踐, in: Paul R. Katz (Kang Bao 康豹) and Vincent Goossaert (Gao Wansang 高萬桑) (eds.), *Gaibian Zhongguo zongjiao de wushinian* 改變中國宗教的 50 年. Taibei: Academia Sinica, 2015, pp. 225-259.

Goossaert, Vincent. *Livres de morale révélés par les dieux*, édités, traduits, présentés et annotés par V. Goossaert. Paris: Belles-Lettres, 2012.

—. "Modern Daoist Eschatology. Spirit-writing and Elite Soteriology in Late Imperial China," *Daoism. Religion, History & Society* 6 (2014), pp. 219-246.

—. "Spirit-writing, Canonization and the Rise of Divine Saviors: Wenchang, Lüzu, and Guandi, 1700–1858," *Late Imperial China*, 36 (2015) 2, pp. 82-125.

—. "Guerre, violence et eschatologie. Interprétations religieuses de la guerre des Taiping (1851-1864)", in: Jean Baechler (ed.), *Guerre et Religion*. Paris: Hermann, 2016, pp. 81-94.

Li Shiwei 李世偉. "Chuangxin shengzhe: *Guansheng dijun shengji tuzhi* yu Guandi chongbai 創新聖者—《關聖帝君聖蹟圖誌》與關帝崇拜," in: Wang Chien-ch'uan 王見川 *et al.* (eds.), *Jindai de Guandi xinyang yu jingdian*, pp. 76-82.

Liu Wenxing 劉文星. "*Guandi jueshi zhenjing* zhushiben chutan. Yi Huang Qishu suoji de sanzhong *Jueshi zhenjing* weili" 《關帝覺世真經》註釋本初探. 以黃啟曙所輯的三種《覺世真經》為例, in: Wang Chien-ch'uan 王見川 *et al.* (eds.), *Jindai de Guandi xinyang yu jingdian*, pp. 47-68.

Sakai Tadao 酒井忠夫. *Zōho Chūgoku zenshu no kenkyū* 增補中國善書の研究. Tokyo: Kokusho kankōkai, 1999.

Takeuchi Fusaji 武內房司. "Shinmatsu Shisen no shūkyō undō" 清末四川の宗教運動, *Gakushūin daigaku bungakubu kenkyū nenpō* 学習院大学文学部研究年報 37 (1994), pp. 59-93.

Ter Haar, Barend. "Divine Violence to Uphold Moral Values: The Casebook of an Emperor Guan Temple in Hunan Province in 1851–1852," in: Jeroen Duindam *et al.* (eds.), *Law and Empire. Ideas, Practices, Actors*. Brill: Leiden, 2013, pp. 314-338.

—. "The Rise of the Guan Yu Cult: the Taoist Connection," in: Jan A.M. de Meyer – Peter M. Engelfriet (eds.), *Linked Faiths. Essays on Chinese Religions and Traditional Culture in Honour of Kristofer Schipper*. Leiden: Brill, 2000, pp. 184-204.

Wang Chien-ch'uan 王見川. "Taiwan 'Guandi dang Yuhuang' chuanshuo de youlai" 台灣「關帝當玉皇」傳說的由來, in: *Hanren zongjiao, minjian xinyang yu yuyanshu de tansuo: Wang Jianchuan zixuanji* 漢人宗教、民間信仰與預言書的探索—王見川自選集. Taibei: Boyang, 2008, pp. 412-430.

—. et al. (eds.). *Jindai de Guandi xinyang yu jingdian. Jiantan qi zai Xin, Ma de fazhan* 近代的關帝信仰與經典—兼談其在新、馬的發展. Taibei: Boyang, 2010.

—. "*Jindai Guandi, Yuhuang jingjuan yu Xuanmen zhenzong wenxian* daoyan" 《近代關帝、玉皇經卷與玄門真宗文獻》導言, in: *id.* (ed.), *Jindai Guandi, Yuhuang jingjuan yu Xuanmen zhenzong wenxian* 近代關帝、玉皇經卷與玄門真宗文獻. 6 vols. Taibei: Boyang, 2012.

—. "Spirit-writing Groups in Modern China (1840-1937): Textual Production, Public Teachings, and Charity," translated by Vincent Goossaert, in: V. Goossaert – Jan Kiely – John Lagerwey (eds.), *Modern Chinese Religion II. 1850-2015*. Leiden: Brill, 2016, pp. 651-684.

Yau Chi-on [You Zi'an] 游子安. "Fuhua yunei. Qingdai yilai Guandi shanshu ji qi xinyang de chuanbo" 敷化宇內—清代以來關帝善書及其信仰的傳播, *Journal of Chinese Studies* 中國文化研究所學報 50 (2010), pp. 219-253.

—. "Ming zhongye yilai de Guandi xinyang: yi shanshu wei tantao zhongxin" 明中葉以來的關帝信仰—以善書為探討中心, in: Wang Chien-ch'uan 王見川 *et al.* (eds.), *Jindai de Guandi xinyang yu jingdian*, pp. 3-46.

—. *Quanhua jinzhen. Qingdai shanshu yanjiu* 勸化金箴—清代善書研究. Tianjin: Tianjin renmin chubanshe, 1999.

ISLAM AND CONFUCIANISM
AN OFFERING TO FR. MALEK

FRANÇOISE AUBIN

I would have liked to offer to Fr. Roman Malek, S.V.D., an original contribution showing the proximity of the written style of Muslim Chinese classical literature with the Christian one during the 17th–18th centuries. Unhappily, great age and bad health impeded me to carry through this project; and I must content myself with taking up again and translating a paper which I submitted recently for publication to Études orientales about "Islam chinois et confucianisme."[1] But it is an immense pleasure and a great honour for me to be given the opportunity of expressing my deep admiration for Fr. Malek's contributions to Chinese studies: first, for the reader's delight, he brought the journal Monumenta Serica to an exceptionally high level of perfection from a material point of view as much as for its content; secondly, he strongly and efficiently advocated the strengthening of Chinese young priests and seminarists' theological culture; and finally, which here concerns us in the most living way, he was actively involved in the recent discovery of the Christian Chinese written literature. I am also pleased to express here to him and to the staff of Monumenta Serica Institute my deep gratitude for the many opportunities this Institute gave me to do research in its library in a pleasant way so that the present paper is one of the results of many years of relationship with the Monumenta Serica Institute library.

When I say that I am interested in Chinese Islam (that is Islam expressed in Chinese for people looking quite Chinese) from the point of view of Confucianism, I generally meet surprise and even scepticism. My approach goes too much against well entrenched and preconceived ideas about Chinese civilization: by nature Confucianism is supposed to be in struggle against Islam. My purpose is now to explain that Islam, which is much more than the Koran, has become in China, since at least the seventeenth century, a religion as Chinese as Buddhism or, more recently, as Christianity has become. And that it did not expand against Confucianism but within it.

Although Islam is solely represented by Sunnism from the Hanafi School in China, it shows some original features which shed light on its flexibility.

---

[1] I deeply thank the responsible staff of *Études orientales* first for stimulating me to carry out my ideas, then for allowing me to present an English translation of my article here.

Historical Overview

There is neither an historical event nor precise date, and particularly no military fact to which to ascribe the entrance of Islam into the Chinese empire. The formation of local Muslim communities all over China has been the result of a long process of anonymous entrances into various places of the country and unassuming continuous settlements.[2] In the first centuries, Near Eastern and Central Asian merchants who set foot on Southern Chinese harbours and Western China were surely not Muslims and even not Arabs: they were more often Persian speaking Mazdean believers. Until the 12th century, they were kept by the Chinese Tang and then Song governments – and by themselves – more or less isolated from the Chinese population. A real Muslim implantation goes back to the Song dynasty, from about the 12th century, as is proved by the existence of mosques and Arabic inscriptions in cemeteries of Southern China and in the 13th–14th centuries, during the Mongolian Chinggisid Yuan dynasty, there are many testimonies of a sudden stream of Arab and Persian speaking helpers of the Mongol government: soldiers, administrators, and various technicians. At that time, Near-Eastern immigrants were generally Muslims integrating rather fast into the host society: already by the third generation, as far as we know, the literate personalities were typical Chinese painters or poets, without a hint of Islam in their artistic expression.

However, during the native dynasty following the Mongol epoch, the Ming Dynasty (1368–1644), Islam obviously had become a Chinese religion followed by believers that were completely sinizised. It was then a religion present in every province and even prefecture, more strongly in north-western provinces at the end of the caravan roads, in Henan province around ancient capitals, and along the seashore. But everywhere it was as unassuming as possible; the mosques around which each local community was evolving were built to look like Chinese popular temples from the outside, although inside they were quite Muslim.[3] A characteristic Muslim literature in the Chinese written language began to appear in the last years of the Ming time, in the mid-seventeenth century, and expanded vigorously during the following Sino-Manchu Qing dynasty (1644–1911), as we shall see.

The main point which Chinese Muslims stood for was that their religion was a Western one, coming from a West different from Europe and superior to that of Christianity. During the Republican time, along with the modern ideas of nationality, ethnicity and the constitution of China as a "Nation-State," they began to put forward their foreign origin and to insist on the fact they were different from the stock of non-believers. The conclusion was that when in the 1930s the Com-

---

[2] For a general basic bibliography see Donald Daniel Leslie – Yang Daye 楊大業 – Ahmed Youssef, *Islam in Traditional China. A Bibliographical Guide*. MSMS LIV (Nettetal: Steyler Verlag, 2006).

[3] One example: Jill S. Cowen, "Dongdasi of Xian. A Mosque in the Guise of a Buddhist Temple," *Oriental Art* XXIX (1983) 2, pp. 134-147.

munist long-marchers stopped at Yan'an in North-West China, proposed to the Muslims to recognise them as an autonomous ethnicity under the name of Hui 回, they accepted. In this way the Communists tried to gain the support of the Chinese Muslims during the war against Japan and the subsequent struggle against the Guomindang – at least they wanted to ensure the neutrality of this considerably large part of the population which appeared so strange to them. For the concerned Muslims, it was a way to have their religious specificity recognised as an ethnic feature. Now eighty years later, an imaginary tradition has been built up and the ten millions or so of Hui are more than ever convinced that they pertain to a distinctive, non-Han nationality (while remaining faithful Chinese citizens).

In the contemporary world, a strategy brought into focus by clever Muslim shopkeepers was to play on the meaning of their self designation as followers of the *Qingzhenjiao* 清真教, "the Religion of the Pure and Real": their main identity is to be "pure," so the food they offer is pure in essence. From this argument results the extraordinary success of Muslim restaurants opened in towns on a background of scandals of food pollution. It is a kind of revenge on centuries of self-segregation owing to their abstinence from pork, an abstinence which sometimes remains now the last mark of their ancestors' Muslim faith.

Various Options

Nevertheless, the Chinese case clearly shows that, as everywhere in the Ummah, Islam is not a unifying factor among believers, as it is divided between diverse options which, although all pertaining to Hanafite Sunnism, may be opposed by rivalry if not by hate. Consequently, some Western specialists are uncertain about the possibility of talking about a "Chinese Islam" as an effective reality of global relevance.

The most widespread form of Muslim religiosity in China, as well as the most ancient one, is called in Chinese *ge-di-mu* 格底木,[4] that is the Arabic word *qadim*, "ancient": it is a more or less strict observance of the *sharī'a* (the Koranic law) and its five commandments taught in a local independent mosque by an imam called *ahong* 阿訇. In some places, this *ahong* inherited his position from his father, but more often he is recruited by the committee of elders of the mosque for a limited period of time so that he moves from one place to another, bringing with him his own library and the knowledge he acquired in China and often in Inner Asia, especially at Samarkand and Bukhara, and now at al-Azhar in Cairo, without the control of any higher ranking religious authority. These intinerant teachers and celebrants helped to maintain a certain unity in theory and rituals.

There were also various Sufi brotherhoods which penetrated into Western China. They spread in successive waves, each under the leadership of a holy

---

[4] The reader may notice that we note with a hyphen between each *pinyin* syllable those Chinese expressions which are only transcriptions from Arabo-Persian words, in order to distinguish them from genuine Chinese locutions, as *heping* 和平 "peace."

shaykh (a Master) announcing that he was reforming an Islam degenerated because of its isolation.

Uprisings

And what about the uprisings involving Muslim villages and places and which ravaged Western China especially at the end of the 18th century (around 1781), in the second half of the 19th (1862–1872) and still disturbed the 20th century? For the Chinese government (and for official literature) troubles were always the work of bandits. For the main foreign witnesses who were Protestant missionaries specializing in the apostolate among Chinese Muslims,[5] it was the living proof that Islam was maladjusted to the Chinese world: the fashionable leitmotiv of "Islam versus Confucianism" prevailed for about a century in Western academic works about Islam in China. But when some decades ago, scholars began to read the multiple Chinese sources available – which had not been done before – a quite different picture appeared. It became obvious that these rebellions were never the result of a call to an anti-Chinese *jihad*, but of a small local incident; very often it was a discord between two small Sufi groups. Then the Qing government sent its army supposedly for "restoring order," in fact for repressing the party which did not buy clemency. Violence provoked violence in reply and finally the official army depopulated entire places. We must recognise that the so-called Muslim rebellions presented all the features of traditional Chinese popular uprisings, all the more so since they occurred at a time of general troubles in a China weary of her Manchu dynasty: for example several surviving leaders of the Taiping rebellion (1850–1864) gave strategic advices to some of the rebellious *shaykhs*.

There are other practical proofs against the theory of an absolute incompatibility of Islam and Chinese civilization. For example there is the well-known fact that in the Chinese countryside Muslim boys very often took a spouse in the non-Muslim neighbourhood: before her entrance into the Muslim family, before pronouncing the *shahāda* which made her a convert, the girl was compelled to accurately wash herself outside and inside of all the pork and fat of pork she was supposed to have eaten in her life. So it commonly happened that a Muslim man had an originally non-Muslim wife, a converted mother, a converted grandmother and a non-Muslim family-in-law whom he met for festive events. For centuries in China the main ways of the demographic increase of the Muslim communities were the marriage of Muslim boys (never the girls) outside their religious social group and the adoption of baby girls rejected by peasants of the vicinity.

Incidentally, the question of polygamy is a good opportunity to see how Chinese Muslims could adapt themselves to precepts of law with which they dis-

---

[5] Françoise Aubin, "L'apostolat protestant en milieu musulman chinois," in: *Chine et Europe. Actes du IVe Colloque international de Sinologie de Chantilly, 1983*. Variétés sinologiques – Nouvelle série, 73 (Taibei 1991), pp. 12-74.

agree. According to an official Chinese principle, a man was allowed to have a main spouse and as many concubines as he could afford, on the condition of a strict hierarchical order between these women, the main wife being the head of the female group. For the Muslims, a man was allowed to have four legal wives, on the condition that they had all equal rights. So what happened in China? In actual practice, this was considered as a family matter and nobody tried to find out what was the real rank of the women inside the family.

Another example of adaptation of the religious Muslim principles with Chinese customs is seen in the funeral rites, so important in Chinese culture. Everything concerning the dead body is scrupulously done in accordance with Muslim rules; but the attitudes of the participants are quite Chinese, especially among the women who play their part loudly with screams, shouts, offering of food and incense, and so on.

Problems of the Transcription of Arabic into Chinese

The best approach for understanding the problem of the integration of Islam into a Chinese environment is to examine the written expression of Islamic thought in Chinese. Here some features mark the essence of Islam in Chinese language:

1. Although Arabic is the sacred language of Islam, the cultural language of educated Chinese Muslims was Persian, because the main stock of literature they were accustomed to use was written by persianised authors from Inner Asia and the Arabic words were received by Muslim Chinese under their Persian form. It is interesting to notice that now in the 21st century, Chinese Islam is undergoing a strong Arabisation under Saudi Arabia's impulse, with the agreement of the Communist government which pushes its "Hui minority" to be an intermediary (especially a commercial intermediary) with rich Near Eastern countries. Under such conditions the Persian language, having lost its cultural value, became the cultural language of female imams (the presence of female imams being a distinctive feature of Chinese Islam).

2. When Islam appeared to really belong to Chinese culture, at least at the turn of the 16th to 17th century, there was no longer any native speaker of Arabic and Persian in the country. For every believer both languages were foreign ones, which had to be learned with painstaking effort.

3. Finally the utmost difficulty that we are not able to fathom adequately was that for the first and unique time in its history Islam (and also Christianity) met with the language of a cultured country devoid of an alphabet. The first solution was to use the pronunciation of some Chinese characters as transcribing units: this was what traditionally Chinese translators of Mongolian,[6] Manchu or Sanskrit texts have done for centuries.

---

[6] On the Chinese transcription of the *Yuanchao mishi* 元朝秘史 (Secret History of the Mongols) see my review of Hitoshi Kuribayashi 栗林均, Genchō hishi *Mongorugo kanji onyaku, bōyaku kanngo taishō go-i* 『元朝秘史』モンゴル語漢字音訳・傍訳漢語対照語彙 – *Word-Index to the* Secret History of the Mongols *with Chinese Transcriptions and Glosses* (Sendai 2009) in *Monumenta Serica* 59 (2011), pp. 555-557.

For example, the welcoming greeting, *al-salāmu 'alaykum*, "Peace with you," is often written (although other transcriptions exist, no more clearer) *an-se-liang-mu a-lai-kong* 安色俩目阿來空; the exclamation *allāhu akbar*, "Allah [is] the greatest," becomes *an-la-hu a-ke-ba-er* 安拉乎阿克巴兒.[7]

One of the basic problems is that Chinese written phonetic misses separate consonants: for example *sunnat* (the Persian form of the Arabic word *sunna* which is in use in China) is written *xun-nai-ti* 孫奈提; the *dhikr* (a repetitive call to God in Sufi ceremonies) is written *qi-ke-er* 弃克爾 or *ji-ke-er* 即克爾.

The second thorny difficulty for us, when trying to reconstruct the original Arabo-Persian word – a genuine nightmare –, is to guess which local, dialectal reading of a Chinese written character has been chosen by the author. As is commonly known, China, being as vast as a continent, is a polyglot country with a host of different dialects and pronunciations.

Anyway, there are some rules for the transcription of Muslim words with Chinese characters:

1. the transcribed word is generally taken under its Persian form;
2. the adopted form is always a singular one: *han kitab*, never *han kutub*;
3. the original notations being, as a rule, unvocalised, the transcribed vowels are only long vowels or initial ones. Example: *'ilm*, "knowledge, science" = *ai-er-mu* 艾爾姆 or *yi-ri-mu* 伊日目 or sometimes *er-lin* 爾林;
4. the dissimilation of the double -l of Allah is rendered by *an-la*. For example, the first part of the *shahāda*, *lā ilāha illā allāhu* is given as *liang yi-la-ha yin-liang an-la* 俩伊拉哈因俩安拉 or *liang yi-liang-hai yin-lan la-hu* 俩伊俩亥印烂拉乎; the pilgrimage, *hajj*, is given either as *ha-ji* 哈吉, *ha-zhi* 哈志 or *han-ji* 罕吉;
5. the dialects used more often are those of Northern and Western China;[8]
6. as a rule, the Chinese character used for a transcription has a neutral meaning; but it may occur that it has by itself a meaning linked to the original word: for example *mai* 埋 "to bury a dead" in the expression transcribed from the Arabic *mai-ti* 埋體 = ar. *mayta*, "mort d'un animal" (David A. King, "Mayl" [declination], *The Encyclopaedia of Islam*, new ed., vol. VI, fasc. 113-114 [Leiden: Brill, 1990], pp. 914-915).

---

[7] There is now a very convenient *Glossary of Chinese Islamic Terms* by Wang Jianping 王建平 (Richmond, Surrey: Curzon Press, 2001).

[8] Cf. Paul Wexler about Jewish and Islamic transcriptions: "The cartography of unspoken languages of culture and liturgy. Reflexions on the diffusion of Arabic and Hebrew," *Orbis* 23 (1974) 1, pp. 30-51; "Research frontiers on Sino-Islamic linguistics," *Journal of Chinese Linguistics* 4 (1976) 1, pp. 47-82; "Jewish languages in Kaifeng, Henan province, China, 1163-1933," *ZDMG* 135 (1985) 2, pp. 330-347; and Ma Shudiao 马树钓, "Hanyu Hezhouhua yu A'ertai yuyan" 汉语河州话与阿尔泰语言, *Minzu yuwen* 民族语文 1984/2, pp. 50-55.

Elementary education was given in Arabic by the imam (then the children were compelled to learn the Koran by heart without understanding its meaning) and the teaching at a higher level was in Persian, in both cases the imam teachers used this system of transcription for Chinese characters. No wonder if later the believers and even the imam(s) spoke Arabic with an incomprehensible way of pronunciation and were laughed to scorn when visiting Mecca. Something better was to be invented.

Around the mid-sixteenth century, at the peak of the Ming Dynasty, when Muslim communities of Chinese-looking adherents, more or less auto-segregated near their mosques, were ubiquitous in China, it happened that China closed its Inner Asian boundaries on international security grounds. Thus direct intellectual connections were severed with the great Inner Asian centers which until then had provided teaching imam(s) with apologetic literature. These imam(s) (*ahong*) started to ponder about the best way for transmitting their religious message directly into a Chinese context, as religious teachers were haunted (until the 20th century) by the fear that the original Koranic message would be lost or misrepresented.

Problems of the Translation of Arabo-Persian into Chinese

So the point was to determine which would be the basic language for teaching and conveying religious matters. The habit to translate original Muslim texts into literary Chinese became implanted somehow in a way which we yet do not know very much about. In one way, according to an inner tradition, the founder of a new method of teaching in the mosque, called *jingtang jiaoyu* 經堂教育, "Education of the Hall of the Book (i.e, the Koran),"[9] was Hu Dengzhou 胡登洲 (ca. 1522–1597), an '*ālim* (Chinese *a-lin* 阿林, specialists of religious questions, *huiru* 回儒 or *shi* 士) teaching in an ancient region of Chinese culture, in the West of the confluence of the Wei to the Yellow River.

In another way, it seems that since the mid-17th and more strongly in the 18th century, Chinese '*ulama*' ('*ulama*' being the plural form of '*ālim*) living in coastal towns, especially Nanjing, draw their inspiration from the example of their neighbours, the Jesuit missionaries and their literate Chinese converts who already had been very successfully translating or writing by themselves Christian literature into literary Chinese for some decades: although we surely cannot suspect that Muslims have "cribbed" from Chinese Christian works, it seems that they were interested in how Christians could present to the cultivated people in an understandable way religious concepts and ideas that, while not identical, were very similar to those of Islam (seen from China, Islam and Christianity look very close to each other). The framework for literary expression in Chinese during the Ming and Qing dynasties was what we call "Neo-Confucianism." In that way, Chinese '*ulama*' wrote their work in the Neo-Confucian style in which they had been educated and their books were collectively called the *Han kitāb* (*Han* mean-

---

[9] Cf. Zvi Ben-Dor Benite, *The Dao of Muhammad. A Cultural History of Muslims in Late Imperial China* (Cambridge, Mass.: Harvard University, Asia Center, 2005).

ing "Chinese" in Chinese, and *kitāb* being the Arabic word for "book," in the singular form).

The first Christian work written in a Neo-Confucian style was *Tianzhu shiyi* 天主實義 (The True Meaning of the Lord of Heaven)[10] published in Peking in 1603 by the famous Jesuit Matteo Ricci (1552–1610), a book which, we know, was read by Muslim scholars. The first known *Han kitāb* was *Zhengjiao zhenquan* 正教真詮 (The Real Commentary on the True Teaching) published in 1642 in Nanjing by the *'ālim* Wang Daiyu 王岱輿 (ca. 1592 – ca. 1658). Although there is a gap of forty years between the publication of the two works, such a time span is normal in terms of literary influence.

Sufism

Generally, a *Han kitāb* includes elementary initiations to compulsory religious rites, and to the holy history of the past, including the mythical heroic founders of the Chinese culture who were supposed to have come from the Near East; then the teaching introduces Confucian ethics which was supposed to be a Muslim moral system which lost its religious dimension, and so on. And finally a *Han kitāb* in general concludes with a Sufi treatise. The Sufism expressed by authors of literary Islam appears devoid of any allegiance to a specific brotherhood.

The diverse ways of worship were classified according to three stages which were described with terms borrowed from Daoism, Buddhism, and Confucianism.

The first lower level is the cult practised in the mosque and based on the *sharī'a*: it is called "the Usual Way" or "the Vehicle of Rites."

The second level, "the Middle Way" or "Vehicle of the Way," is practised inside popular Sufi brotherhood.

Only at the third level, "the Perfect Way" or "the Vehicle of the Transcendental Reality," which is taught in the *Han kitāb*, the believer may reach union with God which is the final goal of his mental process.

	The Three Levels of the Knowledge of God		
	The Way = *dao* 道	The Vehicle = *cheng* 乘	Transmitted through:
1	Usual (*chang* 常)	of Rites (*li* 禮) or of the Teaching (*jiao* 教)	*Sharī'at*
2	Middle (*zhong* 中)	of the Way (*dao* 道)	*Tarīqat*
3	Perfect (*zhi* 至)	of the transcendental Reality (*zhen* 真)	*Haqīqat*

---

[10] Matteo Ricci, *The True Meaning of the Lord of Heaven* (*T'ien-chu shih-i*), translated with Introduction and Notes by Douglas Lancashire and Peter Hu Kuo-chen, S.J. A Chinese-English Edition, edited by Edward J. Malatesta, S.J. Variétés sinologiques N.S., 72 (St. Louis – Taibei: The Ricci Institute, 1985).

Neo-Confucian Expression

It sometimes happens that I am asked what I mean by the expression "Confucian style" and especially "Neo-Confucian" applied to Islamic literature. For understanding it, I advise the reader to refer to the splendid expositions by Anne Cheng in her *Histoire de la pensée chinoise* (Éditions du Seuil, 1997) and Peter K. Bol in his *Neo-Confucianism in History* (2008). The term of Neo-Confucianism is a Western invention for designating an intellectual movement, which appeared in the 11th century and lasted for one millennium with many roundabout ways, splits and various branches, sometimes under the fire of an official condemnation. It is also sometimes called the "Teaching of the Way" (*daoxue* 道學), "Teaching of the Spirit" (*xinxue* 心學), and so on, but Peter Bol prefers the general term of "Neo-Confucianism" for showing the deep unity of the movement that its supporters felt despite their divergences.

It is probably not a matter of chance, that the first great *Han kitāb*, as mentioned above, published in 1642, near the end of the Ming dynasty, was preceded, during some forty years, by a flow of Christian apologetic and theological publications expressed in Confucian terms. The way, opened by Matteo Ricci, was followed by European missionaries, mainly Jesuits, and the first Chinese converts, as Xu Guangqi 徐光啟 (1562–1633), Li Zhizao 李之藻 (1565–1630) or Yang Tingyun 楊廷筠 (1562–1627).[11] When Manchus invaded China and overthrew the Ming dynasty, Christian converts numbered about 70,000, mainly peasants and people of modest means. As for the literati converts, they generally pertained to the local gentry, at Nanjing, Suzhou and other towns of Central and Coastal China, just where these Muslim literati looking for scriptural models lived. In the atmosphere of the philosophical and literary discussions so characteristic of provincial China by the end of the 16th and the first half of the 17th century, we may easily imagine that our Muslim literati, such as Wang Daiyu, were aware of the Christian publications and probably even entertained discussions with their authors as they could have debated with local Neo-Confucians. The new Christian literature proved that it would be possible for them to express in an understandable written language a theology and an ethic very close to theirs. This does not mean that they copied down the Christian literature, but that to them it was a kind of enlightenment and even a catalyst, that is, as a faulty reasoning which had to be corrected.

For which audience did the *'ulama'* write? Christian foreign and native scholars had for their final target the conversion of the whole Chinese population, and, for this, they explained again and again that Christianity did not contradict Confucian tenets and was not a condemned heterodox sect.

---

[11] See an inventory of these Chinese Christian publications of the 17th c. in the "Index of Chinese and Manchu Books," in: *HCC* 1, pp. 936-941. See also Gianni Criveller, *Preaching Christ in Late Ming China. The Jesuits' Presentation of Christ from Matteo Ricci to Giulio Aleni* (Taibei: Ricci Institute for Chinese Studies *et al.*, 1997), for example "*Learned Conversations in Fuzhou* by Giulio Aleni (1582–1649)," pp. 260-280.

Conversely, Muslim scholars did not particularly aim at the conversion of unbelievers. Strangely enough, Islam in China was not a religion of conquest. For example, there is not a single mention of a Confucian scholar's conversion, as there was for Christianity. *Han kitāb* authors blandly announced that they were native Chinese, sons of Chinese, and that from immemorial time Islam was their ancestors' religion. Furthermore, Confucius was a prophet, the only Chinese prophet. Confucianism was an Islamic teaching which forgot the Revelation so that it was the "outer part" (*biao* 表), of the reality, while Islam was its "inner part" (*li* 裏). The main work of the *ulamā'* was the "rectification" (*zheng* 正) of the ideas, the usual duty of Confucian thinkers, and they aimed at educating the rank and file believers, who, living so far away from Mecca, were suspected to have lost the basis of their faith and to be unable to pick up the Sufi message. And as a secondary aim, they intended, as Christians did, to demonstrate to those Confucian literati in a position of power that they were themselves good Confucians and that their religion had nothing in common with forbidden sects. Indeed, their relationship with neighbouring Confucian scholars were sometimes warm and even fruitful, as it happened that some of these literati wrote prefaces for *Han kitāb*, for example for that of the great Liu Zhi 劉智 (ca. 1670 – ca. 1730), introduced below.

We must also underline that the spirituality of the *chan/zen* (*dhyāna*) Buddhism, which permeated the Neo-Confucianism of the Cheng brothers in the Northern Song and Wang Yangming 王陽明 (also Wang Shouren 王守仁, 1472–1529) in the Ming dynasty, suited Chinese Muslim authors very well, as nearly all of them were deeply influenced by Sufism: the Neo-Confucian idea of cosmic unity – heaven, earth and myriad of things, including man – helped them in their meditations about divine immanence or transcendence and mystic unity. The Neo-Confucian processes for understanding the world and acting accordingly were perfectly suitable for Islamic spirituality. Arguments expressed as circles of thought in Chinese as well as in Arabic and the method of a catechism by questions and replies, *wenda* 問答, used in Chinese as well as in Arabic, concurred to bring together *'ulama'* and Neo-Confucianists' reasoning.

There is, too, a matter of compatibility in the statement of acts and facts: for example, the *silsila*, the chain of the Holy men which vindicates the authority of the present head of a Sufi community, is called *daotong* 道統, a term which in the Confucian tradition points out the transmission of a doctrine. Furthermore, mythical Chinese heroes were adopted as Muslim founders who forgot their religion, and so on.

Two recent remarkable books help us now to begin to understand the working mechanisms of the borrowing: it is by Sachiko Murata and her contributors, a commented translation of an emblematic work of the literary Chinese Islam, the *Tianfang xingli* 天方性理 (generally understood as philosophy), published in 1704 by Liu Zhi, the *'ālim* whose thought was till nowadays the most influential in the Chinese speaking Muslim world,[12] and that of the above mentioned founding work of the *Han kitāb* in 1642, by Wang Daiyu.[13]

The Confucian tint of the moral and theological teaching of Chinese *'ulama'* was due to a lot of philological turns, as dichotomies and polarities, for example *ti* 體 (substance) versus *yong* 用 (function); or *yi* 義 (meaning) versus *xing* 形 (form) or *xiang* 象 (images), etc. ... Or a chain of inclusive or exclusive implications (if there is A, there is B, if there is B, there is C), or a vocabulary which looks as a coded language.

We see an identity of the words expressing actions to be performed for fulfilling the *dao* 道. The five rules of propriety, which Confucianism codified early on, the *wulun* 五倫 (relationship between prince and minister or ruler and subject, between father and son or parents and children, between husband and wife, between elder brother and younger brother, and between friends), became in Islam "the five Rules of the Human Way" (*rendao wudian* 人道五典), and they found a parallel at a upper level with "the Five Meritorious Acts of the Celestial Way" (*tiandao wugong* 天道五功), that are the Five Pillars of Faith. The congruity of tenets in the methods of enhancing their faith is striking, for example by self-examination and auto-improvement. One basic operation was designated by the term *gewu* 格物 (investigation of things). It is often associated with *zhizhi* 致知 (expand one's knowledge) and *qiongli* 窮理 (fully fulfil the principle).

Many basic concepts of spiritual expression are here re-used. One example is provided by the title of the work which Murata translated (2009) – *Tianfang xingli*. *Tianfang* literally points out "the square of the Sky," i.e., the place of the Sky, and more precisely the *ka'ba* or more broadly Mecca and generally Arabia, or even in Liu Zhi's age the whole Arabo-Muslim world; the *xing* 性 of *xingli* is one of the central terms of Neo-Confucianism: "the Nature," but which nature? Each Neo-Confucian or Muslim author devotes himself to demonstrate his theory in this matter. It is obvious that for Liu Zhi, *xing* translates the Arabic word *rūḥ*, an equivalent of *nafs* (soul, spirit). As for *li* 理 (the Principle), this is a concept central to every Neo-Confucian discussion. In the end, the concept indicated by the characters *xing li* is generally translated by foreign scholars as "philosophy" and thus the title of Liu Zhi's book is rendered as "Philosophy of Islam." Certainly it is the final meaning of the expression, but as demonstrated by Murata (2009, p. 50), it is not a question of philosophy in the sense of the arabic *falsafa*, but really of "nature and principle."

---

[12] Sachiko Murata – William C. Chittick – Tu Weiming, with a foreword by Seyyed Hossein Nasr, *The Sage Learning of Liu Zhi. Islamic Thought in Confucian Terms* (Cambridge, Mass.: Harvard University Asia Center for the Harvard-Yenching Institute, 2009).

[13] Sachiko Murata, *Chinese Gleams of Sufi Light. Wang Tai-yu's* Great Learning of the Pure and Real *and Liu Chih's* Displaying the Concealment of the Real Realm (Albany, N.Y.: State University of New York Press, 2000).

Conclusion

To sum up in a general way: Although the *Han kitāb* authors borrowed liberally from Neo-Confucian texts, they proposed a perfect Islamic teaching without any heresy. Therefore, it would be a mistake to interpret their works as "syncretism," as certain Western scholars have done somewhat prematurely and in a biased manner, without taking more than a superficial glance at the contents of the *Han kitāb*.[14] As a material proof, we can turn to the *Tianfang xingli* written by one of the greatest *'ulama'*, Liu Zhi, which can be counted among the most popular books giving Muslim lessons in a Confucian language. In fact, it became so popular that an admirer of the author, Ma Lianyuan 馬聯元 (Nûr al-Haqq, 1841–1903) from Yunnan, almost two centuries later, in 1898, prepared an Arabic translation of a part of this work, the *Benjing* 本經 (Root Classic) with the title *al-Laṭā'if* (The Subtleties) which he published with a commentary in India in 1902 as *Sharḥ al-laṭā'if* (An Explanation of *The Subtleties*) in order to introduce Chinese Islamic thought to the greater Muslim world.[15] This Arabic translation lacks many of the Chinese features of the original, but it kept an inner Muslim genuineness. Thus, Literary Confucianism and its imagery were only the tools of communication adequate for the Chinese cultured society. What else could the *'ulamā'* have done apart from following contemporary scholarly trends and making good use of preexisting concepts? As they could not transcribe original terms, they had to translate them. In this they did not differ much from Christian authors like Matteo Ricci and his followers, who certainly could not be accused as advocates of syncretism.

One of the great differences between the efforts of Muslims and Christians to spread their faith in China is that Muslim authors focused on proving that Confucianism did not contradict their religion, while Christian authors had to demonstrate that their faith was not opposed to Confucianism.

Turning to the 20th and the beginning of our 21st century, we can observe that the Koran and Muslim literature were translated into modern spoken language (*putonghua* 普通話). This includes the *Han kitāb*, which on account of their specificity are still respected by the believers as fundamental tools. However, the main current is nowadays the enhancement of teaching in Arabic under the supervision of Saudi Arabia.

---

[14] See James D. Frankel, *Rectifying God's Name. Liu Zhi's Confucian Translation of Monotheism and Islamic Law* (Honolulu: University of Hawai'i Press, 2011).

[15] Cf. Murata *et al.*, *The Sage Learning of Liu Zhi*, pp. 15-19 and Sachiko Murata, "Die drei Dimensionen des konfuzianischen Islam," *Chh* XXXI (2012) 4, pp. 245-249.

The Most Important Books about Islam in China and in Chinese

1 Basic bibliography: Donald Daniel Leslie – Yang Daye 楊大業 – Ahmed Youssef, *Islam in Traditional China. A Bibliographical Guide*. Monumenta Serica Monograph Series LIV (Nettetal: Steyler Verlag, 2006).

2 Inventory of primary sources: Donald Daniel Leslie, *Islamic Literature in Chinese, Late Ming and Early Ch'ing. Books, Authors and Associates* (Belconnen: Canberra College of Advanced Education, 1981).

3 General history of Islam in China by the 18th century: Donald Daniel Leslie, *Islam in Traditional China. A Short History to 1800* (Belconnen: Canberra College of Advanced Education, 1986).

4 The invention of Hui and Han nationalities: Dru C. Gladney, *Muslim Chinese. Ethnic Nationalism in the People's Republic*. Harvard East Asian Monographs, 149 (Cambridge, Mass.: Harvard University Press, 1991; 2nd ed. 1996). Summary of cases analysed by Gladney (1991) in: *id.*, *Ethnic Identity in China. The Making of a Muslim Minority Nationality* (Orlando, Fl.: Harcourt Brace College Publishers, 1998).

5 About the feeling of a Hui ethnicity (and Female Islam): Élisabeth Allès, *Musulmans de Chine. Une anthropologie des Hui du Henan* (Paris: EHESS, 2000).

6 Some typical cases in history: Jonathan N. Lipman, *Familiar Strangers. A History of Muslims in Northwest China* (Seattle: University of Washington Press, 1997).

7 Modernism among Muslim city dwellers: Maris Boyd Gillette, *Between Mecca and Beijing. Modernization and Consumption among Urban Chinese Muslims* (Stanford, Cal.: Stanford University Press, 2000).

8 Female Islam: Maria Jaschok – Shui Jingjun, *The History of Women's Mosques in Chinese Islam. A Mosque of Their Own* (Richmond: Curzon Press, 2000).

9 A case of Muslim uprising in the 19th century: David G. Atwill, *The Chinese Sultanate. Islam, Ethnicity, and the Panthay Rebellion in Southwest China, 1856–1873* (Stanford, Cal.: Stanford University Press, 2005).

10 On Sufi literary Islam there are two remarkable works: Murata Sachiko, *Chinese Gleams of Sufi Light. Wang Tai-yü's Great Learning of the Pure and Real and Liu Chi's Displaying the Concealment of the Real Realm, with a New Translation of Jāmī's Lawā'iḥ from the Persian by William C. Chittick* (Albany, N.Y.: State University of New York Press, 2000); Murata Sachiko, in collaboration with William C. Chittick, and Tu Weiming, *The Sage Learning of Liu Zhi. Islamic Thought in Confucian Terms* (Cambridge, Mass.: Harvard University Asia Center for the Harvard-Yenching Institute, 2009).

11 Internal networks of transmission of Islamic learning: Zvi Ben-Dor Benite, *The Dao of Muhammad. A Cultural History of Muslims in Late Imperial China*. Harvard East Asian Monographs, 248 (Cambridge, Mass.: Harvard University Press, 2005).

DER EINFLUSS DER URBANISIERUNG AUF DIE MUSLIMISCHEN GEMEINSCHAFTEN IN CHINA IM SPIEGEL CHINESISCHER FACHZEITSCHRIFTEN

KATHARINA WENZEL-TEUBER[*]

1. Einführung

Dass Städte modern und deshalb säkular seien, bezeichnet Peter van der Veer in seiner Einleitung zum *Handbook of Religion and the Asian City* als ein besonders hartnäckiges Missverständnis. Soziologen hätten die singuläre europäische Erfahrung von Urbanisierung und gleichzeitiger Entkirchlichung irrtümlich für ein globales Modell gehalten.[1] „If one goes outside the Euro-American space, ignoring religious spaciality is impossible, even in the sanitized urban spaces of China", schreibt van der Veer.[2] Die Stadt sei „the meeting ground of various populations that had been hardly in touch with one another before arriving there, which makes the need to self-identify and connect quite important. This can be done through churches, temples, shrines, or storefront places of worship. The city is thus a theater of religious innovation […]".[3]

Wie wirkt sich die Urbanisierung auf die Religionsgemeinschaften Festlandchinas aus? Führt sie zu Säkularisierung oder zu religiöser Innovation und Erneuerung? Dieser Frage geht der folgende Text am Beispiel des Islam nach. Dabei stützt er sich auf Forschungsergebnisse chinesischer Wissenschaftler, die in den letzten Jahren einiges zu diesem Thema geschrieben haben. Die meisten der benutzten Aufsätze sind in Zeitschriften erschienen, die in der Volksrepublik China an staatlichen Akademien der Sozialwissenschaften und Universitäten oder von der regierungsgestützten Chinesischen Islamischen Vereinigung (Zhongguo yisilanjiao xiehui 中国伊斯兰教协会) herausgegeben werden. Es ist also eine Art Literaturbericht, der einen offiziellen und dabei bemerkenswert vielfältigen Forschungsstand vorstellt. Je nach Fachbereich und Interesse der oft fächerübergreifend arbeitenden Autoren stehen soziologische, ethnologische, anthropologische oder, seltener, religionswissenschaftliche Fragestellungen im Vordergrund. Einige Texte formulieren explizit Empfehlungen für die staatliche Religions- und

---

[*] Bei Reisen nach China im Auftrag des China-Zentrums habe ich in ländlichen Regionen Nordwest- und Südwestchinas die drastischen Veränderungen gesehen, die der katholischen Kirche in China durch Migration und Urbanisierung entstanden sind. Dies weckte mein Interesse für ähnliche Phänomene auch bei anderen Religionen. Mit diesem Beitrag möchte ich P. Roman Malek danken, der mich als Mitarbeiterin in das China-Zentrum und in die Welt der chinesischen Religionen eingeführt hat.

[1] Van der Veer 2015, S. 7-8.
[2] *Ibid.*, S. 6.
[3] *Ibid.*, S. 9.

Minderheitenpolitik.⁴ Ein großer Teil der Autoren gehört den Hui an, der größten muslimischen Nationalität Chinas (was aber keine automatischen Rückschlüsse auf ihre persönliche Religiosität erlaubt).⁵ Im folgenden Text steht also die Situation der Hui-Muslime im Vordergrund. Gezeigt wird eine Außensicht – die muslimischen Geistlichen oder Gläubigen selbst, die möglicherweise vieles anders sehen würden, kommen nicht zu Wort.

Die chinesischen Forscher sehen zwei zentrale Faktoren für die gewaltigen Umbrüche, die die urbane muslimische Kultur seit Beginn der Reform- und Öffnungspolitik und insbesondere seit den 1990er Jahren drastisch verändern: die Auflösung der traditionellen Muslimviertel im Zuge eines tiefgreifenden Umbaus der Städte und die starke Zuwanderung muslimischer Binnenmigranten, meist aus ländlichen Gebieten im Westen Chinas, im Zuge der Urbanisierung.⁶ Während chinesische Politiker und Wissenschaftler – vielleicht unter dem Einfluss des bei van der Veer angeführten „Missverständnisses" – bei Planungen zu Städtebau, Urbanisierung und Umsiedlung den Faktor Religion zunächst kaum berücksichtigten, hat sich dies in letzter Zeit etwas geändert,⁷ was auch die im Folgenden behandelten Texte belegen.

---

⁴ Nach David Palmer gibt es im politischen System Chinas ein „diskursives Netzwerk" zu Religionsfragen, das aus Parteikadern/Religionsbeamten, Wissenschaftlern und staatlich anerkannten religiösen Führern besteht. Über die Rolle der Akademiker in diesem Netzwerk schreibt er: „[A]cademics, no less than the religious leaders, have been active in formulating their visions of how the religion they study should modernize. [...] Scholars typically have a more liberal attitude than the government, but also need to establish and protect the legitimacy of their field of study, and they use academic norms of distance and objectivity to balance their sympathies with the religions they study." Palmer 2009, S. 21. Diese Haltungen chinesischer Religionsforscher spiegeln auch viele der hier besprochenen Artikel wider.

⁵ Viele der herangezogenen Artikel sind in *Huizu yanjiu* 回族研究 (*Journal of Hui Muslim Minority Studies*) erschienen; diese Zeitschrift gibt stets auch die ethnische Zugehörigkeit ihrer Autoren an, die großenteils selbst Hui sind (daher auch das häufige Vorkommen des für die Hui typischen Familiennamens Ma 马 unter den hier besprochenen Autoren). Auffällig ist, dass unter dem in chinesischen Fachzeitschriften reichlich vorhandenen Material kein Aufsatz eines uigurischen Autors zu finden war. – Zitate aus chinesischsprachigen Artikeln werden in deutscher Übersetzung der Autorin wiedergegeben.

⁶ So z.B. Ge Zhuang 2011, S. 157. – Der chinesische Begriff *chengshi gaizao* 城市改造 wird hier mit „Stadtumbau" übersetzt. Für den Begriff „Urbanisierung" verwenden die ausgewerteten Texte unterschiedliche Bezeichnungen: *chengshihua* 城市化 oder (seltener) *dushihua* 都市化 sowie den neueren Begriff *chengzhenhua* 城镇化. Letzterer spiegelt die politische Absicht wider, dass der Zuzug in die Metropolen begrenzt und der Ausbau der kleinen und mittleren Städte gefördert werden soll, wie es das 2014 von der Zentralregierung verabschiedete „Programm für neue Formen der Urbanisierung" (*xinxing chengzhenhua guihua* 新型城镇化规划) vorsieht (vgl. Heilmann 2016, S. 252). Für die muslimischen Binnenmigranten werden hauptsächlich die Begriffe *liudong musilin* 流动穆斯林 (mobile Muslime), *wailai musilin* 外来穆斯林 (auswärtige/zugezogene Muslime) oder die Kombination *wailai liudong musilin* 外来流动穆斯林 verwendet.

⁷ So enthält beispielsweise die Ausgabe 2014/1 von *Zhongguo zongjiao* 中国宗教 (*ZGZJ*), der Zeitschrift des Staatlichen Büros für religiöse Angelegenheiten, einen Themenschwer-

Nach der Vorstellung einiger demographischer Basisdaten in Abschnitt 2 werden in Abschnitt 3 der Stadtumbau, seine Folgen für die Nachbarschaftsviertel der Muslime und einige Reaktionen darauf behandelt. Abschnitt 4 befasst sich mit dem Phänomen des Zuzugs muslimischer Migranten vom Land in die Städte und schildert am Beispiel Shanghais damit zusammenhängende Herausforderungen und Chancen für die urbanen muslimischen Gemeinschaften. Nach einigen grundsätzlichen Überlegungen zur Transformation der muslimischen Gemeinschaften in Abschnitt 5 geht der Blick zurück auf das „Missverständnis", das am Anfang dieses Textes steht.

2. Die muslimische Bevölkerung der Volksrepublik China: Zahlen, geographische Verteilung und Urbanisierungsgrad

Im Vielvölkerstaat der Volksrepublik China gelten zehn Ethnien als muslimisch. Ihre Bevölkerungszahl wird in chinesischen Statistiken im Allgemeinen mit der Zahl der Muslime in China gleichgesetzt. Diese Zahlen lassen keine Rückschlüsse darauf zu, ob die Einzelnen sich tatsächlich zu dieser Religion bekennen. Auch Konversionen zum Islam, die vereinzelt in der Literatur erwähnt werden,[8] sind darin nicht berücksichtigt, ebenso wenig wie Konversionen von Angehörigen der muslimischen Ethnien zu anderen Religionen.[9]

Da die ethnische Zugehörigkeit in den staatlichen Melderegistern erfasst ist, lässt sich die Bevölkerungsstruktur dieser ethnisch definierten Muslime genauer analysieren, als dies bei den Angehörigen anderer Religionen der Fall ist. Liu Xiaochun von der Tangshan shifan xueyuan 唐山师范学院 (Tangshan Normal

---

punkt „Urbanisierung und Religion" (S. 30-43), in dem fünf Autoren aus Wissenschaft und Politik Themen wie die Rolle der Religion für eine nachhaltige Entwicklung urbaner Nachbarschaftsviertel oder die angemessene Berücksichtigung religiöser Stätten in der Stadtplanung behandeln.

[8] Z.B. erwähnen Bai Youtao – Chen Yunchang 2007, S. 80, in einer Studie über Nanjing und Shanghai, dass Einheimische durch Kontakt mit muslimischen Migranten zum Islam konvertiert seien. Fang Gang – Liu Xinlu 2015, S. 22-23, berichten, dass es in der Provinz Guangdong derzeit über 3.000 transnationale Ehen gebe, in denen ein Ehepartner – meist der Mann – ein ausländischer Muslim sei. Die Ehefrauen, meist Han, „konvertieren alle nach islamischem Brauch vor der Ehe". Sie behalten aber nach chinesischem Recht ihre ursprüngliche Ethnienzugehörigkeit und können nicht eine muslimische (etwa Hui) annehmen, ebenso wenig ihre Kinder, die damit auch nicht die Sonderrechte muslimischer Ethnien bezüglich Ausbildung oder Beerdigung in Anspruch nehmen können.

[9] Hierzu ein Beispiel: Ein Forscherteam der Chinesischen Akademie der Sozialwissenschaften, das 2012 eine vergleichende Feldstudie zur religiösen Situation in den Städten Kaifeng und Nanyang (Provinz Henan) durchführte, stellte fest, dass es in Kaifeng unter der Hui-Bevölkerung eine ganze Reihe Buddhisten gab, und in Nanyang entdeckten die Forscher sogar Hui, die buddhistische oder daoistische Mönche oder protestantische Pastoren waren. Die höhere Konversionsrate in Nanyang wurde in dem Bericht darauf zurückgeführt, dass die Muslime dort verstreut leben, in Kaifeng hingegen im Umkreis der Moscheen in der (damals noch vor dem Umbau stehenden) Altstadt; vgl. Duan Qi 2013, S. 276-277. In den nordwestlichen Regionen der Volksrepublik unterbindet die Regierung christliche Missionierung unter Nicht-Han.

University) erstellte eine solche Analyse auf der Basis der Daten der letzten nationalen Volkszählung in China von 2010. Im Folgenden werden daraus einige für unsere Fragestellung relevante Daten vorgestellt: [10]

Nach dem Zensus von 2010 umfasst die muslimische Bevölkerung der Volksrepublik China 23.1421 Mio. Menschen. Ihr Anteil an der Gesamtbevölkerung ist von 1,37% im Jahr 1953 auf 1,74% gestiegen. Zwei Ethnien stellen zusammen fast 90% aller Muslime. Das sind die (überwiegend) chinesischsprachigen Hui (Huizu 回族) mit 10.586 Mio. (45,74% aller Muslime) und das aufgrund einer höheren Wachstumsrate inzwischen fast gleich große Turkvolk der Uiguren (Weiwu'erzu 维吾尔族) mit 10.069 Mio. (43,51%). Es folgen die Kasachen (Hasakezu 哈萨克族) mit 1.4626 Mio. (6,32%) und die Dongxiang (Dongxiangzu 东乡族) mit 621.500 (2,69%). Kirgisen (Ke'erkezizu 柯尔克孜族), Salar (Salazu 撒拉族), Tadschiken (Tajikezu 塔吉克族), Usbeken (Wuzibiekezu 乌孜别克族), Bao'an (Bao'anzu 保安族) und Tataren (Tata'erzu 塔塔尔族) stellen jeweils unter 1% der muslimischen Bevölkerung.[11]

Über die hier interessierende Verteilung der muslimischen Bevölkerung sagt Liu Xiaochun Folgendes: Überall in China leben Muslime, aber in unterschiedlicher Konzentration. Auf Provinzebene ist Xinjiang die einzige Region, in der über die Hälfte der Bevölkerung (58,26%) Muslime sind, gefolgt von Ningxia (34,5%) und Qinghai (16,9%). Die Hui verteilen sich traditionell über ganz China, mit lokalen Konzentrationen: 20,5% aller Hui leben in Ningxia, 11,9% in Gansu, 9,3% in Xinjiang, 9% in Henan, 7,9% in Qinghai, 6,6% in Yunnan, 5,4% in Hebei und 5,1% in Shandong. Die Uiguren hingegen leben zu 99,3% in Xinjiang. Auch die anderen acht muslimischen Ethnien leben überwiegend im Nordwesten der Volksrepublik China.[12]

2010 lebten 21,5% aller Muslime in Städten (*chengshi* 城市), 15% in Großgemeinden (*zhen* 镇) und 63,5% in Dörfern auf dem Land (*xiangcun* 乡村). Damit, so Liu Xiaochun, wiesen die Muslime einen deutlich geringeren Urbanisierungsgrad auf als der Bevölkerungsdurchschnitt der VR China (30,3% Stadt, 20% Großgemeinde, 49,7% Dorf). Hier gab es jedoch deutliche Unterschiede zwischen den Ethnien – so lebten 34,07% der Hui-Bevölkerung in Städten, aber nur 11,53% der uigurischen Bevölkerung.[13]

Im Gegensatz dazu stellte ein Bericht zur religiösen Situation im heutigen China, der 2014 veröffentlicht wurde, einen im Vergleich der fünf großen Religi-

---

[10] Abschnitt 2 folgt im Wesentlichen der Auswertung von Liu Xiaochun 2014 in Wenzel-Teuber 2016, S. 30-32. Dort werden noch weitere Daten zur muslimischen Bevölkerungsstruktur aufgeführt.

[11] Liu Xiaochun 2014, S. 70-71. – Liu Xiaochun (geb. 1968, Hui aus Gansu): Abteilung für Ressourcenmanagement, Tangshan shifan xueyuan, Forschungsgebiet Regionalwirtschaft (Angaben zu den besprochenen Autoren werden hier und im Folgenden aus den Zeitschriften übernommen, in denen die Artikel erschienen sind).

[12] *Ibid.*, S. 71-72.

[13] *Ibid.*, S. 72-73.

onen überdurchschnittlich hohen Urbanisierungsgrad der Muslime fest. Der Bericht basiert auf Daten der Querschnittbefragung China Family Panel Studies, die vom Institute of Social Science Survey der Beijing daxue 北京大学 (Peking University) durchgeführt wird. Demnach betrug der muslimische Bevölkerungsanteil in Städten 1,2%, deutlich mehr als in Großgemeinden (0,3%) und auf dem Land (0,4%). Diese unterschiedlichen Befunde zum Urbanisierungsgrad der Muslime dürften sich zumindest teilweise daraus erklären, dass die China Family Panel Studies in nur 25 Provinzen Chinas Daten erheben und mit Xinjiang, Qinghai und Ningxia gleich drei weniger urbanisierte Provinzen bzw. Autonome Gebiete mit großer muslimischer Bevölkerung ausschließen, was das Ergebnis verzerren dürfte.[14] In den Städten Ost- und Zentralchinas wiederum gibt es historisch gewachsene Muslimgemeinschaften. Bereits 1991 bezeichnete auch der amerikanische Asienwissenschaftler und Anthropologe Dru C. Gladney, Experte für die muslimischen Minderheiten in China, die Hui als „China's most urbanized minority nationality".[15]

3. Die traditionellen Muslimviertel in der Urbanisierung

3.1 Die Auflösung der traditionellen Muslimviertel im Zuge des Stadtumbaus und ihre Folgen für das religiöse und soziale Leben der urbanen Hui-Muslime

Seit Jahrhunderten lebten Hui-Muslime in Chinas Städten in eigenen Vierteln. Sie werden *Huifang* 回坊 (Hui-Viertel) oder *sifang* 寺坊 (Moscheeviertel) genannt, von den Hui-Muslimen selbst *jiaofang* 教坊 oder *zhemati* 哲玛提 (von arab. *jamaat*), was beides die um eine Moschee herum lebende islamische Gemeinde bezeichnet.[16] Die hier ausgewerteten Texte bevorzugen den neuen Begriff *shequ* 社区 (im Deutschen öfter mit „Nachbarschaftsviertel", im Englischen meist mit „community" übersetzt) und sprechen von *Huizu shequ* 回族社区 (Nachbarschaftsvierteln der Hui-Nationalität) oder *musilin shequ* 穆斯林社区 (muslimischen Nachbarschaftsvierteln).[17]

Mittelpunkt der traditionellen Hui-Viertel war die Moschee. Vor 1949 waren die Moscheeverwaltung und die Gilden der Muslime für das gesellschaftliche und

---

[14] Angaben zu den China Family Panel Studies hier nach Wenzel-Teuber 2015, S. 22-23 und 25.

[15] „They constitute the vast majority of minorities in every Chinese city, with the exception of cities in the border regions of Tibet, Xinjiang, and Inner Mongolia." Gladney 1991, S. 171.

[16] Vgl. Tian Haiyan 2013, S. 38; Gladney 1991, S. 404, 420.

[17] Der folgende Text verwendet für *shequ* den Begriff „Nachbarschaftsviertel" oder „Viertel", wenn es tatsächlich um geographisch begrenzte Nachbarschaften oder um die städtische Verwaltungseinheit geht, und den Begriff „Gemeinschaft", wenn die muslimische Gemeinschaft in einem weiteren, nicht territorial begrenzten Sinn gemeint ist.

religiöse Leben im Viertel verantwortlich und vertraten es nach außen.[18] Dem Ethnologen Yang Wenjiong zufolge basierten der kulturelle Zusammenhalt und die Identität der Hui auf fünf Faktoren – auf der um die Moschee herum wohnenden territorialen Gemeinschaft, ihrem traditionellen Religionsunterricht in der Moschee (*jingtang jiaoyu* 经堂教育), der Heirat innerhalb der Ethnie (Religion), einer für die Ethnie spezifischen Wirtschaft und spezifischen Berufen sowie der Selbstverwaltung des Moscheeviertels.[19]

In den letzten Jahrzehnten wurden im Zuge von Stadtumbauprojekten überall in China großflächig ganze Stadtviertel abgerissen und ihre Bevölkerung umgesiedelt. Durch diese Abriss- und Umsiedlungsmaßnahmen sind auch viele der traditionellen Muslimviertel verschwunden oder einschneidend verändert worden. Hier einige von den chinesischen Autoren vorgestellte Beispiele, die das Ausmaß der Veränderungen deutlich machen: Im ostchinesischen Nanjing bestand bereits zur Zeit der Ming-Dynastie (1368–1644) eine große und kulturell bedeutende Hui-Gemeinde. Heute verfügt es mit fast 80.000 Hui über die größte Hui-Bevölkerung einer ostchinesischen Küstenstadt.[20] Qijiawan 七家湾 war das größte von mehreren Hui-Vierteln der Stadt. Wie die Forscher Zhang Cheng und Mi Shoujiang in einem Aufsatz feststellen, spielte es lange Zeit eine unschätzbare Rolle für die Bewahrung der Identität der Hui und war ein wichtiges Symbol für die Weitergabe ihrer Kultur in Nanjing. Nach Darstellung der beiden Autoren zog Qijiawan – ein altes Viertel ohne öffentliche Toiletten, ohne Kanalisation und Straßenbeleuchtung und mit veralteten Stromleitungen – in den 1990er Jahren aufgrund seiner günstigen Lage Immobilienfirmen an. Die neu entstehenden Geschäfts- und Wohnhäuser waren für die ursprünglichen Hui-Bewohner unerschwinglich teuer und sie mussten wegziehen. 1997/1998 wurde der Kern des Viertels mit 200 Hui-Wohnhäusern abgerissen und die Bewohner wurden umgesiedelt.[21] Auch die Caoqiao 草桥-Moschee, früher das Zentrum dieses Viertels, wurde abgerissen und an anderer Stelle wiederaufgebaut, doch leben in ihrem Umkreis inzwischen nur noch wenige Hui.[22] Viele Hui in Nanjing befürchteten nun eine allmähliche Schwächung ihrer kulturellen Identität, schreiben Zhang und Mi.

---

[18] So wird beispielsweise die Organisationsform des Hui-Viertels Qijiawan 七家湾 in Nanjing vor 1949 beschrieben in Zhang Cheng – Mi Shoujiang 2006, S. 56.

[19] Yang Wenjiong 杨文炯, *Hudong, tiaoshi yu chonggou* 互动、调适与重构 (Interaktivität, Adaption und Rekonstruktion) (Beijing: Renmin chubanshe, 2007), S. 364, hier wiedergegeben nach Ma Qiang 2011, S. 112.

[20] Zhang Cheng – Mi Shoujiang 2006, S. 55. Die dort als Beleg für diese Zahl zitierte Quelle stammt aus dem Jahr 2000. – Zhang Cheng (geb. 1982): Jiangsu shengwei dangxiao 江苏省委党校 (Parteischule der Provinz Jiangsu), Forschungsgebiet marxistische Religionswissenschaft; Mi Shoujiang (geb. 1951, Hui aus Shandong): Jiangsu sheng qingnian guanli ganbu xueyuan 江苏省青年管理干部学院 (Akademie für junge Verwaltungskader der Provinz Jiangsu), Forschungsgebiet Ethnologie und Religionswissenschaft.

[21] *Ibid.*

[22] Bai Youtao – Chen Yunchang 2007, S. 79.

Tatsächlich stellen Bai Youtao und Chen Yunchang von der Nanjing shifan daxue 南京师范大学 (Nanjing Normal University) in ihrer Studie über Hui-Nachbarschaftsviertel in Nanjing und Shanghai bei der Mehrheit der jungen Muslime eine Verflachung des Glaubens fest; viele heiraten zudem Han-Chinesen.[23] Tian Haiyan von der Abteilung für Philosophie der Shanghai shifan daxue 上海师范大学 (Shanghai Normal University) spricht, auf Shanghai bezogen, von „Erschütterung und Niedergang" der traditionellen Shanghaier Muslim-Nachbarschaftsviertel. Nur noch ein sehr kleiner Teil der Muslime lebt im Umkreis einer der Hauptmoscheen Shanghais. In der Zerstreuung sei die Gemeinschaft schwer aufrecht zu erhalten und der Assimilationsdruck der „urbanen Mainstream-Kultur" sei groß, schreibt Tian. Beispielsweise ist Tian zufolge die Einhaltung der Speisevorschriften schwierig, wenn es in der neuen Wohngegend keine *halal*-Lebensmittel zu kaufen gibt. Die regelmäßige Teilnahme am gemeinsamen Gebet leidet, ebenso der Religionsunterricht an der Moschee, was laut Tian dazu führt, dass junge Muslime oft keine Gelegenheit haben, systematisches religiöses Wissen zu erwerben. Nach Tians Beobachtung halten viele von ihnen die Speisegebote nicht mehr und interessieren sich nicht für die Moschee.[24]

Angemerkt sei hier noch, dass manche Forscher die Rolle der traditionellen Hui-Viertel – trotz ihrer unbestritten großen Bedeutung für die muslimische Gemeinschaft – nicht ausschließlich positiv sehen. Diese Viertel seien auch abgeschlossen und „konservativ" gewesen, merkt ein Autor an, und hätten den geistigen Austausch mit anderen Gruppen in der Gesellschaft stark eingeschränkt.[25]

Über kurz oder lang werden sich in ganz China im Zuge der raschen Modernisierung die Existenzbedingungen der islamischen Kultur der Hui ändern, schreiben Zhang und Mi – auch in den Städten Nordwestchinas, wo die Hui einen höheren Bevölkerungsanteil aufweisen als im Osten des Landes. Das Verschwinden der Hui-Nachbarschaftsviertel sollte auch der Regierung zu denken geben, mah-

---

[23] Bai Youtao – Chen Yunchang 2007, S. 79. – Bai Youtao (geb. 1963, Hui aus Anhui): Forschungsgebiete Stadtsoziologie und Hui-Nachbarschaftsviertel; Chen Yunchang (geb. 1983, Hui aus Nanjing). Beide gehören der School for Social Development der Nanjing shifan daxue an.

[24] Tian Haiyan 2013, S. 39, 41-42.

[25] Ma Xuefeng 2012, Kapitel 1; die hier benutzte Internetversion des Artikels hat keine Seitenzahlen. – An dieser Stelle sei angemerkt, dass der Soziologe Richard Madsen auf Parallelen zwischen traditionellen katholischen Gemeinden und Hui-Gemeinden in ländlichen Gebieten Chinas hingewiesen hat, was das Verhältnis zu ihrem Glauben und zu Außenstehenden angeht; er bezeichnete die chinesischen Katholiken als „eine Art Ethnie" (Madsen 1998, S. 53-56). Da der Katholizismus in China bis in jüngste Zeit seine Stärke aus den seit Generationen katholischen Familienclans bezieht, die oft in Dörfern oder manchen Stadtvierteln (wie Xujiahui in Shanghai) konzentriert zusammenlebten, haben die Land-Stadt-Migration und in geringerem Ausmaß der Städteumbau teilweise ähnliche Auflösungserscheinungen zur Folge, wie sie hier für die Hui beschrieben wurden. Auch bei den Gegenstrategien lassen sich Parallelen erkennen, worauf hier aber nicht näher eingegangen werden kann. Zur katholischen Migrationsproblematik vgl. auch Zhang 2011 und Wenzel-Teuber 2012.

nen die Autoren. Denn die historisch gewachsenen Viertel seien nicht nur Kulturträger und wichtige Bestandteile der „pluralistischen Kultur der chinesischen Nation". Sie böten auch eine gute Plattform für den Austausch mit der arabischen islamischen Welt.[26]

3.1.1 Fallbeispiel: Veränderungen in der Feier von Id al-Fitr im Niujie-Viertel von Beijing

Aus zwei Gründen wird dem Niujie 牛街 („Ochsenstraßen")-Viertel, dem größten Nachbarschaftsviertel der Hui in Beijing, hier größerer Raum gewidmet. Zum einen liegt eine Studie von Ma Weihua (Nankai daxue 南开大学 [Nankai-University]) vor, in der am Beispiel der Feier des Id al-Fitr konkrete Veränderungen in den Bräuchen der Hui anschaulich werden. Zweitens war man in diesem Fall bestrebt, den Charakter des auch religions- und außenpolitisch relevanten Viertels zu einem gewissen Grad zu erhalten und wirtschaftlich zu nutzen. Für diesen zweiten Aspekt wurde ergänzend zu Mas Studie ein Beitrag des Politologen Reza Hasmath von der University of Alberta (Kanada) herangezogen.

Die in ihren Anfängen auf die Zeit der Liao-Dynastie (907–1125) zurückgehende Niujie-Moschee ist die älteste Moschee Beijings[27] und gehört zu den Touristenattraktionen der Stadt. Im Niujie-Viertel haben außerdem die zentralen Institutionen des offiziellen Islam ihren Sitz – die Chinesische Islamische Vereinigung und das Chinesische Koraninstitut. Das Viertel dient der Regierung als „Schaufenster" des chinesischen Islam – Staatsgäste aus islamischen Ländern werden häufig zur Niujie-Moschee geführt. Ab 1997 begann die Stadtregierung mit einem Umbau des Viertels, von dem 7.500 Haushalte betroffen waren.[28] Die alten ebenerdigen *hutong*-Häuser wurden abgerissen und durch Hochhäuser ersetzt, in die viele der früheren Hui-Bewohner einzogen, während andere auf andere Teile Beijings zerstreut wurden.[29] Offenbar bemühte sich die Regierung, den ethnisch-religiösen Charakter des Viertels zu erhalten: Wie Reza Hasmath darlegt, wurden die neuen Wohnblocks in den „islamischen Farben" grün und weiß gestrichen und mit islamischen Symbolen verziert, und die Ochsenstraße wurde als „Islamic-style commercial street" wiederbelebt.[30] Heute leben im Niujie-Viertel nach Angaben von Ma Weihua 54.000 Menschen mit Wohnsitzregistrierung, von denen

---

[26] Zhang Cheng – Mi Shoujiang 2006, S. 58.

[27] Zum Niujie-Viertel siehe auch Gladney 1991, S. 171-227, zur Niujie-Moschee Shatzman Steinhardt 2015, S. 138-142. Leslie 1986, S. 56, versieht die Liao-Dynastie als Entstehungszeit mit einem Fragezeichen.

[28] Hasmath 2014, S. 12.

[29] Ma Weihua 2015, S. 107; Hasmath 2014, S. 12. Während Ma zufolge „viele" der früheren Hui-Bewohner des Viertels in andere Stadtteile zogen, kehrten laut Hasmath, der sich auf Angaben des Niujie Street Administration Office beruft, 90 % der ehemaligen Bewohner in die Neubauten des Viertels zurück. – Ma Weihua (geb. 1977, Hui aus Ningxia): Zhou Enlai School of Government, Nankai daxue (Tianjin), Forschungsgebiete Ethnologie, religiöse Anthropologie.

[30] Hasmath 2014, S. 12.

12.000 (26%) der Hui-Ethnie angehören.³¹ Hasmath gibt für das Kerngebiet von Niujie eine Bevölkerung von 24.088 Personen an, von denen 54,1% Hui sind.³²

Obwohl man also das Niujie-Viertel heute als eine der „last surviving historical ethnic neighbourhoods in Beijing"³³ bezeichnen kann, haben sich auch dort das religiöse Leben und die Bräuche der Hui stark verändert. Ursachen dafür sind einerseits der generelle Wandel des urbanen Lebensstils, andererseits aber auch die drastische Umgestaltung des Viertels. Ma Weihua zeigt dies in einer Studie zur Feier des Id al-Fitr.

Das „Fest des Fastenbrechens" (Id al-Fitr, *kaizhaijie* 开斋节) am Ende des Ramadan ist einer der höchsten Feiertage des Islam. Heute halten im Niujie-Viertel laut Ma meist nur noch die Älteren, die schon in Rente sind und Zeit haben, das strenge Fasten während des Ramadan ein.³⁴ Zum Festgebet an Id al-Fitr hingegen kommen viel mehr Leute als früher – nicht nur die Muslime des Viertels, sondern auch in Beijing studierende Muslime, muslimische Binnenmigranten, Touristen und ausländische Muslime, die in Beijing arbeiten. An Id al-Fitr 2013 kamen nach Mas Angaben 20.000–30.000 Menschen zum Festgebet zur Niujie-Moschee. Eine Reihe von Bräuchen wurden nach Mas Beobachtung vereinfacht, so beispielsweise die traditionellen Gräberbesuche nach dem Festgebet, die manche Hui jetzt auch schon vor dem Fest absolvieren.³⁵ Da die Menschen weniger Zeit und mehr Geld haben, werden die traditionellen Speisen für Id al-Fitr nicht mehr selbst gemacht, sondern in *halal*-Geschäften gekauft. Wie Ma berichtet, besuchen sich Familienmitglieder und Freunde nicht mehr unbedingt, wie früher üblich, am Festtag selbst (der für Muslime in Beijing, anders als für die Hui in Nordwestchina, nicht arbeitsfrei ist), und man lädt nicht mehr zum Festessen nach Hause ein, sondern eher ins Restaurant. Daran ist nach Mas Einschätzung nicht nur der schnellere Rhythmus des Großstadtlebens schuld, sondern auch die veränderte Wohnstruktur: Die neuen Appartements sind viel enger als die alten Wohnhöfe und bieten kaum Platz für Besucher. Auch den Ahong 阿訇 (Imam) laden fromme Leute jetzt eher ins *halal*-Restaurant als nach Hause zum Essen ein. Im Restaurant – so berichtete Ahong Zhang von der Niujie-Moschee dem Forscher Ma Weihua – rezitiert der Ahong nach wie vor aus dem Koran, wozu in bestimmten muslimischen Restaurants eigens ein Platz vorgesehen ist.³⁶

---

31 Ma Weihua 2015, S. 103. Niujie jiedao 牛街街道 ist ein Unterbezirk des Stadtbezirk Xicheng 西城 (früher gehörte es zum Stadtbezirk Xuanwu 宣武). Gladney 1991, S. 176 gibt, basierend auf dem Zensus von 1982, ähnliche Zahlen für den Bezirk Niujie: 55.722 Einwohner, davon 24,7% Angehörige ethnischer Minderheiten, davon wiederum 96,6% Hui.

32 Hasmath 2014, S. 11.

33 *Ibid.*, S. 10.

34 Ma Weihua 2015, S. 104.

35 *Ibid.*, S. 105-106.

36 *Ibid.*, S. 104-106, 108.

Eine weitere große Veränderung für die Feier des Id al-Fitr wurde von der Beijinger Stadtregierung initiiert. Wie Ma Weihua berichtet, veranstaltete sie 2013 schon zum fünften Mal in Folge an Id al-Fitr ein „*halal*-Spezialitäten-Fest" im Niujie-Viertel, um in der zunehmend internationalen Hauptstadt die Rolle der Niujie-Moschee als „Schaufenster" für die islamische Kultur Chinas zu fördern. Nach dem Festgebet in der Moschee kaufen viele Gebetsbesucher an den Ständen noch etwas zu Essen, Tee oder andere islamische Produkte. Auch Nicht-Muslime besuchen Ma zufolge in großer Zahl das Spezialitätenfest. In gewisser Hinsicht – so Ma Weihua – gleicht Id a-Fitr an der Niujie-Moschee einem Han-chinesischen Tempelfest! Ma bewertet es als bedeutungsvolle Gelegenheit zur Überwindung von Barrieren, dass Menschen verschiedener Ethnien und Religionen anlässlich eines islamischen Feiertags zu einem fröhlichen Fest zusammengebracht werden.[37] „Oberflächlich gesehen ist das *halal*-Spezialitätenfest eine kommerzielle Veranstaltung, doch [...] es zeigt, wie traditionelle Volksbräuche aus der Marktwirtschaft neue Antriebskraft für ihre Entwicklung schöpfen können." Nur durch Anpassung an die gesellschaftliche und wirtschaftliche Entwicklung blieben sie auf Dauer lebendig – meint Ma Weihua.[38]

Reza Hasmath stellt allerdings den Begegnungswert solcher Festivals infrage. Er schreibt:

> [C]elebratory ethno-festivals and ethnic-oriented restaurants that showcase minority traditions serve as a mechanism to encourage Han interactions with ethnic minority groups. However, the attendant risk in utilizing this practice is that the socio-economic struggles of many ethnic minority groups are being masked when a celebratory version of their culture and traditions are presented. This can potentially lead to reduce meaningful Han-ethnic minority interactions in the future.[39]

3.2 Strategien gegen Identitätsverlust und Säkularisierung urbaner Muslime

Einige Autoren machen sich Gedanken über Strategien, mit denen urbane Muslime als soziale Gruppe den oben beschriebenen Auflösungs- und Säkularisierungserscheinungen entgegenwirken können. Drei Beispiele werden im Folgenden vorgestellt. Während die ersten beiden Beispiele im Kern die Frage betreffen, wie die Rolle von Ehe/Familie und Frauen für die Weitergabe von ethnischer Tradition und religiösem Glauben erhalten bzw. wiederhergestellt werden kann, geht es im dritten Punkt um die Nutzung des Internets zur Rekonstruktion muslimischer Netzwerke.

---

[37] Ma Weihua 2015, S. 105.
[38] *Ibid.*, S. 108.
[39] Hasmath 2014, S. 1.

3.2.1 „Blind Date"-Treffen gegen den Trend zu Mischehen zwischen Muslimen und Nicht-Muslimen

Ein Grundpfeiler der traditionellen Hui-Gemeinschaften, die Heirat innerhalb der Ethnie bzw. Religion, ist durch die Entwicklungen der letzten Jahrzehnte ins Wanken geraten.[40] Ma Qiang von der Shaanxi shifan daxue 陕西师范大学 (Shaanxi Normal University) führt folgende Zahlen aus den Eheregistern der Stadt Guangzhou als Beispiel an: Im Guangzhouer Stadtbezirk Haizhu 海珠 wurden zwischen 1996 und 2003 78 Ehen mit Involvierung von Hui als Ehepartner geschlossen, davon waren 76 Ehen interethnisch, also 97,4%; im Stadtbezirk Yuexiu 越秀 waren 92,7% der 1999, 2000, 2001 und 2004 mit Involvierung von Hui geschlossenen Ehen interethnisch, im Stadtbezirk Baiyun 白云 waren alle zwischen 2000 und 2004 von Hui geschlossenen Ehen interethnisch. In ostchinesischen Städten ist dieses Phänomen Ma Qiang zufolge häufiger als im Westen Chinas, allerdings haben nach seiner Beobachtung auch dort in Städten wie Lanzhou und Xining interethnische Ehen von Hui stark zugenommen. Zudem – so Ma – kommt es in den Städten vor, dass Familien im Fall von Mischehen beschließen, ihre Kinder als Han zu registrieren, und so die ethnische Identität und den islamischen Glauben des muslimischen Ehepartners aufgeben, damit die Kinder sich ungehindert von Speisetabus leichter in die Gesellschaft integrieren und im sozialen Konkurrenzkampf besser bestehen können.[41]

Yang Wenbi von der Ningxia daxue 宁夏大学 (Ningxia University) in Yinchuan, wie Ma Qiang ein Angehöriger der Hui-Nationalität, sieht eine der Ursachen für die steigende Zahl der Mischehen darin, dass die von den Hui wie den Han praktizierte Tradition der Ehevermittlung nach 1949 durch die gesetzlich verankerte Freiheit der Eheschließung unter Beschuss geraten ist. Yang zufolge ist es überall in China für unverheiratete Hui schwer, einen passenden Partner finden. Deshalb hätten Personen aus der städtischen muslimischen Elite nach einer Gegenstrategie gesucht, schreibt Yang Wenbi in einem Artikel über die „Neuerfindung" der Heiratsvermittlungtradition der urbanen Hui. Wie Yang berichtet, begann man in den 1980ern in einigen Städten mit ersten Maßnahmen wie der Gründung von Heiratsvermittlungsstellen für Hui sowie Internet- oder Instant Messaging-Partnervermittlungsgruppen für Muslime.[42] Am 17. April 2010 fand nach Yangs Angaben die erste große muslimische Blind-Date-Versammlung mit fast hundert Teilnehmerinnen und Teilnehmern in einem Park in Zhengzhou,

---

[40] Gladney 1991, S. 208-214, beschreibt die Zunahme interethnischer Ehen bereits in den 1980er Jahren: Nach dem Zensus von 1982 waren im Niujie-Viertel von 491 Haushalten 38 gemischte Ehen zwischen Hui und Han, wobei, wie traditionell üblich, häufiger Han-Frauen in Hui-Familien einheirateten als umgekehrt (S. 209-210). In Städten im Süden, beispielsweise in Shanghai, fand Gladney eine weit höhere Rate von Mischehen vor (S. 213).

[41] Ma Qiang 2011, S. 112. – Ma Qiang (geb. 1972, Hui aus Ningxia): Northwest Ethnology Center, Shaanxi shifan daxue, Forschungsgebiete Anthropologie und islamische Kultur.

[42] Yang Wenbi 2015, S. 97. – Yang Wenbi (geb. 1981, Hui aus Ningxia): Institut zur Erforschung der Hui-Nationalität, Ningxia daxue, Forschungsgebiet: Ethnosoziologie.

der Hauptstadt der zentralchinesischen Provinz Henan, statt. Das Echo war so groß, dass an der dritten muslimischen Blind-Date-Versammlung in Zhengzhou Anfang 2011 bereits 500 Heiratswillige teilnahmen. Die Idee breitete sich auch auf Hui-Gemeinschaften in anderen Städten der Provinz Henan aus und ist nach Yangs Darstellung zu einer festen Einrichtung geworden.[43] Die Organisatoren dieser modernen Form der Partnervermittlung sind laut Yang von Ort zu Ort verschieden und umfassen Ahongs und Moscheeverwaltungen, lokale Islamische Vereinigungen, muslimische Ehevermittlungsbüros, Verantwortliche muslimischer Websites sowie in Kultur, Medien oder Handel tätige muslimische Verbände. Der Teilnehmerkreis besteht hauptsächlich aus muslimischen jungen Frauen und Männern aus der Provinz Henan, seltener aus anderen Provinzen oder aus der Gruppe der Hui-Migranten.[44] Zur Erfolgsquote dieser Blind-Date-Versammlungen macht der Autor leider keine Angaben.

3.2.2 Mit Frauenmoscheen und islamischen Frauenschulen gegen die Säkularisierung

Bei der religiösen Erziehung der Kinder und der Weitergabe des islamischen Glaubens spielen die Familien eine entscheidende Rolle – schreibt Ma Qiang in seinem Plädoyer für die islamischen Frauenschulen. Traditionell hätten die Väter oder Söhne religiöses Wissen durch den Religionsunterricht in der Moschee erworben und es in der Familie an Frauen und Kinder weitergegeben. Heute, angesichts des Niedergangs der traditionellen Moscheeerziehung, verfügen die Männer laut Ma Qiang oft nur über einzelne Brocken religiösen Wissens, die sie hier und da aufgeschnappt haben, und sind religiös zu wenig gebildet, um den Glauben systematisch an die Frauen weitergeben zu können. Ein weiteres Defizit ist Ma zufolge dadurch entstanden, dass die neuen Appartements rein privater Wohnraum sind, während die Familien früher in den Wohnhöfen der Muslim-Viertel eigenständig Wohltätigkeitsaktionen, Beerdigungen, Hochzeiten und Festmähler ausrichteten und der Glaube so auch durch gemeinsam begangene Bräuche weitergegeben wurde. Diese Veränderung hat nach Mas Beobachtung dazu geführt, dass, während die Männer ihren Platz in der Moschee finden, den Frauen der Raum für gemeinschaftliche Aktivitäten fehlt. Drittens sind muslimische Frauen – so Ma – aufgrund des Einflusses der Globalisierung, von Medien und Schule selbstbewusster geworden, sie möchten die Monopolisierung der religiösen Ressourcen durch die Männer nicht länger hinnehmen und selbst religiöses Wissen erwerben.[45] Frauenmoscheen und islamische Frauenschulen bieten nach Ansicht des Autors die passende Antwort auf diese Probleme und Entwicklungen.

Frauenmoscheen sind eine Besonderheit des chinesischen Islam. Es gibt sie seit mehreren Jahrhunderten, besonders in der chinesischen Zentralebene, also in Henan und angrenzenden Provinzen. Sie werden von weiblichen Ahongs gelei-

---

[43] Yang Wenbi 2015, S. 98.
[44] *Ibid.*, S. 99-100.
[45] Ma Qiang 2011, S. 113.

tet.⁴⁶ Wie Ma Qiang darlegt, hat ihre Verbreitung in den letzten Jahrzehnten zugenommen. So haben zehn Moscheen in Xi'an seit den 1990er Jahren Frauenmoscheen oder Gebetshallen für Frauen errichtet.⁴⁷ Ma zufolge gibt es sowohl selbständige Frauenmoscheen (insbesondere in Henan, Shandong, Shanxi und Hebei) als auch solche, die einer Männermoschee unterstehen (in allen anderen Provinzen; fast alle seit den 1980er Jahren neu gegründeten Frauenmoscheen gehören diesem zweiten Typ an). Bei den islamischen Frauenschulen unterscheidet er chinesisch-arabische Frauenschulen mit einem Schwerpunkt auf arabischem Sprachunterricht, von Moscheen organisierte sowie privat von Gläubigen organisierte Frauenschulen.⁴⁸

Frauenmoscheen und -schulen seien in einigen Regionen Chinas immer noch umstritten, schreibt Ma, doch die Stadt und die schnelle Urbanisierung hätten ihnen gesellschaftliche Räume der Toleranz eröffnet. „Man kann sagen", so Mas Fazit, „dass das Aufblühen der Frauenmoscheen und -schulen, zu dem die Urbanisierung beigetragen hat, eine Form des Widerstands der urbanen muslimischen Frauen gegen die Säkularisierung und eine Ausdrucksform weiblichen Glaubens ist."⁴⁹

3.2.3 Wiederaufbau und Neugründung vom muslimischen Netzwerken durch Internet und soziale Kommunikationsmittel

Zwei der untersuchten Autoren analysieren die Rolle, die das Internet und soziale Medien für einen erneuerten Zusammenhalt der sich auflösenden urbanen Muslimgemeinschaften spielen können.

Der Soziologe Ma Xuefeng von der Yunnan daxue 云南大学 (Yunnan University) im südwestchinesischen Kunming hat – wie er in seinem hier vorgestellten Aufsatz berichtet – den Zusammenbruch des traditionellen Systems der Muslimviertel durch den Umbau der Altstädte von Beijing und Kunming studiert. Er stellte dabei fest, dass „die Muslime zu atomisierten Individuen geworden waren, denen die notwendigen strukturellen Beziehungen zueinander fehlten". Er entdeckte aber auch zwei Internetforen, die junge Muslime um das Jahr 2005 in Kunming gegründet hatten und die nach Mas Angaben bald mehrere tausend Teilnehmer zählten. Ma Xuefeng sieht in der Gründung dieser Internetforen das Bestreben der jungen Muslime, ihre soziale Gruppe wieder aufzubauen, und zwar in Interaktion zwischen virtueller und realer Welt. Er interpretiert dies als den Versuch, „eine neue Art muslimischer Gemeinschaft in der chinesischen urbanen Gesellschaft aufzubauen, zu der sich die Muslime als Einzelne zusammenschlie-

---

⁴⁶ Vgl. Allès 2005, S. 34, Anm. 24.

⁴⁷ Ma Qiang 2011, S. 113.

⁴⁸ *Ibid.*, S. 111. Ma gibt viele weitere Details zu den unterschiedlichen Arten von Frauenmoscheen und -schulen an. – Guo Chengzhen, Generalsekretär der Chinesischen Islamischen Vereinigung, erklärte im März 2016, dass es in China rund einhundert Frauenmoscheen gebe (vgl. „Quanguo zhengxie weiyuan Guo Chengzhen: Zhongguo musilin zongjiao xinyang ziyou dedao qieshi baozhang"). Die Zahl der islamischen Frauenschulen dürfte allerdings vielfach höher sein.

⁴⁹ *Ibid.*, S. 115.

ßen, wobei das Zusammenwohnen an einem Ort nicht mehr die notwendige Voraussetzung ist, sondern die Verbindung eher auf geistigen Faktoren basiert". Leider, so Ma, sind die beiden Internetgemeinschaften in Kunming gespalten: Die eine hält die Religion hoch („muslimisch"), die andere die Ethnie („Hui"). Einen anderen Nachteil sieht Ma darin, dass diese Gruppen nicht sehr beständig sind. Für mehr Kohärenz bräuchten sie den Rückhalt von Institutionen oder Gruppen, die ihnen die geistigen Elemente liefern, die lebendige intellektuelle Aktivitäten in der Internetgemeinschaft sichern. Nach Ansicht von Ma Xuefeng können die Moscheen und Ahongs in China einen solchen geistigen Input nicht liefern, da sie sich auf rituelle Dienste beschränken. Deshalb ist es seiner Meinung nach notwendig, eine muslimische intellektuelle Gemeinschaft aufzubauen, die dazu in der Lage ist.[50]

Auch Tian Haiyan sieht die Verbreitung des Internets und der anderen sozialen Kommunikationsmittel als eine Art Ausgleich für die Kommunikationsdefizite, die durch die räumliche Zerstreuung, aber auch die zunehmende religiöse Zersplitterung der urbanen Muslimgemeinschaften aufgrund von Migration entstehen. Tian bezeichnet die „Internetgemeinschaft" (*wangluo shequ* 网络社区) als eine Sonderform der muslimischen Gemeinschaft.[51]

4. Land-Stadt-Migration von Muslimen in China

4.1 Präludium im Nordwesten: Muslimische Umsiedler in der Entwicklungszone Hongsibao (Ningxia)

Bevor wir uns den Folgen des Zustroms muslimischer Binnenmigranten in die Metropolen Ostchinas zuwenden, ist der Blick auf ein staatliches Umsiedlungsprojekt im Nordwesten Chinas aufschlussreich. Die Studie von Ding Mingjun (Ningxia daxue) zum Wiederaufbau der Moscheeviertel durch Hui-Umsiedler in Hongsibao 红寺堡 illustriert zum einen die Tatsache, dass die staatlichen Behörden in der Stadt- und Gemeindeplanung bisher oft die religiösen Bedürfnisse der Menschen nicht im Blick haben. Zum anderen macht es anschaulich, wie vielfältig, zersplittert und andersartig die islamische Welt ist, aus der die muslimischen Migranten stammen, die in die Städte Ostchinas ziehen.

Das Autonome Gebiet Ningxia der Hui-Nationalität liegt im Nordwesten der Volksrepublik China. Ab 1983 wurden auf Beschluss der Zentralregierung innerhalb von 30 Jahren über 800.000 Menschen aus Armutsgebieten im bergigen Süden von Ningxia in den Norden des Autonomen Gebiets umgesiedelt. Fast 60% dieser Umsiedler gehörten der Hui-Nationalität an. Für den 12. Fünfjahresplan (2011–2015) war die Umsiedlung von weiteren 350.000 Menschen innerhalb

---

[50] Ma Xuefeng 2012, Kapitel 1 und 2, ohne Seitenangabe. Zu Mas Idee einer muslimischen intellektuellen Gemeinschaft siehe den Abschnitt 5. – Ma Xuefeng (geb. 1978, Hui aus Yunnan): Forschungsschwerpunkte Ethnosoziologie und Religionssoziologie.

[51] Tian Haiyan 2013, S. 43. Tian nennt Zhongmuwang 中穆网 (www.2muslim.com) und Yisilan zhi guang 伊斯兰之光 (Licht des Islam, www.norislam.com) als zwei der landesweit einflussreichsten chinesischsprachigen islamischen Websites.

Ningxias vorgesehen.⁵² Zwar verbesserte sich die wirtschaftliche Situation der Menschen durch die Umsiedlung, schreibt Ding. Doch die Regierung, die bei der Neuansiedlung zwar Han und Hui nach Möglichkeit getrennt hatte (was der Autor begrüßt), hatte Ding zufolge nicht beachtet, dass die Hui-Umsiedler verschiedenen islamischen Gruppierungen und Sufi-Orden angehörten.⁵³

Ding Mingjun schildert diese innerislamische Vielfalt – die nicht nur für Ningxia, sondern auch für andere Regionen im Nordwesten der Volksrepublik charakteristisch ist: Die älteste Form des Islam in China und damit auch in Ningxia wird als Gedimu 格底目 (Qadim) bezeichnet. Ab Mitte des 18. Jahrhunderts kam der Sufismus nach Ningxia. Im Lauf der Jahrhunderte missionierten dort vor allem drei der großen Sufi-Orden (*menhuan* 门宦), die sich nach und nach in zahlreiche weitere Untergruppen aufspalteten – Jahriyya (Zheherenye 哲合忍耶, heute in Ningxia der größte Sufi-Orden), Qadariyya (Gaderenye 嘎德忍耶) und Khufiyya (Hufuye 虎夫耶). In den 1930er Jahren gelangte auch die Ikhwani (Yihewani 伊赫瓦尼)-Bewegung nach Ningxia, eine islamische Erneuerungsbewegung, die im 19. Jahrhundert in China entstand. Sie verbreitete sich schnell und wurde zur islamischen Gruppierung mit den meisten Anhängern und Moscheen in Ningxia.⁵⁴

Hongsibao 红寺堡 ist heute ein Stadtbezirk von Wuzhong 吴忠. Es ist in ganz China die „größte Entwicklungszone für die Armutsminderung von Umweltmigranten".⁵⁵ Ab 1999 wurde das ursprüngliche Wüstengebiet mit Hilfe eines Bewässerungsprojekts urbar gemacht und es wurden systematisch Armutsmigranten aus dem Süden Ningxias dorthin umgesiedelt. Nach dem Zensus von 2010 lebten in

---

52 Zahlen nach Ding Mingjun 2013, S. 81. Nach Angaben des im Januar 2016 vorgelegten Arbeitsberichts 2016 der Regierung des Autonomen Gebiets Ningxia („Ningxia Huizu zizhiqu renmin zhengfu 2016 nian ‚Zhengfu gongzuo baogao'" 宁夏回族自治区人民政府 2016 年《政府工作报告》) wurden in Ningxia in den Jahren 2011–2015 insgesamt 350.000 Umweltmigranten aus der Armut gehoben, was den von Ding genannten Vorgaben des 12. Fünfjahresplans entspräche; siehe http://leaders.people.com.cn/n1/2016/0118 /c58278-28063590.html, aufgerufen am 29. Februar 2016. – Ding Mingjun (geb. 1962, Hui aus Ningxia): Forschungsgebiet Geschichte und Kultur der Hui-Nationalität.

53 Ding Mingjun 2013, S. 81.

54 *Ibid.*, S. 81-83. Ding geht hier auch auf sufistische Untergruppen und historische Entwicklungen ein. Gedimu wird in anderen Texten häufig 格迪目 geschrieben. – Michael Dillon bezeichnet die „tendency to schism and sectarianism" als eine der Charakteristika der muslimischen Gemeinschaften in China. Zwar würden Spaltungen religiös begründet, so Dillon, doch dahinter zeige sich „a complex interplay of religious, personal, family and social factors. [...] In northwest China in particular, after their own immediate family, it is their sect or order with which most Hui people have tended to identify [...]. Membership of a sect or Sufi order could have profound effect on everyday lives of Hui people, their employment prospects and standard of living" (Dillon 1999, S. 91-92). Dillon 1999, S. 91-152, gibt einen Überblick über die wichtigsten Schulen und Orden des Islam in China.

55 Laut dem Kurzportrait „Hongsibao qu jiben gaikuang" 红寺堡区基本概况 auf der amtlichen Website von Hongsibao, www.hspzfw.gov.cn/list.jsp?urltype=tree.TreeTempUrl& wbtreeid=1002, aufgerufen am 2. Februar 2016.

Hongsibao 165.000 Menschen, 60,76% davon Hui. 2012 gab es dort 192 religiöse Versammlungsstätten, von denen 184 Moscheen waren.[56]

Bei der Neuansiedlung in Hongsibao platzierte die Regierung die Hui-Muslime ohne Rücksicht darauf, welcher islamischen Gruppierung sie angehörten. Laut Ding Mingjun wurden dadurch alte Bindungen, Strukturen und soziale Netzwerke zerstört, was die Neubildung der Hui-Nachbarschaften erschwerte. Bei seinen Studien stellte er fest, dass die Muslime in den neuen Siedlungen Hongsibaos meist ebenso viele Moscheen bauten, wie es islamische Sekten und Orden unter ihnen gab. Das führte dazu, dass in vielen der über 50 Dörfer mehrere Moscheen entstanden – teilweise mehr als fünf, in einem Fall sogar 23.[57] Ein Ahong, der in einem Dorf in Hongsibao tätig war, erzählte Dings Forschungsteam, dass es in diesem Dorf vier verschiedene islamische Gruppierungen gebe, die jeweils ihre eigenen Moscheen hätten. Doch sei es immer wieder zu Konflikten gekommen, wenn Gläubige verschiedener Gruppierungen einander den Inhalt der Freitagspredigten erzählt hätten und eine Gruppe sich angegriffen gefühlt habe. Es sei deshalb sehr schwer, überhaupt noch zu predigen, anders als in der alten Heimat, wo es pro Dorf nur eine Moschee gab und alle der gleichen islamischen Gruppierung angehörten. Ein Hui berichtete den Forschern, dass sie lieber bei Wind und Wetter im Freien gebetet hätten, als die dreihundert Meter entfernte Moschee einer anderen islamischen Gruppierung zu besuchen.[58]

Aufgrund der Ergebnisse seiner Studie empfiehlt Ding der Politik, bei künftigen Umsiedlungen von Hui, in Absprache zwischen Herkunftskreisen und Zielgebieten, möglichst Angehörige der gleichen islamischen Gruppierungen gemeinsam anzusiedeln und schon im Vorfeld – unter strenger Einhaltung der einschlägigen Genehmigungsverfahren – den Bau von Moscheen zu planen. Die Koordination der Beziehungen der verschiedenen islamischen Schulen und Sufi-Orden untereinander sei wichtig für die Stabilität der Gesellschaft und die soziale Kontrolle in einem solchen Hui-Immigrationsgebiet.[59]

4.2 Muslimische Migranten aus Nordwestchina in ostchinesischen Metropolen – das Beispiel Shanghai

Seit Beginn der Reform- und Öffnungspolitik und insbesondere seit den 1990er Jahren sind nach Angaben von Mi Shoujiang zwei Millionen Muslime aus den nordwestlichen Regionen der VR China in die wirtschaftlich entwickelten Gebiete Ostchinas migriert, so dass es inzwischen in fast allen Kreisen und Städten im

---

[56] Zahlen nach Ding Mingjun 2013, S. 83.

[57] Ding Mingjun 2013, S. 88. Auf S. 85-87 gibt Ding in tabellarische Übersichten für 52 Dörfer Hongsibaos die Zahl der Moscheen nach Zugehörigkeit zu den verschiedenen islamischen Gruppierungen an. Dabei führt er auch fünf salafistische Moscheen auf.

[58] Ibid., S. 87-88.

[59] Ibid., S. 89.

Osten Chinas muslimische Binnenmigranten gibt.[60] Bai Youtao schätzte die Zahl der „mobilen Muslime" 2012 auf rund 3 Mio.[61] Dabei ist in den Zielorten der Migration die Zahl der zugezogenen Muslime oft ebenso groß oder größer als die der einheimischen. Teilweise entstanden auch muslimische Gemeinden an Orten, in denen es früher keine gab.[62]

Nach Darstellung von Ma Qinghu, der sich auf die Städte im Yangtse-Delta bezieht, verdient ein großer Prozentsatz der muslimischen Migranten seinen Lebensunterhalt mit *halal*-Lebensmitteln, wobei Hui häufig Nudelrestaurants (für *Lanzhou niurou lamian* 兰州牛肉拉面, gezogene Nudeln mit Rindfleisch nach Lanzhou-Art) betreiben, während viele Uiguren Lammspieße und Trockenobst verkaufen. Muslimische Migranten arbeiten dort außerdem häufig für ausländische Firmen und Joint Ventures sowie als Gelegenheitsarbeiter oder Betreiber kleiner Verkaufsstände.[63] Wie andere Migranten ohne städtische Wohnsitzregistrierung genießen sie in den Städten bislang nicht die gleichen Rechte wie die Stadtbürger. Sie haben keinen Zugang zum städtischen Gesundheitssystem und anderen Formen der sozialen Absicherung und stoßen auf große Probleme bei der Wohnungssuche und dem Schulbesuch ihrer Kinder.[64]

Was geschieht, wenn muslimische Migranten aus ländlichen Regionen im Nordwesten der Volksrepublik China, mit ihrem am Beispiel von Hongsibao beschriebenen intensiven und komplexen religiösen Hintergrund, in die ostchinesischen Städte kommen, deren muslimische Gemeinden durch die Auflösung ihrer traditionellen Viertel geschwächt und bei denen Säkularisierung und Assimilation an die „Mainstream-Kultur" weit fortgeschritten sind? Zwei der besprochenen Autoren – Ge Zhuang vom religionswissenschaftlichen Institut der Shanghai shehui kexueyuan 上海社会科学院 (Shanghai Academy of Social Sciences) und Tian Haiyan – gehen dieser Frage am Beispiel von Shanghai nach.

Shanghai, das vor 1949 über 20 Moscheen besaß, hat heute sieben – darunter die in der Yuan-Dynastie gegründete alte Moschee von Songjiang 松江, das heute

---

[60] Mi Shoujiang, „Zhongguo yisilanjiao dushihua de guocheng ji qi fazhan qushi" 中国伊斯兰教都市化的过程及其发展趋势 (The Urbanization Process of Chinese Islam and Its Development Trends), *SJZJWH* 2010/1, hier zitiert nach Fan Lizhu – Chen Na 2014, S. 22.

[61] Bai Youtao 2013, S. 52.

[62] Ein besonderer Fall in dieser Hinsicht ist die Stadt Yiwu 义乌 (Provinz Zhejiang): 1989 waren dort nur 19 Hui fest ansässig; vgl. Ma Qinghu 2015, S. 49. Infolge der Entwicklung des Ortes zum internationalen Umschlagplatz für kleine Gebrauchsartikel gab es um 2007 in Yiwu bereits 20.000 Muslime, davon waren 60% ausländische Muslime aus arabischen, afrikanischen und asiatischen Ländern, 40% waren Binnenmigranten aus ländlichen Regionen im Westen der Volksrepublik China; vgl. Guo Chengmei 2007, S. 120.

[63] Vgl. Ma Qinghu 2015, S. 49; Ma zufolge sind muslimische Migranten teilweise auch als Vertreter oder Dolmetscher von Handelsorganisationen aus dem Nahen und Mittleren Osten, aus Zentralasien und Südostasien tätig. – Ma Qinghu (geb. 1976, Hui aus Ningxia), Institut für Politik und Recht, Ningxia daxue, Anthropologe, Forschungsschwerpunkt ethnische Kulturen.

[64] Am Beispiel Shanghais dargelegt von Ge Zhuang 2014, S. 3-4.

ein Stadtbezirk von Shanghai ist, und eine Frauenmoschee.⁶⁵ Infolge des Stadtumbaus wohnen die rund 70.000 einheimischen Muslime Shanghais nicht mehr wie früher im Umkreis der Moscheen, sondern in allen Ecken Shanghais verstreut. In der Metropole leben außerdem über 100.000 muslimische Binnenmigranten; ihre Zahl ist damit höher als die der einheimischen Muslime.⁶⁶ Der Zuzug der islamischen Migranten aus dem Nordwesten bringt nach Beobachtung von Ge und Tian diverse Veränderungen für das muslimische Leben der Stadt mit sich, die im Folgenden vorgestellt werden sollen.

4.2.1 Veränderungen in den Shanghaier Moscheegemeinden durch den Zuzug muslimischer Migranten

4.2.1.1 (Wieder-)Belebung des religiösen Lebens

Die stark religiös geprägten muslimischen Migranten aus dem Nordwesten halten nach Beobachtung der Autoren meist auch in Shanghai an ihrem Glauben und am Moscheebesuch fest. „Sie bringen den religiös im Niedergang befindlichen urbanen Muslim-Gemeinschaften ihre Glaubensfrömmigkeit mit und stimulieren ein erneutes Aufblühen des religiösen Glaubens in der Stadt. Die bisher an Freitagen recht leeren Moscheen sind wieder voller fromm betender Muslime. An hohen Feiertagen sind alle Moscheen Shanghais überfüllt, die betende Menge reicht bis hinaus auf die Straßen", schreibt Tian Haiyan. Man könne sagen, dass die verunsicherten Stadtmuslime durch die Migranten „die Bedeutung ihrer kulturellen Tradition und ihres Glaubens wiederentdecken".⁶⁷

Besonders die Moscheen in Huxi 沪西 und Pudong 浦东 ziehen aufgrund ihrer Lage viele Migranten an.⁶⁸ Das Publikum dieser beiden Moscheen ist Tian Haiyan zufolge sehr unterschiedlich: In der Nähe der Huxi-Moschee siedelten sich muslimische Wanderarbeiter aus dem Nordwesten an, es entstand ein hauptsächlich aus auswärtigen Muslimen bestehendes, stark vom religiösen Leben des Nordwestens geprägtes und deutlich konservatives Muslim-Nachbarschaftsviertel.

---

⁶⁵ Ge Zhuang 2011, S. 149.

⁶⁶ *Id.* 2014, S. 5. Die einheimischen Muslime waren ab 1843 ebenfalls als Migranten aus Jiangsu, Henan, Shandong, Hubei und Anhui nach Shanghai gekommen, siehe *id.* 2011, S. 149, 152. – Zum Größenvergleich: Ende 2012 hatte Shanghai eine Migrantenbevölkerung von über 9,6 Mio., das waren rund 40% der Gesamtbevölkerung. Die Muslime sind also eine sehr kleine Minderheit unter den Migranten. Vgl. „Shanghai issues report on migrant population", chinadaily.com.cn 2.07.2013 (www.chinadaily.com.cn/china/2013-07-02/content_16710313.htm, aufgerufen am 3. August 2016).

⁶⁷ Tian Haiyan 2013, S. 42. Auch Ge Zhuang 2014, S. 1, spricht davon, dass die muslimischen Migranten „in den Muslimgemeinschaften des ganzen Yangtse-Deltas die religiöse Atmosphäre beleben". Bai Youtao – Chen Yunchang 2007, S. 80, berichten Ähnliches für Nanjing und Shanghai, ihnen zufolge bekehren sich sogar Nichtmuslime durch den Kontakt mit muslimischen Migranten zum Islam.

⁶⁸ Ge Zhuang 2011, S. 151.

Die Moschee in Pudong hingegen ist international und modern, geprägt von der zunehmenden Zahl der in Shanghai tätigen ausländischen Muslime.[69]

Da, wie Ge Zhuang schreibt, die einheimischen Muslime überwiegend keine regelmäßigen Moscheegänger sind, machen die frömmeren Migranten inzwischen den Hauptteil der Gebetsteilnehmer aus. Ge belegt dies eindrucksvoll mit der folgenden Zählung von Moscheebesuchern:

Gruppe / Datum	Einheimische Muslime	Muslimische Migranten [ohne Uiguren]	Uigurische Muslime aus Xinjiang	Ausländische Muslime	Gesamtzahl der Gebetsteilnehmer aller 7 Moscheen Shanghais
Id al-Fitr 1428 (13.10.2007)	2.737 Ps. 17,32%	9.452 Ps. 59,83%	2.750 Ps. 17,41%	859 Ps. 5,43%	15.798 Ps.
Id al-Fitr 1430 (21.09.2009)	1.991 Ps. 18,07%	6.415 Ps. 58,24%	1.505 Ps. 13,66%	1.104 Ps. 10,02%	11.015 Ps.
Opferfest 1430 (28.11.2009)	1.577 Ps. 12,64%	6.939 Ps. 55,61%	2.651 Ps. 21,24%	1.312 Ps. 10,51%	12.479 Ps.

Tabelle: Muslimische Gebetsteilnehmer in Shanghai nach Gruppen.
(Ge Zhuang 2011, S. 152, Tabelle 1. Zahlen: Islamische Vereinigung Shanghai.)

Am Opferfest 2009 machten die einheimischen Muslime also nur noch 12,64% der Gebetsteilnehmer in Shanghai aus. Ihr Anteil lag damit knapp über dem der ausländischen Gebetsteilnehmer und weit unter dem der Uiguren. Die inländischen nicht-einheimischen Muslime aller Ethnien stellten zusammen über drei Viertel der Gebetsteilnehmer.[70]

4.2.1.2 Spannungen und die Entstehung von „Druck auf der religiösen Ebene"

Es wurde bereits erwähnt, dass die muslimischen Migranten die Moscheegemeinden beleben. Es entstehen Ge Zhuang zufolge aber auch Spannungen unter den verschiedenen Gruppen von Muslimen. Einheimische Shanghaier Muslime neigen – nach Ges Beobachtung – zu einer kritischen Einstellung gegenüber den zugezogenen Muslimen, deren Bildung und deren Sinn für Gesetz und Ordnung sie für unzureichend halten. Umgekehrt, so Ge, können sich die zugezogenen Muslime aus dem Nordwesten an die säkulare Atmosphäre und den feierfreudigen Lebensstil der Shanghaier Gesellschaft nur schwer gewöhnen; sie grenzen sich nicht nur

---

[69] Tian Haiyan 2013, S. 39.

[70] Ge Zhuang 2011, S. 151. – Den Rückgang der Gebetsbesucher aus den Reihen der muslimischen Migranten (ohne Uiguren) zwischen Oktober 2007 und November 2009 erklärt *ibid.*, S. 153, mit der Zunahme provisorischer Gebetsstätten in den Außenbezirken Shanghais im gleichen Zeitraum. Nicht begründet wird der drastische Rückgang des Moscheebesuchs bei den einheimischen Muslimen. Die Gesamtzahl der Gebetsteilnehmer in den sieben offiziellen Moscheen – maximal knapp 16.000 – erscheint nicht hoch im Vergleich mit der von *id.* 2014, S. 5 für Shanghai angegebenen Zahl von 70.000 einheimischen und 100.000 auswärtigen Muslimen.

gegenüber den Stadtbewohnern im Allgemeinen, sondern auch gegenüber den einheimischen Muslimen ab.[71]

Durch die Anwesenheit dieser großen, frommen und streng auf die Einhaltung der religiösen Pflichten bedachten Gruppe von Muslimen entsteht laut Ge Zhuang „Druck auf der religiösen Ebene". Dies betrifft nach seiner Einschätzung besonders die Islamischen Vereinigungen und Moscheeverwaltungskomitees der Stadt, die mehrheitlich mit einheimischen Muslimen besetzt sind, und die persönliche religiöse Praxis der Letztgenannten.[72] Wie Ge feststellt, beurteilen muslimische Migranten die Frömmigkeit der einheimischen Muslime und das religiöse Wissen der lokalen Ahongs oft kritisch und lassen kein gutes Haar an deren Predigten. Besonders streng urteilen Ge zufolge jene unter den Migranten, die in ihrer Heimat systematischen Religionsunterricht genossen haben, Koranschüler gewesen waren oder gar selbst einmal als Imam gearbeitet hatten. Das sei eine Herausforderung, die die städtischen Ahongs einerseits dazu anrege, sich um eine Anhebung ihrer religiösen Fähigkeiten zu bemühen, andererseits aber auch zu neuen Konflikten führe.[73]

Konfliktpotential bergen nach Ge Zhuangs Ansicht aber auch die Gegensätze unter den verschiedenen islamischen Gruppierungen. Zwar seien auch schon früher in der Geschichte Anhänger unterschiedlicher islamischer Gruppierungen aus anderen Provinzen nach Shanghai gekommen, diese seien aber friedlich miteinander ausgekommen. Einen Kampf zwischen muslimischen Schulen und Sufi-Orden, wie er in den nordwestlichen Provinzen Gansu, Qinghai und Ningxia üblich sei, habe es in Shanghai nie gegeben. Nun aber seien in den letzten Jahren durch die zunehmende Zahl ausländischer und aus anderen Provinzen Chinas zugewanderter Muslime Glaubensrichtungen aller Art an die Shanghaier Moscheen gelangt. Einige zugezogene Muslime „halten starr an den Vorstellungen ihrer ursprünglichen islamischen Schule fest und können sich an die religiöse

---

[71] Ge Zhuang 2011, S. 153, 155.
[72] Ibid., S. 154.
[73] Id. 2014, S. 3. – Jérôme Doyon macht in seiner Untersuchung über die Islamische Vereinigung der Stadt Nanjing – die wie Shanghai im Yangtse-Delta liegt – auf folgende Zusammenhänge aufmerksam: In Provinzen mit einem geringen Bevölkerungsanteil von Muslimen werden die Moscheen häufig zentral von der lokalen Islamischen Vereinigung kontrolliert, während sich in den Gebieten des Nordwestens mit einem relativ hohen Bevölkerungsanteil von Muslimen die Moscheen dezentral selbst verwalten (Doyon 2014, S. 48). In Nanjing werden die Ahongs von der Islamischen Vereinigung (und nicht wie traditionell üblich von der Moschee) angestellt und sind von ihr abhängig (S. 48-49). Die Führer der Islamischen Vereinigung von Nanjing müssen keine praktizierenden Muslime (aber Hui) sein; zur Zeit von Doyons Untersuchungen waren der Vorsitzende und sein erster Stellvertreter Parteimitglieder (S. 50). Dies schafft „an atmosphere of non-belief. [...] these leaders are generally not considered to be close followers of the religion by members of the community, and especially more by religious migrants from the northwest. [...] They are not demanding in terms of religious aptitude of the *ahong*, instead placing more emphasis on protecting social order" (S. 51). Man kann vermuten, dass die Situation in Shanghai nicht völlig anders ist als in Nanjing, was die kritische Haltung mancher Migranten erklären würde.

Atmosphäre Shanghais nicht gewöhnen", schreibt Ge. Er zählt dies zu den „latenten Gefahren", die durch den Zuzug der auswärtigen Muslime in die Metropole entstehen.[74] Auch unter zugezogenen Muslimen aus unterschiedlichen Herkunftsregionen oder unterschiedlichen religiösen Schulen und Sufi-Orden kommt es laut Ge immer wieder zu Misshelligkeiten.[75]

4.2.2 Gründung provisorischer islamischer Gebetsstätten in den Außenbezirken Shanghais

Viele muslimische Migranten wohnen in den Außenbezirken von Shanghai. Wie Ge Zhuang darlegt, ist der Weg zur Moschee für diese Migranten sehr weit, da alle sieben Moscheen Shanghais im eigentlichen Stadtgebiet liegen. Um das Freitagsgebet in einer der Shanghaier Moscheen besuchen zu können, brauchen sie mit dem Bus oft mehrere Stunden, vom Außenbezirk Jinshan 金山 etwa fünf Stunden.[76] Da kaum einer der Migranten jede Woche so viel Zeit erübrigen kann, gründeten sie in Eigeninitiative in den äußeren Stadtbezirken provisorische islamische Gebetsstätten.[77] Ge Zhuang untersuchte diese provisorischen Stätten im März 2010 in einer Feldstudie. Dabei stellte er Folgendes fest: Die provisorischen islamischen Gebetsstätten in Shanghai werden fast nur von Migranten aus Nordwestchina besucht, und zwar hauptsächlich von solchen, die in Nudelrestaurants arbeiten. Teilweise befinden sie sich in Nebenräumen von Nudelrestaurants. Sie bieten – ganz wie die traditionellen Moscheeviertel – den muslimischen Migranten eine geistige Heimat und die Möglichkeit, sich zu treffen. Nur Hui, Salar, Dongxiang und Bao'an besuchen diese provisorischen Moscheen, nicht aber die turksprachigen Uiguren, Kasachen, Kirgisen, Usbeken, Tataren und Tadschiken. Die Angehörigen der zweiten Gruppe gehen eher in die regulären Stadtmoscheen. Hier zeigt sich Ge zufolge deutlich die Abgrenzung der verschiedenen Ethnien voneinander.[78] Besonders mit den Uiguren haben die anderen Gruppen laut Ge fast keinen Kontakt.[79]

---

[74] Ge Zhuang 2011, S. 155.

[75] *Id*. 2014, S. 3. – In der Provinz Hubei ist auch unter den Ahongs der Anteil der Zugezogenen hoch: Wie Li Anhui und Chen Xiaomin berichten, kommen 65% der Ahongs in Hubei aus anderen Provinzen, 13% davon aus dem Nordwesten. Den Autorinnen zufolge haben die einheimischen Muslime Schwierigkeiten, sich an deren Predigt- und Gebetsstil zu gewöhnen. Zwischen muslimischen Migranten und leitenden Ahongs an den Moscheen bestehen ebenfalls Differenzen bezüglich der religiösen Gruppierungen und Verhaltensnormen. Vgl. Li Anhui – Chen Xiaomin 2015, S. 87.

[76] Ge Zhuang 2011, S. 149. Erschwerend sind die häufigen Staus. Ein Nudelrestaurantbesitzer sagte zu Ge, bei Stau würden sie oft mit dem Moped bei Rot über die Ampeln fahren, um rechtzeitig zum Gebet in die Moschee zu kommen, auch wenn sie wüssten, dass dies dem Ruf der Muslime schade, aber der Weg sei einfach zu weit.

[77] *Ibid*., S. 149.

[78] *Ibid*., S. 149-150.

[79] *Ibid*., S. 153. – Tian Haiyan 2013, S. 44, spricht (als einzige[r] der untersuchten Autoren) von häufiger Diskriminierung uigurischer Migranten in der Shanghaier Gesellschaft, etwa

Außer im Bezirk Jinshan sind die provisorischen islamischen Gebetsstätten bislang (Stand 2010) nicht von den zuständigen Behörden anerkannt und damit nach den einschlägigen Rechtsvorschriften „illegal". Die Behörden vor Ort wissen nicht, wie sie damit umgehen sollen, und ziehen es vor, sie zu ignorieren, stellt Ge Zhuang fest.[80] Er bezeichnet diese behördlich unbeaufsichtigten provisorischen Stätten, die mit dem Netzwerk der über 2.000 muslimischen Nudelrestaurants Shanghais verbunden sind, als „toten Punkt" im Blickfeld der staatlichen Verwaltung und als latente Gefahr für die soziale Stabilität. Wenn Misshelligkeiten mit Behörden oder Nichtmuslimen oder von Muslimen untereinander zu „plötzlichen Zwischenfällen" führen, spielen laut Ge oft die provisorischen Gebetsstätten als Kohäsionspunkte eine Rolle.[81] Ge Zhuang plädiert dafür, die behördliche Verwaltung provisorischer Gebetsstätten zeitnah zu verstärken, sobald sie auftauchen, und gleichzeitig eine Erweiterung des bestehenden Moscheenetzes zu erwägen. Er empfiehlt außerdem, die „Brückenfunktion" des Moscheeklerus, der Moscheeverwaltungskomitees und der Islamischen Vereinigungen zu nutzen, um eine bessere Kommunikation zwischen Behörden sowie zugezogenen und einheimischen Muslimen zu erreichen und „Massenzwischenfälle" zu vermeiden; die Religionsbehörden der Stadt Nanjing etwa hätten mit der Gründung einer entsprechenden Kontaktgruppe bereits gute Erfahrungen gemacht.[82]

---

bei der Wohnungssuche. Tian führt dies darauf zurück, dass Diebesbanden aus Xinjiang in Shanghai ihr Unwesen treiben, wodurch Vorurteile in der Bevölkerung entstehen, unter denen auch die rechtschaffenen Uiguren leiden. – An dieser Stelle vermisst man besonders die Stimme eines uigurischen Wissenschaftlers bzw. eine ausführlichere und differenziertere Darstellung der Situation der uigurischen Migranten.

[80] Ge Zhuang 2011, S. 149, 150. – Möglicherweise sind inzwischen weitere provisorische islamische Gebetsstätten in Shanghai von den Behörden anerkannt. Guo Chengzhen, Generalsekretär der Chinesischen Islamischen Vereinigung, erklärte im März 2016, dass die Moscheen in manchen Städten wegen des Zuzugs von Muslimen aus dem Westen oft gefährlich überfüllt seien, weshalb einige Provinzen und Städte im Osten die Errichtung provisorischer religiöser Stätten genehmigt hätten (vgl. „Quanguo zhengxie weiyuan Guo Chengzhen: Zhongguo musilin zongjiao xinyang ziyou dedao qieshi baozhang").

[81] Ge Zhuang 2011, S. 154-155. – Ge nennt folgende Arten von „sozialen Konflikten, die mit islamischen Faktoren zu tun haben": Konflikte, die die Verletzung religiöser Tabus betreffen; Konflikte in Zusammenhang mit religiösen Aktivitäten, wie die Auflösung illegaler provisorischer Gebetsstätten durch die Behörden; religiöse Infiltration durch Kleriker unter den ausländischen Muslimen in Shanghai oder durch chinesische Rückkehrer aus islamischen Ländern, die radikales religiöses Gedankengut verbreiten; Spannungen zwischen den verschiedenen Ethnien; vgl. *ibid.*, S. 155-156. Häufige Ursachen für Konflikte zwischen muslimischen Migranten und den Behörden auf nicht-religiöser Ebene sind u.a. Gewerbe ohne Gewerbeschein sowie mobile Essbuden und Verkaufsstände, die aus Behördensicht das Erscheinungsbild der Stadt verschandeln; vgl. z.B. Xue Qing – Chen Deyong – Xue Peng 2012, S. 47; Bai Youtao 2013, S. 52-53; Li Anhui – Chen Xiaomin 2015, S. 87.

[82] Ge Zhuang 2014, S. 4. – Solche Kontaktstellen für muslimische Migranten werden in Xue Qing – Chen Deyong – Xue Peng 2012 für die Stadt Yangzhou (Provinz Jiangsu), in Wang Yinjun 2015 für die Stadt Changzhou (ebenfalls Jiangsu) und in Li Anhui – Chen Xiaomin 2015 für mehrere Städte der Provinz Hunan vorgestellt. Diese Stellen haben die Aufgabe, den muslimischen Migranten Dienstleistungen und Hilfestellungen anzubieten, sie zur

4.3 Religion als soziales Kapital der Migranten und ihre zweifache Rolle für die Integration

Welche Rolle spielt nun die Religionszugehörigkeit der Binnenmigranten für ihre Integration in die Städte, und bestehen diesbezüglich Unterschiede zwischen den verschiedenen Religionen? Mit dieser Frage beschäftigt sich ein Artikel der Wissenschaftler Fan Lizhu und Chen Na von der Fudan daxue 复旦大学 (Fudan University) in Shanghai, aus dem hier kurz einige die bisherigen Ausführungen ergänzende Gedanken wiedergegeben werden sollen.

Fan und Chen betonen, dass die Religion zum sozialen Kapital gehört, das die Migranten von ihrem Heimatort in die Stadt mitbringen. Da die Migranten in den Städten nicht chancengleich sind, sind den Autoren zufolge Beziehungen, die auf gemeinsamem Heimatort, familiären Bindungen oder gemeinsamer Religionszugehörigkeit beruhen, sehr wichtig. Sie bieten spirituelle Stütze und Hilfe bei Anfangsschwierigkeiten und sind somit ein erster Schritt zur sozialen Integration der Migranten in den Städten.[83] Während Religion somit ein integrierender Faktor sein kann, nennen Fan und Chen aber auch Konstellationen, in denen Religion eine abgrenzende Wirkung hat. Auf die Muslime bezogen stellen sie Folgendes fest: Bei den muslimischen Migranten aus dem Nordwesten sind Religions- und Ethnienzugehörigkeit oft mit einer auf ein sehr kleines Segment beschränkten Berufswahl verbunden, was ihnen im Vergleich zu Migrantengruppen mit vielfältigeren Berufsmöglichkeiten geringere Chancen bietet, mit der städtischen Gesellschaft in Kontakt zu kommen.[84] Außerdem heben den Wissenschaftlern zufolge besonders bei Protestanten und Muslimen die den beiden Religionen eigenen internen Abgrenzungen – durch unterschiedliche religiöse Untergruppen oder regionale Zugehörigkeiten – die integrierende Funktion der Religion zu einem gewissen Grad wieder auf.[85]

5. Transformation zu einer mobilen geistigen Muslimgemeinschaft?

Bisher wurde dargelegt, wie chinesische Wissenschaftler die zwei zentralen Faktoren – die Auflösung der historischen Muslimviertel im Zuge des Städteumbaus und die starke Zuwanderung muslimischer Binnenmigranten im Zuge der Urbanisierung – für die gewaltigen Umbrüche der letzten Jahrzehnte in der urbanen muslimischen Kultur beschrieben und interpretiert haben. Zwei Autoren stellen sich die übergreifende Frage, wie sich die muslimischen Gemeinschaften in China weiterentwickeln sollten, um angesichts dieser doppelten Herausforderung in

---

Wahrung der Gesetze zu erziehen, Konflikte zu schlichten, Informationen weiterzumelden und die gesellschaftliche Stabilität zu wahren. Dabei kooperieren meist die lokalen Behörden für ethnische und religiöse Angelegenheiten mit der örtlichen Islamischen Vereinigung, wobei Migrantenvertreter einbezogen werden.

[83] Fan Lizhu – Chen Na 2014, S. 23-24.
[84] *Ibid.*, S. 24.
[85] *Ibid.*, S. 26.

der Zukunft bestehen zu können. Ihre Thesen sollen abschließend vorgestellt werden.

Der Glaubenskern des chinesischen Islam sei durch die Geschichte stets gleich geblieben, aber seine gesellschaftliche Organisationsform und sein kulturelles Zeichensystem hätten sich fortwährend gewandelt – ein Zeichen der unerschütterlichen Lebenskraft des Islam, schreibt Tian Haiyan.[86] Tian sieht die Muslimgemeinschaften in den Städten vor einer „Transformationsaufgabe": Die geographischen Grenzen der traditionellen Muslimviertel seien aufgehoben, was die Kohäsionskraft der Gemeinschaften geschwächt habe. Zudem stelle sich auch angesichts des Zuzugs einer großen Zahl muslimischer Migranten aus dem Nordwesten mit ihrem ganz andersartigen religiösen und kulturellen Hintergrund die Frage nach einer neuen Integration.[87] Für Tian besteht die Transformationsaufgabe darin, dass „die Muslimgemeinschaften sich durch Integration und Rekonstruktion der religiösen Kultur von den traditionellen räumlich konzentriert zusammenlebenden Gemeinschaften zu mobilen geistigen Gemeinschaften (*liudongxing jingshen shequ* 流动性精神社区) wandeln".[88] Die muslimischen Migranten kämen gewöhnlich aufgrund starker Beziehungen, die auf Verwandtschaft oder auf lokaler Herkunft basieren, in die Städte, stellt Tian fest. In den urbanen muslimischen Gemeinschaften aber sei meist der Glaube der verbindende und die Gruppenidentität prägende Faktor, während sich die Faktoren von Blutsbeziehung und territorialer Herkunft mit der Zeit abschwächen.[89]

Ma Xuefeng postuliert den Aufbau einer muslimischen intellektuellen Gemeinschaft (*musilin zhishi gongtongti* 穆斯林智识共同体). Eine solche Gemeinschaft ist seiner Meinung nach notwendig, um auf der einen Seite die innere Integration der vereinzelten und untereinander zersplitterten Muslime herzustellen und auf der anderen Seite einen wirksamen Austausch mit der Mainstream-Gesellschaft führen zu können. Ma argumentiert, dass – wenn man die drei „von außen" nach China gekommen Religionen Buddhismus, Christentum und Islam vergleiche – der Islam der Mehrheitsgesellschaft und der akademischen Welt am fremdesten sei, was auch daran liege, dass die chinesischen Muslime traditionell konservativ seien, sehr wenig nach außen missionierten und wenig publizierten. Seiner Ansicht nach sollte die aufzubauende muslimische intellektuelle Gemeinschaft ein Bewusstsein für die gesellschaftlichen Fragen der Zeit haben, wie es beispielsweise, jeweils als Reaktion auf Krisen ihrer Zeit, die muslimischen Gelehrten in der Ming-Zeit und dann wieder ab dem Ende der Qing-Zeit besessen hätten.[90]

---

[86] Tian Haiyan 2013, S. 40.

[87] *Ibid.*, S. 43.

[88] *Ibid.*, S. 41.

[89] *Ibid.*, S. 44.

[90] Ma Xuefeng 2012, Kapitel 4-6, ohne Seitenangabe. Einen Vortrag gleichen Titels hielt Ma auf der Tagung „Urbane Muslime vor dem Hintergrund der Modernisierung", die am 6./7. April 2012 an der Jinyelu 锦业路 -Moschee in Xi'an stattfand; vgl. Ma Qiang – Ma Chao 2012, S. 54.

6. Schluss

Eingangs war von dem „Missverständnis" die Rede, dass Urbanisierung zwangsläufig zu Säkularisierung führt. Wird diese Aussage Peter van der Veers durch die oben vorgestellten Forschungsergebnisse chinesischer Wissenschaftler zu den Auswirkungen der Urbanisierung auf den Islam in China bestätigt? Das Ergebnis ist zweideutig. Während die Auflösung der traditionellen Muslimviertel Säkularisierungstendenzen beschleunigt hat, halten muslimische Migranten aus dem stark religiösen Nordwesten Chinas auch in den Zielstädten ihrer Migration an ihrem Glauben fest, was teilweise zu einer religiösen Rückbesinnung der städtischen Muslime führt. Es entstehen neue Formen der Kommunikation und der Netzwerke.

Einer von manchen Autoren vertretenen These zufolge geht die Entwicklung der urbanen muslimischen Gemeinschaften dahin, dass der Glaube zunehmend zum verbindenden Faktor wird bzw. dass es sich bei neuen Formen von Gruppen (beispielsweise im Internet) um Zusammenschlüsse von Einzelnen auf der Basis von geistigen Gemeinsamkeiten handelt, während Verwandtschaft und Herkunftsort eine immer weniger wichtige Rolle spielen. In diesem Punkt kann man eine Parallele zu einer für die traditionelle chinesische Religiosität festgestellten Entwicklung sehen, die ebenfalls bei van der Veer genannt wird. Er schreibt: „Up to 1949 (when the Communists took over), large Chinese cities were organized as networks of neighborhoods, each with its own territorial god and temple [...]." Diese sozioreligiöse Organisation sei weitgehend zerstört worden. Die Folgen dieser politisch herbeigeführten Säkularisierung manifestieren sich nach van der Veer am tiefsten in „a deterritorialization of religion and a shift toward voluntary association".[91]

Literaturverzeichnis

Allès, Elisabeth. 2005. „Muslimisches religiöses Schulwesen in China", *Chh* 2005/1-2, S. 32-40.

Bai Youtao 白友涛. 2013. „Chengshi shehui guanli zhong de ‚liangge bu shiying'. Jiyu Wuhan, Guangzhou, Nanjing, Yiwu deng di liudong musilin diaocha de sikao" 城市社会管理中的两个不适应—基于武汉、广州、南京、义乌等地流动穆斯林调查的思考 (Two Inadaptations in Urban Social Management. Migrant Muslims in East Urban China), *HZYJ* 2013/1, S. 51-55.

Bai Youtao 白友涛 – Chen Yunchang 陈赟畅. 2007. „Liudong musilin yu chengshi Huizu shequ. Yi Nanjing, Shanghai deng chengshi wei li" 流动穆斯林与城市回族社区—以南京、上海等城市为例 (Migrant Muslims and the Hui Communities

---

[91] Van der Veer 2015, S. 13. – Van der Veer bezieht sich hier besonders auf den Beitrag von Vincent Goossaert im *Handbook of Religions and the Asian City*, der am Beispiel der Stadt Suzhou das Schicksal territorialer Tempelkulte beschreibt, die seit Beginn der Reformbewegung 1898 allmählich eingeschränkt und nach 1949 zunehmend unterdrückt worden waren und nun, auch im Zuge der Einverleibung dörflicher Gemeinden in die Städte, weiter schwinden oder nur in stark veränderter Form fortbestehen.

in Megacities. A Study on Migrant Muslims in Nanjing and Shanghai), *HZYJ* 2007/4, S. 77-84.

DDZJYJ: *Dangdai zongjiao yanjiu* 当代宗教研究 (Contemporary Religious Studies), hrsg. von der Shanghai Academy of Social Sciences, Institut für Religionswissenschaft.

Dillon, Michael. 1999. *China's Muslim Hui Community. Migration, Settlement and Sects*. Richmond, Surrey: Curzon.

Ding Mingjun 丁明俊. 2013. „Yimin anzhi yu Huizu ‚jiaofang' de chonggou. Yi Ningxia Hongsibao yimin kaifaqu wei li" 移民安置与回族"教坊"的重构—以宁夏红寺堡移民开发区为例 (Resettlement of Displaced Residents and the Reconstruction of Ethnic Hui „Muslim Community". Taking Hongsibao Displaced Residents Development Zone as Example), *HZYJ* 2013/1, S. 81-90.

Doyon, Jérôme. 2014. „The Local Islamic Associations and the Party-State. Consanguinity and Opportunities", *China Perspectives* 2014/4, S. 45-52.

Duan Qi 段琦. 2013. „Henan Kaifeng he Nanyang de zongjiao geju ji chengyin baogao" 河南开封和南阳的宗教格局及成因报告 (Field Study Report on the Present State and Pattern of Religions in Kaifeng and Nanyang, Henan Province), in: Jin Ze 金泽 – Qiu Yonghui 邱永辉 (Hrsg.), *Zhongguo zongjiao baogao (2013)* 中国宗教报告. *Annual Report on Religions in China (2013)*. Zongjiao lanpishu 宗教蓝皮书 Blue Book of Religions. Beijing: Shehui kexue wenxian chubanshe, S. 252-280.

Fan Lizhu 范丽珠 – Chen Na 陈纳. 2014. „Zongjiao xinyang yu chengshi xin yimin (xiang – cheng) chuyi. Shehui rongru wenti de ling yige shijiao" 宗教信仰与城市新移民（乡-城）刍议—社会融入问题的另一个视角 (Religion and Rural-Urban Immigration. An Approach to Study Assimilation in China), *SJZJWH* 2014/2, S. 21-26.

Feng Gang 冯刚 – Liu Xinlu 刘欣路. 2015. „Zai Yue waiguo musilin shehui guanli mianlin de wenti yu yingdui" 在粤外国穆斯林社会管理面临的问题与应对 (Problems of Managing Foreign Muslims in Guangdong Province and Countermeasures), *ZGMSL* 2015/3, S. 22-24.

Ge Zhuang 葛壮. 2011. „Hushang wailai liudong musilin qunti de jingshen shenghuo. Guanyu Shanghai zhoubian qu xian yisilanjiao linshi libaidian de kaocha yu fansi" 沪上外来流动穆斯林群体的精神生活—关于上海周边区县伊斯兰教临时礼拜点的考察与反思 (The Spiritual Life of Migrant Muslim Communities in Shanghai – An Investigation and Reflection on Temporary Islamic Worship Places around Shanghai), *Shehui kexue* 社会科学 (Sozialwissenschaften) 2011/10, S. 148-157.

—. 2014. „Changsanjiao qu wailai musilin qunti rongru chengshi de xiangguan wenti ji fansi" 长三角区外来穆斯林群体融入城市的相关问题及反思 (Probleme im Hinblick auf die Integration der auswärtigen Muslime im Yangtse-Delta in die Städte und Überlegungen hierzu), *DDZJYJ* 2014/3, S. 1-8.

Gladney, Dru C. 1991. *Muslim Chinese. Ethnic Nationalism in the People's Republic*. Harvard East Asian Monographs, 149. Cambridge, Mass.: Harvard University Press.

Guo Chengmei 郭成美. 2007. „Dangdai ‚fanfang' de jueqi. Yiwu musilin shequ fazhan licheng de chubu diaocha" 当代"藩坊"的崛起——义乌穆斯林社区发展历程的初步调查 (The Rise of „Fan Fang" in Nowadays. Tentative Investigation of Muslim Community Development History in Yi Wu City), *HZYJ* 2007/2, S. 119-125.

Hasmath, Reza. 2014. „The Interactions of Ethnic Minorities in Beijing". Centre on Migration, Policy and Society Working Paper No. 111. University of Oxford. www.academia.edu/4374023/The_Interactions_of_Ethnic_Minorities_in_Beijing (aufgerufen am 31. Januar 2015).

Heilmann, Sebastian (Hrsg.). 2016. *Das politische System der Volksrepublik China*. 3., aktualisierte Auflage. Wiesbaden: Springer VS.

HZYJ: *Huizu yanjiu* 回族研究 (Journal of Hui Muslim Minority Studies), hrsg. von der Ningxia Academy of Social Sciences.

Leslie, Donald Daniel. 1986. *Islam in Traditional China. A Short History to 1800*. Canberra: Canberra College of Advanced Education.

Li Anhui 李安辉 – Chen Xiaomin 陈晓敏. 2015. „Yisilanjiao xiehui zai chengshi minzu gongzuo zhong de zuoyong yu wenti yanjiu. Hubei sheng yixie zuzhi ge'an diaocha" 伊斯兰教协会在城市民族工作中的作用与问题研究——湖北省伊协组织个案调查 (The Study on the Role and Problems of the Islamic Association in the Working of Urban Ethnic), *HZYJ* 2015/1, S. 84-90.

Liu Xiaochun 刘晓春. 2014. „Jiyu renkou diaocha de Zhongguo musilin renkou tezheng fenxi" 基于人口调查的中国穆斯林人口特征分析 (Traits of the Muslims of China Based on Census Data Analysis), *HZYJ* 2014/1, S. 70-76.

Ma Qiang 马强. 2011. „Dushihua jincheng zhong de qingzhen nüsi he nüxue" 都市化进程中的清真女寺和女学 (Urbanization and the Development of Women's Masjid and Women's School in China), *HZYJ* 2011/2, S. 110-116.

Ma Qiang 马强 – Ma Chao 马超. 2012. „Xiandaihua beijing xia qingzhensi gongneng tuozhan de tansuo yu changshi. ‚Xiandaihua beijing xia de chengshi musilin' xueshu yantaohui zongshu" 现代化背景下清真寺功能拓展的探索与尝试——"现代化背景下的城市穆斯林"学术研讨会综述 (Explorations and Attempts in Expanding the Functions of the Mosques in the Modernization Background. Summary of the Symposium on Urban Muslims in the Modernization Background), *ZGMSL* 2012/4, S. 54-57.

Ma Qinghu 马清虎. 2015. „Liudong musilin renkou yu Changsanjiao chengshi yisilanjiao de xin fazhan. Yi Yiwu, Wenzhou, Shaoxing wei li" 流动穆斯林人口与长三角城市伊斯兰教的新发展——以义乌、温州、绍兴为例 (The Islam Development between the Floating Population and the Yangtze River Delta Muslim – A Case Study of Yi Wu, Wen Zhou, Shao Xing), *HZYJ* 2015/2, S. 48-53.

Ma Weihua 马伟华. 2015. „Chuancheng yu bianqian. Dushi Huizu kaizhaijie xisu de xin sikao. Yi Beijing shi Niujie diqu wei li" 传承与变迁—都市回族开斋节习俗的新思考—以北京市牛街地区为例 (Inheritance and Change. New Thinking on Urban Hui People's Eid al-Fitr. Taking Niujie District of Beijing as an Example), *HZYJ* 2015/1, S. 103-109.

Ma Xuefeng 马雪峰. 2012. „Chongjian Zhongguo musilin zhishi (intellectual) gongtongti. Zhongguo neidi musilin shequn shehui wenti shengsi" 重建中国穆斯林智识 (intellectual) 共同体—中国内地穆斯林社群社会问题省思 (Die intellektuelle Gemeinschaft der chinesischen Muslime wiederaufbauen. Gedanken zu den gesellschaftlichen Problemen der sozialen Gruppe der chinesischen Muslime), *Ningxia shehui kexue* 宁夏社会科学 2012/5. Hier nach www.douban.com/note/240378521/ (aufgerufen am 1. Februar 2016).

Madsen, Richard. 1998. *China's Catholics. Tragedy and Hope in an Emerging Civil Society*. Berkeley – Los Angeles – London: University of California Press.

Palmer, David A. 2009. „China's Religious Danwei. Institutionalising Religion in the People's Republic", *China Perspectives* 2009/4, S. 17-30.

„Quanguo zhengxie weiyuan Guo Chengzhen: Zhongguo musilin zongjiao xinyang ziyou dedao qieshi baozhang" 全国政协委员郭承真：中国穆斯林宗教信仰自由得到切实保障 (Mitglied der Politischen Konsultativkonferenz des Chinesischen Volkes Guo Chengzhen: Glaubensfreiheit der chinesischen Muslime erhält vollen Schutz), *Xinhua* 2.03.2016, nach www.sara.gov.cn/mtjj/332597.htm (aufgerufen am 3. August 2016).

Shatzman Steinhardt, Nancy. 2015. *China's Early Mosques*. Edinburgh Studies in Islamic Art. Edinburgh: Edinburgh University Press.

SJZJWH: Shijie zongjiao wenhua 世界宗教文化 (The Religious Cultures in the World), hrsg. von der Chinese Academy of Social Sciences, Institut für Weltreligionen.

Tian Haiyan 田海燕. 2013. „Cong Shanghai musilin shequ kan zongjiao wenhua de shehuixue chanshi" 从上海穆斯林社区看宗教文化的社会学阐释 (Eine soziologische Interpretation der religiösen Kultur ausgehend von den Shanghaier Muslimvierteln), *DDZJYJ* 2013/1, S. 38-45.

van der Veer, Peter. 2015. „Introduction. Urban Theory, Asia, and Religion", in: *id.* (Hrsg.), *Handbook of Religion and the Asian City. Aspiration and Urbanization in the Twenty-First Century*. Oakland: University of California Press.

Wang Yinjun 王胤骏. 2015. „Lai dao Changzhou cheng bian shi Changzhou ren. Changzhou shi minzongju qingqing fuwu liudong musilin" 来到常州城便是常州人—常州市民宗局倾情服务流动穆斯林 (Changzhou Administration for Ethnic and Religious Affairs Provide Services for the Floating Muslims), *ZGZJ* 2015/2, S. 68-69.

Wenzel-Teuber, Katharina. 2012. „Urbanisierung, Migration und Religion in China am Beispiel der katholischen Kirche", in: Iwo Amelung – Thomas Schreijäck (Hrsg.), *Religionen und gesellschaftlicher Wandel in China*. Frankfurt East Asian Studies Series 2. München: Iudicium Verlag, S. 143-167.

—. 2015. „Statistisches Update 2014 zu Religionen und Kirchen in der Volksrepublik China", *Chh* 2015/1, S. 22-34.

—. 2016. „Statistisches Update 2015 zu Religionen und Kirchen in der Volksrepublik China", *Chh* 2016/1, S. 24-37.

Xue Qing 薛清 – Chen Deyong 陈德勇 – Xue Peng 薛鹏. 2012. „Chuangxin shehui guanli moshi, wei wailai musilin zuohao fuwu" 创新社会管理模式，为外来穆斯林做好服务 (Innovate Social Management for Better Service for Immigrant Muslims), *ZGMSL* 2012/1, S. 47-49.

Yang Wenbi 杨文笔. 2015. „Musilin xiangqinhui. Chengshi Huizu hunjie chuantong de xiandai ‚faming'" 穆斯林相亲会—城市回族婚介传统的现代"发明" (Muslim's Blind Date. A Modern Invention of Hui Matrimonial Tradition in Urban City), *HZYJ* 2015/3, S. 96-101.

Zhang Cheng 张成 – Mi Shoujiang 米寿江. 2006. „Nanjing Huizu shequ de xiaoshi yu Huizu wenhua chuancheng de sikao" 南京回族社区的消失与回族文化传承的思考 (Thinking of Disappearance of Hui Community and Inheritance of Hui Culture of Nanjing), *HZYJ* 2006/4, S. 54-59.

Zhang Jianfang 张建芳 – Wang Lihong 王丽宏. 2007. „Chengshihua jincheng zhong Huizu yisilan wenhua de tiaoshi he fazhan. Yi Ningxia Huizu zizhiqu Wuzhong shi wei li" 城市化进程中回族伊斯兰文化的调适和发展—以宁夏回族自治区吴忠市为例 (The Adjustment and Development of the Hui Islamic Culture during Urbanization. In The Case of the City Wuzhong, Ningxia Hui Autonomous Region), *HZYJ* 2007/1, S. 60-68.

Zhang, John B. 2011. „Antwort der chinesischen Kirche auf die Migration in Festlandchina (I)", *Chh* 2011/3, S. 166-177.

Zhang Ruolin 张若琳 – Chang Jing 常晶. 2015. „Chengshi shaoshu minzu juju shequ zhili de zhidu fenxi. Yi Changzhi shi chengqu Huizu shequ wei li" 城市少数民族聚居社区治理的制度分析—以长治市城区回族社区为例 (Institutional Analysis of the Governance of Urban Ethnic Minority Communities. Taking Urban Hui Minorities in Changzhi as Examples), *SJZJWH* 2015/4, S. 56-61.

ZGMSL: *Zhongguo musilin* 中国穆斯林 (China Muslim), hrsg. Chinesische Islamische Vereinigung.

ZGZJ: *Zhongguo zongjiao* 中国宗教 (China Religion), hrsg. von dem Staatlichen Büro für religiöse Angelegenheiten.

QIANLIYAN UND SHUNFENG'ER IN *XIAOSHUO* UND ANDEREN TEXTEN DER YUAN- UND MING-ZEIT

RODERICH PTAK

1. Einleitung

Über die chinesische Göttin der Seefahrer – weithin bekannt unter den Namen Mazu 媽祖, Tianfei 天妃, Tianhou 天后 etc. – ist während der letzten zwei Jahrzehnte sehr viel geschrieben worden.[1] Das hat unter anderem mit der Wiederbelebung ihres Kultes in den chinesischen Küstenprovinzen zu tun, vor allem in Fujian und Guangdong, aber auch in verschiedenen Orten Zhejiangs und Shandongs, auf Hainan und anderswo. Am wichtigsten bleibt jedoch Taiwan; die Zahl der Gläubigen wird dort auf bis zu zwanzig Millionen Menschen geschätzt.

Zum Inventar der meisten Mazu-Tempel gehören zwei besondere Figuren, welche der Seefahrergöttin zur Seite stehen: Qianliyan 千里眼 und Shunfeng'er 順風耳.[2] In der Regel werden sie neben Mazu, der Zentralfigur, postiert, und

---

[1] Bibliographische Hilfen bieten Zhonghua Mazu wenhua jiaoliu xiehui, Putian xueyuan 中华妈祖文化交流协会, 莆田学院 (Zheng Lihang 郑丽航 et al. [Hrsg.]), *Mazu yanjiu ziliao mulu suoyin* 妈祖研究资料目录索引 (Fuzhou: Haifeng chubanshe, 2004; gedruckt 2005); Zhang Xun 張珣 – Yang Yujun 楊玉君, *Mazu yanjiu shumu* 媽祖研究書目 (Minxing bei Jiayi: Zhongzheng daxue Mazu wenhua yanjiu zhongxin, 2016); die drei „Standardbibliographien" von Laurence G. Thompson et al., *Chinese Religions in Western Languages. A Comprehensive and Classified Bibliography of Publications in English, French, and German through 1980* (Tucson: The Association for Chinese Studies, 1985; Nachfolgewerke mit Gary Seaman 1993 und 1999); Philip Clart, *Bibliography of Western Language Publications on Chinese Popular Religion (1995 to present)*, http://www.uni-leipzig.de/~clartp/bibliography_CPR.html (zuletzt Februar 2014). – Wichtige Überblickswerke sind z.B.: Li Xianzhang 李獻璋, *Maso shinkô no kenkyû* 媽祖信仰の研究 (Studies on Belief of Ma-tsu) (Tokyo: Taisan bunbutsu-sha, 1979), chin. Übersetzung *Mazu xinyang yanjiu* 媽祖信仰研究 (O culto da deusa A-Ma) (Macau: Aomen haishi bowuguan, 1995), und Xu Xiaowang 徐晓望, *Mazu xinyang shi yanjiu* 妈祖信仰史研究 (Fuzhou: Haifeng chubanshe, 2007). Allgemein Roderich Ptak, *O culto de Mazu. Uma visão histórica (Da dinastia Song ao início da dinastia Qing) – Der Mazu-Kult. Ein historischer Überblick (Song bis Anfang Qing)* (Lissabon: Centro Científico e Cultural de Macau, 2012). – Die bislang umfangreichste (gedruckte) Sammlung mit Mazu-Materialien heißt *Mazu wenxian shiliao huibian* 媽祖文獻史料彙編 (nachfolgend *MZWX*); es liegen drei Serien mit verschiedenen Herausgebern vor: Ser. I, 4 Bde. (Beijing: Zhongguo dang'an chubanshe, 2007), II, 5 Bde. (Beijing: Zhongguo dang'an chubanshe, 2009), III, 7 Bde. (Fuzhou: Haifeng chubanshe, 2011). Dieses Werk hat frühere Sammlungen in mancherlei Hinsicht abgelöst, so etwa: Jiang Weitan 蔣維錟 (Hrsg.), *Mazu wenxian ziliao* 媽祖文獻資料 (Fuzhou: Fujian renmin chubanshe, 1990).

[2] Beide werden auf unzähligen Internetseiten und in einer Vielzahl gedruckter Werke erwähnt. Dazu gehören Aufsätze aller Art, die vor allem auf Tempel und Brauchtum eingehen. Beispiele in obigen Hilfsmitteln (Anm. 1) oder seither etwa in dem Sammelband: Ye

auch auf Gemälden entsprechend angeordnet. Beide Figuren lassen sich an bestimmten Merkmalen identifizieren. Qianliyan ist an seiner roten Farbe zu erkennen (aber es gibt Ausnahmen). Oftmals hält er eine Hand vor die Stirn und blickt in die Ferne. Sein Name verrät, dass er Ereignisse in großer Entfernung, gleichsam auf tausend *li*, wahrzunehmen vermag. Darum ist er in deutschsprachigen Werken häufig als „Tausend-Meilen-Auge" (englisch: „Thousand-Miles Eye") zu finden. Shunfeng'er hört jedes Geräusch, kein noch so leiser Klang entgeht ihm. Oftmals liegt eine Hand an seinem Ohr, weil er alle Botschaften erlauscht, die ihm der Wind aus fernen Welten zuträgt. Ihm ist meist die grüne (blaue: *qing* 青) Farbe zugeordnet. In der westlichen Literatur erscheint er als „Mit-dem-Wind-Ohr" bzw. „With-the-Wind Ear".

Nicht selten trägt Qianliyan eine Hellebarde, während Shunfeng'er an seiner Axt zu erkennen ist. Manchmal wirken ihre Gesichtszüge wie bei anderen Wächterfiguren recht grimmig, gelegentlich werden sie sogar ins Groteske übersteigert, zeigen hornähnliche Auswüchse am Kopf und andere furchterregende Merkmale. Kunsthistoriker würden sicher, wollten sie lokale Stile und Varianten definieren, mehrere Grundmuster feststellen können; die vielen Abbildungen im Internet mögen dabei eine gewisse Hilfe bieten, aber dies ist für uns unerheblich.[3] Hingegen wird der Umstand, dass Qianliyan und Shunfeng'er bisweilen auch neben anderen Gottheiten erscheinen, also nicht allein im Umfeld von Mazu zu sehen sind, hier eine gewisse Rolle spielen.

Worum geht es im vorliegenden Beitrag? Nicht um die Darstellung des Trios Qianliyan / Shunfeng'er / Hauptfigur in der bildenden Kunst; auch nicht um quantitative Ermittlungen, die es uns wahrscheinlich erlauben würden, mehr über die Bedeutung der beiden Mazu-Assistenten zu sagen – etwa mit Blick auf regionale und temporäre Varianten; und schließlich ebenso wenig um die Dokumentation ritueller und anderer, eher gegenwartsbezogener Komponenten rund um diese Figuren. Von Interesse sind vielmehr Belegstellen in alten Schriftquellen, besonders in Erzählungen (*xiaoshuo* 小說 im weitesten Sinne), welche Qianliyan und Shunfeng'er oder andere Gestalten, die mit beiden in Zusammenhang gebracht worden sind, en passant erwähnen, kurz beschreiben bzw. in einfache literarische Kontexte stellen. Natürlich wird es nicht möglich sein, alle Werke zu berücksichtigen; die hier vorgetragenen Gedanken beruhen nur auf ausgewählten Texten der Epochen Yuan bis Ming – auf Quellen zumeist, die der Wissenschaft bekannt sind und gerne von Mazu-Experten zitiert werden. Am Rande geht es aber noch um ein anderes Anliegen: Vor allem während der Ming-Zeit wurden gerne literarische Versuche unternommen, buddhistische, daoistische und konfuzianische Elemente zu kombinieren, also in größeren synkretistischen Einheiten zusammenzuführen. Derlei ist besonders bei Erzählungen zu beobachten. Mithin

---

Shushan 葉樹姍 (Hrsg.), *Taizhong Mazu guoji wenhua guanguang wenhuajie, 2012. Mazu guoji xueshu yantaohui lunwenji* 臺中媽祖國際文化觀光文化節, 2012. 媽祖國際學術研討會論文集 (Taizhong: Zhengshi wenhua ju, 2012).

[3] Beispiele nennt auch Klaas Ruitenbeek, „Mazu, the Patroness of Sailors, in Chinese Pictorial Art", *Artibus Asiae* 58 (1999) 3-4, S. 281-329, hier besonders S. 316, 317, 319, 320.

ist zu fragen, in welcher Weise Qianliyan und Shunfeng'er hiervon betroffen waren.

2. Ausgangsepisode: Qianliyan und Shunfeng'er im *Tianfei xiansheng lu*

Beginnen wir mit dem *Tianfei xiansheng lu* 天妃顯聖錄 (Die Aufzeichnungen von der manifestierten Heiligkeit der Himmelprinzessin), einem qingzeitlichen Werk, das in Teilen auf nicht mehr vollständig erhaltenem Material der Ming-Epoche beruht. Für viele Mazu-Gläubige gilt diese Abhandlung als ein zentraler Text, vielleicht als der wichtigste überhaupt, denn er erzählt Mazus Leben im Detail und berichtet von ihren posthumen Wundertaten. Außerdem nennt er offizielle Ehrentitel, die Mazu seit der Song-Zeit erhalten hat, zudem schildert er zeremonielle Belange und zeichnet weitere Einzelheiten auf, die für den Kult von Bedeutung sind.[4]

Aus dem *Tianfei xiansheng lu* erfährt der Leser, dass Mazu im Jahre 960 in eine Familie namens Lin geboren wurde und 987 in den Himmel aufstieg. Schon zu Lebzeiten soll sie nur gute Taten vollbracht und anderen geholfen haben. Dabei werden ihr übernatürliche Fähigkeiten nachgesagt. Diese Geschichten sind weithin bekannt und immer wieder in Wort und Bild dargestellt worden. Eine Episode bezieht sich auf Qianliyan und Shunfeng'er. Beide, so erfährt der Leser, seien böse Geister gewesen, aber Mazu habe sie unterworfen. Hier die wichtigsten Passagen in der deutschen Übertragung von Gerd Wädow (mit leichten Änderungen):[5]

> Vormals gab es zwei Dämonen – des Nordens und Westens, von Venus und Merkur. Der eine besaß ein ausgezeichnetes Gehör und wurde „Mit-dem-Wind-Ohr" genannt, der andere verfügte über eine starke Sehkraft und hieß „Tausend-Meilen-Auge" ... Die Dorfbevölkerung litt sehr unter ihnen und erflehte folglich Hilfe von der Prinzessin (Mazu). Darauf mischte sich diese unter eine Gruppe von Frauen ... [Doch die Geister] hielten sie irrtümlich für ein Mädchen aus dem Volke und wollten auf sie losgehen ..., [als selbige] plötzlich aufsprang und wie ein Feuerrad dahinflog ... [Nun] griffen die beiden zu ihren Eisenäxten und warfen ihr finstere Blicke zu. „Wagt Ihr es etwa, mit

---

[4] Zu den Titeln z.B. Bodo Wiethoff, „Der staatliche Ma-tsu Kult", *ZDMG* 116 (1966) 2, S. 311-357; Cai Xianghui 蔡相煇, *Mazu xinyang yanjiu* 媽祖信仰研究 (Taibei: Xiuwei zixun keji, 2006), S. 113-176; Xu Xiaowang, *Mazu xinyang shi yanjiu*, mehrere Kapitel, sowie Tabelle 1 im Anhang.

[5] Gerd Wädow, *T'ien-fei hsien-sheng lu. „Die Aufzeichnungen von der manifestierten Heiligkeit der Himmelsprinzessin". Einleitung, Übersetzung, Kommentar*, MSMS XXIX (Nettetal: Steyler Verlag, 1992), S. 180-182. Wädow liefert auch den vollständigen chinesischen Text; hier: 先是西北方金水之精，一聰而善聽，號「順風耳」，一明而善視，號「千里眼」。二人以金水生天 ... ...。村民苦之，求治於妃。妃乃雜跡於女流採摘中，... ...。彼誤認為民間女子，將近前，... ...遽騰躍而去，一道火光如車輪飛越，... ...。彼仍持鐵斧疾視。妃曰：『敢擲若斧乎』？遂擲下，不可復起。因咋舌伏法。越兩載，復出為厲。... ... 滾盪於浮沉蕩漾之中，巫覡莫能治。... ... 至次年五、六月間，絡繹問治於妃。乃演起神咒，林木震號，沙石飛揚。二神躲閃無門，遂拜伏願皈正教。時妃年二十三。

Euren Äxten zuzuschlagen?" herrschte sie zurück. Schon ließen sie die Äxte niedersausen – [aber] sie schafften es nicht, [selbige] wieder vom Boden zu lösen! Von Furcht übermannt, beugten sie sich [schließlich] dem Urteil der Prinzessin. [Doch] nach zwei Jahren übten sie [erneut] ihre Tyrannei aus … Sie tobten derart durch die aufgerührte See, dass selbst Hexen und Zauberer ihrer nicht mehr Herr werden konnten. … Im darauffolgenden Jahr, während des fünften und sechsten Monats, erbaten [die Menschen] fortwährend Hilfe von der Prinzessin. Darauf begann sie, göttliche Inkantationen anzustimmen; [bald] erzitterten die Wälder, Sand und Steine flogen umher. Vergebens versuchten die beiden Unholde, sich aus ihrem Blickfeld zu stehlen. Am Ende unterwarfen sie sich, gelobend, von nun an der rechten Lehre zu folgen. Zu dieser Zeit war die Prinzessin dreiundzwanzig Jahre alt.

Der letzte Satz legt nahe, dass Qianliyan und Shunfeng'er im Jahre 982 oder 983 unterworfen wurden, je nach Berechnung von Mazus Alter zum Zeitpunkt ihrer Geburt (im Jahre 960). Weiterhin bringt der Text die beiden Unholde in enge Verbindung mit der See; derlei ist im älteren Schriftgut kaum zu finden. Zudem scheint ihre Bändigung der Fünf-Elemente-Lehre geschuldet: Einmal setzt Mazu Feuer ein, damit werden die Eisenäxte neutralisiert, denn Feuer kontrolliert Metall; bei der zweiten Konfrontation wird das Element Wasser mit Hilfe von Erde und Holz (Wälder, Sand, Steine) eingedämmt. Zugleich können Wasser und Metall dem Norden und Westen zugeordnet werden (der Eingangsteil im Zitat). Auch Venus (Jinxing 金星) und Merkur (Shuixing 水星) passen hierzu.[6] Diese Konstellationen deuten auf eine gewisse Nähe zu daoistischen Vorstellungen.

3. Tempelwächter im nichtliterarischen Kontext

Einige Koordinaten aus der oben zitierten Quelle können in älteren Kontexten aufgespürt werden, doch sind die großen Zusammenhänge fast immer andere. Die folgenden Absätze stellen Texte vor, in denen Qianliyan und Shunfeng'er – oder „verwandte" Figuren dieser beiden – auftreten bzw. kurz erwähnt werden, wobei die Präsentation der Belege einem groben chronologischen Raster folgt. Das impliziert hier und da ein Hin- und Herwandern zwischen verschiedenen literarischen Genres; allerdings stehen, wie eingangs angekündigt, *xiaoshuo*-Werke im Zentrum.

Beginnen wir jedoch mit etwas anderem – mit Beispielen aus der Song-Zeit, und zwar aus der nichtliterarischen Welt. Aus dieser Epoche, wie auch aus früheren Perioden, sind mehrere Tempelwächter bekannt, so etwa eine Figur namens Zhaobao qilang 招寶七郎. Diese wurde gelegentlich, wie Qianliyan, mit einer Hand über dem Auge dargestellt; daher ist sie bisweilen als möglicher Vorläufer Qianliyans in Betracht gezogen worden. Eventuell habe Letzterer mit der Verbreitung des Mazu-Glaubens die Figur des Zhaobao qilang sogar ersetzt.[7]

---

[6] Wädow, *T'ien-fei hsien-sheng lu*, hat auf die zweite Konstellation aufmerksam gemacht. Vgl. dort S. 181, Anm. 316. Die meisten Sekundärwerke übergehen dieses Thema.

[7] Näheres z.B. in Nikaido Yoshihiro 二階堂善弘, *Asian Folk Religion and Cultural Interaction*, Global East Asia 2 (Göttingen: V & R unipress – National Taiwan University Press, 2015), besonders S. 21-24, 27-31. – Über eher unbekannte Götter und Geister in dao-

In die frühe Zeit gehört auch die Verehrung des Nanhaishen 南海神 (Südmeergott). Als wichtigste Kultstätte gilt noch immer ein berühmter Tempel im Osten von Guangzhou.[8] Er ist unzählige Male beschrieben worden und beherbergt viele Inschriften bekannter Literaten, nebst mehreren Götter- und Geisterfiguren. Zu selbigen zählen zwei große Statuen: Qianliyan und Shunfeng'er. Allerdings fehlen bei beiden die gewohnten Gesten. Zwar handelt es sich nicht um alte Kunstwerke, doch hat man vermutet, frühere Qianliyan- und Shunfeng'er-Darstellungen seien den jetzigen wohl ähnlich gewesen. Eine in Sichuan entdeckte Figur aus der Song-Periode (diese Statuette hat nichts mit dem Nanhaishen zu tun) scheint derlei zu bestätigen.[9] Zugleich wurde angenommen, Qianliyan und Shunfeng'er seien vor Beginn der Mazu-Verehrung anderen Tempelgottheiten zugeordnet gewesen, nicht nur dem Nanhaishen; das erkläre wohl auch die nicht vorhandenen Gesten. Freilich, ob dies stimmt, bleibt vorerst offen. Zu ergänzen ist allerdings: Heute wird die scheinbar alte Tradition, den (an sich wenig verbreiteten) Nanhaishen-Glauben mit Qianliyan und Shunfeng'er zu verbinden, in der populären Literatur fortgeführt.[10]

In dem oben genannten Tempel in Guangzhou findet sich eine weitere Statue, die jene Geste ausführt, welche wir beim dortigen Qianliyan vermissen. Es handelt sich um Daxi Sikong 達奚司空, der im 6. Jahrhundert mit Bodhidharma aus Indien nach Guangzhou gekommen sein soll.[11] Ob Daxi gleich zu Beginn seiner posthumen Karriere zu den „Weitblickenden" zählte oder erst allmählich in diesen Kreis aufstieg und die Ikonographie entsprechend angepasst wurde, ist wohl kaum noch festzustellen. Neben Daxi und Zhaobao qilang sind noch andere Figuren bekannt, welche in die Ferne schauen oder, gleich Shunfeng'er, die Hand ans Gehör legen. Entsprechende Beispiele sind sogar in Japan zu finden.[12]

---

istischen und buddhistischen Kontexten geben Handbücher oft gute Auskünfte. Beispiele etwa in: Ma Shutian 马书田, *Huaxia zhushen* 华夏诸神 (Beijing: Yanshan chubanshe, 1990), oder Lü Zongli 吕宗力 – Luan Baoqun 欒保群, *Zhongguo minjian zhushen* 中国民间诸神 (Shijiazhuang: Hebei jiaoyu chubanshe, 2001).

[8] Zu besagtem Tempel siehe z.B. Huang Miaozhang 黄淼章, *Nanhaishen miao* 南海神庙 (Guangzhou: Guangdong renmin chubanshe, 2005), besonders S. 10-11, 48-49. Ferner Wang Yuanlin 王元林, *Guojia jisi yu haishang silu yiji. Guangzhou Nanhaishen miao yanjiu* 国家祭祀与海上丝路遗迹—广州南海神庙研究 (Beijing: Zhonghua shuju, 2006); mehrere Aufsätze in *Haijiaoshi yanjiu* 海交史研究, Nummern für 2006 und folgende.

[9] Vgl. z.B. Hu Wenhe 胡文和, *Sichuan daojiao Fojiao shiku yishu* 四川道教佛教石窟艺术 (Chengdu: Sichuan renmin chubanshe, 1994), S. 16.

[10] Wenigstens ein Beispiel sei genannt: Zeng Yingfeng 曾应枫 *et al.*, *Nanhaishen chuanqi* 南海神传奇 (Guangzhou: Guangzhou chubanshe, 2013). In dieser Erzählung treten Qianliyan und Shunfeng'er auf.

[11] Siehe z.B. Huang Miaozhang, *Nanhaishen miao*, besonders S. 48-49.

[12] Näheres, besonders zu Huaguang dadi 華光大帝, z.B. in Nikaido Yoshihiros *Asian Folk Religion*, v.a. Kapitel 2, und „The Transformation of Gods in Chinese Popular Religion. The Examples of Huaguang Dadi 華光大帝 and Zhaobao Qilang 招寶七郎", unter

In Zhenjiang 鎭江 gab es unter den Song einen Mazu-Tempel, der in einem Text des frühen 14. Jahrhunderts erwähnt ist. Die dortige Beschreibung (*Linghui fei miaoji* 靈惠妃廟記), datiert auf das Jahr 1259, erwähnt zwei Figuren an der Seite Kuixings 魁星, des Literaturgottes. Diese werden als *qingyi shi* 青衣師 und *zhuyi li* 朱衣吏 bezeichnet, also als „Grün gekleideter Lehrer" und „Rot gekleideter Beamter". Es ist möglich, dass beide Vorläufer oder Varianten der (bereits existierenden?) Figuren Shufeng'er und Qianliyan waren.[13] Zu ergänzen noch: Linghui fei steht für Mazu. Dieser Ehrentitel ist ab 1192 belegt.[14]

Zusammengenommen zeigen die obigen Hinweise das Folgende: 1) Es sind frühe Figuren mit übernatürlichen Kräften bekannt, die von ihrer Funktion her – als Späher und Informanten – an die heutigen Mazu-Begleiter erinnern und verschiedenen Tempeln und Gottheiten zugeordnet wurden. 2) Einige wenige lassen sich als Qianliyan und Shunfeng'er identifizieren, wobei keineswegs Klarheit darüber besteht, wann diese „Gleichsetzung" begann. 3) Mazus Rolle bleibt dabei recht verschwommen; erst später lässt sich Genaueres sagen.

4. Die Erzählung *Wu wang fa Zhou*

An dieser Stelle können wir erstmals in die Welt der Erzählungen eintauchen. Aus der Ära Zhizhi (1321–1323) ist ein anonymes *pinghua* 平話 (etwa „volkstümliches Erzählbuch") überliefert, das in Jianyang 建陽 gedruckt wurde.[15] Sein Titel lautet *Wu wang fa Zhou* 武王伐紂 (König Wu bekämpft Zhou). Es handelt vom Krieg der Zhou 周 gegen Zhou 紂, den letzten Herrscher der Shang 商. Dieser wird in konfuzianisch geprägten Geschichtsbüchern bekanntlich sehr negativ dargestellt, während man dem Lande Zhou – und damit König Wu 武 – Legitimität zuspricht. Aufseiten der Shang, so die Erzählung, kämpfen unter anderem zwei Generäle: Li Lou 離婁 und Shi Kuang 師曠. Sie fügen den Zhou eine Niederlage bei und lassen sich auch nicht durch eine List ausschalten. So berät die Zhou-Seite, geführt von Marschall Jiang Shang 姜尚 (Jiang Ziya 姜子牙), über Gegenmaßnahmen.[16] Dabei fällt folgender Satz: „Der mit dem Namen Li Lou –

---

http://kuir.jm.kansai-u.ac.jp/dspace/bitstream/10112/4346/1/06_NIKAIDO.pdf (aufgerufen im August 2016).

[13] Vgl. z.B. *MZWX*, Ser. II, shizhai, Anm. auf S. 6; Ruitenbeek, „Mazu, the Patroness of Sailors", S. 320. – Kuixing: auch Kuixing 奎星 bzw. Dakui xingjun 大魁星君 oder Dakui fuzi 大魁夫子 usw.

[14] Vgl. z.B. Xu Xiaowang, *Mazu xinyang shi yanjiu*, besonders S. 73-74, und Tabelle S. 315 (dort auch Hinweise zum Ausdruck *fei* in diesem und anderen Ehrentiteln). Weiteres etwa in Li Xianzhang, *Mazu xinyang yanjiu*, S. 97-99.

[15] Zu Jianyang als Zentrums des Buchdrucks. Siehe z.B. Lucille Chia, *Printing for Profit. The Commercial Publishers of Jianyang, Fujian (11th–17th Centuries)* (Cambridge, Mass.: Harvard University Asia Center – Harvard University Press, 2002).

[16] Jiang Ziya geht auf eine „historische" Gestalt zurück, die in vielen populären Werken auftritt. Eine der neuesten europäischsprachigen Studien hierzu: Barbara Witt, „General unter Jiang Ziya, göttlicher Beistand für Jin Bifeng. Der Himmelskönig Li im *Fengshen*

das ist ‚Tausend-Meilen-Auge', Shi Kuang ist [niemand anders als] ‚Mit-dem-Wind-Ohr'. Beide haben keine besonderen Gaben, sie [vermögen] nur alles zu hören und zu sehen, auf nah und fern." Am Ende gelingt es dann doch, beide zu fangen. Aber kurz vor ihrer geplanten Hinrichtung entschwinden sie mit einem kräftigen, magischen Wind. Schließlich werden Qianliyan und Shunfeng'er als Torhüter gesichtet – vor einem dem Xuanyuan Huangdi 軒轅皇(黃)帝 gewidmeten Tempel. Hierauf lässt die Zhou-Seite von beiden ab und kümmert sich wieder um ihre militärischen Aufgaben, das heißt, Jiang sendet seine Truppen nach Mianchi 澠池. Dort wird der örtliche Machthaber, Qin Jing 秦敬, durch Prinz Yin Jiao 殷郊, der zum Lager Jiangs gehört, ausgeschaltet.[17]

Xuanyuan Huangdi steht natürlich für den Gelben Kaiser. Er trägt viele Namen und ist mit allerlei Mythen verknüpft. Zugleich gehört er in die Welt des Daoismus. Häufig wird er als Herrscher auf dem Göttersitz Kunlun 崑崙 gesehen, ebenso ist er für die traditionelle Medizin wichtig; man denke nur an das berühmte Werk *Huangdi neijing* 黃帝內經. Kaum verwunderlich also, dass die Zhou keine weiteren Maßnahmen gegen Qianliyan und Shunfeng'er planen; vermutlich ist Huangdis schutzgewährende Position im Pantheon der Unsterblichen zu hoch, als dass man bereit wäre, ihn zu erzürnen.

Nun zu Li Lou und Shi Kuang: Beide finden häufig Erwähnung in alten Texten, so etwa im Buch *Mengzi* 孟子.[18] Dort wird Li Lou als weitblickender Seher genannt – ja, dieses Werk enthält sogar ein zweigeteiltes Segment gleichen Namens. Shi Kuang ist bekannt für sein gutes Gehör. Blind sei er gewesen, aber ein wunderbarer Musiker, deshalb gilt er als Schutzpatron dieser Zunft. Daneben soll er das *Qinjing* 禽經, den „Vogelklassiker", geschrieben haben – in Wirklichkeit wohl ein Text aus späterer Zeit, und von anderer, unbekannter Hand.

Was spätere Literaten dazu bewogen haben mag, Li Lou und Shi Kuang, die in vielen älteren Werken vorkommen und heute vielleicht in die Nähe von Autisten gerückt werden könnten, mit Kriegshandlungen zu verknüpfen, bleibt freilich offen. Einige Quellen deuten an, vor allem Shi Kuang habe für „soziale Harmo-

---

yanyi und *Xiyang ji*", in: Shi Ping 时平 – Roderich Ptak (Hrsg.), *Studien zum Roman Sanbao taijian Xiyang ji tongsu yanyi* 三宝太监西洋记通俗演义之研究, 2 Bde., Maritime Asia 23 und 24 (Wiesbaden: Harrassowitz Verlag, 2011–2013), S. 163–178. Ein kurzer Überblick zu Jiang Ziya findet sich z.B. in: Edward Theodore Chalmers Werner, *A Dictionary of Chinese Mythology* (Neudruck New York: The Julian Press, 1961; ursprüngl. Shanghai 1932), S. 59–65.

[17] Die für uns relevanten Passagen erscheinen z.B. in: *MZWX*, Ser. II, shizhai, S. 5–7. Eine vollständige Ausgabe ist z.B.: Zhonghua shuju Shanghai bianjibu 中華書局上海編輯部 (Hrsg.), *Wu wang fa Zhou pinghua* 武王伐紂平話 (Beijing: Zhonghua shuju, 1959), dort S. 70–71. Englische Übersetzung in Liu Ts'un-yan, *Buddhist and Taoist Influences on Chinese Novels. The Authorship of the Feng Shen Yen I* (Wiesbaden: Harrassowitz, 1962), besonders S. 63–64.

[18] James Legge, *The Chinese Classics,* Vol. 2., *The Works of Mencius* (Neudruck Taibei: Wenshizhe chubanshe, 1971), besonders S. 288, Anfang des Kapitels „Li Lou".

nie" werben wollen – mit Blick auf die Belange des Staates.[19] Daneben ist an mögliche phonetische Brücken zwischen „Li Lou" und „zhuyi li" sowie „Shi Kuang" und „qingyi shi" zu denken; obschon derlei eher unwahrscheinlich ist, völlig auszuschließen sind solche Brücken nicht.

Halten wir also fest: Das Werk *Wu wang fa Zhou* gehört sicher zu den frühesten Erzählungen, in denen Qianliyan und Shunfeng'er auftreten. Mit Mazu hat dies nichts zu tun. Beide Figuren erscheinen dort in einer eigenartigen Zwitterposition: Einerseits stützen sie die „falsche" Seite, andererseits werden sie durch ihre Verbindung mit den eher positiv konnotierten Figuren Li Lou und Shi Kuang vor dem Abgleiten in ein exklusiv negatives Ambiente bewahrt. An anderer Stelle werden wir auf die Rivalität zwischen Zhou und Shang und damit auch auf die Rolle beider noch einmal zurückkommen müssen.

5. Ausgewählte Texte aus dem daoistischen Kanon

Ein ganz anderes Werk ist das *Taishang laojun shuo Tianfei jiuku lingyan jing* 太上老君說天妃救苦靈驗經 (Klassiker über die Worte des Höchsten Ehrwürdigen Alten im Hinblick auf die wunderbare und wirksame Rettung aus dem Leiden durch die Himmelsprinzessin). Sein Erstdruck erfolgte 1416, später wurde es in die Zhengtong-Version des *Daozang* 道藏 (1445) aufgenommen. Diese Sammlung ist weithin bekannt. Die in ihr überlieferte Fassung findet sich auch in der modernen Kollektion *MZWX*.[20]

Auf Basis des *Taishang laojun shuo Tianfei jiuku lingyan jing* entstand 1420 ein ähnlicher Text, der in Japan erhalten ist und einen leicht verkürzten Titel hat: *Taishang shuo Tianfei jiuku lingyan jing*. Ihm gehen einige Illustrationen voran, die unter anderem Mazu und ihr Gefolge zeigen. Von diesem Text existieren im übrigen weitere Varianten. Neben der Version von 1420 orientieren sich noch einige Qing-Werke – etwa das *Tianhou shengmu zhenjing* 天后聖母眞經 (Wahrer Klassiker über die Heilige Mutter Himmelskönigin) – an der Fassung aus dem Jahre 1416. In der europäischsprachigen Sinologie sind vor allem die Ming-

---

[19] Vgl. die vielen Beispiele aus Han- und Vor-Han-Werken in Zhou Xiaowei 周曉薇, *Siyou ji congkao* 四游记丛考 (Beijing: Zhongguo shehui kexue chubanshe, 2005), S. 141-151. Weiteres etwa auch in Roel Sterckx, *Food, Sacrifice, and Sagehood in Early China* (Cambridge: Cambridge University Press, 2011), besonders S. 189-190, oder Erica Brindley, *Music, Cosmology and the Politics of Harmony in Early China* (New York: State University of New York Press, 2012), besonders S. 51-52.

[20] Hierzu und zum Folgenden: *MZWX*, Ser. III, jingchan, S. 1-8. Der Text findet sich in der Sammlung *Zhengtong Daozang*, Abteilung Dong shen bu 洞神部 (*CT* 649; nach Kristofer Schipper et al., *Concordance du Tao-tsang*; Paris 1975). Er ist an vielen Stellen im Internet einsehbar (z.B. http://ctext.org/library.pl?if=gb&file=99390&page=1; aufgerufen im August 2016). Vgl. ferner Kristofer Schipper – Franciscus Verellen (Hrsg.), *The Taoist Canon. A Historical Companion to the* Daozang, 3 Bde. (Chicago – London: Chicago University Press, 2004), II, 3.B.14, S. 1224-1225 (dort datiert auf 1409–1413).

Stücke untersucht worden, besonders in einem längeren Aufsatz von Judith Boltz.[21]

Betrachten wir hier zunächst die früheste Version. Sie gehört zu den wichtigsten liturgischen Schriften des Mazu-Kultes, enthält jedoch einige Details, die späteren Konventionen widersprechen oder gar Fragen aufwerfen. Wenigstens ein Beispiel sei genannt. Die irdische Niederkunft Mazu, so heißt es im Text, habe am 23. Tag des 3. Monats stattgefunden, und zwar in einem Jahr mit den zyklischen Zeichen *jiashen* 甲申. Diese Angabe passt zu den Jahren 984, 1044 und 1104, nicht aber auf das Jahr 960, in welchem Mazu, so die landläufige Vorstellung bis heute, wie schon eingangs vermerkt, geboren worden sei.[22]

Doch nun zu Qianliyan und Shunfeng'er. An anderer Stelle berichtet der Text, Laojun 老君 habe Mazu einen Titel verliehen und sie mit angemessener Kleidung, Utensilien und Gefolge ausgestattet. Zu ihren Gehilfen zählen auch der „Tausend-Meilen-Auge-Übelerspäher" (*qianliyan zhi chajian* 千里眼之察奸) und der „Mit-dem-Wind-Ohr-Berichtende" (*shunfeng'er zhi baoshi* 順風耳之報事). Beide Zeichenkombinationen lassen sich als Namen auffassen, aber ebenso als allgemeine Wendungen lesen, im Singular oder Plural.[23]

In der Version aus dem Jahre 1420 erscheinen die Lesungen in abgewandelter Form, als *qianliyan zhi shen* (神) und *shunfeng'er zhi jiang* (將), also als „Gott"/ „Geist" und „General", wobei die Attribute beibehalten wurden. Wiederum könnte man in diesen Sequenzen Namen erblicken. Im Übrigen stehen sie den späteren Texten durchaus näher.

Aber noch etwas anderes fällt auf, und zwar in beiden Werken. Neben Qianliyan und Shunfeng'er (bzw. ihren Vorläufern/Varianten) erscheinen dort noch Qingyi tongzi 青衣童子, wörtlich „grün gekleideter Junge", und Shuibu

---

[21] MZWX, Ser. III, jingchan, S. 9ff. (dort wesentliche Angaben zur Editionsgeschichte der jeweiligen Texte); Judith Magee Boltz, „In Homage to T'ien-fei", *JAOS* 106 (1986) 1, besonders S. 214-215. Boltz hat die Fassung von 1416 übersetzt; dabei geht sie gelegentlich von einer anderen Interpunktion aus. Zu den Texten ansonsten kurz: Fabrizio Pregadio (Hrsg.), *Encyclopedia of Taoism*, 2 Bde. (London – New York: Routledge, 2008), Bd. II, S. 743-744, oder Ren Jiyu 任繼愈 et al. (Hrsg.), *Daozang tiyao* 道藏提要 (verbesserte Ausgabe Beijing: Zhongguo shehui kexue chubanshe, 1995; nachfolgend: *DT*), Nr. 644. Die Illustrationen des Textes von 1420 sind auch für die Forschung über Zheng He 鄭和 (und seine Verbindung zum Buddhismus) wichtig. Dazu etwa: Chen Yunü 陳玉女, „Zheng He shi yin Fojing yu xingjian Fosi de yiyi" 鄭和施印佛經與興建佛寺的意義, in: Chen Xinxiong 陳信雄 und *id.*, (Hrsg.), *Zheng He xia Xiyang guoji xueshu yantaohui lunwenji* 鄭和下西洋國際學術研討會論文集 (Taibei: Daoxiang chubanshe, 2003), S. 163-200, hier besonders S. 198-199; Jin Qiupeng 金秋鵬, „Qijin faxian zui zao de Zheng He xia Xiyang chuandui tuxiang ziliao. Tianfei jing juanshou chatu" 迄今發現最早的鄭和下西洋船隊圖象資料—《天妃經》卷首插圖, *Zhongguo keji shiliao* 中國科技史料 Nr. 21 (2000) 1, S. 61-64; auch in: Wang Tianyou 王天有 – Wan Ming 萬明 (Hrsg.), *Zheng He yanjiu bainian lunwen xuan* 鄭和研究百年論文選 (Beijing: Beijing daxue chubanshe, 2004), S. 256-259.

[22] MZWX, Ser. III, jingchan, S. 3. Zu den Daten etwa Xu Xiaowang, *Mazu xinyang shi yanjiu*, S. 29-30; ebenso Boltz, „In Homage to T'ien-fei", S. 223-224.

[23] MZWX, Ser. III, jingchan, S. 5; Boltz, „In Homage to T'ien-fei", S. 226.

panguan 水部判官, der „Richter des Wasseramtes", als Mazus Gehilfen. Qingyi tongzi gilt als mächtige Figur in den östlichen Gefilden des Himmels; die zweite Kombination, von Boltz wohl eher allgemein gelesen und in den Plural gebracht, weist auf die Unterwelt, in der besagter Richter über das Schicksal wandernder Seelen entscheidet.[24] Damit stehen Mazu Spezialisten mit unterschiedlichen Fähigkeiten und Funktionen zur Verfügung, wodurch ihre eigene Position sicher zusätzlich hervorgehoben werden sollte. Das Attribut *qing* (grün) im ersten Namen erinnert zudem an die mit Shunfeng'er assoziierte Farbe. Auch wenn dem Wasseramt nichts Vergleichbares zugeordnet werden kann, wäre zu fragen, welche weiteren Überlegungen bestimmend für die Figurenanordnung gewesen sein könnten.

Gleich wie, die beiden *Tianfei ... lingyan jing*-Texte gehören zu den frühesten Stücken, in denen Qianliyan und Shunfeng'er, namentlich genannt, in einen Zusammenhang mit Mazu gebracht werden. Im *Daozang* erscheinen sie allerdings noch in weiteren Texten. Zwei Beispiele seien angeführt: *Dahui jingci miaole tianzun shuo fude wusheng jing* 大惠靜慈妙樂天尊說福德五聖經 und *Taishang dongxuan lingbao Wuxian guan Huaguang benxing miaojing* 太上洞玄靈寶五顯觀華光本行妙經.[25] Das erste Werk enthält die Zeichenfolge „Qianli Shunfeng", und zwar in einer langen Beschwörungsformel. Mit Miaole tianzun 妙樂天尊, oft auch Lingguan dadi 靈觀大帝 genannt, ist eigentlich ein Schüler des (Taishang) Laojun gemeint. Er erscheint auch in der späteren Erzählung *Beiyou ji* 北遊記. Huaguang 華光, der gewissermaßen im Zentrum des zweiten Werkes steht, ist für den Roman *Nanyou ji* 南遊記 wichtig. Darauf wird noch einzugehen sein. Einige der im *Nanyou ji* erwähnten Gehilfen Huaguangs finden in besagtem *Daozang*-Text Erwähnung; das betrifft auch Shunfeng und Qianli (wieder ohne die Zeichen *er* und *yan*), die dort als „Botschafter" (*shizhe* 使者) gelistet sind. Schließlich noch: Hinsichtlich der Datierung beider *Daozang*-Texte herrscht Unklarheit; doch das ist nicht so wichtig, denn mit Qianliyan und Shunfeng'er sind dort keine echte Handlungen verknüpft.

6. Das Theaterstück *Xia Xiyang* und andere Dramen der *zaju*-Kategorie

Von der religiösen Literatur nun zu den Singspielen (*zaju* 雜劇) der Ming-Epoche. Das anonyme Stück *Feng tianming Sanbao xia Xiyang* 奉天命三保下西洋 (Sanbao fährt auf kaiserlichen Befehl ins Westmeer; Kurztitel *Xia Xiyang*), das möglicherweise schon Ende des 15. Jahrhunderts geschrieben wurde – vielleicht in Taicang 太倉 oder einem nahen Ort –, schildert die Seefahrten des berühmten

---

[24] Boltz, „In Homage to T'ien-fei", S. 226. Weiterführende Hinweise dort. – Viele moderne Werke zitieren die betreffende Stelle, gehen aber nicht näher auf sie ein. So etwa Cai Xianghui, *Mazu xinyang yanjiu*, S. 87. – Vgl. ferner weiter oben (Abschnitt 3): *qingyi shi*.

[25] *Zhengtong Daozang*, Abteilung Zheng yi bu 正一部 (*CT* 1192; *DT* 1182), und Abteilung Xu Daozang 續道藏 (*CT* 1448; *DT* 1435). Inhaltsangaben in: Schipper – Verellen, *The Daoist Canon*, Bd. II, 3.B.14, S. 1225, 1229-1230.

Zheng He 鄭和.²⁶ Vor der Abreise bittet Zheng He in einem Tempel um Mazus Hilfe. Es wird ein Gebet verlesen, in dem es unter anderem heißt: „Heute stechen wir im Auftrag des Kaisers mit [unseren] Schiffen in See, um die Barbaren des Westmeeres (Xiyang 西洋) zu befrieden. Mögen die Wellen stets günstig gehen, mögest Du (Mazu) uns beschützen, mögen wir viele seltene Gegenstände sammeln, schnell in die Heimat zurückkehren, mit vollbeladenen [Schiffen] den Rückweg antreten!"

Nach vollzogenem Opfer schläft Zheng He im Tempel ein. Mazu erscheint ihm im Traum und verspricht Schutz. Aus dem Text wird zudem ersichtlich, wenngleich nur durch eine Regieanweisung, dass sie mit zwei Begleiterinnen die Bühne betritt.²⁷ Sollte das Werk tatsächlich noch im späten 15. Jahrhundert entstanden sein, wäre dies nicht nur die früheste heute erhaltene literarische Erwähnung Mazus außerhalb der rein religiösen Literatur, sondern auch der früheste Beleg für Mazus Begleitfiguren im Theater. Jedoch liefert der Text keine Namen oder andere Anhaltspunkte, die es uns ermöglich würden, diese Figuren zu identifizieren.

Dafür fällt etwas anderes auf: Die Seefahrenden bitten um Schutz, aber sie wollen noch mehr – nämlich die „Barbaren befrieden und Schätze sammeln" (*he fan qu bao* 和番取寶). Dabei wird das zweite Anliegen geschickt mit der Bitte um Protektion vermengt. Mazu, unausgesprochen ebenso ihre Begleiterinnen, werden also, abgehoben von der rein religiösen Ebene, für staatliche Belange instrumentalisiert.

Das Theaterstück *Xia Xiyang* hat in der Mazu-Forschung kaum Beachtung gefunden. Weshalb Mazu dort in weiblicher Begleitung erscheint, bleibt darum offen. Gleich wie, vielleicht ist die ungewöhnliche Figurenanordnung als weiteres Indiz für die Annahme zu werten, dass die Verknüpfung von Qianliyan und Shunfeng'er mit Mazu damals noch nicht überall üblich war. Oder aber die Autoren des Stückes, die wir leider nicht kennen, wussten nicht um jene Tradition, die sich schon in den *Tianfei ... lingyan jing*-Texten niedergeschlagen hatte.

---

²⁶ Details, auch zu den chinesischen Ausgaben von *Xia Xiyang*, werden vorgestellt in: Roderich Ptak, *Cheng Hos Abenteuer im Drama und Roman der Ming-Zeit. Hsia Hsi-yang. Eine Übersetzung und Untersuchung. Hsi-yang chi. Ein Deutungsversuch*. Münchener Ostasiatische Studien 41 (Stuttgart: Steiner, 1986). In jüngster Zeit sind einige Aufsätze zu diesem Theaterstück erschienen, die das Datierungsproblem allerdings nicht wirklich zu lösen vermögen. Zum möglichen Entstehungsort z.B. Zhou Yunzhong 周云中, „Mingdai zaju *Xia Xiyang* chengshu didian kao" 明代杂剧《下西洋》成书地点考, *Zheng He yanjiu* 郑和研究 Nr. 81 (2011), S. 53-56.

²⁷ Übersetzt in Ptak, *Cheng Hos Abenteuer*, S. 65. Zu den Begleiterinnen siehe S. 67, 111. Sehr selten erscheint Mazu auch anderweitig in weiblicher Begleitung. Vgl. z.B. Xu Xiaowang, *Mazu xinyang shi yanjiu*, S. 298-299, sowie das kaum bekannte Theaterstück *Xitai ji* 西臺記 von Lu Shilian 陸世廉 (廉) (aktiv um 1640/1650), in: Zou Shijin 鄒式金 (Hrsg.; *jinshi* 1640), *Zaju sanji* 雜劇三集 (Beijing: Zhongguo xiju chubanshe, 1958), Akt 3, 9a (Tianfei tritt in Begleitung auf) bis 10b (ihr Abgang). Dieses Stück, das vermutlich erst unter den frühen Qing entstand, behandelt den letzten Widerstand der Song gegen die Yuan. Über Tianfeis Begleiterinnen wird nichts weiter gesagt.

Wie immer die Antwort ausfallen mag, Qianliyan und Shunfeng'er erscheinen zwar nicht in *Xia Xiyang*, dafür aber an anderer Stelle im *zaju*-Theater. Hiermit sind wir erneut bei Huaguang. In dem meist der Ming-Periode zugeordneten Stück *Shijiafo shuang lin zuo hua* 釋迦佛雙林作化 (Kurztitel *Shuang lin zuo hua*), dessen Inhalt stark buddhistisch gefärbt ist, werden unsere Späher ganz explizit als seine Begleiter genannt.[28] Obschon sie nicht wirklich zum Fortgang der Handlung beitragen, anders als in der schon erwähnten und später noch näher vorzustellenden Erzählung *Nanyou ji*, belegt der Sachverhalt doch, dass die Verbindung zwischen ihnen und Huaguang damals üblich gewesen sein könnte und nicht nur auf das rein religiöse Ambiente beschränkt war. Und noch etwas sei hervorgehoben: Das Umfeld ist ein buddhistisches, bislang hatten wir Qianliyan und Shunfeng'er eher auf daoistischem Terrain erlebt.

Damit ist das Thema *zaju* aber keinesfalls ausgeschöpft. Yang Jingxian 楊景賢 gilt als Verfasser eines Theaterstücks namens *Xiyou ji* 西遊記, in dem die Kombinationen „Qianliyan Li Lou" und „Shunfeng'er Shi Kuang" erscheinen.[29] Yang lebte in der Übergangszeit von der Yuan- zur Ming-Dynastie. Das bedeutet, die Verbindung zwischen Qianliyan/Shunfeng'er und dem *Xiyou*-Stoff könnte recht alt sein. Auch auf das *Xiyou*-Thema werden wir deshalb noch einmal zurückkommen müssen.

7. Das Werk *Xue Rengui kai hai zheng Liao*

Aus der Ära Chenghua (1465–1487) sind mehrere Stücke der Gattung *shuochang cihua* 說唱詞話 (etwa „narrative Balladen") überliefert. Eines dieser Werke mit dem Titel *Xue Rengui kua hai zheng Liao* 薛仁貴跨海征遼 (Xue Rengui überquert das Meer und zieht nach Liao; kurz *Kua hai zheng Liao*), datiert auf das Jahr 1471 und vom Verlagshaus Yongshun 永順 gedruckt, nennt Qianliyan und Shunfeng'er.[30] Die Geschichte berichtet über den Feldzug des Tang-Kaisers gegen Korea. Der Stoff ist durch andere populäre Fassungen bekannt, etwa durch das *zaju*-Stück *Xue Rengui yi jin huan xiang* 薛仁貴衣錦還鄉 (von Zhang Guobin 張國賓, ca. 14. Jahrhundert) oder die anonyme Erzählung *Xue Rengui zheng dong* 薛仁貴征東 aus der Qing-Zeit; außerdem ist im *Yongle dadian* 永樂

---

[28] Das Theaterstück ist z.B. in der Sammlung *Guben Yuan Ming zaju* 孤本元明雜劇, 4 Bde. (Beijing: Zhongguo xiju chubanshe, 1958), in Bd. IV enthalten (dort Akt 3, 8a des Stückes).

[29] Hier benutzte Ausgabe des Dramas: Sui Shusen 隋樹森 (Hrsg.), *Yuanqu xuan waibian* 元曲選外編, 3 Bde. (Beijing: Zhonghua shuju, 1961), Bd. II, Akt 12, Melodie Guisantai 鬼三台, S. 664.

[30] Zum Text z.B.: Zhu Yixuan 朱一玄 (Hrsg.), *Ming Chenghua shuochang cihua congkan* 明成化说唱词话丛刊 (Zhengzhou: Zhongzhou guji chubanshe, 1997), besonders S. 103. In modernen Werken über den Mazu-Kult ist nur selten auf das Stück *Kua hai zheng Liao* aufmerksam gemacht worden. Ein Beispiel: Luo Chunrong 罗春荣, *Mazu chuanshuo yanjiu. Yi ge haiyang daguo de shenhua* 妈祖传说研究：一个海洋大国的神话 (Tianjin: Tianjin guji chubanshe, 2009), S. 191.

大典 ein Werk namens *Xue Rengui zheng Liao shilüe* 薛仁貴征遼事略 gefunden worden.[31] „Liao" im Titel der *shuochang*- und *Yongle dadian*-Versionen bezieht sich auf das Liaodong-Gebiet (遼東), *hai* in ersterer auf das „Ostmeer" zwischen Korea und China. Zu den Generälen, die den Kaiser bei seinem Unternehmen helfen, zählen Zhang Shigui 張士貴 und Xue Rengui, die beide auf historische Figuren (Daten: Xue 614-683; Zhang ?-656) zurückgehen.

Aber bleiben wir beim *shuochang cihua*-Text. Dort tritt Xue in weißer Kleidung auf, ist folglich dem Westen (und dem Element Metall) zugeordnet und wird auch Xifang baihu shen 西方白虎神 bzw. Baipao 白袍 genannt. Außerdem gilt er als hervorragender Kämpfer. Die Bezeichnung „Xifang baihu shen" entlarvt ihn natürlich als Sternengeist; im allgemeinen werden hierunter die sieben westlichen Gestirne subsumiert, die zu den „28 Konstellationen" (*ershiba xingxiu* 二十八星宿) zählen.

Im Verlauf des Feldzuges entpuppt sich Zhang Shigui als hinterhältiger Rivale Xue Renguis. Das ist auch in einigen anderen literarischen Versionen so. In *Kua hai zheng Liao* geschieht das Folgende: Xue und seine Brüder sind in einem engen Tal, und Zhang glaubt sie mit Feuer vernichten zu können (Feuer besiegt Metall). Qianliyan und Shunfeng'er erkennen die Gefahr und erstatten dem Jadekaiser (bekannt als Yuhuang dadi 玉皇大帝 und unter anderen Namen) sofort Meldung. Dieser reagiert, indem er mehrere Geister und Götter auf die Erde schickt, um Xue zu helfen. Damit allerdings erschöpft sich die Rolle Qianliyans und Shunfeng'ers. Interessant ist für uns allein, dass beide in einem daoistisch gefärbten Kontext erscheinen und ihre Warnung den Handlungsverlauf gleichsam auf eine höhere Ebene katapultiert, zumal sich ihr oberster Herr und Gebieter, eben der Jadekaiser, zum Eingreifen genötigt sieht. Dies dürfte im Übrigen eines der frühesten Erzählwerke sein, welches Qianliyan und Shunfeng'er als direkte Gehilfen des Jadekaisers ausweist.

Sofern die Datierungen der bislang vorgestellten Werke stimmen, wäre *Kua hai zheng Liao* ungefähr zur selben Zeit entstanden wie das Theaterstück *Xia Xiyang*; außerdem müsste man Qianliyan und Shunfeng'er im 15. Jahrhundert mehreren Kontexten zuordnen: der Zhou-Shang-Geschichte, dem Huaguang-Stoff, dem *Xiyou*-Zyklus, dem Mazu-Thema und eben Xue Rengui. Rücken wir nun ins 16. Jahrhundert vor, in die Zeit der großen Romane. Innerhalb des

---

[31] Vgl. z.B. Wilt L. Idema, „The Remaking of an Unfilial Hero. Some Notes on the Earliest Dramatic Adaptions of the Story of Hsüeh Jen-kuei", in: Erika de Poorter (Hrsg.), *As the Twig is Bent ... Essays in Honour of Frits Vos* (Amsterdam: J.C. Gieben, 1990), S. 83-111; id., „Fighting in Korea. Two Early Narrative Treatments of the Story of Xue Rengui", in: Remco E. Breuker (Hrsg.), *Korea in the Middle. Korean Studies and Area Studies. Essays in Honour of Boudewijn Walraven*. CNWS Publications, 153 (Leiden: CNWS Publications, 2007), S. 341-368; Thomas Zimmer, *Der chinesische Roman der ausgehenden Kaiserzeit,* in: Wolfgang Kubin (Hrsg.), *Geschichte der chinesischen Literatur*, Bd. 2/1 (München: Saur, 2002), S. 151-152. Zu dem selten zitierten *Yongle dadian*-Werk siehe die Ausgabe von Zhao Wanli 趙萬里 (Hrsg.) (Shanghai: Gudian wenxue chubanshe, 1957).

xiaoshuo-Genres – dies sei schon jetzt vorweggenommen – werden Qianliyan und Shunfeng'er vor allem den ersten drei Bereichen „treu bleiben", während sie dort, wo man sie vielleicht zuerst vermuten würde, eigentlich nichts zu sagen haben.

8. *Lieguo zhi zhuan* und *Fengshen yanyi*

Der Stoff des yuanzeitlichen Werkes *Wu wang fa Zhou* – dies hat Liu Ts'un-yan als einer der ersten nachgewiesen – ist in spätere Erzählungen übernommen worden, etwa in das recht selten rezipierte *Lieguo zhi zhuan* 列國志傳 (Geschichte der Reiche) und den wichtigen Roman *Fengshen yanyi* 封神演義 (Investitur der Götter). Der erste Text, aus unbekannter Hand, dürfte seine Wurzeln im ausgehenden 16. Jahrhundert haben; an seiner Drucklegung im frühen 17. Jahrhundert hat vermutlich Yu Xiangdou 余象斗 (ca. 1561–1637), Verfasser vieler Werke, maßgeblich mitgewirkt. Das zweite Buch, seinerseits vom *Lieguo zhi zhuan* beeinflusst, gehört ins frühe 17. Jahrhundert; die Verfasserschaft ist bis heute umstritten.[32]

In beiden Werken kommen Qianliyan und Shunfeng'er vor. Die betreffenden Passagen greifen einige der im *Wu wang fa Zhou*-Teil geschilderten Elemente auf, doch werden diese jetzt ausgeschmückt, oftmals umgedeutet und in viel komplexere Handlungsabläufe eingebettet. Hierauf werden die folgenden Abschnitte eingehen.[33]

---

[32] Zu beiden Erzählungen: Liu Ts'un-yan, *Buddhist and Taoist Influences*, besonders S. 77, 78, 80. Yu Xiangdou ist auch unter anderen Namen bekannt. Zum *Fengshen yanyi* sind viele Sekundärwerke vorhanden. Hier sei nur verwiesen auf Pin Pin Wan, „Investiture of the Gods (‚Fengshen yanyi'): Sources, Narrative Structure and Mythical Significance" (Ann Arbor: University of Michigan, 1987, Dissertation University of Washington 1987), besonders S. 1-3 (einzelne *Fengshen yanyi*-Ausgaben und die Frage der Verfasserschaft im Überblick), und Mark R.E. Meulenbeld, *Demonic Warfare. Daoism, Territorial Networks, and the History of a Ming Novel* (Honolulu: University of Hawai'i Press, 2015). Zusammenfassendes ansonsten etwa bei Zimmer, *Der chinesische Roman der ausgehenden Kaiserzeit*, S. 354-372. Zu Yu Xiangdou auch L. Carrington Goodrich und Chaoying Fang (Hrsg.), *Dictionary of Ming Biography, 1368–1644*, 2 Bde. (New York – London: Columbia University Press, 1976), Bd. II, S. 1612-1614.

[33] Folgende Ausgaben wurden benutzt: Yu Shaoyu 余邵魚, *Chunqiu wu ba qi xiong lieguo zhi zhuan* 春秋五霸七雄列國志傳. Guben xiaoshuo jicheng 古本小說集成, 2 Bde. (Shanghai: Shanghai guji chubanshe, 1991), Kap. 1, S. 91-97; Xu Zhonglin 許仲琳, *Fengshen yanyi*, 2 Bde. (Neudruck Hong Kong: Zhonghua shuju, 1979), Bd. III, Kap. 89-91, S. 886-914 (vor allem Kap. 90 ist hier wichtig). Gekürzte englische Fassung: Gu Zhizhong (Übers.), *Creation of Gods*, 2 Bde. (Beijing: New World Press, 1992), Bd. II, Kap. 89-91, S. 359-385. Französische Version: Jacques Garnier (Übers.), *L'investiture des Dieux* (Paris: Librairie You Feng, 2002; nicht gesehen). Deutsch: Wilhelm Grube (Übers.), Herbert Müller (Inhaltsangabe der Kapitel 47-100), *Die Metamorphosen der Götter. Historisch-mythologischer Roman ...* (Leiden: Brill, 1912), S. 621-623. – Zum Vergleich zwischen *Fengshen yanyi* und *Lieguo zhi zhuan* siehe etwa Liu Ts'un-yan, *Buddhist and Taoist Influences*, S. 101, ferner S. 208-209. – Eine ältere Sekundärquelle mit einigen

Trotz grundlegender Ähnlichkeiten zwischen allen drei Werken – im *Lieguo zhi zhuan* und *Fengshen yanyi* ist etwas Neues festzustellen: Qianliyan und Shunfeng'er werden dort mit den Brüdern Gao Ming 高明 und Gao Jue 高覺, vermengt, deren Namen eindeutig auf die gesteigerten Wahrnehmungsfähigkeiten der Ausgangspersonen anspielen. Beide unterstützen, wie schon zuvor, die Shang-Seite und sind damit Gegner des Jiang Ziya.

Im ersten Text wird ihre Natur durch einen magischen Spiegel entlarvt. Wichtig dabei: Sie werden mit Shen Tu 神荼 und Yu Lei 鬱壘 assoziiert, also mit zwei bekannten Geisterschergen aus dem Altertum, die am Berge Dushuo 度朔, unterhalb eines Pfirsichbaumes, böse Dämonen einfangen. Neben diesen beiden verrichten dort auch Qianliyan und Shunfeng'er ihre Dienste; ihnen obliegt es, das Treiben anderer zu beobachten und vor allem üble Geister zu erfassen. Eingreiftruppe und Rasterfahnder arbeiten also eng zusammen. Huangdi, so erfährt der Leser ebenfalls, habe die Abbilder aller vier Wächter neben einem Tempeleingang anbringen lassen.

In gewisser Weise instrumentalisieren Gao Ming und Gao Jue also nur die Kräfte Qianliyans und Shunfeng'ers, um gegen die Zhou-Seite antreten zu können. Jiang Ziya durchschaut den Sachverhalt und entwickelt einen Plan, mit dem er beide unterwerfen will. Das gelingt schließlich mit Hilfe verschiedener magischer Tricks. Nach vollzogener Schlacht heißt es entsprechend: Den beiden Holzfiguren im Tempel fehlen jetzt die Köpfe; damit ist das Übel gebannt.[34]

Im *Fengshen yanyi* ist es vor allem der (bisweilen auch in anderen Texten auftretende) Magier Yang Jian 楊戩, welcher Jiang Ziya über die wahre Natur der Gao-Brüder aufklärt. Der Sachverhalt ist ähnlich: Bei beiden handele es sich um Baumgeister (Taojing 桃精 und Liugui 柳鬼) mit weitverzweigtem Wurzelwerk, und zwar am Berge Qipan 棋盤. Dort, so Yang ferner, gebe es auch einen Xuanyuan-Tempel mit Tonfiguren – Qianliyan und Shunfeng'er –, deren Essenz Gao Ming und Gao Jue offenbar viel Kraft beschere. Wolle man ihrem Unwesen ein Ende setzen, seien sowohl die Figuren wie das Wurzelwerk sämtlich zu vernichten. Schließlich werden Gao Ming und Gao Jue nach gründlicher Vorbereitung tatsächlich besiegt und getötet. Ihre Seelen wandern jedoch zur Götterinvestitur-Terrasse (Fengshen tai 封神臺).[35]

Sätzen in Übersetzung: Henri Doré, *Recherches sur les superstitions en Chine*, 18 Bde. (Shanghai: Imprimerie de T'ou-sè-we, 1911–1938), IIème partie, tome IX, S. 661-664.

[34] Hierzu z.B. auch kurz Luo Chunrong, *Mazu chuanshuo yanjiu*, S. 192.

[35] Zu dieser „Terrasse" siehe z.B. Liu Ts'un-yan, *Buddhist and Daoist Influences*, S. 154, 156, 285. Einige der magischen Elemente, die beim Kampf zum Einsatz gelangen, werden in Handbüchern zusammengefasst, so etwa in Werner, *Dictionary*, S. 66-67 (Eintrag zu Qianliyan). Ansonsten finden sich kurze Darstellungen zu den Gao-Brüdern im *Fengshen yanyi* bei Ruitenbeek, „Mazu, the Patroness of Sailors", S. 319-320, und zuvor bereits in J.J.M. de Groot, *Les fêtes annuelles célébrées à Émoui (Amoy). Étude concernant la religion populaire des Chinois*, 2 Bde., Annales du Musée Guimet, 11 und 12 (übersetzt aus dem Niederländischen; Paris: Ernest Leroux, 1886), S. 266-267.

Mehrere Dinge fallen auf. Der Autor des *Fengshen yanyi* beschreibt die Gao-Brüder als hässlich und furchterregend; der eine hat ein blaues Gesicht, glühende Augen und große Fangzähne, der andere einen gehörnten, melonenähnlichen Kopf, ein riesiges Maul mit scharfem Gebiss, zudem eine rötliche Haut. Diese Attribute erinnern an heutige Darstellungen. Ältere Belege aus der Erzählliteratur, die den Paaren Gao Ming / Gao Jue bzw. Qianliyan / Shunfeng'er ähnliche abschreckende Merkmale zuweisen, dürften kaum zu finden sein.

Und Weiteres ist festzuhalten: Das *Fengshen yanyi* deutet an, dass es zwischen den Paaren Gao Ming / Gao Jue bzw. Qianliyan / Shunfeng'er und Li Lou / Shi Kuang Bezüge gibt, und zwar vor allem durch die Überschrift zu Kapitel 90. Außerdem zieht dieser Text, wie das *Lieguo zhi zhuan*, die Auseinandersetzungen deutlich in die Länge. Es finden heftige Kämpfe statt, verschiedene Generäle und Götter kommen zum Einsatz, darunter etwa der mächtige Nazha 哪吒 (unterschiedliche Schreibungen und Transkriptionen). In früheren Werken sind Gao Ming und Gao Jue bzw. Qianliyan und Shunfeng'er keinesfalls so mächtig und gefährlich.

Auch ihr Ende differiert in den Texten: Die *pinghua*-Version verrät nichts Genaues, im *Fengshen yanyi* werden sie physisch vernichtet, nur ihre Seelen scheinen zu überleben. Doch Vorsicht ist geboten: Eigentlich haben wir es hier, wie im *Lieguo zhi zhuan*, mit zwei Gestalten zu tun, die sich nur der Essenz Qianliyans und Shunfeng'ers bedienen, also nicht wirklich mit diesen identisch sind, wie schon vermerkt. Das fügt sich zum Thema beider Erzählungen. Denn viele ihrer Protagonisten, gute wie böse, durchlaufen mehrere Verwandlungen (was bereits Grube zur Wahl entsprechenden deutschen Titels – *Die Metamorphosen der Götter* – veranlasst hat), wobei ihre Existenzen der Vorhersehung unterliegen. Sie sind also in einen größeren Plan eingebunden, der letztlich buddhistische Züge trägt, aber ebenso daoistische Elemente aufweist.

Die Editionsgeschichte des *Fengshen yanyi* ist, wie die der meisten großen Ming-Romane, sehr kompliziert. Ein Vergleich der erhaltenen Ausgaben ließe sicher weitere Rückschlüsse zu. Auch ist der Stoff – also die Auseinandersetzung zwischen Zhou und Shang – noch in andere Werke eingegangen, jedoch meist nur in Teilen und häufig in abgewandelter Form. Ein „Derivat" ist das wenig bekannte *Xia Shang yeshi* 夏商野史 (Inoffizielle Geschichte der Xia und Shang). Zugeschrieben wird dieses Werk einem gewissen Zhong Xing 鍾惺 (1574–1624), den wir aus dem Umfeld des *Fengshen yanyi* kennen; doch der *yeshi*-Text entstand wohl erst in späterer Zeit.[36] In Kapitel 29 desselben helfen Qianliyan und Shunfeng'er dem bedrängten Qin Jing in Mianchi. Der Ablauf des Geschehens ist über weite Passagen wortgleich mit der Darstellung im *Lieguo zhi zhuan*.

Halten wir nun zusammenfassend fest: Der Stoff über Shang und Zhou assoziiert die Namen „Qianliyan" und „Shunfeng'er" mit der negativen Seite. Beide werden in vergleichbaren Konstellationen präsentiert, wobei sie mit den Paaren

---

[36] Zum Text z.B. *Xia Shang yeshi* (Shanghai: Yishu Zhongguo wang, 2001). Zu Zhong Xing siehe z.B. Li Xiangeng 李先耕, *Zhong Xing zhushu kao* 钟惺著述考 (Harbin: Heilongjiang daxue chubanshe, 2008).

Shen Tu / Yu Lei, Li Lou / Shi Kuang und Gao Ming / Gao Jue verknüpft sind, und zwar in unterschiedlicher Weise. Die älteste Fassung, zugleich die kürzeste, geht mit Li Lou / Shi Kuang eher gnädig um – vielleicht weil der Autor hinter diesen Figuren bekannte Personen des Altertums wusste und mit ihnen Gutes verband.[37] Die späteren Versionen ersetzen Li Lou und Shi Kuang durch die Brüder Gao, deuten an, dass diese von den besonderen Gaben ersterer profitieren und strafen sie dann ab. Das ist durchaus folgerichtig, zumal die Shang-Seite als schlecht gilt und – so könnte man meinen – die beiden Gaos den Wesenskern anderer nicht hätten für sich benutzen dürfen. Aber auch ein positiver Schluss ist denkbar, quasi im Sinne des Vorherbestimmten, des Metamorphosen-Motivs: Die Herausforderung der Gao-Brüder stärkt Jiang Ziya, der Hauptheld wächst. Das Gute wird kurzfristig an das (vermeintlich) Negative verliehen, um am Ende wieder Gutes zu befördern.

Nachzutragen wäre noch, dass Shen Tu (das zweite Zeichen bisweilen fälschlich *cha* 茶 etc.) und Yu Lei (statt „Lei" manchmal auch „Lü" 律) sowie viele weitere Gestalten, die im *Fengshen yanyi* und anderen Büchern Erwähnung finden, bisweilen recht eigene Spuren im Schriftgut hinterlassen haben. So findet sich das Paar Shen/Yu in mehreren Werken über Götter und Geister, z.B. im *Soushen daquan* 搜神大全 (Kompendium zur Ermittlung des Übernatürlichen), von dem es wiederum unterschiedliche Editionen gibt, deren Anfänge weit vor die Ming-Zeit reichen.[38] Im Übrigen wird das *Fengsu tongyi* 風俗通義 (Erklärungen zu Sitten und Gebräuchen) des Ying Shao 應劭 gerne als früheste Belegstelle für Shen / Yu angegeben. Selbiges nennt den Dushuo-Berg, den Pfirsichbaum, das Treiben anderer Geister und weitere Elemente.[39] Aus dieser Tradition haben sich verschiedene Türwächter (*menshen* 門神) und deren Bilder entwickelt,

---

[37] Zhou Xiaowei, *Siyou ji congkao*, S. 151. Allerdings interpretiert Zhou die entsprechenden Szenen kaum.

[38] *Sanjiao yuanliu Soushen daquan* 三教源流搜神大全 (ursprünglich 1909; Neudruck Changsha: Zhongguo gushu kanyinshe, 1935), S. 41. Eine neuere Ausgabe: *Huitu sanjiao yuanliu Soushen daquan. Fu Soushen ji* 繪圖三教源流搜神大全—附搜神記 (Taibei: Lianjing, 1985). Zu den teils recht unterschiedlichen *Soushen*-Editionen im Zusammenhang mit Mazu jüngst: Barbara Witt, „The Hagiographies of Tianfei in the *Soushen daquan* and the *Zengbu soushen ji*", Vortrag beim „International Workshop on Mazu/Tianfei: The Chinese Goddess of Seafarers. Regional, Historical, and Comparative Perspectives" (18.–19. März 2016, Institut für Sinologie, München). – Für das „Götterinventar" des *Fengshen yanyi* sind Liu Ts'un-yans *Buddhist and Taoist Influences* und Wei Juxians 衛聚賢 Studie *Fengshen bang gushi tanyuan* 封神榜故事探源, 2 Bde. (Hong Kong: Shuowenshe, 1960), noch immer nützlich.

[39] Ying Shao, *Fengsu tongyi*, Kap. 8 (Sidian 祀典); benutzt: Text der ICS Concordance Series (Hong Kong: Shangwu yinshuguan, 1996), S. 60-61. Wenigstens eine weitere Quelle sei genannt: Wang Chongs 王充 *Lun heng* 論衡; dazu Alfred Forke (Übers.), *Lun-Hêng*, 2 Bde. (Neudruck New York: Paragon Book Gallery, 1962), Bd. I, S. 243 (Ding gui 訂鬼); Bd. II, S. 352 (Luan long 亂龍). Ähnliches im *Shanhai jing* 山海經 und weiteren frühen Werken.

außerdem der Pfirsichtalisman (*taofu* 桃符) zur Dämonenabwehr. Entsprechende Darstellungen sind schon aus alter Zeit bekannt.⁴⁰

9. *Beiyou ji* und *Nanyou ji*

Im späten 16. und frühen 17. Jahrhundert wurden zwei weitere Erzählungen verfasst, die unser Thema berühren: Yu Xiangdous *Nanyou ji* und das *Beiyou ji*. Beide Werke fanden später Eingang in die Sammlung *Siyou ji* 四遊記. Im *Beiyou ji* geht es vor allem um Zhenwu 眞武, den Gott des Nordens, der auch als Xuanwu 玄武 und unter anderen Namen bekannt ist. In Kapitel 23 dieses Buches werden Li Lou und Shi Kuang in einer Götterliste genannt; sie erhalten dort den gemeinsamen Titel *congming er jiang* 聰明二將.⁴¹

Im Mittelpunkt des *Nanyou ji* steht der uns schon bekannte Huaguang (darum der alternative Buchtitel *Wu xian linggong dadi Huaguang tianwang zhuan* 五顯靈公大帝華光天王傳, kurz *Huaguang tianwang zhuan* [Erzählung vom Himmelskönig Huaguang]) bzw. Ma *lingguan* 馬靈官, also „Seelen-Marschall Ma".⁴² Huaguang wird dreimal inkarniert. Das Thema – die Rettung der Mutter – erinnert an den berühmten Mulian-Stoff (*Mulian jiumu* 目蓮救母). Die Handlung wird von daoistischen und buddhistischen Elementen bestimmt, Huaguang begegnet mehreren Göttern und Geistern, so auch Qianliyan und Shunfeng'er. Viele Gestalten treten in bekannten Texten auf – etwa im *Fengshen yanyi*, *Xiyou*

---

⁴⁰ Eine frühe Darstellung z.B. in *Shufa-Zhongguo shuhua bao* 书法一中国书画报, Nr. 49 (26.6.2010; Gesamtnummer 2000). In knapper Form zur Rolle des Pfirsichs in ältester Zeit z.B. Wolfgang Münke, *Die klassische chinesische Mythologie* (Stuttgart: Klett, 1976), S. 262-263.

⁴¹ Benutzt wurde der Text: Yu Xiangdou, *Beifang Zhenwu xuantian shangdi chushen zhizhuan* 北方眞武玄天上帝出身志傳, in: *Siyou ji*, Zhongguo xueshu mingzhu 中國學術名著 172 (Taibei: Shijie shuju, 1962); Übersetzung: Gary Seaman, *Journey to the North. An Ethnohistorical Analysis and Annotated Translation* (Berkeley et al.: University of California Press, 1987), S. 201. Wertvolle Hinweise geben Liu Ts'un-yan, *Buddhist and Taoist Influences*; Zhou Xiaowei, *Siyou ji congkao*; Richard von Glahn, *The Divine and the Demonic in Chinese Religious Culture* (Berkeley et al.: University of California Press, 2004); Noelle Guiffrida, „Representing the Daoist God Zhenwu, the Perfect Warrior, in Late Imperial China" (Dissertation, University of Kansas, 2008).

⁴² Benutzt wurde der Text: Yu Xiangdou, *Wu xian linggong dadi Huaguang tianwang zhuan*, in: *Siyou ji* (wie Anm. zuvor); hier besonders S. 67-68, 73, 75, 77, 84-86 und 95. Weiterhin zum *Nanyou ji* und zum Umfeld: Ursula Angelika Cedzich, „The Cult of Wu-t'ung / Wu-hsien in History and Fiction: The Religious Roots of the *Journey to the South*", in David Johnson (Hrsg.), *Ritual and Scriptures in Chinese Popular Religion. Five Studies*. Publications of the Chinese Popular Culture Project 3 (Berkeley: Institute for East Asian Studies, 1995), S. 137-218, besonders S. 149 und S. 189: Anm. 221; *id.*, „Wu-t'ung: Zur bewegten Geschichte eines Kultes", in: Gert Naundorf et al. (Hrsg.), *Religion und Philosophie in Ostasien. Festschrift für Hans Steininger* (Würzburg: Königshausen und Neumann, 1985), S. 33-60; Werke von Liu Ts'un-yan, Zhou Xiaowei und von Glahn, wie in Anm. 41 – Zu Huaguang z.B. auch *Soushen da quan*, S. 57-58; dort Li Lou und Shi Kuang. Ebenso die oben und in Anm. 25 zitierten *Daozang*-Texte.

ji und *Xiyang ji* 西洋記 –, und es kommt zu zahlreichen Kämpfen. Gegen Ende der Erzählung will Huaguang magische Pfirsiche für seine Mutter beschaffen. Er verwandelt sich in Sun Wukong 孫悟空 und stiehlt die Früchte. Diese Teile sind dem weithin bekannten *Xiyou ji* nachempfunden. Es kommt zu Auseinandersetzungen zwischen Huaguang und dem Affenkönig, doch später vermittelt Huaguangs Lehrer zwischen beiden und sie schließen Bruderschaft.

Qianliyan und Shunfeng'er werden in Kapitel 6 eingeführt. Sie leben in der Hibiskus-Höhle (Furong dong 芙蓉洞) am Lilou-Berg und heißen auch Li Lou bzw. Shi Kuang. Allerdings, so der Text, würden sie Menschen verspeisen, deren Knochen sie in großer Menge gestapelt hätten. Huaguang will sie unterwerfen, doch die beiden *gui* 鬼 (Dämonen) durchschauen den Plan und versuchen ihn zu überlisten. Vergeblich, denn Huaguang setzt sie mit seinem magischen „Anti-Dämonen-Speer" (*jiangmo fugui qiang* 降魔伏鬼槍) fest. Dann bricht er ihren Widerstand mit Hilfe einer „Feuerpille" (*huodan* 火丹), die sie schlucken müssen; beide sind ihm nun untergeben. Anschließend sorgt er dafür, dass die Menschenopfer beendet werden.

Der weitere Handlungsverlauf hat mit Qianliyan und Shunfeng'er selbst nur noch wenig zu tun. Allerdings treten sie hier und da auf, um Huaguang zu beraten; damit treiben sie das Geschehen voran. So empfehlen sie ihm einmal, die Gestalt des Jadekaisers anzunehmen, eine Zeremonie abzuhalten und vereinsamte Seelen herbeizurufen (Kapitel 8). Hierüber ist der Jadekaiser erzürnt und beauftragt Song Wuji 宋無忌, einen der himmlischen Heerführer, Huaguang zu maßregeln (Kapitel 9). Doch Qianliyan und Shunfeng'er wissen darum und warnen ihren Meister. Dieser schmiedet einen Gegenplan, den General Song seinerseits erahnt. So kommt es zu magischen Auseinandersetzungen, wobei Huaguang am Ende die Oberhand behält. An anderer Stelle, noch in Kapitel 9, sollen Qianliyan und Shunfeng beim Einfangen gegnerischer „Feuerkrähen" (*huoya* 火鴉) behilflich sein; dafür müssen sie ein besonderes Netz bereithalten. Das trägt zum erneuten Siege bei. In Kapitel 11 erklären beide, auf welche Weise Huaguang eine seine verlorenen Waffen, den goldenen Ziegel (*jinzhuan* 金磚), ersetzen könne. In Kapitel 12 warnen sie ihn vor dem magischen Fächer einer Gegnerin. Als Huaguang dennoch in die Schlacht ziehen will, springen sie ein; der Fächer katapultiert sie in die Weite, doch sie besteigen eine magische Wolke und kehren zum Lilou-Berg zurück. Gegen Ende der Handlung, in Kapitel 17, werden beide dann noch einmal um Auskunft gebeten.

Im *Nanyou ji* nehmen Qianliyan und Shunfeng'er somit Rollen ein, die vom üblichen Muster etwas abweichen. Zwar sind sie, wie stets, über die Absichten des Gegners im Bilde, aber sie treten zunächst als negative Gestalten auf, obschon der Autor sie mit Li Lou und Shi Kuang gleichsetzt, die ja eigentlich positiv konnotiert sind. Erst Huaguang bereitet ihrem schlimmen Treiben ein Ende. Dessen Geschichte wiederum ist in eine komplexe Erzählstruktur eingebettet, deren Fäden im Götterhimmel zusammenlaufen. Viele Ereignisse sind darum kausal vorherbestimmt. Folglich werden Gut und Böse in gewisser Weise relativiert, das gilt auch für Huaguangs Gehilfen; der Sachverhalt erinnert also an die Interpretationsmöglichkeiten des Shang-Zhou-Stoffes.

Huaguang tritt noch in weiteren Erzählungen auf; diese behandeln aber meist andere Themen.[43] Außerdem finden wir ihn im *zaju*-Theater, wie oben erwähnt. Die Verknüpfung zwischen ihm und dem Duo Qianliyan / Shunfeng'er ist jedoch in den frühen Werken nirgends so ausgebaut worden wie im *Nanyou ji*. Insofern hat das *Nanyou ji* besondere Bedeutung für unser Thema. Wohl in keinem anderen *xiaoshuo*-Werk der Ming-Periode nehmen Qianliyan und Shunfeng'er einen so großen Aktionsradius ein wie in diesem Werk.

10. Der *Xiyou ji*-Stoff

Dass Qianliyan und Shunfeng'er mit dem *Xiyou ji*-Stoff verbunden sind, wurde bereits gesagt. In der Version des Romans von 1592, die gewöhnlich Wu Cheng'en 吳承恩 (ca. 1500 – ca. 1582) zugeschrieben wird, berichten sie dem Jadekaiser über Sun Wukong; erst erläutern sie seine Herkunft, an anderer Stelle fügen sie hinzu, Sun sei zu einem Unsterblichen aufgestiegen und habe inzwischen andere Wesen unterworfen.[44] Auch in der viel kompakteren Fassung des Zhu Dingchen 朱鼎臣 (16. Jahrhundert) dienen Qianliyan und Shunfeng'er als Informanten, jedoch erst, nachdem der Affe für Unruhe im Himmel gesorgt hat. Die Ausgabe des Yang Zhihe 楊致和 (ebenso Ming-Zeit), welche noch knapper ist, nennt die beiden nicht in diesem Zusammenhang.[45]

Über das Verhältnis der drei *Xiyou ji*-Editionen ist unendlich viel geschrieben worden.[46] Sie stammen alle aus der späten Ming-Zeit, doch die weiteren Details sind für uns nicht relevant, zumal mit Qianliyan und Shunfeng'er daselbst kaum Handlung und keine anderen Besonderheiten verknüpft werden. Bemerkenswert ist nur: Bisweilen entbehrt der Kontext nicht eines gewissen Humors. Das trifft auf andere Erzählungen, die unsere beiden Informanten nennen, kaum im glei-

---

[43] Zu weiteren literarischen Werken, in denen Huaguang auftritt, z.B. Nikaido Yoshihiro, „Tongsu xiaoshuo li yuanshuai shen zhi xingxiang" 通俗小說裡元帥神之形象 (http://kuir.jm.kansai-u.ac.jp/dspace/bitstream/10112/868/1/KU-1100-20070900-53.pdf; aufgerufen am 10. August 2016). Siehe ebenso Titel in Anmerkung 12, oben.

[44] Wu Cheng'en, *Xiyou ji*, 2 Bde. (Beijing: Renmin wenxue chubanshe, 1973), Bd. I, Kap. 1, S. 3; Kap. 3, S. 42. Übersetzt z.B. von Anthony C. Yu (Übers., Hrsg.), *The Journey to the West*, 4 Bde. (Chicago – London: The University of Chicago Press, 1977–1984), Bd. I, S. 68, 114.

[45] Zhu Dingchen, *Tang Sanzang Xiyou shi e zhuan* 唐三藏西游释厄传, und Yang Zhihe, *Xiyou ji zhuan* 西游记传, beide in einem Bd., herausgegeben von Chen Xin 陈新, Zhongguo xiaoshuo ziliao congshu 中国小说资料丛书 (Beijing: Renmin wenxue chubanshe, 1984), S. 32 (Zhu), 207-208 (vergleichbare Abschnitte, Yang).

[46] Nur zwei westliche Werke hierzu seien genannt: Glen Dudbridge, „The Hundred-Chapter Hsi-yu chi and Its Earlier Versions", *AM*, New Series 14 (1969) 2, S. 141-191; Nicholas A. Koss, „The *Xiyou ji* in Its Formative Stages. The Late Ming Editions" (Dissertation, Indiana University, 1981).

chen Maße zu; der *Xiyou ji*-Stoff taucht Qianliyan und Shunfeng'er also in ein recht spezielles Ambiente.

Aber damit ist nicht alles gesagt. Wir finden beide Geister ebenso in einem älteren koreanischen Fragment, der sogenannten Pak t'ongsa 朴通事 -Fassung, die ihre Ursprünge wohl im 15. Jahrhundert hat. Hier ist der Zusammenhang ein etwas anderer: Tripitaka und Sun Wukong müssen sich in einem langen Duell gegen ihre daoistischen Rivalen durchsetzen. Wiederum stecken diese Szenen voller Komik. Während des Wettbewerbs ruft Sun etliche Geister herbei, unter anderem Qianliyan und Shunfeng'er. Sie sollen einen Kessel mit siedendem Öl bewachen, in welchem Lupi 鹿皮, einer der Daoisten, baden will, um seine Widerstandskraft zu beweisen. Doch bald ist er der Hitze nicht mehr gewachsen und versucht aus dem Gefäß zu steigen. Die Geister aber hindern ihn daran und er geht auf jämmerliche Weise zugrunde. Sieger des Wettstreits sind am Ende Tripitaka und Sun Wukong.[47]

Über mögliche Verbindungen zwischen der Pak t'ongsa-Version und anderen Fassungen des *Xiyou ji*-Stoffes, die ganz oder auch nur noch teilweise überliefert sind, ist wiederum sehr viel Literatur vorhanden; aber diese Ausführungen können hier übergangen werden.[48] Weniger bekannt ist hingegen, dass der Magier Lupi in mehreren anderen Texten vorkommt, so im *Xiyang ji*, welches im nächsten Abschnitt betrachtet werden wird.

11. Ming-Erzählungen, in denen Mazu auftritt

Dem *Xiyou ji* in gewisser Weise ähnlich, zumindest in struktureller Hinsicht, ist der Luo Maodeng 羅懋登 zugeschriebene Roman *Sanbao taijian Xiyang ji tongsu yanyi* 三寶太監西洋記通俗演義 (Reise des Eunuchen Sanbao ins Westmeer; Kurztitel *Xiyang ji*; Vorwort 1597).[49] Beide Werke können als „Zielsuche"-Erzählungen gelesen werden. Zentrales Anliegen des *Xiyou ji* ist die Beschaffung heiliger Schriften in Indien. Im *Xiyang ji* führt Zheng He eine große Flotte durch das „Westmeer", also den Indischen Ozean, um nach dem verlorenen kaiserlichen Siegel zu fahnden und fremde Länder zu unterwerfen. In diesem Werk, dessen komplexer Aufbau buddhistische, daoistische und konfuzianische Elemente vereint – genau wie das *Xiyou ji* –, tritt Mazu als Schutzpatronin auf. Sie bewacht die Ming-Flotte auf ihrem Weg von China bis nach Mekka, wobei ihre rote

---

[47] Text und Übersetzung in: Glen Dudbridge, *The Hsi-yu chi. A Study of Antecedents to the Sixteenth-Century Chinese Novel* (Cambridge: At the University Press, 1970), S. 182, 187. Dudbridge hat den Nachdruck (1943) einer Version benutzt, deren Vorwort auf das Jahr 1677 datiert ist (S. 60-61).

[48] Das gilt auch für Fragmente des Stoffes im *Yongle dadian* und in einem *baojuan* 寶卷 -Text.

[49] Zu diesem Roman etwa Ptak, *Cheng Hos Abenteuer*. Ferner z.B. Shi Ping 时平 - Ptak (Hrsg.), *Studien*, Bd. 1 und 2. Weiterführende bibliographische Hinweise – auch zu Luo Maodeng, über dessen Leben bislang fast nichts bekannt ist – in: Barbara Witt, „*Sanbao taijian Xiyang ji tongsu yanyi*. An Annotated Bibliography", *Crossroads* 12 (2015), S. 151-243.

Lampe am Mastbaum als Orientierung dient. Hiermit ist natürlich das Elmsfeuer gemeint, das immer wieder im Zusammenhang mit Mazus Wundertaten genannt wird.

Beide Erzählungen weisen der buddhistischen Ebene den höchsten Rang zu. Damit wird das Paradoxe zum literarischen Leitfaden. Raum und Zeit sind zwar gegeben, können aber ebenso negiert werden. Das gilt auch für alle Phänomene und Wesen, deren Lebenswege ohnehin vorherbestimmt sind. Im Rahmen dieser Anordnung spielt Mazu selbstverständlich nur eine Nebenrolle.

Obschon der Roman im späten 16. Jahrhundert entstand, zu einer Zeit also, da der Mazu-Kult schon weit verbreitet war, muss Mazu ohne Begleiter auskommen. Statt dessen finden wir Qianliyan und Shunfeng'er an anderer Stelle: In Kapitel 3 zählt ein Orakelmeister mehrere Geister und Götter auf, darunter auch diese beiden. In Kapitel 37 findet sich die Zeichenfolge *qianliyan* als Attribut in einer Charakterisierung des Ming-Generals Zheng Tang 鄭堂: Hiermit soll offenbar sein scharfer Blick hervorgehoben werden. Und in Kapitel 44 werden Qianliyan und Shunfeng'er vom Jadekaiser beauftragt, Erkundigungen einzuziehen. Diese Szene ist nicht unwichtig, sie bedarf deshalb eines kurzen Kommentars.[50]

Qianliyan und Shunfeng'er berichten, dass Jin Bifeng 金碧峯, die buddhistische Hauptfigur des Romans, ohne die Zheng He sein Unternehmen nicht durchführen könnte, und Lishan laomu 驪山老母, welche über große magische Kräfte verfügt und eigentlich dem daoistischen Lager zuzuordnen ist, in Streit geraten seien. Tatsächlich handelt es sich um eine sehr ernste Situation, die den Jadekaiser dazu veranlasst, Guanyin 觀音 aufzusuchen. Beide schaffen es schließlich, den Streit zu schlichten.[51] Damit wird eine folgenschwere Auseinandersetzung zwischen Buddhisten und Daoisten in den himmlischen Gefilden vermieden. Das ist für den Fortgang der Handlung essentiell. Denn ein Kampf zwischen Jin Bifeng und Lishan laomu würde nicht nur Zheng Hes Unternehmen belasten, zugleich liefe Jin Bifeng Gefahr, spirituell abzusteigen, zumal er als Wiedergeburt des Randeng gufo 燃燈古佛, also des Buddha Dīpaṃkara, an die Vorhersehung und damit an einen höheren Auftrag gebunden ist.

Qianliyan und Shunfeng'er werden zwar nur kurz in den Ablauf des Geschehens eingebunden, aber sie erscheinen, wie das Obige zeigt, in einem äußerst kritischen Moment. Keines der bislang vorgestellten Werke ordnet diese beiden Figuren einem so zentralen Ereignis zu. Luo Maodengs Erzählung nimmt in dieser Hinsicht eine Sonderrolle ein.

Doch noch eine andere Besonderheit fällt auf. In Kapitel 44 werden Qianliyan und Shunfeng'er als *pusa* 菩薩 bezeichnet. Damit wird ihnen ein unerwartet ho-

---

[50] Benutzte Ausgabe: Luo Maodeng, *Sanbao taijian Xiyang ji*. Zhongguo gudian xiaoshuo mingzhu baibu 中国古典小说名著百部 (Beijing: Huaxia chubanshe, 1995), S. 22, 301, 358-359.

[51] Zur besonderen Rolle Lishan laomus im *Xiyang ji* und zu der hier beschriebenen „Kompromisslösung" sowie ihrer möglichen Bedeutung siehe Katrin Weiß, „Lishan laomu im *Xiyang ji*", in: Shi Ping – Ptak, *Studien*, Bd. 2, S. 107-121.

her Rang zugedacht; sie sind also mehr als nur konventionelle Wächter oder Späher. Fast noch wichtiger aber: Die gewählte Klassifikation weist sie dem buddhistischen Lager zu. Anders formuliert: Der Jadekaiser, oberste Instanz der daoistischen Sphäre, bedient sich zweier Figuren, die man eigentlich der „anderen Partei" zurechnen könnte. Zwei Möglichkeiten bieten sich als Erklärung an: Der Autor nahm es mit der Klassifikation *pusa* nicht genau. Oder aber er wollte durch die gewählte Konstellation für formalen Ausgleich sorgen: Jin Bifeng (Buddhismus) ist im Sinne der Gesamtkonstruktion letztlich Lishan laomu und ihrer Gruppe übergeordnet, beim Jadekaiser (Daoist) liegen gleichsam umgekehrte Verhältnisse vor. Natürlich wäre hier noch eingehender über die Rolle Guanyins (Buddhismus) nachzudenken, doch das würde uns zu weit vom Thema fortführen. Halten wir darum nur fest: Qianliyan und Shunfeng'er erhalten im Einklang mit den Vorgaben der Erzählung besonderes Gewicht, zumindest auf symbolischer Ebene.

In der wenig bekannten Erzählung *Tianfei niangma zhuan* 天妃娘媽傳, deren Hauptfigur Mazu ist, treten Qianliyan und Shunfeng'er, entgegen jeder Erwartung, nicht auf. Autor dieses kurzen, aber wichtigen Textes ist ein gewisser Wu Huanchu 吳還初 (Ende Ming). Das Werk enthält einfache Illustrationen und wurde während der Wanli-Epoche (1573–1620) in Fujian gedruckt. Es geriet dann in Vergessenheit und kam erst vor wenigen Jahren erneut in Umlauf.[52] Sein Inhalt ist schnell skizziert: Es geht um Mazus Vorleben, ihre Geburt auf Erden und schließlich um ihren Kampf gegen böse Geister, zum Schutz des Guten. Insgesamt unterscheidet sich der Stoff deutlich von jenen Legenden, die im späteren *Tianfei xiansheng lu* und vergleichbaren Texten überliefert sind.

Ein Merkmal der Erzählung besteht darin, dass die Anfänge der Mazu-Verehrung zeitlich vorverlegt werden. Schon unter dem Han-Kaiser Mingdi 明帝 (reg. 58–75) sei ihr ein Schrein errichtet worden. Zugleich wird Mazu als Tochter des Beitian miaoji xingjun 北天妙機星君 (Sternenfürst des wunderbaren Pols am Nordhimmel) ausgewiesen. Eine andere Besonderheit des Textes: Mazus leibliche Mutter ist eine geborene Cai 蔡. In der Erzählung selbst spielt Lin Erlang 林二郎, Mazus Bruder, eine zentrale Rolle. Außerdem treten ungewöhnlich viele Tiergeister auf, die es zu besiegen gilt.

Diese und andere Besonderheiten sind jüngst recht ausführlich von Cai Jiehua beschrieben worden. Unter anderem lesen wir dort: Mazu wirkt bei Wu Huanchu „mächtiger und stärker als in früheren Texten, obschon sie der überlegenen Guanyin als Schülerin untergeordnet ist". Und mit Bezug auf Qianliyan und Shunfeng'er, die ja nicht auftreten, schreibt Cai: „Fast könnte man meinen, Tianfei bedürfe ihrer Hilfe nicht, sie komme alleine zurecht, Räucherwerk über-

---

[52] Moderne Druckausgabe: Wu Huanchu (Verfasser), Huang Yongnian 黄永年 (Hrsg.), *Tianfei niangma zhuan*, Zhongguo gudian xiaoshuo yanjiu ziliao congshu 中国古典小说研究资料丛书 (Shanghai: Shanghai guji chubanshe, 1990). Eine Fassung des *Tianfei niangma zhuan* ist auch in: *MZWX*, Bd. II, zhulu shang, enthalten, ebenso in der Sammlung Guben xiaoshuo jicheng (Shanghai: Shanghai guji chubanshe, 1991).

nehme die gesteigerte Funktion von Augen und Ohren, sei das geeignete Medium, Warnungen zu übermitteln." Diese Interpretation mag überraschend klingen, würde aber die Abwesenheit der beiden Späher erklären.[53]

12. Schluss

Sicher könnte das Obige um viele weitere Belege aus anderen Texten bereichert werden. Obschon das Dargestellte somit keine endgültigen Schlüsse erlaubt, werden mehrere Sachverhalte doch recht deutlich. Beginnen wir mit Mazu: Nach heutiger Konvention sind Qianliyan und Shunfeng'er aufs Engste mit Mazu verbunden. Aber bis weit in die Ming-Zeit hinein kennen wir nur wenige Textbeispiele für dieses Trio. Die beiden dem Daoismus zugeordneten *Tianfei ... lingyan jing*-Werke aus dem frühen 15. Jahrhundert stehen in dieser Hinsicht fast isoliert da. Im Theaterstück *Xia Xiyang* fehlen die Namen für Mazus Begleitfiguren, außerdem handelt es sich dort um weibliche Rollen. Im *Tianfei niangma zhuan*, in welchem Mazu im Mittelpunkt steht, werden sie überhaupt nicht genannt. Im *Xiyang ji* treten Qianliyan und Shunfeng'er in gänzlich anderen Kontexten auf. Der mutmaßliche Autor dieses Werkes, Luo Maodeng, hat sich auch mit *Soushen*-Texten befasst und gilt als besonders belesen;[54] wäre Mazu damals in der literarischen Tradition – außerhalb der rein religiösen Literatur – schon fest mit Qianliyan und Shunfeng'er verknüpft gewesen, Luo Maodeng hätte es sicher in seinem Roman honoriert.

Es ist mehrfach behauptet worden, etwa von Meir Shahar, *xiaoshuo*-Werke hätten maßgeblich zur Entwicklung religiöser Kulte beigetragen.[55] Das mag für die äußere Gestaltung Qianliyans und Shunfeng'ers gelten – erinnert sei an die Beschreibungen im *Fengshen yanyi* und an das Aussehen heutiger Wächterfiguren –, aber ganz gewiss nicht für die Zuordnung zu Mazu. Erzählungen der Ming-Periode haben die Entstehung dieses Trios keinesfalls befördert. Auch in anderer Hinsicht versagt die obige These: Qianliyan und Shunfeng'er erscheinen heute nur noch selten im Umfeld jener Figuren, denen sie in alten Texten zur Seite stehen. Im übrigen ist nicht zu vergessen, dass der Roman *Tianfei niangma zhuan* recht eigene Vorstellungen mit Mazu verknüpft, die bei der Entwicklung des Kultes, vor allem in Fujian, höchstens am Rande Berücksichtigung fanden.

---

[53] Zum *Tianfei niangma zhuan* letztens z.B. Cai Jiehua 蔡婕华, „*Xiyang ji* und *Tianfei niangma zhuan*. Ein Vergleich", in: Shi Ping – Ptak, *Studien*, Bd. 1, S. 139-154. Ferner Cais *Das* Tianfei niangma zhuan 天妃娘媽傳 *des Wu Huanchu* 吳還初. Maritime Asia, 25 (Wiesbaden: Harrassowitz, 2014). Dort Angaben zur Editionsgeschichte, zu einzelnen Romanfiguren und vieles andere mehr. Zu den zitierten Passagen daselbst S. 23-24.

[54] Luo schrieb ein entsprechendes Vorwort. Vgl. *CT* 1476 / *DT* 1464; Boltz, „In Homage to T'ien-fei", S. 219, Anm. 47; Ptak, *Cheng Hos Abenteuer*, S. 169; Witt, „The Hagiographies of Tianfei".

[55] Meir Shahar, „Vernacular Fiction and the Transmission of Gods' Cults in Late Imperial China", in: *id.* – Robert P. Weller (Hrsg.), *Unruly Gods. Divinity and Society in China* (Honolulu: University of Hawai'i Press, 1996), S. 184-211.

Die Nicht-Mazu-Kontexte, in denen Qianliyan und Shunfeng'er auftreten, sind schnell genannt: 1. Sie werden in der *xiaoshuo*-Welt mit dem Thema der Shang- und Zhou-Dynastie verknüpft. Hierbei ist die Art der Zuordnung zu den Paaren Li Lou / Shi Kuang und Shen Tu / Yu Lei entscheidend. Gao Ming / Gao Jue sind negative Figuren, wie wir sahen, aber Qianliyan und Shunfeng'er werden eigentlich nur von ihnen missbraucht, erscheinen also nicht automatisch in schlechtem Lichte. Die übrigen Geschichten betreffen vor allem 2. Xue Rengui, 3. Huaguang und den 4. *Xiyou ji*-Stoff. Alle Kontexte weisen Ähnlichkeiten auf: Qianliyan und Shunfeng'er (bzw. ihre Pendants) sind stets Späher; ihre Fähigkeiten gehen gewissermaßen auf die Gaben Li Lous und Shi Kuangs zurück. Außerdem greifen beide nur selten aktiv in das Geschehen ein, bisweilen tragen sie aber durch ihre Meldungen zum Fortgang der Handlung kräftig bei. Erzähltechnisch sind sie fast wie Katalysatoren.

Allein Gao Ming und Gao Jue, die sich der magischen Kräfte beider bedienen, füllen eine Sonderrolle aus, denn sie nehmen maßgeblich an mehreren Kämpfen teil und sind im *Fengshen yanyi* über ein ganzes Kapitel erbitterte Gegner Jiang Ziyas. Den längsten Wirkradius haben Qianliyan und Shunfeng'er jedoch im *Nanyou ji*. Yu Xiangdou war, wie Luo Maodeng, mit den Geistern und Göttern seiner Zeit aufs Innigste vertraut. Dass er diesen beiden Figuren entsprechende Rollen zuwies, unterstreicht das Obige: In der damaligen *xiaoshuo*-Welt hatten sie so gut wie nichts mit Mazu zu tun.

Im *Xiyang ji* finden wir Qianliyan und Shunfeng'er in einer Schlüsselszene. Ohne ihre warnenden Meldungen käme es zum Bruch im Himmel, zwischen dem buddhistischen und dem daoistischen Lager, und die gesamte Romanstruktur würde aus den Fugen geraten. Abermals bleibt Mazu außen vor, doch dafür kommt der „Datenbeschaffung im cyber space" größte Bedeutung zu.

Nicht weiter ausgeführt wurde hier die Entwicklung sogenannter Wächterfiguren, derer es viele Varianten im alten China gab. Aufgrund ihrer letztlich von Li Lou und Shi Kuang abgeleiteten Fähigkeiten sind Qianliyan und Shunfeng'er jedoch eher als Informanten zu klassifizieren, also weniger als „Aufräumarbeiter", wie schon erwähnt; fast könnte man sie heute – modern ausgedrückt – als Mazus „NSA" bezeichnen. Alle übrigen Rollen, die ihnen angetragen wurden, lassen sich hieraus ableiten. Damit hatten beide Figuren natürlich auch stets das Potential, andere Gestalten mit ähnlichen Funktionen vom religiösen Markt zu verdrängen.

Die *xiaoshuo*-Literatur der Ming-Zeit ist bekannt für ihre synkretistischen Züge – dafür, dass sie oftmals konfuzianische, buddhistische und daoistische Elemente in ein großes Gerüst zu pressen versucht (*sanjiao he yi* / *gui yi* 三教合一 / 歸一). Mal wird dabei die buddhistische, mal die daoistische Ebene als bestimmend empfunden. Das ist allerdings für Qianliyan und Shunfeng'er – und ihre „Derivate" – ohne Belang, denn sie treten stets nur als untergeordnete Personen auf, sind quasi Spielbälle in der Hand des Schicksals. Vor allem dann, wenn Zeit und Raum relativiert, Sein und Nichtsein, ja selbst die Existenz der Götter in Frage gestellt, aber zugleich bestätigt werden, rücken Qianliyan und Shunfeng'er an den Rand einer imaginierten Welt. Gleichwohl stehen sie dem Jadekaiser wohl etwas näher als der buddhistischen Ebene, und da man ihren Vorläufern, Li Lou und Shi Kuang, unterstellen kann, hin und wieder an das Gemeinwohl gedacht zu haben, sind sie ebenso der konfuzianischen Sphäre verbunden. Zusammenfassend kann man also sagen: Qianliyan und Shunfeng'er oszillieren, wie andere Nebenfiguren auch, zwischen unterschiedlichen Anschauungen hin und her; sie gehören damit zu den vielen Quasten eines bunten Gewebekanons.

Über die Fähigkeiten des Sehens und Hörens wurden sogar Brücken zu der Zeichenfolge *Guanyin* geschlagen. Doch Guanyin ist in der Literatur nicht von Qianliyan und Shunfeng'er abhängig, und Mazu ebensowenig, zumindest nicht bis zur Ming-Zeit. Außerdem werden unsere Späher unterschiedlich klassifiziert; sie erscheinen als *gui* 鬼, *jing* 精, *shen* 神 oder gar als *pusa* 菩薩. Heute wird in Werken über Mazu, die buddhistisch gefärbt sind, auch gerne auf die besonderen Dimensionen des „Buddha-Hörens" und „-Sehens" hingewiesen. Allwissenheit hat viele Gesichter. Entsprechendes findet sich schon in alter Zeit, etwa im *Hua yan jing* 華嚴經.[56] Aber derlei führt weit weg von unserem Thema.

Für andere gilt, dass Qianliyan und Shunfeng'er als Gehilfen Mazus separat zu betrachten sind. Dieses Trio habe, den Bedürfnissen der Gläubigen Rechnung tragend, eine mehr oder minder eigenständige Entwicklung durchlaufen. Shi Kuang / Li Lou und vergleichbare Figuren müsse man wohl ebenfalls in eine unabhängige Tradition stellen.[57] Es ist wahrscheinlich, dass solche Diskussionen in der Zukunft ausgeweitet werden, zumal der Mazu-Glaube expandiert. In unseren Tagen gilt die Kontrolle der Küsten und Ozeane als überlebenswichtig. Sicherheitserwägungen rechtfertigen mehrere Instanzen, an Lauschenden wird es auch künftig nicht fehlen.

---

[56] Weitere Hinweise z.B. in Ruitenbeek, „Mazu, the Patroness of Sailors", S. 320, Anm. 59; Cai Xianghui, *Mazu xinyang yanjiu*, S. 86; Luo Chunrong, *Mazu chuanshuo yanjiu*, S. 189-190.

[57] Vgl. z.B. Shi Houzhong 釋厚重, *Guanyin yu Mazu* 觀音與媽祖 (Xinbei: Daotian, 2005), S. 285-286.

JEWS AND JEWISH STUDIES IN CHINA
NOTES FOR A BIBLIOGRAPHY[*]

Pier Francesco Fumagalli

During the course of Chinese history, dating back several thousands of years, the Jews have been mentioned many times: in the south, at Khanfu (i.e., Canton/Guangzhou), their presence was documented in the 9th century in the Arab *Chronicles* written by Abu Zaid, while in Kaifeng (Henan), the most important Jewish community – its existence known since the 12th century – remained there until the middle of the 19th century; in the 20th century particularly important settlements were to be found in Shanghai, Harbin and Tianjin.[1] Today the Jews in China, although few in number and not officially recognized amongst the 56 Nationalities (*shaoshu minzu* 少数民族, national "minorities") of the People's Republic of China, do, however, constitute a significant presence, and are at the center of a growing interest through seminars, debates and publications, not only of a general and informative nature but also at a specialized scientific level.[2]

---

[*] An Italian version of this article was published in *Asiatica Ambrosiana* 3 (2011), pp. 391-400. – I am particularly grateful to the Monumenta Serica Institute of Sankt Augustin, and to its longtime Director Roman Malek, for the hospitality and assistance received at the Institute and at the Library, where I was able to deepen my knowledge and complete a great part of the present research.

[1] Cf. Xu Xin, *The Jews of Kaifeng, China. History, Culture, and Religion* (Jersey, NJ: Ktav, 2003), where the document of Dunhuang (sec. VIII), the Jewish presence at Khanfu (877/878) and, in subsequent eras, in Beijing (Peking), Canton, Hangzhou, Nanjing, Ningxia, Quanzhou, Shanghai, Yangzhou, Xi'an, are recalled; Irene Eber, *Chinese and Jews. Encounter between Cultures* (London – Portland, OR: Mitchell, 2008); Nadine Perront, *Être juif en Chine. L'histoire extraordinaire des communautés de Kaifeng et de Shanghai* (Paris: Albin Michel, 1998).

[2] Cf. Roman Malek, "*Tiaojinjiao* 挑筋教. 'Die Religion, welche die Sehnen entfernt'. Judentum als 'Fallbeispiel' einer marginalen Fremdreligion im traditionellen China," *minima sinica* 2010/2, pp. 16-52, in particular p. 17, notes 3-5; see also the wide panorama exhibited at the international conference held in Sankt Augustin in 1997 and published by Roman Malek (ed.), *From Kaifeng ... to Shanghai. Jews in China*, MSMS XLVI (Nettetal: Steyler Verlag, 2000); this volume follows another two, also extremely important works in the same series: Donald Daniel Leslie (ed.), *Jews and Judaism in Traditional China. A Comprehensive Bibliography*, MSMS XLIV (Nettetal: Steyler Verlag, 1998) and Irene Eber – Sze-kar Wan – Knut Walf (eds.), *Bible in Modern China. The Literary and Intellectual Impact*, MSMS XLIII (Nettetal: Steyler Verlag, 1999). On the Jewish communities in Kaifeng, Shanghai, Harbin, Tianjin, cf. the recent book by Izabella Goikhman, *Juden in China. Diskurse und ihre Kontextualisierung*, Berliner China-Studien, 47 (Berlin – Münster: LIT, 2007). On the subject of minorities and nationalities, cf. James Stuart Olson, *An Ethnohistorical Dictionary of China* (Westport, CN: Greenwood Press, 1998), where on pp. 409-410 a complete list of the 56 nationalities officially recognized in China is to be found.

Studies – regarding both the Jews in China and also those carried out in China on the subjects of Judaism and Israel – have made remarkable progress since the beginning of the early 1980s, coinciding with the opening of the new phase of modernization and international relations inaugurated by Deng Xiaoping.[3] The literature on this subject, which is examined here, is prevalently American, Chinese, and German, while the referred bibliography in general consists of works in many other languages, including Hebrew, French, Japanese, English, Italian, Dutch, Portuguese, Russian, Spanish, and Yiddish. As to the type of sources taken into consideration, in order to be thorough it must be noted that many other sources of various types, from the traditional to the formal to the most informal and modern, are also to be included: archives and manuscripts, epigraphs and artistic and archeological finds, doctoral theses and dissertations, international seminars, temporary and permanent exhibitions, films and recordings, albums, posters and interviews, up to the most recent internet websites. This introductory explanation allows us to define the limits of the present "Notes."

I. Research Phases and Development

I.1 The Early Phases

There is substantial agreement in indicating the beginning of the 1980s in China – after the failure of the "Cultural Revolution" (1966–1976) and the launching of reforms – as the favourable moment for a deep-rooted renewal, which is still evolving, in the field of Jewish studies.[4] Before that time, the works of Loewenthal (1947) and Kublin (1971)[5] were considered sources of remarkable importance. The Israeli bibliographical reviews also registered an identical tendency: compared with the scarce information shown there until 1975, a remarkable increase in titles and subject matter is to be noted in subsequent bibliographies.[6]

---

[3] Cf. Pan Guang, *The Development of Jewish and Israel Studies in China*, The Harry Truman Research Institute for the Advancement of Peace. Occasional Papers, No. 2 (The Hebrew University of Jerusalem, Spring 1992).

[4] More than 100 monographic studies on the Jews have been published in China since 1980, Cf. Izabella Goikhman, "The Internationalization of Chinese Research on Jews in China since the 1980s," *Berliner China-Hefte (Chinese History and Society)* 31 (2007), pp. 117-139, in particular p. 122; Pan Guang 潘光, *Youtai yanjiu zai Zhongguo. Sanshi nian huigu: 1978–2008* 犹太研究在中国—三十年回顾：1978-2008, CJSS Center of Jewish Studies Shanghai, Jewish and Israeli Studies Series (Shanghai: Shanghai shehui kexueyuan chubanshe, 2008), Bibliographic appendix see pp. 319-367.

[5] According to Michael Pollak, *Mandarins, Jews, and Missionaries. The Jewish Experience in the Chinese Empire* (Philadelphia: Jewish Publication Society, 1980), p. 360, where he refers to Rudolf Loewenthal, "The Nomenclature of Jews in China," *Monumenta Serica* 12 (1947), pp. 91-126 and Hyman Kublin, *Studies of the Chinese Jews. Selections from Journals East and West* (New York: Paragon Book Reprint, 1971).

[6] As far as the period preceding 1975 is concerned, there are few indications in Shlomo Shunami, *Bibliography of Jewish Bibliography*. 2nd ed. enlarged (Jerusalem: The Magnes Press – The Hebrew University, 1965), pp. 108-109, nos. 603-606; p. 150, nos. 844-846; pp. 389-390, nos. 2201-2211; *id.*, *Bibliography of Jewish Bibliography. Supplement to Se-*

The work by Michael Pollak, *Mandarins, Jews and Missionaries* (1980) is representative of the cultural attitude which, at the beginning of the 1980s, only considered Judaism in China in its distant past, as a subject for historical research on the rich in history but now assimilated Chinese Jewish community, a subject on which Pollak supplies a bibliography in various European languages and in Hebrew, from which, however, Chinese authors are absent.[7]

I.2 The Turning Point

The years 1983-1984 mark a turning point, from which subsequent research carried out by Chinese scholars derived a vigorous thrust. The protagonists were Pan Guangdan 潘光旦 (1899-1967) in China in 1983 through a posthumous book, and Sydney Shapiro in America the following year. The former scholar had already concluded his work by 1953, which however had to wait until 1983 before being finally updated and edited.[8] His book, in a version completed by a rich bibliography, together with that of Chen Yuan 陳垣 (1880-1971) dating back to 1920 and approximately ten other articles by Chinese authors, was presented one year later in an American edition by Sydney Shapiro.[9] The bibliographical structure with which Shapiro completes the work by Pan Guangdan is remarkable for the list of manuscript and printed sources, subdivided into 4 sections: Chinese and Japanese, followed by those for English and French, Latin, German, Spanish, Italian, Hebrew, and Yiddish. Within this framework, the role of the Chinese academy seems to be still in the background, and in the years 1981-1983 only eight publications worthy of note that appeared in China on this subject are mentioned by Shapiro.[10]

---

cond *Edition Enlarged 1965* (Jerusalem: The Magnes Press – The Hebrew University, 1975), p. 141, n. 5503. There are more numerous references also in Israel in the following period, cf. the collection of articles available in the series of annual volumes of the רשימת מאמרים במדעי היהדות – *Index of articles on Jewish studies* ("Rambi"), Jerusalem, The Jewish National and University Press, website http://www.jnul.huji.ac.il/rambi/ [accessed 3 May 2016]; worthy of particular note is research such as that by Irene Eber, who published the modern Hebrew translation of her studies on the Jews of Kaifeng and Shanghai, and on Chinese translations of the Bible and of works in Yiddish: איירין איבר ‎»סינים ויהודים. מפגשים בין תרבויות«, ירושלים, מוסד ביאליק. See Irene Eber, *Chinese and Jews. Encounters between Cultures* (Jerusalem: Bialik Institute, 2002).

[7] Pollak, *Mandarins, Jews, and Missionaries*, pp. 356-363.

[8] Pan Guangdan 潘光旦, *Zhongguo jingnei Youtairen de ruogan lishi wenti* 中国境内犹太人的若干历史问题 (Beijing: Beijing daxue chubanshe, 1983).

[9] Sydney Shapiro, *Jews in Old China. Studies by Chinese Scholars* (New York: Hippocrene Books, 1984), presents in English 13 principal works by Chinese scholars, including Chen Yuan and Pan Guangdan, who played an historic role with their publications between 1920 and 1953.

[10] *Ibid.*, pp. 190-191.

I.3 From Studies on the Jews to Jewish Studies in China (1983–1993)

The following decade thrived with initiatives and studies: in 1985 the Jewish Historical Society (JHS) of Hong Kong, founded the previous year, printed the essay by Dennis A. Leventhal, with a bibliography on the Jews in China, of 284 titles in western languages and in Chinese.[11] In 1988 Pollak published the bibliographies that Rudolf Loewenthal had compiled between 1939 and 1946, revising them and integrating them with his own fundamental contribution in the *Critical Bibliography* published in 1993.[12] In the same year the Center for Jewish Studies was opened in Shanghai and not long after Xu Xin founded the Chinese Association of Jewish Studies, which promotes this research on an academic level.

Awareness is now widespread in the academic environment that it is necessary to cultivate studies not only on the Chinese Jews, but on Judaism in general in its various facets and dimensions. In 1991, under the direction of Gu Xiaoming 顾晓鸣 of the Fudan University of Shanghai, the publication of volumes in the series Youtai wenhua congshu 犹太文化丛书 (Jewish Culture) began, which, within the space of a few years, was to print more than twenty works, many of which are translated from American English and which are important for becoming acquainted with Judaism in its various historical, spiritual, social and national aspects. In 1993 the publication of the *Encyclopaedia Judaica* in Chinese can be considered a summary of the path covered, a symbol of the beginning of new studies not only on the ancient Jewish era of the Kaifeng community, but on Judaism in general, and the beginning of a new phase.[13] In the last chapter of his work, dedicated to "Jewish Research in China," Huang Lingyu outlines a complex historical picture and adds an extensive bibliography.[14]

---

[11] Dennis A. Leventhal, *Sino-Judaic Studies. Whence and Whither. An Essay and Bibliography*, Monographs of the Jewish Historical Society of Hong Kong, 1 (Hong Kong: Hong Kong Jewish Chronicle, 1985).

[12] Michael Pollak, *The Sino-Judaic Bibliographies of Rudolf Loewenthal* (Cincinnati: Hebrew Union College Press, 1988); id., *The Jews of Dynastic China. A Critical Bibliography* (Cincinnati: Hebrew Union College Press, 1993).

[13] Xu Xin 徐新 – Ling Jiyao 凌继尧 (eds.), *Youtai baike quanshu* 犹太百科全书 (אנציקלופדיה יודאיקא – *Encyclopaedia Judaica*) (Shanghai: Shanghai renmin chubanshe, 1993); interest in the three Mediterranean monotheistic religions – Judaism, Christianity and Islam – developed in the same period, as can be seen from the fact that in that same year a similar work on Islam was published: Zheng Mianzhi 郑勉之 (ed.), *Yisilanjiao jianming cidian* 伊斯兰教简明辞典 (القموالاسلامي) (Nanjing: Jiangsu guji chubanshe, 1993); another work, useful for an area of contact between Muslims and Jews, was published the following year: Raphael Israeli (ed.), *Islam in China. A Critical Bibliography*, Bibliographies and Indexes in Religious Studies, 29 (Westport CN – London: Greenwood Press, 1994).

[14] Huang Lingyu 黄陵渝, *Youtaijiao xue* 犹太教学. Zhongguo xiandai kexue quanshu. Zongjiaoxue 中国现代科学全书. 宗教学 (Beijing: Dangdai shijie chubanshe, 2000), pp. 370-399, 400-403; the same scholar presents her principal conclusions in English: Huang Lingyu, "Research on Judaism in China," *China Study Journal* 15 (2000) 1, pp. 13-23 (also published in: Malek [ed.], *From Kaifeng ... to Shanghai*, pp. 653-669), where the state of Jewish studies up to 1999 in the following three areas is summed up: 1. Jews and Juda-

I.4 Associations and Study Centers

The three decades 1980–2010 were moreover to be noted for the establishment of Associations and Study Centers on Judaism in its various aspects, somewhat comparable to the way in which similar centers and initiatives, dedicated to other cultural and religious traditions such as Tibetan, Muslim, Buddhist and Christian, often organised thanks to international cooperation,[15] also developed.

Associations for Jewish studies have flourished in Beijing, Jinan, Nanjing, Shanghai and in other universities;[16] sometimes research on Judaism has been carried out within the framework of investigations promoted by study associations on the Middle East, or on Africa and Asia: on other occasions they were conducted within the context of studies on history, international politics, economics or philosophy.

After the foundation of the Jewish Historical Society in 1984, the Sino-Judaic Institute, publisher of the bulletin *Points East*, was set up in California in 1985. The Shanghai Association of Jewish Studies (Shanghai Youtaixue yanjiuhui 上海犹太学研究会) was established in 1988, while the following year the Israel and Judaism Study Center (Yisilie, Youtai yanjiu zhongxin 以色列·犹太研究中心) was founded at the Institute for Studies on Peace and Development (Heping yu fazhan yanjiusuo 和平与发展研究所), within the Social Science Academy at the Fudan University of Shanghai, which produced the journal *Yisilie dongtai* 以色列

---

ism in China; 2. Judaism in the U.S.A. and in Israel; 3. Judaism and Jewish culture in general.

[15] Complex considerations on the socio-cultural relationships and on religions in China today can be read in Chen Cunfu 陈村富, "Dangdai Zhongguo wenhua yu zongjiao de guanxi" 当代中国文化与宗教的关系, in: Chiara Piccinini (ed.), *Culture e religioni in Asia*, Asiatica Ambrosiana, 1 (Milano – Roma: Veneranda Biblioteca Ambrosiana – Bulzoni, 2009), pp. 39-63. Wang Meixiu draws attention to the great changes followed by the opening in the 1990s: Wang Meixiu 王美秀, "Paihuai yu bu kuanrong yu kuanrong zhi jian. Cong Jidujiao yu Zhongguo shehui zhengzhi wenhua de hudong jiaodu kan" 徘徊于不宽容与宽容之间—从基督教与中国社会政治文化的互动角度看, in: Maria Angelillo (ed.), *Culture, religioni e diritto nelle società dell'Asia orientale. Federico Borromeo, uno sguardo volto a Oriente*, Asiatica Ambrosiana, 2 (Milano – Roma: Veneranda Biblioteca Ambrosiana – Bulzoni, 2010), pp. 310-340, in particular pp. 333-337. With regard to studies on Christianity see also Matteo Nicolini-Zani, "L'«accademia» cinese e la cultura cristiana: luoghi e tendenze dell'attuale ricerca sul cristianesimo in Cina," in: Paolo Siniscalco (ed.), *Cristianesimo e storia. Rapporti e percorsi*, Religione e società. Storia della Chiesa e dei movimenti cattolici, 42 (Roma: Edizioni Studium, 2002), pp. 171-198; Pier Francesco Fumagalli, "Gli insegnamenti di storia del cristianesimo e di storia della chiesa in Cina," in: *ibid.*, pp. 161-167.

[16] Pan Guang, *The Development of Jewish and Israel Studies*, pp. 2-3; Huang Lingyu, *Youtaijiao xue*, pp. 378-379. A detailed list of university courses, research organisations and religious study associations, including Jewish, Christian, Taoist, Tibetan, Muslim and Buddhist, is to be found in Wang Leiquan 王雷泉 – Liu Zhongyu 刘仲宇 – Ge Zhuang 葛壮, *Ershi shiji Zhongguo shehui kexue. Zongjiaoxue juan* 二十世纪中国社会科学—宗教学卷 (Shanghai: Shanghai renmin chubanshe, 2005), pp. 435-458.

动态 (*Israel Trends*) and led to the publication of the series Yisilie Youtai yanjiu 以色列犹太研究 (Israeli and Judaic Studies). Again in 1989, *The China Judaic Studies Association* (Zhongguo Youtai wenhua yanjiuhui 中国犹太文化研究会) was set up, which published *Zhong-You lianluo* 中犹联络 (*China-Judaic Connection*).[17] In 1992 – the year in which diplomatic relations between Israel and The People's Republic of China were established – two more important Judaic Studies Centers were founded, one at the University of Nanjing (Nanjing daxue Youtai wenhua yanjiu zhongxin 南京大学犹太文化研究中心), the other at the Henan University of Zhengzhou (Henan daxue Zhongguo Youtai lishi yanjiu zhongxin 河南大学中国犹太历史研究中心). In 1994 the Institute of Jewish Culture was founded in the University of Shandong at Jinan, which in 2003 became the Center for Judaic and Inter-religious Studies (Youtaijiao yu kuazongjiao yanjiu zhongxin 犹太教与跨宗教研究中心); this was to be very active in the organisation of international seminars and in the publication of journals and monographs, directed by Fu Youde 傅有德.[18]

The "Glazer Center for Jewish Studies," founded and directed by Xu Xin 徐新, which promotes studies on Zionism, reformed Judaism, Hebrew literature, American Judaism and philosophy, is active at the University of Nanjing.

II. Research Scope and Prospects

II.1 Principle Sectors and Types

We can distinguish six principal sectors within which research on Hebrew or Jewish matters are presently being carried out in China: 1. General studies on Jewish culture; 2. the Jews in China, according to an historical perspective or to the history of religions; 3. the modern State of Israel and China: studies on politics, economics, society, the Middle East, international relations, Zionism, antisemitism; 4. the Bible, Archaeology, and Medieval Studies; 5. Jewish Thought: Talmud, Qabbalà, Philosophy, and Religion; 6. Studies on Hebrew and Yiddish literature. In 2009, two seminars on Israeli Studies were held, for the first time in China, at the Universities of Beijing and Shandong: in the same year an international seminar was held at the University of Nanjing on "Education and Holocaust," organised jointly by the Universities of Nanjing and Henan.

As to the different types of publications, Pan Guang identifies four main groups in his bibliographical appendix: 1. Translations; 2. monographs; 3. popular works; 4. dissertations and essays.[19] With regard to the specific subject of the Jews in China, Pan Guang, Wang Shuming 汪舒明 and Luo Ailing 罗爱玲 have presented a special bibliography, subdivided by language (Chinese, English,

---

[17] Huang Lingyu, *Youtaijiao xue*, pp. 378-379.

[18] Cf. Fu Youde 傅有德, *Youtai zhexue shi* 犹太哲学史, 2 vols. (Beijing: Zhongguo Renmin daxue chubanshe, 2008); the Centre published the journal *Youtai yanjiu* 犹太研究 (Jewish Studies).

[19] Pan Guang, *Youtai yanjiu zai Zhongguo* (see above, note 4).

German, French, Hebrew and Japanese) and extended also to newspapers, journals, other publications, archives, and interviews.[20] Of particular note for its systematic diligence is the work by Jonathan Goldstein, with a special bibliography by Frank Joseph Shulman, leaning more towards works in the English language, but also with sources in Chinese and modern Hebrew.[21]

II.2 General Outlook

As far as the general outlook surrounding these studies is concerned, the observations of Zhang Qianhong 张倩红, vice chairman of Zhengzhou University and founder and director of the Jewish Studies Institute of Henan University in Kaifeng, are worthy of note. While emphasising the positive aspects of the progress made in the last decades, she also points out the possible risks of negative prejudice on the part of both the Jews and the Chinese.[22] On the same subject, the scholar Zhou Xun refers to a thesis by Jin Yingzhong 金应忠, the secretary general for the Jewish Studies Association and deputy director of the Israel and Judaism Study Center at the Peace and Development Institute in Shanghai: "China is undergoing a period of reform and opening towards the world: Jewish studies in the Chinese academic community are also flourishing and reaching maturity."[23] Zhou proposes to overcome prejudice and commonplaces which surround the concept of "Chinese Jews," through work that is not only historical but also an accurate sociological and political analysis: she therefore takes up the various images of Jews, Zionists and Imperialists, which have been presented in China starting from Matteo Ricci, up to the *Manyou suilu* 漫遊隨錄 (Diaries) by Wang Tao 王韜 (1879), to the ambiguous esteem of Liang Qichao 梁啟超 for the American Jews, and in contrast, to the contempt to which they were subjected during the period of the May Fourth Movement (1919–1930). She examines the concepts, often contradictory, which Chinese intellectuals had about the Jews

---

[20] Pan Guang 潘光 – Wang Jian 王健, *Youtai yu Zhongguo. Jindai yilai liangge gulao wenming de jiaowang he youyi* 犹太人与中国—近代以来两个古老文明的交往和友谊, (*Jews and China. Contact and Friendship between Two Old Civilizations in Modern Times*), (Beijing: Shishi chubanshe, 2010), pp. 314-333; the same authors had previously collected a vast documentation, including films and exhibitions on the subject of Jews in Shanghai: Pan Guang 潘光 – Wang Jian 王建, *Yige ban shiji lai de Shanghai Youtairen. Youtai minzu shishang de dongfang yi ye* 一个半世纪来的上海犹太人—犹太民族史上的东方一页 (Beijing: Shehui kexue wenxian chubanshe, 2002), pp. 277-292.

[21] Frank Joseph Shulman, "The Chinese Jews and the Jewish Diasporas in China from the Tang Period (A.D. 618–906) through the Mid-1990s," in: Jonathan Goldstein, *The Jews of China. Volume Two, A Sourcebook and Research Guide* (New York – London: Sharpe, 2000), pp. 157-183.

[22] Zhang Qianhong, "Some Thoughts on the Enhancement of the Sino-Judaic Relationship," *Points East* 25 (2010) 1, pp. 1, 6-8; cf. also Jordan Paper, "Chinese Policies Regarding Religion and Chinese Judaism," *Points East* 24 (2009) 1, pp. 1, 6-8.

[23] Zhou Xun, *Chinese Perception of the "Jews" and Judaism. A History of the Youtai* (Richmond: Curzon, 2001), p. 1.

between the two World Wars: on the one hand they were considered a "superior race" (Pan Guangdan), yet on the other victims of racial discrimination (He Ziheng 何子恒) and oppressed as much as the Chinese. Finally she puts much emphasis to the illustration of the various assessments of Zionisim and the Arab-Israeli conflict on the part of Chinese politicians and scholars.

Another recent example of the orientation of Chinese Jewish studies can be glimpsed in the work published by Pan Guang, Wang Shuming and Luo Ailing, which includes essays by numerous authors subdivided into four main themes: 1. The Jews in America; 2. Israel; 3. the Jews in China; 4. Jewish history and culture; some of these essays help to assess the Sino-Jewish relationship, compared to the relationships of America and of Israel *versus* Turkey, India, Iran and the Palestinians.[24]

II.3 Multicultural and Multireligious Aspects

Furthermore, from the moment that Judaism can be taken into consideration also from the point of view of being an ethnic and religious "minority" (*shaoshu minzu*), the case which it represents can imply suggestions and consequences for similar relationships between minorities and majorities,[25] from a religious, cultural and in general social and legal viewpoint, not only in China but also in the West. This outlook stretches in a wider Asian horizon, such as for example in the last chapter of the work by David. G. Goodman and Masanori Miyazawa, on the "Jewish Problem in Japan. Implications in a Multicultural World": the authors examine matters such as xenophobia, anti-Semitism, responsibility for the "massacres of the Chinese population – the "Rape of Nanjing" with a bibliography rich in Japanese and English works.[26]

From the religious point of view, the considerations of Donald McInnis, although not updated, are still valid; they extend the analysis of documents to other religions, including not only Judaism but also Islam, Tibetan Buddhism and the

---

[24] Pan Guang 潘光 – Wang Shuming 王舒明 – Luo Ailing 罗爱玲, *Youtairen zai Meiguo. Yige chenggongqun de fazhan he yingxiang* 犹太人在美国：一个成功群的发展和影响 (*The Jews in America. Development and Influence of a Successful Community*), CJSS Jewish and Israeli Studies Series, IV (Beijing: Shishi chubanshe, 2010); Pan Guang 潘光 – Wang Shuming 王舒明 – Sheng Wenqin 盛文沁, *Nacui da tusha de zhengzhi he wenhua yingxiang* 纳粹大屠杀的政治和文化影响 (*The Political and Cultural Impacts of the Holocaust*), CJSS Jewish and Israeli Studies Series, III (Beijing: Shishi chubanshe, 2009). Cf. also a work to which I did not have direct access, *The Jewish-Chinese Nexus. A Meeting of Civilizations*, ed. Mark Avrum Ehrlich. Routledge Jewish Studies (London: Routledge, 2008).

[25] Cf. Roman Malek, "'Marginal religion'. Remarks on Judaism in the context of the history of Chinese religions, in: Raoul David Findeisen – Gad C. Isay – Amira Katz-Goer – Yuri Pines – Lihi Yariv-Laor (eds.), *At Home in Many Worlds. Reading, Writing and Translating from Chinese and Jewish Cultures. Essays in Honour of Irene Eber*, Veröffentlichungen des Ostasiens-Instituts der Ruhr-Universität Bochum, 56 (Wiesbaden: Harrassowitz, 2009).

[26] David G. Goodman – Masanori Miyazawa, *Jews in the Japanese Mind. The History and Uses of a Cultural Stereotype* (New York *et al.*: The Free Press, 1995).

Russian Orthodox Church.[27] A similar and complementary perspective, but from a Chinese viewpoint more oriented towards Eastern Asia, can be seen in works such as the *History of Religions* by Lou Ninglie, who pays close attention also towards Indian Buddhism, to the areas of Korea, Japan and Vietnam, to Muslims and to other religions.[28] Developments can be foreseen also in the field of comparative religious study between the three monotheistic religions, and between oriental and western cultures and their respective systems of values. In concluding a volume that collects essays by various authors, whilst endeavouring to produce an historical summary attentive at sociological, philosophical, religious, ethnic, political and intercultural levels, Robert Elliot Allinson notes that the prescriptive formulation of the Golden Rule chosen by Hillel and Confucius: "Do not do unto others what you do not want others to do unto you,"[29] expresses the fundamental convergence between Jewish and Confucian ethics. Confucianism and Judaism, from this point of view, constitute in effect a field of common study which seems open to a promising future in China, without forgetting the condition mentioned by He Guanghu 何光沪: "If only scholars and religious and irreligious people have the courage to use their own reason and to act accordingly."[30]

---

[27] Donald MacInnis, *Religion in China Today. Policy and Practice* (New York: Maryknoll, Orbis Book, 1989); id., *Religion im heutigen China. Politik und Praxis* (German edition), ed. Roman Malek, MSMS XXXI (Nettetal: Steyler Verlag, 1993), in particular ch. 30, pp. 490-495.

[28] Lou Ninglie 楼宁烈, *Zhong-Wai zongjiao jiaoliushi* 中外宗教交流史 (*A Chinese-Foreign History of Religious Exchange*), Zhong-Wai wenhua jiaoliushi congshu 中外文化交流史丛书 (Changsha: Hunan jiaoyu chubanshe, 2000), in particular pp. 197-208.

[29] Robert Elliot Allinson, "Six Arguments for the Primacy of the Proscriptive Formulation of the Golden Rule in the Jewish and Chinese Confucian Ethical Traditions," in: Peter Kupfer (ed.), *Youtai. Presence and Perception of Jews and Judaism in China* (Frankfurt am Main: Peter Lang, 2008), pp. 289-307, in particular pp. 305-306.

[30] He Guanghu, "Religious Studies in China 1978–1999 and Their Connection with Political and Social Circumstances," *China Study Journal* 15 (2000) 1, pp. 5-13, in particular p. 13.

Chinese Language and Literature
Chinesische Sprache und Literatur

中國語言與文學

TRANSLATING KING DAVID

IRENE EBER

Translations of the scriptures into Chinese were part of the large scale translation activity at the end of the nineteenth and the first half of the twentieth century. Many major works from world literature appeared in Chinese, especially in the 1920s and 1930s, and Bible translations into classical Chinese were gradually replaced by new versions into spoken Chinese.[1] But translating into modern Chinese was not an unusual phenomenon. Recreating an others' creation is a necessary activity at a time of intellectual and literary ferment which certainly characterized China at that time.

If we accept that translation too is an art form, we must also understand its uniqueness as an interpretive art. As such it is both identical with and different from the original. Indeed, George Steiner reminds us that we, in fact, always translate. "The schematic model of translation is one in which a message from a source-language passes into a receptor-language via a transformative process."[2] It is significant, therefore, that translators participate in the concerns of their own culture, are aware of their readership, social problems, and the like.[3] Clearly, a translation in order to succeed should be audience-oriented and its reception in the new culture is what matters.

Keeping in mind these general considerations, let me now turn to some specific issues that will concern us. There is general agreement among biblical commentators that the narrative about King David in Samuel 1 and 2 is a singular masterpiece. Artistically outstanding,[4] Robert Alter considers the Book of Samuel as presenting the reader with "... the first full-length portrait of a Machiavellian prince in Western literature."[5] Shimon Bar-Efrat has argued that David in Sam 1 and 2 is "... richer than any other figure in the Bible. His portrait ... is described

---

[1] For a history of Bible translations, which culminated in the 1919 *Union Version*, still in use today, see Jost Oliver Zetzsche, *The Bible in China. The History of the* Union Version *or the Culmination of Protestant Missionary Bible Translation in China*, MSMS XLV (Nettetal: Steyler Verlag, 1999).

[2] George Steiner, *After Babel. Aspects of Language and Translation* (London: Oxford University Press, 1975), p. 28.

[3] Irene Eber, *Voices from Afar. Modern Chinese Writers on Oppressed Peoples and Their Literature* (Ann Arbor: The University of Michigan, 1980), pp. xv-xvi. See also Hans Joachim Störig, *Das Problem des Übersetzens* (Stuttgart: Goverts, 1963).

[4] David M. Gunn, "David and the Gift of the Kingdom (2 Sam 2-4, 9-20, 1 Kings 1-2)," *Semeia* 3 (1975), pp. 14-45.

[5] Robert Alter, *The David Story. A Translation with Commentary of 1 and 2 Samuel* (New York – London: W.W. Norton, 1999), p. xviii.

as developing and changing enormously in the course of his life."[6] Since it is generally assumed that in the story of David we confront masterful portraits of this man and others as well as problems of history and human conduct, we must ask next whether the various aspects and nuances can be in fact conveyed in translation. This is a crucial question, especially when the translation is from one culture into another.

Before exploring the translation in some detail, it will be useful to take a brief glance at the story told in the two books of Samuel, where it is presented to the reader from two perspectives: the political and the personal. The political content deals with the end of tribal society, where authority was wielded by judges who ruled. It is the beginning of the era of kings, the unification of the two states, Israel and Judah, and the establishment of Jerusalem as the religious capital and seat of the monarchy. All this takes place during the troubled times of the Philistine threat.

Despite Samuel's vociferous opposition to the establishment of a monarchy,[7] Saul is anointed and becomes the new leader. Soon, however, Saul acts contrary to the Lord's commands and falls out of favor with both Samuel and the Lord.[8] At this point David makes his appearance in the story, becoming at first Saul's musician, as the latter increasingly succumbs to mental anguish, and then the hero who kills Goliath with a slingshot.

While wars with the Philistines continue, the story takes a more personal turn. There is the close friendship between Jonathan, Saul's son, and David,[9] and juxtaposed to this is Saul's growing hostility to David causing the latter to escape being killed by Saul. Finally, both Saul and Jonathan perish in the wars and David becomes king. Under him the kingdom is at last united,[10] Jerusalem becomes the capital of the united and growing kingdom as well as the seat of the royal

---

[6] Shimon Bar-Efrat, "From History to Story: The Development of the Figure of David in Biblical and Post-Biblical Literature," in: Graeme Auld – Erik Eynikel (eds.), *For and Against David. Story and History in the Book of Samuel* (Leuven et al.: Peeters, 2010), p. 49.

[7] Samuel's opposition is expressed in his famous anti-monarchy speech in 1 Samuel 8:10-18, when he describes how a king will exploit the people.

[8] The translation of the growing conflict between Saul and Samuel is discussed in my brief essay, "Samu'er ji shang de liangge Zhongwen yiben," 撒母耳記上的兩個中文譯本 (1 Samuel in two Chinese translations), in: Philip P. Chien (Xie Pinran 謝品然) – Chin Kan-pu (Zeng Qingbao 曾慶豹) (eds.), *Zi Shangdi shuo Hanyu yilai. Heheben Shengjing jiushi nian* 自上帝說漢語以來—《和合本》聖經九十年 (Ever since God Speaks Chinese. The 90th Anniversary of the Union Version Bible) (Hong Kong: Centre for Advanced Biblical Studies, 2010), pp. 91-98.

[9] See Orly Keren, "David and Jonathan. A Case of Unconditional Love?" *Journal of the Old Testament* 37 (2012) 1, pp. 3-23. The author points out that the love between the two men is not mutual, but more of Jonathan's for David. The relationship has, therefore, political implications. Jonathan assumes the role of David's vassal, who is the future king.

[10] That is, Israel and Judah are joined. See Albrecht Alt, "Das Großreich Davids," in: *id., Kleine Schriften zur Geschichte des Volkes Israel* (München: C.H. Beck, 1959), vol. 2, pp. 66-75.

residence. In addition, David establishes orderly dynastic succession in place of the arbitrary emergence of a leader. These successes are, however, accompanied by a troubled family life. There is the Bathsheba affair and David's calculated murder of her husband, Uriah. There is the disgraceful behavior of his sons and the nasty Tamar and Amnon episode (2 Samuel 13:1-14)[11] which leads to Absalom's rebellion, civil war, and Absalom's death. The narrative of Solomon's succession to the kingship and David's death are not told in 2 Samuel but in the subsequent book of Kings (1 Kings 1 and 2-10).

In this article two Bible translations into vernacular Chinese will be examined with regard to the two Books of Samuel, the 1875 translation by S.I.J. Schereschewsky in its 1899 revision and the 1919 *Union Version*.[12] Several reasons determined this choice. Together with consulting previous translations into classical Chinese, Schereschewsky rendered his version from Hebrew.[13] To help the Chinese reader with this text from another culture, the translator included interlinear notes. These warrant a closer look to determine whether they indeed ease the reader's way into the culturally alien text. No question, the *Union Version* is a linguistically updated text, but to what extent can it be said to depend on the earlier work? To attempt even only a preliminary comparison of a tiny portion of the earlier and the later text will be useful in gaining a better understanding of the translating process. Furthermore, translating scriptures often involves more than linguistic competence in the original and receptor language. Several examples cited below will illustrate the problem.

Translation Issues: Saul, David, and Jonathan

Despite Samuel's opposition, God decides to acquiesce to popular demand for a king and Samuel duly anoints Saul *nagid* (1 Samuel 10:1), that is leader (*jun* 君) over his inheritance. Schereschewsky apparently interpreted inheritance as people (*min* 民) and translated accordingly. The *Union Version* translators, on the other hand, considered inheritance as possessions (*chan* 產). A minor difference, but a difference nonetheless.

---

[11] The drama in which Xiang Peiliang 向培良 (1905–1959; other dates: 1901–1961) wrote about the Tamar and Amnon episode is discussed by Marián Gálik, *Influence, Translation, and Parallels. Selected Studies on the Bible in China* (Nettetal: Steyler Verlag, 2004), pp. 237-250. – On Xiang Peiliang, see also the contribution of Marián Gálik in the present volume (pp. 649-664) [Eds.].

[12] For Schereschewsky's translation I used his *Jiuxinyue Shengjing* 舊新約聖經 (Shanghai: British and Foreign Bible Society, 1899) (rev. ed.) and for the Union Version I consulted the *Jiuxinyue quanshu* 舊新約全書 ([Shanghai]: China Bible House, 1939).

[13] As a boy and teenager Schereschewsky had a traditional Jewish education, which would have endowed him not only with a thorough biblical Hebrew background but also with a solid background in traditional Jewish commentary tradition. For his biography, see Irene Eber, *The Jewish Bishop and the Chinese Bible. S.I.J. Schereschewsky (1871–1906)* (Leiden: Brill, 1999), pp. 19-163.

However, the question of people or possessions is less problematic than the translation of *nagid* (leader) as *jun*. In accordance with general usage, the term *jun*, or *junzi* 君子 especially in Confucian tradition, refers to an accomplished person, a Superior Man of outstanding moral character and manifold abilities, who is not always necessarily a ruler. From a Chinese point of view, Saul, even before his mental deterioration sets in, would be hardly considered such a man and a Chinese reader might very well question Samuel's action. When Saul disobeys the Lord he is rejected (1 Samuel 16:1) and Samuel is commanded to anoint one of Jesse's sons. He anoints David, but not as someone specific (1 Samuel 16:13). In this place the *Union Version* uses a similar wording, including *jun*, or Superior Man in the case of Saul.

Still another problem occurs in the same chapter when Samuel promises that the spirit (*ruakh*, 1 Samuel 10:6) of God will come on Saul. Schereschewsky translated the Tetragrammaton generally but not always with *zhu* 主 and for *ruakh* he used *shen* 神. In distinction to Schereschewsky, the *Union Version* translators transliterated the name of the Lord (YHVH: *Yehehua* 耶和華) and translated His spirit with *ling* 靈. Both *shen* and *ling* are accurate renderings here. The Hebrew *ruakh*, however, has various connotations and Schereschewsky paid special attention to the differing nuances of the term in portions of the Bible.

David the Man and the King

As it is generally the case in Chinese traditional fiction, the protagonists are not known by means of authorial description, but from what they do, how they do it, and what they say. A similar literary device is used in the biblical narrative. The reader gets to know the protagonists by means of their actions, how they conduct themselves, and what they say. Saul was mortally wounded in battle with the Amalekites. The Amalekite who delivered the mercy blow to Saul now brings David the king's crown and bracelet. David, overwhelmed by sorrow over Saul and Jonathan's death, says, "your blood is on your head because your own mouth testified against you when you admitted, 'I killed the Lord's anointed.'" (2 Samuel 1:16), that is for telling him that it was he who delivered the deadly blow. To make it perfectly clear who has been killed, Schereschewsky translates the "anointed" with *jun* 君, or Superior Man. However, the blood on the head part is omitted and the Amalekite is told he must die. The omission has not damaged the narrative and David's lament that follows, it can be argued, is clearer as a result. David emerges here as a ruthless but also as a highly emotional man.

In comparison the *Union Version*'s more literal translation continues to use "the anointed" and merely modifies the subsequent clause as the blame being returned to the Amalekite's head. Despite Saul's pursuit of David and his attempts to kill him, David expresses genuine sorrow at the news of Saul's and Jonathan's death. Among many others, it provides an example of how inner feelings are outwardly expressed telling the reader something about what the man is like by means of his actions.

David is often portrayed as a kindly and generous man as, for example, in his relationship with Jonathan's crippled son, to whom he promises to restore all of Saul's lands as well as nourish him at his table. The son humbles himself before David, referring to himself as a dead dog (2 Samuel 9:8). Both the 1899 revised version and the *Union Version* translate this literally, thus highlighting David's generosity.

Where other biblical figures tend to see David's cruelty, David often evades the issue, pointing to the Lord having commanded the person to revile him. Such is the case of the man from Saul's family who curses David, calling him a bloody man (2 Samuel 16:7). This is an unlikely curse in Chinese and seems much stronger and apt as *canren de ren* 殘忍的人 (in Schereschewsky's translation as "brutal man"). The *Union Version* translators, however, apparently preferred the more literal expression *liuren xue de huairen* 流人血的壞人 (blood-spilling bad man).

Yet there are also many portions where both translations agree and where the earlier and later Chinese versions convey an accurate meaning. Such is, for example, the instant when Saul, unable to make contact with the Lord, decides to consult a woman soothsayer (the *ba'alat-ov* of Endor). Saul asks a servant to find him this kind of person (1 Samuel 28:7), despite the fact that he had earlier forbidden such practices. Both Chinese texts here translate clearly *jiaogui de furen* 交鬼的婦人, that is, a woman who communicates with spirits of the dead.

The reader who might also consult the Hebrew version will encounter an interesting question in David's heartbroken lament when informed of Absalom's death. In the Hebrew text (2 Samuel), David's famous cry, "Absalom, my son, my son" occurs in chapter 19:1 and 19:5. In both Chinese translations, however, the lament is divided between chapters 18 and 19. Verse 1 of chapter 19 occurs as chapter 18:33 and verse 5 of chapter 19:4. Schereschewky in this instance obviously followed the chapter division of the Protestant Bible. The question, therefore, is whether he consistently translated the Hebrew text, or whether he was occasionally persuaded perhaps to deviate from the Hebrew by his colleagues in the Peking Translating Committee.[14]

The Lord's Name

In the Hebrew Old Testament three different names are used for God and Schereschewsky with few exceptions adhered to these different usages. Although the Peking Translating Committee had decided to use *tianzhu* 天主 (Lord of Heaven) for their translation of the Tetragrammaton, in the two books of Samuel

---

[14] The work of this committee is discussed in Irene Eber, "The Peking Translating Committee and S.I.J. Schereschewsky's Old Testament," *Anglican and Episcopal History* 67 (1998) 2, pp. 212-226. The committee constituted itself in 1864 with five members. Four were assigned to the New Testament and Schereschewsky was responsible for the Old Testament. They met for regular discussions of their work and proposed revisions. Their working method is described by Henry Blodget, "Occasional Notes," American Board of Commissioners for Foreign Missions, Letters and Papers Addressed to the Board, Houghton Library, Harvard University, vol. 302:I, ms. 181, 6 pp.

Schereschewsky generally used only *zhu* 主 (Lord).¹⁵ Still, in 1 Samuel 1:26-28 for both the Lord (*Adonai*) and the Tetragrammaton he used *zhu*. On the other hand, in 1 Samuel 2:30, "the Lord, God of Israel" is translated with *zhu* as the Lord and *shangdi* 上帝 as the God of Israel. The inconsistency is perpetuated elsewhere, as for example, in 2 Samuel 5:10 where the "Lord, God of Hosts" is translated as *zhu shangdi*, with hosts being entirely omitted, and the Tetragrammaton is transcribed as *Yehehua* 耶和華. In David's long praise song (2 Samuel 22) both the Tetragrammaton and *El* are used. The distinction is carefully preserved in Schereschewsky's translation by using *zhu* for the first and *shangdi* for the second. The same distinction is retained in the *Union Version*.

The Interlinear Notes

The notes are an interesting part of the translation, allowing for glimpses into the translators' ways of thinking – where and in which parts they thought it important to elucidate the text. Or where they believed the reader needed to understand why the text was rendered in the way it was. Schereschewky's translation has more notes than the *Union Version*, thirty notes altogether in 1 and 2 Samuel whereas in the later book are only ten. One reason for the larger number of notes in the first translation is that he frequently explained the meaning of names in the notes. Some examples are 1 Samuel 1:1 where he told the reader that the Hebrew word for Ephraim is *Yifata* 以法他, and it can also be *Yifalian* 以法蓮. In 1 Samuel 4:21, the newborn is named *I-khabod* ("Without honor" [*rong* 榮], that is, having lost honor), or 1 Samuel 23:15, 19, 28 where Schereschewsky clarifies place names.

At times the translator had to choose between translating and transcribing. An example of this is 1 Samuel 7:12. Samuel marks a place with a stone and calls it *Even-ha'ezer*. Schereschewsky chose to transcribe the name in the text, but in a note he explained the meaning. Saul's son, Jonathan, reassures David of his loyalty (1 Samuel 20:12-15), and asks David at the end to continue to show kindness to his house, that is his family. To make this amply clear, a long note is appended to 1 Samuel 20:15 underscoring the family relationship. Sometimes alternative translations are suggested by the notes as in 2 Samuel 8:6 where *fangbing* 防兵 (a defensive army) can be also considered *guanzhang* 官長 (official). After killing Absalom and throwing him into a pit, the people fled to their tents (2 Samuel 18:17). Here the note tells the reader that this implies the people's return to their families.

---

15 Actually *tianzhu* was used in the Catholic Church, whereas Protestants had decided to use *shangdi* 上帝 – Supreme God. Which term to use involved a prolonged controversy. The so-called Term Question is discussed by Irene Eber, "The Interminable Term Question," in: Irene Eber – Sze-kar Wan – Knut Walf – Roman Malek (eds.), *Bible in Modern China. The Literary and Intellectual Impact*, MSMS XLIII (Nettetal: Steyler Verlag, 1999), pp. 135-161.

As mentioned earlier, the *Union Version* contains fewer notes than Schereschewsky's translation. Although none of the notes repeat those of the earlier translation, the *Union Version* translators were concerned with similar issues, alternative wording or elucidation of the text.

Concluding Remarks

No attempt was made in this brief essay to evaluate the quality of one translation or the other. Rather the aim was to demonstrate by means of several examples the extent to which interpretation plays a role in translation. Not only linguistic competence, but a thorough acquaintance with the text to be rendered into another language is mandatory. Schereschewsky said when he wrote in 1890 that literal translation is mistranslation. Faithfulness to the original text is certainly required, but the text must be transposed into an idiomatic style of the target language. Although he did not write it so explicitly, he implied that the translated text must fit into the new cultural context.[16]

Reading the two Books of Samuel about King David more than one hundred years later one cannot but be impressed by the extent to which the translator eased it into another culture. There is the literary attraction of a story about a man who rises from humble beginnings to greatness, a leader of his people. Yet he is not the ideal monarch, a man without human failings. All this is faithfully reproduced in the earlier and later translation. Nonetheless, still another investigation is needed to determine to what extent the *Union Version* relies on the earlier translation of Schereschewsky for revealing the various aspects of the king.

The present discussion has been more concerned with how certain crucial terms and phrases were rendered into the receptor language as a result of interpretation. Equally important in the translating enterprise, however, was also the work and contribution of the Chinese co-workers. It was these men, no doubt, who helped the missionaries appreciate the nuances of such terms as *jun* or *shen*. The different terminology for God used in both translations is intriguing. Is it due to his Jewish background that Schereschewsky seems to have avoided as much as possibly using the Tetragrammaton? Clearly the *Union Version* translators freely used YHVH (*Yehehua* 耶和華). By the time the *Union Version* was under way, of course, a multiplicity of terms had become acceptable.[17]

The Bible is both a literary and a religious text. As such it has been translated many times and into many languages. In China, the translation uniquely coincided with times of great changes in intellectual and political life. How a text is translated and subsequently received is, therefore, a crucial issue related to the time when it takes place. To be sure, much more work must be done to determine

---

[16] S.I.J. Schereschewsky, "Translating the Scriptures into Chinese," *Records of the General Conference of the Protestant Missionaries in China,* 1890 (Shanghai: American Presbyterian Mission Press, 1890), pp. 41-42.

[17] The early history of the problem of which name to use is discussed in my essay, "The Interminable Term Question," in: *Bible in Modern China*, pp. 135-161.

to what extent both Schereschewsky's translation and the *Union Version* had undergone a transformative process in translation. Could a story like that of David evoke a response in the reception culture at either time?

SHANDONG DRUM SONGS OF THE BIBLE

Monika Motsch

It is a great joy for me to make a contribution to a "Festschrift" in honour of Professor Malek's 65th birthday. I have known Father Malek for many years, first as a lively and intelligent student, and later as an eminent scholar and warm-hearted friend.

I met Father Malek in 1976 in the "Seminar für Orientalische Sprachen" of Bonn University where I was teaching at that time. He was only 25 years old, a young, dynamic Polish priest, who had just been ordained. Starting on his Chinese studies, he showed great talent, picking up the Chinese language at an amazing speed. But that did not mean that he was a bookworm who spent all his time studying. Quite the contrary, he possessed great social gifts and had a wide circle of friends. This meant that he sometimes had to skip lessons in order to entertain friends from Poland, from China, and from all over the world. When he went to Fu Jen Catholic University in Taiwan in 1978 to complete his studies, we all missed him. Fortunately, after two years we could welcome him back and admire his progress: He was now able to speak, read and write colloquial and even classical Chinese beautifully.

In later years, after becoming a distinguished scholar and professor, he never lost his youthful liveliness and sense of humour. I remember him telling me that writing his dissertation on Daoist fasting and purification practices[1] always made him so awfully hungry that he had to eat something immediately. He loved to take part in joyous parties, and described with gusto the banquets in his Kashubian native country with its abundant food and drink.

Schoolbooks of the Shandong Mission

Father Malek, working as a professor in Bonn and Münster, as director of the China-Zentrum (China Centre) and of the Monumenta Serica Institute, engaged in a broad range of projects and showed admirable courage and energy in tackling almost "impossible missions." One of these is his ambitious plan to publish a general catalogue of all publications of the Steyl Missionaries (S.V.D.)[2] in China, on which he is currently working. In 2007 he wrote a stimulating article on this subject, an introduction to the educational material published by the S.V.D. Shandong mission, followed by a detailed biographical list.[3] It was this article by Father Malek that inspired me to collect more information on the subject. The Shandong teaching material Father Malek describes in the article covers many

---

[1] Malek, *Das Chai-chieh lu*.

[2] Steyl Missionaries (S.V.D.), i.e., Divine Word Missionaries or Societas Verbi Divini, *Shengyanhui* 圣言会. They were founded in 1875 in Steyl in the Netherlands.

[3] Malek, "Christian Education," pp. 79-155.

subjects: Chinese grammar, Western geography, Latin and Greek, mathematics, philosophy, psychology and even some popular stories with a literary flavour. Attached was a photo of the title page of such a booklet with the intriguing title: "Fei Jinbiao's Drum Songs to the Old Testament (1918)."[4] This title especially awakened my interest. With the help of the staff of the Monumenta Serica Institute, the original and many other similar little booklets were found, and I was allowed to use them for this article.[5] Father Malek generously granted me access to his personal library and let me use an unpublished article on this subject.[6] There must have been many such popular little stories, yet they are now scattered in various places. I myself have seen fifteen of them. They fall into three groups:

Drum Song Stories from the Old Testament
Stories about Roman Martyrs
Children's Books.

Most booklets were published at the beginning of the 20th century between 1915 and 1920 and were printed by the Yanzhou Catholic press of the S.V.D., famous for its wide range of Catholic and scholarly publications.[7]

The stories were helpful for Chinese and for Western readers, since they had a double function: First, they served as schoolbooks for Chinese children, in elementary as well as in middle schools. Following the abolition of the Chinese civil service exams in 1905, there was a great demand for modern, i.e., Western education, including world history, modern science, Western geography, and Western culture and literature. Much educational material of the Shandong mission was written for the German-Chinese school in Taikia (Daijia 戴家) and the college in Tsining (Jining 济宁). Secondly, being written in easy colloquial Chinese, they provided lively teaching material for missionaries who needed to learn the difficult Chinese language. The stories are not only instructive but also very entertaining. The authors use traditional Chinese storytelling modes, like Shandong Drum Songs and Chinese Opera.

In this article I have used a comparative approach, contrasting the Chinese stories with their European sources and showing how Chinese authors and Western priests of the Shandong mission successfully combined elements of their two traditions, found points of contact between Chinese and Western cultures and created interesting and original stories.

---

[4] Illustration 12: Fei Jinbiao's *Shengjiao gushi xiaoshuo guci* 聖教古史小說鼓詞 (1918), in: Malek, "Christian Education," p. 154.

[5] Barbara Hoster (Monumenta Serica, Editorial office) first introduced me to this theme and helped me to find relevant material. My sincere thanks go to her and to the staff of the Monumenta Serica Institute.

[6] This article has been recently published in *Monumenta Serica* 64 (2016) 1, pp. 137-172, see Malek, "The Bible at the Local Level" [Eds.].

[7] Yanzhou Catholic press of the S.V.D. (Yanzhoufu Tianzhutang yinshuju 兗州府天主堂印书局). Yanzhou 兗州, Shandong Province, is nowadays called Jining 济宁. For the history and activities of the printing house see Huppertz, *Katholische Verlagsarbeit in China*.

Eight Drum Songs of the Old Testament[8]

Father Joseph Hesser (1867–1920), director of the Catechist's School of S.V.D. in Yanzhou, had already translated the stories of the Old and New Testament into Chinese prose in the early 1900s.[9] A decade later they were transformed into "Shandong Drum Songs" (*Shandong dagu* 山东大鼓), a traditional form of storytelling with a history of many centuries, which was and still is very popular in Shandong.[10] There are various styles of performance. Usually the storyteller will accompany himself on a drum, but there can also be other instruments and female singers as well. Popular themes are hero stories like *Sanguo yanyi* 三国演义 (The Three Kingdoms) or *Shuihu zhuan* 水浒传 (Water Margin), love stories like *Hongloumeng* 红楼梦 (Dream of the Red Chamber) or *Xixiang ji* 西厢记 (West Chamber), criminal stories like *Baogong an* 包公案 (Judge Bao) and humorous clown stories and satires (*huaji fengci* 滑稽讽刺). The Drum Songs were performed in temples or the market place, the audience being mostly farmers and poor people. But they were also popular among the educated, who admired their literary charm and vigour.

At the beginning of the 20th century the Yanzhou Press published a cycle of eight stories from the Old Testament under the title *Shengjiao gushi xiaoshuo guci* 聖教古史小說鼓詞. The author was Fei Jinbiao 费金标 (dates unknown), a traditional scholar (*xiucai* 秀才) and famous storyteller of the times:

1. *Chuangshi ji* 創世紀 (Genesis)
2. *Chugu ji* 出谷紀 (Exodus), *Huji ji* 戶籍紀 (Numbers), *Shenming pian* 申命篇 (Deuteronomy)
3. *Yuesuwei zhuan* 約穌位傳 (Joshua), *Zhanglao zhuan* 長老傳 (Judges), *Lude zhuan* 盧德傳 (Ruth)
4. *Qianliewang zhuan* 前列王傳 (First book of Kings)
5. *Zhongliewang zhuan* 中列王傳 (Second book of Kings)
6. *Houliewang zhuan* 後列王傳 (Third book of Kings)
7. *Dani'er zhuan* 大尼爾傳 (Daniel), *Ruobo zhuan* 若伯傳 (Job), *Rudide zhuan* 儒第德傳 (Judith), *Duobiya zhuan* 多俾亞傳 (Tobit), *Yuena zhuan* 約納傳 (Jonah)
8. *Aiside zhuan* 愛斯德傳 (Esther), *Aisitela zhuan* 愛斯忒辣傳 (Ezra), *Naheimi zhuan* 納黑彌傳 (Nehemiah), *Majiabo zhuan* 瑪加伯傳 (Maccabees).[11]

---

[8] For all Bible references I have used the *Holy Bible, New International Version* (Anglicised edition).

[9] Father Joseph Hesser (transl.), *Gujing lüeshuo* 古經略說 (Yanzhou 1905). Father Hesser translated Ignaz Schuster's (1838–1869) *Biblische Geschichte des Alten und Neuen Testaments* from German into Chinese. See Malek, "Christian Education," p. 111; Malek, "The Bible at the Local Level," p. 145.

[10] Zheng Zhenduo 郑振铎, *Zhongguo suwenxue shi* 中国俗文学史 (History of China's Popular Literature), vol. 2, chs. 8, 13.

[11] Detailed list in Bibliography A of the present article. See Malek, "Christian Education," pp. 112-113; Malek, "The Bible at the Local Level," pp. 167-168, figs. 3 and 4; Hup-

The stories are translated into colloquial Chinese and adapted to Shandong Drum Songs, with a narrator alternately speaking in prose and singing in rhyme. As is usual in traditional Chinese storytelling, the performer will appeal to his audience in a familiar way, asking listeners for their opinions and comments on the action. Important details will be repeated several times, so that a noisy and fluctuating audience on a market place will be able to catch up with whatever they have missed. The narrator will always inform his listeners about sudden turns in the story, i.e., if he leaves aside one thread of his tale and takes up a new one. At exciting moments he is sure to pause and ask his audience "to wait for the next scene," thus increasing the suspense, while he himself can take a rest and collect some money:

> *The moon rises in the west on the river/ Let us tell again a story of old times*
>
> Dear audience ... guess who is that person?
>
> Telling a story, I have not two mouths. I must leave this, and tell the other.
>
> Let's have a rest and smoke a pipe.
>
> Let me now string the *pipa* and continue the music.
>
> If you want to know how this meeting went, you have to wait for the music in the next scene. [12]

Regularly, jokes and funny scenes are added to enliven the biblical stories. For instance, the prophet Elisha's servant Gehazi appears as a comic figure, creating chaos and making the audience laugh (vol. 6, pp. 34f.)

Often details are added, connecting the old Bible stories with present Shandong life, i.e., a song about a terrible famine:

> (song): *In a year of great famine the troops had encircled the capital / Food in the town was a hundred times more expensive / One donkey's head was worth 80* diao */ Dove's droppings cost 5* diao */ The people could really not keep their existence / People would devour people to keep alive /* [13]

There are many allusions to traditional Chinese culture: For instance the palace of Babylon looks very similar to the court of the Chinese emperor, with palace ladies singing "Ten thousand Years" (*wansui* 万岁) three times and kowtowing in honour of the emperor (vol. 6, p. 96). The audience is told that some biblical events "happened at the time of our Zhou dynasty" (vol. 6, p. 101). There are also many popular proverbs and quotations from the classics.

---

pertz, *Katholische Verlagsarbeit in China*, p. 53. Kang Zhijie 康志杰, "Tianzhujiao yinglian chuyi 天主教楹联刍议," p. 86 (notes 7 and 8).

[12] In the present translation, all songs are printed in italics, prose passages in normal script. 提罢西江月，再把古传明 ("Judith," vol. 7, p. 60). 列位，你说 ... 是谁? (vol. 6, p. 7). 说书没有贰咀。得丢下文头。再说那头 (vol. 8, p. 65). 好歇歇喘喘吸袋烟 (vol. 6, p. 94). 再拧拧琵琶继续红绒 (vol. 6, p. 114). 要说是见面怎么样 / 只得是下回续纶音 (vol. 6, p. 16).

[13] 凶荒年大兵围京城 / 城里的吃物贵百成 / 一驴头值钱八十吊 / 鸽子粪五吊钱一升 / 百姓们实在不能过 / 人吃人好夕顾生命 (vol. 6, p. 49).

While in the Old Testament Israel is punished for worshipping Baal and other wicked gods, in the Chinese text these deities look like devils from Buddhist hells or like monsters in the fantastic archaic geography *Shanhaijing* 山海经 (The Classic of Mountains and Seas):

> (Song): *Some adore Yaksha devils / With red beard, green eyes and red lips / Others worship evil monsters / They believe those with black faces and red hair to be gods / Worship those with pig's snout and vampire's teeth / Or with legs of wild beasts and bird's body / With human head and fish body / With bull's face and horse face horrible / Countless all those statues of wicked gods.*[14]

When Moses is born, the Bible characterizes him as "a fine child" (Exodus 2). Fei Jinbiao, on the other hand, adorns his baby features with the physiognomy of the Chinese future hero: "Square face, big ears. More intelligent than others, has all the talent for great deeds."[15] As a boy Moses gets a model Chinese education: "First classic poetry and history, then essays; having only once skimmed through a text, he already could recite it."[16]

In his "Third Book of Kings," Fei Jinbiao, himself a scholar who passed the exams of the Qing Dynasty, even added a letter in classical Chinese (*wenyan* 文言) with learned allusions, in order to appeal to the more educated members of his audience. While the Bible says only:

> At that time Marduk-Baldan son of Baladan king of Babylon sent Hezekiah letters and a gift, because he had heard of Hezekiah's illness (2 Kings, 20: "Envoys from Babylon").

Fei Jinbiao writes:

> I, Baladan, King of Babylon, have many times visited His Majesty Hezekiah, king of Juda. I have heard that your might shakens the world, and your virtue moves the whole earth. The Barbarians pledge their allegiance. The Golden Crow (the sun) obeys you. The shadow of the sun has gone back ten degrees, thus every day is five hours longer. This is unheard of since thousand antiquities! Your imperial body has suffered from heavy illness, but is now happily healthy and can do without medicine. This gives royal me boundless consolation. I send my congratulations and a small present. I pray that you kindly accept this. With respect I send this.[17]

---

[14] 有的是供着夜叉鬼 / 红胡子绿眼睛红嘴唇 / 有的是供着恶模样 / 那青脸红发也当神 / 那猪嘴獠牙他也供 / 还有那兽蹄是鸟身 / 那人头鱼尾也都有 / 那牛头马面恶狠狠 / 数不尽多少邪神像 (vol. 6, p. 86).

[15] 方面大耳精明过人。将来是个有大能为的材料 (vol. 2, p. 7).

[16] 读过了诗书念文章,真正是过目能成诵 (vol. 2, p. 11).

[17] 巴比隆王柏落大。百拜右达王厄则下陛下。侧闻我王威震人寰。德感地。夷狄归心。金乌顺命。晷影倒退十度。一日转长五时。此千古未闻之事也。且御体沉疴。立占勿药之喜。寡人不胜欣慰。爱肃贺函。并呈薄礼。乞笑纳。诸惟钧鉴 (vol. 6, p. 96). *Jinwu* 金乌 (Golden Crow): In legend it is said that there is a three-legged golden-coloured crow in the sun, so in antiquity people called the sun "golden crow." *Guiying* 晷影 is an instrument, which measures the time of day according to the shadow of the sun (sundial).

It is quite impossible to translate the classic beauty of style and learned allusions into plain English, the letter should really be translated into Latin.

In order to adapt the Bible text to Chinese customs, Fei Jinbiao sometimes feels free to change the content of the stories a bit. For instance, the biblical story of "Ruth" describes how Ruth, having lost her husband while still very young, decides to stay with her mother-in-law, which is in accordance with the Confucian ethical code. On the other hand Ruth, on the advice of her mother-in-law, finds herself a second husband, which is certainly not the way that a chaste Chinese widow should behave. Fei Jinbiao first quotes a popular Chinese proverb criticizing this act:

A good horse does not carry two saddles /
How can this good woman marry two men?[18]

Then the narrator explains that Ruth values most the Confucian virtues of "chastity and filial piety" (*jiexiao* 节孝), that she married not for lust but in order to give birth to a son, whose offspring will be the famous king David. The scene in which Ruth lies down at night at the feet of her future husband on the threshing floor is discreetly left out.

Fei Jinbiao is fond of making jokes and sometimes engages in mock learned discussions. According to him there are, compared to the Bible, many wrong traditions about the beginning of the world: In China the first men were created from mud as in the Bible, but the historians forgot to mention the names of Adam and Eve, a big mistake. In Chinese history there is also a Great Flood, but the waters were regulated by the Chinese emperor, the Great Yu (Da Yu 大禹), thus Noah and his family of eight on the Ark were not mentioned, another big mistake. But, so Fei Jinbiao argues, the Chinese at least preserved the character *chuan* 船 (ship). He first criticizes the scholars of the Ming dynasty for their incorrect analysis of this character and then gives his "correct" interpretation: *chuan* 船 "ship," when split into its three parts "boat," "eight," "mouth" is proof that in antiquity the Chinese already knew about Noah and the Great Flood – long before Christian missionaries told them about it:

船 *chuan* (ship)

舟 *zhou* (boat) — 八 *ba* (eight) — 口 kou (mouth or person)

"Noah on his Ark with his family of eight" (vol. 1, p. 20)[19]

---

[18] 好马还不背双鞍鞯 / 这好女怎么嫁二夫男? (vol. 3, p. 95).

[19] This traditional method of fortune telling by dissecting Chinese characters called glyphomancy was already employed by a group of Jesuit missionaries, the so-called Figurists, in the 18th c. to prove that biblical events can be traced in ancient Chinese texts. See *HCC* 1, p. 675 [Eds.].

The Shandong Opera *Hongshui mieshi* (The Great Flood)

Hongshui mieshi juben 洪水滅世劇本. *The Great Flood*. Opera. Written by Fei Jinbiao (Yanzhou 1921).

Fei Jinbiao made the story of Noah into a veritable Chinese opera. The work must have been very well received, since it soon went into a second edition (see Figure 1). As the Yanzhou Press announced:

> The author is Fei Jinbiao. He adapted "The Great Flood" of the *Old Testament* to the style of a Chinese opera, describing feelings and scenes which captivate the heart of the reader.[20]

Fei Jinbiao certainly can captivate the hearts of his audience – his opera is full of suspense. The basic facts are the same as in Genesis 6-9: Noah was a good man, and so were his three sons and family. But since the people of the world were wicked, God decided to destroy them all except Noah. God told Noah to build the Ark, thus saving him, his family and all the animals.

In the Chinese version, every scene starts in the traditional opera style with a short poem foreshadowing and summing up the main content. The actors first introduce themselves, alternately singing in rhyme and speaking in prose. First Noah appears, informing the audience about all his ancestors, longing for the peaceful old times of Adam and lamenting about the present wickedness of the world. After Noah has left the stage, the "Angel" appears (for the Chinese text, see Figure 3):

> I am the Angel telling you that God will reward the good and punish the wicked. God has made Heaven and Earth for the use of men. He commands men to cultivate virtue and do good deeds, so that after their death they can go to Heaven and enjoy happiness as rightful sons of God ... God has ordered me (*an* 俺) to appear to Noah in a dream and save him and his family of eight ... God will destroy everything with a Great Flood. That is such a pity![21]

In Chinese folklore, we find an abundance of gods, fairies, ghosts, devils, animal, and flower spirits – but no angels. For a Chinese rural audience of that time the Christian God and his angels were something new and had to be explained in more detail. The Chinese Angel in Fei Jinbiao's opera speaks to his audience in a relaxed familiar way, using Shandong dialect, often saying *an* 俺 ("I") instead of *wo* 我. The Angel – like the Buddhist Goddess of Mercy Guanyin Pusa 观音菩萨 – is full of pity for the people of the world who are going to perish in the Great Flood. When the Angel tells his audience that God commands men "to cultivate virtue and do good deeds" (*xiude ligong* 修德立功), this not only sounds Christian but also has a Buddhist flavour. Before leaving, the Angel sings in poetic verse: "*Having told you this, I will now fly up to Heaven.*" And then in

---

[20] 此书系费金标，将古经灭世纪，按戏剧体裁，描情画景，读之令人心惊。

[21] 我乃天上天神。告明天主赏善罚恶。天主造了天地万物为人享用。命人在世修德立功。死后升天享福。当作天主义子 ... 天主命俺。托给诺厄一梦。救他一家八口不死 ... 天主要用洪水灭绝。真可惜呀 (p. 2).

colloquial prose: "Noah, Noah, do not believe that this dream will not come true!"[22]

Realistic details make the story livelier and closer to Shandong life: For instance, there is a scene in which Noah's son Shem tries to hire a carpenter to build the Ark, and haggles about the money:

Carpenter sings: *If you want me make an ark, the price is one hundred sixty, if less, I won't do it!*

Shem sings: *I will give you exactly 100 copper coins / In bad weather and rain the same.*

Another man comes in admonishing them: *The government price is one hundred and twenty / You two should be fair and don't quarrel!*

Shem sings: *Well, well, well, you come with me / Let us select some wood in the mountains.*[23]

There is much fun and comedy, when Noah tries in vain to admonish the wicked people of the world. While good Noah sings in majestic rhymes, the unrepentant people make fun of him in colloquial prose, with disrespectful jokes and plays on words:

People speak: This old guy really becomes more peculiar the older he gets. Who can ever drown the world?

Noah sings: *Last night I had a dream*

People speak: I knew that it was a dream!

Noah sings: *This dream was really nightmarish*

People speak: True, you certainly had a nightmare!

Noah sings: *A Great Flood* (hongshui) *will cover the whole earth*

People speak: Don't bother about green floods or red floods *(hongshui)*, the more water we get the better![24]

The last passage is a pun, *hongshui* meaning "Great Flood" (洪水) as well as "red flood" (红水).

There follows a bloodcurdling attempted murder scene, recalling the famous Shandong robbers of the *Shuihu zhuan*: A man persecutes and threatens another with a knife, claiming that this scoundrel rapes virtuous girls and women. When Noah tries to admonish the knife bearer, this man gets furious and turns against Noah himself, singing: *"You try this knife – see whether it's sharp or not / I'll*

---

[22] 唱:说此话我就要升天而去 / 白: 诺厄呀，诺厄，切莫要当梦中是些虚言 (p. 3).

[23] 木工唱：你要造船是一百六 / 价钱少了俺不行 / 生唱：铜钱给你一百整 / 阴天下雨一般同 / 出来一人劝着唱：官价原是一百二 / 两家公道不必争 / 生唱：是是是来随我去 / 拣选材料到山中 (p. 5).

[24] 众人说：这个老头子越老越古怪。你还能灭这个世界不成。唱：昨夜里三更天我偶作一个梦。众人说：我知道你是做梦咧。唱：这一梦做的那真是不强。众人说：不错。你做的梦不强是就啦。唱：普世上下大雨洪水落地. 众人说：别管绿水红水。下的越大越好。如今天旱的很了。不下大雨还不行咧？(pp. 5f.).

raise my weapon and crack your head!"[25] Happily, the Angel appears and covers the world in darkness so that the murderer can see nothing and Noah escapes at the very last moment.

After Noah and his family have entered the Ark and no rain comes for seven days, the Angel reassures the audience (Angel sings):

> *Our Lord is just sitting on the colourful rainbow / Making calculations that the day for the Great Flood has come*[26]

The Great Flood is described with vivid images, showing how the water, step by step, rises from the ground up to the sky:

> (Angel sings): ... *Just see how the people on the ground are all drowned / Those who climbed trees are now rolling like dragons in the waves / Those who climbed the summits could first save their life / But later the flood killed all of them / This rain fell forty days / Forty days and forty nights, incessantly / Not only the ground flooded / Even the high mountains were all covered / Ants wanting to go into their holes found them full of water / Winged birds could reach no sky ...*[27]

When the water finally recedes and the bird comes back to the Ark with a green branch, Noah is full of joy, which breaks out in spontaneous exclamations of happiness: "Hooray! Lord, oh my Lord, I really must praise you!"[28]

The Chinese opera *The Great Flood* adapted the biblical text to the level of Shandong farmers, most of whom could probably not read or write. But since their childhood they had often listened breathlessly to the traditional stories of Old China, which the storytellers would recite to drum music in front of temples and in market places. Here the Chinese "translator" – or perhaps we should say "author" – Fei Jinbiao combined this tradition with the Bible text, writing in a lively and colourful style, full of fun and laughter, tragedy and compassion.

Yet we should also admire the Western priests of the Shandong mission for their tolerance. Fei Jinbiao was taking great liberties with the Holy Bible, adding elements that could be criticized as irreverent, too Chinese, too funny or even unchristian.[29] Yet the Catholic priests of the Shandong mission saw no problem here. Both Father Peter Röser (in 1916) and Bishop Augustin Henninghaus (in 1921), leading Divine Word missionaries in Shandong, gave their permission, written in Latin, to print *The Great Flood* (see Figure 2):

---

[25] 凶人唱：你试试这把刀快呀不快 / 举钢刀要劈开你的天门 (p. 8).

[26] 我的主正坐在五彩云霄 / 算一算灭世界日期到了 (p. 14).

[27] 天神唱：有天主罚世界显了全能 / 下大雨只下的普世皆平 / 只见那地上的人都淹死 / 上树的也如同水里滚龙 / 上山的爬岭的先也有命 / 到后来一个个水把命倾 / 这场雨只下了四十天整 / 四十天四十夜没有少停 / 不必论平地里水有多大 / 就让那高山上水也皆蒙 / 是蚂蚁要入地穴中有水 / 是飞禽有翅膀也难腾空 / 这一次灭世界作表记 / 到后来再有人也许惊醒 (p. 14f.)。

[28] 白：哈哈哈哈！天主呀。天主。真是可赞美的了！(p. 16).

[29] Kang Zhijie mentions that in Southern China religious couplets were banned, if they did not conform strictly to the Catholic faith (*id.*, "Tianzhujiao yinglian," p. 86).

Nihil obstat. Yenchowfu, die 17. m. Januarii 1916. P. Roeser. Reimprimatur, Yenchowfu, die 2. Sept. 1921. † A. Henninghaus.

As Father Malek has pointed out, the theatre was considered to be dangerous for Christians and was therefore not used for evangelisation for a long time, except in Shandong:

> It is all the more interesting, then, that the Divine Word Missionaries used this medium at the beginning of the 20th century in their work. They broke new ground with this initiative, at least in China, and at the local level, at that. [30]

As it worked out, the little stories were a very successful Chinese-Western cooperation, creating rather enjoyable reading.

We might well ask why Fei Jinbiao added the "Angel" and gave him such a leading role in his opera. No angel appears in the Bible text, and there are no angels in Chinese folklore. I suggest that Fei Jinbiao did this for artistic reasons: The Christian God was high and almighty and not easy to impersonate on the stage. Instead, the Angel, who is much more human and close to the audience, takes His part. Besides, the Angel is sometimes very good fun, because he is charmingly naive, for instance, when he tells the audience that God is sitting on his rainbow doing his calculations. Fei Jinbiao with his classical education was certainly not naive himself, but his Angel is. However that may be, the Angel is certainly an interesting addition to the Chinese opera "The Great Flood."

Roman Martyrs' Stories

The Shandong mission published quite a few stories about Christian martyrs, among them even a Latin-Chinese edition *Acta Sanctorum Martyrum*.[31] Many stories were adapted from Jesuit sources. For Shandong missionaries at the beginning of the 20th century, the old theme was again of topical interest, because of their own suffering during the Boxer Rebellion.

1. *Zhiming xiaozhuan guci* 致命小傳鼓詞 **(Drum Songs about Martyrs). 2 volumes (Yanzhou 1915)**

On the cover of the little booklet there is no name of a writer or translator. Luckily, an advertisement by the Yanzhou Press (see Figure 4) helped me to find the names of both the author of the English source of the story and the Chinese translator:

> This is a famous novel of Cardinal Wiseman. It was translated and adapted to Drum Song by Mr. Fei Jinbiao, in two volumes. The price is 15 cents.[32]

---

[30] Malek, "The Bible at the Local Level," p. 155.
[31] Malek, "Christian Education," p. 108.
[32] 乃枢机主教 Wiseman 所作著名小说，经费金标先生用鼓词体裁译出，分两册共二四四页，定价一角五. Advertisement in Svensson, *Icelandic Boys Meeting Danger* (see Bibliography A).

Nicholas Wiseman (1802–1865) was an Irishman, who was educated in Rome, became archbishop of Westminster and Cardinal in Rome. In his leisure time he wrote a historical romance, *Fabiola. A Tale of the Church of the Catacombs* (1854; see Figure 5), which became immensely popular. It was translated into many European languages, made into two films and has just been reprinted.[33] It was this novel which was made into a Shandong Drum Song by Fei Jinbiao.

Fabiola is set in ancient Rome before and after the victory of Constantine. Some characters of the book are based on biographies of Christian Saints such as St. Agnes, St. Sebastian, and St. Pancratius, while others, like the main character Fabiola, are fictitious. Fabiola is a beautiful but spoilt young lady from an aristocratic Roman family, who later reforms and becomes a Christian.

In his version (for the Chinese cover, see Figure 6), Fei Jinbiao has left out a great number of historical chapters, in which Wiseman describes the antique Roman theatres and baths, the development of the "Church of the Catacombs," gives graphic plans of the underground graves etc. Fei Jinbiao also ignores the many learned Latin and Greek references to the "Acts of Martyrs" (*Acta Sanctorum Martyrum*) and other historical material.

But all of the highlights are kept, following one another in much more rapid succession than in the original: The Chinese audience is introduced to daring heroes, wily fortune hunters, devilish poisoners, arrogant young ladies and saintly Christian slave girls. Religious devotion and sacrifice contrast with the perennial greed for sex and money. Like a film camera, the story moves quickly between different places, different people and different threads of action: The narrator tells us about the splendours of Rome, takes us into the labyrinth of the catacombs, shows how the martyrs were tortured and sent to fight with wild animals, describing saints and villains, and showing us visions of Heaven and Hell.

Fei Jinbiao often builds bridges between China and the West. Just like the Jesuits many years before him, he sets the Christian God and Confucius side by side, as in this poem:

> *The great Christian God is the principle of Truth / Confucius declared, if he heard in the morning about the True Way, he would gladly die in the evening / Being suddenly enlightened about the Right Way / And not wavering till death, that is a True Man.*[34]

On the other hand, the typical Chinese ideal of the "filial son" (*xiaozi* 孝子)[35] is dramatized in quite a different way from the original. In *Fabiola* two Christian boys are in prison awaiting execution. Parents and friends implore them to save

---

[33] Nicholas Patrick Wiseman, *Fabiola. Or the Church of the Catacombs* (London 1854), Classic Reprint Series, published by Forgotten Books, Great Britain 2012.

[34] 诗曰： 皇皇天主道理真 / 朝闻夕死孔子云 / 豁然贯通识正路 / 至死不变成好人, vol. 5, p. 23. Quote from *Lunyu* 论语, "Liren" 里仁: 朝闻道，夕死可矣. A still better quote in the martyr context would be *Lunyu*, "Weilinggong," 卫灵公: 杀身成仁 ("To die for humanity").

[35] For attempts to interpret Confucian teachings and "filial piety" in the light of the Bible see Malek, "The Bible at the Local Level," p. 157.

their lives by apostasy, and they seem to waver. The Christian officer, the holy Sebastian, rushes into their prison "like an angel of light," rebuking them sternly with the Bible words: "He that loveth father or mother more than Me, is not worthy of Me." The two boys "hung their heads and wept in humble confession of their weakness" and quickly resolve not to renounce their faith.[36]

Fei Jinbiao describes a much more heartrending scene:

> (The father Tang Guilin speaks to Sebastian): "Save the life of my sons! See the tears of their mother and my earnest exhortations. I have exerted all my strength, till my sons finally wanted to reform. But with your intimidation and deception you send them again to death! You let them forsake father and mother and become unfilial sons (*buxiao zhi zi* 不孝之子)! What kind of sense does this make? Besides, all others urge them to live, you alone want them to die! This is not only unreasonable, it is a crime against all human feelings (*dafan renqing* 大反人情)!"[37]

Even the Christian general, the saintly Sebastian, agrees that it is the duty of every filial son to be obedient to his parents. Only much later does he add that an even better way to serve one's parents would be to persuade them to become Christians and enjoy eternal happiness together. In the Chinese version the conflict is not between black and white, right and wrong – there is understanding for both sides.

The story of the great villain Fulvius (Fu Feisi 傅斐斯), a spy and unscrupulous fortune hunter who has sent many Christians to their death, is also treated differently than in the original. After the victory of Constantine, he has lost everything and desperately breaks into the house of young, rich and beautiful Miss Fa Bila 法壁辣 (Fabiola) extorting money from her and threatening her with death: "… this is my day of Nemesis. Now die!" (Wiseman, *Fabiola*, p. 426).

Fei Jinbiao's villain, like the wild Shandong robbers of the Liangshan marshes, not only wants to kill but also to rape Miss Fa:

> (Fu Feisi sings) *"To heaven I have no way/ To earth I have no door/ You even want to drive me away quickly/ Where should I go for shelter …*
>
> (prose) "Do not tell me to go away, even you will not be able to go." Saying this, he threw Miss Fa on the bed …[38]

At the end of the story, after twenty years, a "stranger from the east" appears who turns out to be none other than the villain Fu Feisi/Fulvius. In *Fabiola* this is not so very surprising, since the Christian reader is often reminded that the Shep-

---

[36] Wiseman, *Fabiola*, pp. 73ff.

[37] (父亲唐桂林说) ... 来救俺那儿的活命。还有他娘的眼泪。我的苦口。费了多些功夫。俺那儿才说有了回心转意。叫你这一番吓诈。又把俺儿送到死地去了。叫俺儿舍了爹娘。成个不孝之子这算什么道理呢。况且人都劝他活。你偏劝他死。别说与理不合。也算大反人情了 (vol. 5, p. 25).

[38] (傅斐斯) ... / 你叫我升天没有路 / 你叫我入地没有门 / 你还要快快捻我走 / 你叫我哪里去存身。... 别说我不走。连你也走不了。一面说着。一面用手把法小姐推倒床上了 (vol. 5, p. 42).

herd will bring back the lost sheep and that a loving God can pardon all sinners. In the Chinese version this comes as a real surprise. Fei Jinbiao keeps the reader in suspense about the identity of the "stranger from the east" to the very last, thus making the story much more dramatic.

Sure of his talents as an artist, Fei Jinbiao often takes liberties with his text and looks down on pedantic realism. An example is the description of Maximian (Marcus Aurelius Valerius Maximianus, ca. 240–310), the barbarian West King of Rome. In *Fabiola* he is characterised thus:

> Gigantic in frame ... with eyes restlessly rolling in a compound expression of suspicion, profligacy, and ferocity, this almost last of Rome's tyrants struck terror into the heart of any beholder, except a Christian. Is it wonderful that he hated the race and its name?[39]

This is certainly frightening, yet without transgressing the bounds of reality. Not so Fei Jinbiao who indulges freely in fantasy, scoffing at all would-be critics:

> *(sings) This West King had a depraved heart / And looked horrible/ People would be frightened to death / He was actually a giant measuring one* zhang *and twenty /* [about three metres twenty]
>
> (speaks) Dear audience, you will ask me, was he really so huge? I tell you, I am talking about Chinese *chi*, in the West they are *mida* (metre) – to make absolutely sure, you should really check yourselves. But don't be so pedantic and listen again:
>
> *His shoulders were broad three* chi *and three tenth*
>
> There you go again and say, "three inches" are enough, why add "three tenth"? Let me tell you, there are fat ones and skinny ones, the fat ones are three inches three tenth. As a narrator and singer I do not care for such narrow-minded pettiness ...
>
> *His pig's snout and vampire's teeth were not like those of men / His steely protruding eyes spit fire ...*[40]

Cardinal Wiseman wanted to write the history of the first Christians, of the "Church of the Catacombs." Therefore in *Fabiola* the historical element plays a central role. In Fei Jinbiao's version, history gives way to artistic aims, i.e., to entertain by a thrilling story.

---

[39] Wiseman, *Fabiola*, p. 212.

[40] 他坐在西京是狠心 / 生就的面貌凶恶样 / 说起来真是吓死人 / 果然是身高一丈二 /
列位，您说真这么高么。我说这是论的中国尺子。要说西国是论米达。您到那里量量才算准。这不过是说他身量很大就是了。杠要少抬。慢慢的往下听罢。
那膀宽三尺零三分 / 这又是抬杠。敢说。 人家都说膀宽三尺。你怎么说三尺零三分呢。叫我说呀。人有瘦的时候。也有胖的时候呢。光胖这三分么。说书唱戏。不兴抬杠的。慢慢往下听罢。那猪嘴獠牙不像人 / 明煌煌一对钢铃眼 / .... (vol. 5, p. 44).

2. *Kuming darong* 苦命大榮 (From Misery to Glory). By Luo *siduo* 羅司鐸 (Father Luo; Yanzhou 1916)

As author only the name Luo *siduo* 罗司铎 (Father Luo) was given, which is the Chinese name of Father Peter Röser, S.V.D. (Chinese name: Luo Sai 罗赛, 1862–1944). By luck I found a slip of paper in German stuck on the cover of the booklet indicating that the author was R.D.A. de Waal.[41] This helped me to find the German source of the story, *Valeria oder der Triumphzug aus den Katakomben* (Valeria or the Triumphal Procession out of the Catacombs; Regensburg 1884), by Anton de Waal (see Figure 7).

Monsignor Anton de Waal (1837–1917) was a German priest and Church historian, who spent most of his life in Rome. He carried out archaeological excavations in the catacombs and established the Collegio Teutonico del Campo Santo in the Vatican. His novel treats the same theme as Cardinal Wiseman's *Fabiola*, again using the Roman persecutions of Christians followed by the conquest of Rome and the victory of Emperor Constantine in the year 337 as the historical background. The story centres on a noble Roman family: The father, Rufinus, is Lord Mayor of Rome and believes in the old Roman gods. Both the mother, Sophronia, and the daughter Valeria are secretly Christians. At the beginning of the story, Sophronia, in order to avoid being raped by the depraved Roman emperor Maxentius (Marcus Aurelius Valerius Maxentius, 278–312), takes her own life. Later her husband and their daughter Valeria are sent to prison and threatened with a cruel death, but are saved in the end by Emperor Constantine. Like *Fabiola* the story includes many learned historical annotations about ancient Rome and the catacombs. Yet the style of the narration is very different, i.e., rather full of an exalted Christian fervour and pathos. Nowadays the story cannot be read for literary enjoyment, but rather as a historical document giving information about the spirit of the times.

Although the Chinese version (see Figure 8) names only Father Röser as translator, he certainly had a Chinese native speaker at his side whose name we do not know. At the beginning there is a reproduction of a dark and gruesome picture showing Christians burying their martyrs in Rome's catacombs. As in the Chinese *Fabiola*, all learned references and descriptions of ancient Rome are left out. The style is more moderate, lacking the Christian pathos of the original.

There are some variations in view of the different cultural backgrounds of the readers. One example is the controversial theme of suicide. In our story the Christian lady Sophronia (Soufouniya 叟否尼亞) kills herself, in order not to be raped. This was praiseworthy in Rome as the case of Lucretia shows, yet for Christians it was a mortal sin. In his foreword to the third edition of 1896 de Waal mentions that he got many complaints about this "unchristian" suicide and therefore made some modifications – for example, adding a note quoting St.

---

[41] The slip reads: "Khu min da jung. Erzählung aus dem 4. Jht. v. R.D.A. de Waal, übersetzt v. P. Roeser."

Augustine's *De Civitate Dei* who generally condemned suicide but made some exceptions.[42]

For most Chinese readers suicide under such circumstances was praiseworthy. As was the case in ancient Rome there are also many stories about suicides of chaste Chinese women. Thus, Sophronia writes a letter to her husband justifying her deed as God's will: If she was raped, she would be ashamed to look her husband in the face or to look into God's holy face. In her heart she has heard a voice: It is God's will that you free yourself from this villain. At this point the Christian narrator comments: Since Sophronia was unaware that the Christian religion forbade suicide she did not commit a sin (pp. 9f.). Though this may sound a bit like sophistry, yet the translators found a way not to condemn the Roman lady to hell.

Sometimes different Chinese and Western images and values are successfully blended. An interesting example is a strange miraculous scene in the Mamertine dungeon, when Valeria baptizes her father and in a religious rapture (Verzückung) suddenly sees her mother Sophronia in heaven:

> Soon, Valeria with divine eye (*shenmu* 神目) saw men and women in paradise, among them her mother, who asked her and her father to come to Heaven. But in between was a deep abyss with an enormous dragon who opened his mouth wide to devour them. Valeria spoke like in a dream (*rutong mengli* 如同梦里), her father could hear her, when she said suddenly: "Dada, don't be afraid. If you stamp your foot on the dragon's head and trust Jesus' holy name, he will not hurt you. Let us pass quickly, my mother is waiting for us. The misery is temporary, happiness will be eternal."[43]

In Europe expressions like "spiritual eye" (in German "geistiges Auge") mean seeing things beyond reality. On the other hand, the Chinese *shenmu* (divine eye) alludes to the magic "third eye" (*disan zhi yanjing* 第三只眼睛) on the forehead of the god Erlang (Erlangshen 二郎神), which enabled him to see invisible things. Even though the Chinese and Western images evoke different associations, the visionary experiences are very much alike. Talking in a trance, crossing an abyss or stamping on a dangerous dragon's head are also dreamlike experiences not difficult to understand either for Europeans or for Chinese.

Children's Stories

Western missionaries in China founded many schools, for primary as well as for higher education. In Shandong, a most active organizer was the Divine Word Bishop Johann Baptist Anzer (1851–1903), who with the help of the Chinese and

---

[42] *Valeria*, p. IX (Foreword to the third edition), p. 44, p. 46 (note 5).

[43] 不久，瓦肋利亚神目见了天堂上的圣人圣女。其中也有他的母亲。请他同他父亲升天。到底有个深渊隔着。也有个大龙张口伸舌要吞他们。瓦肋利亚如同梦里说话一样叫他父亲都听见。忽然他说。大大你别害怕。使脚跐大龙的头。赖耶稣的圣名他不能害你。咱们快快的过去罢。我的母亲等候我们。苦是暂苦。福是总福 (p. 32). De Waal, *Valeria*, pp. 143f.

German governments, opened the first Chinese-German school in 1902 in Jining.[44] His successor, Bishop Augustin Henninghaus (1862–1939), asked Father Georg Maria Stenz (1869–1928) to become director, first of the school in Daijia (1904–1909) and afterwards of the Chinese-German College in Jining (1909–1927).[45] Stenz was a lively and successful writer, who published widely about his life in China and about Chinese culture.[46]

1. *Xiaozi zhuan* 孝子傳 **(The Filial Son).** *Collectio narrationum* **P. G.M. Stenz S.V.D. Published by Jining Western-Chinese Middle School (Yanzhou 1920)**

The story is about a young Indian prince, who – despite the strong resistance of his father – finally succeeds in being baptized and becoming a Christian (for the book cover, see Figure 9). Since his father is a devout Brahmanin, the son faces the typically Chinese dilemma of filial piety vs. Christian faith: Should he be obedient to his father and follow Brahmanism? Or should he rebel and follow the Christian God? The Catholic priest advises the son to be patient and tolerant, using his "divine eye" (*shenmu*) and praying constantly. Thus, the Christian baptism of the prince first takes place only spiritually, i.e., in a dream. When the son is imprisoned by his angry father, the narrator asks the readers:

> Dear believers, think about it. Is it possible that God will desert such a devout filial son? One evening, God showed himself before Xidi'ang (the son) in a dream. In his dream he saw the priest Ao, who stood smiling before his bed, holding a crucifix and saying to him: Xidi'ang, you can now follow Jesus and carry the cross of the world. God loves you and fulfills your prayer. Come, I will baptize you, so that later you can go to heaven and enjoy eternal happiness. Xidi'ang was so overjoyed that he could not speak … Only when he awoke, he realized that it was a dream.[47]

The end is similar to a famous scene in the *Shuihu zhuan*. The father is captured by robbers and about to be hanged on a tree, but just as the rope is already around his father's neck, the filial son hurries to his side, heroically sacrificing himself in order to save his father's life. The son goes to Heaven, moving the father so deeply that he converts to the Christian faith as well.

---

[44] For Catholic western schools see Rivinius, *Johann Baptist Anzer*, chap. 15, pp. 725-761.

[45] Puhl, *Georg M. Stenz SVD*, pp. 85-128.

[46] Among other works: *Reise-Erinnerungen eines Missionars, Ins Reich des Drachen unter dem Banner des Kreuzes, In der Heimat des Konfuzius, Beiträge zur Volkskunde Süd-Schantungs* (see Bibliography B).

[47] 众位教友。你想想。天主能舍了有信德的孝子么。有一晚上。天主发现给西地盎（儿子）。他做了南柯一梦。梦见奥神父。笑嘻嘻的。站在床前手拿苦像。对他说。西地盎你能效法耶稣表样。背你世俗的十字架。天主爱怜你。允了你的祈求。你来罢。我给你领洗。叫你将来升天国。享无穷的福乐。西地盎喜出望外。乐不可言 … 西地盎醒了。才知是南柯一梦 (*Xiaozi zhuan*, pp. 40f.).

2. *Heitaizi* 黑太子 *(The Black Prince). Collectio narrationum* P. G.M. Stenz S.V.D. Published by Jining Western-Chinese Middle School (Yanzhou 1920)

Heitaizi also takes place in India and treats a similar theme (for the book cover, see Figure 10). Again the story centres round the father-son relationship. Since the prince becomes very attached to a Catholic priest, his Brahamin father allows him to go to a Christian school, but he must swear never to be baptized. The school life described in the story seems to be an idealized picture of life in the Chinese-German School in Shandong, where Father Stenz was director. Again, dramatic elements from the traditional Chinese adventure story are introduced. This time the help comes, surprisingly, from the British army. When the Catholic priest is captured and tortured, the British army marches in like a *deus ex machina*. The priest, instead of becoming a martyr, is saved from his tormentors. He generously forgives them and when even the English Queen sends a reprieve, the criminals are spared the death penalty.

This is a rather interesting mixture of fiction and truth. In reality, such incidents with missionaries were often unscrupulously used by the foreign powers to extort huge compensations from China. [48]

3. *Yisilan tongzi yuxianji* 伊斯蘭童子遇險記 (Iceland Boys Meeting Danger). Yanzhou 1931

The Yanzhou Catholic Printing House published quite a few children's stories, which were very much in demand, since there were practically no such books in traditional China at that time. At a very early age the children would start to memorize classical texts like Tang poems and the Confucian classics in order to pass exams and become officials later. There were of course interesting novels like *Xiyouji* 西游记 (Journey to the West) or *Sanguo yanyi*, but for these a fairly good command of Chinese characters was needed. And as for the many stories about love and adventure – they were thought unsuitable for children and therefore generally forbidden.

On the cover of *Yisilan tongzi yuxianji* no author is named. Yet there is a preface by Liu Baohua 刘保华, who introduces himself as translator. Liu tells his little readers about the strange and beautiful country called Iceland, and especially emphasises the fact that he has translated this tale not into classical Chinese (*wenyan* 文言), but into colloquial language (*baihua* 白话):

---

[48] In two of them Fr. Stenz was involved personally. In 1897, the Divine Word missionaries P. Richard Henle and P. Franz Xaver Nies while spending the night in Stenz's house, were killed by the Chinese "Society of Broad Swords" (Dadaohui 大刀会). Afterwards, the German Government used this as a pretext to occupy the Jiaozhou 膠州 peninsula and make it a German colony (cf. Rivinius, *Johann Baptist Anzer*, pp. 487-627). In another such incident in 1898, Fr. Stenz himself was captured and tortured for three days. Though this had been caused by the wrongdoing of some Christian converts, there followed a punitive expedition of the German army, which Fr. Stenz accompanied, in the course of which two Chinese villages were completely demolished (cf. Rivinius, *Johann Baptist Anzer*, pp. 589-615).

This story has been written in colloquial language, in a vulgar and unadorned style, very easy to understand. When you read it you will not be able to stop, the intelligent will be instructed and the stupid will be enlightened. It will open heart and eyes, it is really a treasure for all times and a world rarity.[49]

He also mentions that the author is Siwensong 斯文松 (Svensson). I found out that Jón Svensson (Jón Stefán Sveinsson, 1857–1944) was a Jesuit priest from Iceland and a famous writer of children's stories. His boy hero's name Nonni is the familiar form of Svensson's first name Jón. In his books Svensson writes about his childhood in Iceland, his life in a fishing village and his adventures on the ocean and in the mountains. His stories were written in German, translated into several languages and made into films and TV serials.[50] After some searching I discovered the original German stories, which Liu Bohua had translated into Chinese.

The Chinese version has two parts. In the first, *Naoni ji Mani* 腦尼及馬尼 (Nonni and Manni) Nonni tells about his life as a fisher boy, about a "magic flute" which was supposed to attract fish and about an adventurous boating trip with his little brother Manni. When in mortal danger, the two boys take a vow, promising that if God saved them, they would later become missionaries. They are saved by a French ship and escorted home to their happy parents.

In the second part, *Naoni ji Aili* 腦尼及愛立 (Nonni and Elis), Nonni sets out with friends to enjoy "the ocean on fire," i.e., a spectacular marine phosphorescence. When he is accidentally hit on the head by an iron anchor, Nonni falls into the sea. Praying to God, they are all saved by an Irish ship.

The Chinese version (see Figure 12) is a quite faithful translation of two German stories.[51] Yet there are some alterations. Foreign languages and customs receive particular emphasis. While Nonni and Manni are rowing on the ocean, they come into contact with foreign warships and commercial ships from France and England. First the little boys just shout the only French word they know: "Napolun!" 拿破仑 (Napoleon). Later they learn the French words "non" and "bonsoir," to be pronounced through the nose. When they come to an English boat, they even manage a real dialogue with the foreign sailors: "Good evening," "Who are you?", "We are Icelandic boys" etc. This is done with the help of an older boy who translates from "Islandic" – i.e., Chinese – to English and back to Chinese. The little readers are even informed that Irish is different from English and are given an onomatopoetic imitation of Irish sounds:

---

[49] 此篇小说，系用白话著作，粗俚不文，最易明悉，令人阅读，难以释手，智者蒙诲，愚者启迪，开其心，明其目，确系古今奇观，世所罕有。Preface by Liu Baohua 刘保华, from Ganling, province Hebei (Hebei sheng Ganling 河北省甘陵), dated Dec. 15, 1929. Catholic Church in the district Xian (Tianzhutang Xianxian 天主堂献县).

[50] His grave is in the Jesuit cemetery in Cologne where there is a "Nonni Fountain" showing a young boy reading a book (see Figure 11).

[51] Jón Svensson, *Neue Abenteuer auf Island*, pp. 82-127; id., *Ein Priester erzählt von seiner Heimat. Nonni*, pp. 157-173.

The (Irish) captain smiled to me, placed his hand on my head and "*diliandulu*" talked a while. Even though we could not understand it, yet reckoned he talked well, since we heard him repeat many times "Poor little boy."[52]

In a short epilogue we are told that the early vow of the two boys to become missionaries was not fulfilled later. The younger brother Manni died early, the older studied a long time and forgot about it:

> Since he (Nonni) has not even achieved the grade of a priest and is now already middle-aged, it would be a bit late to set out to foreign parts and preach to the people there.[53]

This is a bit of self-irony, since Svensson actually became a priest, though not a missionary. In this little story praying to God is important, but missionary work is no longer the only theme. Just as important is imparting knowledge about foreign countries and about their languages, i.e., English and French.

Translators are Matchmakers

We have seen that the Chinese and Western translators of our little stories worked for a better understanding between China and Europe in many ways. Thus, the Shandong Fathers, in Father Malek's words, "continued the accomodation tradition of the Jesuits."[54] Instead of one-sidedly forcing the Chinese into European ways, they tried in their translations to understand and adapt themselves to Chinese culture.

In China, such mediation by translation has a history of nearly two thousand years. Qian Zhongshu 钱锺书 (1910–1998) produced illuminating research in this field. In his article "Lin Shu de fanyi" 林纾的翻译 (The Translations of Lin Shu), Qian comes to the conclusion that one important job of the translator is the art of "matchmaking."

In ancient China – just as in ancient Greece – foreigners were looked down upon as wild beasts or birds. Their – for the Chinese incomprehensible – language was called "bird-talk" or "croaking." Quoting from the Han dynasty dictionary *Shuowen jiezi* 说文解字 (Explaining and Analyzing Characters, early 2nd c.), Qian starts from an explanation of the etymology of the Chinese character for "translation":

> *E* 囮, means "to translate." The bird-catcher enchains a living bird to tempt others. ... (Qian comments): Since the Southern Tang dynasty etymologists

---

[52] （船长）向我笑了一笑，两手扶在我头上，低廉嘟噜的说了一套，我们虽然不懂，大估量他说的不错，因为许多次我们听见他重说"可怜的孩子" (Poor little boy), Jón Svensson, *Yisilan tongzi yuxianji*, pp. 135, 136.

[53] 到如今连司铎的品位也没有得到，大如今数十岁了，再想上外教人地方传教去，也就晚一点了. Jón Svensson, *Yisilan tongzi yuxianji*, p. 153.

[54] Malek, "Christian Education," pp. 99-101. For the history of "accommodation" see Knöpfler, "Die Akkomodation im altchristlichen Missionswesen," pp. 41-51.

explained "translate" as translating into the "language of barbarians, birds and wild beasts" – just like "a bird-catcher lures birds."[55]

Thus a basic job of the translator is to attract and to seduce. He has to keep an eye on his public and play the part of the matchmaker between the two cultures. In the same vein, many centuries later we find Goethe's famous saying: "Übersetzer sind als geschäftige Kuppler anzusehen ..." ("Translators are to be seen as busy matchmakers").[56]

When in the second century Indian Buddhist monks came to China and translated the Buddhist scriptures, they developed new and more sophisticated theories of translation. Three different schools were founded, which exist to this day: The school of faithful translation (*zhiyi* 直译), the school of elegance (*yayi* 雅译) and the school of popular translation (*suyi* 俗译).

The Chinese monk Dao An 道安 (314–385) was among the first to advocate the "faithful translation." He wanted to translate the holy Buddhist scriptures into Chinese without changes. Yet he soon found that this was impossible. In his treatise "Wu shiben" 五失本 (Five Treasons) he wrote: If one follows faithfully the Sanskrit, the Chinese sentences would be upside down, this is the first treason. Then, there would be cultural differences:

> The Buddhist scriptures are deep and simple. But we Chinese love a beautiful style. If we want to convert the Chinese ... this is impossible without Chinese rhetoric. This is the second treason.[57]

The Jesuit missionaries, the Shandong S.V.D. Fathers, and most translators all over the world have come to the same conclusion: A verbatim translation would very quickly scare away all believers and readers.

After Dao An, the famous Indian monk Kumārajīva (Jiumoluoshi 鸠摩罗什, 344–413) propagated and practised a different strategy. Kumārajīva cultivated an elegant style, which won him many believers among the educated Chinese. Stylistically bad translations he criticized passionately without mincing words:

> When translations from Sanskrit, even though the sense is correct, are lacking in literary beauty, this is like offering your guests already chewed food; it is not only tasteless, it also makes you vomit.[58]

---

[55] "囮"译也。... 率鸟者系生鸟以来之，名曰"囮"... 南唐以来，小学家都申说"翻译"就是"传四夷及鸟兽之语"，好比"鸟媒"对"禽鸟"的引诱 (Qian Zhongshu, "Lin Shu de fanyi", p. 89). Cf. Motsch, "Lin Shu und Franz Kuhn," pp. 78f.

[56] Goethe, „Maximen und Reflexionen", *Kunst und Altertum*, vol. 5, no. 3 (1826): "Übersetzer sind als geschäftige Kuppler anzusehen, die uns eine halbverschleierte Schöne als höchst liebenswürdig anpreisen: sie erregen eine unwiderstehliche Neigung nach dem Original."

[57] "五失本"之一曰："梵语尽倒，而使从秦"。"失本"之二曰："梵经尚质，秦人好文，传可众心，非文不合". Quoted from Qian Zhongshu, *Guanzhuibian*, vol. 4, p. 84 (*Quan Jinwen juan* 全晋文卷 158:"翻译术开宗明义"). For the three schools of Chinese translation see Motsch, "Zwischen Indien und dem Westen," pp. 2-5.

Kumārajīva used a method which more or less is followed in China to this day: He first recited a *sūtra* in Sanskrit. Then translators translated it orally into Chinese. Afterwards the different versions were discussed by hundreds of monks and corrected. Only then was the translation written down.

Apparently the Shandong priests adapted a similar method, naturally with some variations. The little stories are written in simple, but fluent Chinese, certainly not by German priests, but by Chinese native speakers. On the flyleaf, before the name of German priests like Father Stenz or others, one often finds the term *shuyi* 述译, i.e., "oral translator." Thus we can surmise that the German priests would translate a text from German into Chinese orally, while at the same time their Chinese partners would write it down in fluent, idiomatic Chinese. This written version was afterwards discussed and corrected by the German Fathers. A confirmation of this can be found in a foreword by Fei Jinbiao, in which he thanks Father Röser for helping him with the sometimes problematic translation of names of cities or persons in the Old Testament.[59]

The third school is that of "popular translation." After Kumārajīva, the monks addressed themselves not to the educated, but mainly to the common people in the market place. Usually, the Buddhist monk would first recite the scripture in classical Chinese. Then followed popular explanations, often accompanied by music, pictures, songs, comic scenes, theatre plays – the famous, all-beloved storytelling and story singing (*shuoshu* 说书, *shuochang* 说唱). We have seen that the Shandong priests, and especially the talented storyteller Fei Jinbiao, used this tradition with great success.

Admittedly this art of matchmaking was not always the guiding principle. Even in our little stories quite a few prejudices and limitations can be detected. For instance, in schoolbook stories like *Xiaozi zhuan* or *Heitaizi*, Christian priests, Chinese converts and Christian schools are very much idealized, while believers of other religions are usually in the wrong and often come to a bad end.

In some rare cases there is even a total lack of esteem for the other culture: In *Fabiola* as well as in the Chinese adaption, there is a scene in which a cultured Roman, after becoming a convert, smashes all the beautiful statues of Greek and Roman gods in his park. This is done, I am sorry to say, on the good advice of his Christian priest, and as a reward for this barbarian behaviour the Roman gentleman is promptly cured of his gout.[60]

Another debatable point is the passionate glorification of martyrdom. Dying a martyr's death is described as something very desirable for Christians, being the key to paradise. It is like "going to a great feast," and one victim even goes so far as to kiss the instruments of torture. Nowadays hearing about such heroic deeds, we would be more likely to associate this spirit of self-sacrifice with fa-

---

[58] 但改梵文为秦，失其藻蔚虽得大意，疏隔文体，有似嚼饭与人，非徒失味，乃令呕秽也 Quoted from Qian Zhongshu, *Guanzhuibian*, vol. 4, p. 85 (*Quan Jinwen juan* 158).

[59] *Shengjiao gushi xiaoshuo guci*, vol. 1 (Genesis), Fei Jinbiao's Preface.

[60] Wiseman, *Fabiola*, pp. 135-138. Fei Jinbiao, *Zhiming xiaozhuan guci*, p. 35.

natic Islamic terrorists than with so-called "civilized Christians." Yet such views were rather typical for the times. Many young European missionaries, setting out for China at the beginning of the twentieth century, were eager to fight as "soldiers of Jesus" and to become martyrs.[61] On the other hand, there is even now a strange attraction in reading these little stories about the cruel fate of the early Christians. What could be the reason for this sympathy? For one thing, reading a martyr's story is something very different from really dying as a martyr. It is rather like seeing a Greek tragedy. It helps to see our own life in a new perspective, and this can be a great solace.

However that may be, we certainly can see that the longing for martyrdom did not turn the Christian authors into inhuman fanatics. On the whole, the Chinese little stories analyzed above are free from too much moralising or heavy missionary bias. The authors not only preached, they also wanted to entertain and to inform about foreign customs and languages. We can see that Chinese and Western authors respected each other and were trying to draw East and West together.

This worked especially well in the stories of Fei Jinbiao, a creative writer who transformed the old Bible and martyr stories into lively Shandong Drum Songs, with scenes full of fantasy, shocking suspense and humorous relief. And it is just as admirable that the Divine Word priests had the courage to print these texts without fear that somebody might accuse them of lacking respect for the Holy Bible and the memory of Christian martyrs.

It is certainly a pity that we know so little about the Chinese translators who did such an important job. Even about so brilliant a writer as Fei Jinbiao we have very little information.

We can be truly grateful to Father Malek, since he has done most of the work of collecting the booklets, doing research on them and saving them from oblivion. Father Malek's very ambitious project – to publish a general catalogue of all S.V.D. publications of the China Mission – will certainly bring to light many other hidden treasures.

So let me conclude with my best wishes for Father Malek and his work as a "matchmaker" – furthering Sino-Western understanding and drawing China and Europe together!

---

[61] Rivinius, *Anzer*, pp. 395-400 ("Missionaries seeing themselves"). Stenz wrote: The blood of martyrs had to flow everywhere, in order to fructify the teachings of Christendom (*Ins Reich des Drachen*, p. 250). In the same vein the Steyler General Superior P. Janssen: "And would it not be a great blessing, if one had the fortune to become a martyr?" (Henninghaus, *P. Jos. Freinademetz*, p. 137).

Bibliography A

Drum Songs of the Old Testament:

Shengjiao gushi xiaoshuo guci 聖教古史小說鼓詞 *Drum Song Stories from the Old Testament*. Shandong Shouzhang Fei Jinbiao zhu 山東壽張費金標著, written by Fei Jinbiao from Shouzhang in Shandong. Yanzhou: Tianzhutang yinshuju huoban 兗州天主堂印書局活版, published by the Catholic Yanzhou Press with movable types. 8 booklets, 1918.

1. *Chuangshi ji* 創世紀 (Genesis), 79 pp.
2. *Chugu ji* 出谷紀 (Exodus), *Huji ji* 戶籍紀 (Numbers), *Shenming pian* 申命篇 (Deuteronomy), 68 pp.
3. *Yuesuwei zhuan* 約穌位傳 (Joshua), *Zhanglao zhuan* 張老傳 (Judges), *Hude zhuan* 戶德傳 (Ruth), 54 pp.
4. *Qianliewang zhuan* 前列王專 (First Book of Kings), 138 pp.
5. *Zhongliewang zhuan* 中列王傳 (Second Book of Kings), 126 pp.
6. *Houliewang zhuan* 後列王傳 (Third Book of Kings), 121 pp.
7. *Dani'er zhuan* 大尼爾傳 (Daniel), *Ruobo zhuan* 若伯傳 (Job), *Rudide zhuan* 儒第德傳 (Judith), *Duobiya zhuan* 多俾亞傳 (Tobit), *Yuena zhuan* 約納傳 (Jonah), 134 pp.
8. *Aiside zhuan* 愛斯德傳 (Esther), *Aisitela zhuan* 愛斯忒辣傳 (Ezra), *Naheimi zhuan* 納黑彌傳 (Nehemiah), *Majiabo zhuan* 瑪加伯傳 (Maccabees), 119 pp.

The Shandong Opera *Hongshui mieshi* (The Great Flood):

Hongshui mieshi juben. 洪水滅世劇本. *Chinese Opera: The Great Flood*. Shandong Shouzhang Fei Jinbiao zhu 山東壽張費金標著. Written by Fei Jinbiao from Shouzhang in Shandong. Yanzhou: Tianzhutang yinshuju huoban 兗州天主堂印書局活版, published by the Catholic Yanzhou Press with movable types. 2nd ed. 1921 (1st ed. 1919), 67 pp.

Stories about Roman Martyrs:

Zhiming xiaozhuan guci 致命小傳鼓詞 (Drum Songs about Martyrs). Shandong Nanjie zhujiao Han zhun 山東南界主教韓准. Imprimatur Bishop Han [Henninghaus] from Nanjie in Shandong, 2 vols. Yanzhou 1915. Translator Fei Jinbiao 費金標. Adapted from *Fabiola: Or the Church of the Catacombs* (1880) by Cardinal Nicholas Patrick Wiseman.

Kuming darong. 苦命大榮 (From Misery to Glory). By Luo *siduo* 羅司鐸 (Father Röser). Adapted from *Valeria oder der Triumphzug aus den Katakomben* (1884) by Monsignor Anton de Waal. Yanzhou 1916.

Children's Books:

Xiaozi zhuan 孝子傳. *The Filial Son. Collectio narrationum* P. G.M. Stenz S.V.D. Author: P. Geyser S.Y. [*sic*] Oral translator (*yishuzhe* 譯述者): Father Stenz S.V.D. *Jining Zhong-Xi zhongxue chuban* 濟寧中西中學校出版. Published by Jining Western-Chinese Middle School, Yanzhou 1920.

Heitaizi 黑太子. *The Black Prince. Collectio narrationum* P. G.M. Stenz S.V.D. Author: P. A.v B. S.Y. [*sic*.] Oral translator: Hantschau. Published by Jining Western-Chinese Middle School, Yanzhou 1920.

Yisilan tongzi yuxianji 伊斯蘭童子遇險記. *Iceland Boys meeting Danger*. Author: Ion Svensson. Translator: Hebeisheng Ganling Liu Baohua 河北省甘陵刘保华 (Liu Baohua from Ganling in Hebei). Yanzhou 1931.

Bibliography B

Holy Bible, New International Version (Anglicised edition). London: Hodder and Stoughton, 1979, 1984, 2011.

Fischer, Hermann SVD, *Augustin Henninghaus. 53 Jahre Missionar und Missionsbischof*. Kaldenkirchen: Steyler Missionsbuchhandlung, 1946.

Hartwich, Richard (Hrsg.), *Steyler Missionare in China*, Bd. 1: *Missionarische Erschließung Südshantungs 1879–1903. Beiträge zu einer Geschichte*. Sankt Augustin: Steyler Verlag, 1983.

Henninghaus, Augustin, *P. Joseph Freinademetz SVD. Sein Leben und Wirken. Zugleich Beiträge zur Geschichte der Mission Süd-Schantung*. Yenchowfu: Verlag der Katholischen Mission, 1920.

Huppertz, Josefine, *Ein Beispiel katholischer Verlagsarbeit in China. Eine zeitgeschichtliche Studie*, Studia Instituti Missiologici Societatis Verbi Divini, 54. Nettetal: Steyler Verlag, 1992.

Kang Zhijie 康志杰, "Tianzhujiao yinglian chuyi" 天主教楹联刍议 (Catholic Couplets), *Xueshu tansuo* 学术探索 (Academic Exploration), 2012/5, pp. 84-88.

Knöpfler, Alois, "Die Akkomodation im altchristlichen Missionswesen," *Zeitschrift für Missionswissenschaft* 1 (1911), pp. 41-51.

Malek, Roman, *Das Chai-chieh lu. Materialien zur Liturgie im Taoismus*. Frankfurt a.M. *et al.*: Peter Lang, 1985.

—, "Christian Education and the Transfer of Ideals on a Local Level: Catholic Schoolbooks and Instructional Material from Shandong (1882–1950)," in: *Jiang gen zhahao. Jidu zongjiao zai Hua jiaoyu jiantao* 将根扎好—基督宗教在华教育的检. *Setting the Roots Right. Christian Education in China and Taiwan*, ed. Wang Chengmian 王成勉. Taibei: Liming wenhua, 2007, pp. 79-155.

—, "The Bible at the Local Level. Notes on Biblical Material Published by the Divine Word Missionaries (S.V.D.) in Shandong (1882–1950)," *Monumenta Serica* 64 (2016) 1, pp. 137-172.

Pieper, Rudolph, *Unkraut, Knospen und Blüten aus dem "blumigen Reich der Mitte."* Steyl: Verlag der Missionsdruckerei, 1900.

Puhl, Stephan, *Georg M. Stenz SVD (1869–1928). Chinamissionar im Kaiserreich der Republik*. Mit einem Nachwort von R.G. Tiedemann (London): "Der Missionspolitische Kontext in Süd-Shandong am Vorabend der Boxer." Ed. Roman Malek. Nettetal: Steyler Verlag, 1994.

Motsch, Monika, "Lin Shu und Franz Kuhn – zwei frühe Übersetzer," *Hefte für Ostasiatische Literatur* 5 (1986), pp. 76-87.

—, "Zwischen Indien und dem Westen. Neue Tendenzen chinesischer Übersetzungstheorie und Übersetzungspraxis," *Orientierungen* 1995/1, pp. 1-12.

Qian Zhongshu 錢鐘書, "Lin Shu de fanyi" 林紓的翻譯 (The Translations of Lin Shu), in: *Qian Zhongshu ji. Qizhuiji* 錢鐘書集—七缀集 (Works of Qian Zhongshu. Seven Essays). Beijing: Sanlian shudian, 2001, pp. 89-133.

—, *Guanzhuibian* 管錐編 (*With Pipe and Awl*), in: *Qian Zhongshu ji* 錢鐘書集, vol. 4. Beijing: Sanlian shudian, 2001.

Rivinius, Karl Josef SVD, *Die katholische Mission in Süd-Shantung. Ein Bericht des Legationssekretärs Speck von Sternburg aus dem Jahr 1895 über die Steyler Mission in China*. Sankt Augustin: Steyler Verlag, 1979.

—. *Im Spannungsfeld von Mission und Politik. Johann Baptist Anzer (1851–1903), Bischof von Süd-Shandong*. Nettetal: Steyler Verlag, 2010.

Stenz, Georg M., *Reise-Erinnerungen eines Missionars. Meine Fahrt von Steyl (Holland) nach Shanghai (China) und ins Innere von China*. Trier: Verlag der Paulinus-Druckerei, 1894.

—. *Ins Reich des Drachen unter dem Banner des Kreuzes*. Ravensburg: Friedrich Alber Verlag, 1906.

—. *In der Heimat des Konfuzius. Skizzen, Bilder und Erlebnisse aus Schantung*. Steyl: Missionsdruckerei, 1902.

—. *Beiträge zur Volkskunde Süd-Schantungs*, hrsg. und eingeleitet von A. Conrady. Leipzig: R. Voigtländers Verlag, 1907.

Svensson, Jón, "Nonni und Manni in Seenot," *Neue Abenteuer auf Island mit Nonni und Manni*. Freiburg i.Br. – Basel – Wien: Herder, 2008, pp. 82-127.

—. "Abenteuer auf dem Meer," *Nonni*, Bd. 2: *Ein Priester erzählt von seiner Heimat*. Leipzig: St.-Benno-Verlag, 1981, pp. 157-173.

Waal, Anton de, *Valeria oder der Triumphzug aus den Katakomben*, 3rd ed. Regensburg: Pustet, 1896.

Wiseman, Nicholas Patrick, *Fabiola. Or the Church of the Catacombs*. London: Burns and Oates, 1854, Classic Reprint Series, published by Forgotten Books, London 2012.

Zheng Zhenduo 郑振铎, *Zhongguo suwenxue shi* 中国俗文学史 (History of China's Popular Literature), 2 vols, Shanghai: Shanghai shudian, 1984.

Figures

Fig. 1. Drum Song *The Great Flood* by Fei Jinbiao

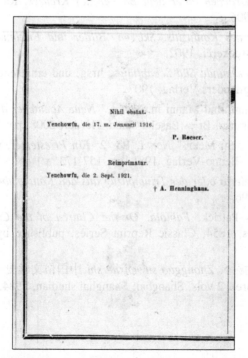

Fig. 2. Latin imprimatur for *The Great Flood*

Fig. 3. The scene "I am the Angel" in Drum Song *The Great Flood*

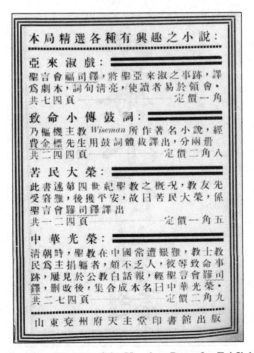

Fig. 4. Advertisement of the Yanzhou Press for Fei Jinbiao

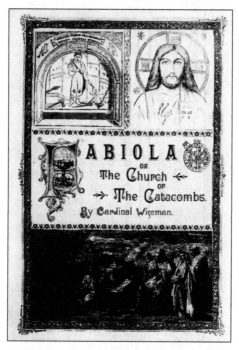

Fig. 5. *Fabiola* by Cardinal Wiseman (New York 1886)

Fig. 6. Chinese Drumsong of *Fabiola* by Fei Jinbiao

Fig. 7. *Valeria* by de Waal (Regensburg 1884)

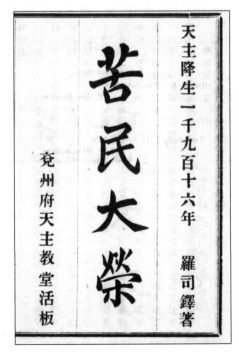

Fig. 8. The Chinese *Valeria*, ed. Fr. Röser

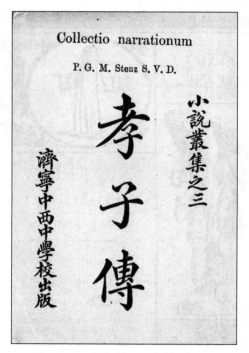

Fig. 9. *The Filial Son*, ed. Fr. Stenz

Fig. 10. *The Black Prince*, ed. Fr. Stenz

Fig. 11. The Nonni Fountain in Cologne

Fig. 12. The Chinese *Iceland Boys* of Jón Svensson

"OMNIA CONSUMMATA SUNT"[1]
XIANG PEILIANG'S VERSION OF THE BIBLICAL STORY OF JESUS BETWEEN BETHANY AND GETHSEMANE

MARIÁN GÁLIK

At present, Xiang Peiliang 向培良 (1901–1961) is little known among students of modern Chinese literature. To the best of my knowledge, only in the year 2013 did a group of scholars around Professor Cao Shunqing 曹順清, Sichuan University, Chengdu, decide to search for, collect, and finally study in scholarly fashion a body of materials of this prominent Chinese playwright, writer, translator, theoretician of drama and art, and theatre director.[2] Because of his anti-Communist orientation, Xiang has been neglected in the PRC.[3] At first a good student and collaborator of Lu Xun in the 1923–1925, after Lu Xun's transition to a Marxist position and his persuasion of the necessity to judge literature and art according to the needs of "class struggle," young Xiang Peiliang, who believed in their all-human mission,[4] could not cooperate any further with Lu Xun. Following the great author's fierce attack, Xiang separated himself from Lu Xun. Among the final reasons for their definitive split was the publication of Xiang Peiliang's *Renlei de yishu* 人類的藝術 (The Art of Humankind) in May 1930. This turning point for the two of them, Xiang and Lu Xun, coincided with the founding of the Zhongguo zuoyi zuojia lianmeng 中國左翼作家聯盟 (League of the Chinese Leftist Writers), with close ties to the CCP in the Guomindang 國民黨 owned Bati 拔提 Publishers. It is my understanding and view that Xiang Peiliang's literary theory has not been sufficiently studied as of yet.[5] We do know,

---

[1] Cf. "Postea sciens Jesus, quia omnia consummata sunt, ut consummaretur Scriptura, dixit: Sitio." *Biblia Sacra Vulgatae Editionis* (Jn 19:28) – "After this, Jesus knowing that all things were now accomplished, that the scriptures might be fulfilled, saith, I thirst." *The Holy Bible. King James Version* (hereafter: KJV). All translations from the Bible in this essay are from this version.

[2] Information according to email from Professor Liao Jiuming 廖久明, Leshan Normal University, March 17, 2013.

[3] Only in 2013 after the decision of Professor Cao Shunqing, the first essays about Xiang Peiliang's life and work began to appear in the PRC, published in the electronic media. The best according my opinion is from Deng Hongshun 郑宏顺: "Bei Lu Xun yingxiang yi sheng de Xiang Peiliang" 被鲁迅影响一生的向培良 (Lu Xun's Influence upon Xiang Peiliang's Life). See http://www.frguo.com/info.aspx?ModelId=1&ID=6710 (May 18, 2016).

[4] For more, see Deng Hongshun, "Bei Lu Xun yingxiang."

[5] There is one exception: Hong Hong 洪宏, "Lun Xiang Peiliang de xiju lilun" 論向培良的戲劇理論 (On Xiang Peiliang's Theory of Drama). *Xiju yishu* 戲劇藝術 - *Theatre Arts*, No. 6 (2000), pp. 49-58. http://www.cqvip.com/qk/81960x/200006/12523922.html (May 18, 2016).

however, of at least three concrete sources for Xiang's ideas: the books by George P. Baker, *Dramatic Technique*, William Archer's, *Playmaking,* and Archibald Henderson's *The Changing Drama*.[6] Much attention he devoted also to Gordon Craig.[7] We may at least specify two main features of his creative writings, one of which is connected with European literary Aestheticism or Decadence, mostly in relation to Oscar Wilde[8] and Gabriele D'Annunzio.[9] To this kind of literature, whether in the genre of drama or short story, we may also add the works concerned with Freudian psychology, mainly the first section of Freud's work *Three Contributions to the Theory of Sex*.[10] Xiang Peiliang was an avid reader about sexual matters in both English and Chinese literature. He appreciated two books by Marie Carmichael Stopes, *Married Love. A New Contribution to the Solution of Sex Difficulties,* and *Wise Motherhood*.[11] He read also Havelock Ellis's (1859–1939) *Sex Education* in Chinese translation (*Xing de jiaoyu* 性的教育),[12] although he was not enthralled by the author's convictions. It

---

[6] See Xiang Peiliang, *Lun juben* 論劇本 (On Drama) (Shanghai: Shangwu yinshuguan, 1936). It seems to him, not only as playwright, but also a director and theatre manager, that the most important source was George P. Baker, to whom he was mostly indebted when writing this booklet (p. 63).

[7] Xiang Peiliang, *Renlei de yishu* 人類的藝術 (The Art of Humankind) (Nanjing: Bati shudian, 1930), pp. 89-92, 114-115, *Lun juben,* pp. 15-16.

[8] Cf. his drama *Annen* 暗嫩 (Amnon) with the biblical motif of the tragic love of King David's eldest son Amnon and his step-sister Tamar, which is a good example of this kind of literary creation. More on this specific concern is available in Marián Gálik, "Temptation of the Princes. Xiang Peiliang's Decadent Version of Biblical Amnon and Tamar." In: *id., Influence, Translation and Parallels. Selected Studies on the Bible in China*. Collectanea Serica (Nettetal: Steyler Verlag, 2004), pp. 231-250. See also a shorter treatment by Xie Zhixi 解志熙: *He er bu tong. Zhongguo xiandai wenxue pianlun* 和而不同—中国现代文学片论 (Harmony but not Uniformity. Studies in Modern Chinese Literature) (Beijing: Qinghua daxue chubanshe, 2002), pp. 41-43.

[9] Xiang Peiliang translated into Chinese Gabriele D'Annunzio's (1863–1938) tragedy *La Città morta* (The Dead City), using the English translation by Mantellini, in 1927 and published it in Shanghai 1929.

[10] Sigmund Freud, *The Basic Writings of Sigmund Freud*. Translated and edited with an Introduction by Dr. A.A. Brill (New York 1938), pp. 553-569. Such is, for instance, Xiang Peiliang's short story "Rou de chu" 肉的觸 (Touching of the Flesh), *Mangyuan* 莽原 (Wilderness) 1 (1926) 16, pp. 674-680. See Marián Gálik, "Temptation of the Princes," pp. 247-248. A similar character appears also in another story "Youyin" 誘引 (Temptation), in Xiang Peiliang's collection *Piaomiao de meng* 飄渺的夢 (Floating and Vague Dreams) (Shanghai: Beixin shudian, 1926), pp. 151-160. This piece seems of lesser literary value than the one just mentioned.

[11] Xiang Peiliang, "Guanyu xingyu ji ji bu guanyu xingyu de shu" 關於性慾及幾部關於性慾的書 (On Sexual Desire and on Some Books Concerned with It), *Kuangpiao zhoukan* 狂飆週刊 No. 17 (January 1927), p. 507.

[12] See *ibid.,* p. 506. The translation of Ellis's work was probably done on the basis of the long Chapter II, entitled "Sexual Education" from the well-known collection *Studies in the Psychology of Sex*. Vol. II (Philadelphia: F.A. Davis Company, n.y.), pp. 33-93. The

is necessary to say that Xiang Peiliang's words about Ellis's work were not convincing, since he did not have the translation in his hands when writing his essay, and was caught up in "very confused impressions" which must be taken *cum grano salis*.

Two of his drama collections are probably best. Their titles are very similar to each other, but their contents are quite different. The first, *Shenmen de xiju* 深悶的戲劇 (Melancholic Plays), present plots related to the dark side of human existence. *Guangming de xiju* 光明的戲劇 (Straightforward Plays) offers a bright, promising side. The best specimen of the first is the play *Annen* 暗嫩 (Amnon) depicting the tragic love between two children of King David (ca. 1037 – ca. 967 B.C.), Amnon and Tamar, on the basis of 2 Samuel, 13:1-18, not taking into account the verses that follow, 19-38. In this place the impact of Sigmund Freud's treatise entitled "Sexual Aberrations" from the above mentioned *Three Contributions to the Theory of Sex,* and of the famous decadent play *Salome* by Oscar Wilde (1854–1900), is most obvious.[13] The second dramatic work is *Sheng zhi wancheng* 生之完成 (Life Mission Accomplished), which focuses on the last days of Jesus Christ as he moved between Bethany and the Garden of Gethsemane.[14] The drama consists of three acts, of which the first and second are situated in Bethany in the house of Simon the Leper (Mt 26:6 and Mk 14:3). The third act is set in the Garden of Gethsemane (Mt 26:36-56, Mk 14:32-50, Lk 22:39-53 and Jn 18:1-12).

1

Nothing is known about Simon the Leper. Perhaps he was the leper whom Jesus restored to health. Here on the stage, in addition to Simon the Leper, we also meet Lazarus and his sisters Martha and Mary, a Samaritan, and several disciples of Jesus, Peter and Judas Iscariot at the beginning, and later also John, James and Matthew.

Before the analysis of this drama, it is necessary to say a few words about Xiang Peiliang's theory of drama which, as far as I know, has not been adequately studied until now.[15] From his *Renlei de yishu* we may deduce that Xiang's literary theory begins with the book of Genesis 5:12-16 in the Old Tes-

---

translator was Pan Guangdan 潘光旦 (1899–1967). About his life, work and death during the cruelest of times of the Cultural Revolution, see Wang Youqin 王友琴, "Pan Guangdan zhi si" 潘光旦之死 (Pan Guangdan's Death), in Gongshi wang 共識網 21ccom.net. 9 pp. See https://t2.shwchurch.org/2013/04/19/潘光旦之死-王友琴/ (May 18, 2016).

[13] For the study of Xiang Peiliang's accomplishments in the Chinese theatre of the 1920s and 1930s, see Ding Mingyong 丁明拥 – Ma Baomin 马宝民, "Zuo wei xiju huodongjia de Xiang Peiliang" 作为戏剧活动家的向培良 (Xiang Peiliang – Master of Theater), *Yihai* 藝海 *Arts-Sea* 2011/12, pp. 18-22. The two collections of plays are merely mentioned in this study, not analyzed.

[14] *Sheng zhi wancheng* 生之完成 was published in 1929 by Nanhua shuju (Shanghai).

[15] Apart from Hong Hong's "Lun Xiang Peiliang de xiju lilun."

tament. This marks the story of Mahalalel,[16] the son of Cainan, in the fourth generation after Adam and Eve, and his younger sister Madala.[17] Dramatic activity grows out of the process in which the characters try "to express themselves fully in order to know each other."[18] Allegedly, in the year 437 following the act of creation by God, on an evening in spring, the romantic couple met and expressed their love to each other. Their loneliness was the first deep sentiment in the hearts of Mahalalel and Madala. Both needed to feel human tenderness, to see the faces of one another, and to hear their voices. At a time when human civilization lacked scripts, paintings, architecture, and so forth, here we discover already the germs of theatrical art and music.[19]

On the second page of Xiang Peiliang's essay we read his prayer in front of a sacrificial altar. It is very similar to the prayers in the Book of Psalms, but no single source is evident.

> You most honoured and highest God, unveil yourself to us. We are your servants from the oldest times, and we shall sincerely proceed in serving you. All our joys and mournful feelings, and all our lives as well we have submitted to you on the sacrificial altar, you who are the most honored and highest God. But we are still blind (*mengmei* 朦昧). We do not see. O God, reveal Yourself to us![20]

This prayer is to some extent similar to Psalm 28, attributed to David.

> Unto thee I cry, O LORD my rock. Be not silent to me, lest, *if* thou be silent to me, I become like them that go down to pit. Hear the voice of my supplications, when I cry unto thee, when I lift my hands toward thy holy oracle ... The LORD *is* my strength and my shield; my heart trusted in him, and I am helped; therefore my heart rejoiceth; and with song I praise him.

It is, of course, possible that Xiang Peiliang, when writing his prayer of supplication, had in mind also the words of the Apostle Philip, who said to Jesus, "Lord, shew us the Father, and it sufficeth us" (Jn 14:8). It is likewise possible that Psalm 28 was sung or recited as part of a liturgical ceremony in the Temple.[21]

From what has been said thus far, we may deduce that Xiang Peiliang was a follower of the theory of the ritual origin of theatre and its practitioners. This is

---

[16] In Xiang Peiliang's treatise *The Art of Humankind* there are no Chinese characters for Mahalalel. In the KJV it is Mahalaleel and in the *Hehe ben* 和合本 (Union Version) Maleili 玛勒列.

[17] There is no such name in the Scripture. She is Xiang's invention, and can be most likely regarded as similar to the character of Bianca Maria from D'Annunzio's *La Città morta* or to the Antigone of Sophokles (497–405 B.C.).

[18] Xiang Peiliang, "Zai women de jitan xia qidao" 在我們的祭壇下祈禱 (We Pray under the Sacrificial Altar), in: *Renlei de yishu,* p. 101.

[19] *Ibid.*, p. 100.

[20] *Ibid.*, p. 84.

[21] Carol Stuhlmueller, *Psalms 1 (Psalms 1-72)* (Willmington, Del.: Michael Grazier 1983), p. 167.

true at least with the drama *Annen,* where the actual performance occurs in the House of David, the anointed, i.e., the Messiah of God, and in *Sheng zhi wancheng,* where precisely the same scene is performed in the presence of Jesus Christ, likewise anointed, from the House of David, the Son of God according to the belief of Christians.

Xiang Peiliang had hardly read about Jesus Christ and Jewish history. The exception to this fact was that he read the Old and New Testaments in the Chinese Protestant Union Version from the year 1919. Certainly he was not familiar with the Apocrypha of the Old Testament, which were not included in the Union Version (as the Apocrypha were considered non-canonical by most Protestants). It is also probable that he did not read the critical works on Jesus written by David Friedrich Strauss (1808–1874) and Ernest Renan (1823–1892), which were probably not accessible on the Chinese book-market, and perhaps also not available for, or in libraries at the time.

Simon the Leper was similar to many who invited Jesus to their homes. It was not only with Peter (Mt 8:14), but also the apostle Matthew, that he "sat at meat in the house, [and] behold, many publicans, and sinners came and sat down with him and his disciples" (Mt 9:10). Perhaps Jesus did enter the house of the centurion in Capernaum, and heard him say, "I am not worthy that thou shouldest come under my roof, [but] speak the word only, and my servant shall be healed" (Mt 8:8). Well-known are the reports of Jesus and his visits to Bethany and meetings with Lazarus, Mary and Martha (Mt 21:17, 26:6, Mk 14:3 and Jn 11:1-17).

The meeting of Jesus and his disciples in the house of Simon the Leper was put into Xiang Peiliang's drama after the triumphal entrance of Jesus into Jerusalem and the Temple, and later during the eventide of that day when "he went out unto Bethany with the twelve" (Mk 11:11).

The first act of the drama *Sheng zhi wancheng* begins with Simon the Leper meeting a Samaritan who was present in Jerusalem as a witness of the arrival of Jesus at Jerusalem the same day. Here Xiang Peiliang alludes to Jesus's conversation with a woman in the Samaritan city of Sychar at Jacob's well, during which he asks her to give him ordinary water in exchange for the living water he can give to her. In John's Gospel we read the words of Samaritan woman, "I know that Messiah cometh, which is called Christ; when he is come, he will tell us all things. Jesus saith unto her, I that speak unto thee am he" (Jn 4:25-26). This woman was one of the first who presupposed that Jesus is the Messiah to come.[22] Many Samaritans began to believe "on him for the saying of the woman" (Jn 4:39) and after a two day stay there, "many more believed because of his own word" (Jn 4:41). It is of course possible that Xiang Peiliang had in mind also Jesus's parable about the Good Samaritan from Lk 10:33-35. The Samaritan acted in an exemplary way, taking care of a man coming from Jerusalem to Jericho upon whom thieves had fallen, leaving the poor victim half dead on the street.

The Samaritan reached Bethany before Jesus and the twelve. Then Jesus met Simon the Leper, who invited him to come under his roof. He was astonished

---

[22] Cf. Mt 16:14-16.

because friendly relations did not exist between the Jews and Samaritans. Simon the Leper said however to him, "Are not Samaritans the children and grandchildren of God? It is only necessary to have this faith (*xinxin* 信心). Jesus Christ, the Prophet, said it to me. In his name I shall treat you. Please come in with your servant."[23] The Samaritan says that he saw Jesus in Jerusalem, the future King of the Jews, and the great multitude crying, "Hosanna to the Son of David: Blessed is he that cometh in the name of the Lord; Hosanna in the highest" (Mt 21:9). The quotation from Matthew is verbatim from the Chinese Union Version translation, and another similar passage pronounced by Simon the Leper about Jesus. Simon's quotation concerns Jesus as, in keeping with the Old Testament prophecy by Zechariah, he sits upon an ass. The reference is somewhat like it. "He said to the daughter of Zion, your King comes to you. He is gentle and riding upon an ass."[24] Both agree that Jesus will be the King of the Jews, the Samaritans, this is to say, and of the people of the whole world. He will be King of Kings, and in his Kingdom there will be no blind, deaf, nor dumb, nor persons possessed by demons.[25]

Chinese readers of Xiang Peiliang were probably greatly surprised that among the disciples of Jesus, the greatest attention is devoted to Judas Iscariot. Perhaps this attention was nothing extraordinary for European readers, but it had to stand out as a bit of a shock, especially for German readers after Johann Wolfgang Goethe's *Der Ewige Jude* (The Wandering Jew), a fragment from the years 1774–1775, where Ahasverus is very similar to Judas Iscariot. According to an impressive number of German writers, Judas Iscariot was a patriot or, better said, a greatly disappointed patriot. According to this view, he was not one to betray Jesus for money, but because of fear of Roman aggression in the case of Jewish insurrection against the foreign rule.[26] Also, according to Anglo-Catholic theologian Henry Ernest William Turner (1907–1995) Judas Iscariot and another, the Apostle Simon the Cananaean or Zealot[27] "seem to belong to the nationalist wing of Judaism." Turner also asserts that "political or national hopes were probably

---

[23] *Sheng zhi wancheng*, p. 2.

[24] *Ibid.*, p. 5. Zechariah's prophecy in the KJV is as follows, "Rejoice greatly, O daughter of Zion; shout, O daughter of Jerusalem: behold, thy King cometh unto thee: he *is* just, and having salvation; lowly, and riding upon an ass, and upon a colt the foal of an ass (Zechariah 9:9).

[25] *Sheng zhi wancheng*, p. 6. Cf. Mt 11:5; 12:22-30 and Mk 3:22-27.

[26] See entry "Judas Ischarioth," in: Elisabeth Frenzel, *Stoffe der Weltliteratur. Ein Lexikon dichtungsgeschichtlicher Längsschnitte* (Stuttgart: Kröner, 1981), pp. 376-377. The text mentions no less than ten literary works of German authors from 1774–1911. They analyze the motives for why Judas acted as he did, as well as the outcome of his treachery.

[27] Cf. Mt 10:1-4; Mk 3:14-18 and Lk 6:15. Simon the Cananean was a member of the sect of Zealots, who often were violent nationalists with an agenda to fight against the Romans. For more about them, see Marcel Simon, "Judaism. Its Faith and Worship," in: Harold Henry Rowley (ed.), *A Companion to the Bible. Second Edition* (Edinburgh: T. and T. Clark, 1963), pp. 402-404.

present in the minds of other disciples as well (Mk 10:35-40) and contributed to their misunderstanding of the nature of the coming Kingdom."[28]

Judas Iscariot was the first of the twelve to be welcomed to the house of Simon the Leper. Like the Samaritan, Judas Iscariot was a witness of the Triumphal Entry of Jesus into Jerusalem, which may be explained as a Messianic ovation, as the patriotic Jews, including Jesus's disciples, had in mind. The short record in the Gospel of Mark may be understood in a broader way. There is yet another possibility of a more appropriate understanding than what we can find in the Scriptures. The whole discussion in the house of Simon the Leper was around a promising Messianic movement which was typical for Galilee. Significantly, many a Galilean pilgrim came to Jerusalem before the Passover.

One of the first questions the Samaritan puts to Judas Iscariot is as follows: "What time will he [Jesus, M.G.] become King of the Jews? Now the Temple has been cleansed." The answer of Judas is short. "The Jews do not need a King."[29] According to Judas, the Jews may not need a King, for they have God on High Yahweh (Yehehua 耶和華), a title used for God in the Union Version. Yahweh should rule over the Jews as he has done over the Hebrews before King Saul (r. ca. 1012–1004 B.C.). The Samaritan then asks, "Jesus Christ will not become the King of the Jews?" "He will not," is Judas's answer. "But the people very much hope in him. If the Lord will become our King [i.e., King of the Jews, Samaritans and the peoples of the world, M.G.] then we shall have better times. There will not be troubles, weeping, illnesses, we shall not pay the duties and always higher revenues," says the Samaritan. Judas contradicts him with the words, "It will not be like this. Only under Yahweh's administration (*guanli* 管理), not under the King, is it possible to have such times. The Jews do not need a King."[30]

After the dialogue between the characters Judas and the Samaritan, at first Martha and Lazarus come to the house of Simon the Leper. More or less, Martha and Lazarus merely repeat the same words that the Samaritan and Simon the Leper had earlier spoken. Judas, hearing their pronouncements, agrees with the words to an extent, but solely under the condition that Yahweh alone may make their countrymen happy. The point is that happiness will not come from Jesus serving as their king. Lazarus (Nasalu 拿撒路, for Xiang Peiliang reads "L" as "N," as is usual in the southern part of China) asserts that if Jesus will not become the King of the Jews, God will renounce his chosen people (Psalm 89:3-4) and the foreigners will bully them (*qifu* 欺負). According to Judas Iscariot, only the blind would try to offer resistance to Roman power, and if that were to happen, self-destruction was sure to follow.[31]

---

[28] See H.E.W. Turner, "The Life and Teaching of Jesus Christ," in: Rowley, *A Companion to the Bible*, p. 443.

[29] *Sheng zhi wancheng*, p. 10.

[30] Ibid., pp. 10-12.

[31] Ibid., p. 18.

Lazarus is the first who asks Jesus about his *guodu* 國度, which may mean "country," "state," "nation," but here signifies "kingdom," or *guo* 國, as it is translated in the KJV or in Union Version. This is understandable during the period before the death of Jesus because, as we know from Mk 8:27-30 and Mt 16:14, we see that his disciples were not quite sure about the identity of Jesus. It is even possible that Peter's confession, "Thou art the Christ, the Son of the living God," was not fully in agreement with the mission of Jesus. Only from Pilate's question, "Art thou the King of the Jews?" (Jn 18:33) do we know Jesus' answer: "My kingdom is not of this world; if my kingdom were of this world, then would my servants fight, that I should not be delivered unto the Jews; but now is my kingdom not from hence" (Jn 18:36).[32] Answering the question of Lazarus, Jesus explains that in his Kingdom, it will not be necessary to pay taxes. In addition, in his kingdom there will be no foreigners and natives, no knives and swords. Children will play with wild animals, and lions with the lambs. Tigers and leopards will stroll with the roes, and angels will sing their songs among the people.[33] These words may remind the reader of the Old Testament prophesy, "The wolf also shall dwell with the lamb, and the leopard shall lie down with the kid; and the calf and the lion and the fatling together; and the little child shall lead them" (Isaiah 11:6).

After Jesus goes to the house of Simon the Leper, Judas leaves with the intention to do something for the cause of the "kingdom." Peter tries to hinder him from carrying out the plan, Jesus lets him go, and announces to all that he came to this world to atone for sins (*shuzui* 贖罪). Mary in Xiang Peiliang's drama was not the woman who in this house took "an alabaster box of very precious ointment, and poured it on the head, as he sat at meat" (Mt 26:7). Martha was not the one to whom Jesus said, "Martha, Martha, thou art careful about many things" (Lk 11:41). Mary, instead of sitting at Jesus' feet and hearing his word (Lk 11:30), asked him about the very important and very painful event (*duome zhongda duome jiankude yijian shi* 多麼重大多麼艱苦的一件事) that awaits him soon. He did not specify what it should be. She was alone among the present that

---

[32] A truly excellent essay on Jesus as a Messiah and hope for the Jews of Jesus' time was written by Wang Xuecheng 王學晟, "Misaiya mimi xinjie" 彌賽亞祕密新解 (New Interpretation of Messianic Secret), *Shengjing wenxue yanjiu* 聖經文學研究 - *Biblical Literary Studies* No. 7 (2013), pp. 354-379. Cf. earlier books by William Wrede: *Das Messiasgeheimnis in den Evangelien* (Göttingen: Vandenhoeck und Ruprecht, 1901) and its translation by J.C.G. Greig, The Messianic Secret (Cambridge - London: J. Clarke, 1971) and Alfred Edward John Rawlinson, *The Gospel according to St. Mark* (London: Methuen, 1936). All these works point to the interesting "claim" that Jesus during his ministry did not like to be characterized, and especially resisted being highlighted, honoured and praised as Messiah. See also Marián Gálik, "Wang Meng's *On the Cross* (1988) after 25 Years," *Asian and African Studies,* n.s. (Bratislava) 23 (2014) 2, pp. 274-287. As for different interpretation(s) of the Messiah in the times of the Old Testament, see John Day (ed.), *King and Messiah in Israel and the Ancient Near East, Journal for the Study of the Old Testament. Supplement Series 270* (Sheffield: Sheffield Academic Press, 1998).

[33] *Sheng zhi wancheng*, p. 20.

would be prepared to face with him what in the end was the mission given him by Yahweh. The word *wancheng* 完成 (to complete, or accomplish), referred to all that preceded the death of Jesus on the Cross.³⁴ Mary did not imagine the kind of suffering that awaited Jesus. As in Jn 12:3 she took "a pound of ointment of spikenard, very costly, and anointed the feet of Jesus, and wiped his feet with her hair: and the house was filled with the odour of the ointment."³⁵

2

The second act of the drama takes place in the same house of Simon the Leper. Only Judas Iscariot left and "went to the chief priests" (Mt 26:14). This act begins with John, Jesus' beloved disciple, and with the phrase "Here am I" (*Wo zai zheli* 我在這裏). John responds to Jesus' call. In the Bible this same response was used always when, for instance, God spoke to Abraham, before the burnt offerings of Isaac in the land of Moriah (Genesis 22:1), or in the moment with Samuel, called by God to be one of his prophets (1 Samuel 3:10). God called Samuel three times, and here John three times is calling Jesus the Lord (*zhu a* 主啊). Jesus answers with the same words as Abraham or Samuel.³⁶ Repetition is one of the literary methods we often find in the construction of biblical texts. Xiang Peiliang uses repetition as well, but in the most simple of ways.³⁷ John observes that Messiah Jesus is sad or distressed (*youchou* 憂愁). Jesus answers that he feels only a bit uncomfortable (*nanshou* 難受). Jesus admits John's assertion fully later in Gethsemane when he says to him, his brother James, and Peter, "My soul is exceedingly sorrowful, even unto death; tarry ye here, and watch with me" (Mt 26:38). Together with John, Mary is engaged in dialogue with Jesus. Now Jesus explains to both what is necessary for him to complete or accomplish his given task. He came to this world to fulfil the will of his Heavenly Father as we read in Jn 6:38: "For I came down from heaven, not to do mine own will, but the will of him that sent me," and this will (*zhiyi* 旨意), written in the Scriptures, he will fulfil: to die on the Cross to atone for the sins of mankind, to be resurrected from the dead on the third day, to be received into Heaven, and to bestow the Holy Spirit upon all his followers that they may believe what he said. Jesus does not want that his disciples and friends be participants in his suffering and death. He asks from them and needs a strong faith (*xinxin* 信心) in him, and in all that is his Father's will. Faith, God's will, and completing or accomplishing his mission are the most repeated words in Xiang Peiliang's

---

[34] *Sheng zhi wancheng*, p. 25.
[35] Ibid., p. 27.
[36] Ibid., pp. 29-33.
[37] Many forms of more complicated and literarily more successful repetition appear in Robert Alter's *The World of the Biblical Literature* (New York: Basic Books, 1991), pp. 35-40, 42 and 72-75.

drama. After the dialogue, Jesus and Mary leave the stage to pray, but John, the "disciple whom Jesus loved" (Jn 21:20) was not invited to join them.[38]

The first question of Peter for John after their departure is the reason for that departure. John answers that it is the bitter grief in Mary's heart. Peter asks about Jesus' moods during their dialogue. According to him, the Lord should be happy, having witnessed the whole of Jerusalem calling him the King of the Jews! John answers that Jesus is not happy. The second question of Peter is, when will Jesus be anointed as king, when will he govern over his people as did King David? John does not have the time to answer by the moment that Judas Iscariot, James, Andreas, Matthew and other disciples of Jesus arrive. James puts the same question to the disciples who are present in the scene. Judas's assertion is as it was in the first act of the drama. The Lord will not be the king of the Jews. Peter, the rock on which Jesus wants to build his church (Mt 16:18), responds with impolite words, "You say nonsense" (*hushuo* 糊說), a brushing aside of Judas's reasoning.

How could Peter know this better than the other disciples of the Lord? Judas says that the sons and grandsons of Abraham do not need a king. Not having a king is the will of Yahweh. Peter denounces this view as blasphemy. At this point, in the longest monologue in the drama, Matthew claims that since the time of the Babylonian invasion, the Jews have not had a king, and now they are as ill-treated by foreigners as they were the time of Egyptian rule. At that time, Yahweh sent Moses to save his people. Now he sends Jesus Christ to do the same. David's descendant will govern us.

According to James, Jesus will be a military leader in the way that Joshua was. David and the Jews will follow in war chariots as their ancestors once did. Once again, faith is highlighted as the most important of all priorities. Peter and James assert that Judas Iscariot does not have faith, and those who are faithless are both blind and deaf. It is necessary to wait for an anointing ceremony. That ceremony is to occur on a day that will resemble the day of anointing for King David. Judas tells the other apostles that they do not know the Scriptures. He points to 1 Samuel 15:1, where Samuel anoints Saul as king over the Hebrews, but does so not because of the Amalekites, as Xiang Peiliang writes in this act of the drama,[39] but because the Philistines are hostile to the Jews, and the people want a king as the Gentiles have, although it is not the will of God (1 Samuel 8:4-20). Peter contradicts Judas. God rejected Saul as king, he says, because he did not like him, but did not say that the "LORD of hosts" ordered him, "Now go and smite Amalek, and utterly destroy all that they have, and spare them not; but slay both man and woman, infant and suckling, ox and sheep, camel and ass" (1 Samuel 15:2-3). James adds to Peter's claim that after Jesus is king of their nation, all Jews will rise (*qilai* 起來) and cast off foreign shackles. Yahweh's hand will help his people as it did during the Egyptian yoke. Judas insists that Roman power is much stronger than that of the Assyrians and Babylonians. Two times in his short

---

[38] *Sheng zhi wancheng*, p. 37.
[39] *Ibid.*, p. 42.

comment Peter accuses Judas of lacking faith in Yahweh, who could again divide the waters of the sea and come to help his anointed. Did not our Lord Jesus say to us, "If you have faith and you say to the mount that it should move to another place [and] you will see that it did"?[40] Judas then similarly responds as Caiaphas, the High Priest, said, "Don't you think that it is better if one man dies for the people and obviates thus the death of the whole population?"[41] To this John remarks, "Not only the death of the whole nation, but of the whole world. One man dies for the atonement of the sins of all nations." To this Judas makes no comment. Both these judgments are concerned with Jesus, but they contain completely different messages.

Jesus returns to his twelve without Mary. Even Lazarus, the Samaritan and Martha do not appear on the stage during the remaining part of the play. Peter tells Jesus that Judas Iscariot does not believe that He will become the King of the Jews, or that he wants this to happen. Jesus agrees with Judas's judgment: "He is right because the Jews do not want to recognize (*renshi* 認識) their king."[42]

The Last Supper is not even mentioned in Xiang Peiliang's drama. The second act ends with the washing of the disciples' feet and Jesus' admonishment to love each other as he has loved them. The drama at this point emphasizes that in his Heavenly Kingdom "many that are first shall be the last; and the last shall be the first" (Mt 20:30, Mk 10:31). Judas does not allow Jesus to wash his feet. He simply leaves the stage. Jesus warns him that although he may act according to his own intentions, he is responsible for his deed. Judas will regret it, but it will be too late.

3

In the third act, a High Priest, probably Caiaphas, according to Xiang Peiliang's reasoning, one of the Elders, Jesus, Peter, John, James and Mary are all present on the stage. This act is divided into two parts, both in the Garden of Gethsemane. In the first part, we meet the High Priest, one of the Elders, and Judas Iscariot. The time ought to be late at night, before Jesus and his three disciples, "who often attended him on a number of occasions," pray in an "agony of spirit that the cup of suffering may pass from him" (Mk 5:57, 9:3, 14:33).[43] Judas informs the High Priest that Jesus will certainly come to this place. Both the High Priest and the Elder are quite sure that it is necessary to arrest him during the

---

[40] *Sheng zhi wancheng*, pp. 44-45. Peter has in mind Jesus' saying from Mt 21:21-22 or Mk 11:22-23. It is said in a figurative language and is hardly believable. According to the RSV The Oxford Annotated Bible with the Apocrypha. Revised Standard Edition (New York: Oxford University Press, 1965; hereafter: RSV) where is maintained that "Jesus emphasizes not power in faith but the power of God" (p. 1230).

[41] "... it is expedient for us, that one man should die for the people, and the whole nation perish not" (Jn 11:50).

[42] Jesus foresees the words of the chief priests: "We have no king but Caesar" (Jn 19:14).

[43] Turner, "The Life and Teaching of Jesus Christ," p. 448.

night. Judas is interested how much he will receive for his delivery (Mt 26:15). According to Xiang Peiliang Judas asks for more than thirty pieces of silver, but the High Priest says that it is not possible. The Elder asks about Jesus' relation to him and the other disciples. Judas answers that the Lord is good to him, as he is to all. Why then he is prepared to deliver Jesus to them? Judas answers that he has a reason for doing so. Later in the dialogue, he explains that notwithstanding the fact that Jesus is his rabbi, he is dangerous for the whole nation, because he proclaims himself as the King of the Jews. What is more, his disciples and people around him want to support him as a real king.

Yahweh, however, does not want kings to reign over Jews. Should they have a king, Yahweh will reject him as he rejected King Saul (1 Samuel 15:26). In addition, the followers of Jesus want to begin an anti-foreign uprising, which includes a movement against Caesar and Rome.

Both the High Priest and the Elder suppose that they are the best choices to govern their nation. An insurrection against Rome would be fatal for all concerned. Caesar would with a single finger push the entire country into the sea. All three unanimously proclaim it as their duty to prevent such destruction. The High Priest views Judas Iscariot as "the greatest patriot (*aiguozhe* 愛國者)." For the Elder, he is the greatest good man (*haoren* 好人). Judas agrees with them. In this way, he justifies his treachery.[44] The High Priest asserts that for betraying Jesus, the whole nation will excuse him or even sing praises (*chengzan* 稱讚) of him. The Elder adds that the entire world will eulogize him. Neither the servants of the High Priest nor of the Elder have ever met Jesus. They therefore ask how to recognize him. Judas's answer in Xiang Peiliang's drama is only a slightly different paraphrase of Mk 14:44: "Whomsoever I shall kiss, that same is he; take him, and lead him away safely."[45]

After they leave the scene, Jesus comes to Gethsemane together with his three most preferred apostles, Peter, John and James. Jesus asks them if they are not too tired. He seems to enjoy the murmur of the trees and of Cedron Brook (Jn 18:1). He speaks about life, about the creation of humankind. He speaks of human souls. Life is everywhere, even in the gurgle of the flowing water and the rustle of tree branches. Repetitive words on the arrival of spring occur three times. Jesus speaks about the green leaves of grapes, of young grass, the cedars of Libanon, the swift waves dancing on both banks of the Cedron. But this spring, the Son of Man will not witness any of this.

Peter and John do not believe his words. Then Jesus three times repeats why he must leave them soon to realize (*shixing* 實行, the same as "to consummate") the will of his Father. All the other *shiming* 使命 missions are to be handed over to them. John is surprised that Jesus would respond to all this in a tone that is so cool (*lengleng qingqing* 冷冷清清). How can he so quietly leave them? Peter and James say that they are prepared to die with Jesus, who declares that for him they will suffer, be attacked, and even killed. This night he will leave them. Later

---

[44] *Sheng zhi wancheng*, p. 58.
[45] *Ibid.*, p. 60.

they will meet in Galilee, where he will go before them.⁴⁶ John sees him very distressed (*youshang* 憂傷). Jesus answers that this is so because he is very fond of all who follow him. Still, this parting must soon happen. As regards the question John asks, if he in this situation thinks also about his Mother and brother, Jesus answers that he has no mother or brother.⁴⁷ He has his mission, and he belongs to mankind (*shiren* 世人).⁴⁸ When Peter says that death on the cross involves terrible emotions, and the punishment on the body is like a nightmare (*emeng* 噩夢), Jesus simply adds to Peter's words: "Assuming that the spirit is involved, it is nothing frightening." To Peter's question how death on the cross relates to the body, Jesus does not answer.⁴⁹ But he characterizes the death as it is expressed in the Gospels.⁵⁰

Before Judas Iscariot arrives at the Temple to make the arrest, probably in the company of officers of the law, Jesus asks three disciples to watch with him. He prays two times in petition, asking his Father take away this "cup of suffering," but not according to his will, but as his Father wants it to be done.⁵¹

At moments between these scenes, his friend Mary appears at the side of the praying Jesus. He at first does not notice her, and she waits until he finishes. She approaches him, kneels down, and kisses his feet. Then she stands and embraces him. Jesus puts his hands on her shoulders and kisses her hair. Tenderly, he then pushes her away, saying, "Now I may reach out my hand for that bitter cup. You may go."⁵² (p. 75). This scene is not found in the Gospels. It is very possibly according to the understanding that Xiang Peiliang reached after a deduction from Jesus' own characterization of Mary in Lk 10:42: "But one thing is needful, and Mary hath chosen that good part, which shall not be taken away from her." From these words we may see that Jesus "approved Mary's preference [in contrast to

---

⁴⁶ Cf. Mt 26:32, 28:7 and Mk 14:28, 16:7.

⁴⁷ In Mt 12:48-50 we read: "Who is my mother? And who are my brethren? And he stretched forth his hand toward his disciples, and said, 'Behold my mother and my brethren! For whosoever shall do the will of my Father which is in heaven, the same is my brother, and sister, and mother'." Here in Xiang Peiliang's text the word "brother" is in the singular form. He had in mind one of the brothers (or cousins) of Jesus. According to Mt 13:55 they were four: James, Joses, Simon and Judas. In later translation, for instance, in the RSV Joses is transcribed as Joseph. It is also possible that Xiang Peiliang made a mistake when writing in this way.

⁴⁸ *Sheng zhi wancheng*, p. 67.

⁴⁹ *Ibid.*, p. 68.

⁵⁰ Cf. Mt 26:41: "Watch and pray, that ye enter not into the temptation: the spirit indeed is willing, but the flesh is weak" and Mk 14:38: "Watch ye and pray, lest ye enter into temptation. The spirit truly is ready, but the flesh is weak."

⁵¹ *Sheng zhi wancheng*, pp. 70-71. Cf. Mt 26:39: "O my Father, if it be possible, let this cup pass from me: nevertheless not as I will, but as thou wilt." And again Mt 26:42: "O my Father, if this cup may not pass away from me, except I drink it, thy will be done."

⁵² *Sheng zhi wancheng*, p. 75.

Martha, M.G.] for listening to his teaching"[53] and approved as well her chaste love for him.[54]

Jesus calls Peter after Mary leaves. Jesus says to him and the two sons of Zebedee: "You have to watch (*liuxin* 留心)!" This is one of the four warnings of Jesus from his earlier teaching and he addresses his words also to the three disciples during his time of prayer in Gethsemane (Mt 26:41, Mk 13:33, 35:37 and 14:38). At that moment it is possible to hear the voices of the multitude coming to arrest him, and to see the light of their torches. The last words of Jesus in the play under analysis are, "You may go. My hour is at hand."[55]

*

Jesus Christ is the protagonist of this modern Chinese drama. His antagonist is Judas Iscariot. But we may see that Judas is only partly antagonistic, since he has a high esteem for the ethical teachings of Jesus and for the humane behaviour he observes in Jesus toward neighbours, including his disciples. He does not betray his rabbi for the money, but for the idea of the preservation of the Jewish people in the case of insurrection against the Roman Empire, which was to some extent foreseeable and even possible after Jesus' miracles, the results of his ministry, and his fame as a Messiah. The Galilean kind of Judaism, quite pietistic, and to which Jesus probably belonged was widespread at that time. Also, presumably the impact of the nationalism of the Zealot type was great upon the inhabitants of Galilee.[56] Zealotic and nationalistic aspirations were present in the minds of others among the apostles of Jesus as well, especially John and James.[57]

It may seem strange that Simon the Cannanean is not even mentioned in Xiang Peiliang's drama. This is probably because his name is only found a few times in the Bible and Xiang Peiliang tried to be "faithful" as much as possible to the text of the Gospels.

Xiang Peiliang was a follower of that trend of literary theory and criticism of which the most important representatives were Lu Xun's brother, Zhou Zuoren 周作人 (1885–1967) and Liang Shiqiu 梁實秋 (1903–1987).[58] *Renlei de yishu* appeared only one month before "Zhongguo minzu wenyi yundong xuanyan" 中國民族文藝運動宣言 (A Manifesto of the Chinese National Literary Move-

---

[53] In the RSV comment we see that "Jesus approved Mary's preference for listening to his teaching as contrasted with Martha's unneeded acts of hospitality," p. 1260.

[54] For more about Mary, Martha and Jesus, see Francis Moloney, "The Faith of Martha and Mary. A Narrative Approach to Jn 11, 17-40," *Biblica. Commentarii Periodici Instituti Biblici* 75 (1994) 4, pp. 471-493.

[55] *Sheng zhi wancheng*, p. 76. Cf. Mt 26:45-46 and Mk 14:41.

[56] On Zealotism, see a short explanation in: Johann Maier, *Judentum von A bis Z. Glauben, Geschichte, Kultur* (Freiburg: Herder, 2001), pp. 435-436.

[57] See Mk 10:35-40.

[58] Marián Gálik, *The Genesis of Modern Chinese Criticism (1917-1930)* (Bratislava – London: Veda-Curzon Press, 1980), pp. 17-24 and 285-307.

ment)[59] and it is possible that Xiang Peiliang was among those who felt sympathy with it, or was its fellow-traveller. In any case, later he was the author of a long five act drama entitled *Minzu zhan* 民族戰 (National War), a very free imitation of Friedrich Schiller's *Wilhelm Tell*[60] brought into Manchuria during the Sino-Japanese War after the Mukden Incident on September 18, 1931. Xiang Peiliang is also the author of the short story "Sansun yu Delina" 叁孫與德麗娜 (Samson and Delilah), published in *Xiandai wenxue* 現代文學 (Modern Literature) No. 3, (Sept. 16, 1930), pp. 95-119. This story also evidences an anti-Japanese orientation. To the best of my knowledge, it has not yet been studied.[61]

Xiang Peiliang's sympathy for "national problems" is understandable. His deciphering of an antagonistic relation between Jesus and Judas Iscariot is likewise not surprising. Jesus was aware of his mission as a Messiah of another kind, and popular reactions to the drama are typical for Jews of that time and later. Jesus himself indeed had nationalists in his vicinity. He did not approve, however, of insurrection against the Romans which could end, as later occurred during the Jewish War (66–73), with the fall of Jerusalem, the destruction of the Temple under Titus in the year 70, and other strongholds, including Masada in 73. The last attempt to restore an independent national Jewish state ended with the insurrection of Simon bar Koseba (alias Bar Cochba, "Son of the star") in 132–135. Jesus' prophecy on the day of his Triumphal Entry to Jerusalem was only partly realized when he said at the sight of several Pharisees weeping over Jerusalem:

> For the days shall come upon thee, that thine enemies shall cast a trench about thee, and compass thee round, and keep thee in on every side, and shall lay thee even with the ground, and thy children within thee; and they shall not leave in thee one stone upon another; because thou knewest not the time of thy visitation (Lk 19:43-44).

Numerous other writers after Friedrich Gottlieb Klopstock (1724–1803) in his *Messias* used the Messianic mission of Jesus as the *Stoff* for their works. In Klopstock's drama, Judas Iscariot believes in messianic rule over Jews, and tries to derive profit from it. The hero of Goethe's *Der ewige Jude* is a disappointed patriot, not an apostate, and does not betray because of money.[62]

---

[59] Wang Yao 王瑤, *Zhongguo xin wenxue shigao* 中國新文學史稿 (Draft of History of Modern Chinese Literature), vol. 1 (Shanghai: Xin wenyi chubanshe, 1953), p. 156.

[60] Xiang Peiliang, "Zixu" 自序 (Self-Preface, pp. 1-7) in the mentioned drama published in 1939 by the Huazhong tushu gongsi in Chongqing. See the excellent study by Barbara Kaulbach where at least accessible materials for the study of Xiang Peiliang's piece are shortly analyzed: "Schillers *Wilhelm Tell* im Chinesischen Widerstand. Zur Rezeption von Schiller's Helden in China," *TRANS Internet-Zeitschrift für Kulturwissenschaften* No. 17 (March 2010), see http://inst.at/trans/17Nr/3-2/3-2_kaulbach17.htm (May 20, 2016). I am very much indebted to Dr. Kaulbach for providing me with a xeroxed copy of this drama.

[61] Herewith I thank Professor Xie Zhixi 解志熙 for presenting this story to me on the occasion of my 80th birthday on February 21, 2013.

[62] See "Judas Ischarioth," in: Elisabeth Frenzel, *Stoffe der Weltliteratur. Ein Lexikon dichtungsgeschichtlicher Längsschnitte* (Stuttgart: Alfred Kröner Verlag, 1976), p. 376.

Renlei de yishu is a very important contribution to the understanding of literature and art prevailing in China in the beginning of 1930s and partly in the world. Differently than authors such as James George Frazer, *The Golden Bough,* 12 vols. (London 1913–1915), Ernest Alfred Wallis Budge, *Osiris and the Egyptian Resurrection,* 2 vols. (New York 1911), Ivor Brown, *The First Player. The Origins of Drama* (New York 1928), Loomis Havemeyer, *The Drama of Savage People* (New Haven 1916), who saw the beginning of theatre in the rituals and myths of ancient peoples, Xiang Peiliang strongly emphasizes the importance of the Bible, and elaborates the story of Mahalalel and Madala we mentioned above. The beginning of poetry, according to him, is however even earlier, and begins with Eve's retelling of the stories of Eden to her son Cain with the instruction that he should tell them for posterity. According to Xiang Peiliang, in this way allegedly "literature began. From this we may know that the literature has its origin in a woman, a woman who was a mother."[63] We should of course, be critical of such statements.

In any case we should see the germs of his theory of art and literature as set directly in the Bible. This work of drama about Jesus is a kind of parable, and shows us a pattern or a memorial similar to what we find in Joshua 22:28: "Behold the pattern [or copy, M.G.] of the altar of the LORD, which our fathers made, not for burnt offerings, nor for sacrifices ..." not so much for praying, but for producing literature and art for mankind. The sacrificial altar mentioned above is within the Great temple (Dadian 大殿), or God's temple (Shendian 神殿), which is very probably an allusion to the First and Second Temple. In addition to the briefly analyzed, "We Pray under the Sacrificial Altar," another study from the *Renlei de yishu* entitled "Renlei – yishu – wenxue" 人類—藝術—文學 (Humankind – Art – Literature) is also deserving of careful study.

But this is beyond the scope of the present essay.

---

[63] *Renlei de yishu*, p. 152.

"A FORTUNATE ENCOUNTER"
SU XUELIN AS A CHINESE CATHOLIC WRITER*

BARBARA HOSTER

Su Xuelin 蘇雪林 (1897–1999) belongs to the first generation of women writers in modern Chinese literature.[1] She is also one of the rare examples of a May Fourth intellectual who converted to the Catholic faith. In this respect she is often compared to her male contemporary, the well-known writer and legal scholar Wu Jingxiong 吳經熊 (John C.H. Wu, 1899–1986).[2]

In this article, I show that Su Xuelin's conversion was by no means a mere biographic episode, but left a lasting imprint on her life and works. Traces of her Catholic faith can be found in her fictional as well as her non-fictional writings. Although she once described her conversion as "a fortunate encounter" (*yizhong qiyu* 一種奇遇),[3] her life as a Catholic intellectual in 20th century China was not without trial and made her an outsider in the literary scene.

Su Xuelin was a versatile writer, who has left quite a large body of works, including fiction, poetry, literary criticism, autobiographical works, translations, diaries, obituaries, travelogues, and texts on diverse topics. A collection of her

---

* A previous version of this article was presented at the international workshop "'I Have Called You by Name' – Contribution of Chinese Women to the Church," Sankt Augustin, Germany, 25–26 September 2014. I owe a debt of gratitude to Fr. Roman Malek, whose participation in a research project on religious change and conversion at the University of Basel (see Malek 2012) aroused my interest in Su Xuelin and her conversion to the Catholic faith. Having worked together with Fr. Malek for more than two decades, in particular during his time as director of the Monumenta Serica Institute and editor-in-chief of its publications, has been a rewarding experience. His extraordinary vigor, creativity, and dedication to his work will remain a source of inspiration for me.

[1] Usually counted among this group are Bing Xin 冰心 (1900–1999), Chen Hengzhe 陳衡哲 (1890–1976), Ding Ling 丁玲 (1904–1986), Feng Yuanjun 馮沅君 (1900–1974), Ling Shuhua 凌叔華 (1900–1990), Lu Yin 盧隱 (1898–1934) and a few others. – On Su Xuelin's biography, see, e.g., Lee – Stefanowska 2003, pp. 489-495, Wu San-san 2012, pp. 383-389, and Chen Changming 2014, pp. 17-40. See also her autobiographies *Wo de shenghuo* 我的生活 (1971) and *Fusheng jiusi* 浮生九四 (1991; in the following abbreviated as *FSJS*).

[2] See, e.g., Monsterleet – Gu Baogu, n.d., on Su Xuelin and Wu Jingxiong. On the latter, see Guo Guoqi 2006.

[3] Su Xuelin, "Yige guiyi Tianzhujiao Wusi ren de zibai" 一個皈依天主教五四人的自白 (Confession of a May Fourth Person Who Converted to Catholicism), first published in a collection edited by the priest Li Dianran 李奠然 entitled *Guiyi zishu* 皈依自述 (Personal Accounts of Conversion; Taibei: Guangqi, 1958; new ed. Xinzhuang: Furen daxue chubanshe, 1983), p. 102. In the following, this text is cited as "Zibai." Page numbers refer to the version included in *Linghai weilan* 靈海微瀾, vol. 3, pp. 74-106.

articles on religious themes and personalities, originally published in newspapers and journals, was issued by the Catholic publisher Wendao 聞道 in Tainan under the title *Linghai weilan* 靈海微瀾 (translated into English as *Some Thoughts of Mind*).[4]

"A Spiritual Odyssey" – The Theme of Conversion in the Novel *Jixin*

For Su Xuelin, her conversion to Catholicism as a student in France in 1924 was beyond doubt a crucial event in her life. Her conversion experience is most clearly reflected in her only novel *Jixin* 棘心 (Heart of Thorns), written a few years after her return from France and first published in 1929.[5] Like the heroine of *Jixin*, a young woman named Xingqiu 醒秋, Su Xuelin had studied French language and literature at the Institut franco-chinois in Lyon from October 1921 to May 1925.[6] The novel can be read as a kind of "Entwicklungsroman,"[7] a "coming-of-age story" that describes the protagonist's psychological development during her stay abroad and her struggles with a number of crises. The question of love and marriage is addressed, as well as the relation between mother and daughter and the encounter with French culture. Yet the most important topic in this work is that of conversion, making the text unique in the literature of the Republican period. As the plot centers on the protagonist's spiritual development from her rejection of religion to her commitment to the Catholic faith, I read the

---

[4] 5 vols., 1978–1996. I am indebted to Wu San-san 吳姍姍, Tainan, for drawing my attention to this collection, and to Wang Mei-ling 王美玲, Taibei, for making it available to me.

[5] The title of the novel alludes to a poem in the Chinese classic *Shijing* 詩經 (Book of Songs) about the loving care and sorrows of a mother for her child ("Beifeng" 北風 32). The compound *jixin* 棘心 can be literally translated as "heart of the thorn bush," but it is also a metaphor for the child and its affection towards its mother (see *Grand dictionnaire Ricci de la langue chinoise*, vol. I, p. 461, entry no. 823). Su Xuelin dedicated the novel to the memory of her mother, who died shortly after Su Xuelin's return home.

[6] This newly founded Chinese–French institution of higher learning was designed to prepare Chinese students for their studies at regular universities in France. For a history of this institution, in Chinese also known as Zhong-Fa daxue 中法大學, Haiwai daxue 海外大學 or Li'ang daxue 里昂大學, see Pinet – Li 2001. According to Su Xuelin's "Bulletin d'Identité," kept in the Archives of the Fonds chinois in the Bibliothèque municipale in Lyon, she enrolled at the Institut franco-chinois under the name Su Mei 蘇梅 on 3 October 1921, initially to study Fine Arts. Without having finished her studies, she departed on 22 May 1925 to return to China; see "Liste des noms des étudiants de l'Institut franco-chinois de Lyon (1921–1946)," in: Boully – Li 1987, p. 29.

[7] This literary genre presents, with psychological consistency, the inner and outer development of a person's character until reaching maturity, see Wilpert 1989, pp. 238-239. Novels of this genre are sometimes also labelled as "Bildungsroman" ("formation novel"). On the latter term, see Cuddon 2013, p. 77. In English literature, Charles Dickens's novel *David Copperfield* is regarded as one of the foremost examples of this genre. Su Xuelin refers to *David Copperfield* in her preface to the revised version of *Jixin* and compares it, with regard to its blend of fictional and autobiographical elements, to her own novel (*Jixin zengdingben* 1957 [hereafter: JXZDB], p. 5).

novel as a "conversion narrative."[8] This reading is supported by Su Xuelin's remark in her autobiography *Fusheng jiusi* 浮生九四 (Ninety-four Years of a Floating Life) that *Jixin* recounts the story of her conversion.[9]

As the process of Xingqiu's conversion is fairly complicated, with many twists and turns, the novel has been aptly called the depiction of a "spiritual odyssey."[10] Xingqiu comes to Lyon as a young intellectual deeply imbued with the spirit of the Chinese May Fourth Movement, a cultural renaissance movement that, among other things, advocated rationalism and rejected religion as superstitious. In this atheist vein, she exchanges her views on religion in her correspondence with Shujian 叔健, her fiancé who is studying in the United States. She also sends him an anti-religious journal published in Chinese at her school. In fact, the Institut franco-chinois in Lyon was a stronghold of the anti-religious movement among the Chinese students in Europe.[11] To her surprise, her sober and rational fiancé, a student of engineering, speaks strongly in favor of religion, advocating religious freedom and praising Christian virtues as useful for society. His views clearly reflect some of the pro-religious positions in the contemporary debate on religion among Chinese intellectuals.[12] In the correspondence exchange, as well as in other passages of the novel, Su Xuelin proves herself to be well versed in the ideological discourses of her time.

The protagonist, Xingqiu, not only rejects religion on rational grounds, she is also prejudiced against the manifestations of Catholic life she encounters in Lyon on a more emotional level. At the time of her arrival, she associates the notions of "darkness" (*hei'an* 黑暗) and "corruption" (*fubai* 腐敗) with the Catholic faith. When she sees priests in the streets wearing their black cassocks, she resentfully comments on them as "black crows that will be wiped away by the tides of time."[13] The liturgy during a Catholic mass she attends strikes her as awkward and artificial.

Her negative attitude towards religion in general and Christianity in particular gradually changes after she becomes acquainted with two French Catholic women, a nun named Masha 馬沙 and a teacher called Bailang 白朗. Both of them are fervent believers and embody Christian virtues such as charity and self-sacrifice in their daily life. Xingqiu is deeply impressed by their "Christian spirit

---

[8] On conversion narratives cf. Stromberg 2014.

[9] See *FSJS*, p. 93.

[10] See Monsterleet 1953, p. 87.

[11] A number of authors in a collection of anti-religious articles in Chinese published in France were students of the Institut franco-chinois in Lyon. On this work entitled *Wusuowei zongjiao* 無所謂宗教 ("No Religion!"), see Boully 1995, p. 291 (no. 2158). On the anti-religious movement, see Bastid-Bruguière 2002.

[12] On this debate, see Chow Tse-tsung 1960, pp. 320-327 and Siebenhandl 1982.

[13] *Jixin*, p. 124. In this paper I refer to the following edition of the novel: *Jixin* 棘心 (Shanghai 1987; facsimile of the original edition, Shanghai: Beixin shuju, 1929), hereafter abbreviated as *JX*.

of active service and the virtue of love"[14] and becomes close friends with them. The two women, on their part, try to convince Xingqiu to adopt the Catholic faith. In the novel, this gradual process of Xingqiu's approach to Christianity is reflected in several stages.[15] An important part in this process is played by the discussions she has with Masha and Bailang on matters of faith, for example about the immortality of the soul.

Lengthy excerpts from Xingqiu's diary document her spiritual change. She starts to reflect more thoroughly on the phenomenon of religion and begins to realize its positive effects on human life. She is attracted to the clarity of Christian values and to the "uncompromising spirit" of many Christians, who are determined to fight for their convictions. She compares the Christian spirit to the Chinese pursuit of harmony and balance represented in the Confucian ideal of *zhongyong* 中庸, the "golden mean of moderation."[16] Xingqiu criticizes the Chinese for being too materialistic and hedonistic, only striving for short-lived personal wellness. She blames their egoistic attitude in life for the deplorable state of the Chinese nation, where corruption and injustice reign. She demands "a reformation of souls" (*xinling gaizao* 心靈改造) to save China.[17]

In her diary, Xingqiu only suggests that the solution for China's national crisis could be the spreading of the Christian faith. She is more outspoken in a conversation with Chinese fellow students in Lyon when she announces that if China had more Christian role models like Masha and Bailang, who were willing to sacrifice themselves and serve society, the country would turn from a weak into a strong nation.[18]

Through the influence of Masha and Bailang and her intellectual preoccupation with the Christian faith, Xingqiu becomes an advocate of Christianity, but she is still not ready to convert. Among other reasons, she has strong reservations about some Christian doctrines, in particular Jesus Christ's divinity and miracles. The decisive turn in her conversion process is triggered by two personal crises. First, she receives news from home about her mother's serious illness. In her desperation, she agrees with Bailang's proposal to pray to God for her mother's health and she promises to convert if her mother is healed. But when Xingqiu hears of her mother's recovery, she breaks her promise and refuses to receive baptism because she fears being slandered as a national traitor by her Chinese fellow students.

Then a second crisis makes her renew her decision to become a Catholic. Her fiancé Shujian rejects her invitation to join her in France and marry her. In-

---

[14] *JX*, p. 147.

[15] For a detailed analysis of the conversion process in the novel, see my study *Konversion zum Christentum in der modernen chinesischen Literatur. Su Xuelins Roman* Jixin *(Dornenherz, 1929)* (Hoster 2017).

[16] Cf. *JX*, p. 152. – On the concept of *zhongyong*, see Yao Xinzhong 2003, p. 832.

[17] *JX*, p. 160.

[18] Cf. *JX*, p. 184.

stead, he coolly informs her that he will return directly to China after his graduation in the United States and wait for her until she finishes her studies in France. Deeply hurt by his lack of romantic feelings towards her, she stages a "family rebellion." In a letter to her parents she categorically states that she will break off the engagement. As her parents refuse to give their consent, Xingqiu sees only one way out of her crisis. In order not to marry her fiancé, whom she now deeply despises, she is finally resolved to adopt the Christian faith and subsequently become a nun together with her friend Bailang. By joining a religious order she hopes to save her family's face, as, in China, this was an accepted means of avoiding an arranged marriage.[19] At the end of her winding path towards Christianity, Xingqiu is baptized in the Basilica Notre-Dame de Fourvière in Lyon.[20]

Su Xuelin devotes the remaining chapters of her novel to the description of Xingqiu's initial euphoria about her conversion, which is followed by severe doubts about her newly adopted faith. The reasons for this "post-conversion crisis"[21] are manifold. They lie, among others, in Xingqiu's unruly personality and her unwillingness to submit herself to the rules and regulations of a Christian lifestyle. For fear of the strict monastic life, she eventually gives up her plan to become a nun. After being once more confronted by the hostile attitude of her Chinese fellow students in Lyon towards her conversion, she plunges into deep despair. She regains strength in prayer and in her friendship with Bailang. Xingqiu ultimately decides to return to China because her mother has fallen fatally ill again. Upon leaving France, Xingqiu solemnly pledges to Bailang that she will never betray her faith.

The end of the novel is open with regard to the protagonist's conversion. In the last chapter, the reader is informed in retrospect that Xingqiu and her fiancé were reconciled and got married at the deathbed of her mother. There are only few allusions to the Christian faith. In a letter to her husband, Xingqiu expresses her gratitude for having seen her mother pass away peacefully. Was this made possible by the "compassion of the Holy Mother" or by the "protection of supernatural beings"?[22] The answer is not given. We do not know if Xingqiu still believes in the Catholic faith or if she has returned to the traditional Chinese belief in spirits. One may speculate on the reasons for this open end. Although Su Xuelin's novel shows many characteristic traits of a typical conversion narrative, she did not entirely construct *Jixin* along the lines of this kind of narrative that

---

[19] In imperial China, it was not uncommon for women to enter a Buddhist monastery if they did not want to marry. This is depicted, e.g., in the 8th chapter of the late Ming, early Qing novel *Xingshi yinyuan zhuan* 醒世姻緣傳 (Marriage Destinies to Awaken the World). Cf. Motsch 2003, p. 204.

[20] Like her protagonist, Su Xuelin was also baptized in this Basilica, namely on 15 August 1924, the Feast of the Assumption. See *FSJS*, p. 86.

[21] I employ Lewis Rambo's term, see Rambo 1993, p. 136.

[22] *JX*, p. 320.

usually "calls for a conversion."²³ Obviously she did not intend to convince her readers to follow her protagonist in becoming a Christian.

Regarding its religious character, the reception of the novel by contemporary critics was equivocal: While *Jixin* was labelled as "a literary work with Catholic colour" (*gongjiao secai de wenyi zuopin* 公教色彩的文藝作品) by a Chinese critic,²⁴ a Belgian missionary in China, Jean Monsterleet S.J., expressed his regret that the novel did not meet the expectations of an outstanding work of Catholic literature in China. Such a work, in his opinion, should compare with the writings of Ba Jin 巴金 (1904–2005) and Mao Dun 茅盾 (1896–1981) in depicting the social reality and historical background of China. Furthermore, it should have a deeper psychological dimension, as it is commonly found in French literature. Though Monsterleet's judgment on *Jixin* is not enthusiastic, he still calls it a "unique document of the history of religious feeling" in China.²⁵ With regard to a more elaborate description of the historical background, he might have evaluated the novel more favorably, had he known the revised and enlarged version *Jixin zengdingben* 棘心增訂本 that Su Xuelin published in Taiwan in 1957, almost three decades later than its original edition. In her preface to this revised edition Su Xuelin clarifies her view on the novel. According to her

> the gist of this book is the introduction of a young woman, an intellectual living in an epoch of political transformations in China, who has been deeply influenced by the ideas of the May Fourth Movement, but who eventually converts to Catholicism. With the unfolding of the plot, the novel reflects the changes and upheavals in the conditions of the family, society, nation and the world of its time. The novel also shows the vexations, distress, aspirations and hopes of contemporary intellectuals.²⁶

In other words, in her revised novel Su Xuelin wanted to paint a portrait of a distinct period in Chinese history, her female heroine representing a typical Chinese intellectual of that time. The story of her conversion unfolds against this backdrop. To achieve her narrative goal, Su Xuelin added many new passages explaining historical circumstances such as the Work-Study Movement, the May Fourth Movement and the various associations of Chinese students in France.²⁷ She also included four entirely new chapters, some of which introduce additional characters, e.g., Chapter 7 entitled "Two ideologically advanced female stu-

---

[23] Rambo 1993, p. 159.

[24] Pan Ji 1931, p. 193.

[25] Monsterleet 1952, p. 15. – For an evaluation of the critical accounts on Su Xuelin and her novel *Jixin* by three francophone China missionaries, including Monsterleet, see my article "Zai Hua Ouzhou chuanjiaoshi dui Su Xuelin de xiaoshuo *Jixin* zhi pingjia" 在華歐洲傳教士對蘇雪林的小說《棘心》之評價 (Hoster 2015).

[26] *JXZDB*, p. 5.

[27] Cf. *JXZDB*, pp. 84-87, 90-91, and 158-159, respectively.

dents" who represent the communist faction among the Chinese students in France.[28]

Though historically more elaborated, the expansion of *Jixin* somewhat hampers its readability. The voice of an omniscient narrator nearly drowns the personal perspective of the protagonist Xingqiu, making the revised version of the novel at times appear more like a lecture on history than a piece of literature. With regard to the theme of conversion, Su Xuelin introduced a decisive change in the closing chapter of the novel, letting Xingqiu convert her mother at her sickbed and baptizing her with the name Mary.[29] This unexpected turn of the plot emphasizes that the protagonist not only remains loyal to her Catholic faith after her return to China but also develops a "sense of mission" and proclaims the Gospel to others.[30] Su Xuelin thus reduced the ambiguity of the last chapter in the original version of *Jixin* that lacks such a clear commitment to the Catholic faith.

Spiritual Companions and Role Models

The names of two Catholic priests are closely linked with Su Xuelin's life and her novel: the Chinese Jesuit Xu Zongze 徐宗澤 (1886–1947) and the Belgian missionary Vincent Lebbe (Chinese name Lei Mingyuan 雷鳴遠, 1877–1940).

Xu Zongze, one of the most prolific Catholic scholars of 20th century China,[31] obviously played an important part in the genesis of *Jixin* and influenced Su Xuelin deeply in questions of faith. She once called him her "only spiritual companion" and her "second father."[32]

Su Xuelin became acquainted with Xu in 1926 while she was teaching in Suzhou after her return from France. At that time the Jesuit priest worked as a religious tutor at a Catholic girls' school in Shanghai. He also edited the Catholic journal *Shengjiao zazhi* 聖教雜誌 (*Revue catholique*), to which Su Xuelin con-

---

[28] "Liang wei sixiang qianjin de nütongxue" 兩位思想前進的女同學, Chapter 7 of *JXZDB*. Because of its anticommunist stance, this chapter is left out in recent editions of *Jixin* in the PR China.

[29] *JXZDB*, p. 251.

[30] In her feminist interpretation of the revised version of *Jixin*, Ni Zhange claims that the conversion of the mother by her daughter implies that Su Xuelin's "[e]xistential feminism further evolved into religious feminism" (Ni Zhange 2014, p. 87).

[31] Xu Zongze was a descendant of the famous Ming Catholic convert Xu Guangqi 徐光啟 (1562–1633). After studies in Europe and the United States he obtained a doctorate in Philosophy and returned to his native Shanghai to teach at the Jesuit campus in Xujiahui 徐家匯 (in Western sources also known as Zikawei). Among other duties, he was director of the famous library Xujiahui cangshulou 徐家匯藏書樓. Today he is still noted for his academic works, in particular *Ming Qing jian Yesuhuishi yizhu tiyao* 明清間耶穌會士譯著提要 (Survey of the Translations by Jesuits of the Ming and Qing, Shanghai 1949). On Xu Zongze, see Fang Hao 1969.

[32] "Yuan wei Tianzhu hao nü'er – wo yu Xu Zongze shenfu" 願為天主好女兒—我與徐宗澤神父, p. 102.

tributed a number of articles, mainly on Chinese literature, in the following years.³³

In her novel *Jixin*, Su Xuelin shows a great familiarity with Christian language and doctrine. The authentic Catholic tone of many passages probably owes a lot to her cooperation with Xu Zongze. In an obituary on him, she recalls that he had encouraged her to write the novel and personally edited two thirds of the manuscript.³⁴ It is difficult to estimate Xu's actual share in the composition of *Jixin*, as no letters between Su Xuelin and Xu Zongze apparently survive.³⁵ However, Su Xuelin's obiturial remark attests that Xu had actively participated in the creative process of writing this novel. He also helped to make it known in Catholic circles.³⁶ Su Xuelin maintained a correspondence with Xu for more than twenty years, until his death in 1947, and she declared that his letters had been most precious to her as a spiritual guidance.³⁷ In her preface to the revised version of the novel, written ten years after his death, she says that Xu had a special liking for this work and she therefore dedicates this version to him, as a tribute to his soul in heaven.³⁸

The second priest to be mentioned in the context of *Jixin* is the Belgian Vincent Lebbe, one of the most famous European missionaries to China of the 20th century.³⁹ During an interim stay in Europe in the 1920s, he pursued all kinds of activities to help Chinese students in need and to preach the Gospel to them. In her autobiography *Fusheng jiusi* Su Xuelin relates that after her baptism became known rumors were spread among the Chinese students in Lyon that she had been bribed into conversion by Lebbe. Although she claims that she had hardly known him and was not in need of financial support because she received a scholarship from the department of education of her native Anhui province, these slanderous accusations persisted and were a heavy blow to her self-esteem.⁴⁰ Back in China she apparently was in touch with Lebbe, as she mentions that he invested a larger sum of money to buy the rights of her novel *Jixin* back for her from the publisher Beixin shuju 北新書局 in Shanghai after the Sino-Japanese

---

33 E.g., "Wusi shidai de jige shiren" 五四時代的幾個詩人 (Some Poets of the May Fourth Movement), *Shengjiao zazhi* 24 (1935) 9, pp. 327-330 and pp. 380-391 (published under the name Lingfen 靈芬). – Thanks are due to Tang Yaoguang 唐耀光, Sankt Augustin, for pointing these articles out to me.

34 Su Xuelin, "Wo de shenshi Xu Zongze shenfu" 我的神師徐宗澤神父, p. 68.

35 According to information provided to me by Wu San-san, Tainan, and Tang Yaoguang, Sankt Augustin.

36 "Wo de shenshi Xu Zongze shenfu," p. 68.

37 The duration of their correspondence is mentioned in "Wo de shenshi Xu Zongze shenfu," p. 61 (originally published in 1947). The remark on the high esteem she held this exchange of letters is to be found in *Yiduo xiao baihua*, "Zixu," p. 1.

38 *JXZDB*, p. 7.

39 Lebbe is mainly commemorated for promoting the indigenization of the Catholic Church in China. On Lebbe, see Leclercq 1961 and Wiest 1999.

40 *FSJS*, pp. 71-73.

war.⁴¹ Maybe out of gratitude she later dedicated a new chapter in the revised version of *Jixin* to him. The chapter is called "The Religion of Love and Priest Lai"⁴² and features a Belgian missionary named Lai 賴, whose name bears a close resemblance to Lebbe's Chinese surname Lei 雷. In a hagiographical manner Su Xuelin describes the priest's tireless and self-sacrificing activities to help financially troubled Chinese students in France and other European countries. The episodes recounted in this chapter testify to Su Xuelin's familiarity with the legend and lore of Lebbe's life.⁴³ The figure of Priest Lai functions as a kind of role model, a contemporary saint. Through his deeds, he embodies the "religion of love." To the heroine Xingqiu his personal example is more convincing than that of the Christian saints introduced to her by her French teacher because "a teaching with words is inferior to a teaching with one's own life" (*yanjiao buru shenjiao* 言教不如身教).⁴⁴

Apart from this literary homage to Vincent Lebbe in the revised edition of *Jixin*, Su Xuelin also wrote a number of articles commemorating him, in which she praises the Belgian missionary for his dedication to the Chinese people and his ultimate self-sacrifice.⁴⁵ His greatest achievement, in her opinion, lies in his efforts to promote the establishment of a Chinese clergy.⁴⁶

Cooperation with the Catholic Clergy in Mainland China

As a teacher, translator and literary historian, Su Xuelin took part in some academic activities of the Catholic Church in China. In February 1948, while teaching as a professor of Chinese literature at the University of Wuhan, she attended the "National Catholic Education Congress" in Shanghai, which had been convened by Msgr. Antonio Riberi, the Internuntio Apostolic to China.⁴⁷ On this occasion she delivered a speech on "The importance of the Chinese language and literature in our Catholic schools," which was later published in English and in French.⁴⁸

---

⁴¹ *FSJS*, p. 93. Lebbe had also returned to China in 1928 to serve under a Chinese bishop in Hebei province.

⁴² "Ai de zongjiao yu Lai shenfu" 愛的宗教與賴神父, ch. 13 of *JXZDB*, pp. 154-167.

⁴³ Cf. the episode of Lebbe failing to get off the train in time because he has fallen asleep out of exhaustion (see *JXZDB*, p. 162 and Leclercq 1961, p. 242).

⁴⁴ *JXZDB*, p. 164.

⁴⁵ Cf. *Linghai weilan*, vol. 3, pp. 12-35.

⁴⁶ Su Xuelin, "Yuan Lei gong wei muqian duonan de Zhongguo sheng jiaohui qidao," 願雷公為目前多難的中國聖教會祈禱, p. 17.

⁴⁷ For a detailed report on this congress, see Kao 1948.

⁴⁸ Su Hsiue-lin [*sic*], "Chinese Literature in Catholic Schools," *China Missionary Bulletin* 1 (1948) 3, pp. 272-279; Sou Hsue-ling [*sic*], "La place que doivent occuper la langue et la littérature chinoise dans nos écoles catholiques," *Bulletin de l'Université l'Aurore*, Série III, Tome IX, No. 33-34 (1948), pp. 39-48. – The Chinese title of the conference paper is

In her paper, she strongly advocated the teaching of *baihuawen* 白話文, the modern literary language, in class and urged "a course of modern literature ... to be included at once in our Catholic schools."[49] With the help of such a course, both teachers and writers are to be formed to "propagate our Holy Religion by writings and thus consolidate the apostolate of our missionaries."[50] She thus took a clear stance on the use of literature for spreading the Christian faith.

Around the same time, Su Xuelin, being a noted expert on modern Chinese literature, contributed an extensive introduction to a handbook entitled *1500 Modern Chinese Novels and Plays*, compiled by the Belgian Scheut missionary Joseph Schyns and his confreres.[51] In her introduction entitled "Present Day Fiction and Drama in China" (pp. iii-lviii), Su Xuelin presents the most important writers and literary groups that had emerged in the previous three decades, a period of an intensive search for new forms of literary expression. Her overview stresses the diversity of Chinese writers, who despite ideological differences have in common "a burning desire for the betterment of humanity."[52] In contrast to Su Xuelin's rather pluralistic and objective approach, the handbook judges the individual literary works from a rigid moral point of view on the grounds of Christian doctrine.[53] A case in point is Su Xuelin's treatment of Mao Dun. Regarding his worldview, she clearly characterizes him as a leftist writer who is convinced of the "inevitable triumph of Communism," a political movement she condemns, but from an artistic point of view, she calls him "a literary giant." She also briefly relates, among some of his other works, the contents of his representative novel *Ziye* 子夜 (Midnight).[54] In the main part of the handbook, written by Schyns and his confreres, Mao Dun's novel is not recommended at all: "Everyone should be warned against reading it" because of its "socialistic outlook" and its "immoral descriptions."[55] Other examples of such vastly differing judgments of Su Xuelin on the one side and of the compilers of the handbook on the other could easily be found.

---

given in the preface to the French translation as "Guoyu ji guowen zai gongjiao xuexiao zhong yingyou de diwei" 國語及國文在公教學校中應有的地位 (p. 39).

[49] Su Hsiue-lin, "Chinese Literature in Catholic Schools," p. 277.

[50] *Ibid.*

[51] This handbook was first published in 1946 in a shorter version in French under the title *Romans à lire et romans à proscire* (see Schyns 1948, p. ii, note 3). A Chinese translation of this French edition appeared as *Wenyi yuedan. Jia ji* 文艺月旦—甲集 in Beiping in 1947. For this Chinese edition, see Liu Lixia 2006, pp. 214-224. Both the French and the Chinese edition did not include Su Xuelin's preface.

[52] *Ibid.*, p. lviii.

[53] All works are classified in four categories, ranging from "for everyone" to "proscribed." See the appendix, pp. 470-484.

[54] "Present Day Fiction and Drama in China," pp. x-xi.

[55] Schyns 1948, p. 260.

It comes as no surprise that the literary historian C.T. Hsia (Xia Zhiqing 夏志清, 1921–2013) commends Su Xuelin's introduction, whereas he denounces the handbook as "an uncritical companion."[56]

Working for the Catholic Truth Society in Hong Kong

For fear of political persecution after the communist takeover on the Chinese mainland, Su Xuelin, an outspoken anticommunist, joined the editorial office of the Catholic Truth Society (Zhenli xuehui 真理學會) in Hong Kong in 1949, having been introduced to this institution by Father Lebbe.[57] The Society had been founded in 1934 for the publication and distribution of Catholic works in Hong Kong and on the Chinese Mainland.[58]

During her brief stay in Hong Kong from 1949 to 1950, two monographic works from Su Xuelin's pen were published there. The first one is a religious tract entitled "Traditional Chinese Culture and the Ancient Belief in the Lord of Heaven."[59] It represents an attempt to reconcile the most representative world views of Chinese and western culture, Confucianism on the one hand and Catholicism on the other. Su Xuelin claims the existence of an early Chinese monotheism she calls *Tianzhu gujiao* 天主古教.[60] In her view, it shows influences of Hebrew and Greek thinking and can be regarded as the predecessor of Confucianism.[61] By pointing out these traces of an "ancient belief in God" in Chinese tradition, Su Xuelin hoped to contribute to a more positive Chinese attitude towards Christianity.[62] This religious tract expresses her strong conviction of the mutual influence of the Eurasian and Chinese civilizations, a hypothesis she also tried to prove in her lifelong research on the poetry of Qu Yuan 屈原 (ca. 340–278 B.C.).[63]

Su Xuelin's second monographic publication with the Catholic Truth Society is her Chinese translation of the autobiography of Saint Thérèse of Lisieux, *Histoire d'une âme*. The translation is entitled *Yiduo xiao baihua* 一朵小白花 (A

---

[56] Hsia 1999, p. 627.

[57] See Su Xuelin, "Zai Zhenli xuehui de yinian" 在真理學會的一年 (One Year at the Catholic Truth Society), p. 217.

[58] For the beginnings of the Catholic Truth Society, see the memoirs of its founder, Nicholas Maestrini, an Italian missionary of the congregation Pontificio Istituto Missioni Estere (P.I.M.E.), Maestrini 1990, pp. 133-142.

[59] *Zhongguo chuantong wenhua yu Tianzhu gujiao* 中國傳統文化與天主古教.

[60] Leopold Leeb claims that this term of Su Xuelin comes close to the concept of a "prisca theologia," which denotes a "true theology" that existed in all religions in ancient time. This concept was adapted to China by the Jesuit Figurists (see Leeb 2000, pp. 218-219).

[61] Cf. *Zhongguo chuantong wenhua yu Tianzhu gujiao*, p. 2.

[62] *Ibid.*, p. 47.

[63] On this research, see her own account in *FSJS*, pp. 133-143; for an academic introduction, see Wu San-san 2012, pp. 153-246.

Little White Flower. The Autobiography of Saint Therese of Lisieux).⁶⁴ In her preface, Su Xuelin declares that the autobiography of Saint Thérèse belonged to her favorite books and had helped her to hold on to her Catholic faith. She had read it at least five times in an earlier translation by Ma Xiangbo 馬相伯 (1840–1939).⁶⁵ No wonder that she immediately took the challenge and embarked on retranslating the book, when she heard of the plan of the Catholic Truth Society to publish a new translation of it. On another occasion, Su Xuelin said that she had admired Saint Thérèse of Lisieux all her life and took her as an example of how to resist temptations.⁶⁶

When Su Xuelin left Hong Kong in 1950 to study comparative mythology at the University of Paris, she continued to write for the Catholic Truth Society in order to earn her living abroad. Shortly after her arrival in France she went on a pilgrimage to Rome, Lisieux and Lourdes. Her travelogues were later published in book form under the title *San da shengdi de xunli* 三大聖地的巡禮 (Pilgrimage to Three Holy Sites).⁶⁷

Conversion to Catholicism as a Personal Experience

How did Su Xuelin assess the meaning of her conversion to the Catholic faith for her personal life? She has left several autobiographical texts that provide us with answers to this question. In an important text entitled "Confession of a May Fourth Person Converted to Catholicism," she declares that she has suffered a number of hardships in her life, namely her failed marriage and the violent repercussions on her commitment to Catholicism. Both of these experiences spurred her ambition to devote herself to literature and scholarship.⁶⁸

According to this "Confession," Su Xuelin's conversion seems to have been a fairly traumatic experience. She says that she was exposed to fierce attacks by her Chinese fellow students in the anti-religious atmosphere of the Institut franco-chinois in Lyon. The original version of her novel only hints at these circumstances. In the revised edition of *Jixin*, Su Xuelin became more outspoken and admitted that she had even received death threats at that time.⁶⁹ For the period after her return to China she recalls several incidents that illustrate the animosity

---

⁶⁴ The autobiography was translated and edited with the authorization of the Lisieux Central Office and carries the imprimatur of the bishop of Hong Kong, Henricus Valtorta. The Chinese title follows the English translation.

⁶⁵ *Yiduo xiao baihua*, "Zixu" 自序 (Preface by Su Xuelin), p. 1. – The translation by Ma Xiangbo was published under the title *Lingxin xiao shi* 靈心小史 in Shanghai (Tushanwan 土山灣) in 1928.

⁶⁶ Cf. "Zibai," p. 102.

⁶⁷ By Guangqi chubanshe in Taizhong in 1957. In a later edition, the title was changed to *Ouyou liesheng* 歐遊獵勝 (Highlights of a Trip to Europe), see Chen Changming 2014, p. 58.

⁶⁸ "Zibai," p. 90.

⁶⁹ Cf. *ibid.*, pp. 82-83. This is described in the sixteenth chapter of *JXZDB*.

she was confronted with as a convert, as the political climate prior to the Sino-Japanese war was not favorable towards Catholicism. The publication of her novel in 1929, in which she clearly stated the motives of her conversion, won her esteem, as the wild speculations about these motives ceased. Su Xuelin states that her motives were of a merely private nature, arising from the conflict with her family about her marriage.[70] Having made this clear in her novel, she could no longer be suspected of political reasons for her conversion or other ulterior motifs.

Su Xuelin's conversion has been the subject of dispute and bewilderment not only in the time following her baptism, but also later in her life. As an adult, she answered the question "Why I believe in the Catholic faith" in an interview.[71] She emphasized that "the reason why I converted to Catholicism was not because I enthusiastically read the Bible or because I was convinced of the doctrine, but because I was converted by the example of believers and by certain events related to the faith."[72] These believers, she explains, are the two women fictionalized in the novel as Bailang, her French teacher, whose real name was Elisabeth Raymond,[73] and the nun Masha, whom she met at a Catholic boarding house for girls in Lyon. The tireless efforts of these women, who became her close friends, in convincing her to become a Christian, were a crucial factor in her conversion process. In this interview, Su Xuelin also mentions an incident during her stay at the boarding house, when she felt guilty of having committed a big mistake, but instead of being blamed she was pardoned. This experience showed her the Christian virtue of forgiveness and was one of the factors that prompted her to convert to the Catholic faith.[74]

Apart from these personal experiences, family matters were the most important reason for Su Xuelin's conversion, namely the dispute she had with her family about her marriage arrangement.[75] Yet there were also many impediments to her conversion, among them her scientific worldview. In her youth she had been deeply influenced by the radical ideas of the May Fourth Movement in China, which promoted rationalism, atheism, and evolutionism, so Su Xuelin could not easily accept the Catholic doctrine.[76] In fact, she had to struggle hard to adapt her worldview to the Catholic faith, e.g., her knowledge of scientific cosmology

---

[70] Cf. "Zibai," pp. 87 and 81.

[71] "Wo weishenme xinyang Tianzhujiao. Da xinwenju jizhe" 我為什麼信仰天主教—答新聞局記者, in: *Linghai weilan*, vol. 5, pp. 84-105. Although the year of the original publication of this interview is not given, it is mentioned in the beginning that Su Xuelin was already hard of hearing at the time of the interview.

[72] *Ibid.*, p. 84.

[73] *Ibid.*, p. 85.

[74] *Ibid.*, p. 104.

[75] *Ibid.*

[76] *Ibid.*, p. 94.

to the Christian belief in a creator.[77] From this perspective, she regarded her conversion as an intellectual challenge. She said that instead of a "physical martyrdom" God had granted her a kind of "mental martyrdom" to sharpen her. The pains she had endured made her loyal to her faith. It was a faith acquired through reason, not a "blind faith."[78]

What made Su Xuelin hold on to her faith despite all impediments? One reason is that she felt inspired by numerous eminent Christians of the past and the present, among them Saint Augustine, Saint Thomas Aquinas and the Belgian missionary Father Vincent Lebbe.[79] Throughout her life, she also maintained friendship with members of the Catholic clergy and cooperated with them in different ways. This was also a way for her to live the Catholic faith.

In many ways, Su Xuelin remained an outsider for most of her life. Because of her conversion to Catholicism as a student in France, she was harassed by her anti-religious Chinese fellow students in Lyon. After her return to China she still had to fight rumors about ulterior motives for her conversion. As a Catholic she became a staunch anticommunist, a political position that ultimately forced her to leave the Chinese mainland and live in Taiwan for the second half of her life. Partly for religious reasons, she chose not to divorce her husband.[80] Instead they separated after a few years of a failed marriage and Su Xuelin later lived together with her elder sister.

As one of the pioneer woman writers in modern China literature, she earned a reputation as an outstanding prose writer for her first literary works, but on account of the growing ideological tensions in China from the 1930s onward she was often criticized for her narrow individualistic outlook and her lack of social concern.[81]

As a literary scholar, she was renowned as an expert for contemporary literature, but her harsh criticism of Lu Xun 魯迅 (1881–1936),[82] the icon of the "literary revolution" in the wake of the May Fourth Movement, made her a longtime *persona non grata* in Mainland China from the late 1930s to the late 1980s.

It has been suggested that Su Xuelin had an independent and strong personality, thus her conversion to Catholicism can be seen as a highly individualistic move, a conscious decision not for eternal life but in search of spiritual salvation in the present world.[83] Whatever may have been the reasons for her adoption of

---

[77] "Zibai," pp. 103–105.
[78] Ibid., p. 106.
[79] Ibid., p. 101.
[80] See *FSJS*, pp. 196–197.
[81] A typical representative of this kind of criticism is He Yubo 1936.
[82] A collection her criticisms, *Wo lun Lu Xun* 我論魯迅, was published in Taibei in 1967. There are numerous articles in Chinese on this controversial topic. For an analysis in English, see Kowallis 2010.
[83] Wu San-san (forthcoming), p. 314.

the Christian faith, the gains must have outweighed the losses, as she termed her conversion "a fortunate encounter."

References

1. Works by Su Xuelin:

"Chinese Literature in Catholic Schools," *China Missionary Bulletin* 1 (1948) 3, pp. 272-279 (French version: "La place que doivent occuper la langue et la littérature chinoise dans nos écoles catholiques," *Bulletin de l'Université l'Aurore*, Série III, Tome IX, No. 33-34 [1948], pp. 39-48).

FSJS. Fusheng jiusi. Xuelin huiyi lu 浮生九四—雪林回憶錄. 1991. Taibei: Sanmin shuju.

JX. Jixin 棘心. 1987. *Zhongguo xiandai wenxueshi cankao ziliao* 中國現代文學史參考資料. Shanghai: Shanghai shudian. Facsimile (*yingyin* 影印) of the original edition (Shanghai: Beixin shuju, 1929).

JXZDB. Jixin (zengdingben) 棘心 (增訂本). *A Pricked Heart.* By Su Hsüeh-lin. *Xiaoshuo congkan zhi yi* 小說叢刊之一. Taizhong: Guangqi chubanshe, 1957.

Linghai weilan 靈海微瀾 (*Some Thoughts of Mind*). 1978-1996. 5 vols. Tainan: Wendao chubanshe.

"Present Day Fiction and Drama in China," in: Schyns 1948, pp. iii-lviii.

"Wo de shenshi Xu Zongze shenfu" 我的神師徐宗澤神父, in: *Linghai weilan* 靈海微瀾, vol. 2, pp. 59-74.

Wo de shenghuo 我的生活. 1971. Taibei: Zhuanji wenxue chubanshe.

"Wo weishenme xinyang Tianzhujiao. Da xinwenju jizhe" 我為什麼信仰天主教—答新聞局記者, in: *Linghai weilan*, vol. 5, pp. 84-105.

Yiduo xiao baihua 一朵小白花. *A Little White Flower. The Autobiography of Saint Therese of Lisieux.* 1950. Xianggang: Zhenli xuehui.

"Yige guiyi Tianzhujiao Wusi ren de zibai" 一個皈依天主教五四人的自白, in: *Linghai weilan*, vol. 3, pp. 74-106.

"Yuan Lei gong wei muqian duonan de Zhongguo sheng jiaohui qidao. Lei Mingyuan shenfu shishi shisi zhounian jinian" 願雷公為目前多難的中國聖教會祈禱—雷鳴遠神父逝世十四週年紀念, in: *Linghai weilan*, vol. 3, pp. 17-19.

"Yuan wei Tianzhu hao nü'er – Wo yu Xu Zongze shenfu" 願為天主好女兒—我與徐宗澤神父, *Yishi zhoukan* 益世周刊 29 (1947) 7, pp. 101-104.

"Zai Zhenli xuehui de yinian" 在真理學會的一年, in: *Su Xuelin zuopin ji* 蘇雪林作品集, *Duanpian wenzhang juan* 短篇文章卷, vol. 6, ed. Chen Changming 陳昌明. Tainan: Chenggong daxue, 2011, pp. 217-219.

Zhongguo chuantong wenhua yu Tianzhu gujiao 中國傳統文化與天主古教. 1950. *Zongjiao yanjiu congshu* 宗教研究叢書. Xianggang: Zhenli xuehui.

2. Secondary Sources:

Bastid-Bruguière, Marianne. 2002. "La campagne antireligieuse de 1922," *Extrême-Orient, Extrême-Occident* 24 (2002), pp. 77-93.

Boully, Jean Louis. 1995. *Ouvrages en langue chinoise de l'Institut franco-chinois de Lyon 1921-1946. Faguo Li'ang shili tushuguan guancang Li'ang Zhong-Fa daxue 1921 nian zhi 1946 nian Zhongwen shumu* 法國里昂市立圖書館館藏里昂中法大學 1921 年至 1946 年中文書目. Lyon: Bibliothèque municipale de Lyon.

Boully, Jean Louis – Danielle Li. 1987. *Catalogue des Thèses de Doctorat des étudiants de l'Institut Franco-chinois* (*Li'ang Zhong-Fa daxue boshi lunwen mulu* 里昂中法大學博士論文目錄). *Liste des noms des étudiants de l'Institut Franco-Chinois de Lyon (1921-1946)* (*Li'ang Zhong-Fa daxue haiwaibu tongxue lu* 里昂中法大學海外部同學錄). Lyon: Bibliothèque municipale de Lyon.

Chen Changming 陳昌明 (ed.). 2014. *Su Xuelin* 蘇雪林. Taiwan xiandangdai zuojia yanjiu ziliao huibian 臺灣現當代作家研究資料彙編 51. Tainan: Guoli Taiwan wenxueguan.

Chow Tse-tsung. 1960. *The May Fourth Movement. Intellectual Revolution in Modern China*. Cambridge, Mass.: Harvard University Press.

Cuddon, J.A. 2013. *The Penguin Dictionary of Literary Terms and Literary Theory*. Revised by M.A.R. Habib. London: Penguin Book.

Fang Hao 方豪. 1969. "Wo huainian Xu Runnong shenfu" 我懷念徐潤農神父, in: *Fang Hao liushi ziding gao (bubian)* 方豪六十自定稿(補編). *The Collected Works of Maurus Fang Hao Revised and Edited by the Author on His Sixtieth Birthday (Supplement)*. Taibei: Xuesheng shuju, pp. 2571-2574.

Grand dictionnaire Ricci de la langue chinoise, ed. Institut Ricci, 7 vols. Paris – Taipei: Instituts Ricci – Desclée de Brouwer 2001.

Guo Guoqi 郭果七. 2006. *Wu Jingxiong. Zhongguoren yi Jidutu* 吳經熊—中國人亦基都徒. Taibei: Guangqi wenhua.

He Yubo 賀玉波. 1936. "Ziran de nü'er Lü Yi nüshi" 自然的女兒綠漪女士, in: *id.*, *Zhongguo xiandai nü zuojia* 中國現代女作家, Shanghai: Fuxing shuju, pp. 115-134.

Hoster, Barbara [Ba Peilan 巴佩蘭]. 2015. "Zai Hua Ouzhou chuanjiaoshi dui Su Xuelin de xiaoshuo *Jixin* zhi pingjia – yi Bi Baojiao (Octave Brière SJ, 1907-1978), Wen Baofeng (Henri Van Boven CICM, 1911-2003) yiji Ming Xingli (Jean Monsterleet SJ, 1912-2001) wei li" 在華歐洲傳教士對蘇雪林的小說《棘心》之評價—以畢保郊 (Octave Brière SJ, 1907-1978)、文寶峰 (Henri Van Boven CICM, 1911-2003) 以及明興禮 (Jean Monsterleet SJ, 1912-2001) 為例, in: Caituan faren Su Xuelin jiaoshou xueshu wenhua jijinhui 財團法人蘇雪林教授學術文化基金會 (ed.), *Su Xuelin ji qi tongdai zuojia guoji xueshu yantaohui lunwenji* 蘇雪林及其同代作家國際學術研討會論文集. Tainan: Guoli Chenggong daxue, pp. 21-39.

—. 2017. *Konversion zum Christentum in der modernen chinesischen Literatur. Su Xuelins Roman* Jixin *(Dornenherz, 1929)*. Deutsche Ostasienstudien, 27. Gossenberg: Ostasien Verlag.

Hsia, C.T. 1999. *A History of Modern Chinese Fiction. Third Edition. With an Introduction by David Der-wei Wang*. Bloomington et al.: Indiana University Press [1st ed., New Haven, Conn.: Yale University Press, 1961].

Kao, John B. "National Catholic Educational Congress. Shanghai, February 15–21st, 1948," *China Missionary* 1 (1948) 2, pp. 133-148.

Kowallis, Jon Eugene von. 2010. "The Enigma of Su Xuelin and Lu Xun," *Wen yu zhe* 文與哲. *Literature and Philosophy* 16 (2010), pp. 493-528.

Leclercq, Jacques. 1961. *Vie du Père Lebbe. Le tonnerre qui chante de loin*. Tournai: Casterman.

Lee, Lily Xiao Hong – A.D. Stefanowska (eds.). 2003. *Biographical Dictionary of Chinese Women. The Twentieth Century 1912–2000*. Armonk, NY: Sharpe.

Lei Libo 雷立柏 (Leopold Leeb). 2000. *Lun Jidu zhi da yu xiao. 1900–1950 nian Huaren zhishi fenzi yanzhong de Jidujiao* 论基督之大与小—1900~1950 年华人知识分子眼中的基督教. *De quantitate Christi. Christianity in the Eyes of Chinese Intellectuals*. Beijing: Shehui kexue wenxian chubanshe.

Liu Lixia 刘丽霞. 2006. *Zhongguo jidujiao wenxue de lishi cunzai* 中国基督教文学的历史存在. *Historical Existence of Chinese Christian Literature*. Beijing: Shehui kexue wenxian chubanshe.

Maestrini, Nicholas. 1900. *My Twenty Years with the Chinese. Laughter and Tears 1931–1951*. Avon, NJ: Magnificat Press.

Malek, Roman. 2012. "Zur Heterotopie der Konversion im chinesischen Kontext. Skizziert am Beispiel des Christentums," in: Christine Lienemann-Perrin – Wolfgang Lienemann (eds.), *Religiöse Grenzüberschreitungen. Studien zu Bekehrung, Konfessions- und Religionswechsel – Crossing Religious Borders. Studies on Conversion and Religious Belonging*. Wiesbaden: Harrassowitz, 2012, pp. 632-679.

Monsterleet, Jean. 1952. "De l'amour d'une mère à l'amour de Dieu. Sou Siue-lin (Sou Mei), Témoin de son temps," *China Missionary Bulletin* 1 (1952), pp. 8-15.

—. 1953. *Sommets de la littérature chinoise contemporaine*. Paris: Editions Domat.

Monsterleet, Jean (Ming Xingli 明興禮) – Gu Baogu 顧保鵠. *Xiandai Zhongguo de liang wei xianshi* 現代中國的兩位賢士 (Two virtuous personalities of modern China). Tianjin, n.d. [ca. 1950].

Motsch, Monika. 2003. *Die chinesische Erzählung. Vom Altertum bis zur Neuzeit*. Geschichte der chinesischen Literatur, vol. 3. München: Saur.

Ni Zhange. 2014. "Making Religion, Making the New Woman. Reading Su Xuelin's Autobiographical Novel *Jixin* (Thorny Heart)," in: *Gendering Chinese Religion. Subject, Identity, and Body*. Ed. Jinhua Jia, Xiaofei Kang and Ping Yao. Albany: State University of New York Press, pp. 71-99.

Pan Ji 磐基. 1931. "Wo suo kandao guoqu de Zhongguo wentan" 我所看到過去的中國文壇, *Shengjiao zazhi* 聖教雜誌 20 (1931) 8, pp. 183-196.

Pinet, Annick – Danielle Li. 2001. *L'Institut franco-chinois de Lyon (1921–1950). L'ancien: 1921–1950. L'actuel: depuis 1980. Li'ang Zhong-Fa daxue jin yu xi.* 里昂中法大學今與昔. Lyon: Institut franco-chinois de Lyon.

Rambo, Lewis W. 1993. *Understanding Religious Conversion.* New Haven – London: Yale University Press.

Schyns, Joseph *et al.* (eds.). 1948. *1500 Modern Chinese Novels and Plays*, Scheut Editions, Series I, Critical and Literary Studies, 3. Peiping: Verbist Academy.

Siebenhandl, Hans. 1982. "Zur geistigen Auseinandersetzung der chinesischen Intelligenz mit dem Christentum zwischen 1915 und 1927." Ph.D. diss., University of Vienna.

Stromberg, Peter G. 2014. "The Role of Language in Religious Conversion," in: *The Oxford Handbook of Religious Conversion.* Eds. Lewis R. Rambo and Charles E. Farhadian. Oxford – New York: Oxford University Press, pp. 117-139.

Wiest, Jean Paul. 1999. "The Legacy of Vincent Lebbe," *International Bulletin of Missionary Research* (Jan. 1999), pp. 33-37.

Wilpert, Gero von. 1989. *Sachwörterbuch der Literatur*, 7th ed. Stuttgart: Kröner.

Wu San-san 吳姍姍. 2012. *Su Xuelin yanjiu lunji* 蘇雪林研究論集. Taibei: Taiwan xuesheng shuju.

—. (forthcoming). "Lun Su Xuelin de zongjiao qinghuai" 論蘇雪林的宗教情懷 (A Study of the Religious Outlook of Su Xue-lin), in: *Furen daxue di yijie chuanjiaoshi Hanxue guoji huiyi. Chuanjiaoshi dui renshi Zhongguo yu Taiwan de gongxian* 輔仁大學第一屆傳教士漢學國際會議—傳教士對認識中國與台灣的貢獻 – *First Symposium of Missionary Sinology. The Contribution of Missionary Sinology to the Knowledge of China and Taiwan.* Taibei: Furen daxue chubanshe, pp. 303-314.

Yao Xinzhong. 2003. *RoutledgeCurzon Encyclopedia of Confucianism*, 2 vols. London – New York: RoutledgeCurzon.

„ERST JETZT WUSSTE ER, DASS ES KEINE EINFACHE SACHE WAR, AN GOTT ZU GLAUBEN"
DIE RELIGION IN DER GEGENWARTSLITERATUR CHINAS

Thomas Zimmer

Der zitierte Satz aus der Überschrift zu diesem Artikel stammt aus dem Munde einer Figur in dem 2009 erschienenen Roman *Yi ju ding yiwan ju* 一句顶一万句 (Ein Satz toppt zehntausend Sätze) des chinesischen Schriftstellers Liu Zhenyun 刘震云.[1] Warum tauchen religiöse Motive und Figuren in der gegenwärtigen Literatur Chinas auf und welche Rolle spielen sie? Diesen Fragen widmet sich der vorliegende Beitrag. Zunächst erscheint es allerdings notwendig, einige grundsätzlichere Überlegungen zum Problem der Religion und Literatur mit Blick auf China anzustellen.

Traditionell hat sich China immer als ein Land der religiösen Toleranz verstanden. Es mag immer wieder Konflikte zwischen den einzelnen Religionen und ihren Vertretern im Reich gegeben haben, aber Glaubenskriege des Ausmaßes, wie wir sie aus der europäischen Geschichte kennen, waren in China unbekannt. Dies änderte sich in der Mitte des 20. Jahrhunderts auf ganz drastische Weise: Nach der Ausrufung der Volksrepublik 1949 wurde die Religion zu einem „Aberglauben" der zu bekämpfenden feudalistischen Klasse erklärt und unterlag der Lenkung durch Organe der KPCh. Angepasst an die Verhältnisse in China folgten die chinesischen Parteikader weitgehend der grundlegenden These des dialektischen Materialismus, wonach das gesellschaftliche Sein das gesellschaftliche Bewusstsein bestimmt. Einer geläufigen These zufolge unterstreiche der dialektische Materialismus „auch das Spezifische des gesellschaftlichen Bewusstseins, seine relative Selbständigkeit und seine Fähigkeit, auf das gesellschaftliche Sein zurückzuwirken".[2] Dieser Auffassung zufolge besitzt „Religion" einen ausgeprägt phantastischen, der Erfahrung feindlichen, geistig-metaphysischen Cha-

---

[1] Liu Zhenyu, *Yi ju ding yiwan ju* (Wuhan: Changjiang wenyi, 2009). Zu dem Zitat siehe *ibid.*, S. 115. Mit *Yi ju ding yiwan ju* hat Liu Zhenyun ein faszinierendes Zeitportrait über menschliche Beziehungen geschaffen, welche vom Sprechen, dem Kommunizieren mittels der Schrift und einem dabei nahezu immer zustande kommenden Missverstehen bestimmt werden. *Yi ju ding yiwan ju* ist fraglos einer der wenigen welthaltigen Romane Chinas, von denen man sich mehr wünschte. Man liest von den skurrilsten Typen, die kulturell kaum noch eingebettet sind, da es sich um Charaktere handelt, die auf die verschiedensten, jedoch vermutlich überall auf der Welt zustande kommenden Situationen stoßen. „Moses Yang", so die zitierte Romanfigur, ist von einem italienischen Geistlichen bekehrt worden, der nach mehreren Jahrzehnten weitgehend erfolgloser Missionarsarbeit in China vor Ort nur eine winzige Gemeinde von acht Mitgliedern schaffen konnte.

[2] Ich beziehe mich hier auf Ausführungen des Bulgaren Todor Pawlow (1890–1977) in seinem Aufsatz „Kunst und Religion", in: *id.*, *Aufsätze zur Ästhetik*, hrsg. von Erhard John (Berlin: Dietz, 1975), S. 199-227, hier zitiert nach S. 205.

rakter. Die Annahme eines „Gottes", so die Folgerung weiter, ist demnach stets die Idee eines „‚Jenseitigen', eines ‚Überirdisch-Geistigen', irgendeiner mystischen ‚geistigen Kraft' oder ‚Vernunft', eines ‚Schicksals' oder ‚Geistes'." Religion bedeutet demnach „stets eine Flucht aus der realen, irdischen Wirklichkeit in die Sphären phantastischer und metaphysischer Träume, Luftschlösser, Wünsche und Ideale." Religion habe einen „lähmenden Charakter".[3] Angesichts dieses einseitigen Blicks ist es nicht verwunderlich, dass der hier zitierte Pawlow und andere marxistische Theoretiker freilich immer mit Bezug auf die Verbindung zwischen der Kunst und der Religion die „Dienerrolle" der Kunst gegenüber der Religion betonten, „um der Idee Gottes einen sinnlich wahrnehmbaren, konkreten Charakter zu geben".[4] Hervorgehoben wurde daher von den Theoretikern gerne, dass die Kunst nur eine nach marxistischen Maßstäben angemessene Zukunft besitzen könne, wenn sie sich von jeder Religion emanzipiere.[5] Auf etwas wie die religiösen Bedürfnisse der Menschen und die gestaltenden Räume, über die Literatur verfügt, wurde angesichts dieser starren weltanschaulichen Bindung kein Wert gelegt.

Im Laufe der Jahrzehnte hat sich nun freilich auch gezeigt, dass die strenge weltanschauliche Schulung den Menschen in China kaum einen Ersatz für die Möglichkeit einer gelebten Religion bieten kann; das entstandene geistige Vakuum in der Gesellschaft hat zu neuen Formen der Suche nach geistig-moralischer Orientierung geführt.[6] Auf diese Weise boten sich auch in der Literatur mit der Zeit neue Möglichkeiten für den Umgang mit „Religion" im weitesten Sinne, wie noch zu zeigen sein wird. Dabei kann allerdings in der Gegenwart ebenfalls nichts anderes gesagt werden, als dass die Religion in China auch drei Jahrzehnte nach dem Beginn der Öffnungspolitik einen schweren Stand hat. China ist zurzeit (Winter 2014/2015), weiterhin und wieder einmal ein gutes Stück davon entfernt, zu einer pluralistischen, religiös-toleranten Gesellschaft zu werden. Seit gut einem Jahrzehnt wird von höchster Stelle die Schaffung einer „harmonischen Gesellschaft" (*hexie shehui* 和谐社会) gepredigt. Im Herbst 2014 gab der chinesische Präsident Xi Jinping den Anwesenden auf einer Sitzung des Parteiforums für Kunst und Kultur den Wunsch mit auf den Weg, Literatur und Kunst mögen – ausgestattet mit „positiver Energie" (*zheng nengliang* 正能量) – „sein wie der Sonnenschein, wie der blaue Himmel und eine Frühlingsbrise, um den Geist anzuregen, die Herzen zu erwärmen und den Geschmack zu kultivieren". Vage

---

[3] Zu den hier angeführten Zitaten vgl. Pawlow: „Kunst und Religion", S. 213.
[4] Vgl. *ibid.*, S. 226.
[5] Vgl. *ibid.*, S. 227.
[6] Eine sehr eindringliche Schilderung gerade der Entwicklung des Christentums in China nach 1949, mit der freilich auch auf die Schwierigkeiten der Religion seit dieser Zeit hingewiesen wird, bietet Liao Yiwu, *God Is Red. The Secret Story of How Christianity Survived and Flourished in Communist China*, translated by Wenguang Huang (New York: HarperOne, 2011). In der Zwischenzeit liegt auch eine deutsche Übersetzung vor, vgl. Liao Yiwu, *Gott ist rot. Geschichten aus dem Untergrund. Verfolgte Christen in China*. Aus dem Chinesischen von Hans Peter Hoffmann (Frankfurt a.M.: Fischer, 2014).

deuten sich hier Spielräume für religiöse Themen und Motive an. Doch wo es dann nahezu zeitgleich auch schon wieder Äußerungen gibt, denen zufolge selbst intime Gefühle wie die Liebe (*ai* 爱) nicht nur dem Mitmenschen und Partner oder dem Vaterland gehören, sondern eins zu sein haben mit den Gefühlen für die Partei, da stellt sich natürlicherweise die Frage: welchen Stellenwert können die Religion und der Glaube da überhaupt einnehmen?[7]

Trotz des offiziell verkündeten Harmoniestrebens ist in China mittlerweile freilich hin und wieder auch von der Krise die Rede, und zwar nicht von einer wirtschaftlichen, sondern von einer mentalen Krise, die ausdrücklich in einer „umfassenden geistig-seelischen Leere" (*zhengti jingshen kongxu* 整体精神空虚) zum Ausdruck kommt.[8] Der „Glaube", hier in einem zunächst einmal ganz allgemeinen Sinne und ohne Bezug zur Religion verstanden, wird als ein Mittel zur Behebung der „Krise" gesehen, die ihre Ursache zu einem guten Teil in dem großen wirtschaftlichen Erfolg der Vergangenheit hat: „Obwohl es bei der materiellen Lage in China große Verbesserungen gegeben hat, so können doch Geist und Glaube nicht in der Folge der materiellen Verbesserung von alleine entstehen." Daraus zieht der Verfasser einen interessanten Schluss: „Für die Gemeinschaft (*qunti* 群体) ist der Glaube ein geistiges Band (*jingshen niudai* 精神纽带), das die gemeinsamen Gruppen (*gongtong zuqun* 共同族群) miteinander verbindet." Der Glaube, so die These weiter, sei für die Blüte und das beständige Wachstum der Menschheit eine wichtige geistige Stütze. Unterschiedliche Glaubensformen könnten auch die voneinander abweichenden Weltanschauungen und Lebenskonzepte der verschiedenen Gruppen wiederspiegeln. Derzeit befinde sich China in einer entscheidenden Phase des nationalen Wiederaufstiegs. Die rasante wirtschaftliche Entwicklung habe die von einem Mangel an Glauben (*xinyang queshi* 信仰缺失) verursachte geistig-seelische Krise (*jingshen weiji* 精神危机) noch stärker zum Ausdruck gebracht. Angesichts der Krise sei es notwendig, bei der Schaffung eines Glaubens (*shuli xinyang* 树立信仰) neues Denken zu praktizieren und neue Formen zu finden. Nach Hinweisen auf den Glauben in religiöser und nicht-religiöser Form hebt der Verfasser hervor, dass die Hauptströmung des traditionellen Glaubens in China ein nicht-religiöser Glaube war. Von zentraler Bedeutung sei die Weltlichkeit des Konfuzianismus gewesen: dort habe sich im

---

[7] Vgl. zu den Ausführungen von Xi Jinping http://beforeitsnews.com/china/2014/11/positive-energy-a-pop-propaganda-term-2450256.html, eingesehen am 18.8.2016, und zur Liebe gegenüber der Partei den Artikel „Aiguo he aidang zai Zhongguo shi yizhide" 爱国和爱党在中国是一致的 (Die Liebe zum Vaterland und zur Partei sind in China eins), von Chen Xiankui 陈先奎, einem Professor für Marxismus an der Volksuniversität Peking, in *Huanqiu shibao* 环球时报 / *Global Times* (chin. Ausgabe) vom 10.9.2014.

[8] Ich beziehe mich bei der Konstatierung der Krise auf einen kürzlich in der Wochenzeitung *Nanfang zhoumo* 南方周末 erschienenen Artikel von Zeng Bowei 曾博伟, „Jiangou Zhongguo shi xinyang" 建构中国式信仰 (Die Schaffung eines Glaubens mit chinesischen Merkmalen) vom 9. Oktober 2014. Der Artikel ist in einem rational-materialistischen Ton abgefasst; für wesentlichen Gefühle, die im Zusammenhang mit Glauben eine wichtige Rolle spielen – etwa Leidenschaft und Hingabe – ist demgemäß kein Platz.

Patriotismus das Schicksal des Kleinen Ich (*xiao wo* 小我) auf natürliche Weise mit dem Schicksal des Großen Ich (*da wo* 大我) von Staat und Nation verbunden. Obwohl es in diesem Konzept keinen Gott oder göttlichen Willen gebe, werde in der über-individuellen Allgemeinheit die Rolle eines Gottes ausgeübt. Der Glaube in China sei eher auf die überindividuelle Allgemeinheit und das Diesseits gerichtet. Die wirtschaftliche Vorherrschaft des Westens bringe, so der Verfasser des Artikels weiter, viele Menschen dazu, die Kultur und den religiösen Glauben des Westens zu überhöhen. Vereinfachend werde daraus der Schluss gezogen, der entwickelte Westen beruhe auf der Religion und dem Glauben der Menschen:

> Ich bin davon überzeugt, dass wir in dem neuen Zeitalter (*xin de shiqi* 新的时期) eine Wahl treffen sollten: Beruhend auf der Tradition die fortschrittlichen Erfolge anderer Kulturen vollkommen aufnehmen und einen Glauben mit chinesischen Merkmalen schaffen, der von der Mehrzahl der Menschen in unserem Land akzeptiert wird.[9]

Daran schließen sich Vorschläge an, wie solch ein Glaube herzustellen ist: 1. Durch Toleranz: ein Glaube mit chinesischen Merkmalen sei nicht religiös, schließe aber anderen religiösen Glauben nicht aus. Es folgt wie selbstverständlich der Hinweis auf das friedliche Nebeneinander der verschiedenen Glaubensformen und Religionen in China über lange Perioden hinweg. 2. Erziehung/Bildung/Unterweisung (*jiaoyu* 教育): maßgeblich darauf fußend „soll der Glaube nach und nach in die Herzen der Menschen eindringen" (*rang xinyang zhujian shenru renxin* 让信仰逐渐深入人心). Insgesamt stelle der Glauben einen wichtigen Beitrag zur Entwicklung des Einzelnen und zum Fortschritt von Staat und Gesellschaft bei.

Streng genommen lassen sich die vorstehenden Bemerkungen in der Vermutung bündeln, dass damit ein Scheitern des Strebens nach einer „harmonischen Gesellschaft" angedeutet wird. Wäre die Harmonie mit den vor geraumer Zeit verordneten Mitteln erreicht, dann erübrigte sich auch die Anregung zu mehr glaubensfester Innerlichkeit. Die „harmonische Gesellschaft" chinesischer Prägung ist keine von inneren Werten und Idealen getragene Vision. Am Himmel der Visionen chinesischer Glaubenshüter taucht allenfalls vage das Streben nach etwas auf, das William James vor mehr als hundert Jahren einmal als die „unsichtbare Ordnung" bezeichnete. Danach wird das religiöse Leben in der spätmodernen Gesellschaft des Westens von der Überzeugung getragen, dass das höchste Gut in einer harmonischen Anpassung an eben diese Ordnung besteht. Der wesentliche Unterschied besteht in den gesellschaftlichen und politischen Gegebenheiten: der Wunsch nach mehr Spiritualität mag in China vorhanden sein, der freie Raum, dies auch zu praktizieren, jedoch nicht.[10]

---

[9] Siehe den in Fußnote 8 angeführten Artikel.

[10] Ich beziehe mich mit dem Hinweis auf William James auf die Ausführungen in dem Abschnitt „Kulte und Neureligionen" (S. 13-36) in: Douglas E. Cowan – David G. Bromley, *Neureligionen und ihre Kulte*, aus dem Amerikanischen von Claus-Jürgen Thornton (Berlin: Verlag der Weltreligionen, 2010), S. 23.

Ich will es zunächst bei diesen kurzen einleitenden Bemerkungen zu den allgemeinen Problemen der Religion in China belassen, denn das Thema meines Artikels ist schließlich die Literatur. Warum? Gründe gibt es wohl viele, mit *ein* Grund, der mir bedeutsam erscheint, ist, dass es gerade die Literatur und zumal Erzählliteratur fertig bringt, geistig-spirituelle Räume auf ihre ganz eigene Art und Weise auszudeuten. Es ist die in der Literatur angelegte Vielsinnigkeit und Mehrdeutigkeit, die es für Interpreten egal welcher Couleur interessant macht, auch dort theologisch-symbolische und möglicherweise sozial relevante Deutungen zu wagen, wo dies nicht auf direkterem Wege möglich ist.[11] Ein schönes aktuelles Beispiel, das weit mehr als nur „Unterhaltung" darstellt, ist die herrliche kleine Satire von Ma Boyong 马伯庸 mit dem Titel „Yi ge shenzhi renyuan yu ta de ping'anye" 一个神职人员与他的平安夜 (Ein Geistlicher und sein Heiligabend), die zum Ende des Jahres 2014 auf Weibo 微博, dem chinesischen Mikroblogging-Dienst ähnlich Twitter, verbreitet wurde und auf köstliche Weise die fragwürdige Verbindung von Staat und Kirche in China beschreibt: die „christliche Botschaft" formuliert im Parteijargon und der Kirchenbetrieb in China, getrieben von dem landläufigen Streben nach Pomp und Selbstdarstellung.

Anders als man vielleicht erwarten würde, wird die Literatur in den meisten Arbeiten zu Fragen der Religion im China der Gegenwart weitgehend ausgespart. Adam Chau nennt in seinem Beitrag zum religiösen Leben in China zwar fünf Formen des „Umgangs" mit der Religion, doch „Literatur", wie ich sie in diesem Beitrag verstehe, spielt dabei allerhöchstens indirekt eine Rolle.[12] Anders als hier, wo der künstlerischen Fiktion und Erzählung Raum gegeben wird, geht es bei Chau um die Beschäftigung mit in einer bestimmten Überlieferung stehenden religiösen Texten sowie den daraus entwickelten Diskursen.

---

[11] Vgl. die Interpretation durch Hans Küng in Bezug auf Kafkas *Das Schloss*: „Das Schloß ist somit nicht Ausdruck der Gnade, wohl aber einer chiffrierten, änigmatischen Transzendenzerfahrung, wo die Transzendenz rätselhaft, undurchsichtig, ängstigend bleibt, dem Menschen aber ein Weg offengelassen, eine Hoffnung nicht verunmöglicht wird. Das ‚Schloß' also ein religiöses Werk? Antwort: ein direkt religiöses nicht, wohl aber ein religiös höchst relevantes Werk!" Zitiert aus Hans Küng, „Religion im Zusammenbruch der Moderne", in: Walter Jens – Hans Küng, *Dichtung und Religion. Pascal, Gryphius, Lessing, Hölderlin, Novalis, Kierkegaard, Dostojewski, Kafka* (München: Kindler, 1985), S. 286-305, hier S. 297.

[12] Vgl. dazu Adam Chau, „Modalities of Doing Religion", in: David A. Palmer – Glenn Shive – Philip L. Wickeri (Hrsg.), *Chinese Religious Life* (Oxford: Oxford University Press, 2011), S. 67-84. Angeführt werden dort fünf „Formen" (modalities), mit denen Religion in China ausgeübt wird: 1. „the discursive or scriptural", „based on the composition and use or religious texts2; 2. „the personal-cultivational", „involving a long-term interest in cultivating and transforming oneself"; 3. „the liturgical", „which makes use of procedures conducted by priests, monks, or other ritual specialists"; 4. „the immediate-practical", „aiming at quick results making use of using religious or magical techniques", 5. „the relational", „emphasizing the relationship among humans, deities, ghosts, and ancestors as well as among people in families, villages, and religious communities". Zitiert aus Philip L. Wickeri, „Introduction", in: *Chinese Religious Life*, S. 4.

Die Literatur ist sicherlich in China nach wie vor kein besonders geschützter Raum, doch sie ist angesichts der anhaltenden Debatte in China über das Wesen, die Rolle und die Notwendigkeit der Religion eine Form von Öffentlichkeit, mittels der sich möglicherweise atmosphärisch zum Thema etwas erschließt und Eindrücke auf die eine oder andere Art und Weise bestätigen lassen. Der Erzählkunst als einer proteischen Kunst, welche keinen strengen Repräsentationsregeln unterliegt, kommt hierbei eine, wie ich meine, herausragende Bedeutung zu.[13] Ziel des vorliegenden Beitrags kann nicht die Analyse eines angenommenen Ist-Zustandes sein, vielmehr geht es um die Beschäftigung mit der Frage, in welchem Maße die Auseinandersetzung mit „Religion" in der Literatur Chinas heute möglich ist und was dort über „Religion" ausgesagt wird. Im Mittelpunkt der Betrachtungen steht dabei allgemein die Thematisierung des Christentums in einer Reihe von neueren Werken der Vertreter der Erzählliteratur. Wo „Religion" lediglich in generellem Sinne thematisiert wird oder von anderen als den christlichen Religionen die Rede ist, wird das entsprechend angemerkt. Die Beschäftigung mit dem Christentum und Fragen des christlichen Glaubens ist vor allem deshalb auch interessant und wichtig, weil das Christentum sich einer kulturellen Vereinnahmung durch China weitgehend entziehen konnte, von den Staats- und Kulturbehörden Chinas bis heute weitgehend als „fremd" (und „bedrohlich") eingestuft wird und in dieser Hinsicht auch von chinesischen Schriftstellern immer wieder gerne als eine authentische Folie benutzt wird, um auf den Zustand der eigenen chinesischen Kultur, Gesellschaft und Sprache hinzuweisen. Ziel ist es, auf Facetten „literarischer Religiosität" hinzuweisen.[14]

„Religiöses Setting" oder die Autorität der fremden Religion?

In einer ganzen Anzahl von Romanen und Erzählungen im China der Gegenwart ist nicht immer klar auszumachen, zu welchem Zweck die Namen und Begriffe aus der Religion bzw. dem Christentum letzten Endes dienen. Mitunter wird der Versuch erkennbar, in allgemeiner Form oder auch ganz direkt auf religiöse Probleme anzuspielen oder so etwas wie eine „religiöse Atmosphäre" zu verbreiten. Die beim Leser damit hervorgerufene Wirkung bleibt dabei eher oberflächlich. Als Beispiel für diese Form von Literatur sei hier die kurze Erzählung eines nur unter seinem Pseudonym „ShakeSpace" (vermutlich eine Verballhornung von „Shakespeare") genannten Schriftstellers mit dem Titel „Godelized" genannt, in der es um einen Hexenmann und eine Hexenfrau geht.[15] Der genaue Handlungs-

---

[13] Vgl. zum Repräsentationscharakter und dem Umgang mit der „Wirklichkeit" ausführlicher Albrecht Koschorke, *Wahrheit und Erfindung. Grundzüge einer Allgemeinen Erzähltheorie* (Frankfurt/M.: S. Fischer, 2012), S. 109.

[14] Vgl. dazu die Bemerkungen zum Verhältnis von Religion und Öffentlichkeit in China bei Philip L. Wickeri, „Introduction", in: Palmer – Shive – Wickeri, *Chinese Religious Life*, S. 5.

[15] Der Text der Erzählung findet sich in dem von Pan Haitian 潘海天 herausgegebenen Band *Qixuan juan* 奇玄卷 (Fantasy) in der neunbändigen Reihe *Xin shiji xiaoshuo daxi* 新世纪小说大系 2001–2010 (Große Reihe Erzählliteratur des neuen Jahrtausends, 2001–2010), Ge-

hintergrund ist unklar, ebenso wie die Zeit, in der sich die Ereignisse zutragen. Neben den beiden Hexengestalten ist u.a. von einem „heiligen Ritter" sowie von der – hier bereits in ihrer literarisierten Form auftretenden – religiösen Figur Mephisto sowie von Gott die Rede.

In anderen Erzählungen, die gar nicht mehr in China, sondern in Gegenden Europas vor langer Zeit spielen und exotistisch angehaucht sind, ist ein konkret religiös-historisches Setting notwendigerweise mit der Handlung gegeben: Beispielhaft sei hier nur Li Duo 李多 mit *Guancai li de shengnü* 棺材里的圣女 (Die Heilige im Sarg) angeführt.[16] Offenbar ist die Erzählung ganz im europäischen Mittelalter angesiedelt. Hauptfigur ist die junge schwachsinnige Emmily: die Frau muss auf den Befehl der Religionsrichter, welche im Auftrag des Papstes handeln, als Vampirfrau herhalten und wird gepfählt. Als ihre Leiche jedoch nach längerer Zeit immer noch nicht verwest ist, sondern von Tag zu Tag an Schönheit gewinnt, kommt es zum Konflikt zwischen den Dorfbewohnern und den päpstlichen Truppen.

Bei Yu Hua 余华 und einigen seiner neueren Werke wird ein weiterer Aspekt des Umgangs mit „Religion" erkennbar, nämlich die Berufung auf eine „fremde Autorität" wie die Bibel, um kontrastiv und vor dem Hintergrund eines vollkommen anderen Wertesystems auf die Mängel in China aufmerksam zu machen. Es könnte sich hierbei um eine – bei einem Schriftsteller wie Yu Hua durchaus nicht verwunderliche – besondere Form des Protestes gegen die Propaganda und das immer wieder lauthals beschworene Glück der Menschen in China handeln.

In seinem 2005 und 2006 in zwei Teilen erschienenen Roman *Xiongdi* 兄弟 (Brüder) greift der Autor Yu Hua das in der zeitgenössischen chinesischen Literatur weit verbreitete Thema der Kulturrevolution (1966–1976) wieder auf, das bereits den Hintergrund einer Reihe seiner Erzählungen aus den späten 1980er Jahren bildete.

Hauptfiguren des Romans sind die beiden Stiefbrüder Song Gang 宋钢 und Li Guangtou 李光头 („Glatzkopf Li"). In schonungsloser Genauigkeit beschreibt Yu Hua die Gewalt und Demütigungen, die den Brüdern, Lis Mutter, Songs Vater und anderen Bewohnern der kleinen Stadt Liuzhen widerfahren, und zeichnet damit ein Bild des schmutzigen Erbes aus der Vergangenheit, angereichert durch zahllose Szenen der ungezügelten Gewalt, des Vulgären und Triebhaften. China erscheint als Irrenhaus, das sich nach dem verrückten Revolutionsgehabe der 1960er und 1970er dem ebenso verrückten kapitalistischen Geldscheffeln der Gegenwart verschrieben hat. Besonders im zweiten Romanteil setzt der Autor dieses China des beginnenden 21. Jahrhunderts in Form immer bizarrerer Bilder eindrucksvoll in Szene.

---

samtherausgeber Chen Sihe 陈思和 (Shanghai: Shanghai wenyi, 2014), S. 89-122. Eine genaue Namensangabe zum Autor fehlt im Vorspann zu der Geschichte, es ist nur von seiner Herkunft aus Shanghai die Rede.

[16] Die Erzählung findet sich in *Qixuan juan* auf S. 369-373.

Mit der Steigerung der realistischen Details ins Grotesk-Absurde fängt er eine Stimmung ein, die in drastischen Bildern die chinesische Gesellschaft bloßstellen will. Mehr als drei Jahrzehnte nach dem Ende der Kulturrevolution fragt Yu Hua nach ihren Folgen für das Leben der Menschen in China und schlägt so einen Bogen von der Vergangenheit in die Gegenwart, wie sich dies in keinem anderen Werk der chinesischen Literatur findet. Der Roman bringt etwas von den Extremen und der Zerrissenheit Chinas zum Ausdruck und schafft es damit als Kunstwerk viel eher, als dies einem Werk der politischen, historischen oder der Sozialwissenschaft gelingen könnte, ein überaus facettenreiches Bild der chinesischen Gesellschaft zu zeichnen. In seinem auf das Jahr 2005 datierten Nachwort kommt Yu auf den Prozess des Schreibens zu sprechen und erläutert,[17] wie er bei der Abfassung des ursprünglich viel kürzer angelegten Romans plötzlich die Gewalt über die Geschichte verlor, so dass sich der Inhalt um ein Vielfaches verlängerte. Die Erfahrung, wie man sich auf wunderbare Weise vom Kleinen schreibend aufmacht hin zum Großen, bringt Yu Hua schließlich zu dem Vergleich mit dem Leben schlechthin: Wenn Menschen auf einem vermeintlich großen und prächtigen Weg voranschreiten, um sich plötzlich in einer Sackgasse wiederzufinden, anstatt besser vorsichtig und klein anzufangen, um dann zur rechten Zeit ganz plötzlich vor einem weiten Horizont stehen. Als moralische Instanz für diese literarisch-poetische ebenso wie für das Leben gültige Weisheit der Demut und Bescheidenheit beruft sich Yu Hua auf niemand anderen als Jesus, den Mahner: „Geht hinein durch die enge Pforte! Denn weit ist die Pforte und breit der Weg, der zum Verderben führt, und viele sind, die auf ihm hineingehen. Denn eng ist die Pforte und schmal der Weg, der zum Leben führt, und wenige sind, die ihn finden."[18] Yu Hua verzerrt, ob absichtlich oder aus Unwissenheit sei dahingestellt, das Bibelzitat, indem er das für den gläubigen Christen Wesentliche – die Berufung auf die Autorität Gottes – auslässt: nämlich dass Gottes Wahrheit keinem Kompromiss unterworfen werden kann. Die Straße, die hin zur Zerstörung führt und mit weltlichen Vorstellungen gefüllt ist, ist nicht der Weg des Christen.

Noch deutlicher – nämlich bereits im Titel – bezieht sich Yu Hua mit seinem 2013 erschienenen Roman *Di qi tian* 第七天 (Der siebte Tag) auf das Christentum.[19] Dem Romantext vorangestellt ist – bei Yu verkürzt – ein Bibelzitat aus dem Schöpfungsbericht:

> Danach betrachtete Gott alles, was er geschaffen hatte. Und er sah, dass es sehr gut war. Und es wurde Abend und Morgen: der sechste Tag [...] Am siebten Tag vollendete Gott sein Werk und ruhte von seiner Arbeit aus. Und

---

[17] Vgl. dazu das Nachwort in der Ausgabe Yu Hua, *Xiongdi* (Beijing: Zuojia chubanshe 2013), S. 631f.

[18] Siehe Matthäus 7:13-14. Die Bibelstelle klingt in der von Yu zitierten Fassung etwas anders, hier die Rückübersetzung der Zeilen auf S. 632 mit dem Jesus in den Mund gelegten Spruch: „Die Straße in den Tod führt durch ein breites Tor für viele. Der kleine Weg in die Ewigkeit ist eng, er wird nur von wenigen gefunden."

[19] Vgl. Yu Hua, *Di qi tian* (Beijing: Xinxing, 2013).

Gott segnete den siebten Tag und erklärte ihn für heilig, weil es der Tag war, an dem er sich von seiner Schöpfungsarbeit ausruhte.[20]

Yu Hua konterkariert in seinem Roman freilich die christliche Schöpfungsvorstellung; geboten wird das krasse Gegenteil des von Gott (bei Yu Hua *shen* 神) geschaffenen Paradieses und einer gelungenen Schöpfung: Im Buch geht es um die Seelen der Toten und der „Verlierer" in der heutigen Gesellschaft. Gott und sein Dichter Yu Hua sind letzten Endes sprachlos angesichts der katastrophalen Zustände, die sich kaum in Worte fassen lassen: Mord und Gewalt, Korruption und Lebensmittelskandale, Organhandel und Betrügereien im Nachrichtenwesen.

Einen äußerst interessanten Versuch von symbolistischer Literatur stellt die Beschäftigung mit der Religion in dem Buch *Fayuan* 法院 (Das Gericht) des 1964 geborenen Schriftstellers Zhang Xiaobo 张小波 dar.[21] In den Bericht des Ich-Erzählers, einem Arzt, dem vorgeworfen wird, er habe seine Praxis eröffnet, um Patientinnen sexuell zu belästigen und der nun auf seinen Prozess wartet, ist die Geschichte von einem früheren Seemann eingeflochten, der sich als Barmixer in einem Seemannsclub einen Namen gemacht hat, da er sehr kreativ Dutzende verschiedener Cocktails und Drinks herzustellen versteht. Er befindet sich in Untersuchungshaft, da er einen Bischof umgebracht haben soll. Folgendes spielte sich nach dem Bericht des Barmixers an den Ich-Erzähler ab: Bei den Gesprächen mit den Gästen in dem Seemannsclub wurde der Barmixer auf eine alte Legende aufmerksam, die sich um den Kirchenschatz von Shanghai dreht. Berichtet wird nun von dem alten Bischof Gong Pinmei 龚品梅, der 1954 verhaftet und wegen Landesverrats zu einer lebenslänglichen Haft verurteilt wurde.[22] In den folgenden Wirren sei u.a. ein aus dem Vatikan stammendes wertvolles Messkännchen verloren gegangen, das auch nicht wieder auftauchte, als Bischof Gong Pinmei später in die USA reiste und nicht mehr nach Shanghai zurückkehrte. Erzählt wird in dem Zusammenhang auch von der heimlichen Ernennung von Gong zum Erzbischof durch Rom während seiner Haft.[23] Das Gerücht besagt nun, dass das Messkännchen in einem Kellergewölbe der Kirche entdeckt worden sei. In dem Seemann/Barmixer kam nun, nachdem er von dieser Geschichte erfahren hatte, die Idee auf, sich das sakrale Gerät anzueignen („Ich ging einen Pakt mit dem Teufel ein").[24] Er drang daher in die Kirche ein, in der Hand einen Strauß Rosen. Dort

---

[20] Genesis 1:31-2:3 (1. Mose 1-2).

[21] Nanjing: Jiangsu wenyi, 2012.

[22] Die von dem Seemann/Barmixer erzählte Geschichte über den historischen Bischof findet sich größtenteils auf den Seiten 109-118. Die grob angeführten Tatsachen aus dem Leben des Bischofs entsprechen weitgehend den Fakten; hier ergänzend einige Stichpunkte: Bischof Gong Pinmei (1901–2000) wurde 1955 inhaftiert und reiste 1988 nach seiner endgültigen Entlassung aus der Haft in die USA aus. Bereits 1979 war er zum Kardinal ernannt worden. Vgl. *Christus in China. Der Bischof von Shanghai. Aloysius Jin im Gespräch mit Dominik Wanner und Alexa von Künsberg, mit Begleittexten von Thomas Zimmer* (Freiburg: Herder, 2012), S. 160.

[23] Zu diesen Angaben siehe Zhang Xiaobo, *Fayuan*, S. 167.

[24] Ibid., S. 114.

trat ihm der Bischof entgegen, erkannte ihn aber zunächst nicht als Verbrecher. Der Bischof lud den Räuber auf einen Kaffee in seine Wohnung ein, doch nach dem Messkännchen befragt, antwortete er:

> Er sagte, mein Kind, auch wenn du in dieser Nacht nicht der erste bist, der mich nach irgendeinem Messkännchen fragt, so ist deine Art, dies zu tun, mit einem Rosenstrauß in der Hand, sehr ungewöhnlich. Er sagte, mein Kind, nimm ruhig alles von den Dingen hier um dich herum mit, gerne gehe ich mit dir auch in die Kellerräume, dann wird dir bewusst werden, dass es kein Messkännchen gibt. Bei der Sache mit dem Messkännchen, das angeblich ein Geschenk aus dem Vatikan ist, handelt es sich um ein Gerücht. In dem biblischen Buch der Weisheit heißt es, dass sanfte Zungen Knochen brechen können, und weiter wird dort gesagt, dass ein Mensch, dem es nicht gelingt, sein Herz zu kontrollieren, einer zerstörten Stadt gleicht, die von keinen schützenden Mauern mehr umgeben ist. Herr, Du darfst deine Kinder nicht aufgeben ...[25]

Der Erzähler sei darüber so erbost gewesen, dass er den Bischof erstach. Noch im Sterben vergab der Bischof seinem Mörder und forderte diesen auf, die Momente vor dem Tod des Geistlichen noch zu nutzen, damit dieser ihm die Beichte abnehmen könne. Im Folgenden wird der Seemann/Barmixer verhaftet und wartet auf seinen Prozess wegen Mordes. Der Ich-Erzähler im Buch rät dem Seemann, der befürchten muss, zum Tode verurteilt zu werden, sich den Dingen zu stellen – Gerechtigkeit und Vergebung seien zwei unterschiedliche Dinge: Der Bischof als Geistlicher hat seinem Mörder vergeben, nun ist es an den weltlichen Instanzen, der Gerechtigkeit Genüge zu tun.

Bemerkenswert sind an dieser nur wenige Seiten langen Geschichte mehrere Aspekte. Da ist zum einen die Schilderung über den in China heute vermutlich nur noch einem kleineren Kreis von Gläubigen bekannten Bischof Gong Pinmei. Die Erzählung steckt voller Symbole und möglicher Anspielungen. Deutliche Bezüge werden im Text vor allem zu Kafka hergestellt (genannt werden die Erzählung „In der Strafkolonie" und *Das Schloss*). Wie bei Kafka sind dabei mehrere Lesungen möglich, eine weltimmanente und eine metaphysische. Im Mittelpunkt steht die vergebliche Suche nach einem Sinn des Daseins, das letzten Endes durch die ausschließliche Orientierung an materiellem Wohlstand und der rein oberflächlichen Bedürfnisbefriedigung verloren zu gehen droht. Eher andeutungsweise bleiben die Hinweise auf Verbindungen zwischen Religion und Gesetz. Der Mord an einem Bischof aus Habgier könnte sich eventuell als eine fundamentale Kritik an der Profanität der chinesischen Kultur verstehen lassen.

Auf einen letzten und wie mir scheint besonders wichtigen Aspekt bei der Beschäftigung einiger Autoren mit dem Christentum in ihren Werken soll hier noch hingewiesen werden, nämlich auf die Auseinandersetzung mit christlichen Motiven sowie der durch Übersetzungen der Bibel aus den klassischen abendländischen Sprachen ganz eigene Sprachstil des im christlich-religiösen Kontext verwendeten Chinesisch.

---

[25] Vgl. Zhang Xiaobo, *Fayuan*, S. 116f.

Die 1982 geborene Zhang Yueran 张悦然 gehört zu den gefeierten Jungautoren Chinas und erreicht mit ihren Werken ein riesiges Publikum unter den jungen Lesern. Zhangs bereits 2004, zunächst in einem anderen Verlag erschienener Roman *Yingtao zhi yuan* 樱桃之远 (Fern der Kirschen) entstammt noch der von ihr selber als Sturm- und Drangphase bezeichneten Zeit.[26] Umso beachtlicher sind die stilistische Sicherheit und das hohe Sprachvermögen. Es ist etwas Natürliches, Selbstverständliches und Unbefangenes an Zhangs Buch, das zeigt, welchen rasanten Wandel auch die Literatur Chinas in den letzten Jahren durchgemacht hat: unvorstellbar, dass ein chinesischer Schriftsteller vor zehn oder zwanzig Jahren so freimütig über die Liebe einer Romanfigur zu Gott geschrieben hätte, wie Zhang das mit ihrer Duan Xiaomu 段小沐 in *Yingtao zhi yuan* tut. Zhang kennt ihre vielleicht etwas sentimentale junge Leserschaft, und sie trifft den richtigen Ton: Die kleine Duan Xiaomu kommt, nachdem sie ihre Mutter bei einem Unfall verloren hat, zunächst in ein Heim. Nach zwei Jahren holt ihr Vater sie dort ab, um mit ihr nach Nordchina zu fahren. Doch auch dort, in Licheng 郦城, bleibt die Lage der beiden unsicher. Zwar geht Xiaomu jeden Tag in einen Kindergarten, doch der Vater kehrt von einer Geschäftsreise, die er angeblich unternehmen muss, nie wieder zu ihr zurück. Xiaomu gelangt in die Obhut einer christlichen Nonne. Sie ist gerade einmal sieben, als sie von einem anderen Mädchen namens Du Wanwan 杜宛宛, das Xiaomu zu hassen scheint, von der Schaukel gestoßen wird und sich dabei so stark verletzt, dass sie für den Rest ihres Lebens gehbehindert bleibt. Als Xiaomu aus dem Krankenhaus entlassen wird, ist Wanwan bereits in eine andere Stadt gezogen, doch die beiden Mädchen sind einander sehr eng verbunden, ohne dass sie es richtig wissen. Da ein Studium für Xiaomu nicht in Frage kommt, bricht sie den Schulbesuch nach der Mittelschule ab und wird eine geschickte Näherin. Sie verliebt sich ausgerechnet in den kriminellen Halbstarken Xiao Jiezi 小杰子 aus der Nachbarschaft, der sie ausnützt und dem die seit ihrer Kindheit herzkranke Xiaomu das eigentlich für ihre bald notwendige Operation gedachte Geld überlässt. Parallel dazu wird das lange Zeit oberflächlich bleibende Leben Du Wanwans in einer anderen Stadt geschildert, bis die beiden Frauen am Ende nach einigen Verwicklungen doch noch zusammenfinden. Doch die Zeit, die sie die gemeinsame Freundschaft genießen können, währt nur kurz, denn Xiaomu stirbt im Alter von gerade mal zwanzig Jahren, nachdem Xiao Jiezi ihr auf eine grausame Art klar gemacht hat, dass er sie nicht liebt.

Erste Freundschaften, Liebeskummer, Trennung, Tod sind die Themen des Romans, aber nicht alle werden gleichermaßen stark ausgeführt. Was beeindruckt, ist die Anstrengung Zhang Yuerans, Innerlichkeit und die Suche nach einem inneren Halt und Spiritualität am Beispiel der zentralen Helden des Buches plastisch zu machen. Spiritualität ist nun etwas, das auch in der chinesischen

---

[26] Vgl. Zhang Yueran, *Yingtao zhi yuan* (Jinan: Mingtian chubanshe, 2007); der engl. Titel auf dem Buchcover lautet *The Doom of Bloom*, in Online-Ankündigungen einfach mit *Cherry* (Kirschen) übersetzt.

Kultur und Literatur nichts Fremdes darstellt, doch das vielfach in der schwierigen, heute schon dunkel wirkenden Sprache des klassischen Chinesisch wiedergegeben wird. Das wirkt stilistisch unzeitgemäß. Zhang Yueran erfindet nun freilich keine neue Sprache, doch sie tut etwas Mutiges: Sie bringt das Christentum ins Spiel. Um verständlich zu sein und den (chinesischen) Leser zu überzeugen, muss die Autorin genug Raum bieten für die Erläuterung von Vorstellungen wie Liebe, Gnade, Schuld, Reue, Güte und Selbstüberwindung in der Sprache von heute. Diese Sprache klingt (zurückübersetzt) für den westlichen Leser vertraut, doch in China ist sie ein Novum. Zhang thematisiert diese Eigenartigkeit und anfängliche Fremdheit der christlichen Religion auch im Roman: Schwester Lis Gebet bleibt Duan Xiaomu zunächst unverständlich, sie wundert sich über die vielen fremden Worte. Doch es bleibt nicht bei Worten und Begriffen, mit denen das Christentum umschrieben wird, es kommt zu einer Welt ganz neuer Vorstellungen, wenn zum Beispiel davon die Rede ist, den Reichtum des Lebens zu preisen, den Glauben in sich zu spüren, Gott als Lenker zu erkennen, innere Ruhe zu finden usw. An Duan Xiaomu verdeutlicht die Autorin, was es heißt, im Glauben und mit dem Glauben zu leben und daraus die Kraft zu gewinnen, das Leben auch als behinderter Mensch zu bejahen, anderen Liebe zu geben, obwohl man von ihnen gehasst wird.

Wie anregend die Beschäftigung mit der durch die Bibelübersetzungen beeinflussten chinesischen Schriftsprache sein kann, zeigt der kräftige epische Stil in *Sishu* 四书 (Vier Bücher) des 1958 geborenen Schriftstellers Yan Lianke 阎连科, das auf unglaublich eindringliche Weise die Hunger- und Naturkatastrophen in China am Ende der 1950er Jahre behandelt.[27]

Religion und Geschichte

Der bekannte chinesische Schriftsteller Li Rui 李锐 hat vor kurzem mit dem Roman *Zhang Mading de di ba tian* 张马丁的第八天 (Martin Zhangs achter Tag) ein eigentlich ganz beachtliches Echo hervorgerufen,[28] was vor allem Thema liegen dürfte:[29] *Zhang Mading de di ba tian* hat als historischen Hintergrund den

---

[27] Hongkong: Mingbao, 2010.

[28] Zu Li Ruis ansonsten ganz beachtlichem Werk aus den letzten Jahren vgl. die Besprechungen von Thomas Zimmer, „Li Rui, *Taiping fengwu* (Friedliche Landschaften)", in: *Orientierungen, Themenheft* 2009 (*Chinesische Gegenwartsliteratur. Zwischen Plagiat und Markt?*), S. 122-124. und „Li Rui, *Renjian. Chong shu Baishe zhuan* (In der Menschenwelt. Der Mythos von der Weißen Schlange neu erzählt)", in: *ibid.*, S. 124-126.

[29] Erschienen in Nanjing: Jiangsu wenyi, 2012. Dem Roman vorangestellt ist ein längerer wissenschaftlicher Essay mit dem Titel *Yi ge ren de chuangshiji* 一个人的'创世纪' (Der „Schöpfungsbericht" eines Menschen) des ebenfalls bekannten amerikanischen Sinologen und Literaturwissenschaftlers David Der-wei Wang (chinesisch Wang Dewei 王德威) aus Harvard. Im Anhang finden sich Angaben zum Schöpfungsbericht aus der Bibel und aus chinesischen Klassikern sowie eine Reihe von historischen Dokumenten zum Boxeraufstand. Ebenfalls angefügt ist weiterhin ein längeres Interview mit dem Journalisten einer Literaturzeitschrift, in der Li Rui historische Hintergründe des Romans erläutert.

Boxeraufstand 1900/1901, der aufgrund von Konflikten zwischen den von ausländischen Missionaren betreuten chinesischen Christen und Kreisen der einheimischen lokalen Bevölkerung in Nordchina ausbrach. Der Unmut im Volk trieb den Boxern als einer teilweise aus religiösen Zusammenhängen entstandenen Kampfkunstgruppe zahlreiche Anhänger zu. Die Ermordung des deutschen Gesandten Clemens Freiherr von Ketteler führte zum Einmarsch alliierter Streitkräfte unter der Führung des „Weltgenerals" Alfred Graf von Waldersee und zur Besetzung der Hauptstadt Peking.

Der schwierige Stoff stellt für Autoren fraglos eine große Herausforderung dar: China kurz vor dem Sturz des Kaiserhauses, ein zerrissenes Land, nahezu führerlos, gepeinigt von Korruption und Unfähigkeit, ein Spielball der imperialistischen Mächte; die komplexe religiöse Komponente – hier die vielen indigenen lokalen Kulte und volkstümlichen Praktiken, dort die Anstrengungen der christlichen Missionare, ihre Ziele durchzusetzen. Ein insgesamt äußerst sensibler Stoff mit einem hohen aktuellen Wertgehalt, bei dem aus chinesischer Sicht schnell die nationalen Gefühle hochkommen, da stets die Erinnerung an die „Erniedrigung" durch die Mächte des Westens mitklingt.

Selbstverständlich hat der reiche Stoff vielen chinesischen Autoren über die Jahre immer wieder die Gelegenheit geboten, ihre Kunst unter Beweis zu stellen. Einen sehr gelungenen Versuch lieferte etwa Mo Yans 莫言 vor mehr als einem Jahrzehnt erschienener Roman *Tanxiang xing* 檀香型 (Die Sandelholzstrafe).[30] Doch während Mo Yan den Stoff kunstvoll auskleidet, die verschiedenen Stimmen und Tonlagen der Kunstgattungen aus Theater, Oper und Gesang einfängt und daraus inhaltlich wie formal ein vielstimmiges Werk komponiert, begibt sich Li Rui auf das wohl schwierigste aller möglichen Gebiete – die Religion: Chinas Volksglaube in der Auseinandersetzung mit der christlichen Religion. Der für das Vorwort gewonnene David Wang soll dem Roman ganz offensichtlich ein größeres Gewicht verleihen, doch überzeugt auch das nicht. Die Anstrengungen, Li Ruis Werk im Lichte der Theorien schwergewichtiger Vertreter der Moderne wie Max Weber, Frederic Jameson oder Giorgio Agamben zu spiegeln, wie David Wang das tut, wirken nach der Lektüre des Romans vollkommen hilflos und hanebüchen.

Zhang Mading de di ba tian erzählt die Geschichte eines jungen italienischen Geistlichen, der seinem Bischof nach China folgt. Während eines tätlichen Angriffs durch die örtliche Bevölkerung, die dem Glauben an die Wirkkraft einer lokalen Göttin anhängt, verliert der junge Italiener das Bewusstsein und wird für tot erklärt. Der vermeintliche Tod eines christlichen Mitbruders wird vom Bischof dazu genutzt, um seiner Forderung nach einem Kirchenbau bei den Provinzbehörden nachdrücklich Ausdruck zu verleihen. Als der wieder zu Bewusstsein gelangte Geistliche den Einheimischen sein Verschwinden erklärt, wird er vom Bischof verstoßen. Die verzweifelte Witwe eines lokalen Religionsführers glaubt in dem Ausländer die Wiedergeburt ihres Mannes gefunden zu haben.

---

[30] Beijing: Zuojia, 2001. Deutsche Übersetzung: *Die Sandelholzstrafe*. Aus dem Chinesischen von Karin Betz (Frankfurt/M. – Leipzig: Insel, 2009).

Selbstverständlich war Li bekannt, auf was für ein komplexes Thema er sich einlässt, die bemühten Erläuterungen im Interview machen das nur allzu deutlich. Der Autor lässt zum Beispiel erkennen, wie problematisch es für Schriftsteller in China heute immer noch ist, das offizielle Geschichtsbild zu verändern (etwa indem er zugesteht, dass die Christen in China durchaus nicht zum Glauben gezwungen wurden, sondern sich freiwillig dazu bekannten). Freilich macht es sich Li Rui zu einfach, wenn er die offensichtliche Unfreiheit, in der die chinesische Gegenwartsliteratur existiert, knapp mit Anspielungen auf die Kontrolle durch Geld und Macht abtut.[31] Lis Bedauern über den Mangel an Ausdruck von geistiger Tiefe im chinesischen Gegenwartsroman ist sicherlich ehrlich und richtig, aber einen überzeugenden Weg, diese zwangsläufig entstehende Flachheit zu überwinden, zeigt Li Rui mit *Zhang Mading de di ba tian* nicht auf. Dabei scheint er – glaubt man seinen Ausführungen in dem Interview – auf die Konzeption des Werkes und die Suche nach einer geeigneten „Form" durchaus erhebliche Mühe verwendet zu haben.[32] Auch Li ist wie zuvor Mo Yan darum bemüht, Vielstimmigkeit herzustellen, doch entsteht daraus nichts Ganzes, Geschlossenes. Die durchaus interessanten Hinweise von Li im Interview zeigen, mit was für einem hohen Maß an Bewusstheit er an den Stoff herangegangen ist, doch es stellt sich heraus, dass der Versuch interessanter ist als das Ergebnis. Li ist ganz einfach an seinem Stoff gescheitert, die Materie der christlichen Religion bleibt ihm fremd,[33] das meiste wirkt aufgesetzt und mühsam angelesen. Tiefe und Ergriffenheit teilen sich nicht mit, alles bleibt seltsam floskelhaft und dünn. Die Figuren leben das Gefühl der Religion nicht; um dennoch alles auf irgend eine Weise „verständlich" und „glaubwürdig" zu machen, bittet Li seine Leser darum, die im Anhang angeführten Dokumente aus der Bibel und chinesischen historischen Quellen zu konsultieren. Das Gespräch zwischen Li und seinem Interviewpartner über die Verdrängung der Religion aus dem Leben der Menschen aufgrund der Fortschritte in der Wissenschaft und die Verbreitung des Christentums im Kontext der blutigen Geschichte des westlichen Kolonialismus wirkt klischeebehaftet.[34]

Ganz anders im Vergleich dazu Mo Yans Roman *Fengru feitun* 丰乳肥臀 (Große Brüste und fette Hintern).[35] Ähnlich kritisch wie bei vielen anderen Werken Mo Yans fielen die Reaktionen auf dieses im Jahre 1995 zunächst als Fortsetzungsroman in der Zeitschrift *Dajia* 大家 erschienene Werk aus: Anhand der Romanfigur Shangguan Jintong 上官金童 (einem Mann, der aus der Verbindung einer chinesischen Mutter mit einem Missionar hervorgegangen ist) thematisiert Mo Yan die traditionelle Rolle des Katholizismus in seiner Heimat Gaomi 高密 in der Provinz Shandong. In den Erläuterungen zu seinem Werk betonte Mo Yan

---

[31] Vgl. *Zhang Mading de di ba tian*, S. 246.
[32] Vgl. *ibid.*, S. 228f.
[33] Vgl. dazu *ibid.*, S. 230.
[34] Vgl. *ibid.*, S. 240.
[35] Vgl. dazu die Ausgabe Shanghai: Shanghai wenyi 2012.

dabei gelegentlich die Notwendigkeit einer differenzierten Betrachtung des Wirkens von Missionaren in der Vergangenheit – ein für ein Mitglied der KPCh durchaus mutiges Verhalten. Im Jahr 1895, so Mo Yan, seien Missionare aus Schweden und Norwegen nach Gaomi gekommen. Mit dem Eisenbahnbau 1900 seien entlang der Bahnstrecke mehr und mehr katholische und evangelische Gotteshäuser errichtet worden, in deren Folge eine größere gesellschaftliche Vielfalt anzutreffen gewesen sei. Der Verfasser weist auf die oft klischeebehaftete Beurteilung des missionarischen Wirkens hin, dem gebetsmühlenartig Imperialismus und Ausbeutung, Unterdrückung usw. unterstellt werden. Mo hebt dagegen positive Aspekte des missionarischen Wirkens hervor. Richtig stellt er dabei heraus, dass Missionare oft ein einfaches und karges Leben gefristet hätten.[36] In China blieb der Roman nach seinem Erscheinen lange umstritten, Mo Yan musste sich gegen eine Reihe von Angriffen seitens der Leser und Kritiker zur Wehr setzen. Dies führte auch zu Schwierigkeiten mit seiner Arbeitseinheit, der Armee. Auf Druck seiner Vorgesetzten und Kollegen wurde Mo Yan 1996 zur Abfassung eines Briefes an den Verlag gedrängt, in dem er die Einstellung des weiteren Drucks und die Vernichtung der noch nicht ausgelieferten Titel verlangte. Wie in zahlreichen seiner Romane und Erzählungen stellt Mo Yan am Beispiel seiner Figuren in *Fengru feitun* das individuelle Gedächtnis dem kollektiven Gedächtnis gegenüber und hinterfragt dabei immer wieder die „Interpretationsmuster der offiziellen Vergangenheitskonstruktion."[37]

Weniger literarisch-historisch als auf einen kulturellen Diskurs hin angelegt ist dagegen die Erzählung „Shengying" 圣婴 (Heiliges Baby) des bekannten chinesischen Horrorschriftstellers Cai Jun 蔡骏.[38] Es bietet sich dabei keine religiöse, sondern vielmehr eine postkolonialistische Lesart der Geschichte an. Der Autor spannt in ein zeitlich-räumliches Gerüst eine verwickelte Geschichte ein. Die zeitlichen Koordinaten bewegen sich zwischen den Jahren 1900 und 2000, der Handlungsraum umfasst zur gleichen Zeit Italien und China, womit eine zeitliche und räumliche Parallelität angedeutet wird. In der gewagten Story ist ein häretischer Missionar aus Italien der Impulsgeber: Mazzolini, die Gestalt ist Lesern bekannt aus Cai Juns Roman *Diyu di 19 ceng* 地狱的第19层 (Die 19. Ebene der Hölle; 2004), kommt im Jahr 1900 nach China. In seinem Besitz hat er eine Christusstatue mit verstümmeltem Unterleib, die für ihn zum Symbol seines von Rom nicht geduldeten Glaubens wird, welchen er in China verbreitet. Im religiö-

---

[36] Vgl. dazu die Ausführungen in „Yu Wang Yao changtan" 与王尧长谈 (Langes Gespräch mit Wang Yao), datiert auf Dezember 2002, in: Mo Yan, *Suiyu wenxue* 碎语文学 (Fragmentarische Betrachtungen zur Literatur; Beijing: Zuojia, 2012), S. 54-228, hier S. 147f.

[37] Vgl. den Beitrag von Pan Lu, „Der Roman *Üppiger Busen, dicker Hintern*. ‚Ein Buch für die Mutter und die Erde'. Die Erinnerungsarbeit in Mo Yans Familiensaga", in: Ylva Monschein (Hrsg.), *Chinas subversive Peripherie. Aufsätze zum Werk des Nobelpreisträgers Mo Yan* (Bochum – Freiburg: Projektverlag, 2013), S. 223-247, hier zitiert nach S. 240.

[38] Cai Jun, *Shengying* 圣婴 (Haikou: Nanhai chuban gongsi 2014), S. 1-34; die englische Übersetzung auf dem Buchtitel lautet *Holy Baby*.

sen Kern der Geschichte geht es um die Frage der Allmacht und Fruchtbarkeit Gottes, die hinführt zu der Überlegung, dass Gott der Vater mehrerer Kinder gewesen sein könnte und nicht nur den Sohn Jesus, sondern auch eine Tochter gezeugt hat. Damit taucht logischerweise auch die Möglichkeit auf, dass der Papst als irdischer Stellvertreter Jesu Christi (bzw. als dessen weiblichem Pendant) auch eine Frau sein könnte.[39] Mittels der Figur einer – wie sie selber angibt – aus unerklärlichen Gründen schwangeren Chinesin in der Gegenwart und ihrem Beharren darauf, Maria zu sein („In meinem Bauch ist ein anderer Jesus, ein jüngerer Bruder oder eine jüngere Schwester des Jesus Christus"; „Ich bin die neue Mutter Gottes" [*shengmu* 圣母]) wird vom Autor der Herkunftsmythos des Christentums dekonstruiert.[40] In der Gegenüberstellung von „falscher" Maria und „echter" Jesusstatue ergibt sich eine Anspielung auf die „Wahrheit" der religiösen Lehre und die Authentizität ihrer Symbole. Hinter dem unerhört bleibenden Schrei der vermeintlichen chinesischen Maria („Mein Kind wird die Welt verändern") deutet sich der Wunsch an,[41] das Christentum bereits von seinem Ursprung her als nicht mehr notwendigerweise an „andere", „westliche" Bilder, Traditionen und Missionen gebunden zu verstehen, sondern daraus etwas vollkommen „Eigenes", „Chinesisches" zu machen. In Cai Juns Roman lassen sich durchaus Ähnlichkeiten zu den am Beginn dieses Beitrags angeführten Bestrebungen in China feststellen, auf der Grundlage der eigenen Traditionen neue quasireligiöse Kulturangebote zu entwerfen. Mit der der Literatur innewohnenden Relativität und vieldeutigen „Softpower" wird in Cai Juns „Shengying" die „Wahrheit" und „Vision" letzten Endes aber wieder in Frage gestellt, als sich zeigt, dass es sich bei der chinesischen Maria um eine Verrückte handelt, die seit 20 Jahren erfolglos davon spricht, die Jungfrau Maria zu sein und den Heiland zur Welt zu bringen.

Atheisten und christliche Schriftsteller – zwei Beispiele

Als im Titel eines Buches des chinesischen Literaturnobelpreisträgers von 2000, Gao Xingjian 高行健, die Bibel genannt wurde, rief das in der Öffentlichkeit großes Erstaunen hervor. Gao ist ein erklärter Atheist. *Yigeren de shengjing* 一个人的圣经 – so der Titel des Originals – ließe sich,[42] bleibt man nah am Wort, etwa mit „Die Bibel eines Einzelnen" oder „Die Bibel nur für den einen" übersetzen.[43] Überträgt man freier und versteht *shengjing* nicht im Sinne der judäo-

---

[39] Vgl. zu diesen Erörterungen *Shengying*, S. 26.

[40] Vgl. alle Zitate in *ibid.*, S. 30.

[41] Vgl. *ibid.*, S. 30.

[42] Zur chinesischen Ausgabe vgl. Gao Xingjian, *Yigeren de shengjing* (Hongkong: Tiandi tushu, 2000). Alle Zitate beziehen sich – sofern nicht anders angegeben – auf diese chinesische Fassung.

[43] Auch Wolfgang Kubin arbeitet mit dem Begriff der „Bibel", variiert aber leicht, indem er übersetzt „Die Bibel eines Mannes". Vgl. *id.*, *Die chinesische Literatur im 20. Jahrhundert*, Geschichte der chinesischen Literatur, Bd. 7 (München: Saur, 2005), S. 373.

christlichen Heiligen Schrift, so könnte man den chinesischen Titel auch im Sinne eines „Leitfadens für einen Menschen" verstehen: jemand jedenfalls, der mit seinen Vorstellungen und Grundsätzen an die Öffentlichkeit tritt, um Autorität zu beanspruchen. Der Titel der deutschen Übersetzung – *Das Buch eines einsamen Menschen* – hat sich dem gegenüber schon sehr weit vom Original entfernt und interpretiert: so kommt in *shengjing* mehr als nur „Buch" zum Ausdruck.[44] Eventuell könnte man mit Begriffen wie „Glaubenssätze" oder „Bekenntnisse" arbeiten. In britischen und amerikanischen Texten über Gao und sein Werk findet sich meist die Übersetzung als *One Man's Bible* – vermutlich eine Anspielung auf die „Mao-Bibel".[45]

Die judäo-christliche Bibel dient Gao in seinem Buch jedenfalls immer wieder als Metapher für ideologische Macht und Autorität, und es ist vielleicht vor allem dieser Aspekt, der sein Werk auch eineinhalb Jahrzehnte nach seinem Erscheinen noch aktuell wirken lässt. So spürt Gao den Mechanismen der Machtkontrolle in China nach: *Yigeren de shengjing* liest sich an vielen Stellen – und Gaos Angaben in Interviews belegen, dass es ihm tatsächlich auch in hohem Maße um die Aufarbeitung von persönlichen Erlebnissen mittels der Literatur ging – wie ein biographisches Zeugnis.

Aus der Distanz und mit Nüchternheit kommt Gao zu dem Urteil, dass die Partei in China – der Vergleich mit der Kirche im Abendland drängt sich buchstäblich auf – quasi gottgleiche Kontrolle ausüben kann: Die Parteibeschlüsse sind unwiderruflich und – hier nun kommt der christliche Klassiker ins Spiel – „tausendmal genauer als alle Vorhersagen in der Bibel".[46] Gaos Wahl des Namens der Bibel im Titel seines Buches ist mehr als nur ein Wortspiel. Die Explikationen im Verlaufe des Romans zeigen zum einen, dass der Autor mit Kultur und Geschichte des Abendlandes vertraut ist, machen jedoch ebenfalls deutlich, wie sehr er um Distanz und Vagheit weiterhin bemüht bleibt. Diese vermutlich gewollte Disparität, der indirekte Hinweis darauf, dass sich vieles aus Ost und West nicht in Deckungsgleichheit bringen lässt, bildet als Botschaft die große Antithese zum Titel des Romans: der einzelne Mensch auf der ständigen, jedoch vergeblichen Suche nach Grundsätzen und Lösungsvorschlägen für sein Leben.

Es gibt vermutlich nicht viele chinesische Schriftsteller in der Gegenwart wie den weiter unten näher beschriebenen Bei Cun 北村, die sich ausdrücklich zu ihrer Glaubenszugehörigkeit bekennen, und eine absolute Seltenheit dürften zudem solche Autoren sein, die in essayistischer Form auf die Probleme der Religion im Umfeld der chinesischen Kultur eingehen. Ein solcher Autor ist – quasi als „muslimisches Gegenstück" zu dem christlichen Schriftsteller Bei Cun – der 1948 in einer muslimischen Familie in Peking geborene Schriftsteller Zhang Chengzhi

---

[44] Zur deutschen Ausgabe vgl. Gao Xingjian, *Das Buch eines einsamen Menschen*, aus dem Chinesischen von Natascha Vittinghoff (Frankfurt/M.: Fischer, 2006).

[45] Vgl. dazu Noël Dutrait, „'Without ism'. An Ism for One Man", *China Perspectives* 2010/2, S. 9.

[46] 比《圣经》中的预言要准确一万倍. Siehe *Yigeren de shengjing*, Kap. 18, S. 151.

张承志. Zhang hat vor allem in seinem frühen Werk seinen religiösen Wurzeln nachgespürt und löste damit in den 1990er Jahren eine große Debatte aus.[47] Er beeindruckt dabei vor allem durch seine Beharrlichkeit, und seine Bemerkungen in seinem auf das Jahr 1999 datierten Essay „Zai Zhongguo xinyang" 在中国信仰 (Der Glaube in China) sind nicht nur als Problem im Zusammenhang mit dem Islam zu verstehen. In China, so Zhang, bedarf es des Mutes, wenn man sich zu einem Glauben bekennt: „In China heißt Glauben nicht nur, der Macht mit Humanität zu begegnen, vielmehr heißt es, eine kritische Haltung gegenüber der Kultur zu bewahren."[48]

Zhang äußert sich insgesamt vorsichtig, beschreibt jedoch immer wieder auch mit großer Prägnanz die Probleme, etwa wenn er auf die Rolle und Position der Religion und der Religiosität sowie der Glaubensanhänger in der Gesellschaft eingeht: „Es dürfte sich vielmehr um eine Freude am Widerstand handeln, wie bei den Anhängern und Kämpfern einer häretischen Lehre. Widerstand meint dabei zweierlei: sowohl den Widerstand gegenüber einem grausamen System wie den Widerstand gegenüber dem Herdentrieb der Intellektuellen."[49] Doch bei Zhang Chengzhi findet sich mehr: in klaren Worten beschreibt er einerseits die Tendenzen unserer Zeit, die leer ist und der neuen Formen des Glaubens bedarf. Der Mensch in seinem Allmachtswahn ist sich selbst genug, doch das reicht nicht, und so erklärt Zhang:

> Alles, was es früher einmal gab, steht einer Verwandlung gegenüber. Es sind neue Formen und Zeremonien des Glaubens willkommen zu heißen. […] Aus einer tief verwurzelten Philosophie der Dinge (*baiwu zhexue* 拜物哲学) und einer Welle der Anbetung des Mammon ist nach und nach ein unterdrückerischer Ismus entstanden, der der Wissenschaft und Technik huldigt. Du wirst

---

[47] Zu näheren Angaben über Zhang Chengzhi und sein Werk vgl. den Eintrag in Marc Hermann – Weiping Huang – Henriette Pleiger – Thomas Zimmer, *Biographisches Handbuch chinesischer Schriftsteller. Leben und Werke*, Geschichte der chinesischen Literatur, Bd. 9, hrsg. von Wolfgang Kubin (München: Saur, 2011), S. 353ff.

[48] Vgl. Zhang Chengzhi, „Zai Zhongguo xinyang" in: *id.*, *Zai Zhongguo xinyang* (Changsha: Hunan wenyi, 1999), S. 142-150, hier zitiert nach S. 149. In dem Essay gibt Zhang in reflektierend-erzählerischer Form seinem Glauben Ausdruck. Er geht der Frage nach, warum er glaubt, was er glaubt und wie er glaubt. Diese Fragen sind ihm direkt auch von den Hui gestellt worden, mit denen er zu tun hat. Er gesteht sich ein, dass es schwierig ist, auf diese Fragen zu antworten. Dem Essay haftet etwas Tastendes, Versuchendes, sich um Klärung und Ausdruck Bemühendes an: „Der Grund, warum ich einer Antwort auswich, war, entspannt (*qingsong* 轻松) zu bleiben. Ich fürchte mich vor diesem schrecklichen China (*kongbu de Zhongguo* 恐怖的中国). Ich brauche gar nicht zu sagen, dass es mir an der Kompetenz mangelt, dazu etwas zu sagen. Selbst wenn ich diese Kompetenz besäße, würde ich immer noch mit lauter Stimme verkünden, nicht nur kein Priester zu sein, sondern auch kein Religionswissenschaftler und absolut kein Schriftsteller zu sein, der religiöse Literatur hervorbringt. Auch dies hier ist kein Traktat, das sich ganz und gar nur mit der Erörterung religiöser Vorstellungen beschäftigt. Alles muss die Bedingungen berücksichtigen, mit denen wir in der grausamen Realität Tag für Tag konfrontiert sind." Vgl. *ibid.*, S. 144.

[49] Vgl. *ibid.*

in all dem trainiert, und innerhalb dieses Vorgangs des Schmiedens entwickelst du nach und nach eine einfache, plane Form der Vernunft (*jianpu de lixing* 简朴的理性). [...] Du bist das Universum, die Zeit, das Nichts und das Sein; du bist das Ideal und die Hoffnung, du bist der einzige Geist, der alles umfasst.[50]

Doch wo ist der Raum für die Religion in China, zumal dann, wenn es sich um keine autochthone, sondern eine fremde Religion handelt? Zhang beschreibt intensiv den auch am eigenen Leib erlebten Konflikt zwischen den Kulturen und den Möglichkeiten, die sich bieten würden. Zwei Seiten stehen sich gegenüber, da ist zunächst China:

> China hat es beginnend mit dem Altertum geschafft, eine reife Zivilisation zu entwickeln, die es mit jeder Religion aufnehmen kann. Diese Zivilisation ist von großartiger Tiefe und Geistigkeit, sie ist vielfältig und schön, doch dabei neigt sie allzu sehr dem Profanen zu. Sie hat einen Hang dazu hervorgebracht, absolut dem Materiellen zu huldigen und durch und durch den Pragmatismus zu pflegen. Die Mühseligkeit der Erfahrungen, die ein von religiösem Glauben Erfüllter, und jede Philosophie, welche Anklänge zum Glauben zeigt, in einer derartigen Umgebung wie in China machen, ist unmöglich zu beschreiben. [...] in jedem Moment steht man dieser riesenhaften Kultur gegenüber, dazu gezwungen, mit ihr im Zustand der Diskriminierung in einen Dialog zu treten. Gerade die Hoffnungslosigkeit, die sich sprachlich nicht richtig ausdrücken lässt (*yuyan butong de juewang* 语言不通的绝望), ist schrecklich.[51]

Und dann auf der anderen Seite die Gefahren, die sich bei einer nicht friedlichen Begegnung ergeben können:

> In China sind die Umstände im Großen und Ganzen überall ähnlich – aus Diskriminierung wird Unterdrückung. Bei Anstiftung fließt Blut. Gefühle stärken den Zusammenhalt. Die metaphysische Welt zeigt sich ständig sehr konkret. Der Nutzen von hier teilt sich auf die so genannten zwei Welten. Die eigene Religion wird von der fremden Kultur zersetzt und von ihr assimiliert. Die Herzen der Menschen versinken im Schmerz, die irdische Welt funktioniert weiter so wie vordem.[52]

Man wird die Botschaft, die Zhang in seinem Essay verkündet, wohl in einem eher pessimistischen Sinne zu verstehen haben, er deutet Möglichkeiten für einen fruchtbaren Austausch zwar an, doch die gelebte Wirklichkeit scheint das zu widerlegen.

Das Pseudonym des 1965 in der südchinesischen Provinz Fujian geborenen Schriftstellers Bei Cun 北村 (wörtl. „Norddorf"), der mit eigentlichem Namen Kang Hong 康洪 heißt, ist vielleicht mit Bedacht und aus Gründen der Werbewirksamkeit gewählt worden. Die Ähnlichkeit des Namens zu Bei Dao (wörtl. „Nordinsel") ist nicht zu verkennen. Doch anders als Bei Dao 北岛, der in der Vergangenheit immer wieder einmal als chinesischer Kandidat für den Nobelpreis

---

[50] Vgl. Zhang Chengzhi, „Zai Zhongguo xinyang", S. 146f.
[51] Vgl. *ibid.*, S. 149.
[52] *Ibid.*, S. 148.

gehandelt wurde, muss sich Bei Cun wenigstens international erst noch einen Namen machen. Seine Chancen dazu stehen vielleicht nicht schlecht. Innerhalb Chinas wird vor allem der frühe Bei Cun mit Titeln wie *Dao* 岛 (Insel), *Boli* 玻璃 (Glas) oder *Zhang Sheng de hunyin* 张生的婚姻 (Die Heirat Zhang Shengs) der Avantgarde um Ma Yuan 马原, Su Tong 苏童, Yu Hua und Ge Fei 格非 zugerechnet, sein Stil erinnert an Isaac Singer.

Von Bei Cun, der mit seiner Bindung an das Christentum an eine vor 1949 in China nicht unübliche Tradition anknüpft,[53] heißt es bis in die Gegenwart, dass er auch als Pfarrer einer Gemeinde tätig ist. Bei Cun hat sich Mitte der 1990er Jahre zum Christentum bekannt und sorgte damit damals für einige Aufregung.[54] Die zeitgenössische chinesische Literaturkritik hat Bei Cun vorgeworfen, seine „christliche Schreibe" sei vor allem taktisch motiviert, er strebe nach einer „Sprache des Erlöstwerdens".[55] Fast alle seiner Protagonisten geraten in eine sehr schwierige Lage, aus der sie dann von der Ausweglosigkeit durch den Glauben an Gott inneren Frieden finden. Beispiele sind die Figuren von Liu Lang in „Shixi de he" 施洗的河 (Der getaufte Fluss, 1993), Zhang Sheng in der weiter unten noch näher zu untersuchenden Erzählung „Zhang Sheng de hunyin" 张生的婚姻 (Zhang Shengs Heirat, 1993) und „Sun Quan de gushi" 孙权的故事 (Die Geschichte von Sun Quan, 1994). Der Verfasser deutet mit dem Scheitern des Lebens seiner Protagonisten an, dass man sich ohne Gottes Hilfe beziehungsweise ohne den Glauben an Gott zumeist nicht selbst aus einer schwierigen Lage retten kann. Bei Cuns Geschichten sind nicht in einem missionarischen Sinne zu lesen, doch scheint er durchaus darum bemüht, dem Leser die Vorzüge der christlichen Weltanschauung nahezubringen. Ein Beispiel hierfür ist die oben angeführte Erzählung „Sun Quan de gushi", in der ein Dichter wegen Mordes im Gefängnis landet, dort das Christentum kennenlernt und schließlich ein gläubiger Christ wird.[56]

Bei Cun steht mit seinem Werk durchaus für einen Trend, bei dem Intellektuelle gelegentlich mittels der Religion und eines moralisch-spirituellen Geisteslebens den sich in China ausbreitenden Materialismus zu überwinden suchen.[57]

---

[53] Vgl. Yang Jianlong 杨剑龙, „Lun Bei Cun de chuangzuo yu jidujiao wenhua" 论北村的创作与基督教文化 (Das Werk von Bei Cun und die christliche Kultur), *Ningxia daxue xuebao (Renwen shehui kexueban)* 宁夏大学学报(人文社会科学版) 22 (2000), S. 32.

[54] Vgl. Bei Cun, „Wo yu wenxue de chongtu" 我与文学的冲突 (Mein Konflikt mit der Literatur), *Dangdai zuojia pinglun* 当代作家评论 1995/4, S. 65-67.

[55] Vgl. Qian Xuchu 钱旭初, „Bei Cun de shijie" 北村的世界 (Die Welt des Bei Cun), *Jiangsu shehui kexue* 江苏社会科学 1997/6, S. 112-116.

[56] *Huacheng* 花城 1994/1, S. 56-87 und 96.

[57] Hierzu und zu dem oben bereits im Zusammenhang mit Zhang Chengzhi erwähnten Bestreben einiger Schriftsteller, mittels ihrer Werke ihrer Konfession Ausdruck zu verleihen siehe Li Qiaomei 李俏梅, „Lun Zhongguo dangdai zuojia de ‚zongjiaore'" 论中国当代作家的"宗教热" (Religion als beliebtes Thema bei den zeitgenössischen Schriftstellern Chinas), *Guangdong shehui kexue* 广东社会科学 1996/4, S. 106-111.

Daher zieht er oft Zitate und Geschichten aus der Bibel in seinen Erzählungen heran, mit denen er die Themen der Erzählungen und die Bedeutung des Christentums zu erläutern versucht.

Nur wenige Erzählungen schließen mit einem glücklichen Ende für den Protagonisten. Das Werk „Sun Quan de gushi" ist eine solche Ausnahme. Aber auch in dieser Erzählung gelingt es dem Protagonisten nicht aus eigener Kraft, dem Leben in der kapitalistischen Gesellschaft einen neuen Sinn zu geben. Vielmehr findet er seinen Frieden erst wieder, als er den christlichen Glauben entdeckt. Das Werk stellt in Form einer Ich-Erzählung die Frage nach dem Sinn des Lebens und den Defätismus eines Künstlers dar, der erst durch das Entdecken des christlichen Glaubens überwunden wird. Dies erscheint vor allem vor dem Hintergrund interessant, dass der christliche Glaube in China zwar geduldet wird, aber nur solange er sich der Kontrolle der kommunistischen Partei unterwirft. Die Lösung gesellschaftlicher Defizite, die auf die Reformpolitik zurückzuführen sind, überlässt man aber nur ungern der Religion oder religiösen Bewegungen, wie das Beispiel des Verbots der Falun-Gong-Sekte im Jahr 1999 beweist.

Bemerkenswert bei Bei Cun und seinem Werk ist auf jeden Fall, dass er trotz der Kritik und den anhaltenden Schwierigkeiten im Zusammenhang mit „Religion" in China seinem Stil und vor allem dem Thema treu geblieben ist. Womöglich hat es mit der weiterhin schwierigen Lage der christlichen Kirche in China zu tun, dass Bei Cuns Auskünfte auf Nachfragen hin eher zurückhaltend bleiben.[58]

In seinen Geschichten beschreibt Bei Cun im Wesentlichen Menschen, die sich im Alltag bewähren und seinen Anforderungen auf die verschiedensten Arten

---

[58] Im Anhang zu dem Erzählband mit dem Titel *Gongmin Kai'en* 公民凯恩 (Citizen Kane; Wulumuqi: Xinjiang renmin, 2002) findet sich der Text eines kurzen Interviews, das Bei Cun im Januar 2002 gegeben hat (S. 315-318). Interessant wird der Band, weil er auf der Titelseite angekündigt wird mit dem Hinweis, es handele sich um „die erste chinesische Sammlung von religionistischen Erzählungen" (中国第一部宗教主义小说集). Auf bestimmte Themen angesprochen, weicht Bei Cun in dem Interview aus: Von den Interviewern auf deren Lesart hingewiesen („Nach der Lektüre beinahe aller Ihrer Novellen und Kurzgeschichten sind wir zu der Auffassung gelangt, dass Ihr Werk durchdrungen ist vom Geiste der umfassenden Liebe im christlichen Sinne [充满了基督教的博爱精神] und dass damit einer ‚religionistischen Schreibe' in China ein Weg geebnet worden ist", S. 315), reagiert Bei Cun eher zurückhaltend und gibt an, mit dem Begriff des Religionismus nichts anfangen zu können. Er hält dagegen, dass Literatur nicht für einen „Ismus" stehe. In kurzer Form wird Bei Cuns literarische Entwicklung beschrieben, wie sie sich aus Sicht der Interviewer ergibt: vom Avantgardisten die Rückkehr zum Realisten und der weitere Weg zum Religionisten. Bei Cun akzeptiert offenbar diese Einteilung, widerspricht ihr auf jeden Fall nicht und macht zu jedem Punkt kurze Erläuterungen. Zu dem „Religionismus" in seinem Werk heißt es dabei kurz und knapp: „Der Glaube an Gott verändert den Menschen, wodurch sich auch die Ergebnisse seines [künstlerischen] Schaffens ändern. Dieser Prozess läuft vollkommen individuell ab" (S. 316). Eine Frage zielt direkt auf Bei Cuns Auffassung in Bezug auf das Verhältnis von Literatur und Politik. Dazu Bei Cun: „Da der Mensch sich im politischen Umfeld befindet (人在政治中), lebt auch die Literatur in einer politischen Umgebung, doch sie ist nicht Politik (它不是政治)" (S. 317).

standhalten müssen. „Religion" und religiöser Glauben kommen – abgesehen von einer Ausnahme – nicht vor, allerdings zielen die beschriebenen Inhalte auf Dinge, die mit der Religion zu tun haben. Beispielsweise ist in der Erzählung „Luwei Chen Lin" 芦苇陈林 (Chen Lin, ein Mann wie das Schilf) von einem ängstlichen Großstadtmenschen die Rede, der „daran glaubt, dass das Schicksal gerecht zu den Menschen ist", dass jeder seinen Anteil an dem von Gott (Lao Tianye 老天爷) zugemessenen Glück erhält, nur dass das nicht immer sichtbar wird.[59] Chen erkrankt, beschäftigt sich mit dem Tod und bleibt optimistisch. Er geht von der Annahme einer unsterblichen Seele aus, die nicht so genannt wird, sondern ein unkonkretes „Etwas" (*dongxi* 东西) ist, das nach dem Tod gleich einem Vogel die Flügel ausbreitet und davonschwebt.

Den stärksten Bezug zum Thema Religion/Religionismus weist wohl die oben bereits kurz erwähnte Geschichte „Zhang Sheng de hunyin" auf:[60] Sie erzählt von dem etwas lebensfremden, dafür aber durchaus liebenswerten Philosophieprofessor Zhang Sheng und seinen Bemühungen um seine Braut Xiao Liu: Sie sind eines Tages bereits auf dem Weg zum Standesamt, als Xiao Liu plötzlich die Lust verliert und Zhang einen Korb gibt. Gesellschaftlich gesehen sind die beiden ein eigenartiges Paar (Xiao Liu arbeitet als Animierdame in einem großen Hotel) und scheinen nicht recht zusammen zu passen, doch haben beide eben auch ihre ganz individuelle Entwicklung durchgemacht und finden letzten Endes einen Zugang zueinander. Man schwört einander Liebe und will sich Halt geben. Vor allem Zhang fühlt sich dank der Entwicklungen wohl, gestärkt zudem durch seine Philosophie: Er verfügt über, wie er das nennt „das Glück des Denkens" (*sixiang de kuaile* 思想的快乐).[61] Allerdings verliert er den inneren Halt, als er von Xiao Liu auf einmal sitzen gelassen wird, er spürt eine Leere, eine innere Erschütterung. In der Erzählung erfolgt dabei ein Spiel mit Begriffen aus der chinesischen „Moderne" nach 1949, die Lehrer/Philosophen in ihrer überheblichen Vorstellung der totalen Machbarkeit als „Ingenieure der Seele der Menschheit" bezeichnet (人类灵魂的工程师). Zhang ist verwundert über den Wandel von Gefühlen und darüber, wie schnell Liebe in Hass (er fühlt sich von Xiao Liu gehasst) umschlagen kann. Befragt nach den Gründen für ihre „Entscheidung", zeigt sich Xiao Liu einsilbig. Sie gibt ihm – ohne Worte – auf seine Frage hin zu verstehen, dass sie nicht genug Vertrauen (*xin* 信) zu ihm aufbauen könne. Es folgt ein vager Hinweis von Zhang gegenüber einem Freund, sich „vom Schicksal" (Zhang zeigt hinauf zum Himmel über sich) missverstanden zu fühlen und den Geschicken des Himmels nichts entgegensetzen zu können. Der Vater von Xiao Liu hält ihr eine „Strafpredigt" angesichts des „Verrats" an Zhang: die Liebe sei etwas Heiliges (爱情是很神圣的东西). Die Rede bewirkt bei Xiao Liu das Gefühl einer wachsenden Abneigung gegenüber Zhang. Diesem offenbaren Scheitern im persönlichen Verhalten und in den profanen Dingen des Lebens, in dem nur we-

---

[59] Vgl. Bei Cun, *Gongmin Kai'en*, S. 16-29, das Zitat findet sich auf S. 16.
[60] Vgl. *ibid.*, S. 128-183.
[61] *Ibid.*, S. 146f.

nig Raum für Spiritualität zu sein scheint, wird als intellektueller Kontrast das akademische Wirken Zhangs entgegen gehalten, der im Vorlesungsbetrieb über Nietzsche („Gott ist tot") spricht und den „Übermenschen" erwähnt. Auf die Fragen von Studenten nach dem Status der Religion ihrer Heimat gibt Zhang die folgende Erklärung: „In China gibt es keine Vorstellung von Gott (中国是一个没有神观念的地方), es fällt uns daher schwer, den Schmerz, den Nietzsche innerlich verspürte, nachzuvollziehen."[62] Man kann weiter interpretieren: In einer vornehmlich weltlich orientierten Gesellschaft, wie man sie in China findet, fehlt die Grundlage für einen metaphysischen Schmerz angesichts des Gottesverlustes, wie er im Westen erlebt wurde. Und eine noch weit wichtigere Frage drängt sich auf: wie ist es in China angesichts des Mangels an metaphysischem Schmerz um die Fähigkeit bestellt, Mitleid für die Schmerzen der Mitmenschen zu empfinden?

Zhang Sheng gelingt es nicht, die theoretischen Überlegungen zu Gott und dem Schicksal mit seinem Leben in Übereinstimmung zu bringen. Nach und nach verliert er bei gelegentlichen Treffen mit Xiao Liu die Kontrolle über sich: er wird – anders als in der Vergangenheit – wütend auf sie, neigt zu Handgreiflichkeiten. Zhang nimmt einen Wandel an sich wahr, spürt, dass er nicht, wie er früher immer geglaubt hatte, ein milder und ausgeglichener Mensch ist. Er verspürt ein Gefühl von Verlorenheit und Hoffnungslosigkeit, in ihm entsteht Eifersucht auf die Männer in Xiao Lius Umgebung. Gedanken an den Tod befremden ihn, er unternimmt einen Selbstmordversuch, spielt mit dem Gedanken, Xiao Liu zu ermorden.

Die „Rettung" kommt am Ende durch die Bibel, die er bis dahin nicht eingehender gelesen hat und die ihm fremd und verschlossen geblieben ist. Zhang befindet sich an einem Wendepunkt in seinem Leben. Ging für ihn bisher von der Bibel eine Kraft aus, die ihn nervös machte und abzustoßen schien, geschieht nun etwas Eigenartiges: „Jetzt, in dem Moment, da Hoffnungslosigkeit und Ausweglosigkeit Zhang Sheng überkamen, schien eine Kraft seine Hand in Bewegung zu setzen, und er griff nach dem Buch."[63] Sätze aus der Bibel beginnen Zhang anzusprechen, in denen von der Kraft und der Lenkung durch Gott die Rede ist, ebenso von Gnade und Frieden. Zhang wird gefangen von der Bibel, er kniet nieder, faltet die Hände und bittet um Hilfe. Er nimmt ein Strahlen in sich wahr, ein Leuchten, liest Markus 14 (Mk 14:34; Mk 14:37; Mk 14:38). Weinend verrichtet er ein Gebet: „Die Tränen des Philosophen Zhang Sheng, sein Gebet und seine Zuwendung zu Gott, können in Zeiten wie diesen als Wunder betrachtet werden."[64] Die Geschichte lässt sich auch als Beispiel dafür verstehen, dass das Christentum vor allem für die „Intellektuellen" in China ein hohes Maß an Attraktivität besitzt.

---

[62] Bei Cun, *Gongmin Kai'en*, S. 162.
[63] Vgl. *ibid.*, S. 180.
[64] *Ibid.*, S. 183.

Eines der neueren Werke von Bei Cun, der Roman *Wo he shangdi you ge yue* 我和上帝有个约 (Ich habe eine Verabredung mit Gott),[65] erzählt die Geschichte eines schrecklichen Mordes in einer kleineren chinesischen Stadt. In einem der unerkannt bleibenden Täter kommt nach dem Verbrechen Reue auf, er sucht die Nähe der Angehörigen des umgebrachten Opfers, liebt und wird geliebt, bereut und leistet ein Geständnis. Deshalb wird er zunächst verachtet und gehasst, nimmt jedoch die Verantwortung für sein Verbrechen auf sich. Er akzeptiert die Todesstrafe und findet Trost in der Gewissheit, dass ihm auch die, die ihn einst für seine Tat hasste, am Schluss vergeben hat. Die Frau, die der Verbrecher Chen Busen 陈步森 zur Witwe machte, fühlt ganz am Schluss des Buches, dass der mittlerweile hingerichtete Mörder sich im Himmel aufhält. „Sie ging davon aus, dass er in diesem Augenblick bereits in den Himmel aufgestiegen war. Das war vollkommen außerhalb jeden Zweifels. Denn er hatte das gesagt. Er würde vom Himmel aus auf sie herabblicken. Sie glaubte jedes Wort von ihm. In dieser Form von Ruhe und Gelassenheit wurde jeder Grashalm, den man vom Boden auflas, schön."[66] „Himmel" als Metapher für eine bessere, jenseitige Welt drückt deutlich Bezüge zu dem ansonsten ungenannt bleibenden Christentum aus. Bei Cuns Roman ist deshalb interessant, weil er Gott zwar im Titel des Buches anführt, die Religion aber dann nicht expliziter behandelt, sondern als eine von den Protagonisten verinnerlichte Lebenseinstellung beschreibt. Man kann darin den Versuch sehen, das Christentum in die offizielle Vorstellung von der im Aufbau begriffenen „harmonischen Gesellschaft" einzupassen. Bemerkenswert ist das Buch auch deshalb, weil es – zumindest im Titel – die „Religion" ohne den sichtbaren und ausdrücklichen Glauben an Gott thematisiert. Gemeint ist das Gutsein ohne jeden erkennbaren religiösen Bezug. Die „gemeinte" Religiosität erscheint ohne jede erkennbare Form von Spiritualität und „Jenseits". Dem Leser teilt sich im Buch der Versuch mit, sich dem Thema „Religion" begrifflich-emotional zu nähern, nicht konstitutionell: Reue, Vergebung, Vergeltung, Sünde, Hölle, nichts wird konkreter „ausgeführt", erläutert, anschaulich und nachvollziehbar gemacht. Ohne „Religion" ausdrücklich zu thematisieren, wird die Notwendigkeit von „Religiosität" und „Liebe" angedeutet.

Aus der tödlichen Not geborener Glaube?
Ein Stück aus der Reportageliteratur

Das vielleicht eindringlichste von den hier angeführten Beispielen der chinesischen Literatur der vergangenen Jahre ist vermutlich Zhou Guozhongs 周国忠 im Jahre 2013 erschienenes Buch *Didi zuihou de rizi* 弟弟最后的日子 (Die letzten Tage meines Bruders).[67] Darin beschreibt Zhou die letzten Jahre seines jüngeren

---

[65] Bei Cun, *Wo he shangdi you ge yue* (Wuhan: Changjiang wenyi, 2006).
[66] Ibid., S. 291.
[67] Zhou Guozhong, *Didi zuihou de rizi* (Beijing: Zuojia chubanshe, 2013). Der 1956 geborene Zhou ist Schriftsteller und Mitarbeiter des Schriftstellerverbandes von Wuxi, von ihm liegen eine Reihe von Prosa- und Lyrikbänden vor. Der Verfasser des Vorworts, der bekann-

Bruders, bei dem im Alter von 38 Jahren eine Krebserkrankung im späten Stadium diagnostiziert wurde und der Ende 2005 im Alter von 41 Jahren starb. Interessant und eindrucksvoll ist das Buch vor allem deshalb, weil der erkrankte Bruder aus dem Christentum Kraft schöpfte und die wuchernde Krankheit damit lange Zeit in Schach halten konnte. Aufgezeigt werden ein Weg und eine Entwicklung, die im privaten Umfeld ihren Anfang nimmt: die Zuwendung zu Gott.[68]

Zhou Guozhongs jüngerer Bruder Zhou Jiazhong glaubte – folgt man den Ausführungen in dem Buch – aktiv, d.h. er glaubte nicht nur für sich, sondern teilte seinen Glauben mit und „missionierte" damit in gewissem Sinne. *Didi zuihou de rizi* ist in der Form von Werken der Reportageliteratur (*baogao wenxue* 报告文学) abgefasst, doch liest es sich wie eine umfassende Predigt. Wesentliche Teile des Buchinhalts bestehen aus den Manuskripten, die Zhou Jiazhong hinterlassen hat und in denen er in eloquenter und eindringlicher Form seine Erfahrungen mit dem Glauben mitteilt.[69] Dazu kommen zum Teil über viele Seiten hinweg laufende Protokolle in wörtlicher Rede, die ganz offensichtlich auf den Gesprächen der Brüder fußen. Ein großer Teil hat naturgemäß mit der schweren Krankheit Zhou Jiazhongs zu tun sowie mit dem Trost und der Kraft, die er aus dem christlichen Glauben gewinnt. Allgemeingültigkeit für die Bedeutung der Religiosität wird beansprucht durch den Hinweis auf Persönlichkeiten aus China und dem Ausland (darunter Sun Yat-sen und Zhang Xueliang, Newton und Napo-

---

te Schriftsteller/Philosoph Zhou Guoping 周国平, betitelt dieses mit „Xinyang de qiji" 信仰的奇迹 (Das Wunder des Glaubens) und meint damit, wie er auf S. 2 erklärt, dass der Glaube Wunder bewirken könne. Für die Popularität und die Attraktivität des Buches spricht, dass die erste Auflage nach dem Erscheinen im August 2013 innerhalb kürzester Zeit vergriffen war und binnen eines Monats eine zweite Auflage erschien.

[68] Die Brüder, so erfährt man, stammen aus einer christlich-protestantisch geprägten Familie. Der Glaube war bis dahin vorhanden, wurde aber nicht gelebt. Man betete ab und zu, las in der Bibel, hielt sich an die Gebote, versuchte, nichts zu tun, was dem Glauben widersprach: es werden Beispiele angeführt wie etwa, dass man bestimmte Speisevorschriften einhielt, nicht in Tempel ging, keine Götzen anbetete, den Ahnen keine Opfer darbrachte, bei Hochzeiten kein Feuerwerk abbrannte usw. Dennoch findet sich an einer Stelle die Feststellung, dass man nur an der Oberfläche des christlichen Glaubens blieb (S. 44). Aus den Aufzeichnungen des Bruders heißt es dazu: „Gott (*shen* 神) war so gut wie nicht in unseren Herzen" (S. 44). Erst mit dem Ausbruch seiner Krankheit wendet sich Zhou Jiazhong dann ganz bewusst Gott zu (S. 43).

[69] In den letzten drei Jahren seines Lebens verfasste der Todkranke wohl Dutzende von Redemanuskripten zu religiösen Themen, die auf eine fast missionarische Tätigkeit schließen lassen. In vielen Titeln geht es um die Frage von Autorität. Auf den S. 65-67 des Buches findet sich eine Liste mit 46 Manuskripttiteln und dem Datum der Abfassung, in Auswahl: „Respekt gegenüber der Macht Gottes" (2003); „Gott ist das Licht" (2003); „Was der Mensch gilt" (2003); „Was ist ein gläubiges Herz" (2004); „Der gesegnete Weg des Christen" (2004); „Die Ausweglosigkeit des Menschen ist der Rettungsweg Gottes; wo der Mensch an sein Ende kommt, ist der Beginn Gottes" (2004); „Der Herr ist mein Hirte" (2004); „Wie man Sorgen begegnet" (2005); „Wie man Gottes Weisungen erkennt" (2005); „Die Haltung des Christenmenschen gegenüber dem Geld" (2005); „Die einzige Sünde des Menschen" (2005).

leon), denen der Glaube angeblich Kraft verliehen habe.[70] Angelesenes steht neben den Berichten über selbst Erlebtes.[71] Im Umfeld der Familie entsteht ein Gemeindeleben, es gibt Zusammenkünfte, wobei auf die „Planlosigkeit", den „Zufall" und die „Absichtslosigkeit" der Zusammenkünfte aufmerksam gemacht wird, wohl um den Anschein zu vermeiden, man habe eine „Untergrundkirche" betrieben. Nutznießer, so heißt es weiter, sei nicht nur der kranke Bruder gewesen.[72] Es ist angesichts der bekannten Konkurrenz zwischen Staat und Familie und der weiterhin sehr großen Zuständigkeit staatlicher bzw. der Partei unterstehender Instanzen sowie die dadurch entstehenden Einflüsse auf Privat- und Familienleben beeindruckend, wie klar Präferenzen gesetzt werden, etwa wenn es heißt:

> Der Staat oder die Familie – was das Wichtigere von den beiden ist, das weiß jeder in seinem Herzen. Es ist gut möglich, dass andere Dinge für einen Moment oder auch langfristig alle möglichen Veränderungen bei uns hervorbringen, doch die Familie ist letzten Endes der wichtigste Hort (*guisu* 归宿).[73]

Es wird zwar keine ausdrückliche Gegnerschaft zum Staat beschworen – vielmehr geben die Brüder in kluger Weise ein indirektes Bekenntnis zur „harmonischen Gesellschaft" ab („Eine harmonische Familie ist an sich schon ein positives gesellschaftliches Element und eine gesunde Kraft; Treue gegenüber der Familie ist ein Ausdruck der Treue gegenüber dem Staat");[74] doch es wird ebenso klar, dass man nur *einem* Herrn dient – nämlich Gott: „Gott dienen" (*wei shen fuwu* 为神服务) heißt die Devise an einer Stelle, die frappierend an die maoistische Parole vom „Dienst für das Volke" (*wei renmin fuwu* 为人民服务) erinnert.[75] Den Worten Gottes – und, so liest man im Stillen mit, nicht der Partei – ist Respekt zu erweisen:

> Wie lange ein Mensch lebt und ob er am Leben bleibt, das ist zweitrangig. In den Jahren des Lebens den Weisungen Gottes folgen, das zu tun, was einem der Herr aufträgt, was bedeutet angesichts dessen der Tod? Daher muss jeder den Glauben festigen, immerfort den Worten Gottes antworten, sich auf dem Weg des Glaubens üben, um unseren seelischen Fortschritt zu fördern.[76]

Dabei wird schnell spürbar, dass es den Brüdern um mehr als „nur" die Familie geht, man will die Mitmenschen erreichen und „missioniert": Immer wieder gibt es allgemeine Appelle zur Rettung durch das Christentum und die Lektüre der

---

[70] Vgl. Zhou Guozhong, *Didi zuihou de rizi*, S. 91.

[71] Vgl. den Hinweis auf die innere Stärkung, die der Kranke regelmäßig durch die Lektüre von Bibeltexten verspürt, so etwa die Beschäftigung mit der Geschichte von Hiob (S. 46) und die daraus erwachsene Erkenntnis: „Die Ausweglosigkeit des Menschen ist der Weg Gottes (人的绝路，是神的出路)" (S. 47).

[72] Vgl. Zhou Guozhong, *Didi zuihou de rizi*, S. 48.

[73] Ibid., S. 77.

[74] Ibid.

[75] Ibid., S. 136.

[76] Ibid., S. 175.

Bibel. Aus dem Krankenhaus entlassen, spricht Zhou Jiazhong per Anruf oder SMS kranken Freunden Trost zu, leistet seelische Unterstützung, unterstützt kranke Freunde durch die christliche Liebe, damit sie einen seelischen Halt finden. Es gelingt ihm sogar die „Bekehrung" eines kranken Verwandten zum Christentum und Feier eines „Gottesdienstes" daheim für den Todkranken. Der kranke Zhou Jiazhong sieht in allem Fügungen und Werke des Herrn.[77] Zwangsläufig kommt an einer Stelle die Frage nach dem kulturellen und religiösen Boden Chinas auf, auf dem „Religionen" gedeihen oder auch nicht. Die Brüder ziehen sich hier auf das altbekannte Argument zurück, „[...] dass China keine einheimischen Religionen besitzt."[78]

Es folgen die üblichen Hinweise auf die bereits vor langer Zeit nach China gelangten Fremdreligionen wie den Buddhismus und das Judentum, ebenso werden Konfuzianismus und Taoismus als Philosophien und Gesellschaftslehren angesehen, denen der für die Religion unbedingt notwendige Kern des Metaphysischen fehle.[79] Geradezu zwangsläufig läuft das alles darauf hinaus, lediglich dem Christentum eine glaubhafte religiöse Substanz zuzuschreiben: Der Buddhismus wird als pessimistisch aufgefasst, das Christentum als optimistisch. Der Leib sei zwar vergänglich, doch die Seele existiere weiter. Während das Christentum das Sein (*you* 有) und das Glück (*le* 乐) betone, hebe der Buddhismus das Nichtsein (*wu* 无) und das Leid (*ku* 苦) hervor.[80]

Nach diesem Exkurs wird deutlich, worum es in dem Buch eigentlich geht: nämlich zu verdeutlichen, dass Stärke und wahrer Glauben von jedem Menschen selber erfahren und gefühlt werden müssen, und zwar in einem Zustand der Freiheit und Selbstbestimmung („Der Glaube ist vollkommen dem freien Verhalten des einzelnen Menschen überlassen; nur jeder selbst kann bewusst werden und verstehen").[81] Erst auf der Basis dieser wirklich erlebten und gespürten Kraft ist es – so wird deutlich – möglich, eine wenn nicht vollkommene, so doch zumindest stark von dem geläufigen Diskurs in der chinesischen Gesellschaft abweichende Haltung zum Ausdruck zu bringen. Als die Brüder über den Unterschied zwischen dem politischen und dem religiösen Glauben sprechen, nehmen sie eine feine Differenzierung vor: der politische Glaube wird als etwas angesehen, das

---

[77] Zhou Guozhong, *Didi zuihou de rizi*, S. 116f.

[78] *Ibid.*, S. 92.

[79] Vgl. zu diesen Ausführungen *ibid*.

[80] *Ibid.*, S. 99.

[81] *Ibid.*, S. 91. Zur Frage der unbedingt eindringlich erlebten Innerlichkeit und Spiritualität heißt es an einer anderen zentralen Stelle: „Auf dem spirituellen Weg (属灵的道路上) kann einen niemand ersetzen. Niemand kann für einen selbst Gott bejahen, niemand kann für einen Reue angesichts der Sünden empfinden [...] niemand kann für einen in den Austausch mit Gott treten [...] Das alles muss man selbst tun. Jeder muss für sich einzeln und direkt in den Kontakt mit Gott treten. Das ist eine vollkommen individuelle Angelegenheit und der einzige Ausweg. Erst mit dem Ausbruch der Krankheit begann ich wirklich an Jesus zu glauben und Jesus Christus als meinen lebenslangen Retter anzunehmen. [...] Jetzt glaube ich, dass Gott mein eigener Gott ist und dass ich ein Kind Gottes bin" (S. 44f.).

auf der gesellschaftlichen Ebene angesiedelt ist; der religiöse Glaube als etwas, das sich auf der geistigen Ebene abspielt. Es gibt, so die These, keinen Konflikt zwischen beiden: werden die staatlichen Gesetze und die Parteidisziplin eingehalten und werden auf der anderen Seite die religiösen Vorschriften und die Moral beachtet, dann gewinnt der Mensch an persönlicher Vollkommenheit: nicht streiten, nicht neidisch sein, anderen nichts schuldig bleiben, sich der Partei und der Gesellschaft nicht widersetzen etc.[82] Doch bei allen Kompromissen steht fest: „Der Mensch muss nicht nur über Wissen verfügen, noch mehr bedarf er des Glaubens."[83] Und wo gewusst und geglaubt wird, da sollte auch Kritik an Unvollkommenheiten möglich sein – etwa am wissenschaftlichen und technologischen Fortschritt in der Gegenwart, an der Abhängigkeit von der Technik und daran, wie wirtschaftliche Blüte zur Gier führen kann und was für ein verfehltes Leben das ist, wenn die Natur hemmungslos ausgebeutet wird, wenn man sich alleine an Maßstäben des Nutzens und des materiellen Reichtums orientiert und die Menschen sich fremd werden.[84] Die Klage erstreckt sich auf die „menschliche Halbheit", den „Machbarkeitswahn" und die fehlende Ehrfurcht gegenüber den Geheimnissen des Universums – der Mensch der Gegenwart in dieser Welt ist ungesund und entbehrt der menschlichen Vollkommenheit, da er der inneren Welt nicht genug Wert beimisst. Zur Schaffung einer erfüllteren Welt und Gesellschaft bedarf es den Brüdern Zhou zufolge der Dreiheit aus Philosophie, Religion und Wissenschaft, denn nur so sind seelische ebenso wie geistige und materielle Bedürfnisse zu befriedigen.[85]

Daraus kann, so darf man das wohl verstehen, für den einzelnen Menschen wie für die Gesellschaft eine neue und glaubwürdigere Form der „Vollkommenheit" und des Optimismus entstehen, die nicht nur verordnet, sondern gelebt und empfunden werden:

> Einmal abgesehen vom Glauben bin ich der Ansicht, dass in dieser Gesellschaft ein Mangel bei der Beschäftigung mit dem Tod besteht. Es wird immer groß vom Leben gesprochen, der Tod wird tabuisiert, manche weichen dem Gespräch darüber geradezu aus. Bei mir löst das ein großes Bedauern aus. Dabei bedeutet doch Klarheit über den Tod, dass der Mensch ruhiger wird, dass er den Dingen und dem Leben aufrichtiger gegenübersteht, dass er das Leben und die Existenz mehr schätzt, dass er aktiver, optimistischer und gesünder lebt.[86]

Über die Logik und die Herleitung der einzelnen Tatsachen mag man ggfs. anderer Auffassung sein,[87] doch lassen sich – so darf man das sicher als Fazit lesen –

---

[82] Zhou Guozhong, *Didi zuihou de rizi*, S. 91.
[83] *Ibid.*, S. 131.
[84] Vgl. *ibid.*, S. 49.
[85] Vgl. *ibid.*, S. 50.
[86] *Ibid.*, S. 179f.
[87] Z.B. wenn es sehr vereinfachend heißt: „Das dem Menschen zugehörige Wahre, Gute und Schöne stammt ursprünglich von Gott; durch die Sünde kam es zur Trennung von Gott;

seitens des Staates und seiner Vertreter kaum wirklich und glaubwürdig Einwände gegenüber der Vorstellung einer allumfassende Liebe erheben, wenn es heißt: „[...] der zentrale Punkt der Religion sind Liebe und Güte (*ai shan* 爱善), mit unserem Glauben Gott und die Menschen lieben [...] Die Verbindung von Liebe und Güte bringt Wahrheit und Schönheit hervor [...]."[88]

Fazit

Im religiösen Glauben werden Wahrheiten ausgedrückt, die meist nicht verhandelbar sind, da sie auf einen Schöpfer zurückgeführt werden. Bei dem Kampf um die spirituelle und weltanschauliche Wahrheit treffen der Marxismus und das Christentum aufeinander. Die Literatur als Erzählkunst kann hier eine Mittelposition einnehmen, indem sie die hinter der Religion und der Weltanschauung auftauchenden „großen Erzählungen" beschreibt und in einen Dialog miteinander treten lässt. Die in diesem Beitrag angeführten Belege aus der chinesischen Literatur der Gegenwart verdeutlichen den Spielraum, in dem sich Literatur *und* Religion auch heute noch zwischen den durch staatliche Kontrolle bestehenden Behinderungen und dem Bedürfnis nach einer ungehinderten Betätigung bewegen müssen.

Die Beispiele machen deutlich, dass „Religion" und insbesondere das Christentum oftmals als Folie für den chinesischen Diskurs von „Fortschritt" und „Erneuerung" dienen. Die dabei getroffene Themenwahl bleibt beschränkt und ist in hohem Maße den chinesischen Bedürfnissen angepasst. Die offiziell akzeptierte Erscheinung der Religion in China als weitgehend säkularisierte Praxis wird von zahlreichen Schriftstellern akzeptiert, indem sie Religion als „Kultur" in Szene setzen.[89] Vieles von dem, was „Religion" und „Christentum" ausmachen, viele Fragen, die die Gläubigen betreffen, werden ausgespart, ein „Problem" wie die Rolle des Papstes und seiner Bischöfe, findet nur eine historische Erörterung. Es erfolgt in der Regel keine thematische Zuspitzung, ideologische Machtfragen werden nur angedeutet. Interessant ist dabei die Artikulation des Bedürfnisses nach einer „anderen", „neuen" Wahrheit. Zwischen den Zeilen klingt eine Mahnung an die (immer noch) nicht eingelösten Versprechen an, an eine Umsetzung der Ideale des „Sozialismus chinesischer Prägung". Die Suche nach „neuen", „fremden" Wahrheiten klingt wie ein Abgesang auf die vergangenen Zeiten.

---

    erst so kam es, dass der Mensch machtlos wurde und der Macht und Gewalt durch die satanischen Sünden ausgesetzt war." Zhou Guozhong, *Didi zuihou de rizi*, S. 129.

[88] *Ibid.*

[89] Vgl. zur Säkularisierung und „Kultivierung" der Religion in China Glenn Shive, „Conclusion. The Future of Chinese Religious Life", in: Palmer – Shive – Wickeri, *Chinese Religious Life*, S. 241-253, insbesondere die Bemerkungen auf S. 247 und S. 250.

THE COMPETITIVENESS OF MODERN HAN-CHINESE

LEOPOLD LEEB

I have known Fr. Roman Malek since summer 1988, when I had decided to study Chinese in Taiwan, and he has always inspired me as a great researcher and admirable editor. In 1999 I saw him again, and he suggested to me to translate Latourette's A History of Christian Missions in China *into Chinese. This was a good suggestion although the translated version was published only as late as 2009 and in Hong Kong. I am also indebted to Fr. Malek for having drawn my interest to the Chinese translation of Thomas Aquinas'* Summa theologiae *from 1654 (by Luigi Buglio S.J.). The interest in this translation has propelled my interest in Latin translations into Chinese. Thus, Fr. Malek has somehow directed and inspired my studies and my work in China, and I am very grateful to him. Thus I want to dedicate this short essay on the "competitiveness" of the Chinese language to him. I hope that this idea may contribute to build more bridges between China and other nations.*

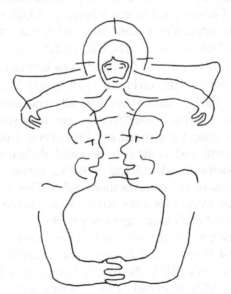

"Yan: Goutong" 言：沟通 (Word: Communication)
Words can bring people together, but they can separate, too. According to the New Testament, Jesus, the Word of God, made communication possible. "He is the peace between us, and has made the two (Jews and gentiles) into one entity and broken down the barrier which used to keep them apart by destroying in his own person the hostility ... and through the cross to reconcile them both to God in one Body" (Eph 2:14-16)
Drawing by Leopold Leeb in: Lei Libo 雷立柏, *Xifangren kan Hanzi de aomiao. Han-Ying duizhao* 西方人看汉字的奥妙—漢英對照. *How a Westerner Sees the Mysteries of Chinese Characters* (Beijing: Zhongguo shuji chubanshe, 2012), p. 13.

Han-Chinese – One of the World Languages

My history with China and the Han-Chinese language is longer than 25 years now, and I have never stopped thinking about the relationship between Han-Chinese and the European languages.[1] I also have often been thinking about the possibility of modern Han-Chinese becoming a major world language, that is to say, Han-Chinese could be spoken and read throughout the world by Chinese and non-Chinese, similar to English, Arabic, French, or German.

China's great achievement of the past 100 years is that through the indefatigable work of many translators Mandarin Chinese has become a language that is now able to convey exact information from all fields of knowledge, including biology, law, philosophy, or grammar. Innumerable modern new words have been adopted from the modern Japanese language about 100 years ago or were invented during the past decades in order to describe the modern world: *kexue* 科学 – science, *shehuizhuyi* 社会主义 – socialism, *guanxi congju* 关系从句 – relative clause, *yongdongji* 永动机 – perpetuum mobile, etc. The fact that today there are Chinese dictionaries and encyclopedias covering almost all fields of knowledge is remarkable and shows that Han-Chinese has become a modern language capable of describing the universe in a scientific way.

In other words, Chinese has become a language which is strictly normed and defined according to international standards, which was not the case before the publication of the *Mashi wentong* 马氏文通 in 1897, the first ground-breaking work on Chinese grammar. Today the distinctions between, e.g., *guojifa* 国际法 (international law), *xingfa* 刑法 (criminal law), *xianfa* 宪法 (constitutional law) and *ziranfa* 自然法 (law of nature) are basically understood by urban Chinese people, but at the final period of the Qing Dynasty most scholars of China would have been unable to grasp the differences.[2] From being a poetic, vague language lacking academic terms and commonly accepted definitions, Han-Chinese has become a clearly defined and efficient tool that serves to translate technical knowledge and philosophical considerations alike. This is the result of a long process of translation work, ever since Ricci, Aleni, Buglio, Varo, and Morrison compiled their bilingual dictionaries and other works.

After many changes in the terminology of translated western concepts throughout the past 400 years most academic and scientific terms are settled and will probably not change much in the future. For example the Italian missionary Luigi Buglio (1606–1682) translated "ethics" with *kejixue* 克己学 and "philoso-

---

[1] In a short article I have reflected on my process of learning the Han-Chinese language, see "Wo xuexi Hanyu zhi lu" 我学习汉语之路, *Guoji Hanyu jiaoxue dongtai yu yanjiu* 国际汉语教学动态与研究 2008/4, pp. 90-93.

[2] For the differences in the understanding of basic philosophical ideas see the revealing article of Deng Xiaomang 邓晓芒, "Zhongguo bainian xifang zhexue yanjiu zhong de shi da wenhua cuowei" 中国百年西方哲学研究中的十大文化错位 ("Ten Big Cultural Misunderstandings in the Chinese Study of Western Philosophy during the Last Hundred Years"), *Shijie zhexue* 世界哲学 2002, (special edition), pp. 7-17.

phy" with *xingxue* 性学, but today the commonly used words are *lunlixue* 伦理学 and *zhexue* 哲学,[3] and these words will probably not undergo major changes any more. If it is true that modern Han-Chinese is a scientific language capable of clear description, we may ask: What prevents Han-Chinese from becoming one of the leading and academically influential languages in the world? To me the main problem seems to be the writing system of Han-Chinese, namely the Chinese characters.

The Obstacle: A Cumbersome Writing System?

A Japanese expert on Plato has complained that the academic achievements of Japanese scholars in the field of classical studies are practically ignored by European colleagues: "Whereas all Japanese scholars (without exception) read and study works written in European languages (usually English, German, French, and sometimes, Italian), not a single western scholar has so far read – or even tries to read – the products of Japanese scholarship on Plato and other Greek philosophers in our own language."[4] The main reason for the isolation of Japanese scholarship might be their script which uses three different writing systems (*hiragana*, *katagana*, Chinese characters) at the same time. A script that is so complicated scares away many would-be students. Probably there exists a similar problem of isolation and inbreeding for Chinese scholarship today, and for the very same reason: a cumbersome writing system prevents efficient communication.

If modern Han-Chinese is to be learned by many people in the whole world, it should be a language that is "user-friendly," that is to say, if somebody wants to find a word in a dictionary or encyclopedia he should be able to do so in an easy way. Only in this way a student of the language can gradually extend his vocabulary and read more texts. And here is the main problem: the Han-Chinese characters are cumbersome and difficult to remember, even for the Chinese people themselves. Wu Yuzhang 吴玉章 (1878–1966) often pointed out that "the Chinese characters have many shortcomings ... and for practical use the Chinese characters entail many inconveniences."[5] Here are some examples:

The character 工 is pronounced *gong*, but it can produce the combinations 攻 *gong* ("attack"), 空 *kong* ("empty"), 红 *hong* ("red"), 扛 *kang* ("to shoulder"), 杠 *gang* ("lever"), 江 *jiang* ("river"), 腔 *qiang* ("cavity"), 式 *shi* ("mode"), 筑

---

[3] Compare my study of Buglio's translation "Qing chu Hanyu shenxue shuyu cidian" 清初汉语神学术语辞典 ("A Dictionary of Early Qing Chinese Theological Terms"), in: Lei Libo 雷立柏 (Leopold Leeb), *Hanyu shenxue shuyu cidian* 汉语神学术语辞典 (Beijing: Zongjiao wenhua chubanshe, 2007), pp. 215-418.

[4] See Noboru Notomi, Kyushu University, "Plato in Japan: Past, Present and Future," *Journal of the International Plato Society* 1 (2001), http://www3.nd.edu/~plato/notomi.htm (access: 12 May 2016).

[5] See Wu Yuzhang 吴玉章, *Wenzi gaige wenji* 文字改革文集 (Beijing: Zhongguo renmin daxue chubanshe, 1978), p. 91.

zhu ("construct"). These examples show the strength of the Chinese writing system, because even if you are not yet acquainted with these words you can guess from the radical signs that 扛 (*kang*) has something to do with hands and might thus be an action or a kind of work; 江 (*jiang*) has to do with water, and 杠 (*gang*) has to do with wood, it might be something like a rod or a branch. On the other hand, these words also show the weakness of the characters, because the pronunciation of the symbol 工 changes, it may be *gong*, *kong*, *hong*, or *gang*, etc. Some may say that this is exactly the beauty of Han-Chinese, but in the first place it is a big burden on all who want to learn Chinese. In fact everyone who learns Mandarin has to learn two languages: spoken Chinese and written Chinese, because the written signs do not converge with the pronunciation: you write *gong*, but you say *gang*, *jiang*, *kong*, *qiang* etc.

I believe very few foreigners and even native Han-Chinese speakers will be able to render the correct spelling of all the characters listed below although these are words that can be found in any pocket dictionary in China:

combinations with 斤 *jin*: 近 *jin*, 折 *zhe*, 析 *xi*, 逝 *shi*, 忻 *xin*, 沂 *yi*, 听 *ting*, 芹 *qin*, 颀 *qi*, 所 *suo*, 断 *duan*, 拆 *chai*, 诉 *su*, 栃 *tuo*;

combinations with 西 *xi*: 牺 *xi*, 栖 *xi/qi*, 茜 *qian/xian*, 洒 *sa*, 晒 *shai*, 贾 *jia*, 要 *yao*, 票 *piao*, 覃 *qin/tan*, 粟 *su*, 覆 *fu*;

combinations with 台 *tai*: 胎 *tai*, 怠 *dai*, 治 *zhi*, 冶 *ye*, 始 *shi*, 笞 *chi*, 迨 *dai*, 绐 *dai*, 怡 *yi*, 骀 *dai*, 饴 *yi*.

If a student of Han-Chinese is confronted with the task to memorize these and many similar rows of words, this student will inevitably ask the following question: "Why is it that the graph *jin* 斤 is pronounced so differently when it has a different radical? Why is there no reliable and simple guide as to the pronunciation of a Han-character?" And if the character does not tell you the exact pronunciation, it will be difficult to look it up in the dictionary.

During the last 25 years I tried many times to encourage foreign friends to learn Chinese, but my experience was always the same: as soon as I started to explain the way of looking up an unknown character in a dictionary, the would-be student turned away: "This is too difficult." And it was no use that I repeated my explanations: "You just need to (1) analyse which part is the radical, then (2) go to the list of radicals in the beginning of the dictionary and find the radical there, then (3) go to the list of characters connected with that radical (also in the front part of the dictionary), then (4) count the number of strokes of that character, then (5) look for the character among the other characters with the same amount of strokes, find it, ascertain the page number, and then (6) you will find the character in the dictionary." I have not succeeded to persuade even one person to learn Chinese yet. To my disappointment my own sister turned to Japanese and never started to learn Chinese. And I must say that I myself have been disappointed too often by the Chinese characters, I do no longer feel the same enthusiasm for the characters that I had 25 years ago. How often did it take me 5 minutes or more to find a character in the dictionary? How often was I unable to find difficult words in the dictionary? It is also hard for the native speakers to work with the Chinese characters. Whenever I come across a more difficult character in the underground or in a shop, I ask the Chinese around me, and often they are unable to analyze the radical part of the character or know its exact pronunciation.

Knowing the Pronunciation Does Not Imply Understanding the Meaning

In private conversations with Arnold Sprenger (1929–2015), who taught English and German in China and Taiwan for 45 years, he sometimes mentioned the differences in language learning for students in Europe and in China. He said that the ability to spell a word and read out a text correctly would be something very simple and basic in a European country, and soon the teacher would start a conversation with the students about the contents of the text, about whether the ideas and expressions conveyed in the text would make sense or should find disapproval. The main aim of education would thus be a critical understanding and analysis of the meaning of a text. In China on the other hand many years would be spent on teaching the students the correct pronunciation and writing of the characters and the memorization of apt phrases and idioms. The critical analysis of the meaning would only come much later, if at all. This was the observation of somebody who had long years of teaching experience. Perhaps Chinese characters do not necessarily preclude creative thought, but possibly too much mental energy is wasted by memorizing the difficult writing system.

In 2008, when the Olympic Games in Beijing were held, there were huge posters alongside the road. One of them read: *bu yao xun xin zi shi* 不要寻衅滋事, which means "Do not provoke anyone or create problems!" using a phrase which is not very common but can be understood by someone who has a good command of Chinese. Sitting in a bus and seeing these words written on a big advertisement board, I asked the young man beside me what these characters meant. (The bus was caught in a traffic jam and stopped just beside the huge inscription.) The young man said he was unable to read the phrase and did not know what it meant. Then I asked another man sitting in front of us. He said he was not sure about the second character in the phrase but he said he had a vague grasp of the meaning. Both of them were between 20 and 25 years old and were dressed like office workers or students, not like farmers or laborers. At class I told this story to my students and added jokingly that nobody in China would be able to write the traditional form of the character *xin* (provocation) without looking it up in the dictionary first. It is a difficult character indeed, a real provocation. It is difficult to convince a foreigner to learn the Han-Chinese characters well if they are so difficult that not even the natives have a good command of them.

Coming from Europe, part of my cultural heritage is the maxim "The letter kills, but the spirit gives life."[6] One possible understanding of this proverb is that the writing style is not important at all, letters are only a vehicle of meaning. The ideas conveyed by a text are central and actually life-giving, inspiring and exciting. Another understanding would be that a culture confined to a set of canonical books is doomed to death if it does not enter a dialogue with other cultures, if it does not receive new ideas and challenges from other languages. Applied to the Han-Chinese language I would say that spoken Chinese is more important than written Chinese, or in other words: the Chinese language that is alive in the minds of the people and inspires their actions is more important than the written texts, and it does not matter at all whether these texts are written in simplified Chinese characters or in traditional Chinese characters. The characters are not as important as the creative understanding of the reader.

After studying the Bopomofo phonetic writing system used in Taiwan, after learning Mandarin Chinese, and the Minnan language used in Taiwan, after struggling with Japanese and with the Korean, Vietnamese, and Mongolian scripts, I discovered that there are many different ways of writing or transliterating Han-Chinese characters. To me all these ways of writing are in a sense equally good or bad. I like the beauty of the traditional characters which I learned in Taiwan, but they are not fast enough for making notes at class. When I started to learn the simplified Chinese characters I was quite enthusiastic about them, but one day an Austrian friend who had lived in Japan remarked that the Japanese simplified characters are more beautiful. He used the example of the word *guang* (traditional form: 廣, Japanese simplified form: 広, Chinese simplified form: 广) and said the Chinese simplification looks like standing on one leg. I have to admit that he is right: the Japanese characters are more balanced. On the other hand, it could also be said of some letters of the western alphabet that they are "standing on one leg", for example the "P" or the "F", they are also "imbalanced." No writing system is perfect, and every system can be improved. However, here is a big difference: few people have been thinking about "improving" the Latin ABC, it would be hard to improve it; but many people have been thinking about changing and improving the Chinese characters, not only during the last 100 years.

The Japanese, Koreans and Vietnamese have been using Chinese characters for centuries, but they all developed their own writing systems (in Vietnam obviously under European influence). Why did these writing systems evolve? Because the users of the Chinese characters in those countries wanted to "improve" the writing system. Therefore they invented scripts that are much easier to learn and

---

[6] Second Letter to the Corinthians, chapter 3, verse 6. The Greek original uses the prefix "apo-", thus it is an emphatic expression, which may be translated as "kills totally." For the Latin and Chinese translations cf. Lei Libo 雷立柏 (Leopold Leeb), *Gu Xila Luoma ji jiaofu shiqi mingzhu mingyan cidian* 古希腊罗马及教父时期名著名言辞典 (*A Dictionary of Famous Works and Words of the Classical and Patristic Periods. Dictionarium librorum et sentiarium auctorum veterum et partum ecclesiae*), Greek – Latin – English – Chinese (Beijing: Zongjiao wenhua chubanshe, 2007), p. 258.

to use than the Chinese characters. However, the "chopstick countries" are somewhat united by a basic knowledge of the ancient Chinese characters, and this tradition will be kept alive by calligraphy, just like in Europe there will always be people who like to study Byzantine manuscripts, calligraphic inscriptions on Russian icons, classical Hebrew texts, Babylonian inscriptions or Egyptian hieroglyphs.

Punctuation Marks and Intelligibility

Once a Chinese friend who helped me with translation work remarked that any "ABC-expression" in a Chinese text would destroy the beauty and harmony of the text, thus foreign words should be limited as much as possible. I know that most Chinese know little about or look down on Western calligraphy, but I was still very surprised to hear this statement from him. However, it is a fact that most publication houses in China still try to keep the ABC out as much as they can. On the other hand they accept "western" punctuation marks, the semicolon, hyphenation, quotation marks, question marks, etc. without feeling that these symbols "destroy the beauty of the text." In the European tradition these marks were added in late antiquity and in the Middle Ages. Old Greek or Hebrew manuscripts are like ancient Chinese books: no blanks between words, no clear divisions between word groups and sentences. There is no doubt that punctuation marks help a lot to enhance the intelligibility of a text. In Europe the efforts to produce new editions of ancient texts in the Middle Ages went along with the invention of abbreviation systems and new letter types, namely the minuscule which was used together with the traditional capital letters. The new letters were doubtless an improvement.

Letters and writing systems are not unchangeable or eternal; they can be adapted to special needs, improved and be made more user-friendly. The change to the simplified Han-Chinese characters during the 1950s and 1960s also shows that the characters are neither eternal nor unchangeable. If hyphenations, brackets, question marks or a blank space can enhance the intelligibility of a text, then they should be used. I would even advocate the use of blanks in Chinese texts which might force the writers and readers to think in clearer terms. Since 2008 most public busses in Beijing have bilingual charts of the route of the bus. The ABC spelling of place names was put beside the Chinese characters, although often in a confusing way. Long words without separating spaces were created like "Chaoyanggongyuanqiaodong." The use of spaces would help to clarify ideas, it would force people to reflect better on the words they use every day.[7]

---

[7] In fact the problem of spaces in a Chinese text has already been solved by Wu Yuzhang, see his *Guanyu dangqian wenzi gaige gongzuo he Hanyu pinyin fang'an de baogao* 关于当前文字改革工作和汉语拼音方案的报告 (Beijing: Wenzi gaige chubanshe, 1958).

A New Way of Writing

In the eyes of many, the traditional Han-Chinese characters are too unsystematic and too irregular to be learned. If the writing system of the Han-Chinese language is so difficult, cumbersome and discouraging, it should be simplified in order to make it more accessible, attractive, and user-friendly. Only in this way more Chinese and non-Chinese will be able to get a good grasp of the Chinese language and literature. Based on this conviction the traditional Han-Chinese characters have been simplified in the 1950s and 1960s, and in 1958 Wu Yuzhang, the president of Renmin University and president of the Committee for the Reform of the Chinese Characters, suggested the Romanization of the Chinese characters. In his report of 1958 he consequently used a writing system that had the ABC on top and the Chinese characters below. Wu believed that international communication is a very important value, thus he stated: "We can even say that the languages and writing systems of all the nations in the world will in the future gradually converge and be unified."[8]

From many discussions I know that most Han-Chinese people would object to giving up the Chinese characters totally and just substituting them with the ABC. I support this view, because I myself appreciate the beauty of Chinese characters and their relative usefulness: the radical sign can give you a clue to the meaning of the word, thus you can guess that a character with the radical "hand" could mean something like "to push", even if you have never seen this character before. However, I think it is not necessary to keep the confusing "phonetic part" (*shengpang* 声旁) of the characters (see the examples above). Why should we not keep what is good (the radicals) and try to correct the troublesome *shengpang*? One way of doing this would be to substitute the *shengpang* with ABC symbols and thus create a very efficient and easy-to-learn writing system. I have heard that many Chinese intellectuals today would like to revive the traditional Han-Chinese characters, and one reason they give is that many simplified characters have changed the original radical of the character, for example the character *ting* (to hear) used to have an "ear" 耳 (聽), and now it has a "mouth" 口 (听), and the character for the word "grain" should be written with the radical 禾 (full form: 穀), and not 谷. I would prefer to keep the original radical, thus preserving some elements of the traditional meaning. Here are some examples:

The word *dong*, "east" was originally written as a combination of a tree 木 and the sun 日, thus: 東. Most people in China do not think of a "sun rising above a tree" when they see the character for *dong*, but it might be good to remember that the radical of the word originally is the "tree," and thus the word could be written like this: 木 *dong*. This means we give up the "sun" (日) contained in the traditional form of the character, which has already been done by the simplified Han-Chinese characters; thus it makes no big difference if we write 东 or 木 *dong*. The only difference would be that the expression 木 *dong* shows

---

[8] Wu Yuzhang, *Guanyu dangqian wenzi gaige gongzuo*, p. 21.

the radical and the pronunciation and thus provides a convenient way to look the word up in the dictionary. This way of writing Chinese characters would make the language more competitive in the international arena of languages.

I want to add that this way of writing Chinese characters is not changing them, it is not the "invention of a new writing system," but it is only a way of expressing what has always been there: the original radical (which has sometimes been changed or omitted in the simplified characters) and the pronunciation. Similar examples would be like this:

Traditional form	Simplified form (since the 1950s)	Radical plus ABC (with indication of the tones)
勞	劳	力 *láo*
聽	听	耳 *tīng*
東	东	木 *dōng*
禮	礼	示 *lǐ*
體	体	骨 *tǐ*
開	开	門 *kāi*
關	关	門 *guān*
讓	让	言 *ràng*
誼	谊	言 *yì*
議	议	言 *yì~*
譯	译	言 *yì#* [9]

Learning Chinese in this way should of course only be a first step to enter more deeply into the Chinese world of thought. Those who study Chinese literature or history should also know the traditional Chinese characters, and one day they may come to know that *láo* is composed of the characters for "fire," a "roof" and "force," but for daily use it is probably enough to remember the radical "force" and the pronunciation *láo*. Thus the ABC writing system will greatly enhance the competitiveness of the Chinese language. Historically speaking, the use of the simplified Chinese characters since the 1950s was a big progress in terms of the popularization of the Chinese characters, but another step has to be made, because even the "simplified" Han-characters are still too difficult for the wider international readership to learn. Only if there is an even more user-friendly way of expressing Chinese thought, Chinese literature will have a better standing in the international academic world. Then one day many people in Europe or India or the Americas might read Confucius' or Lu Xun's works not in an English or Spanish translation but in the "original": 月 *yǒu* 月 *péng* 自 *zì* 辶 *yuǎn* 方 *fāng* 人 *lái*, 一 *bù* 亠 *yì* 木 *lè* 丿 *hu*?[10] Would this not be a step ahead in the communication between the peoples in the world?

---

[9] The symbols ~ and # could be added to distinguish between characters which have the same radical and the same pronunciation, such as the last three in this list.

[10] In simplified characters this quotation reads: 有朋自远方来，不亦乐乎?

Losing Contact to Tradition or Keeping Proper Distance?

Many Chinese might object that changing the Han-Chinese characters would necessarily imply a loss of tradition, because less people would be able to read Confucius' texts in the original. This argument is doubtless true, but I prefer to look at it from a comparative view. If you ask any European whether he or she is able to read the canonical texts of his/her own culture in the respective original language, it might be difficult to find anybody. I think not even one out of 1,000 Europeans would be able to read and understand the Hebrew text of Isaiah's prophecies, Plato's dialogues in Greek and Augustine's *Confessions* in Latin. And yet, these canonical texts are the basis of European culture and literature. If on the other hand one would do a similar research in China and ask literate Chinese whether they would be able to read Confucius' and Laozi's texts in the original, one would find out that quite many people are not only able to read the texts but have actually memorized a good number of proverbs from these works – in the original language. In this sense the Chinese are much closer to their ancient texts than the Europeans to theirs, although the distance to these texts has been constantly increasing since the abolition of the old education system and the establishment of a modern ministry of education in 1905.

The ancient texts and writing systems will not be lost, and in the future there will probably not appear a second Qin Shihuang who destroys old traditions in order to achieve an absolute unification of the writing system. Therefore the old classics are always available and ready to be revived in a renaissance movement of any kind, it is just a question of whether it is worthwhile to stay close to a certain classical tradition and demand that many (or all) children memorize certain texts in a certain language. On the way to modernity the reflection on the good or bad influence of classical literature will naturally produce a certain distance to the old texts. In the European tradition, the discernment process concerning the question which scriptures should be read and taught may be found in an exemplary form in St. Augustine's critique of the old mythology and the education he received.[11] In China certain popular sayings dissuade from reading certain literary works considered to be "classical works," for example the proverb "Shao bu kan *Shuihu*, lao bu kan *Sanguo*" 少不看水浒，老不看三国 ("When young, don't read the *Rebels of the Liangshan Moor*, and when old don't read the *Three Kingdoms*"). Augustine and the Chinese proverb express the same concern: certain texts may undermine moral standards. These worries are justified, and the "proper distance" to certain traditions should be discussed.

One Easy Step towards Higher Competitiveness

As everyone knows Chinese newspapers transliterate the names of all foreigners into Chinese and very seldom keep or add the original ABC. This makes it quite

---

[11] Cf. Augustinus, *Confessiones* (Chin. title: *Chanhui lu* 忏悔录), chapter 1, 6-8, Latin-German edition (München: Kösel, 1960), pp. 46ff.

difficult for foreigners to understand what they read. In June 2009 I finished the course "Theory and Practice of Translation" at Renmin University of China, and one of the questions on the exam paper was: "Do you think that Chinese newspapers should more often use the ABC to express foreign personal names and place names, or do you oppose this suggestion? Please offer at least three arguments to support your viewpoint!" Out of 21 students 2 opposed the ABC, 19 supported the ABC in Chinese newspapers. The arguments of the latter were the following (I have subsumed similar answers under one category):

> The ABC writing of personal and place names often contains information about the respective culture, and if one can analyze the word roots one can get a glimpse of the cultural background. (17 students)
>
> The Chinese transliterations of western names are chaotic and lack unification. (13)
>
> The ABC can arouse the interest of the reader and whet their intellectual appetite. (9)
>
> It is easier to verify or check ABC names. If there is only the Chinese transliteration, one cannot find them on the internet. (8)
>
> The ABC can speed up internationalization. Pure Chinese transliteration may be an obstacle to cultural exchange. (7)
>
> The Han-Chinese translations may produce wrong associations. The ABC names are closer to the original image of foreign cultures. (5)
>
> Chinese transliterations are often too long and without meaning, the ABC is easier to use. (3)
>
> The use of the ABC will make it easier for foreigners in China to read Chinese books. (3)
>
> Chinese are not afraid of the ABC, since their grasp of foreign languages is quite good. (1)
>
> The use of the ABC will help to foster international acceptance. (1)
>
> Respect for the original language. (1)
>
> Ensure the copyrights. (1)

The arguments of those who objected were: "The Chinese do not have a good command of foreign languages and might not be able to read the ABC." "The wider society will not accept the ABC in a Chinese newspaper." "It will create problems for the layout of the newspaper, because more space is needed." "It is necessary to take into account the national feelings of the Chinese." However, one of them also conceded that "the ABC is no cultural aggression, it is rather an internationalization of the language."

Even if the great majority of the students support the "pro-ABC" view, the propaganda ministry and thus all newspaper editorials still support the "anti-ABC" stance. Scientific journals and translations systematically disregard the original names of foreign persons, places, book titles etc. I have voiced my opinion concerning the Chinese version of the *Encyclopedia Britannica* some years ago, because the translation of this wonderful reference book was done without retaining ABC names and book titles.¹² As I mentioned this fact to Guy Alitto (Ai Kai 艾恺) from Chicago, he said dryly: "If there is no ABC, then the translation has not much academic value." Old habits die hard, and old customs are "like a tyrant" ("Usus tyrannus," as the Latin proverb has it). Thus the consequent resistance against a simpler writing system and the objections against the Latin ABC inserted in Chinese texts will probably continue for some time in the future.¹³ However, there is no doubt that in the future ever more Chinese will be educated in a bilingual or multilingual way and thus be able to appreciate the advantages of a simpler writing style. They might use the ABC in a free and creative way and thus enhance the competitiveness of modern Han-Chinese.

Transcending History, Opening up New Horizons

Looking back on the centuries that have passed since Matteo Ricci (1552–1610) tried to introduce the Latin script to China, it can be seen that Chinese scholars and publishers were very slow to accept any new writing system. First, Ricci's way of using the Latin ABC to write the pronunciation of Chinese characters was practically ignored by Chinese intellectuals until around 1900, when more Chinese students needed to communicate with foreigners or went abroad to study. Early in the 1620s the Jesuits Zhong Mingren 鍾鳴仁 (1562–1621) and the trained musician Lazzaro Cattaneo (1560–1640) developed a system to mark the five tones, but only in the 20th century Chinese dictionaries started to use these basic tools. Even until today (2016) it is quite difficult to write the symbols for the tones on the computer and Latinized road signs in Beijing do not use them either. Neither did the Chinese switch to a horizontal writing habit before the 1950s. In a private talk with a western author who publishes in Taiwan in 1999 I came to know that as late as 1995 it was still very difficult to persuade the (Taiwanese) editors of a dictionary that contains many ABC-written western names and terms to give up the vertical way of writing and write horizontally. Likewise, one of my translations (on Chinese history) was re-edited and published in Hong Kong in 2009, but almost all the Arabic numbers were changed into the Chinese numeric symbols. This reveals the same conservative attitude that would immediately return to the traditional vertical writing style if this was possible.

In the last years of the 19th century several Chinese (like Wang Bingyao 王炳耀, Cai Xiyong 蔡锡勇 and others) imitated the method of Christian missionaries who had produced ABC texts in the local dialects (like Bibles in the Suzhou colloquial, Shanghai colloquial languages etc.).¹⁴ Between 1892 and 1910 Chinese

---

[12] See "Zhizao zhang'ai de Hanyi" 制造障碍的汉译, *Bolan qunshu* 博览群书 (*Chinese Book Review Monthly*) 2005/7, pp. 31-33.

[13] These objections were raised after the publication of Trigault's *Xiru ermu zi* 西儒耳目资 in the 1620s, see Fang Hao, "Ladingwen chuanru Zhongguo kao" 拉丁文傳入中國考 (A Study on the Introduction of Latin to China), in: *Fang Hao liushi zidinggao* 方豪六十自定稿 (Taibei: Taiwan xuesheng shuju, 1969), p. 3.

[14] See Wu Yuzhang, *Wenzi gaige wenji*, p. 54.

scholars developed 28 different new scripts to improve the Chinese characters, out of which five made use of the Latin ABC.[15] Not long after, in 1900 Wang Zhao 王照 invented the *Zhuyin zimu* 注音字母, a new script borrowing some signs from the Japanese symbols. This script was promoted by the newly established ministry of education in 1912 and was supported by the Nationalist government since the 1920s. In Taiwan it is still in use under the name Bopomofo, but it has not been very successful internationally. On the other hand, in Mainland China the different Latinized phonetic scripts of Mandarin Chinese were replaced by a standardized *Hanyu pinyin* 汉语拼音 form in the 1950s. At the same time, the simplified Chinese characters were widely propagated, and the use of the traditional characters was discouraged. In other words, 350 years after Ricci's death the government of China realized how useful the Latin script could be for people learning, reading, or writing Chinese characters. Another 50 years later a good percentage of the Chinese population has been equipped with mobile phones and sends millions of short messages through the ether, all of them written by an ABC input system.

All four writing systems are used simultaneously in China today, for example in the popular *Xiandai Hanyu cidian* 现代汉语词典 and in the *Xinhua zidian* 新华字典 one can find simplified characters and *Hanyu pinyin*, but also the traditional Chinese characters and the *Zhuyin zimu*. However, for ordering characters in a dictionary the most important of these writing systems nowadays is the Latin alphabet: most dictionaries start with "A," "Ai," "An," "Ao" etc. In Taiwan or Hong Kong the number of strokes or the radicals would still determine the place of a word in a dictionary or in an index, whereas in China most encyclopedias and dictionaries have adopted the order of Chinese words according to the ABC. This arrangement according to the alphabet was used by the early bilingual Chinese dictionaries in the West, for example the "Dictionnaire Chinois & François [sic]" in the appendix of the 1670 edition of Athanasius Kircher's *China Illustrata* ordered the Chinese words according to their phonetic script, that is, according to the alphabet.[16] Thus after being almost totally ignored and neglected for 300 years, the Latin script wields considerable influence in China today, although conservative forces cling to the old tradition of keeping the ABC out of printed Chinese texts, for example newspapers. The official phrase for this policy is "to protect the purity of Han-Chinese" (*baowei Hanyu de chunjiexing* 保卫汉语的纯洁性). This policy can succeed to keep the ABC formally out of some Chinese texts, but in fact the Latin way of thinking has already pervaded the language. The expression "purity" (*chunjiexing* 纯洁性) is a western concept not found in traditional Chinese, and the metaphorical application of "purity" to a

---

[15] See Yin Li 尹力, *Tushuo Hanzi de gushi* 图说汉字的故事 (Beijing: Renmin ribao chubanshe, 2008), p. 370.

[16] See the Chinese edition of *China Illustrata*, *Zhongguo tushuo* 中国图说, transl. Zhang Xiping 张西平 et al. (Zhengzhou: Daxiang chubanshe, 2010), Appendix: Chinese-French Dictionary, pp. 426-521.

language is not found in old Chinese texts either. This metaphor was first used by St. Jerome (350-420) who talked about the "puritas Hebraica" when translating from Hebrew to Latin. Ironically, the users of modern Chinese language are talking and thinking in Latin terms, even when they try to prevent the use of the Latin script. This example may show to which extent modern Chinese has already been "westernized" (or "internationalized"), and that means of course, Chinese has been "Latinized." If the Chinese do not learn Latin, they will never understand where the metaphors and concepts of their modern language come from.

Encounter of Cultures

Begegnung der Kulturen

文化之間的相遇

BUDDHISTISCHE MALEREI IM MINGZEITLICHEN BEIJING
BEGEGNUNGEN VON VÖLKERN UND KULTUREN IM SPIEGEL DER KUNST

Ursula Toyka

Die chinesische Kunst war in vielen Etappen ihrer Geschichte nicht nur Ausdruck eines bestimmten Gestaltungsauftrages oder eines individuellen Gestaltungswillens, sondern auch der Begegnung vielfältiger kultureller Strömungen, die sich mehr oder weniger erkennbar mischten und mehr oder weniger nachhaltigen Einfluss nahmen. Eine in dieser Hinsicht besonders fruchtbare Periode begann mit der Gründung des Ming-Reiches, nachdem im Weltreich der Mongolen neue Verbindungen zum Vorderen Orient bis hin zum Abendland geknüpft wurden, neue Errungenschaften verschiedenster Art und Menschen, die sie beherrschten, ihren Weg ins Reich der Mitte gefunden hatten. Dazu gehörte auch ein genialischer Künstler newarischer Herkunft, Anige (1243–1306), der einem Ruf an den Hof des zum tibetischen Buddhismus bekehrten Kubilai Khan folgte, um dort die religiösen Bildwerke des neuen Glaubens zu schaffen. Er blieb bis zu seinem Lebensende dort und begründete eine künstlerische Schule, die in den religiösen Gemälden und Skulpturen seiner chinesischen Nachfolger weit über seinen Tod hinaus Nachhall fand. Einflüsse der anmutigen und sinnlich geprägten künstlerische Sprache Nepals entfalteten sich in der buddhistischen Kunst Chinas augenfällig, seitdem der Yongle-Herrscher die Ming-Hauptstadt 1421 von Nanjing nach Beijing hatte verlegen lassen und nach der inneren Konsolidierung des Reiches auch die Sicherung nach außen auf die politische Agenda nahm. Hierbei erkannte man in Tibet einen wichtigen potenziellen Partner und entwickelte eine rege Gesandtschaftsdiplomatie, die zwecks Austausch von adäquaten Geschenken auch die Produktion der höfischen Werkstätten anregte.

Es war die Zeit, als nepalesische und chinesische Künstler auch für Klöster in Tibet arbeiteten, wo sich ihre verschiedenen Stilsprachen mit der tibetischen auf ästhetisch höchst ansprechende Weise mischten, was sich besonders in den Wandgemälden des Stūpa von Gyantse bis heute so eindrucksvoll erleben lässt. Damals entstanden in Beijinger Werkstätten Bronzeskulpturen von transportabler Größe mit chinesischen Datierungen bis in die Mitte des 15. Jahrhunderts, deren Grazie und dekorative Eleganz sich von den bis dahin über ein Jahrtausend entwickelten Traditionen chinesischer Metallskulptur frappierend unterschied. Heather Karmay erforschte wegweisend ihren historischen Kontext und Zusammenhang mit Blockdruckillustrationen buddhistischer Texte, die seit der Yuan-Zeit in China entstanden.[1]

---

[1] Karmay 1975.

In der Malerei aber waren lange keine vergleichbaren Zeugnisse bekannt, bis in den vergangenen Jahrzehnten im Abstand von mehreren Jahren an verschiedensten Stellen der Welt Rollbilder in der Form eines tibetischen *thangka* auftauchten, die eine erkennbar tibetisch-buddhistische Ikonographie in ästhetisch höchst ansprechender, aber rätselhaften Fusion diverser Stiltraditionen zeigen und in den meisten Fällen in Gold geschriebene chinesische Datierungen aus den Jahren zwischen 1474 und 1516 tragen. Ihre religiöse Funktion, die Entstehungsumstände sowie die Frage, wer sie geschaffen haben könnte, blieben bis heute mehr oder weniger im Dunkeln. Licht hierauf wirft die Entdeckung eines 1479 datierten exquisit gemalten, ikonographisch komplexen, großformatigen Maṇḍala des Buddha Vajaradhara aus insgesamt 42 Figuren, das wissenschaftlich bisher nicht beachtet wurde (Abb. 2; siehe Appendix, S. 901-907). Meine dank Roman Malek und Zbigniew Wesołowski 2014 in der Monumenta Serica Monograph Series publizierte Untersuchung der Wandgemälde und Inschriften im mingzeitlichen Kloster Fahai si 法海寺 bei Beijing lässt nun den Schluss zu, dass diesem ikonographisch einzigartigen Gemälde eine Schlüsselrolle zukommt.[2] Die dazu führenden Überlegungen geben im Nachfolgenden zugleich Einblicke in eines der spannendsten Kapitel der Erforschung asiatischer Kunstgeschichte in unserer Zeit.

Es begann 1969 mit einer New Yorker Ausstellung tibetischer Kunst, in der unter anderem erstmals ein „Maṇḍala of Vajranairātmā 1479 A.D., Gouache on cotton" aus der Sammlung des Boston Museum of Fine Arts der Öffentlichkeit als „earliest known dated painting from Tibet" präsentiert wurde.[3] Die Maße des Gemäldes (145 x 92,5 cm) und seine Darstellung von Gottheiten des tibetischen Buddhismus, die chinesische Datierung (entsprechend 1479) und die ungewöhnliche Machart insgesamt zogen über mehrere Jahre die Aufmerksamkeit der Fachwelt und manche wissenschaftliche Kontroverse auf sich. Unbemerkt blieb hingegen die Entdeckung eines mit dem Bostoner Gemälde gleich datierten, in Ikonographie, künstlerischer Gestaltung, Maltechnik und Größe nahezu identischen Pendants im Peabody Museum, Salem, das noch nicht publiziert wurde und daher hier abgebildet ist (Abb. 1).

Im Zentrum der Schaufläche stehen drei Erscheinungsformen der „Himmelswandlerinnen" (Ḍākiṇī) tantrisch geprägter Tradition des Vajrayāna-Buddhismus, der geistiges Erlösungsstreben mit sexuellen Praktiken verbindet. Sie werden besonders in Tibet oft paarweise mit esoterischen Gottheiten aber auch als einzelne Manifestation in der Funktion von Schutzgottheiten hoch verehrt. Die Gemälde in Boston und Salem zeigen jeweils als Hauptfigur inmitten der oberen Bildhälfte die Göttin Nairātmyā und in der unteren Bildhälfte zwei ihr im Pantheon „untergeordnete" Ḍākiṇī. Die in Größe und Ausführung prominenten drei Hauptfiguren sind umgeben von weiteren 39 Gottheiten in einheitlich kleinerem Maßstab, alle wie die Hauptgottheiten getragen von Lotosblüten, die durch ein üppiges Rankenwerk durchsetzt mit farbigen Knospen und Blättchen miteinander ver-

---

[2] Toyka 2014.

[3] Pal 1969: Inv.Nr. 06.1901, H 145 x B 92,5 cm. Malerei in Gouache-Farben auf grundierter Baumwolle.

bunden sind. Die Konfiguration veranschaulicht eine vorgegebene rituelle Platzierung der einzelnen Sakralgestalten im virtuell erfahrbaren Raum, den der Gläubige sich bei der Visualisierung von Gottheiten gemäß tradierter Anrufungstexte (sādhanā) während einer Meditation vorstellt. In diesem Sinne entspricht die auf einem räumlich gedachten Grundkonzept zweidimensional dargestellte Konfiguration dem Konzept eines Maṇḍala, wie in vielen Beispielen auf portablen Rollbildern und Wandgemälden in Zentral- und Ostasien überliefert. Zum Zeitpunkt der Bostoner Ausstellung stand die Erforschung der tibetischen Malereigeschichte noch am Anfang, doch hatte man die Relevanz des Maṇḍala erkannt in Bezug auf den Stil der Ornamentik, die Form der Lotosblüten und die Darstellung der Dämonen unter den Füßen der Hauptgottheiten. In der Farbpalette konstatierte man Einflüsse nepalesischer Malerei und verband damit die Vermutung, das Gemälde sei von einem wohlhabenden chinesischen Gläubigen in einem zentraltibetischen Kloster gestiftet worden.[4]

Vor allem letztere Vermutung reflektiert die nach damaligem Forschungsstand verständliche Ratlosigkeit betreffend die Provenienz des Stückes innerhalb der mit dem Vajrayāna-Buddhismus in Zusammenhang gebrachten Regionen Nepal und Tibet in Verbindung mit einer chinesischen Inschrift. Der ungewöhnliche Malstil des Stückes stellte daher ein Rätsel dar, das die Fachwelt zunehmend faszinierte in einer Zeit, als man auch in den großen Museen Europas begann, die Bestände außereuropäischer Sammlungen systematisch zu sichten und wissenschaftlich zu bearbeiten. In London publizierte zunächst 1973 John Lowry, Kurator für indische Kunst im Victoria and Albert Museum, drei 1907 in Beijing für sein Haus erworbene, stilistisch verwandte Gemälde, deren Ikonographie ebenfalls auf den tibetischen Buddhismus verweist, jedoch in wesentlich kleinerem Bildformat und anderer Komposition. Es steht jeweils nur eine Gottheit prominent im Zentrum, umgeben von weiteren 4 bzw. 17 oder 23 kleineren Gottheiten.

Ähnlich wie das Bostoner Gemälde tragen zwei dieser Thangkas eine in Gold geschriebene chinesische Inschrift:[5] Eine Darstellung der löwenköpfigen Göttin Siṃhavaktrā (61x 47,5 cm, Inv. Nr. IS 14-1969) ist auf das Jahr 1477 datiert und ein Mahākāla (63 x 47,5cm, Inv. Nr. IS 15-1969) entsprechend auf 1478. Lowry wies auf ihre Übereinstimmung mit dem Bostoner Stück in Hinblick auf Details der figürlichen Formulierungen, der Schmuckzeichnung in Gold, der Palette aus vorwiegend roten Farbtönen, der Darstellung der Ranken und Lotossockel sowie der rautenförmig gemusterten dunkelroten Umrandung hin. Das dritte Gemälde mit Darstellung des Totengottes Yama (63 x 40 cm, Inv. Nr. IS 16-1969), aber ohne Inschrift, stellte er in einen Zusammenhang mit einem 1949 vom Tibet-Forscher Guiseppe Tucci erstmals abgebildeten Thangka der Sammlung Barluzzi.[6] Es zeigt ebenfalls die Göttin Siṃhavaktrā, aber in etwas schlichterer Ausführung und mit einer etwas späteren chinesischen Datierung auf das Jahr

---

[4] Pal 1969.
[5] Lowry 1973, S. 306-314.
[6] Tucci 1949, Taf. 205.

1513. Lowry entschied die selbst gestellte Frage, ob die stilistisch offenbar zusammenhängenden Stücke seines und des Bostoner Hauses in China, Tibet oder Nepal geschaffen worden seien, mit „slightly in favor of China" und vermutete als Herkunftsort „a region north of the capital".[7]

Dieser noch vagen Vermutung gab der in Japan lebende Sammler David Kidd 1975 in einem Artikel vehementen Nachdruck mit seiner These, es handle sich um Werke nepalesischer oder tibetischer Künstler, die zuvor nach Beijing geholt worden seien. Dem 1513 datierten Gemälde aus der Sammlung Barluzzi ordnete er zwei weitere bis dahin unbekannte Thangkas mit tibetisch-buddhistischer Ikonographie zu, die in einer ähnlichen Umrandung eine nahezu identische chinesische Aufschrift plus eine Zeile in tibetischer Schrift tragen:[8] eine Darstellung der Sarvabuddhaḍākiṇī (125 x 102 cm) seiner eigenen Sammlung und ein Yamāntaka (122 x 93 cm) im University of California Art Museum. Kidd sah in der künstlerischen Gestaltung aller drei Gemälde eine verwandte, aber im Vergleich mit den Stücken in Boston und London sichtlich geringere künstlerische Qualität. Er holte Rat von sinologischer und tibetologischer Seite zu den Aufschriften ein und publizierte folgende Ergebnisse: Die Bildnisse der Sarvabuddhaḍākiṇī und des Yamāntaka tragen die gleiche chinesische Datierung – „Geschaffen am 24. Tag des 9. Monats im 7. Jahr der Ära Zhengde [正德, 1505–1516] der Großen Ming(-Dynastie) [i.e., 1513] nach einem Gelübde des Glückseligen Gesetzeskönigs Bandan Rinchen im „Landesbeschützenden und friedensbewahrenden Kloster" (Huguo Bao'an si 護國保安寺), und die chinesische Aufschrift des Gemäldes der Siṃhavaktrā Ḍākiṇī aus dem Jahre 1513 aus der Sammlung Barluzzi ist bis auf den Hinweis auf das Gelübde ebenfalls identisch. Letzteres Gemälde und die Sarvabuddhaḍākiṇī-Thangka trugen, wie Kidd entdeckte, darunter noch eine tibetische Aufschrift. Ein von Kidd konsultierter tibetischer Gelehrter stellte fest, dass es sich um eine Übersetzung der chinesischen Aufschrift in dem in Tibet für offizielle Dokumente genutzten dBu-med-Schreibstil handelte. Sie wurde offenbar aber nicht von einem Muttersprachler verfasst, sondern enthält einige linkische Transliterationen des Chinesischen ins Tibetische. So sind Name und Titel des tibetischen Stifters dPal-ldan Rinpoche (dessen Titel „Rinpoche" in den chinesischen Schriftzeichen *lingzhan* 領占 anklingt) zwar dem üblichen tibetischen Sprachgebrauch entsprechend transkribiert, aber für den Begriff „Gesetzeskönig", für den es im Tibetischen einen eigenen Ausdruck (*chos-kyi rgyal-po*) gegeben hätte, nutzte man eine Transliteration des chinesische Begriffes *fawang* 法王. Dank einer Recherche von Michele Strickman erfuhr damals Kidd, dass im Jahr 1512 „the Great Felicitous Dharma-King from Tibet, whose name was Lingchen Pan-tan ... as well as a second Dharma-King named Cho-hsiao Tsang-pu and other Tibetans" in dem 1472 mit dem Titel „Huguo" ausgezeichneten „Lan-

---

[7] Lowry 1973, S. 314.

[8] Kidd 1975a, S. 56-60. Beide Gemälde sollen eine japanische Montierung haben, im Falle der Vajrayogini seit ca. 200 Jahren, was die interessante Frage aufwirft, ob die Ikone damals von Shingon-Mönchen mit nach Japan gebracht wurde.

desbeschützenden Kloster vom Drachenberg" (Huguo Longshan si 護國龍山寺) residierten, wo sich laut mingzeitlichen Quellen tibetische Patriarchen aufhielten, wenn sie die chinesische Hauptstadt besuchten.[9] Kidd folgert, dass die chinesisch datierten Thangkas zum Besitz dieses Großklosters gehörten, das später als Huguo si 護國寺 (Landesbeschützendes Kloster) aus einem westlichen und einem östlichen Teil bestanden haben soll, von denen möglicherweise einer im 15. Jh. den Namen Bao'an si (Friedensbewahrendes Kloster) trug, wie er in Aufschrift erscheint.[10]

Zwei Jahre später, 1977, konnten die beiden 1477 und 1478 datierten, von Lowry publizierten Londoner Thangkas erstmals einer breiteren Öffentlichkeit gezeigt werden, und zwar in der viel beachteten ersten großen Tibet-Ausstellung Europas, die im Grand Palais in Paris stattfand und von dort weiter ins Münchner Haus der Kunst wanderte, wo der französische Katalog[11] ins Deutsche übersetzt wurde. Er beschreibt die Siṃhavaktrā-Thangka zusammen mit dem Bostoner Maṇḍala und dem Yama-Gemälde im Victoria and Albert Museum als die „älteste Gruppe datierter Malereien ... zweifellos für das von Qubilai (1271–1294) gegründete Kloster Hu-kuo-szu in Peking geschaffen".[12] Attestiert werden damit verbunden eine „enge Verwandtschaft mit zeitgenössischen, von der nepalesischen Kunst beeinflussten und im südlichen Tibet ausgeführten Werken" und eine „recht freie Interpretation nepalesischer Motive, die dem chinesischen Geschmack angepasst wurden".[13] Zum Beleg dienen „die Ausführung der Lotosranken im Hintergrund ... das Kollier mit vielfachen Gehängen, die Frisur, die aus nebeneinander gesetzten Spiralen gebildet ist, und die Ornamente, die die Ränder der Lotosblütenblätter des Thrones schmücken".[14] Darüber hinaus ist vermerkt: „Eine zweite, aus vier Malereien bestehende Gruppe, die in der Ausführung plumper ist, datiert aus den Jahren 1513 und 1516 und wurde für das gleiche Kloster hergestellt."[15] Zur Person der Künstler ist lediglich angemerkt, es müsse damals in Beijing zahlreiche Nepali, Tibeter und Mongolen in der Umgebung der Repräsentanten der tibetischen Kirche am chinesischen Hofe gegeben haben. Damit schien ein spannendes Kapitel Forschungsgeschichte zunächst abgeschlossen.

---

[9] Kidd 1975b, S. 158-159, resümiert damit *Dijing jingwu lüe* 帝京景物略 (Liu Tong – Yu Yizheng), Nachdruck aus Taibei 1969, Kap. I, S. 57a-62b, die sich in der hier konsultierten Ausgabe von 1992 auf S. 33 findet, wo Titel und Namen der genannten tibetischen Patriarchen mit Xifan daqing fawang lingzhan Bandan 西番大慶法王領占班丹 und Dajue fawang Zhexiao Zangbu 大觉法王着肖藏卜 verzeichnet sind, siehe auch unten Fn. 58.

[10] Kidd 1975b, S. 160.

[11] Béguin 1977.

[12] Haus der Kunst München 1977, S. 112, Kat. Nr. 80; die Maße werden fälschlich mit 1,11 x 0,67 (Meter) angegeben und das Datum der Inschrift mit „1477 oder 1468".

[13] *Ibid.*

[14] *Ibid.*

[15] *Ibid.*

Überraschend aber wurde es 1991 wieder aufgeschlagen mit einer Publikation der China-Sammlung des Victoria and Albert Museums. Der neue *Catalogue of Chinese Art* führte unter anderem ein bis dahin unveröffentlichtes Gemälde mit chinesischer Datierung ins Jahr 1479 unter der Bezeichnung „Buddhist Scroll, 151 x 99,1 cm, Inv. Nr. E.61-1911" auf. Es sei vermutlich 1911 im nordwestlich vor Beijing gelegenen „Temple of Great and Mighty Benevolence which protects the dynasty" (Da Longshan huguo si 大龍山護國寺) erworben worden, geschaffen wohl von einem dort in der Ming-Zeit lebenden tibetischen Mönch: „It is executed in a style which owes much more to Tibetan (and through them, Nepalese) styles of Buddhist iconography than it does to the Chinese styles ... ."[16] Da nun erstmals dem Text auch eine farbige Abbildung des Stückes beigefügt war, ließ sich auf den ersten Blick eine frappierende Ähnlichkeit mit dem 1969 publizierten Nairātmyā-Maṇḍala im Boston Museum of Fine Arts feststellen, das auch in der Größe übereinstimmt. Dies fand jedoch keine Erwähnung, ebensowenig die beiden von Lowry als Kurator bereits 1975 mit Bezug auf eben dieses Bostoner Stück publizierten Gemälde in der Indien-Sammlung des eigenen Hauses. Dort hatte es offenbar bei den Bearbeitungen der indischen und der chinesischen Sammlungen keinen Austausch gegeben – ein Indiz dafür, dass die heute unter verschiedenen Aspekten kulturwissenschaftlich beachteten interkulturellen Wechselbeziehungen damals noch kein Forschungsthema waren. Das Museum gestattete mir 1998 eine eingehende kunsthistorische Untersuchung der offenkundig zusammengehörenden Thangkas beider Abteilungen, deren Ergebnisse 2002 publiziert wurden.[17] Wesentlich war, dass das 1479 datierte Stück der chinesischen Sammlung im Victoria and Albert Museum ikonographisch dasselbe aus 42 Sakralgestalten bestehende Nairātmyā-Maṇḍala zeigte wie das Bostoner Gemälde. Untersuchungen im Detail ergaben zudem die gleiche Komposition, künstlerische Gestaltung und Maltechnik bis hin zu Einzelheiten der Strichführung, Farbgebung und Materialien. Insbesondere ließ die auf den Tag übereinstimmende Datierungsinschrift besondere Entstehungsumstände im Sinne eines hochrangigen Stiftungsauftrages vermuten.

Erste Hinweise darauf ließen sich indirekt aus dem 1995 erschienenen ersten Bestandskatalog der Tibet-Sammlung im Pariser Musée des Arts Asiatique Guimet erschließen.[18] Darin präsentierte der Kurator Gilles Béguin ein 1979 – kurz nach der oben erwähnten Tibet-Ausstellung im Grand Palais – für sein Haus erworbenes Gemälde der Schutzgottheit Hevajra in 16-armiger Manifestation als Kapāladhara umgeben von 18 begleitenden Gottheiten. Das Gemälde (62 x 47,5 cm, Inv. MA 4838) trägt ebenfalls eine chinesische Inschrift in Gold, die bei genauer Lesung lautet: „Am frühen 2. Tag des 11. Monats im 10. Jahr (der Ära) Chenghua 成化 [1465–1487] [i.e. 1475] der Großen Ming gestiftet." Der Autor

---

[16] Kerr 1991, S. 100, Taf. 38.

[17] Toyka-Fuong 2002, S. 283–297.

[18] Béguin 1995, S. 224–225, Nr. 141, datiert die Ära Chenghua fälschlich 1464–1486 und somit die Malerei in das Jahr 1474.

aber übersetzt den „1. Monat ... Chenghua", lässt das Wort „gestiftet" aus und schließt fälschlich auf das Jahr 1474. Dies gab den Anlass, in meiner Publikation des Londoner Maṇḍala die Formulierung der Inschrift genauer zu hinterfragen, die zudem die Stiftung auf genau denselben Tag datiert wie die Inschrift der 1477 entstandenen Siṃhavaktrā-Thangka im Victoria and Albert Museum, aber zwei Jahre früher, auf 1475. Dass es sich damit um das älteste noch erhaltene Thangka mit chinesischer Inschrift handelt, betont auch Béguin, der die Malerei aus Leimfarben („détrempe") eingehend untersucht. Er weist hinsichtlich des Formats, der Randmusterung und der dunklen Farbpalette Übereinstimmungen mit den kleinformatigen Londoner Vergleichstücken auf bis hin zu der Beobachtung, dass die bis dato bekannten kleinformatigen Maṇḍalas mit chinesischen Datierungen der frühen 1470er Jahre alle eine relativ flüchtige Ausführung in den Details und auffallend kursorische Linienführung in der Goldfassung zeigen. Von der figuralen Komposition her aber verkörpert das 1475 datierte Gemälde des Kapāladhara, in dem die prominente Zentralfigur umrandet von gleichmäßig unterteilten Friesen mit Begleitfiguren erscheint, die im *pradaksinam,* dem Uhrzeiger gegenläufigen Sinne von links unten nach links oben und weiter nach rechts oben und rechts unten angerufen werden, gegenüber den Londoner Vergleichsstücken einen orthodoxeren, stärker indisch inspirierten Maṇḍala-Typus. Béguin erkannte, dass die auf dem Pariser Gemälde dargestellten Gottheiten – über Kapāladhara die fünf Buddhas der Himmelsrichtungen, unter ihm fünf Schutzgottheiten sowie flankierend je vier der acht Ḍākinī aus dem Gefolge der Göttin Nairātmyā – alle spezifisch vom Śaskya-pa-Orden des tibetischen Buddhismus verehrt wurden. Die Tatsache, dass Nairātmyā als Gefährtin des Hevajra hier gar nicht erscheint, deutet der Autor als Ergebnis ihrer damals möglicherweise abgewandelten religiösen Bedeutung.[19] Belege dafür, dass darüber hinausgehend wohl Nairātmyā eine im Pantheon herausragende Bedeutung erlangt hatte, die in großformatigen Darstellungen ihres eigenen Maṇḍalas und mit ihr selbst im Zentrum einer komplexen Konfigurationen zum Ausdruck kam, liefern die beiden 1479 datierten Maṇḍala in Boston und London.

Wie weitgehend diese beiden Stücke mit jeweils 42 Figuren bis ins Detail miteinander und mit dem Gemälde des Peabody Museums (Abb. 1) übereinstimmen, konnte ich im Zuge meiner Untersuchungen feststellen.[20] Dabei wurde auch ihre aufwändige Machart deutlich, die offensichtlich hohen ästhetischen und repräsentativen Ansprüchen genügen sollte. Sie verleiht diesen Ikonen eine ungewöhnliche Ausstrahlung, die einen Wandel im Verständnis, in der Funktion und in der Entstehung religiöser Malerei zur damaligen Zeit reflektiert. Im Zentrum des Maṇḍala (s. Abb. 2) tanzen drei Göttinnen in zorniger Erscheinungsform jeweils auf einem Feind der buddhistischen Lehre. Ganz oben ist Nairātmyā zu erkennen, unten links die rote Kurukulla mit Pfeil und Bogen, unten rechts ist vermutlich

---

[19] Eine stilistisch durchaus vergleichbare andere Darstellung des solitären Hevajra (Kapāladhara) in derselben Sammlung, allerdings ohne Inschrift, datiert Guilles Béguin konsequent ins 15. Jahrhundert, siehe Béguin 1990, S. 62, Nr. 25.

[20] Toyka 2002, S. 287ff.

Vārāhi darstellt. Sie sind umgeben von 39 kleineren Figuren des Pantheons, im Zentrum der obersten Reihe an wichtigster Stelle Buddha Vajradhara und am unteren Bildrand eine Reihe von Schutzgottheiten in zornigen Manifestationen sowie weitere Ḍākiṇī. Sie alle thronen auf Lotosblüten, die untereinander durch ein dichtes Rankenwerk aus kleineren Lotosblüten und -blättern verbunden sind. Die goldene Zeichnung der Konturen und Binnenstrukturen hebt seine dekorative Wirkung hervor, ebenso die in Rosa- und Rottönen changierenden Blätter der Blüten und Knospen. Die ungewöhnliche Ikonographie der Konfiguration warf vor allem die Frage nach der religiösen Funktion des Maṇḍala auf, die ich auf textlicher Grundlage zu entschlüsseln versuchte. Demnach dienten Darstellungen dieser Art wahrscheinlich einem Ritual der Göttin Nairātmyā, das vor allem von Mönchen des Saskya-pa-Ordens vollzogen wurde. Auf die ihnen bekannterweise wichtige Tradition der religiösen Genealogie verweist eine Textstelle, wonach das Nairātmyā-Maṇḍala offenbar speziell zur Verehrung der Lehrer dargebracht wurde. Die Bedeutung, die ein solches im Kern tibetisch geprägtes Ritual augenscheinlich im mingzeitlichen China erlangte, mag durchaus verwundern. Doch könnte sich ein Grund darin finden lassen, dass für Anhänger des tibetischen Buddhismus im fernen China gerade dieses Thema einen besonders tiefen Sinn erlangte und zur Verbreitung des Rituals beitrug. Denn schon damals – und verstärkt seit Entdeckung des dritten Thangka dieser Art im Peabody Museum (Abb. 1) – stellt sich die Frage, warum dieses Konzept des Ḍākiṇī-Maṇḍala 1479 in nahezu identischer Form mehrfach ins Bild gesetzt wurde und ob diese Gemälde ursprünglich zu einem noch größeren Satz mit einer anderen Hauptgottheit im Zentrum gehörte.

Tatsächlich war zuvor im Kunsthandel ein weiteres Thangka mit chinesischer Datierung ins Jahr 1479 aufgetaucht, das ich 1997 kursorisch vorgestellt hatte (Abb. 2).[21] Es handelt sich um ein Maṇḍala des Buddha Vajradhara, des höchsten, im Zenit des Universums gedachten Wesens des buddhistischen Pantheons, Ādi- oder Ur-Buddha als Verkörperung des Ursprungs allen Seins. Dass entsprechend seiner herausragenden inhaltlichen Bedeutung das Gemälde alle anderen bis dato bekannten Vergleichsstücke auch in der exquisiten Qualität der Malerei übertraf, stand schon damals außer Frage. Die Schönheit seiner künstlerischen Gestaltung zeigt alle Qualitäten eines Andachtsbildes, das an zentraler Stelle, aus einem besonderen religiösen Anlass und an geweihtem Ort verehrt wurde. Nach eingehender Analyse des Originals kann ich nun nachfolgend auf die kunsthistorische Bedeutung des Stückes, seine Entstehungsumstände und künstlerische Provenienz eingehen.

Der Erhaltungszustand des Gemäldes von 153 cm Höhe und 102 cm Breite ist exzellent. Das Material besteht aus Leimfarben auf fein gewebtem Leinen oder Baumwolle, jedenfalls einem Stoff, der durch eine harzartige Grundierung fest präpariert wurde und dadurch den Farben eine mehrere Jahrhunderte überdauernde Haltbarkeit gab. Auch die Farben selbst – vermutlich aus Mineralien hergestellt – müssen mit einem speziellen Bindemittel in einer opaken, stark deckenden

---

[21] Toyka-Fuong 1997, S. 30.

Qualität angemischt worden sein. Sie beugen dem Verlaufen an den Rändern vor und verleihen durch die dadurch kaum wahrnehmbaren schwarzen Konturen der Malerei eine weiche, dem Auge angenehme und integrierende Wirkung. Die Palette fein abgestufter Nuancen von Zinnoberrot, Karminrot und Braunrot wirkt warm und suggestiv. Geschickt gesetzte Kontraste in Orangerot, Rosa, Hellrosa bis hin zu strahlendem Weiß beleben und akzentuieren die Schaufläche rhythmisch nach Art eines gewirkten Stoffes oder Teppichs. Die gedämpften Farben und ihre hellen Glanzpunkte wirken so in sich stimmig und geschlossen, gewinnen einen ansprechenden und doch verhaltenen, ruhigen Charakter. Die großzügig verwendete Goldzeichnung und ihre vor allem in der zentralen Triade filigrane Dichte verleiht der Gesamtdarstellung eine augenfällige Qualität, die zum einen den religiösen Inhalt überhöht und in der Prachtentfaltung zugleich auf dekorative Wirkung zielt.

Die Komposition ist ähnlich angelegt wie die drei oben genannten Nairātmyā-Maṇḍala, zeigt aber eine völlig andere Ikonographie. Buddha Vajradhara ist hier an der Spitze einer Triade mit den Bodhisattvas Mañuśrī und Avalokiteśvara in einer der meistverehrten Konfigurationen des buddhistischen Pantheons zu sehen. Alle drei Sakralgestalten thronen jeweils im Meditationssitz auf einer opulent gestalteten Lotosblüte vor einer delikat ziselierten Strahlenmandorla. Sie sind umgeben von 39 kleineren Nebenfiguren, jede ebenfalls vor einer Strahlenmandorla auf einer Lotosblüte thronend und kreisförmig umrahmt von einer Ranke aus Blüten und Blättern. Alle Figuren sind wie auf den Nairātmyā-Maṇḍalas im dichten, rhythmisch geschwungenen Rankenwerk miteinander verbunden. Vor diesem Hintergrund hebt sich die Triade in ihrer Größe und aufwändig dekorierten Umrandung deutlich ab. An denselben Positionen sind auf den Thangkas in Boston, London und Salem die Göttin Nairātmyā und ihre Begleiterinnen dargestellt, allerdings sichtlich weniger prächtig als die Triade des Vajradhara-Maṇḍala, das abgesehen davon mit den Nairātmyā-Maṇḍala in Material und Größe, Inschrift und vielen stilistischen Details übereinstimmt. Inhaltlich besteht ein enger Bezug insofern, als Göttin Nairātmyā die geheime Lehre von Vajradhara, ihrem spirituellen Vater, empfangen haben soll, der auf den Nairātmyā-Maṇḍala im Zentrum der obersten Figurenreihe direkt über dem Kopf der Göttin, also an der Spitze der gesamten Konfiguration zu sehen ist. Nach der Tradition des Śākyapa-Ordens gab Nairātmyā diese Lehre an den indischen Siddha Virupa weiter, der die spezielle Doktrin des Ordens begründete. Bezüge zu diesen Lehren deuten sich an verschiedenen Stellen der Konfiguration an. Die von Shen Weirong vertretene These, dass der religiöse und politische Einfluss des Śākyapa-Ordens zwar nach Bekehrung des Kubilai Khan 1270 zunächst einen Niedergang erfuhr, jedoch im 15. Jh. wieder Aufschwung nahm, findet hier einen bildlichen Beleg. Wie sich zuletzt auch aus den im Fahai si erhaltenen Inschriften ergab, ist davon auszugehen, dass unter den Vertretern verschiedener Schulrichtungen des tibetischen Buddhismus der Einfluss dieses Ordens am chinesischen Kaiserhof des 15. Jahrhunderts vorherrschend war.[22]

---

[22] Shen Weirong 2002, S. 41ff. und S. 68.

Die ikonographisch vorgeschriebene dunkelblaue Körperfarbe des Buddha Vajradhara (Abb. 3) in der oberen Hälfte des Bildes ist vom dunkelgrünen Untergrund kaum zu differenzieren, wohl aber seine in Gold gezeichneten charakteristischen Attribute Donnerkeil (*vajra*) und Glocke (*ghanta*), die er in der linken und rechten Hand vor der Brust kreuzt. Im Zustand der Verklärung (*samboghakāya*) manifestiert sich hier Vajradhara nicht in schmuckloser Mönchsgestalt, sondern in der prächtigen Erscheinung eines Cakravartin, einer königlichen Symbolgestalt aus vorbuddhistischer Zeit, „die das Rad dreht" – in wörtlicher Übersetzung.[23] Wie ein indischer Herrscher trägt Vajradhara Krone, Brustschmuck, Ohrgehänge, Arm- und Beinbänder. Sein Ornat besteht aus einem dunkelroten Hüftgewand (*dhoṭi*), das über und über mit einem Muster aus goldenen Lotosblüten verziert ist. Eine dunkelgrüne, in Gold gemusterte Stola liegt über beiden Schultern und schwingt sich von dort in großen Bögen um die Ellbogen, als schwebe der Buddha gerade rauschend aus Himmelshöhen hernieder. In der Schaufläche unter ihm (Abb. 2) thronen auf gleicher Höhe nebeneinander Vajradharas „geistige Söhne": rechts zu seinen Füßen der rote Bodhisattva Mañuśrī in seiner Manifestation als Dharmacakramañjuśrī ('Jam-dbyans chos-'khor-ma). Seine beiden vor der Brust überkreuzten Hände halten je einen Lotos. Einer öffnet seine Blüte, die das Buch der Erkenntnis (*pustaka*) trägt, neben Mañuśrīs linker Schulter. Die Blüte neben der rechten Schulter trägt das alle Unwissenheit vernichtende Schwert (*khadga*). Links zu Vajradhara's Füßen thront der weiße Bodhisattva Avalokiteśvara in seiner vierarmigen Gestalt als Saḍakṣarilokeśvara (sPyan-ras-gzigs phyag-b'zi-pa) (Abb. 4). Das Hauptpaar seiner Hände ist vor der Brust zur Geste der Anbetung (*anjali mudrā*) gefaltet. Das Nebenpaar hält an seiner linken Schulter eine Lotosblüte (*padma*) und neben der rechten Schulter einen Rosenkranz (*akśamala*).

Die drei gleichgroßen Hauptgottheiten sind von der gleichen prachtvollen Mandorla in spitz zulaufender Hufeisenform gerahmt. Ihre Umrandung trägt rot und grün alternierenden Besatz in dichter Linienzeichnung, die das Gold zum Strahlen bringt. Solch feingliedrige Ornamentik verweist auf die Tradition des Ziselierens in der nepalesischen Metallkunst, wie sie schon in frühen buddhistischen Gemälden Nepals zu finden ist, z.B. in der Mandorla des Sonnengottes Sūrya auf dem von Kitaharasa signierten, vermutlich 1379 entstandenen Thangka (92 x 53,3 cm, 36,5 x 21 inches) der Sammlung Zimmermann.[24] Im Vajradhara-Maṇḍala zeigen die Mandorlen zum nepalesisch inspirierten Goldrand im Innern ein barockes, in Gold auf Dunkelrot gezeichnetes Rankenmuster aus offenen Lotosblüten mit -blättern, wie es in der chinesischen Ornamentik seit der Tang-Zeit in vielerlei Varianten auf Keramik, Stoffen und anderem Kunsthandwerk etabliert ist. Wie aus Goldbrokat gewebt umgibt dieser Hintergrund die innere Umrandung der drei Figuren, einen kleinen dunkelgrünen Nimbus und einer Art „Rückenlehne" mit weißem Rand, beide in Hufeisenform und schmal eingefasst mit einem

---

[23] Dagyap Rinpoche 1992, S. 94.
[24] Pal 1991, S. 70-71, Taf. 33.

ähnlichen Strahlenkranz wie die Mandorla. Diese innere Umrandung, die sich bei den Bodhisattvas kaum vom goldenen Rankengeflecht abhebt, ist bei Vajradhara deutlicher zu sehen, dessen Figur insgesamt durch einen eleganteren Hintergrund betont ist: die breitere „Rückenlehne" zeigt oberhalb der Schultern weiße Schlaufen und erinnert damit an die weißen Schärpen, die auf nepalesischen Gemälden gelegentlich den Thronsitz rahmen. Der Kopf des Buddha wird durch die goldenen Bänder, mit denen seine Krone festgebunden ist, und größere Ohrgehänge stärker betont als bei den begleitenden Bodhisattvas. Sein gebauschtes Beinkleid aus roter Seide ist mit goldenen Lotosranken prächtig verziert, während die Muster im Gewand der Bodhisattvas schlichte Kreise zeigen. Alle drei Figuren tragen dazu die gleiche golddurchwirkte dunkelgrüne Stola, die breit über die Schultern fällt und an den Ellbogen ausschwingt – eine Bewegung, die jeweils von zwei lang gelockten Haarsträhnen aufgegriffen wird, sowie dem gleichen goldenen, mit roten und grünen Edelsteinen besetzten Gürtel und reichem Körperschmuck, der die Symbolik der heiligen Zahlen drei, fünf und neun impliziert: Die Kronen bestehen aus einem breiten Diadem mit fünf Spitzen und einer weiteren dreifachen Spitze darüber. Die Halskette aus fünf großen Edelsteinen trägt neun lange Ketten, die die ganze Brust bedecken neben einer langen roten und einer grünen Perlenkette, die am Bauch in einem Mittelstück aus fünf Medaillons zusammenlaufen.

Das üppig den Oberkörper bedeckende Geschmeide zeigt eigenartige Formen, die sich von den zahlreich erhaltenen Metallskulpturen des sino-tibetischen Stils mit chinesischen Datierungen des frühen 15. Jahrhunderts, von denen eingangs die Rede war, unterscheiden. Dennoch klingt deren Stilsprache an anderen Stellen des Vajradhara-Thangka an, so z.B. in der Darstellung der Köpfe. Besonders gut ist die feine dunkle Gesichtszeichnung auf der weißen Körperfarbe des Bodhisattva Sadakṣarilokiteśvara zu erkennen, dessen Züge eine vergleichbar hohe, eckige Stirn, tief gerundeten Wangen und ein kurzes rundes Kinn zeigen. Die Stirnmitte wird durch zwei runde Locken am Haaransatz akzentuiert. Darunter sind die mit einem dünnen Strich gezogenen Brauen vorn an der Nasenwurzel in hohem Bogen geschwungen. Die Augen zeigen ein fein gezeichnetes doppeltes oberes Lid, das in der Mitte leicht über die Pupille nach unten fällt und dadurch einen sanft verschleierte Blick erhält, der durch rote Akzentpunkte in den inneren und äußeren Ecken belebt wirkt. Die dreifach geschwungene Konturlinie de Nasenspitze ist schmal und tief gesetzt, dicht über einem winzigen Mund, der stark geschürzt ein kaum wahrnehmbares Lächeln zeigt. Ein deutlich mit spitzem Pinsel auf das Kinn gesetzter kreisrunder Punkt mag ein individuelles Memento des Künstlers mit einer ganz privaten Anspielung sein.

Insgesamt aber spiegelt diese Art der Gesichtsdarstellung mit einem Ausdruck vollkommener innerer Ruhe und nahezu kindlicher Unschuld eine außerordentlich anmutige Mischung aus verschiedenen Stiltraditionen. Sie findet sich in den Illustrationen zu *Zhu Fo Pusa miaoxiang minghao jingzhou* 诸佛菩萨妙相名號經咒 (Abbildungen, Namen und Sutrās aller Buddhas und Bodhisattvas), einem zweibändigen Blockdruck mit buddhistischen Texten und Abbildungen in der Sammlung Guimet wieder.[25] Die Texte in Chinesisch, Tibetisch, Mongolisch und Sanskrit sind 1431 datiert und nennen als Entstehungsort die „umwallte, kosmopolitische Stadt Beijing"[26] – was ein Licht auf die damals herrschende interkulturelle Atmosphäre der Hauptstadt als Nährboden für Begegnung und Austausch verschiedener künstlerischer Traditionen wirft. Vor allem aber findet sich der in der Darstellung des Bodhisattva Saḍakṣarilokeśvara präzise erkennbare Gesichtstypus frappierend ähnlich im Wandgemälde eines zweiarmigen Avalokiteśvara in der monumentalen Bodhisattva-Triade des Fahai si.[27] Verwandte Züge verraten auch manche Gesichter von Buddhas und Bodhisattvas der um 1427 entstandenen Wandgemälden im Stūpa (vor allem Kapelle 3) von Gyantse, Zentraltibet, mit Ausnahme des kleinen Kirschmundes der bei Saḍakṣarilokeśvara ganz dem chinesischen Schönheitsideal entspricht. Seine deutlich geöffneten Augen unter stark geschwungenen Brauen aber lassen sich typologisch bis zu den ältesten erhaltenen nepalesischen Thangkas zurückverfolgen, wie das besagte Thangka des Sonnengottes Sūrya und eine 1379 datierte Darstellung der Prajñāpāramitā (64 x 54 cm) im Musée Guimet veranschaulicht.[28] Eine 1403 datierte Darstellung der Göttin Vasudhara (86,4 x 73,7 cm) mit Gefolge in der Sammlung Zimmermann[29] lässt den in der nepalesischen Malerei meist breiteren und stärker lächelnden Mund besonders deutlich erkennen und zeigt zudem beispielhaft auch die rot ausgemalten Innenflächen der Hände und Füße, die uns an anderer Stelle auch im Vajradhara-Maṇḍala begegnen. Dort spricht ähnlich wie in den erwähnten Wandgemälden des Fahai si vieles in der Darstellung der Sakralgestalten für eine nepalesisch inspirierte Körperauffassung, die sich nicht zuletzt in der Betonung breiter Schultern gegenüber einer sehr schlanken Taille, schmalen Hüften und stärker geschwungenen Konturlinien äußert. Diese stilistischen Merkmale gehen letztlich auf den im Spätmittelalter am mongolischen Hof wirkenden nepalesischen Meister Anige zurück. Aus dieser Quelle speisen sich, wie an anderer Stelle ausführlich dargelegt, nicht nur die besagten buddhistischen Metallskulpturen mit chinesischen Datierungen seit der Yongle-Ära, sondern auch im Umfeld des Kaiserhofes geschaffene buddhistische Wandgemälde und Rollbilder bis ins ausgehende 15. Jahrhundert hinein.

Die 39 Nebenfiguren des Vajradhara-Maṇḍala sind wesentlich kleiner als die zentrale Triade aber untereinander gleich groß dargestellt und setzen sich bis auf acht zornig erscheinende Schutzgottheiten in der unteren Schaufläche aus Buddha- und Bodhisattva-Manifestationen zusammen. Alle Nebenfiguren sind auf einer voll geöffneten Lotosblüte dargestellt, deren Farbe im Ensemble symmetrisch zwischen Dunkel- und Hellrot, Rosa und Grün ohne erkennbaren Bezug

---

[25] Karmay 1978, S. 61-64, Abb. 44-47.

[26] Ibid., S. 71, Fn. 2.

[27] Toyka 2014, Bd. 2, Taf. 68.

[28] Béguin 1989, S. 126, Abb. 61.

[29] Pal 1991, S. 72, Abb. 34.

zum Charakter der jeweiligen Gottheit variiert. Die friedlichen Manifestationen thronen im Meditationssitz vor einer hufeisenförmigen, dunkelgrünen Thronlehne, die oben in einen dunkelgrünen Nimbus übergeht. Während dieser bei den drei Hauptfiguren zwar schmal aber doch deutlich in Hufeisenform gehalten ist, wie in vielen buddhistischen Wandgemälden und Blockdrucken seit dem Spätmittelalter tradiert, scheint sich der Maler der begleitenden Bodhisattva-Figuren beim Nimbus mal nicht recht zwischen der Hufeisenform und einer runden Kontur entscheiden zu können, mal willkürlich eine von beiden Varianten zu wählen. Die äußere dunkelrote Mandorla zeigt dieselbe spitz zulaufende Form wie bei den drei Hauptfiguren, aber mit schlichter in Gold gezeichneten „Strahlen" und ist bei den zornigen Schutzgottheiten mit züngelnden Flammen gefüllt. Die Darstellungen der Nebenfiguren sind formal so weit wie möglich vereinheitlicht, was sich auch in den Details der lockeren und dabei auffallend ebenmäßigen Linienführung beobachten lässt. Die unterschiedliche inhaltliche Bedeutung der Figuren lässt sich in vielen Fällen – leider nicht mehr in allen – an ikonographischen Merkmalen erkennen.

In der obersten Figurenreihe königlich geschmückter Erleuchtungskörper sind die fünf Dhyani-Buddhas zu erkennen, die nach der Lehre des Diamantweges (Vajrayana) als Repräsentanten der fünf Weltsphären alle kosmischen Kräfte in sich bündeln: In der Mitte der weiße Buddha Vairocana mit seiner charakteristischen *thathāgata mudrā*, bei der die rechte Hand als sogenannte „Diamant-Faust" mit aufwärts gerichtetem Zeigefinger den Daumen der linken, zur sog. „Lotos-Faust" geschlossenen Hand umschließt (Abb. 5). Zu seiner Rechten den dunkelblauen Buddha Akṣobhya – meditierend mit der linken Hand im Schoß und mit der Rechten die Erde anrufend – und links der dunkelrote Buddha Amithāba mit beiden Händen in Meditationshaltung. Links daneben ist der grüne Buddha Amogasiddhi zu sehen, ebenfalls beide Hände in Meditationshaltung. Rechts neben Buddha Akṣobhya thront Buddha Ratnasambhava mit brauner Körperfarbe, rechts die Geste des Gebens des Besten ausführend und die linke Hand meditierend in den Schoß gelegt. Flankiert werden die Thathāgata außen in der rechten oberen Ecke der Schaufläche von Akaśagarbha mit einem Vajra in der linken Hand und rechts einer geöffneten Lotosblüte, die eine Mondscheibe trägt, und in der linken Ecke von einer weißen Manifestation des Avalokiteśvara mit einer Lotosblüte in der Rechten, während die Linke ein Juwel vor dem Schoß hält.

Buddha Vajradhara im Zentrum der oberen Bildhälfte ist von sechzehn Bodhisattvas umgeben, die auf beiden Seiten in vier Paaren untereinander gereiht sind. Zur Rechten des Buddha (links vom Betrachter) gruppieren sich oben vier Manifestationen des Bodhisattva Ratnapaṇi mit brauner Körperfarbe: links außen mit der zur Lehre erhobenen rechten Hand, die Linke mit einem flammenden Juwel im Schoß, daneben innen mit der Linken ein flammendes Juwel und mit der Rechten eine Lotosblüte mit einem Buch erhebend (Abb. 6), außen darunter mit der rechten Hand Segen spendend und links ein flammendes Juwel im Schoß haltend sowie innen mit der linken Hand ein flammendes Juwel und rechts einen Pflanzenstiel haltend. Auf der gegenüberliegenden Seite sind vier Manifestationen des Bodhisattva Vajrapani zu sehen, die jeweils einen Donnerkeil (*vajra*) halten.

Innen oben liegt die Linke mit Vajra im Schoß, während die Rechte einen Doppelvajra (*viśvajra*) auf einem Juwel vor die Brust hebt (Abb. 7). Darunter sowie bei beiden daneben thronenden Figuren ist die Rechte lehrend erhoben und die Linke hält ein Vajra im Schoß. Darunter gruppieren sich rechts und links je vier Bodhisattvas in Meditationshaltung, alle mit unterschiedlicher Körperfarbe und Handhaltungen. Alle halten ein Vajra oder ein Doppelvajra, manche ein zusätzliches Attribut. Am rechten Bildrand zeigt der zweite Bodhisattva von unten mit einem Dreizack möglicherweise Bodhistattva Vajravidārana, darunter die Figur mit Glocke und Vajragriff wohl eine Form des Bodhisattva Samantabhadra. Die vier unteren Bodhisattvas am linken Bildrand halten ebenfalls alle einen Vajra im Schoß sowie diverse Attribute, die meist nicht mehr erkennbar sind.

Genau in der Mitte zwischen den untersten vier Bodhisattvas ist im Zentrum des Maṇḍalas die Göttin Nairātmā mit blaugrüner Körperfarbe auf einem Feind der Religion tanzend dargestellt. Ihre Haupthände heben Schädelschale und Hackmesser vor die Brust, die zweite Rechte schwingt ein Vajra, die zweite Linke hält eine Lanze (*khaṭvāṅga*). Darunter erscheint die Gottheit in derselben Körperfarbe aber zweiarmiger Manifestation, im Ausfallschritt mit jedem Fuß einen Dämon niedertretend, ähnlich mit Gold und Juwelen geschmückt wie die drei Hauptikonen. Schmuck und Attribute sind in opaker Goldauflage fein gezeichnet wie bei der vierarmigen Manifestation darüber. Unter den beiden Ḍākiṇī-Figuren ist der stierköpfige Schutzgott Bhairava ('Jigs-byed) zu sehen (Abb. 8) – ähnlich mit Gold und Juwelen geschmückt aber mit drohend aufgerissenem Maul, links eine Fangschlinge und rechts einen Spieß mit dem abgehackten Kopf eines Feindes der Religion schwingend. In der untersten Reihe sind die drei meistverehrten Manifestationen des Mahākāla aufgereiht: im Zentrum hervorgehoben durch eine hellrosa Lotosblüte positioniert sich der mächtige Prañajara Mahākāla (Gur-gyi mGon-po) (Abb. 9), eine spezifisch vom Śaskyapa-Orden verehrte Schutzgottheit, deren Darstellung in dreidimensionaler Form bis zu ihrer Zerstörung diese besondere Bedeutung auch im Sanktuarium des Fahai si zukam.[30] Gur-gyi mGon-po zur Linken wacht Ye-śes mGon-po und zur Rechten Kuro Mahākāla (mGon-po nag-po) (Abb. 10) je auf dunkelroten Lotosblüten. Diese Triade besonders wichtiger Schutzgottheiten wird von zwei kleinen in den Hintergrund versetzten, in Tibet ebenfalls hoch verehrten Schutzgottheiten begleitet; rechts neben mGon-po nag-po ist dies der Todesgott Yama (Śin-rje) und links neben Ye-śes mGon-po ist dies Śrīdevi (dPal-ldan lHa-mo), die auf ihrem Maultier über ein Meer aus dem Blut der Feinde der Religion reitet. Alle hier dargestellten zornigen Schutzgottheiten des tibetischen Buddhismus sind von züngelnden Flammen umgeben, die in opakem Gold auf Dunkelrot sehr fein und lebendig gezeichnet sind. Auch in den Gesichtszügen, Brauen und Bärten fällt die minutiös genaue Goldzeichnung auf, die in der tibetischen Malerei des 14. und 15. Jahrhunderts vielfach belegt ist. Sie verleiht als Ausdruck religiöser Verehrung denjenigen Schutzgottheiten, denen mit ihrer furchterregenden Erscheinung und kriegerischen Bewaffnung eine apotropäische Funktion zukommt, um als Vorhut des Maṇḍala alle bösen Einflüs-

---

[30] Toyka 2014, Kap. IV. 1.4.

sen zu wehren, eine sakrale Aura, die sich jedoch durch die dunklen Körperfarben auf dunklem Bildgrund nur verhalten strahlend abhebt.

Im Gegensatz dazu leuchtet entlang der beiden unteren Seiten der Schaufläche die strahlend weiße Körperfarbe von vier untereinander gesetzten Figurenpaaren, die am rechten und linken Bildrand dem Betrachter jeweils spiegelbildlich entgegengesetzt im Dreiviertelprofil zugewandt sind und auf keiner der anderen chinesisch datierten Thangkas vorkommen. Eine größere und eine kleinere Figur trohnt jeweils ähnlich den Buddha- und Bodhisattva-Figuren der oberen Bildhälfte auf einem voll erblühten Lotos, umgeben von Nimbus und Mandorla vor einer Thronlehne, die seitlich mit weißen Schärpen geschmückt ist. Die größere Figur erhebt spiegelbildlich am rechten und linken Bildrand jeweils eine Hand zum Segen und die andere zur Geste der Furchtlosigkeit (*abhaya mudrā*). Ihre Positur, Krone, Ohrgehänge, Ketten, Arm- und Beinbänder aus juwelenbesetztem Gold und der aufwändig gemusterte Dhoti, entsprechend einem weltlichen Herrscher, kennzeichnen einen Bodhisattva. Ihm zu Füßen kniet jeweils in stark verkleinertem Maßstab und mit gefalteten Händen ein ebenfalls mit Gold geschmückter Adorant, der einen wohlhabenden Gläubigen, vermutlich den Stifter des Gemäldes darstellen soll. Die Anzahl der Figurenpaare verweist auf die Acht Großen Bodhisattvas (*aṣṭa mahā-bodhisattva*), deren Darstellungsform indische Vorbilder anklingen lässt. Die Bodhisattvas mit ungewöhnlich kräftig vorspringenden Nasen sitzen in „königlich vergnügter Haltung" (*rājalalitāsana*) am rechten Bildrand mit aufgestelltem linken Bein und erhobener rechter Hand (Abb. 11) und am linken Bildrand mit aufgestelltem rechten Bein und erhobener linker Hand (Abb. 12). Sie tragen einen weißen Rock mit roten, geometrischen Streifenmustern und darüber ein golden gemustertes rotes Lendentuch wie auf mittelalterlichen indischen und nepalesischen Illustrationen zu buddhistischen Palmblatt-Manuskripten.

Dort finden sich auch Bodhisattva-Darstellungen mit ritueller rotbrauner Färbung der Hand- und Fußflächen wie auf dieser Thangka sowohl bei der großen Figur des Ṣaḍakṣarilokeśvara als auch den miniaturhaften segnenden Bodhisattvas. Die letztgenannte Figuration findet sich häufig in der mittelalterlichen indischen Kunst, so auf einer um 1073 in Bihar, Nālāndā, entstandenen Palmblatt-Illumination des Aṣṭasāhasrikā Prajñāparamitā-Manuskriptes[31] und Beispielen des mittleren 12. Jahrhunderts n.Chr. aus derselben Region[32] oder Bangladesh.[33] Besonders nahe an die hier behandelte Thangka kommt eine Illustration zum Gaṇḍavyūtha-Text, die vermutlich im 11. Jahrhundert im Tal von Kathmandu entstand.[34] In dreidimensionaler Form sind solche Figurenpaare bekannt, wie z.B. auf einem Tonamulett (*sāccha*) des 8. Jahrhunderts aus Ost-Indien oder Bangladesh mit dem Relief eines Bodhisattva in königlich vergnügter

---

[31] Huntington – Huntington 1990, Taf. 58b.
[32] *Ibid.*, Taf. 58c.
[33] *Ibid.*, Taf. 59.
[34] *Ibid.*, Taf. 89.

Haltung, vor dem ein Gläubiger kauert[35] oder auf einer Stele des frühen 9. Jahrhunderts wohl aus Bihar (Region Magadha, möglicherweise Kurkihār), die einen Bodhisattva mit einem knieenden Adoranten zeigt.[36] Auch die buddhistische Skulptur und Malerei Chinas kennen seit der Mitte des 1. Jahrtausends n.Chr. derartige Konfigurationen, wobei es sich bei den Adoranten meist um Stifter der Ikone handelt. So könnten sich die acht Adorantenfiguren auf dieser Malerei auf die Person ihres Stifters oder ihrer Stifterin beziehen und die achtfache Wiederholung die Anrufung der Acht Großen Bodhisattvas veranschaulichen, deren besonderer Schutz mit dieser kostbaren Werkspende erlangt werden sollte.

Dass eine solche Darstellung in der mittleren Ming-Zeit kein Einzelfall war, belegt die Existenz einer bisher von der Fachwelt unbemerkten, aber bemerkenswerten Malerei auf Seide (139,5 x 81 cm) im Special Japanese Fund (Inv. Nr. 06.1902) des Boston Museum of Fine Arts, wo sie bisher ins 16. Jahrhundert datiert wird (Abb. 13). Seitlich neben der zentralen Figur eines Bodhisattvas sind am rechten und linken Bildrand in acht kreisrunden Medaillons die gleichen Figurenpaaren in strahlendem Weiß zu sehen, zwar nicht zum Bildinneren sondern nach außen gewandt, aber in ähnlicher Haltung, ähnlichem Dhoṭi und mit ähnlichem Schmuck. Obwohl diese Bildrolle keinerlei Inschrift trägt, kann aus stilistischen Gründen kein Zweifel an ihrer chinesischen Provenienz bestehen, die auch in der Ikonographie Bestätigung findet. Dargestellt ist Bodhisattva Guanyin 觀音 in elfköpfiger Manifestation und mit tausend Händen, deren oberste ein Bildnis des Buddha Amitābha hoch über das Haupt heben. Diese umstrahlt vom Vollmond meditierende Bodhisattva-Gestalt wird in China besonders verehrt und füllt hier von einem voll erblühten Lotos auf einem Thronaltar getragen fast die gesamte Breite der Schaufläche. Über ihr schweben zwei himmlische Genien aus den Wolken herab, die Schalen für das Blumenopfer in Händen tragen. Unten vor dem Thron stehen in stark verkleinertem Maßstab zwei im chinesischen Buddhismus populäre Wächtergottheiten in Gestalt eines Generals mit Helm und Panzer: links der kraftstrotzende Beschützer Vajrapaṇi mit grimmig funkelnden Augen und wildem Bart, sein mächtiges Zeremonialschwert drohend erhoben, rechts General Weituo, ein jung verstorbener Heerführer, der ins Pantheon erhoben wurde und mit gefalteten Händen sein Kampfschwert quer über den Armen trägt. Beide Gottheiten verkörpern die Ideale, die sich nach chinesischer Tradition in einem siegreichen Charakter verbinden, Körperkraft und innere Güte. Ihre dynamische Darstellung hier in prachtvollen Rüstungen über flatternden Seidengewändern und Schärpen in detailreicher, feiner Zeichnung und bunter Farbigkeit mit Verwendung von Gold erinnert an bekannte 1454 datierte Seidengemälde aus einem Bildrollen-Satz zum *shuilu*-Ritus (*shuiluzhai* 水陸齋), die in den kaiserlichen Werkstätten unter Aufsicht der Eunuchen Shang Yi und Wang Qin entstanden.[37]

---

[35] Huntington – Huntington 1990, Taf. 55.

[36] Ibid., Taf. 5.

[37] Toyka 2014, Bd. 2, Taf. 43, 51, 61, 63, 65, 134.

Darüber hinaus sind stilistische Verbindungen zur monumentalen Bodhisattva-Triade auf den Wandgemälden im Sanktuarium des Fahai si erkennbar, die verwandte Gesichtszüge zeigt, ähnliche Gewandmuster und Schmuckformen sowie den charakteristischen überlangen kleinen Finger. Nicht zuletzt ist dort wie hier die Farbpalette von dunklen bis hellen Rot- und Rosatönen neben Dunkelgrün und Dunkelblau bestimmt zu Gold und Weiß als Kontrastfarben. Die auf dem Hauptaltar des Fahai si einst verehrten Buddhas der drei Zeitalter (Sanshi Fo) schweben auf dem Bostoner Seidengemälde hoch oben im Himmel: im Zentrum Buddha Śākyamuni, rechts neben ihm der zukünftige Buddha Maitreya und links Buddha Kaśyapa des vergangenen Zeitalters. Unverkennbar sind auch stilistische Querverbindungen vom Gesicht der Bostoner Guanyin mit hoher Stirn, doppelt gelocktem Haaransatz, lang und schmal gezogenen Augen, am Nasenansatz besonders hoch gebogenen Brauen und einem winzigen Kirschmund zum Antlitz von Ṣaḍakṣari Lokeśvara auf dem Vajradhara-Maṇḍala. Hier wie dort akzentuieren die seitlich hinabfallenden Haarsträhnen den Oberkörper mit breiten Schultern und kräftigen Armen, der sich der Taille zu stark verjüngt. Die Analyse der Bostoner Malerei weist eindeutig darauf hin, dass sie um die Mitte des 15. Jahrhunderts am Kaiserhof der Ming im direkten Umfeld der Meister des Fahai si und mit großer Wahrscheinlichkeit von Wang Fuqing, Wang Shu oder ihren Schülern geschaffen wurde. Wie an anderer Stelle ausgeführt, lassen sich nun bislang anonyme exquisite Gemälde auf Seide wie das Bostoner Stück ohne jeden Zweifel den Meistern dieser Werkstatt zuordnen.[38]

Während die besagte Bostoner Bildrolle ebenso wie die Wandgemälde des Fahai si das Pantheon auf den Wolken des Universums zeigen, ist der Bildraum des Vajradhara-Maṇḍala vollständig mit Lotosranken in elegant geschwungener Zeichnung in Gold auf Grün ausgefüllt. Ungewöhnlich dabei ist vor allem die Gestaltung der Lotosblüten, auf denen die drei in Größe und Ausführung prominent hervorgehobenen Hauptikonen thronen: im Lotossitz meditierend auf einem weiß-rot gemusterten Teppich über einem dunkelgrünen Kissen, das über den hauchfein in Gold gezeichneten, aufgerichteten Samenfäden der Lotosblüten schwebt. Für die überaus dekorative Stilisierung der großen Blüten in mehreren Blattschichten, mit kontrastierenden Konturen, delikaten Farbabstufungen und Hell-Dunkel-Schattierungen der Rosapalette sind Vergleichsbeispiele in der chinesischen Malerei bislang nicht bekannt. Doch zeigt der Lotossockel eines stehenden Buddha Śākyamuni in der Sammlung des British Museum (Höhe 12 7/10 inches, Inv. Nr. 1942, 4-17.I) mit der Inschrift „Hergestellt im 4. Jahr (der Ära) Chenghua" (i.e., 1468) eine ähnliche musterhaft aufgebrochene Form der obersten Blattschicht.[39] Dieser elf Jahre vor der Vajradhara Thanka entstandenen Metallskulptur kommt auch die Gestaltung des Lotosthrones einer bronzenen Śākyamuni-Statue nahe, die laut Inschrift im 4. Jahr der Ära Zhengtong 正統 (i.e.,

---

[38] Toyka 2014, Bd. 2, Taf. 132, Darstellung des Moxishouluo 魔醯首羅 (Maheśvara) im Capital Museum, Beijing.

[39] Jin Shen 1994, S. 419, Abb. 323.

1439) gestiftet wurde.[40] Ansätze ähnlicher stilistischer Formulierung finden sich darüber hinaus auf einigen sino-tibetischen Skulpturen mit chinesischen Datierungen der Yongle 永樂 und Xuande 宣德 -Perioden.[41] Es ist also anzunehmen, dass sich in den höfischen Werkstätten in Beijing, die seit dem ersten Viertel des 15. Jahrhunderts in zunehmenden Maße buddhistische Ikonen herstellten, nicht nur generell eine zunehmend dekorative Gestaltung der Lotossockel entwickelte, sondern diese ähnlich wie die immer üppiger verzierten Darstellungen von Thronaltären zugleich eine hierarchische Prominenz von Figuren im Ensemble der himmlischen Heerscharen zum Ausdruck bringen sollte.

Die Idee, buddhistische Gottheiten nicht nur auf einzelnen Lotosblüten als Symbol für den Buddha und seine Lehre darzustellen sondern diese Blüten durch ein Rankenwerk untereinander zu verbinden, ist mit der Verbreitung der Buddha-Legenden seit der formativen Phase buddhistischer Kunst dokumentiert. Wie viele andere buddhistische Bildmotive erfuhr die Lotosranke über Jahrhunderte hinweg infolge der buddhistischen Missionierung Zentral- und Ostasiens vielfältige Abwandlungen. Seit rund Mitte des 1. Jahrtausends entstanden in Ostasien buddhistische Konfigurationen auf Lotosblüten mit ausgeprägten Stielen, die dreidimensional, im Relief, graviert oder in kombinierter Technik miteinander verbunden sind. Eines der frühesten Beispiele ist die berühmte Amitābha Triade der Hakuhō (645–710) Periode im Schrein der Dame Tachibana, der im Hōriyuji bei Nara erhalten ist. Auch in der chinesischen Skulptur und Malerei der Tang-Zeit sind zahlreiche Beispiele überliefert. Für die hier behandelte Vajradhara-Thangka ist ein im Museum für Ostasiatische Kunst, Köln, aufbewahrtes Metallfragment des 7./8. Jahrhunderts besonders aufschlussreich, das die Sieben Buddhas des vergangenen Weltzeitalters je auf einer Lotosblüte inmitten dynamisch ondulierender Blattranken zeigt, deren Stiele in einen Zapfen zusammenlaufen, der wiederum in den Kopf einer Bodhisattva-Figur zu stecken war. Am Beispiel einer tangzeitlichen Standfigur des Avalokeśvara (Höhe 21,5 cm) im City Art Museum, St. Louis ist zu sehen, wie aus dem Kopf ein solches Rankenwerk mit kleineren Buddha-Figuren kronenförmig herauswächst, als ob der Bodhisattva das Wesen der Buddhas in sich aufgenommen habe und wieder ausströme.[42]

Auch in der buddhistischen Kunst Tibets finden sich buddhistische Sakralgestalten im Lotosrankenwerk, so z.B. auf einer Thangka mit dem Götterpaar Saṃvara und Vajravārāhī zwischen lebensgroßen Fußabdrücken vermutlich des heiligen Lama Tang-pa chen-po (1142–1210), der 1180 das Kloster sTag-lung gründete.[43] Die zentrale Darstellung wird gerahmt von kleineren Figuren des Buddha Śākyamuni, Bodhisattva Avalokiteśvara sowie verschiedener Lamas und

---

[40] Barrett 1957, S. 94, Abb. 11.

[41] Vgl. eine Skulptur des Amitāyus mit Datierungsinschrift der Xuande-Ära (1426–1435) in der Sammlung des Pekinger Palastmuseums, Jin Shen 1994, S. 416, Abb. 320.

[42] Munsterberg 1967, S. 61-62 und S. 79, Taf. 36.

[43] Béguin 1990, S. 20, Nr. 2, Taf. 2, bezieht sich *ibid.* auf eine Deutung von Heather Stoddard-Karmay.

Schutzgottheiten, die je wie ein Medaillon eingefasst sind von kräftigen Lotosstielen, zwischen denen kleine weiße Blüten erscheinen. Die 1427 vollendeten Wandgemälde im Stupa von Gyantse, Zentraltibet, zeigen mehrere Varianten von Lotosranken mit kleinen eingestreuten Blüten und Knospen, z.B. als Umrahmung von Buddha Vajrasattva und Buddha Amoghasiddhi in Kapelle 3. Über der Eingangstür von Kapelle 2/14 sind oberhalb eines Textbandes mit Sanskrit-Silben einige auf Lotosblüten thronende Pancarakṣas von Rankenwerk umgeben zu sehen.[44] Im Gegensatz zu solchen Beispielen aber lässt das Vajradhara Maṇḍala die eingestreuten Lotosblüten besonders wirkungsvoll zwischen und auf den Ranken hervortreten, sei es in Aufsicht mit weit geöffnetem Blütenkranz oder im Profil als Knospen. Als sei dies alles nicht genug des Dekors, entfalten die Knospen mit hellgrünen und hellblauen Blättchen eine fast musterhafte Ornamentik. Sie wirken in hellen und dunklen Rosatönen, mit weißen Konturen oder ganz in Deckweiß wie rhythmische Lichtakzente in einem dunklen, mit Goldfäden durchwirkten Rankenteppich. Tatsächlich lassen diese musterhaften Strukturen an einen kostbar gemusterten Gewandstoff denken. Und so erstaunt es kaum, dass ein Wandgemälde im Fahai si den Bodhisattva Samantabhadra in einem roten Seidenrock mit genau diesem in Gold eingewirkten Lotosrankenmuster zeigt.[45] Solche Textilien gehörten vermutlich um die Mitte des 15. Jahrhunderts in Beijing zum Feinsten, was an edlen Stoffen für höfische Gewänder gewebt wurde. Doch erfreute sich das Lotosrankenmotiv auch im Kunsthandwerk großer Beliebtheit. Ein ursprünglich wohl zu einem größeren Altaraufsatz gehörendes blau-weißes Räuchergefäß aus Porzellan der kaiserlichen Sammlung des Nationalen Palastmuseums in Taibei zeigt Lotosranken derselben Art in Kobaltblau unter der Glasur fortlaufend um die gesamte Wandung, auf der auch eine Datierung in die Ära Xuande (1427-1436) steht.

In der hier behandelten Thangka (Abb. 2) umrankt der Lotos jedoch nicht nur die Sakralgestalten, sondern auch diverse Symbole des Glaubens und der Macht, die aus dem buddhistischen Motivkanon mehr oder weniger bekannt, jedoch in dieser Kombination höchst ungewöhnlich sind. Bei genauem Hinsehen sind in den Vajradhara umgebenden Ranken an gleicher Stelle wie in den Nairātmyā umgebenden Ranken auf den Maṇḍalas in Boston, London und Salem dreizehn gegenständliche Motive auf kleinen Lotosblüten erkennbar, von denen die meisten zu den volkstümlichen Acht Symbolen des Buddhismus zählen: beginnend neben der Ḍākinī im Bildzentrum unter Vajradhara nach rechts aufwärts sind dies der Baldachin, die Schneckenmuschel, das achtspeichige Rad der Lehre und oben rechts über dem Kopf des Buddha eine geöffnete Lotosblüte. Gegenüber, von der zentralen Ḍākinī-Figur nach links aufwärts befindet sich der endlose Knoten, ein Paar Fische und darüber die Schatzvase. Das in dieser Aufzählung fehlende Siegeszeichen, Symbol für den Sieg des Buddhismus über die Unwissenheit der Welt, findet sich hier nicht auf den ersten Blick, was damit zusammenhängen mag, dass

---

[44] Lo Bue – Ricca 1990, S. 215, Taf. 66.
[45] Toyka 2014, Bd. 2, Taf. 74.

sich in China keine bestimmte Funktion dieses Symbols im buddhistischen Ritus tradiert zu haben scheint. Stattdessen haben sich von seiner ursprünglich schmalen zylindrischen Grundform verschiedene Varianten entwickelt, von denen hier aber keine zu sehen ist.

Interessant erscheint daher ein Hinweis von Loden Sherab Dagyab Rinpoche, wonach dem Siegeszeichen (*rgyal-mtshan*) – das in der klassischen tibetischen Literatur nicht behandelt wird – auch außerhalb der Symbolgruppe verschiedene Bedeutungen zukamen.[46] Es hing beispielsweise in der Hauptversammlungshalle eines Klosters am zentralen Punkt der Decke oder stand genau darüber außen auf dem Dach einer Tempelhalle oder eines Gebäudes, in dem ein vollständiger kanonischer Text bewahrt wurde. Eine vergleichbare Hinweisfunktion könnte sich im hier behandelten Gemälde andeuten: über der Spitze von Vajradharas Mandorla ist ein kleiner Sockel mit einem zylindrischen Aufsatz zu sehen, aus dem eben jene Lotosranke sprießt, deren Blüte im Zentrum der obersten Figurenreihe Buddha Vairocana trägt: die Verkörperung aller Kräfte in der östlichen Sphäre des Universums. In den Nairātmyā-Maṇḍalas ist an derselben Stelle ein ganz ähnliches Motiv dargestellt, aus dem die Lotosranke entspringt, die Buddha Vajradhara im Zentrum der obersten Reihe trägt. Wenn man dieses zylindrische Motiv als eine Variante des alten „Siegeszeichens" versteht und als Hinweis auf die höchste Divinität in der speziellen Lehrtradition dieses Maṇḍala (gedacht an oberster Position im Universum), wäre darin für die nach Orientierung suchenden Gläubigen ein genereller Grundsatz der buddhistischen Lehrtradition symbolisiert: Nur die Nachfolge der obersten Lehr-Autorität verleiht den wahren „Sieg" der Erkenntnis, prominent verkörpert durch die in der Spitze der zentralen Triade des betrachteten Maṇḍala dargestellten Hauptgottheit. Letztere ist darüber hinaus hier mit noch weiteren ungewöhnlichen Bildzeichen umgeben, denn die verbleibenden fünf scheinen aus traditionellen tibetischen und chinesischen Symbolgruppen gemischt zu sein. So sind links vom „Siegeszeichen" über Vajradhara von den in Tibet bekannten „Fünf Qualitäten des Genusses" (*hDod-yon sNa-lNga*) für den Geruchssinn eine Duftschale in Form einer liegenden Muschel und für den Geschmackssinn drei wohlschmeckende Früchte zu erkennen. Unten rechts von Vajradhara ist zwischen Schneckenmuschel und Baldachin das Symbol für den Tastsinn, kostbarer Stoff, um eine Schale drapiert zu finden. Die beiden übrigen Symbole für Gehör (Laute oder Klangplatten) und Sehkraft (Spiegel) fehlen. Stattdessen ist oben rechts über Vajradhara in Gold gezeichnet eine Koralle in Form einer Hand zu sehen – nach chinesischer Tradition das Symbol für gute Regentschaft eines Königs oder einer Königin – und links unter der Schale mit Früchten das von Strahlen umgebene Horn eines Einhorns – Symbol für das unbesiegbare Reittier eines siegreichen Herrschers. Koralle und Horn gehören zu Chinas berühmten „Sieben Juwelen" (*qibao* 七寶), die auch im buddhistischen Motivschatz Tibets Verbreitung fanden und als Opfergaben häufig auf Thangkas ihren Platz haben.[47] Im vorliegenden Falle könnte die Vermischung der Symbol-

---

[46] Dagyab 1992, S. 42-46.
[47] *Ibid.*, S. 125.

gruppen als Hinweis auf die Person des Stifters gemeint sein, auf die Intention seiner Stiftung oder die rituelle Funktion des Maṇḍala selbst. Diese Form der „interkulturellen" Symbolsprache mag zudem eine der religiösen Kunst jener Zeit erlaubte Offenheit reflektieren.

Vergleicht man die Nairātmyā-Maṇḍalas mit dem Vajradhara-Gemälde im Hinblick auf die Integration fremdländischer Elemente, so zeigt letzteres einige Motive, die bei den Nairātmyā-Maṇḍalas gar nicht vorkommen, aber einen direkten Bezug zur tibetischen Malerei der Zeit offenbaren, wie die Stolas aus grüner Seide mit goldenen Muster, die zwei hinter den Schultern der Hauptfiguren lanzettförmig von der Rückenlehne abstehenden kleinen weißen Zierelemente[48] und die Ränder der Strahlenmandorlas mit blattförmigen, in einer Folge von Blau, Rot, Grün, Rot gefüllten Aussparungen, die sich überall in den Wandgemälden des Stūpa von Gyantse finden.[49] Verbindungen zur nepalesischen Metallkunst wurden bereits im Kontext der in Gold gezeichneten filigranen Ornamentik angesprochen. Möglicherweise ebenfalls nepalesisch inspiriert ist die Musterung des Bildrandes bei den 1479 datierten Maṇḍalas: Sie sind alle auf dunkelrotem Grund innen mit drei parallelen goldenen Linien umrandet und außen mit schwarz aufgemalten Rauten, die beim Vajradhara-Thangka jede noch das Attribut der Hauptgottheit, ein goldenes Doppelvajra, tragen. Rautenmuster kommen gelegentlich in der nepalesischen Malerei wie z.B. auf einem 1403 datierten Thangka mit der Göttin Vasudhārā und Begleitern (86,4 x 73,7 cm, 34 x 29 inches) der Sammlung Zimmermann als Umrandung bzw. Hintergrund einzelner Bildsektionen vor.[50] Rautenfriese fanden in der chinesischen Malerei keinen nachhaltigen Eingang, lassen sich aber in der Gefäßkunst der Ära Xuande belegen, als ausländische Motive im Porzellandekor beliebt waren. Dies bezeugt eine überraschend „modern" wirkende in ihrer Bemalung heute einmalige Deckeldose in der Sammlung des Palastmuseums Taibei. Sie zeigt in Kobaltblau auf Weiß um die bauchige Wandung verlaufend einen breiten Fries aus Ranken, der eingefasst ist mit einem Rautenmuster, bei dem Partien aus dichtem Liniengitter und großflächige Dreiecke mit Punkten in der Mitte alternieren – ein Muster, das der ca. 50 Jahre später entstanden Umrandung aus Rauten mit Punkten und Vajra hier behandelten Maṇḍala frappierend ähnlich ist.[51]

Der Rautenrand der 1479 datierten Maṇḍalas trägt unten in der Mitte ihre Datierung im Duktus der Standardschrift, jedes Zeichen in Gold exakt in einer Raute, wie auf dem Vajradhara-Thangka besonders klar zu erkennen (Abb. 14). Die Inschrift lautet wie auch auf den Nairātmyā-Maṇḍala: „Am 15. Tag des 4. Monats im 15. Jahr (der Ära) Chenghua der Großen Ming(-Dynastie) gestiftet." Der 15. Tag ist jener Vollmondtag, an dem buddhistische Klostergemeinschaften traditionell den Geburtstag des Buddha begehen, und auffallend ist hier, dass auch

---

[48] Lo Bue – Ricca 1990, Mahāvairocana-Darstellung in Tempel 3 E, Taf. 4.

[49] *Ibid.*, Vairocana, Kapelle 3 EB, Taf. 14, vgl. auch Taf. 7-10.

[50] Pal 1991, S. 72, Nr. 34, Taf. 34.

[51] Kunst- und Ausstellungshalle der Bundesrepublik Deutschland 2003, S. 310, Abb. 221.

die Jahreszählung innerhalb der Regierungsperiode die Zahl 15 wiederholt. Dahinter darf ein günstiges Omen im Zuge einer astrologischen Divination vermutet werden. Ein weiterer Grund für die Datierung mag im Zusammenhang mit der Stiftung der Gemälde gelegen haben, worauf die Formulierung der Inschrift einen wichtigen Hinweis gibt: Das letzte Schriftzeichen *shi* 施 bedeutet „schenken", „stiften", „gewähren" und drückt die Erteilung einer großen Gunst durch hochgestellte Persönlichkeiten aus. Der Begriff unterscheidet sich diametral vom Schriftzeichen *zao* 造 für „hergestellt", das in den meisten Inschriften buddhistischer Ikonen Verwendung findet, die Stifter nennen, die um ihres oder eines anderen Seelenheils willen eine Ikone in Auftrag gaben. Bei den 1479 datierten Thangkas klingt an, dass es sich um eine herausragende Stifterpersönlichkeit gehandelt haben muss – was auch die exquisite Qualität und großzügige Verwendung von Gold insbesondere des Vajradhara-Maṇḍala erklären würde. Vieles spricht dafür, dass es sich um eine besondere Stiftung des Kaiserhofes gehandelt haben muss, wahrscheinlich sogar im Auftrag des Kaisers oder der Kaiserin selbst. Darauf deuten Details wie die acht Darstellungen der segnenden Bodhisattvas und die beiden Sinnbilder für Herrscherin und Herrscher im Symbol-Ensemble um Vajradharas Haupt. Dafür spricht auch, dass die Herstellung der Gemälde mit dem Einsatz erheblicher finanzieller Mittel verbunden gewesen sein muss, denn es handelte sich um einen Gemäldesatz monumentalen Charakters, der vielleicht noch weitere Stücke umfasste. Zweifellos dachte man einem solchen Stiftungsauftrag speziell im Kontext der chinesisch-tibetischen Beziehungen eine besonders segenspendende Wirkung zu, die zugleich eine wichtige religionspolitische Dimension hatte im Sinne eines öffentlichen Bedeutungszuwachses für diejenige religiöse Einrichtung, der diese Stiftung zu Gute kam.

Es spricht vieles dafür, dass die 1479 entstandenen Thangkas als Stiftung des Kaiserhauses der Chenghua-Ära für das Kloster mit den engsten Beziehungen zur tibetisch-buddhistischen Kirche in der Hauptstadt, dem Huguo Longshan si, bestimmt waren, auch wenn nicht völlig ausgeschlossen werden kann, dass spätere Stücke, von denen wie im Falle der Ḍākinī-Maṇḍala mehrere Varianten geschaffen wurden, auch dem in den 1513 datierten Inschriften genannten Landesbeschützende Kloster zum Schutz des Friedens, Huguo Bao'an si 護國保安寺 oder anderen Institutionen geschenkt wurden. Ein solcher hochoffizieller Stiftungsakt wäre jedoch für den Huguo Longshan si auch mit Blick auf die seit Anfang des 15. Jahrhunderts von den Ming-Herrschern praktizierte Religionspolitik gegenüber Tibet am stimmigsten. Ihm wäre neben der religiösen auch eine machtpolitische Symbolkraft in Bezug auf die Erstarkung des Han-Reiches nach der Fremdherrschaft der Mongolen zugekommen. Kubilai Khan, der 1270 durch den Śakyapa-Lama 'Phagspa zum Buddhismus tibetischer Schule bekehrt worden war, gründete bereits in 1285, wenige Jahre nach dem Sieg über China (1279), ein Kloster nördlich von Beijing, nannte es bezogen auf das von ihm errichtete politische Herrschaftsgebiet Chongguo si 崇國寺 („Kloster der Verehrung des Reiches") und stellte es unter die Verwaltung des Śaskyapa-Ordens des tibetischen Buddhismus.

Es wurde nach Gründung der Ming-Dynastie vom Herrscher der Ära Xuande 1425 umbenannt in „Kloster vom Drachenberg" (Longshan si 龍山寺), und der Herrscher der Ära Chenghua verlieh 1472 den Ehrentitel „Landesbeschützendes Kloster vom Drachenberg" (Huguo Longshan si). Dort residierten bis mindestens 1520 die aus Tibet nach Beijing reisenden und dort meist über mehrere Jahre lebenden Großlamas und Mönche. Das Kloster war zugleich Sitz des Amtes für buddhistische Religion (Senglou si 僧樓寺) und diente hochrangigen Kirchenfürsten tibetischer Delegationen als offizieller temporärer Amtssitz. Die engen Beziehungen des Han-chinesischen Hofes zum tibetischen Buddhismus unter dem Mäzenatentum der Herrscher im 15. Jahrhundert sind Gegenstand zahlreicher Untersuchungen und inzwischen vielfach belegt. Dass prominente Persönlichkeiten bei Hofe Anhänger oder Förderer dieser religiösen Schulrichtung waren, geht auch aus den Wandgemälden und Inschriften im Fahai si hervor, zu dessen 1443 gegründeter Mönchsgemeinschaft neben Han-Chinesen auch Tibeter gehörten. Zu den Sponsoren dieser Klostergründung zählten ranghohe Patriarchen der tibetischen Kirche und Vertreter der kaiserlichen Regierung wie Hu Ying 胡濙 (1375–1463), Minister für Ritenwesen, der während der Regierungsperioden Xuande und Zhengtong auch kaiserlicher Beauftragter für die Region Tibet war.[52] In diesem Amt war er u.a. zuständig für die statusgerechte Unterbringung hoher tibetischer Kirchenvertreter und Lamas, die seit dem Umzug des Hofes aus Nanjing in immer größerer Zahl nach Beijing kamen, während ihres Aufenthaltes in der Hauptstadt. Dort lebten laut Huang Hao bereits 1436 in vier Klöstern 450 tibetische Mönche. Laut *Mingshilu* 明實錄 soll der Kaiser daraufhin dem Patriarchen Shijia Yeshi 釋迦也失 (i.e., Shākya ye-shes) und anderen „Westlichen Söhnen des Buddha vom 2. Grade" kundgetan haben, dass ihnen die Rückkehr in die Heimat jederzeit frei stehe (!), wenngleich sie auf Wunsch auch weiter in den prächtigen Tempeln der Hauptstadt verweilen könnten, wozu ebenfalls der damalige Longshan si gehört haben muss. Den offiziellen Gesten der Verbundenheit tat der Wink mit dem kaiserlichen Zaunpfahl offenbar aber keinen Abbruch, denn Kaiser Xianzong 憲宗 der Chenghua-Ära schenkte 1481 dem bis Ende des 15. Jahrhunderts vom Śakya-pa Orden geführten Wenshu si 文殊寺 (Kloster des Mañuśrī) auf dem Berg Wutai 五臺 in Shanxi insgesamt 80 buddhistische Bildrollen.[53] Diese Gemälde dürften Sujets des tibetischen Buddhismus dargestellt haben, und es kann nicht ausgeschlossen werden, dass die 1479 datierten Thangkas dazu gehörten – ebenso wenig, dass um 1480 andere Klöster des tibetischen Buddhismus außerhalb der Hauptstadt wie der Qutan si 瞿曇寺 am Kokonor als Empfänger einer repräsentativen kaiserlichen Stiftung in Frage kamen. Der oben erwähnte 1911 dokumentierte Ankauf des im Victoria and Albert Museum bewahrten Nairātmyā-Thangka im Huang si 黃寺 (Gelber Tempel) – bis heute Residenz des Panchen Lama in Beijing, die 1652 für den inzwischen erstarkten dGelugpa-Orden des tibetischen Buddhismus, dem der Qing-Hof nahestand, erbaut wurde –

---

[52] Toyka 2014, Bd. 1, III.7.
[53] Huang Hao 1987, S. 63 und Fn. 4, 5.

weist allerdings eine andere Spur.⁵⁴ Die kostbaren Thangkas wurden mit großer Wahrscheinlichkeit aus dem Huguo Longshan si zur Einweihung in den unweit gelegenen Huang si verbracht, dessen Rolle in der späteren Ming-Zeit wenig erforscht ist und vermutlich an Bedeutung verlor. So ist über den Verbleib des Thangka-Satzes bis zum Ende des Kaiserreiches nichts weiter bekannt, wohl aber, dass der Huguo Longshan si 1919 in Trümmern lag.⁵⁵

Die Frage nach dem konkreten Anlass der Stiftung bleibt unklar, bis die Auswertung weiterer Quellen zur Geschichte chinesischer Tempel im 15. Jahrhundert und die Umstände ihrer Gründungen Aufschluss gibt. Grundsätzlich mag eine solch wertvolle Gabe ebenso im Zusammenhang mit einem baulichen wie mit einem politischen oder persönlichen Datum in Zusammenhang stehen. Angenommen, Kaiser Xianzong der Chenghua-Ära stiftete die Gemälde dem Huguo Longshan si, so könnte der Anlass der Besuch eines führenden tibetischen Kirchenfürsten gewesen sein, der üblicherweise dem Hof eine Fülle von Gastgeschenken mitbrachte, über die in früheren chinesischen Quellen einiges verzeichnet ist. Leider ist für das Jahr 1479 kein Ereignis bekannt wie das aus dem Jahr 1458, als laut *Dijing jingwu lüe* 帝京景物略 der Großlama (*da lama* 大辣麻) Sangkebala 桑渴巴辣 und der Große Reichspräzeptor (*da guoshi* 大國師) Zhiguangong 智光功 in Beijing verweilt haben sollen.⁵⁶ Es ist aber mit Blick auf den oben erwähnten Zustrom tibetischer Mönche sehr wahrscheinlich, dass der Huguo Longshan si 1472 mit dem Ehrentitel „Reichsbeschützendes" Kloster auch die Erlaubnis für bauliche Erweiterungen erhielt. Vermutlich wurden dem Bedarf entsprechend sukzessive neue Gebäude errichtet, eingeweiht und mit Ikonen ausgestattet – diese Reihenfolge geht zumindest aus der Gründungsgeschichte des Fahai si hervor, der 1443 eingeweiht wurde aber erst 1444 die Fertigstellung durch Künstler und Handwerker verzeichnet. So könnte für die erste nach 1472 neu errichtete Tempelhalle des Huguo Longshan si das 1474 datierte Thangka des Musée Guimet gestiftet worden sein und die 1477 und 1478 datierten Thangkas nach Fertigstellung weiterer Bauten.

Die vier Thangkas aus dem Jahr 1479 könnten anschließend in Auftrag gegeben worden sein, um als geschlossener Satz den Abschluss aller baulichen Ergänzungen zu würdigen und waren vermutlich zur Verehrung im Sanktuarium der Klosteranlage bestimmt. Dass alle vier Gemälde außer der Ikonographie der Hauptfiguren kaum voneinander abweichen, vielmehr in der Anzahl, Komposition und Darstellung der übrigen Figuren sowie in Material, Größe, Farbpalette und Goldfassung, im Malstil, in der dekorativen Gestaltung, in der Umrandung und der Formulierung der Inschrift übereinstimmen, liefert gute Gründe für eine solche Annahme, ebenso wie die Tatsache, dass keines der anderen bekannten Thangkas mehr als einmal erhalten ist. Es ist allerdings anzunehmen, dass ursprünglich vier Nairātmyā-Maṇḍalas geschaffen wurden mit dem Vajradhara-

---

⁵⁴ Toyka-Fuong 2002, S. 294-295.
⁵⁵ Bredon 1920, resümiert bei Kidd 1975a, S. 58.
⁵⁶ Liu Tong – Yu Yizheng 1992, S. 33.

Maṇḍala als zentralem Bildnis des Satzes. Eine solche Konfiguration aus fünf Teilen würde der obersten Reihe auf den Nairātmyā-Maṇḍalas entsprechen, wo Buddha Vajradhara rechts und links von je zwei Ḍākiṇī flankiert ist. Allerdings lässt das Auftauchen eines stark beschädigten weiteren Maṇḍalas in gleicher Größe und Ausführung, mit exakt demselben chinesischen Datum nicht ausschließen, dass seinerzeit ein noch größerer Gemäldesatz geschaffen wurde. Es zeigt an den Positionen der drei Manifestationen der Göttin Nairātmyā drei tantrische Schutzgottheiten in Umarmung mit ihren Partnerinnen (Tib. *yabyum*): Oben in der Spitze des Maṇḍalas erscheint Nairātmyā als Partnerin des Hevajra, zu Füßen des Paares links unten der stierköpfige Yamantaka mit Vajravetali und rechts unten Paramasukha-Saṃvara mit seiner Partnerin, der Himmelswandlerin Vajravāhārī.[57]

Ein solch monumentaler Bildsatz könnte im Zusammenhang mit der oben erwähnten Passage im *Dijing jingwu lüe* entstanden sein, wonach 1512 das Landesbeschützende Kloster vom Drachenberg (Huguo Longshan si) für den Aufenthalt des Großen Glückseligen Gesetzeskönigs Bandan Rinpoche und des Großen Erleuchteten Gesetzeskönigs Zhexiao zangbu 着肖藏卜 erweitert wurde bis auf einen gesamten Bestand von drei Tempelhallen auf der zentralen Achse, je vier an beiden Seiten, sowie einer weiteren Tempelhalle im hinteren Teil.[58] Für die darauf folgende feierliche Einweihung solcher Erweiterungsbauten könnten die mit chinesischen Inschriften der Jahre 1513 und 1516 datierten Thangkas der Sammlungen Barluzzi und Kidd sowie des California Art Museums und der Nelson Gallery Kansas City vom Großlama in Auftrag gegeben worden sein (siehe auch die „Liste der Gemälde" im Anhang). Ihre Inschriften verwenden bezeichnenderweise nicht das Schriftzeichen *shi*, sondern das Schriftzeichen *zao* für „anfertigen", „herstellen".

Maltechnisch zeigen die mit chinesischen Daten der 1470er Jahre ausgewiesenen Thangkas eine sichtlich bessere zeichnerische Qualität als die später datierten Gemälde und einen mit Ausnahme der 1475 datierten Thangka im Musée Guimet haltbareren Auftrag der Farben. Das Vajradhara-Maṇḍala zeichnet sich durch eine vergleichsweise feinere Linienführung und Applikation der Farben bis ins Detail aus und verkörpert auch durch die extensive und sorgfältige Verwendung von Gold den künstlerisch-handwerklichen Höhepunkt. Vor allem die drei Hauptikonen zeigen in den feinen Konturlinien sowie den Binnenlinien wie Faltenstrukturen oder Ornamentik einen gleichmäßig straffen Duktus und kontinuierlich fließenden Verlauf. Eine ähnliche Qualität ist auch in der Darstellung der Göttin Kurukulle auf den Nairātmyā-Maṇḍala festzustellen, wo allerdings insgesamt die Linienführung etwas ungenauer ist und kleine Ausrutscher vorkommen. Auch im Vajradhara-Maṇḍala gibt es vereinzelt solche Unregelmäßigkeiten und Deformationen in kleinen Details, doch wurde dort sorgfältig retouchiert, wo es wichtig erschien, z.B. in der Figur des weißen Buddha Vairocana in der Mitte der obers-

---

[57] *Christie's New York: Indian and Southeast Asian Art Including 20th Century Indian Paintings*, 2000, S. 64-65, Nr. 59.

[58] Liu Tong – Yu Yizheng 1992, S. 33, siehe auch oben Fn. 9.

ten Figurenreihe. Interessant für die Geschichte der Maltechnik solcher Thangkas aber sind die an vielen Stellen zu entdeckenden Vorzeichnungen. Besonders unter der weißen Gesichtsfläche von Avalokiteśvara schimmern schwarz skizzierende Linien durch. Darüber weichen die schwarzen Linien der Hauptzeichnung stellenweise stark ab. Die segnenden Bodhisattvas zeigen z.B. am Hals rot nachgezogene Strukturlinien über der schwarzen Grundlineatur. An vielen Stellen überlagern die farbigen und auch goldenen Flächen die Konturen der Vorzeichnung. Auch die Grundierung scheint je nach der finalen Farbfassung zu variieren: so ist unter den Gewändern der Hauptgottheiten eine rötliche und unter den dunkelfarbig gefassten Körpern nicht selten eine türkisblaue Grundierung zu erkennen. Diese findet sich auch auf dem Nairātmā-Maṇḍala, ebenso die offensichtlich zuletzt aufgetragene und in den Nebenfiguren sichtlich lockerere Goldzeichnung. Die Thangkas mit chinesischen Datierungen bis 1513 zeigen eine insgesamt gröbere handwerkliche Ausführung, flüchtigere Zeichnung und weniger sorgfältigen Farbauftrag.

Stilistisch verweisen sie auf andere Traditionen, die mehr oder weniger deutlich erfassbar bzw. gemischt sind. Die drei 1475, 1477 und 1478 datierten Maṇḍala stehen ikonographisch, farblich und stilistisch unverkennbar in der indisch-nepalesisch geprägten Tradition der Darstellung einer großen zentralen Figur bzw. einer Figurengruppe umgeben von einer deutlich kleineren Konfiguration in separaten Registern entlang den Bildrändern. Dieser Anordnung der Schaufläche entsprechen die Konfigurationen der 1479 datierten Thangkas, zeigen aber abgesehen von dem ungewöhnlich großen Format eine lockere, auf Register verzichtende Komposition, eine andere Farbpalette und sind repräsentativer und dekorativer gestaltet. Bemerkenswert ist auch, dass die Bemalung mit Gold von den 1470er Jahren bis ins frühe 15. Jahrhundert zunehmend sparsamer angewandt wird. Dies steht sicher einerseits mit der finanziellen Investition des Stifters in Zusammenhang, zum anderen aber auch mit einem regressiven Einfluss der tibetischen Stiltraditionen in der buddhistischen Malerei nach dem Ende der Ära Chenghua. Diese Tendenz veranschaulicht ein Gemälde aus der Sammlung John W. Gruber, San Juan, Puerto Rico (heute in der Nelson Gallery, Kansas City), das drei Jahre nach den von Kidd 1975 publizierten, oben bereits erwähnten Maṇḍalas der Sarvābuddha-Ḍākiṇī und des Yamāntaka aus dem Jahr 1513 datiert ist, davon abgesehen aber eine mit jenen identische Inschrift trägt. Das spätere Gemälde reflektiert einen zunehmenden Synkretismus der religiösen Schulen in China.[59] Dargestellt ist nicht mehr ein Maṇḍala, sondern ein beim *shuilu*-Ritus angerufenes Pantheon aus Gottheiten des Buddhismus wie des Daoismus. Im Zentrum ist der im tibetischen wie im chinesischen Buddhismus besonders verehrte König der nördlichen Himmelsregion und des Reichtums, Vaiśravaṇa (rNam-thos-sras), umgeben von einem Gefolge daoistischer Gottheiten mit ihren charakteristischen Insignien und Erscheinungen. Die gesamte Malerei zeigt einen unverkennbar chinesischen Darstellungsstil. Es ist durchaus bemerkenswert, dass laut Inschrift der Stifter, ein hoher tibetischer Geistlicher in China, ein solches Gemälde in Auftrag gab und damit der fortgesetzten Annäherung im Bereich der buddhisti-

---

[59] Kidd 1975b, S. 160.

schen Kunst ein Zeichen setzt, die sich schon in den Wandgemälden des Stūpa von Gyantse durch die Zusammenarbeit von tibetischen, nepalesischen und chinesischen Malern spiegelt.

Wer aber die chinesisch datierten Thangkas tatsächlich schuf, blieb bislang ungeklärt. Die Vermutung Kidds, dass nepalesische oder tibetische Künstler dafür eigens nach Beijing verbracht worden waren,[60] überzeugt nicht. Seit dem Mittelalter bereits waren namhafte Künstler zwischen allen drei Kulturregionen unterwegs, um allein oder zusammen Aufträge potenter Mäzene und Stifter auszuführen. Seitdem der nepalesische Meister Anige im ausgehenden 13. Jahrhundert am mongolischen Kaiserhof wirkte, hinterließ der Einfluss seiner Schule Spuren in der religiösen Kunst Chinas ähnlich wie sich seit dem 15. Jahrhundert der Einfluss chinesischer Kunst in der religiösen Malerei Tibets immer unverkennbarer nachvollziehen lässt. Die drei nach dem chinesischen Kalender auf 1479 datierten Thangkas lassen in der Darstellung der zornvollen Gottheiten, der Kronen und anderer Schmuckelemente Querverbindungen zur nepalesischen und tibetischen Malerei erkennen und zeigen im Falle des Vajradhara-Maṇḍala beim Gesichtstypus der Hauptfiguren und der fein ziselierten Gestaltung der Nimben und Mandorlas manchen Anklang an die Wandgemälde von Gyantse. Bei Betrachtung im Einzelnen aber dominieren die chinesischen Traditionen sowohl in der Gesamtkonzeption der Schaufläche als auch im dekorativen Detail. Betrachtet man das Vajradhara-Maṇḍala, wird gerade in den drei Hauptfiguren jenes Moment der Bewegung spürbar, dass die zeitgenössische buddhistische Malerei Chinas wie ein Leitmotiv durchzieht: die Schärpen schwingen seitlich kräftig aus – während sie in Gyantse ruhig abwärts fließen, die Ranken der Mandorlas wirbeln in rhythmisch strukturierten Kreisen – während in Gyantse solche Flächen in gleichmäßigen Mustern gefüllt sind. Nicht zuletzt das Rankenwerk mit Lotosblüten betont auf allen drei 1479 datierten Maṇḍala in seiner leuchtenden Goldzeichnung und mit strahlend kolorierten Blättern und Blüten eine sanfte Bewegung von nahezu wundersamer Mystik.

Dass die vom Kaiser beauftragten religiösen Maler die besten ihrer Zeit waren und in den höfischen Werkstätten arbeiteten, steht auch beim Anblick des Vajradhara-Maṇḍala außer Zweifel. Es lässt zudem erkennen, dass mehrere Maler daran gearbeitet haben müssen, die sich die Zeichnung der Figuren, des Beiwerkes und die Kolorierung teilten. Deutlich ist das unter anderem an der Darstellung der segnenden Bodhisattvas auf dem Vajradhara-Maṇḍala, denn sie sind am linken Bildrand sichtlich feiner, fließender gemalt als am rechten Bildrand und zeigen einen sichtlich weiblicheren Gesichtstypus. Ähnliche – wenngleich geringe – Abweichungen lassen denselben Schluss für die Nairātmyā-Maṇḍalas zu. Die stilistische Ähnlichkeit mit den früheren und späteren Maṇḍala-Thangkas mit chinesischen Datierungen über mehr als vier Jahrzehnte legt nahe, dass es

---

[60] Kidd 1975a, S. 60. Das unlängst aufgetauchte, ebenfalls 1479 datierte Maṇḍala-Fragment der Triade tantrischer Götterpaare lässt aufgrund der starken Beschädigung erkennen, dass die Grundierung nicht die in Tibet tradierte Rasterzeichnung zur exakten Festlegung von Größen- und Raumrelationen aufweist.

sich nicht um dieselbe Gruppe von Malern handelte, sondern dass sich in den höfischen Werkstätten die Kompetenz tradierte, nach Auftrag und Bedarf verschiedene Stiltraditionen kreativ zu nutzen und zu mischen. Die nachweislichen Stilbezüge zu den Wandgemälden des Fahai si sprechen dafür, dass in den 36 Jahren zwischen 1443 und 1479 eine Gruppe von Künstlern zusammen arbeitete, die vermutlich unter der Leitung besonders talentierter Persönlichkeiten allmählich ihre eigene „Handschrift" entwickelte und über eine Generation hinweg in der religiösen Malerei herausragende künstlerische Höhepunkte erreichte.

Wie die Fallstudie des Fahai si erwies, erreichten die Künstler dieser höfischen Werkstatt nicht nur als Wandmaler ein herausragendes Niveau, sondern schufen auch Meisterwerke im Format portabler Bildrollen. Der seltene Glücksfall ihrer Namensnennung im Fahai si lässt nun auch die Maler der 1479 datierten Maṇḍala aus der traditionellen Anonymität religiöser Malerei treten. Mit großer Wahrscheinlichkeit darf angenommen werden, dass die um die 1. Hälfte des 15. Jhds. am Hofe tätigen Meister des Fahai si, Wan Fuqing 宛福清, Wang Shu 王恕 und ihre Schüler auch verantwortlich waren für die Gestaltung der Maṇḍala-Gemälde mit chinesischen Stiftungsinschriften der 1470er Jahre, insbesondere des hier behandelten Vajradhara-Maṇḍala. Die Tradition ihres Malstils lässt sich bei den Nachfolgern in der Ära Zhengde weiterverfolgen, ohne dass ihr Können erreicht wird. Sie verdienen deshalb einen besonderen Platz in der Geschichte der chinesischen Malerei nicht nur hinsichtlich ihres künstlerisch-handwerklichen Schaffens, sondern auch aufgrund ihres interkulturell orientierten, universell inspirierten Ansatzes, der ihren Werken eine so einmalige Ausstrahlung gibt. Insbesondere das hier vorgestellte Vajradhara-Maṇḍala bezeugt, dass die kosmopolitische Atmosphäre der Metropole Beijing im 15. Jahrhundert aus der Begegnung der Völker und der Mischung der Kulturen eine höchst kreative Inspiration schöpfte, die auf dem Gebiet der Kunst innovative Ideen und wahre schöpferische Glanzleistungen hervorbrachte.

Liste der Gemälde

1475 „Hevajra", Musée des arts asiatiques Guimet, 62 x 47,5 cm, Gouache mit Gold auf präparierter Baumwolle, Inv. Nr. MA 4838

Inschrift in Gold: „Am 2. Tag zu Beginn des 11. Monats im 10. Jahr (der Ära) Chenghua der Großen Ming gestiftet" 大明成化十年十一月初二日施

1477 „Siṃhavaktrā", Victoria and Albert Museum, 61 x 47,5 cm, Gouache mit Gold auf präparierter Baumwolle, erworben Beijing 1907, IS 14-1969

Inschrift in Gold: „Am 2. Tag zu Beginn des 11. Monats im 13. Jahr (der Ära) Chenghua der Großen Ming gestiftet" 大明成化十三年十一月初二日施

1477 „Cakrasamvara", Privatsammlung New York (62,8 x 48,2 cm), Gouache mit Gold auf präparierter Baumwolle (?)

Inschrift in Gold: „Am 2. (?) Tag zu Beginn des 11. (?) Monats im 13. Jahr (der Ära) Chenghua der Großen Ming gestiftet" 大明成化十三年十一月 (?) 初二 (?) 日施

1478 „Mahākāla", Victoria and Albert Museum, London, 63 x 47,5 cm, Gouache mit Gold auf präparierter Baumwolle, erworben in Beijing 1907, IS 15-1969

Inschrift in Gold: „Am 21. Tag des 12. Monats im 13. Jahr (der Ära) Chenghua der Großen Ming gestiftet" 大明成化十三年十二月二十一日施

1479 „Vajradhara Triade mit Mañuśrī und Saḍakṣarilokeśvara", Verbleib unbekannt, 153 x 102 cm, Gouache mit Gold auf präparierter Baumwolle, erworben in Peking um 1910

Inschrift in Gold: „Am 15. Tag des 4. Monats im 15. Jahr (der Ära) Chenghua der Großen Ming gestiftet" 大明成化十五年四月十五日施

1479 „Vajranairatm(y)a", Museum of Fine Arts Boston, 145 x 92,5 cm, Gouache mit Gold auf präparierter Baumwolle, 06.1901

Inschrift in Gold: „Am 15. Tag des 4. Monats im 15. Jahr (der Ära) Chenghua der Großen Ming gestiftet" 大明成化十五年四月十五日施

1479 „Vajranairātmyā", Victoria and Albert Museum, London, 151 x 99,1 cm, Gouache mit Gold auf präparierter Baumwolle, E. 61-1911

Inschrift in Gold: „Am 15. Tag des 4. Monats im 15. Jahr (der Ära) Chenghua der Großen Ming gestiftet" 大明成化十五年四月十五日施

1479 „Vajranairātmyā", Peabody Museum, Salem, 151 x 99,1 cm, Gouache mit Gold auf präparierter Baumwolle, E. 61-1911

Inschrift in Gold: „Am 15. Tag des 4. Monats im 15. Jahr (der Ära) Chenghua der Großen Ming gestiftet" 大明成化十五年四月十五日施

1513 „Sarvabuddhaḍākiṇī", Sammlung David Kidd, 125 x 102 cm, Gouache mit Gold auf präparierter Baumwolle

Inschrift in Gold: „Am 24. Tag des 9. Monats im 7. Jahr (der Ära) Zhengde der Großen Ming nach einem Gelübde des Großen Glückseligen Gesetzeskönigs Lingzhan [i.e. Rinpoche] Bandan (im) Landesbeschützenden Bao'an si geschaffen" 大明正德七年九月二十四日大護國保安寺大慶法王領占班丹发心造 (es folgt die tibetische Übersetzung der Inschrift wie bei Siṃhavaktrā aus der Sammlung Barluzzi)

1513 „Yamāntaka", University of California Art Museum, Los Angeles, 122 x 93 cm, Gouache mit Gold auf präparierter Baumwolle

Inschrift in Gold: „Am 24. Tag des 9. Monats im 7. Jahr (der Ära) Zhengde der Großen Ming nach einem Gelübde des Großen Glückseligen Gesetzeskönigs Lingzhan [i.e. Rinpoche] Bandan (im) Landesbeschützenden Bao'an si geschaffen" 大明正德七年九月二十四日大護國保安寺大慶法王領占班丹发心造

1513 „Siṃhavaktrā", Sammlung Barluzzi, Gouache mit Gold auf präparierter Baumwolle

Inschrift in Gold: „Am 24. Tag des 9. Monats im 7. Jahr (der Ära) Zhengde der Großen Ming (für den) Großen Glückseligen Gesetzeskönigs Lingzhan [i.e. Rinpoche] Bandan (im) Landesbeschützenden Bao'an si geschaffen" 大明正德七年九月二十四日大護國保安寺大慶領占班丹发心造 (es folgt die tibetische Übersetzung der Inschrift wie bei der Sarvabuddhaḍākiṇī-Thangka von 1513 der Sammlung David Kidd)

1516 „Vaiśravana", Nelson Gallery Kansas City, aus der Sammlung John W. Gruber, San Juan / Puerto Rico, 50 x 40 inches, Gouache auf präparierter Baumwolle (?)

Inschrift in Gold: „Am 24. Tag des 9. Monats im 7. Jahr (der Ära) Zhengde der Großen Ming nach einem Gelübde des Großen Glückseligen Gesetzeskönigs Lingzhan [i.e. Rinpoche] Bandan (im) Landesbeschützenden Bao'an si geschaffen" 大明正德七年九月二十四日大護國保安寺大慶領占班丹发心造

Ohne Inschrift, „Yama", Victoria and Albert Museum, London, 63,5 x 40 cm, Gouache auf präparierter Baumwolle, erworben in Beijing 1907, IS 16-1969

Der abgeschnittene untere Rand trug vermutlich eine um 1513 datierte Inschrift

Bibliographie

Barrett, Douglas. 1957. „The Buddhist Art of Tibet and Nepal", *Oriental Art*, N.S., III (1957) 3, S. 90-95.

Béguin, Gilles. 1990. *Art ésotérique de l'Himālaya. Catalogue de la donation Lionel Fournier*, Musée national des arts asiatique Guimet, Paris: Edition de la Réunion des musées nationaux.

—. 1977. *Dieux et demons de l'Himalaya*. Musée national des arts asiatique Guimet, Paris: Édition de la Réunion des musées nationaux.

—. 1995. *Les Peintures du Bouddisme Tibétain*. Musée national des arts asiatique Guimet, Paris: Édition de la Réunion des musées nationaux.

Bredon, Juliet. 1920. *Peking. A Historical and Intimate Description of Its Chief Places of Interest*. Shanghai et al.: Kelly – Walsh.

Christie's New York: Indian and Southeast Asian Art Including 20th Century Indian Paintings, Wednesday 20 September 2000. Auktionskatalog. Christie's International Media Division: London.

Dagyab Rinpoche – Loden Sherap. 1992. *Buddhistische Glückssymbole im tibetischen Kulturraum*. München: Diederichs.

Haus der Kunst München. 1977. *Tibet. Kunst des Buddhismus*. Ausstellungskatalog, Deutsche Bearbeitung Helga Uebach. Paris – München: Réunion des musées nationaux – Ausstellungsleitung Haus der Kunst.

Huang Hao 黄颢. 1987. „Beijing Fahai si Zangzu zhuyuan sengren kao" 北京法海寺藏族助缘僧人考 (Investigation in the Listed Tibetan Buddhist Monks Supporting the Fahai si in Beijing), in: *Lasa Zangxue taolunhui wenxuan* 拉萨藏学讨论会文选, Lhasa, S. 59-82.

Huntington, Susan L. – John C. Huntington. 1990. *Leaves from the Bodhi Tree: The Art of Pāla India (8th–12th Centuries) and Its International Legacy*. Seattle – London: The Dayton Art Institute in Association with the University of Washington Press.

Jin Shen 金申. 1994. *Zhongguo lidai jinian foxiang tudian* 中国历代纪年佛像图典. Beijing: Wenwu chubanshe.

Karmay, Heather. 1975. *Early Sino-Tibetan Art*. Warminster: Aris and Phillips.

Kerr, Rose (ed.). 1991. *Chinese Art and Design. The T.T. Tsui Gallery of Chinese Art*. Trustees of the Victoria and Albert Museum. London: Victoria and Albert Museum.

Kidd, David. 1975a. „Tibetan Painting in China", *Oriental Art* XXI (1975) 1, S. 55-60.

—. 1975b. „Tibetan Painting in China. Author's Postcript", *Oriental Art* XXI (1975) 2, S. 58-160.

Kunst- und Ausstellungshalle der Bundesrepublik Deutschland (Hrsg.). 2003. *Schätze der Himmelssöhne. Die kaiserliche Sammlung aus dem Nationalen Palastmuseum, Taipeh*, Buchkonzept Ursula Toyka. Ostfildern-Ruit : Hatje Cantz.

Liu Tong 劉侗 – Yu Yizheng 于奕正. 1969. *Dijing jingwu lüe* 帝京景物略 (Zusammenfassung der Szenarien und Sehenswürdigkeiten in der Kaiserstadt). Vorwort datiert 1635, Erstausgabe Beijing 1957, Zweitausgabe Beijing 1988, hier: Nachdruck Taibei 1969.

Lo Bue, Erberto F. – Franco Ricca. 1990. *Gyantse Revisited*. Firenze: Casa Ed. Le Lettere.

Lowry, John. 1973. „Tibet, Nepal or China? An Early Group of Dated *Tangkas*", *Oriental Art*, N.S. XIX (1973) 3, S. 306-314.

Munsterberg, Hugo. 1967. *Chinese Buddhist Bronzes*. Rutland – Tokyo: Tuttle.

Pal, Pratapaditya. 1969. *The Art of Tibet*. Exposition catalogue. New York: Asia Society.

—. 1991. With contributions from Ian Alsop, Heather Stoddard, and Valrae Reynolds. *Art of the Himalayas. Treasures from Nepal and Tibet*. New York: Hudson Hills Press in Association with the American Federation of Arts.

Shen Weirong 沈微荣. 2002. *Leben und historische Bedeutung des ersten Dalai Lama dGe 'dun grub pa dpal bzang po (1391–1474). Ein Beitrag zur Geschichte der dGe lugs pa-Schule und der Institution der Dalai Lamas*. Monumenta Serica Monograph Series XLIX. Nettetal: Steyler Verlag.

Toyka-Fuong, Ursula. 1997. „Reflections of Heavenly Bliss", *Christie's Magazine* 14 (November 1997).

—. 2002. „Göttinnen des heiligen Zornes. Ein 1479 n.Chr. datiertes Ḍākiṇī-Maṇḍala", in: Karénina Kollmar-Paulenz – Christian Peter (Hrsg.), *Tractata Tibetica et Mongolica. Festschrift für Klaus Sagaster zum 65. Geburtstag*. Wiesbaden: Harrassowitz , S. 283-297.

—. [Toyka]. 2014. *Splendours of Paradise. The Buddhist Monastery Fahai Si, Murals and Epigraphical Documents*, 2 Bde. Monumenta Serica Monograph Series LXIII/1-2. Nettetal: Steyler Verlag.

Tucci, Guiseppe. 1949. *Tibetan Painted Scrolls*, 3 Bde., Roma: Istituto Poligrafico e Zecca dello Stato.

COMMUNICATION AND EXCHANGE OF KNOWLEDGE BETWEEN WEST AND EAST (17TH AND 18TH C.)
THE ROUTES, ILLUSTRATED BY THE CASE OF THE "VIA OSTENDANA"*

Noël Golvers

The missions of the Jesuits and of other congregations had various commitments: diffusion of the Gospel and catechization; pastoral and organizational aspects; intellectual encounters; scholarly projects; the economic survival of the mission; and propaganda in Europe (fundraising, inspiring new recruits, reporting on results, apology for the methods used). For these two-sided activities (West to China; China to the West), a reliable communication system was absolutely essential in order to acquire personnel and financial resources, as well as to promote and keep updated the exchange of knowledge between West and East through books and other forms of information. Beside the risks "in via," the main problem was the factor of distance (in space and, by consequence, also in time). This article will illustrate the various material obstacles "en route" and the means the Jesuits developed to counter them in one rather underestimated secondary route: the "Via Ostendana" (especially active between ca. 1718–1728). I will describe the material circumstances (tracks, timing, periodicity, etc.) and their impact on the scientific and scholarly exchange between East and West and vice versa (books, products, both artificialia and naturalia).

This *Festschrift* for Fr. Roman Malek offers me the occasion for a synthetic reflection on my research of the last 15 years, combining and comparing the observations and conclusions of my study on the distribution of Ferdinand Verbiest's S.J. (1623–1688) astronomica[1] in European collections with those on the spread and impact of Western books in China.[2] This is a too ambitious project for the present contribution, but still I will try to subsume the main analytical facts and phenomena on this West- and East-bound distribution which I collected under one common concept, as two complementary facets of one and the same

---

* This is the revised text of my communication on the Workshop "The Materiality of Chinese-Western Relations in the Ming-Qing Periods: Methodological Approaches, Empirical Cases" (Leuven, 26–27 May, 2014). I thank Nicolas Standaert (Leuven) and Eugenio Menegon (Boston University), and the other participants for their stimulating remarks and suggestions.

[1] Father Roman Malek S.V.D. was the first to publish the results of this research, by accepting the copiously annotated edition of Ferdinand Verbiest's *Astronomia Europaea* (Dillingen: C. Bencard, 1687) in his Monumenta Serica Monograph Series; for his support and other contributions, I am much indebted to him.

[2] N. Golvers, *Libraries of Western Learning for China. Circulation of Western Books between Europe and China in the Jesuit Mission (ca. 1650 – ca. 1750)*, 3 vols (Leuven; F. Verbiest Institute, 2012-2015).

phenomenon, i.e., the communication and circulation of scholarly materials between Europe and China and vice versa in the early 17th–18th centuries

This inter- or transcontinental exchange of information can be described or analyzed mainly under the perspectives of four different components:
1. The media (bearers of the communication): especially correspondence – books – periodicals – illustrations – oral information;[3]
2. The routes of circulation. The "routes of Learning"[4] coincided with the seven main commercial routes ("via Lusitana," etc.), oversea or over land, Minerva following or accompanying Mercurius, to use a metaphor by Verbiest; for the 'scholarly' communication temporarily important were less well-known *viae* such as the "via Trans-Siberica" linking the Peking Jesuits and the *Academia Imperialis Petropolitana* (established St. Petersburg, 1725), – reflected in the correspondence of the French Jesuits (Antoine Gaubil [1689–1759], among others) and the letters and the academic reports in the Academic archives in St. Petersburg; but also the more ephemeral "Via Ostendana" (especially between 1718–1728), especially revealed in 118 letters (autographs and copies) which I could connect with this track in Belgian archives, and mostly unknown until now;
3. Particular places on these routes, where this knowledge was either *a)* produced, and collected (Astronomical Bureau in Peking and its library/archives; the Court, including the Emperor's collections, Jesuit residences and colleges in China, their libraries and Musea, especially in the Nantang and the Beitang, both in Peking; other – also private – meeting points with Chinese scholars, *b)* temporarily stocked (and sometimes definitely withheld, as in Macao and Canton) or *c)* complemented with other information, communicated with local people, etc. In the Far East such places were – in different degrees – Peking,[5] Macao (as the transit place par excellence for cultural and commercial products shipped between East and West, in both directions, of which the impact in the scholarly communication is not yet comprehensively described,[6] Canton (with an apogee of scholarly activities during the "Canton banishment");[7] Ba-

---

[3] See my complimentary contribution: "Globalization and Exchange of Knowledge between West/East, Mainly Considered from the Perspective of Communication" (presented in Lisbon in October 2012; forthcoming in the Proceedings).

[4] For this term, see the edition of Ferdinando Abbri and Marco Segala, *The "Route of Learning." Italy and Europe in the Modern Age* (Firenze: Olschki, 2004).

[5] Catherine Jami, "Pekin au début de la dynastie Qing. Capitale des savoirs impériaux et relais de l'Académie royale des Sciences," *Revue d'histoire moderne et contemporaine* 2008/2, pp. 43-69.

[6] But see Ugo Baldini, "The Jesuit College in Macao as a Meeting Point of the European, Chinese and Japanese Mathematical Traditions (...)," in: Lúis Saraiva – Catherine Jami, *The Jesuits, the Padroado and East Asian Science (1552-1773)* (New Jersey: World Scientific, 2008), pp. 33-79.

[7] See my paper presented on the Symposium of the Centro Científico e Cultural de Macao (CCCM) in Lisbon (2013): "The Canton-Macao Area as a 'lieu de savoir'. The Western Missionaries' Detention in the Canton Jesuit Residence (1665-1671) and Its Written and

tavia-Ambon; Pondicherry, Goa and the rest of India.[8] As constitutive elements, which shaped the intellectual import of these places, one could refer to the presence of 1) Western (mostly Jesuit) and native libraries and other private collections, to which the Jesuits could get some access;[9] 2) of productive scholars, collectors, readers, who were the virtual interlocutors of the Jesuits and constituted a potential readership of their Chinese publications; 3) the presence of book sellers, if not printers – Chinese and Western, the latter for instance in Macao ("livreiros," still largely unknown), Batavia, Goa; 4) the presence of – Jesuit and/or native institutes of instruction or research (Macao, for instance).

In the West – the other end of the communication line – the main places were obviously the academic centers of early modern Europe (Paris, London, Berlin, St. Petersburg, etc.) but also – despite its somewhat peripheral position with respect to the intercontinental routes – Rome (with the Papal Court as collector of Chinese texts, Christian and other; the Collegio Romano and the Musaeum Kircherianum, with Athanasius Kircher (1602–1680) as collector, commentator and publisher of incoming knowledge[10] and other private collections, such as that of Cassiano dal Pozzo (1588–1657), etc.;[11] European Jesuit colleges where the knowledge was gathered, the information was – publicly or privately – read (in libraries, recreation rooms and refectories), commented, copied and transmitted,[12] and a series of private collections; the remarkable analogy between Chinese collectors of Western curios and Western collectors of Sinica was recently put in evidence by Anna Grasskamp (Heidelberg).[13]

---

editorial output," in: Luís Filipe Barreto – Wu Zhiliang (eds.), *Macao Past and Present* (Lisbon: CCCM, 2015), pp. 215-233.

[8] See Virendra Nath Sharma, *Sawai Jai Singh and His Astronomy* (Delhi: Motilal Banarsidass Publ., 1995).

[9] One could refer to the fact, that the presence of a flourishing book and library culture in Nanking prompted the French Jesuits to ask the Kangxi Emperor for a settlement in Nanking, which the Emperor granted them.

[10] By oral reports of visiting procurators (Martino Martini [1614–1661], Johann Grüber [1623–1680], Michael Boym [1612–1659], etc.) and other Jesuits (Johann Schreck Terrentius [1576–1630], etc.), and written documents and communications, partly found on the shelves of the "Cubiculum Mathematicum" (...), partly directly addressed to him in person.

[11] On this aspect of early modern Rome, see Elisabetta Corsi, "Editoria, lingue orientali e politica papale a Roma tra Cinquecento e Seicento," in: Lúis Filipe Barreto – Wu Zhiliang (eds.), *Port Cities and Intercultural Relations, 15th–18th Centuries* (Lisbon: CCCM, 2012), pp. 179-206.

[12] See the books of collected letters, mostly selected on the topics of the mission's progress as well as ethnographic and other curiosities. See for this circuit some first observations in: N. Golvers, *Building Humanistic Libraries in Late Imperial China* (Rome: Nuova Cultura, 2011), pp. 117-120.

[13] Anna K. Grasskamp, *Cultivated Curiosities. A Comparative Study of Chinese Artefacts in European Kunstkammern and European Objects in Chinese Elite Collections* (Leiden: Universiteitsbibliotheek), forthcoming.

The position and role of Lisbon in this scholarly communication, i.e., to what extent the Portuguese capital had actively contributed in the spread of knowledge between Europe and China, is to my knowledge not yet sufficiently mapped in all its aspects.

4. The people involved, either particular groups or individual *dramatis personae* operating for them, both inside and outside the Jesuit circuit. These are very heterogeneous, in very different positions: I refer, e.g., to *a)* European academies, the academicians and their secretaries;[14] *b)* to commercial enterprises, their Governors, in Europe and the Far East, and their personnel, including preachers, physicians, botanists, and ministers: in the Vereenigde Oostindische Compagnie (VOC),[15] where, among others, Nicolas Witsen was the collector in whose *Noord en Oost Tartarye* converged Far Eastern and Siberian materials from Chinese, Jesuit and other informants;[16] the English East India Company (EIC), including captains and officials, and many free merchants working in the Company's margin, who independently brought Chinese materials and knowledge about the country to England;[17] the French Compagnie des Indes;[18] the three-year Transsiberian commercial route (until ca. 1755) and its German physicians. It was indeed such individuals, with their own connections who fueled this communication, from various positions, also in

---

[14] Most important were the *Académie des Sciences* in Paris, with Marquis de Louvois (i.e., François-Michel Le Tellier, 1641-1691) and his program for the "Cinque mathématiciens du Roy," incl. Cassini's astronomical databank, etc.; the *Royal Society* in London (since Oldenburg); the *Academia Imperialis* in St. Petersburg, etc.

[15] See the recent Ph.D. dissertation of Frasie Hertroijs, "Hoe kennis van China naar Europa kwam. De rol van jezuïeten en VOC-dienaren circa 1680-1795" (How Knowledge Came from China to Europe. The Role of Jesuits and VOC-officials, between 1680-1795), Vrije Universiteit Amsterdam, 2014.

[16] His network of informers extended right to Peking; see Marion Peters, *"Mercator sapiens" (De Wijze Koopman). Het wereldwijde onderzoek van Nicolaes Witsen (1641-1717), burgemeester en VOC-bewindhebber van Amsterdam* (s.l. 2008). Other people involved in the communication on this line were the Protestant minister Theodor Sas (Sax) Sr. (d. 1704), the physicians Andreas Cleyer (1634-1698); Willem ten Rhyne (1647-1700); Jacobus Bontius (1592-1631); Engelbert Kämpfer (1651-1716); the botanists Adrian R(h)eede tot Drakenstein (1636-1691) and Georg Eberhard Rumphius (1627-1702) as well as Johan Van Hoorn (1653-1711), Gouvernor-general of the Dutch East Indies from 1704-1709.

[17] Revealing are the names in the correspondence between Shen Fuzong 沈福宗 (d. 1691) and Thomas Hyde (1636-1703), and in other letters in the MSS. Sloane (British Library, London).

[18] Members of the EIC as well as those of the French Compagnie had direct contacts with Jesuits in the port cities, as we occasionally read in the correspondence (cf., among others, the report about French Jesuits distributing copies of the *Spiritual Exercises* among the French officials arriving in Canton), but also in some book inscriptions, still extant in the Peking-centred "Beitang" collection, referring to some members of the crew of both companies as first owners: see my *Libraries of Western Learning for China*, vol. 2, pp. 460-462.

Europe. Here I think of private (including "royal") confessors and other counselors (Antoine Verjus [1632-1706]; Giovanni Battista Carbone [1694?-1750]), the missionaries themselves, their Chinese companions (Shen Fuzong 沈福宗 [d. 1691]),[19] common travelers (Gemelli Carreri [1651-1725]; Evert Ysbrant Ides [1657-1708]), etc.), European collectors who ordered on command,[20] and the book donators. The role of the latter emerged very clear through the identification of the inscriptions in the extant books of the Beitang and the analysis of a series of letters: further research often revealed direct personal links between individual senders in Europe (representing sometimes an entire local milieu, a college, etc.) and Jesuit addressees in China. The incitements behind these donations appeared to lie precisely in the personalized atmosphere, in pre-existent relations between relatives (Pieter Van Hamme), "condiscipuli" (Antonio Nunes Ribeiro Sanchez [1699-1783] to Policarpo de Sousa [1697-1757]; Antoine de Laval, S.J. [1664-1728] to Antonio Provana, S.J. [1662-1720]); Daniel Papebrochius [1628-1714] to Philippe Couplet [1622-1693]); former teachers and "discipuli" (Valentim Nogueira [d. 1646] to Wenzel Pantaleon Kirwitzer [1588 or 1590-1626]); Jean de Saint Bonnet [ca. 1640-1703] to Jean-Baptiste Régis [1663-1738] and Dominique Parrenin [1665-1741]; Jean Hellot [1685-1766] to Pierre d'Incarville [1706-1757], etc.); local Jesuit communities or nobility and a member of their community (see the series of letters from Sicilian and Palermitan nobles to Prospero Intorcetta and Dazio Agliata). On the basis of this material, it was possible to recognize some 20 smaller networks linking particular centers in Europe directly to a Jesuit place in China.[21]

There are of course also the normal institutional and professional networks, either among Jesuits (especially in the mission procurator's relation vs. the missionaries) or between Jesuits and academicians – the latter mostly turning on the principle of reciprocity (exchange of European books etc. against Chinese curios). I am convinced that it is possible to describe all the known contacts within one of these types. In addition, the recognition of such a connection may also point to the inspiration behind the communication.

These four components – in various forms of mutual interaction – constituted the framework and the space in which knowledge – of very different character (geographical, botanical, astronomical, cultural, historical, ethnographical, etc.) was produced and circulated, in both directions. As a basically dynamic process this circulation was the product of various incentives. I recognize here: First, the challenge from the Chinese context (Court, courtiers, and the common literati): Western materials (books, images, prints) were bought or collected through or-

---

[19] As informer on Chinese items in Paris (in the Bibliothèque du Roy) and London – Oxford (Thomas Hyde).

[20] E.g., the Dutch Gisbert Cuper (1644-1716) and others through Witsen's connections in Batavia.

[21] *Libraries of Western Learning for China*, vol. 1, pp. 386-391.

ders in the West to the mission procurators, provincials, fellow fathers, relatives, authorities, scholars and other benefactors, according to the particular preferences in interest and taste of the Chinese clients, in order to answer to the endless demands of Chinese literati, inspired by feelings lingering between sincere interest, curiosity and suspicion, and to these questions the Jesuits answered not only by commands of products in Europe, but also:
- by producing similar products in the East Asian area or even on the spot (e.g., paintings, made in Goa/Macao or in China; automata etc. in the Peking Imperial ateliers, incl. the "verreries" of Stumpf);
- by technological achievements: in the field of mechanics and general engineering, including hydraulics, in answer to (mostly) official orders in the public, but sometimes also the private sphere (echoes in *Taixi shui fa / Qiqi tushuo*; diversified since Kangxi – Verbiest [see, a.o., *Astronomia Europaea*, some letters [1670] and *Qionglixue*);
- by demonstrations: in particular in the fields of astronomy [instrumental demonstrations; the general exactitude and reliability of Western methods and their cosmological background, with regard to eclipse predictions; the production of a reliable calendar]; geography [the earth's sphericity; the location of the Western countries, the real place of China, etc.].

Second, their own not too secret agenda (even to the members of the Chinese Ministry of Rites [Libu 禮部]): There was the purely missionary agenda of using science and curiosity as a means to get in contact with Chinese literati, as interested and curious clients of Western curiosa, mechanical devices, medicine in order to win them over as converts. In addition, the Jesuits pursued a scholarly agenda which also somewhat served the missionary aims, rather often in view of harmonizing Chinese and Western traditions, see, e.g., the project of a world chronology as a tentative harmonization of Biblical and Chinese chronology, which was put forth by Martino Martini, Antoine Gaubil, and others, or the search for echoes of a proto-revelation (Figurists).

This scholarly agenda was manifested on the one hand by purely academic, i.e., not mission-related commitments, either as official orders (cf. the program of the "mathématiciens du Roy") or self-imposed, often also as statutory members (Paris, London, St. Petersburg, Lisbon): aimed at collecting local materials, often books, but also terms, adages, etc. from native sources and diffusing them to the European academic centers, contributing by this in creating a world-spanning network of observation data:
   a) In the field of astronomy and geography, e.g. with the verification of calculations and hypotheses with data from places all over the earth, with regard to longitude and latitude, discussions on the shape of the earth, measuring the earth radius, magnetic measurements, correcting the map of the world, and describing new areas. Protagonists in this field were Ferdinand Verbiest, Antoine Thomas (1644–1709), Jean-François Gerbillon (1654–1707), Pierre Jartoux (1669–1720), Johann Grüber (1623–1680), and Ippolito Desideri (1684–1733);

b) in the medico-pharmaceutical sphere, by exchanging medical observations (on the historical origin of venereal diseases: reported by Dominique Parrenin to Jean Astruc and Antonio Nunes Ribeiro Sanches), diagnostics (pulse), therapies (moxibustion), and medicaments (medicinal plants).

On the other hand, Jesuit activities to rally support for the missionary method of using science, especially astronomy, started to gain momentum from the 1660s on. This was most eagerly put forth by Ferdinand Verbiest and Antoine Thomas: who reported on their scholarly achievements to European ecclesiastical authorities (the Pope included), secular "principes" (from the Duke of Tuscany to the Holy Roman Emperor), and scholars, in order to:

a) Convince them of the efficiency and results of this method (the "media humana" of the Jesuit sources) for the progress of the mission and against the opposition from the Missions Etrangères de Paris (M.E.P.), the Congregatio de Propaganda Fide (CPF), and some other Jesuits;

b) get official backing from the ecclesiastic authorities for this "mission by the sciences" (see the letters of Verbiest and Couplet to Pope Innocent XI [1676–1689]);

c) obtain active diplomatic support (from Emperor Leopold I [1640–1705], also and especially with regard to the "route de Moscovie");

d) raise funds and other forms of material support (from the Portuguese King and others).

By this, the Jesuits were mediators in a two-sided communication process they had created themselves, in which they tried to realize their goals in China with the means they received from Europe, and tried to engage the European (political and economic, but mainly intellectual) establishment with information and exotica from China to create better conditions for the China mission. Both aspects of their work were thus organically connected. Obviously the entire enterprise in both directions was completely relying on the routes of communication, either overseas or overland: these routes – and the companies which served them – created the material circumstances of the communication, i.e., the continuity; the regularity; the reliability and the technological comfort which differed according to the company. At the same time, these routes had a considerable impact on the transfer of knowledge as they influenced:

a) The speed by which books, information and important decisions arrived in China (which in consequence facilitated or complicated the decisions themselves);

b) the material losses during shipping. Entire cargoes were lost by accident, such as the study library of Hudde, or by human intervention, i.e., mutual interceptions by members of CPF or the Jesuits English ships;

c) the rationalization (for reasons of taxes, budget and volume) in the selection of materials to carry from Europe to China and vice versa.

From this cluster of four components (media, routes, places, and people), for the Symposium of the Centro Científico e Cultural de Macao (CCCM, October 2013) I selected the latter, focusing on the means of communication (correspondence, books, periodicals, oral information); on this occasion I would like to complement these observations, reflecting on the part the transatlantic and transcontinental routes played, more precisely with regard to the lesser well-known "Via Ostendana" i.e., the maritime route which started in the Flemish port of Oostende/Ostend (North Sea) and connected Flanders and part of northwestern and even Central Europe – via the Cape – with the Bengal and Canton.

This route was served by the Ostend Company, with its official name the "Generale Keijserlijcke Indische Compagnie," shortly Oostendsche Compagnie, which was based in Ostend. This port was rebuilt after the 16th-century destruction of this "City of the Protestants" by the Spanish troops after a cruel siege (1601-1604) which was compared in the contemporary newspapers and pamphlets with the "Fall of Troy" hence the name "New Troy" for Ostend. The Company itself was founded in 1715 for the commerce with the (East) Indies and the Far East; the products of this commerce were silk, porcelain, tea, coffee, and textile. Although its activities were apparently preceded by some years of private expeditions, especially since 1717, the first ship under the Flag of the Ostend Company proper left the port only in 1724, and the last one left Canton in 1735; during this barely eleven to eighteen years, it connected the port of Ostend with that of Canton (not Macao), as an alternative for the other, pre-existing lines such as the "Via Goana" or "Via Lusitana" (Lisbon – Goa – Macao), the "Via Batavica" (VOC, Amsterdam – Batavia), the "Via Gallica" (Compagnie des Indes, based in Lorient/Port St. Louis) and the English East India Company. In this short period, the "Via Ostendana" made enormous profits, with a yearly return of 13% for the shareholders during the period 1723-1734, while from 1726 on the dividends raised up to a total of 166% (*sic*)! This unprecedented maritime and mercantile success story provoked also its decay when, after much pressure from the surrounding countries on the Habsburg Emperor Carlos (or Karel/Charles) VI (1685-1740), he cancelled its charter in 1731,[22] and liquidated the Company in 1734, for fear of loosing his international prestige and political influence. Individual cargoes, however, continued to be sent out and to gain huge profits for its shareholders.

Little wonder that this route and its economic success has been studied by many historians, especially within the perspective of economic history, on the basis of its archives, which are now kept in the University Library of Ghent[23]: I refer here especially to the studies of E.J. Baels and Karel Degryse from the 1970s and especially to the more recent books by Jan Parmentier on the Flemish East Asia

---

[22] Curiously enough, as early as 19 November 1728 Antoine Gaubil reports: "La Comp.e d'Ostende est suspendue." See *id.*, *Correspondance de Pékin, 1722-1759*. Ed. Renée Simon. Études de philologie et d'histoire, 14 (Genève: Droz, 1970), p. 211.

[23] See the ms. Index Compagnie des Inde à Ostende. Inventaire, Index. Catalogue (cf. Paul A. Van Dyke, *Merchants of Canton and Macao* [Hong Kong: Hong Kong University Press, 2011]).

trade.²⁴ None of these studies, however, paid any attention to its secondary role, as a highly important and intensively used means of communication for the Jesuit Mission in both directions between Europe and China. In this, it was not different from other parallel routes, as especially the "Via Lusitana" and the VOC.²⁵

In the following, it is my intention to illustrate this role also for the Ostend Company, on the basis of archival evidence no one has reviewed from this angle so far.

One could be tempted to attribute the origin of this involvement, and the appeal of the Jesuits in the Belgian Provinces, in the first place those of the Provincia Flandro-Belgica, but also those of the Provincia Gallica (Paris) and even the Provincia Germania (Inferior and) Superior (Munich) to this Company for their contacts with China and the China mission, simply to this line's quality of service and reliability, with very regular departures and return times.

But there is, in all probability another, more personal reason, which can better explain the intense involvement of both Companies, the Mercantile and the Spiritual one. This key I found in a so far overlooked onomastic correspondence, which, if correct, would explain a lot of phenomena, which look otherwise as isolated facts. It can indeed hardly be a pure accident that among the main shareholders of this Ostend Company were two brothers from Ghent, called Carlos and Jacomo Maelcamp, whose Spanish first names, due to a long stay in Sevilla,²⁶ can not conceal they were scions of a Ghent family, their "official" names being Charles Antoine Maelcamp (1677-1764) and Jacques Fortunatus Maelcamp (1683-1741). Their family name is the same as that of Petrus Maelcamp, a strong Jesuit personality of the first half of the 18th century, based in Antwerp, but born in Ghent in 1679. He entered the Societas Jesu in the Novitiate of the Provincia Flandro-Belgica in Mechelen in 1697, made his fourth vow in the Collego San Ermenegildo in Sevilla on 2 February 1715, returned afterwards to Flanders. He then held a whole series of official functions within the Province, always based in the Antwerp Professed House: first as a procurator of the Provincia Flandro-Belgica (since 1717?), as the Provincial (1727-1731), and as Praepositus of the House (1731-1734). He died in the Jesuit College of Antwerp in 1741.²⁷ As my prosopographical studies in the past taught me well how

---

²⁴ See Eduard J. Baels, *De Generale Keizerlijke en Koninklijke Indische Compagnie, etc.* (Oostende: Erel, 1972), Karel Degryse, "De Oostendse China-handel, 1718-1735," *Belgisch Tijdschrift voor Filologie & Geschiedenis* LII (1974) 2, pp. 306-347, and Jan Parmentier, *Thee van Overzee. Maritieme en Handelsrelaties tussen Vlaanderen en China tijdens de 18e eeuw* (Brugge: Ludion, 1996) and *id.*, *Oostende. Het Verhaal van de Zuid-Nederlandse Oost-Indiëvaart 1715-1735* (Brugge: Ludion, 2002).

²⁵ As concerns the latter in the perspective of the circulation of knowledge, see Frasie Hertroijs, "Hoe kennis van China naar Europa kwam."

²⁶ Idesbald Goddeeris, *Het wiel van Ashoka. Belgisch-Indiase contacten in historisch perspectief* (Leuven: Leuven University Press, 2013), p. 36.

²⁷ Prosopographia Iesuitica Belgica Antiqua, Heverlee-Leuven: Philosofisch en Theologisch College SJ), II, p. 88; many obituaries are preserved in KBR: see PIBA, III, p. 255.

dangerous it is to build conclusions purely on onomastic homonymy, I made some genealogical research, which confirmed, that Petrus Maelcamp was indeed a full brother of both aforementioned shareholders; all three, with their sister Agnes Françoise Maelcamp were the legitimate children of Jean Baptiste Maelcamp (?-1702) and Agnès Françoise de Donckers (1646-1690), a Ghent family of entrepreneurs. This personal link – and the almost complete simultaneity between the activity of the Company (roughly 1718-1731/1734) and Petrus Maelcamp's responsibilities within the Jesuit province (1717-1734) – delivers the final reason why the Jesuits of the Flemish-Belgian Province used the ships of this Company for their contacts with the China Mission, and especially why Jesuits from neighboring Provinciae entrusted their communication with China to this Company.

As for the Flemish-Belgian Province one could even go a step further, and speculate about the financial participation of the Jesuits – especially those of Antwerp – in the commercial enterprise; we should keep in mind that some other wealthy Antwerp families were among the shareholders, both before and after the liquidation, such as Johannes Jacobus Moretus (1690-1757), a rich entrepreneur and heir of the world famous "Officina Plantiniana" (i.e., Plantin printing press), and the banker Jacob de Coninck (1661-1724); but to confirm such a Jesuit partnership I have not yet found the necessary documentary support, also because sources on the financial situation of the pre-Suppression Antwerp Jesuits have not been located yet.

A personal engagement of Petrus Maelcamp, with this primarily commercial enterprise based on direct family ties would also explain why, among the collection of "Autografi" of the Biblioteca Nazionale Centrale Vittorio Emanuele II (BVE, Rome) – a mostly overlooked and neglected collection – I was able to find some letters, in which Maelcamp discusses at length, in an answer to a not yet identified Flemish correspondent at the Collegio Romano a series of rather intimate details of the Company's life: *a*) the problem of the sandbars ("banck van zavel") which blocked the free entrance to the Ostend harbor; *b*) the reasons why a canal between Bruges and Ostend was no good solution; *c*) the spectacular dividends returned to the shareholders, with round but clear numbers which illustrate how well he was informed on this aspect of the route;[28] *d*) the rules of international law on which the establishment of the Ostend Company was based, with reference to a not yet identified publication;[29] all this seems too detailed and well founded, and sufficiently personally engaged, and resuscitates the assumption that Maelcamp – or the Antwerp Professed House – was probably financially engaged in it himself.

Other letters addressed to Maelcamp I found in Berlin, another large collection, since the end of the 18th-century split and distributed over at least four dif-

---

[28] BVE, Autografi (alphabetical order).

[29] "Hinc videt R(everentia) V(est)ra non immerito aegre ferre Anglos et Batavos, quod imperator ita suos subditos protegat; prodiit modo iterum tomus in folio latine, qui demonstrat hanc societatem bene stabilitam esse (?) naturae gentium positivo etc."

ferent locations, three unpublished in the Municipal Library of Antwerp (now: Erfgoedbibliotheek, EBA),[30] the University Library of Leuven,[31] and the Royal Library of Brussels (Koninklijke Bibliotheek van België, KBR)[32] and one published of which the originals are lost now.[33] I have demonstrated elsewhere that these collections once belonged together, as part of the Jesuit archives of either the Antwerp Professed House itself, or the separate archive of the Bollandist fathers,[34] living within the walls of the same Jesuit compound.[35] The other addressees of the letters in question are, among others: Daniel Papebrochius (d. 1714), Franciscus Van Callenberghe (d. 1719), and Conrad Janning (d. 1723), all three Bollandist specialists and living in the Professed House of Antwerp. In total, my census has some 180 items, which span a period between 1683 and 1727.

Two further observations may be added here: *a*) the first reference to Ostend ships and their involvement in the missionary communication between China and Europe stems from Pieter Van Hamme's letter of 10 October 1718, and refers to his initiative to use the "navis Ostendana" for the first time – parallel to or even substituting the "via Goana" (or "Lusitana"), "Anglicana" or "Manilana";[36] as it left the Port of Ostend in January of the same year 1718; the chronological parallel with Maelcamp's appointment as a procurator is remarkable; *b*) the entire archive illustrates again and again that the start of this direct exchange of books, letters etc. between Antwerp and China antedates the establishment of the Ostend Line, and goes back to the relations between the Flemish fathers (Couplet, François de Rougemont [1624–1676] etc.) and the "Officina Plantiniana" in the 1660s.

Finally, some other letters of and to Maelcamp I found in the Bayerisches Hauptstaatsarchiv (BHStA), which stem from the Jesuit college of Munich.[37]

From these letters it appears that, under Maelcamp – and in direct cooperation with the Ostend Company – Antwerp became temporarily a dispatching center in the communication between the Jesuits from large parts of Germany, France and the Low Countries, and the missionaries in China. In this communication, books,

---

[30] Cod. 21 (B 431): "Litterae et Instrumenta circa Res Sinenses."

[31] Leuven, Universiteitsarchief: OU/G/D 126.

[32] Brussels: KBR, Ms. 4096 (Inv. 16691-93) and Ms. 4097 / Inv. 10550-54.

[33] Pieter Visschers, *Onuitgegeven brieven van eenige paters der Sociëteit van Jesus* (sic), *Missionarissen in China, van de 17e en 18e eeuw, met aanteekeningen* (sic) (Arnhem: Josue Witz, 1857).

[34] The successors of Jean Bolland (1596–1665), who continued (and still are continuing) the critical edition of hagiographical sources (*Acta Sanctorum*) according to strong historical critical principles.

[35] See N. Golvers, "The pre-1773 Bollandist Archives and Their Evidence for the Relation between Antwerp and the Jesuit Mission in China," in: Rob Faesen – Leo Kenis (eds.), *The Jesuits in the Low Countries. Identity and Impact (1540–1773)* (Leuven: Peeters, 2012), pp. 269-282.

[36] Visschers, pp. 168ff.

[37] BHStA, Jes. 590.

letters and other documents, and "imagines" were exchanged. Ignaz Kögler explains this role very clearly, in a letter to Maelcamp of 9 November 1726. He also refers to the vicinity of Antwerp as another main advantage of this city compared to others. The fragment runs as follows:

> I explained my desire for good and new books, and I also informed Father Maelcamp about this; because of his vicinity, he could more readily have these things (i.e., books) within his reach, which could satisfy us.[38]

This (alleged?) ease to get books from Europe in China over Antwerp was already mentioned some years earlier, in his letter of 21 November 1724:

> If it is permitted to propose to Y(our) R(everence) a particular petition, [I would ask] that good books be procured by Y(our) R(everence); either sacred ones or books on (profane) sciences, of the sort that appear almost daily in Europe, and usually can easily be obtained, especially in Belgium, in whatever language, and be transmitted here to me.[39]

This statement refers to the central position of Antwerp within Europe, and especially its position with regard to France, Germany, England and Holland, especially the latter being the main book market of contemporary Europe.

In addition, Antwerp offered especially for the German Jesuits the best facilities to communicate with their colleagues in China, and vice versa. One factor in this might have been the commercial network of the "Officina Plantiniana" with which the Jesuits always were quite well-connected – also in terms of vocations in the gremium of the family. For Holland in all probability also the Fathers of the "Missio Hollandica" – which was based in Antwerp – will have been instrumental.

As to the identification of the books, which were transmitted to China by this way, I can enumerate among the examples from the correspondence of Pieter Van Hamme (d. 1727), both published (P. Visschers) and unpublished (KBR Ms. 4096) the following books:

Bourdaloue's *Sermones*, in 3 vols, publ. in Antwerp;

Bellarmini, *Controversiae*;

Milice de France;

Diertins' *Explanatio Exercitiorum S.P.N.*;

J.-A. d'Averoult, *Catechismus Historialis*, in 4 vols.;

Andreas Tacquet, *Opera Omnia* (Antwerp 1669);

---

[38] "Explicavi quoque desiderium meum pro novis et bonis libris, de eoque etiam monui Reverentiam Patrem Maelcamp, qui ob viciniam promptius ad manum habebit quod satisfacere queat." ARSI, JS 183, f. 304v.

[39] "Quod si licebit peculiarem petitionem apud Rev(eren)tiam V(est)ram [P.M] proponere (...) bonos aliquot ab R(everenti)a V(estr)a libros procurari, sive sacros sive de scientiis agentes, cuiusmodi ferme quotidie in Europa prodeunt ac praecipue in Belgio facile ad manum haberi solent, quâcumque demum sint linguâ, atque huc ad me transmitti." Leuven, BUAR, OU/G/D 126.

Institutum SI / *Corpus Institutorum*, vol. 1 and 2 (Antwerp 1702);

Breviarium maius quadripartitum cum officiis Sanctorum Hispanorum;

Missale parvulum cum Rituali Romano;

Horae Diurnae;

12 *Missales novi*;

Libri novi de machinis, instrumentis aut curiosis inventis tractantibus;

Acta Sanctorum;

Opera Pragae Impressa (F. Noël);

Libri novi atque utiles;

Missa nova Hollandica impressa;

Bonos aliquot libros sive sacros sive de scientiis agentes;

Le Clef du Cabinet, 12 vols, publ. in Paris;

Relatio Missionis Sinensis, sent by Slaviçek, with annotations of Maelcamp;

(Baronius), *Martyrologium*;

Exercitia (sc. *Spiritualia*), ed. Diertins;

This is not a really impressive list, and certainly not suited to underpin Kögler's aforequoted observation on Antwerp as a gateway to neighboring European book markets; on the contrary, these dispatches seem to have promoted especially the local book production; other elements are polemical books and Jesuitica. Revealing are also some letters Maelcamp exchanged with the procurators in Munich (Franciscus Xaverius Hallauer [1674-1740], Jacobus Unglert [1679-1744], Mauritius Lergien [1679-1737], among others), now in the collection, called Jesuitica in the BHStA. Maelcamp reports: "misi libros de Auxiliis, Acta Sanctorum, Constitutionem Unigenitus Patris nostri de La Fontaine,"[40] i.e., in addition to the issues of the *Acta Sanctorum*, he sent a copy of the first or second edition of *De auxiliis* (Eleutherius),[41] Jacques de La Fontaine, *S(anctissimi) Dom(i)ni Nostri (...) Clementis Papae XI Contitutio Unigenitus theologica Propugnatus* (Rome 1717), and *Corpus Institutorum S.I.*, 2 vols, Antwerp, 1721.

Compare, from the same collection, a letter of Balthasar Miller (1683-1741) to Maelcamp, Macao, 24 November 1725:

Ex Belgio expecto a R(everenti)a V(estr)a [i.e., Maelcamp] viâ nostrorum Patrum Gallorum Corpus Institutionum Soc(ieta)tis Jesu volumen 1um et 2um

---

[40] BHStA, Jes(uits) 590/41: Antwerp, 1723.

[41] Eleutherius was the pseudonym of Lievin de Meyere S.J. (1655-1730); apparently a direct acquaintance of Petrus Van Hamme to Jean-Baptiste Du Sollier in Antwerp (4. Oct. 1723): "Gratias ago maximas R(everenti)ae V(estr)ae pro novis, quae mihi scribere dignata est de R(everen)do Patre Livino de Meijere, P(at)re Alexandro Blitterswijck et paucis aliis mihi notis, etc."

Antwerpiae 1721 impressum; item 12 libellos La Clef du Cabinet. Item fusum et frequens litteratum R(everenti)ae V(estr)ae commercium."[42]

Certainly less welcome in Jesuit China was the large series of Jansenistic tracts, discovered by João Mourão S.J. (1681-1726) in the Ostend ships arriving in Canton in 1722, which he confiscated, and of which we have detailed lists and descriptions, dated 1 September 1722: "Catalogus librorum qui mittebantur ad Dominum Guigne," i.e., Antoine de Guigne, M.E.P. (d. 1741).[43]

An interesting example of book exchange in the reverse direction, as part of the acquisition process of Chinese books in Europe, also using the Ostend ships we find in the case of the CPF, which had built up a complex network, as follows: Chinese books sent by Procurator Domenico Perroni (1674-1729) to Ostend, then to the Papal Nuntius in Brussels, Giusepe Spinelli (1694-1763) and from there to Cesare Sardi (1654-1731), an Italian banker in Amsterdam, who transmitted them to Leghorn / Livorno with destination Rome.[44]

From the same and other, parallel sources we know that also "naturalia" and "artificialia" were transmitted through this way, continuing directions and routes which existed already before the Company officially existed.

The "naturalia" were mostly seeds and tea (*cha* 茶) leaves sent from China to Europe;"[45] The "artificialia" consisted in various objects:

a) in particular European "imagines," i.e., prints, plates and etchings for the Chinese market, and Chinese (Manchu) prints for European collectors, of which many are mentioned already in the pre-1618 correspondence of Pieter Van Hamme and others. In a letter of 4 November 1726, Kögler gives also some practical suggestions for the dispatching of this kind of "imagines," which can be inserted in books: "Libris porro facile ini addique possent imagines, picturae et huiusmodi," in this way they escaped from being taxed;

b) "curiosa Bertolsgadensia in capsa anni 1724 penitus confracta": these were curios of an unknown character,[46] but apparently artifacts, as they were broken at arrival in China;

---

[42] BUAR, OU/G/126.

[43] ARSI, JS 196, f. 21r/v; cf. Noël Golvers, *Libraries of Western Learning for China*, vol. 1: 3.24, 3.75.7, 6.3.

[44] See especially Hertroijs, "Hoe kennis van China naar Europa kwam."

[45] Cf. P. Van Hamme, in Visschers, pp. 173, 182; especially Romain Hinderer to Maelcamp on 23 November 1722: "His addo tres globos foliorum Po ul cha, sive Po ul the ex praetiosioribus Provinciae Yun nan" and Pierre de Goville on 27 November 1722 to the same, both in BUAR, OU/G/D 126. The letters indicated contain some information on the price of tea. It appears that already in 1722 the two European variants of the name, the Port. *cha*, and the Engl. *tea* were known, reflecting two different areas of orgin. For the Chinese characters in *pinyin*, i.e., *Pu'er cha* 普洱茶, cf. *Mingwu dadian*, vol. 1, p. 666 (with thanks to Ad Dudink).

[46] As far as I can see, Bertolsgaden (Bergtoldsgaden), is a 17th-18th c. variant of the actual Berchtesgaden near Salzburg which is mainly know for a geo-physical curiosity – salt.

c) stationery and boxes (in cardboard?), sent from China as a present of de Goville to Maelcamp: "Munusculi loco V(estra) R(everentia) ne gravetur acceptare ex 100 foliis papyri Nankinensis, quinquaginta et 4 pyxides tcha bouy. Cetera folia aliasque 4 pyxides rogo ut tradat R(everendus) P(ater) de Brettonville, Rectori Domûs Probationis"; from Canton, 27 November 1722).[47] In this context the dispatch of Chinese ink ("atramantum") should also be mentioned, e.g., to Filippo Bonanni;

d) on the other hand, Chinese porcelain was transported to Europe, and we can assume that at least part of the historical Chinese porcelain collections in the Southern Low Countries stem from this route. Some of these precious pieces are preserved in the Bijloke Museum in Ghent. I recently saw, during a private visit to the Rockox Museum in Antwerp (Koninklijk Museum voor Schone Kunsten Antwerpen collection) a porcelain object, with the "Lans-steek" ("lance stitch") of Rubens, made ca. 1710–1720 in Jingdezhen 景德鎮, and another one in the (now closed) private Museum of Smidt van Gelder,[48] both in Antwerp; the chronology may point to a relation with the activities of Antwerp shareholders in the Ostend Company.

e) particular products of Jesuit scientific activities transferred to Europe include, among others, stellar maps made by the Jesuits of the Chinese heaven,[49] a "planisphaerium" drawn by Ferdinand-Bonaventura Moggi (1684–1761) and Ignatius Kögler, and sent to Maelcamp with an accompanying letter, dated 12 November 1725;[50]

f) requested was also a "horologium pro turri campanaria Collegii Macaensis solidum, exactum et durabile, quod horas et quadrantes pulsu campanarum designet" (a solid watch for the bell tower of the Macao college, perfect

---

Since the mid-18th century it was also famous for the production of wooden nut-crackers or nut-biters, which spread over Germany and Europe. Are these the "curiosa" mentioned in Kögler's letter?

[47] On the reverse, particular types of European paper were much appreciated in China: "variegata papyrus seu Turcica (papyrus), ut ibi vocant, et quae auratis vel argentatis floribus modulisque exprimitur" (BHStA 590/82); also "charta pargamena quâ Sinae omnino carent" (ibid. 590/84). "Bouy" is probably Port. boyão: "cylindrical vase, indeed used for the transport of tea" – "uma panela ou boyão de barro parta uso do seu cha,": see Sebatião Rodolfo Dalgado, Glossario luso-asiatico (Coimbra: Imprensa da Universidade, 1919), vol. I, p. 135. I have not yet been able to identify the Jesuit rector de Brettonville (Bretonneau?).

[48] See the folder of the Rockockx-museum (Antwerp): Zaal Z. Koninklijk Museum voor Schone Kunsten Antwerpen 2 (2013–2014) 7, p. 3.

[49] Ignatius Kögler to Maëlcamp (sic), Peking, 12 November 1725: "PS. Accludo hîc binas mappas stellati caeli Sinici pro R(everend)a V(estr)a ac D(omi)no Fratre (?) Directore." Id., 6 December 1725.

[50] "Accludo Planisphaerium Caeleste sculptum in Collegio Pekini a Chr.mo Moggi, dirigente opus P(at)re Ignatio Kögler."

and durable, which should indicate hours and quarters with a hit of its bell);

g) elsewhere it appears that Romain Hinderer (1668–1744) also expected to receive from Munich – through Maelcamp – scales of different types: "10 stateras sive bilances ternos [i.e., 3] quibus una libra ponderare possit; ternas [+3] alias (bilances) quae decem libris ponderandis sufficient; reliquas quatuor [+4 = 10] pro libitu vel prioribus pars vel certe intermedias" (10 steelyards or 3 balances, by which one pound can be weighed out; 3 other balances which will suffice to weigh out 10 pounds).

Among the addressees in Europe of this kind of dispatches are mentioned: Maelcamp, the Antwerp Jesuits, Father Nicolaus (i.e., in all probability Nicolas Grammatici [1684–1735]), Pieter Van Hamme's relatives (Visschers, p. 173; cf. 56; 123), more precisely his sister and her husband in Ghent, Van Hamme's letter communication with this relative became the basis of a monographic manuscript biography by a nephew-by-marriage, Robrecht Willem Van der Heyden ("nepoti meo Dno Vander Heyden"),[51] which was printed by Constant Philippe Serrure in 1871,[52] and which contains many unknown biographical details of Van Hamme's life;[53] further addressees were Filippo B(u)onanni (1638–1723) and the Museum Kircherianum (pp. 173; 184);[54] Julius Zwicker SJ (1667–1738) in the Collegium Clementinum in Prague; "benefactores" in general. Among the addresses in China was the Emperor himself: "duo R(everendi) P(atres) Carmelitae, Ostendanâ navi advecti cum muneribus & duplici Brevi Pontificis ad Imperatorem Sinicum" (6 December 1725); François Noël (1651–1729) in Prague, and Ehrembert Fridelli (1673–1743), 1725, to Maelcamp.

Finally, in this period also personnel, in the first place from the Provincia Germania Superior was sent to China through Antwerp and the North Sea. This less common route was already mentioned by Oskar Münsterberg in 1894.[55] This directs our attention also to the position of Bruges in this network, as the Jesuit

---

[51] Apparently Maelcamp had contacted Van der Heyden, to teach him how to address letters for Van Hamme in China: "Gratias ago maximas R(everend)ae V(estr)ae quod scribere dignata sit nepoti meo D(omi)no V(an)d(er)Heyden, quomodo inscribi debeant epistolae ad me mittendae." It is not without relevance to recall that these relations were between citizens of the same city, Ghent, the native place of the brothers Maelcamp and Pieter Van Hamme with his relatives. On 2 August 1719 it is "cha" and "scyphi" (i.e., cups) which were sent to his sister; in her absence: "mittat (sc. Conrad Janning) omnia D(omin)o V(an) d(er) Heyden, sororis meo genero in eodem domo Gandavi." BUAR, etc.

[52] Constant Philippe Serrure, *Het leven van Pater Petrus-Thomas Van Hamme, missionaris in Mexico en in China* (Ghent: C. Annoot – Braeckman, 1871).

[53] It is probably nothing but a strange coincidence that his brother was married with one Theresa-Isabella Van Alstein in Ghent, which is the same name as one of the most prolific collectors of Asiatica and Sinica in 19th century Ghent, Leopold Van Alstein (1791–1862).

[54] This constitutes a part of a more systematic series of contacts between Pieter Van Hamme with Filippo Bonanni, on which I will return at another occasion.

[55] Oskar Münsterberg, "Bayern und Asien im XVI., XVII. und XVIII. Jahrhundert," *Zeitschrift der Münchener Althertumsvereins* 6 (1894), pp. 12-37.

college which was closest to Ostend, an aspect which Pieter Van Hamme pointed out as early as 1718:[56] the local College was therefore used as a kind of "waiting room" for the missionaries till the ships would leave the Ostend harbor, when the weather was favorable. I found some remarkable testimonies of this stay in some letters now preserved in the "Jesuitica" collection of the BHStA. Three of them were written by the German Jesuit Victor Walter (1689–1745) – whose destination was afterwards changed to Micronesia – and sent from Bruges in December-January 1721/1722 to Franciscus-Xaverius Hallauer (1674–1740), the then Procurator in Munich. In these letters especially three topics are described at length:

a) the route they were following from Bavaria passing through Frankfurt/Main, and the Main valley, Coblenz (*Confluentia*), the Rhine valley via Bonn, Cologne, Liège, Tienen ("Dirlemont"), Louvain, Brussels, Alost, Ghent, Bruges to Ostend;

b) a very long and detailed description on the harsh winter of 1721/1722 they spent among the Bruges fathers, in a residence without any heating in the individual rooms;[57]

c) a list of books he was waiting from Munich, such as unspecified "musicalia"; a "promptuarium philosophicum of Johann Baptist Hofer", and unspecified theological items.

That in all these aspects P(ater) Maelcamp was personally and directly involved is clear, from various indications: As he was the "nominatim" mentioned addressee of a whole series of letters from China by "Galli, Itali & Germani" (apostrophes of the type: "Rev(eren)do Patri in Christo Patri Petro Maelcamp Soc(ietatis) Jesu Collegiorum Prov(inciae) Flandro-Belgicae Procuratori Antwerpiae"). Other letters arrived from Europe, especially from the Procurator of Munich. In one of these letters Maelcamp describes the route to be followed from Ostend for documents, letters etc. for Munich, that is, from Ostend via Bruges and Gent to Antwerp, from where they were transmitted by means of an "auriga" to Cologne (with the address: P. Gabriel Dulman);[58] another interesting aspect are the prices he gives for these episodes.

From another letter we learn that Maelcamp in person transmitted letters, addressed from China to him, to their real German addressee (see, among others, a letter of Romain Hinderer, sent from Canton, 23 November 1722, arrived in Antwerp on 11 September 1723 and transmitted by him to Munich).[59]

---

[56] "R(everend)a V(estr)a [i.e., Conrad Janning] annis singulis poterit intellligere ex nostris Patribus Brugensibus an aliqua navis in Sinas itura sit, necne. Ut autem R(everend)a V(estr)a mature suas litteras praeparet, et Brugas mittat, moneo naves Ostendanas debere mense Januario discedere Ostendâ, si velint habere navigationem felicem." Visschers, p. 170.

[57] See my note: "De betrekkingen tusen de Zuidelijke Nederlanden en de Chinamissie in de 17e en 18e eeuw: enkele Brugse connecties," *Verbiest Koerier* 20 (March 2008), pp. 13-15.

[58] BHStA, Jes. 590, no. 39-40; another letter by Maelcamp of the same date is in the same collection, no/ 41.

[59] *Ibid.*

In many other cases we see his remarks, in his characteristic, awful handwriting jotted down on the sheets themselves, with the fragment of an answer (e.g., "Accepi," "Respondi," "Misi," – "I have already answered" etc.). To give one example in detail, more precisely from Karl Slaviçek's [1678–1735] letter of 4 December 1721, which has the following postscripts:

(on top of the letter)

1723 7 Jan(uarii) misi ipsi duas epistolas a P(atre) Wenzel substituto et unam a R(everendo) Patre, etc. <...>. 4 Dec. 1721. Scripsi Pekinum ad P(atrem) Kegler [sic]. Etiam Pekinum R(everendo) P(atre) Henrico Carvalho[60] procuratore Vice Provinciae Pekini de 1000 flo(renorum) Rhen(orum) Patris Molitor[61] in Sinis me <.......>;

(below)

Patri nostro et P(atri) Julio Zwicker [1667–1738] Pragae inscriptas misi 31 Julii 1722. Litteras inscriptas R(everen)do Patri Antonio Azwanger Soc(ietatis) Jesu Prov(inciae) Germ(ani)ae Sup(erioris) procuratori [1659–1728] misi 29 7bris *(in the margin) flavam illam cistulam misi autem ad R(everendum) P(atrem) Franciscum Xav(erium) Hallauer Monachii, et petii qui (?) transmitteret.

From all these remarks we can verify how intensive and direct his follow-up was in both directions. That it was mostly the (Flandro-Belgian and) German province which took profit from this exchange is clear; that occasionally also the French (Provincia Gallica) were the beneficiaries of his services we hear from the following letter of thanks sent by De Goville: "Iteratas (sc. gratias) ago pro cista librorum nomine totius Missionis Gallo-Sinicae. Utinam occasio se offerat gratum animum exhibendi" (3 November 1721).

As we see in this fragment, Maelcamp occasionally received gifts and presents from the Far East in return for these services. In at least one case this was a copy of a printing, that is, the xylographically printed *Relatio Sepulturae magno Orientis Apostolo S(ancto) Francisco Xaverio erectae in Insula Sanciano Anno Saeculari 1700* of Kaspar Castner (1665–1709), now one of the copies in the KBR, with the provenance (or dedicatory?) inscription: "(A) Domino P(atre) Petro (?) Maelcamp Societatis Jesu Anno 1723."[62] In the same sense, he received two copies of a stellar map of China, one copy for himself, another one for "D(omi)no Fratre Directore," i.e., Carlos (Charles) or Giacomo (Jacques) Maelcamp (Kögler, Peking, 12 November 1725); also the copy of Moggi's planisphere was sent to Europe and accepted as a personal present ("Accepi") (Fridelli, Peking, 14 November 1725).

---

[60] Henrique de Carvalho S.J., procurator of the Far Eastern Mission in Lisbon, and later privre Confessor of João V.

[61] In all probability Kaspar Molitor (1697–1750).

[62] CF. II 87.353°-c A RP. For an incomplete census of these copies (KBR only has five copies), see C[harles] R[alph] Boxer, "Some Sino-European Xylographic Works, 1662–1718," *JRAS* 1947/3-4, pp. 199–215, here pp. 203 and 214.

Thanks to these letters, we also get very precise information on the material circumstances of this communication route, far more than we have on the other routes (except for the "Via Sibirica"). The letters offer precise details on the names of the ships, the captains, some chaplains, problems with the crew, which makes them a relevant though overlooked source for the history of the Ostend Company.[63]

Among all these material details, some are relevant for the dossier of the Jesuit Mission as well: here I think, for instance, of the dates of departure or arrival of the ships; from a comparison we can infer that the average pace to span the distance between Ostend and Canton was 5½ to 6 months:

- Pieter Van Hamme on 10 October 1718: a ship leaving Ostend in January 1718 arriving in Canton in July, after some 6 months (this must be the "Prince Eugenius");
- Pieter Van Hamme on 14 October 1719: a ship which left Ostend on 7 February 1719 and arrived in Canton on 25 July, after barely 5 months and a half.

This was very quick – especially when compared to the average of eight months on the turn of the 17th/18th century, not to mention the two to three years calculated in the early 17th century by Terrentius; especially this speed made this 'line' very attractive to the Jesuits, as these were always in need for a quicker communication of papers, letters, money, books etc. some problems on board, etc., cf. also this remark: "Viae enim Lusitanicae tardissimae sunt, & tarditas plurimum nobis nocet" (Kögler, Peking, 1 November 1724).

In addition some names of European (book) donators are mentioned in the letters: the unidentified "clericus" Antonio Diaz in Bruges and the Jesuit Franciscus Van Callenberghe in Antwerp. Names of intermediaries are especially the Dutch Protestant minister Theodorus Sax, Sr. in Batavia (Visschers, pp. 127/128), who deserves a separate research; Royal Confessors in Europe, such as Anton Stieff ([1660-1729]: Balthasar Miller, from Canton, 5 Jan. 1720) and Vitus Tönneman ([1659-1740]: "Vito Ten(n)eman [sic] ... Maiestatis Caesareae Confessarius"; Ehrembert Fridelli from Peking, 23 November 1725; Giampaolo Gozani, from Canton, 20 December 1725); the Japan Provincial Domingos de Britto ([1674-1742]: Romain Hinderer from Hangzhou, 10 October 1725), and Giuseppe Candone ([1636-1701]: Fridelli, from Peking, 25 November 1719).

Quite unexpectedly we hear some complaints about the poor preparation of the Jesuit missionaries on what the China mission in fact was; see the unusually frank remark of Kögler, in his letter to Maelcamp of 14 October 1723 (Kögler, Peking, 14 October 1723), which seems to break with the myth of the optimal preparation of Jesuit candidates of the mission:

> I had read a lot in Europe, and still more I had heard. I thought that I knew all about Chinese customs. But when I arrived here (in China) I understood that I

---

[63] The data useful in this respect will be subject to a forthcoming study.

knew almost nothing, because I had learned it all only through European conceptions, in a very wrong way, because of the [cultural] difference.⁶⁴

On the costs for the maritime transfer between Europe and China, and for the transport of books within China we receive some information. Books were not considered commercial ware and could be imported for free, i.e., without fare costs: "Libri autem nec speciem commercii faciunt, et intra Sinam saltem a vectigalibus immunes omnino sunt; quod merito exemplo debeat esse Europaeis"⁶⁵; elsewhere we hear that the expenses – if there were any – to be paid to the postmen would be compensated: "Sumptus in cursores postarios, si qui fiunt, iidem utique compensabunt" (Karl Slaviçek, Nanchang, 15 November 1723). Other aspects of the budgetary dossier we find scattered over some other letters, see, among others, Pierre de Goville (from Paris, 24 November 1724), with reference to an amount of 26 Spanish "patacas" to be paid to Petrus Geelhand (ca. 1664–1717), an Amsterdam merchant in Canton, although the situation is not wholly clear); the amount of 34 "scuta, ecus vel piastres" to be paid to one Johannes Tobias (De Goville, from Paris, 24 January 1725). Apparently under normal conditions payment was organized in Canton itself (Fridelli, from Canton, 28 November 1720). Returns from the Paris procurator (namely Louis-François de Orry [1671–1726]) to the Antwerp Procurator Maelcamp are mentioned by De Goville (without date); returns from the German procurator are mentioned, e.g., on 28 November 1720 (Fridelli), from Peking).

We learn about the need of bookbinders and booksellers in China, and on the way books should be sent from Europe to China: "Caret China bibliopolis qui libros compingant cum operculo suo. Satisfuerit si V(estra) R(everenti)a [i.e., Maclcamp?] jubeat saltem folia alligari filo, vocamus 'brocher', ne forte dissipentur ac pereant" (P. de Goville, Canton, 7 December 1721).

Kögler spends a long paragraph on his working with Chinese astronomical works to the General, 23 October 1723 (Peking, 23 October 1723).

Some marginal but substantial information on geographical work on the China atlas ("Tartaro-Sinici Imperii descriptio geographica") is given on 25 November 1719 by Fridelli to Conrad Janning.

Finally in order to function well, this communication had to fit neatly within the Jesuit network inside China. What was needed in the first place were reliable local contact persons based in Canton. In this evidence are mentioned:

- Philippe Cazier (1677–1722), from Menen (Menin), Father of the Gallo-Belgian Province in Canton (1711–1722), mentioned by Visschers,⁶⁶ from him Pieter Van Hamme heard about the "infortunium" that happened to

---

⁶⁴ "Legeram in Europa plurima, plura audieram, rebarque me cuncta nôsse quae apud Sinas moris sunt. Hûc [i.e., in China] autem delatus, perspexi me nihil ferme scire, quia cuncta per species dumtaxat Europaeas erronee nimis ob diversitatem adprehenderam." BUAR, OU/G 126.

⁶⁵ KBR Ms. 4097, f. 6r./v.: Kögler to Maelcamp: Peking, 4 November 1726.

⁶⁶ P. Visschers, p. 173.

the Antwerp Professed House, that is its near-destruction by lightning fire on 18 July 1718.[67] It was also Cazier who reported about the arrival of Ostend ships to his fellow fathers in China, so that they could timely prepare letters and boxes to be sent through these ships to Europe;
- Julien-Placide Hervieu (1671–1746), Superior of the French mission (1719–1731 and 1732–1745): see his letter 14 December 1724 and 24 December 1725;
- Pierre de Goville (1668–1758), procurator in Canton between1707–1724: mentioned, among others, in letters by Balthasar Miller on 5 January 1720 and Karl Slaviçek, on 8 October 1723 (it appears that the latter sometimes withheld copies or transmitted them with much retardation);
- Joseph Labbe (1677–1745), superior of the French Mission in China between 1722–1725: cf. letters of 20 February 1724 and 22 December 1725;
- Giampaolo Gozani (1659–1732), in Canton in 1724–1725.

Conclusion

These so far overlooked letters contain substantial information on one line of communication between China and Europe, through the small-sized Ostend Company, which was active with a huge efficiency and impact, albeit in a short period, between ca. 1718–1730. From this first overview the contribution of this Company may become apparent (always to be considered parallelly and simultaneously with that of the other "Viae") in terms of books, naturalia and artificialia transmitted in both directions, but also a series of details on the practical aspects of the line. This was linked to the presence, the activity and – not in the least – the direct family ties of the then procurator-provincial, Petrus Maelcamp with the main shareholders of this company. The attractiveness of this line relied not only on its good functioning, but also on the Jesuit control over it through Maelcamp, and the geopolitical position of Antwerp and Ostend with regard to the main contemporary European book markets, especially Holland, with which Antwerp was linked through very good relations, e.g., to the "Missio Hollandica" but also other. In addition, this letter corpus and the communication route Canton – Antwerp to which it lends a voice represent the background for the presence of "Sinica" in Belgium (both books and artifacts), mentioned in historical collections now spread over Belgian collections, which have no clear provenance, due to their removal from their original site, and the redistribution in new collections, after the end of the Ancien Régime (due to the Suppression of the Jesuit Society in the Austrian Netherlands in 1773, etc.).

---

[67] Visschers, p. 174.

Appendix

Anon., Macao, 28 Nov. 1721: KBR, Ms. 4097, f. 1-5;

Amiani, Carlo, S.J. (1661–1723), to Orazio Olivieri, in Macao, 20 October 1718: BUAR;

—, to Orazio Olivieri, in Macao, 12 January1719: BUAR;

—, to Orazio Olivieri, in Macao, 4 November 1720: BUAR;

—, to Orazio Olivieri, in Macao, 7 November 1720: BUAR;

Boddens, Johannes Baptista, S.J. (1596–1638), from ?, to (Guilielmus) Paludanus, Hasleti (i.e., Hasselt), 15 November 1634: Visschers, pp. 1-2;

Bouwens, Gerard, S.J. (1634–1712), from the Island Guahan (Mariana Islands), to Conrad Janning, 20 November 1698: Visschers, pp. 33-42;

Boym, Michael, S.J. (1612–1659), from Tonkin, November 1658 (17 pp.): BUAR;

Cazier, Philippe, S.J. (1677–1722), from Canton, 4 November 1718: BUAR;

Couplet, Philippe, S.J. (1622–1693), from Canton, to Godfried Henschenius, 23 November 1670: Visschers, pp. 6-8;

Dentrecolles, François Xavier, S.J. (1664–1741), from Jiujiang, to Conrad Janning, in Antwerp, 20 Sptember 1718: BUAR;

De Rougemont, François, S.J. (1624–1676) from Macao, to Jean Bollandus, 23 December 1658: KBR, Ms. 4096, f. 1;

Emmanuel e Jesu et Maria, to José Suarez: BUAR;

Episcopus Lorimensis, i.e. Francesco Saraceni, OFM (1679–1742) from Shaanxi, to José Suarez, in Peking, 6 July 1726: KBR, Ms. 4097, f. 12;

Fridelli, Xavier Ehrembert, S.J. (1673–1743), from Peking, to Conrad Janning, 25 November 1719: BUAR;

—, from Peking, to Conrad Janning, 28 November 1720: BUAR;

—, from Peking, 28 October 1723: BUAR;

—, from Peking, to Petrus Maelcamp, 14 November 1725: BUAR;

—, from Peking, 23 November 1725: BUAR;

Goville, Pierre de, S.J. (1668–1758), from Paris, 10 May 1726: BUAR;

—, from Paris, 10 May 1726: BUAR;

—, from Canton, 3 November 1721: BUAR;

—, from Canton, 3 November 1721: BUAR;

—, from Paris, to Petrus Maelcamp, 24 November 1724: BUAR;

—, from Canton, to Conrad Janning, 10 November 1718: BUAR;

—, from Canton, to Petrus Maelcamp, 27 November 1722: BUAR;

—, from Canton, 4 November 1721: BUAR;

—, from Canton, 4 November 1721: BUAR;

—, from Canton, 5 November 1720: BUAR;

—, from Canton, 7 December 1721: BUAR;

—, from Canton, 7 December 1721: BUAR;

—, from Paris, to Petrus Maelcamp, 10 May 1726: BUAR;

—, from Paris, to Petrus Maelcamp, 10 May 1726: BUAR;

—, from Paris, 24 January 1725: BUAR;

Gozani, Giampaolo, S.J. (1659–1732), from Canton, to Petrus Maelcamp, 20 December 1725: BUAR;

—, from Canton, to Petrus Maelcamp, 22 December 1725: BUAR;

—, from Canton, 29 December 1725: BUAR;

Hamme, Pieter Van, S.J. (1651–1727), from Rome, to ?, 22 December 1685: KBR, Ms. 4096, f. 11-12;

—, from the Philippines, to Conrad Janning, in Antwerp, 28 June 1689: KBR, Ms. 4096, f. 13r./v.;

—, from Manila, to Conrad Janning, in Antwerp, 8 September 1689: KBR Ms. 4096, f. 14;

—, from Canton, to Franciscus Van Callenberghe, 25 March 1690: Visschers, pp. 16-32;

—, from Canton, to ?, 4 January 1690: KBR, Ms. 4096, f. 16-17;

—, from Nanking, to Conrad Janning and Daniel Papebrochius, in Antwerp, 5 May 1691: KBR, Ms. 4096, f. 18;

—, from Nanking, to the same, 5 May 1691: KBR, Ms. 4096, f. 19 (another item as the former one);

—, ex Regno Sinensi, to Conrad Janning, in Antwerp, unknown date: KBR, Ms. 4096, f. 20;

—, ex Metropoli Huguang [i.e., Wuchang], to Franciscus Van Callenberghe and Conrad Janning, 24 October 1694: KBR, Ms. 4096, f. 21r/v;

—, ex Metropoli Prov. Huguang, to the same, in Antwerp, 28 October 1694: KBR, Ms. 4096, f. 24;

—, ex Metropoli Prov. Huguang, to Johannes de Brier and Conrad Janning in Antwerp, 8 November 1694: KBR, Ms. 4096, f. 22;

—, ex Metropoli Prov. Huguang, to Conrad Janning, in Antwerp, 8 November 1694: KBR, Ms. 4096, f. 23;

—, from Huguang, to Franciscus Van Callenberghe and Conrad Janning, 29 December 1694: KBR, Ms. 4096, f. 26r/27;

—, ex Metropoli Huguang, to the same, 4 October 1695: KBR, Ms. 4096, f. 27-28;

—, ex Metropoli Huguang, to the same, in Antwerp: KBR, Ms. 4096, f. 29;

—, ex Metropoli Huguang to the same, in Antwerp: KBR, Ms. 4096, f. 30 (another item);

—, Huguang, to the same, 21 January 1696: KBR, Ms. 4096, f. 31r;

—, ex Metropoli Prov. Huguang, to the same, in Antwerp: KBR, Ms. 4096, f. 32;

—, ex Prov. Huguang, to the same, in Antwerp, 8 July 1696: KBR, Ms. 4096, f. 33r;

—, ex Imperio Sinensi (Huguang), to the same, 25 February 1697: KBR, Ms. 4096, f. 34-35;

—, ex Petropôli Prov. Huguang ex Imperio Sinensi, 2 July 1697: KBR, Ms. 4096, f. 38;

—, ex Imperio Sinensi (Huguang), to Franciscus Van Callenberghe and Conrad Janning, 4 January 1698: KBR, Ms. 4096, f. 39/40;

—, ex Huguang, to the same, in Antwerp, 8 October 1698: KBR, Ms. 4096, f. 41;

—, ex Imperio Sinensi, to the same, 21 February 1699: KBR, Ms. 4096, f. 44r;

—, ex Imperio Sinensi, to the same, 8 June 1699: KBR, Ms. 4096, f. 45;

—, ex Imperio Sinensi, to the same, in Antwerp, 25 August 1700: KBR, Ms. 4096, f. 46;

—, ex Metropoli Prov. Huguang, to the same in Antwerp, 10 October 1700: KBR, Ms. 4096, f. 50;

—, ex Imperio Sinensi, to the same, in Antwerp, 18 December 1700: KBR, Ms. 4096, f. 47;

—, ex Imperio Sinensi, to Conrad Janning and Daniel Papebrochius, in Antwerp, 10 February 1702: KBR, Ms. 4096, f. 51;

—, from Peking, to the same, 15 October 1702: KBR, Ms. 4096, f. 52;

—, from Peking, to the same, 26 October 1702: KBR, Ms. 4096, f. 53;

—, from Peking, to the same, in Antwerp, 27 November 1702: KBR, Ms. 4096, f. 54;

—, from Peking, to the same, 14 January 1703: Visschers, pp. 43-45;

—, from Peking, to the same, in Antwerp, 3 November 1703: KBR, Ms. 4096, f. 55;

—, from Peking, to Franciscus Van Callenberghe, 16 October 1704: Visschers, pp. 45-49;

—, from Peking, to Conrad Janning and Daniel Papebrochius, 15 January 1706: Visschers, pp. 49-53;

—, from Peking, to Conrad Janning, Libertus de Pa(e)pe, and Franciscus Van Callenberghe, 20 January 1706: Visschers, pp. 54-56;

—, from Peking, to Conrad Janning and Daniel Papebrochius, 18 October 1706: Visschers, pp. 56-57;

—, from Peking, to the same, 16 October 1707: Visschers, pp. 57-68;

—, from Peking, to Aurelianus de Baenst, 20 October 1707: Visschers, pp. 69-70;

—, from Peking, to Conrad Janning and Daniel Papebrochius, 22 October 1707: Visschers, pp. 77-78;

—, from Peking, to the same, 9 January 1708: Visschers, pp. 70-76;

—, from Peking, to the same, 26 October 1710: Visschers, pp. 78-84;

—, from Peking, to the same, 5 November 1710: Visschers, pp. 84-86;

—, from Peking, to?, 5 October 1711: Visschers, pp. 86-96;

—, ex Imperio Sinensi, to Conrad Janning, Daniel Papebrochius, and Joannes Baertius, in Antwerp, 2 October 1712: KBR, Ms. 4096, f. 48-49;

—, from Peking, to the same, 10 October 1713: Visschers, pp. 108-122;

—, ex Imperio Sinensi, to the same, 26 January 1714: Visschers, pp. 122-126;

—, ex Imperio Sinensi, to the same, 12 November 1715: Visschers, pp. 127-129;

—, ex Imperio Sinensi, to ?, 26 September 1716: Visschers, pp. 129-137;

—, from Peking, to Conrad Janning, Daniel Papebrochius, and Joannes Baertius, 25 January 1717: Visschers, pp. 138-157;

—, ex Imperio Sinensi, to Conrad Janning, 11 October 1717: Vissschers, pp. 158-167;

—, ex Imperio Sinensi, to Conrad Janning and the Fathers "hagiographi," 10 October 1718: Visschers, pp. 167-172;

—, ex Imperio Sinensi, to Conrad Janning, 14 October 1719: BUAR;

—, ex Imperio Sinensi, to Conrad Janning, 2 October 1719: BUAR;

—, ex Imperio Sinensi, to Conrad Janning and the Fathers 'hagiographi', 16 January 1720 (23.II.1720): Visschers, pp. 173-182;

—, ex Imperio Sinensi, to the same, 14 September 1720: Visschers, pp. 182-185;

—, ex Imperio Sinensi, to Conrad Janning, 5 October 1722 (?): BUAR;

—, ex Imperio Sinensi, to Petrus Maelcamp, 4 October 1723: BUAR;

—, ex Imperio Sinensi, to Jean-Baptiste du Sollier, 4 October 1723: BUAR;

—, ex Imperio Sinensi, to Petrus Maelcamp, 1 November 1724: BUAR;

—, ex Imperio Sinensi, to the same, 6 Octobr 1725: BUAR;

—, ex Imperio Sinensi, to the same, 30 May 1726: BUAR;

Hervieu, Julien-Placide, S.J. (1671-1746), from Jiujiang, to Petrus Maelcamp, 14 October 1721: BUAR;

—, from Canton, to Petrus Maelcamp, 14 December 1724: BUAR;

—, from Canton, to Petrus Maelcamp, 14 December 1724: BUAR (second letter);

Hinderer, Romain, S.J. (1668-1744), from Canton, to Petrus Maelcamp, 23 November 1722: BUAR;

—, from Canton, to Petrus Maelcamp, 7 October 1723: BUAR;

—, from Hangzhou, to ?, 1725: BUAR;

—, from Hangzhou to ?, August 1725: BUAR;

—, from Hangzhou fu, to Petrus Maelcamp, 10 October 1725: BUAR;

Jannsens, Franciscus, S.J. (1671-1716), to Jacques de la Fonteyne and Conrad Janning, 9 April 1700: KBR, Ms. 4096, f. 8;

Kögler, Ignaz, S.J. (1680-1746), from Peking, to Petrus Maelcamp, 14 October 1723: BUAR;

—, from Peking, to ?, 23 October 1723: BUAR;

—, from Peking, to Petrus Maelcamp, 28 October 1723: BUAR;
—, from Peking, to ?, 21 November 1724: BUAR;
—, from Peking, to ?, March 1724: BUAR;
—, from Peking, to ?, July 1724: BUAR;
—, from Peking, to ?, September 1724: BUAR;
—, from Peking, to some procurator, 22 October 1724: BUAR;
—, from Peking, to some procurator, 12 November 1724: BUAR;
—, from Peking, to ?, 2 November 1724: BUAR;
—, from Peking, to some Superior, 2 November 1725: BUAR;
—, from Peking, to some Superior, 5 November 1725: BUAR;
—, From Peking, to Petrus Maelcamp, 6 December 1725: BUAR;
—, from Peking, to the same, 12 November 1725: BUAR;
—, from Peking, to the same, 28 October 1726: KBR, Ms. 4097, f. 46-53;
—, from Peking, to the same, 4 November 1726: KBR, Ms. 4097, f. 6;
—, from Peking, to Michelangelo Tamburini, in Rome, 5 November 1726: KBR Ms. 4097, f. 22-25;
—, from Peking, to Pater Praepositus (i.e., Petrus Maelcamp), 9 November 1726: KBR, Ms. 4097, f. 8;
—, from Peking, to the Assistant, 14 November 1726: KBR, Ms. 4097, f. 32-33;
—, from Peking, to Nicolo Giampriamo, in Rome / Naples, 26 November 1726: KBR, Ms. 4097, f. 10-11;

Labbe, Joseph, S.J. (1677-1745), from Canton, to ?, 22 December 1725: BUAR;
—, from Canton, to Petrus Maelcamp, 20 February 1724; BUAR;

Leblanc, Philibert, MEP (1644-1720) from Middelburg, to ?, 10 November 1689: KBR, Ms. 4096, f. 15r/v;

Maldonado, Jean-Baptiste (1634-1699), from Macao, to Prospero Intorcetta, in Flanders, 10. December 1671: Visschers, pp. 11-14;
—, from Macao, to Godfried Henschenius, 20 February 1672: Visschers, p. 15;
—, from ?, to ?, 29 September 1690: KBR, Ms. 4096, f. 2 r/v;

Mezzabarba, Carlo Ambrosio, (1686-1741), from Peking, to ?, 4 March 1721: KBR, Ms. 4097, f. 43;

Miller, Balthasar (1683-17419, from Canton, to C. Janning, 5 January 1720: BUAR;
—, from Xinhui, to Petrus Maelcamp, 14 September 1721: BUAR;
—, from Xinhui, to ?, 10 August 1723: BUAR;
—, from Shangchuan, to Petrus Maelcamp, 5 September 1723: BUAR;
—, from Shangchuan, to Petrus Maelcamp, 6 December 1724: BUAR;
—, near Shangchuan, to Petrus Maelcamp, 6 December 1724: BUAR;
—, from Macao, to Petrus Maelcamp, 24 November 1725: BUAR;
—, from Canton, to Petrus Maelcamp, 3 December 1726: KBR, Ms. 4097, f. 9;

Morabito, Antonio Saverio (1691–1769), from Canton, to Petrus Maelcamp, 2 November 1721: BUAR;

Mourão, João (1681–1726), from Xi da tong, to ?, 2 April 1725: BUAR;

—, from Xi da tong, to ?, 15 April 1725; BUAR;

—, from Xi da tong, to Michelangelo Tamburini, 26 July 1725: KBR, Ms. 4097, f. 26-30;

—, from Xi da tong, to ?, 8 July 1725: KBR, Ms. 4097, f. 54-71;

Noël, François (1651–1729), from Macao, to ?, 9 September 1695: KBR, Ms. 4096, f. 4;

Pedrini, Teodorico (1671–1746), from ?, to Dominique Parrenin, 12 December 1723: BUAR;

—, from Peking, 19 September 1725: BUAR;

Pereira, Jose, S.J. (1674–1731), from Canton, to Petrus Maelcamp, 24 December 1724: BUAR;

Roveda, Benedetto, to Dominique Parrenin, in Macao, 8 October 1721: BUAR;

Sibin, Philipp, S.J. (1679–1759), from Macao, 11 November 1721: BUAR;

Slaviçek, Karl, S.J. (1678–1735), from Peking, to Conrad Janning, 27 October 1718: BUAR;

—, from Peking, to Conrad Janning, 2 November 1719: BUAR;

—, from Canton, to Petrus Maelcamp, 4 December 1721: BUAR;

—, from Nanchang, to Petrus Maelcamp, 15 November 1723: BUAR;

—, from Nanchang, to Franciscus Rets, 8 October 1723: BUAR;

—, from Nanchang, to Petrus Maelcamp, 8 October 1723: BUAR;

—, "Relatio de missione Sinensi ad annum 1725," from ?, to ?, 20 November 1725, BUAR;

—, from Peking, 20 November 1725: BUAR;

Suarez, José, S.J. (1656–1736), from Peking, to Teodorico Pedrini (?), 17 September 1725: BUAR;

Van Callenberghe, Franciscus, S.J. (1643–1719) from Rome, to Conrad Janning, in Antwerp, 6 January 1703: Brussels, KBR, Ms. 4096, f. 9;

Van der Beken, Willem, S.J. (1659–1702), from Huai'an, to Johannes Van der Beken, 7 September 1698: KBR, Ms. 4096, f. 7;

Verbiest, Ferdinand, S.J. (1623–1688), from Peking, to François de Rougemont, 23 January 1670: Visschers, pp. 3-5.

—, from Peking, to Tommaso Valguarneira, 1 (10?) July 1671: Visschers, pp. 9-10;

Visdelou, Claude de, S.J. (1656–1737), from ?: 1686: EBA

明清之际"西学汉籍"的文化意义

张西平、任大援

English Abstract

Cultural Significance of the "Chinese Books on Western Learning" in Late Ming and Early Qing

ZHANG XIPING, REN DAYUAN

Among numerous intercultural activities between China and other peoples and countries, the communication between China and Europe during the late Ming dynasty and the beginning of the Qing dynasty is one of the most significant events. The European missionaries in China provoked a large-scale encounter of ideas and cultures. A new type of literature, the *Xixue Hanji* 西学汉籍 (Chinese Books on Western Learning) emerged in historical studies, which aimed to translate and introduce Christianity as well as the science, history, and philosophy of Europe into Chinese.

Already since the late Ming dynasty, scholars tried to classify and compose bibliographies for *Xixue Hanji*. For some reasons, Chinese scholars formerly neglected these *Xixue Hanji*. Since 2008, a Chinese scholar team cooperated with the Vatican Library to reproduce and compose a comprehensive bibliography on the Vatican *Xixue Hanji* collections. After seven years the publication of the first 44 volumes of *Xixue Hanji* preserved in the Vatican Library came out. Successive publications are forthcoming.

The value of the reproduction of *Xixue Hanji* in the Vatican Library can be reflected in the following field of studies: 1. the politics and society of the Ming and Qing Dynasty; 2. the history of Christianity in China; 3. the history of translation and linguistics in China; 4. the intellectual history of China, the philosophical notions and their exchange between China and Europe; 5. the transmission of Chinese Classics to the West; 6. the scientific history of mathematics, astronomy, and geography etc.; 7. the history of Sinology in Europe.

The reproduction of *Xixue Hanji* carries significance especially when China explores into the concept of Chinese characteristics, universal values, and the common destiny of mankind. The historical heritage from these in-depth cultural communications between China and Europe can still provide wisdom and shed light on the on-going reforms in China.

明清之际从时间上说大体是中国晚明崇祯朝到清顺治、康熙时期。黄宗羲用"天崩地解"来形容这一时期的早期阶段，所言极是。这一时段，明清鼎革，历经满汉政权转化与文化巨变，世界范围正经历从15世纪末期的地理大发现带来的西方文化与体制在全球的扩张。文化相遇与冲突以多重形式展开，其影响波及今日之世界。

对中国和西方关系来说，最重要的事件是葡萄牙和西班牙从印度洋和太平洋来到东亚以及耶稣会入华。由此，拉开了中华文明和欧洲文明的在文化与精神上真正相遇。著名汉学家许理和认为，17 至 18 世纪的中西文化交流史是"一段最令人陶醉的时期：这是中国和文艺复兴之后的欧洲高层知识界的第一次接触和对话。"[1]

一

正是在这次文化相遇与对话中，来华的传教士将书刊作为传教的重要手段。利玛窦说："基督教信仰的要义通过文字比通过口头更容易得到传播，因为中国人好读有任何新内容的书。"[2] "任何以中文写成的书籍都肯定可以进入全国的十五个省份而有所获益。而且，日本人、朝鲜人、交趾支那的居民、琉球人以及甚至其他国家的人，都能像中国人一样地阅读中文，也能看懂这些书。虽然这些种族的口头语言有如我们可能想象的那样，是大不相同的，但他们都能看懂中文，因为中文写的每一个字都代表一样东西。如果到处都如此的话，我们就能够把我们的思想以文字形式传达给别的国家的人民，尽管我们不能和他们讲话。"[3] 梵蒂冈图书馆所藏的《天主聖教書目·曆法格物窮理書目》中明确说出传教士刻书传教之目的是："夫天主圣教为至真至实，宜信宜从，其确据有二：在外，在内。在内者则本教诸修士著述各端，极合正理之确，论其所论之事虽有彼此相距甚远者，如天地、神人、灵魂、形体、现世、后世、生死等项，然各依本性自然之明，穷究其理。总归于一道之定向，始终至理通贯，并无先后矛盾之处。更有本教翻译诸书百部一一可考，无非发明昭事上帝，尽性命之道，语语切要，不设虚玄。其在外之确据以本教之功行踪迹，目所易见者，则与吾人讲求归复大事，永远固福辟邪指正而已。至若诸修士所著天学格物致知，气象历法等事，亦有百十余部，久行于世，皆足徵。天主圣教真实之理，愿同志诸君子归斯正道而共昭事焉。"[4]

由此，明清之际开始，在中国的历史文献中出现了一批新的类型的书籍，即以翻译和介绍欧洲文化宗教的汉文书籍。[5]

梁启超在《中国近二百年学术史》中说：

> 明末有一场大公案，为中国学术史上应该大笔特书者，曰：欧洲历算学之输入。先是马丁·路得既创新教，罗马旧教在欧洲大受打击，于是有所谓"耶稣会"者起，想从旧教内部改革振作。他的计划是要传教海外，中国及美洲实

---

[1] 许理和《十七—十八世纪耶稣会研究》，载任继愈主编《国际汉学》第四期，大象出版社 1999 年。第 429 页。

[2] 利玛窦、金尼阁著，何高济等泽《利玛窦中国札记》，北京：中华书局，1983 年，第 172 页。

[3] 利玛窦《中国札记》，第 483 页。

[4] 梵蒂冈图书馆藏 Raccolta Generale Oriente – Stragrandi. 13a，据 CCT-Database 数据库著录，编撰者为比利时耶稣会士安多 (Antoine Thomas, 1644–1709).

[5] 与此同时，在欧洲的文献中出现了大量的关于东亚和中国的报导与研究的书籍，中国古代文化典籍被译成各种欧洲语言，中国的思想和文化开始进入欧洲思想家和民众的视野，从此逐渐形成 18 世纪欧洲中国热。鉴于本文的主题所限，这里不做展开。

为其最主要之目的地。于是利马窦、庞迪我、熊三拔、龙华民、邓玉函、阳玛诺、罗雅谷、艾儒略、汤若望等,自万历末年至天启、崇祯间,先后入中国。中国学者如徐文定,名光启,号元扈,上海人、崇祯六(1633)年卒,今上海徐家汇即其故宅。李凉庵名之藻,仁和人等都和他们来往,对于各种学问有精深的研究。先是所行"大统历",循元郭守敬"授时历"之旧,错谬很多。万历末年,朱世堉、邢云路先后上疏指出他的错处,请重为厘正。天启、崇祯两朝十几年间,很拿这件事当一件大事办。经屡次辩争的结果,卒以徐文定、李凉庵领其事,而请利、庞、熊诸客卿共同参豫,卒完成历法改革之业。此外中外学者合译或分撰的书籍,不下百数十种。最著名者,如利、徐合译之《几何原本》,字字精金美玉,为千古不朽之作,无庸我再为赞叹了。其余《天学初函》、《崇祯历书》中几十部书,都是我国历算学界很丰厚的遗产。又《辨学》一编,为西洋论理学输入之鼻祖。又徐文定之《农政全书》六十卷,熊三拔之《泰西水法》六卷,实农学界空前之著作。我们只要肯把当时那班人的著译书目一翻,便可以想见他们对于新智识之传播如何的努力。只要肯把那个时代的代表作品—如《几何原本》之类择一两部细读一过,便可以知道他们对于学问如何的忠实。要而言之,中国智识线和外国智识线相接触,晋、唐间的佛学为第一次,明末的历算学便是第二次。中国元代时和阿拉伯文化有接触,但影响不大。在这种新环境之下,学界空气,当然变换,后此清朝一代学者,对于历算学都有兴味,而且最喜欢谈经世致用之学,大概受利、徐诸人影响不小。[6]

梁任公这段论述有两点十分重要:一是,明清之际的中西文化交流是继佛教传入中国后,中华文明与外部世界知识最重要的一次接触。他从中国历史的角度将明清之际的中西文化交流史定位,对其评价的视野与高度都是前所未有的;其二,对传教士与文人所合作翻译的"西学汉籍"给予了高度的评价,认为是"字字精金美玉,为千古不朽之作。"

梁启超对这批书籍并未统一定义,学界也有用"汉文西书"来定义,[7] 这个定义尚不能全面概括这类文献的特点,因为一是在文献呈现形式上并非全部是以书的形式出现,其中含有大量手稿、舆图等;二是从文献内容上不仅有大量向中国介绍西方的学术和知识的内容,也有传教士用中文写作,研读中国文化的文献,例如白晋的汉文《易经》手稿。我们认为用"西学汉籍"较为稳妥。"汉籍"一语,学术界已经不再将其仅仅理解为中国士人在历史上的出版物,凡是用汉文书写的历史文献都可称为汉籍。[8] 这些我们将在下面介绍梵蒂冈图书馆藏明清中西文化交流史文献时再具体展开。

对这批文献的整理史,最早可以追溯到1615年(万历四十三年)杨廷筠所编的《绝徼同文纪序》,书中收入了包括部分来华耶稣会士在内的中国文

---

6 梁启超《中国近三百年学术史》第9页,东方出版社,2004年。

7 "今天我们也用该词来泛指16-19世纪通过西方传教士介绍给中国的西方学术、西方知识或西方的知识体系自成反映这一部分内容的文献,可以统称为"汉文西书"。见邹振环《晚明汉文西学经典:编译、诠释、流传与影响》,第6页,复旦大学出版社2013年。书中邹振环认为"西学"一词最早出现在中国人的著述中,可能是南宋李心传(1167-1244)记述高宗一代史事的史书《建炎以来系年要录》,其中卷116记载了载曹冠在廷试对策中所言:"凡为伊川之学者,皆德之贼也。又曰:自西学盛行,士多浮伪,陛下排斥异端,道术亦有所统一矣。"

8 张伯伟编《域外汉籍研究集刊》,第1-4辑,中华书局,2005-2008年。

人为西学汉籍所写的 70 篇序言和 7 篇明朝关于处理来华传教士的公文,这些序言涉及到传教士所出版的西学汉籍 25 部。杨廷筠在序言中说:"知六经之外自有文字,九州之表更有畸人,由是纪以索观其书,由读书以接通其人。"[9] 尽管《绝徼同文纪序》以西学汉籍的题跋序言为主,但开启了对西学汉籍的整体收集与整理之先河。

李之藻在 1623 年(天启三年)的《天学初函》书中收录了传教士和中国文人的著作二十篇,其中"理编"十篇,"器编"十篇。收入理编的有:《西学凡》(《唐景教碑附》),《畸人十篇》(附《西琴曲意》),《交友论》,《二十五言》,《天主实义》,《辩学遗牍》,《七克》,《灵言蠡勺》,《职方外记》;收入器编的有:《泰西水法》,《浑盖通宪图说》,《几何原本》,《表度说》,《天问略》,《简平仪说》(附《测量法义》),《同文算指》,《圆容较义》,《勾股义》,《测量异同》。他在《天学初函》的序中说:"时则有利玛窦者,九万里抱道来宾,重演斯义,迄今又五十年;多贤似续,翻译渐广,……顾其书散在四方,愿学者每不能尽睹为憾!"康熙朝后,西学影响日益扩大,后因"礼仪之争",特别是雍乾禁教后,西学日渐式微,但作为一种新的知识,这批文献官方仍不能忽视,在《四库全书》中就说"西学所长在于测算,其短则在于崇奉天主,以炫惑人心"。这样它仅收入西学汉籍 22 种。对于西学汉籍中的非科学类书籍,《四库全书》"止存书名",不收其书。这样有 15 部西学汉籍被入《四库存目》之中,其中收入子部杂家类的 11 种,收入史部地理类的 2 种,收入经部小学类的 2 种。[10]

生于 1620 的中国文人刘凝,一生未得功名,弱冠入县学。[11] 他编辑的《天学集解》,涉及西学汉籍的有 284 本,分为首集、道集、法集、理集、器集、后集。[12] 尽管是手稿,尚未出版,但却是当时收集的最全面的西学汉籍的序跋。[13]这些序跋的大部分撰写于 1599–1679 年间。

"刊书传教"已成为利玛窦所确立的"适应路线"的重要举措,从教内各类书目也可以看出这批"西学汉籍"的传播,上面提到的梵蒂冈图书馆所藏的中文书中有两份文献专门记载了这批书目[14]。编号"R.G. Oriente – Stragrandi 13 (a)有两个书目,《天主圣教书目》著录了宗教类著作 123 种,《历法格物穷理书目》,著录了 89 种西学汉籍文献,两份文献共收录了 212 种文献。

9　杨廷筠《绝徼同文纪序》,钟鸣旦 杜鼎克、蒙曦编《法国国家图书馆藏明清天主教文献》第 6 卷,第 10 页,台北利氏学社,2009 年。

10　参阅计文德《从四库全书探究明清间输入之西学》,台湾济美图书有限公司,1991 年。

11　肖清和著《清初儒家基督徒刘凝生平事迹与人际网络考》,《中国典籍与文化》,2012 年第 4 期。

12　参见 Ad Dudink, "The Rediscovery of a Seventeenth-Century Collection of Chinese Christian Texts: The Manuscript *Tianxue jijie*," SWCRJ 15 (1993), pp. 1-26.

13　胡文婷《明清之际西学汉籍书目研究初探》抽印本。

14　伯希和 (Paul Pelliot) 著、高田时雄补 (Takata Tokio) 编, *Inventaire sommaire des manuscrits et imprimés chinois de la Bibliothèque vaticane: A Posthumous Work*, Tokio: Istituto italiano di cultura, Scuola di studi sull'Asia orientale, 1995. 有关这个目录的情况下面我们还要专门介绍。

《圣教信证》是张赓和韩霖合写的一部书，书中编入来华传教士的汉文著作，以表达"续辑以志，源源不绝之意。"全书收录 92 个明代传教士的简要生平和 229 部汉文西书。同治年间的胡璜著《道学家传》有着很高的文献学价值。全书共收录了传教士 89 人，其中有中文著述的 38 人，共写下中文著作 224 部。

与此同时，在中国文人所编的各种书目和丛书中也开始著录西学汉籍的图书。[15] 初步研究大约有 15 种书目著录了各种西学书籍，共收录的西学汉籍约 138 部。[16]

同时随着欧洲天主教修会进入中国，各地教徒的增加，各地修会也开始翻刻耶稣会所出版的书籍，同时，中国信徒也开始翻译和编写出版各类西学书籍。[17]

在西方汉学界最早注意来华耶稣会中文著作的是基歇尔（Athanasius Kircher，1602-1680），由于他和来华耶稣会士有着密切的关系，他于 1667 年在阿姆斯特丹出版的《中国图说》首次向欧洲介绍了入华传教士的中文著作，其中包括利玛窦、罗雅谷、高一志等人的书籍。[18]

明末清初来华传教士究竟出版了多少西学汉文书籍？写作并留下多少西学汉文手稿？这些学术界至今尚无定论。

亨利·考狄（Henri Cordier, 1849-1925）1901 年所编写的《十七十八世纪欧洲人在中国的出版书目》(*L'Imprimerie sino-européenne en Chine: bibliographie des ouvrages publiés en Chine par les Européens au XVIIe et au XVIIIe siècle*)书目中收录了明清之际的西学汉籍有 363 种。

法国汉学家，著名的中国基督教史研究专家裴化行（Henri Bernard, S.J.）1945 年在《华裔学志》（*Monumenta Serica*）第 10 卷上发表了《从葡萄牙人到广东至法国传教士到北京期间欧洲著作的中文编译书目 1514-1688》("Les adaptations chinoises d'ouvrages européens: bibliographie chronologique depuis la

---

[15] 徐宗泽的《明清间耶稣会士译著提要》统计，共有 13 种丛书收录了西学文献，而据郑鹤声，郑鹤春《中国文献学概要》（上海书店，1990 年），共有 11 种丛书收录了西学文献。

[16] 见赵用贤 (1535-1596)《赵定宇书目》，祁承㸁 (1565-1628)《澹生堂藏书目》，赵琦美(1563-1624)《脉望馆书目》，徐𤊹 (1570-1642)《徐氏家藏书目》，陈第 (1541-1617)《世善堂书目》，董其昌 (1556-1636)《玄赏斋书目》，无名氏(明末)《近古堂书目》，钱谦益 (1582-1664)《绛云楼书目》，季振宜 (1630-?)《季沧苇书目》，钱曾 (1629-1699 之后)《也是园藏书目》，黄虞稷 (1629-1691)《千顷堂书目》，徐乾学 (1631-1694)《传是楼书目》。钟鸣旦（Nicolas Standaert）、杜鼎克（Ad Dudink）《简论明末清初耶稣会著作在中国的流传》。

[17] 张淑琼《明末清初天主教在粤刻印书籍述略》，图书馆论坛，2013 年第 3 期；

[18] 基歇尔著、张西平、杨慧玲等译，《中国图说》（*China monumentis, qua sacris qua profanis, nec non variis naturae & artis spectaculis, aliarumque rerum memorabilium argumentis illustrata*"，中文为《中国宗教、世俗和各种自然、技术奇观及其有价值的实物材料汇编》，简称《中国图说》即 "*China illustrata*"），大象出版社，2013 年；张西平《国外对明末清初天主教中文文献的收集和整理》，刊于《陈垣先生的史学研究与教育事业》，北京师范大学出版社，2010 年，页 234-238。

venue des Portugais à Canton jusqu'à la mission française de Péking 1514–1688"）的论文[19]，在这篇文章中，刊登出 38 位传教士名单，其中 36 人有中文著作，共 236 种。1960 年在《华裔学志》的第 19 期，他又发表了《从法国传教士到北京至乾隆末期欧洲著作的中文编年书目 1869–1799》("Les adaptations chinoises d'ouvrages européens: deuxième partie, depuis la fondation de la Mission française de Pékin jusqu'à la mort de l'empereur K'ien-long 1689–1799") 的论文，并整理出《北京刊行天主圣教书板目》《历法格物穷理书板目》《福建福州府钦一堂刊书板目》《浙江杭州府天主堂刊书板目录》四篇目录。这四个目录共刊录了 303 种文献。

由冯承钧所译的法国中国基督教史研究专家费赖之（Louis Pfister, S.J.）1932 年所做的《在华耶稣会士列传及书目》（*Notices biographiques et bibliographiques sur les jésuites de l'ancienne mission de Chine (1552–1773)*，是一部研究入华传教士的重要的工具书，他把传教士的中文和西文的文献统一编目，提供了入华耶稣会士中文文献的重要而又丰富的信息。《在华耶稣会士列传及书目》中共有 63 人写了 366 种中文文献。[20]

《法国国家图书馆馆藏中国图书目录》（*Catalogue des livres chinois, coréens, japonais, etc.*）这个目录是 1912 年由法国人古郎（Maurice Courant）所做，古郎书目共收入了 99 名作者的明清天主教文献 374 种，[21] 这些作者中耶稣会的传教士 56 人，方济各会，道明会，奥斯定会等其他修会的传教士 15 人，中国士人 28 人。这 374 部文献中署名作者的文献有 278 种，无作者署名的文献 96 种。[22]

徐宗泽在《明清间耶稣会士译著提要》[23] 第十卷的《徐家汇书楼所藏明末清初耶稣会士及中国公教学者译著书目》达 402 种，其中基督教宗教类书目达 296 种，占总数的 74%；属于自然科学技术方面的书目共 62 种，占总数的 15%；关于中西哲学、政治、教育、社会、语言文学艺术方面的共 31 种，约占总数的 8%；传教士奏疏等历史文献共 13 种，约占 3%。译著书籍的主体是宗教类文献，其次是自然科学技术类文献。在第十卷的《巴黎国立图书馆所藏明末清初耶稣会会士及中国公教学者译著书目录》中著录了 760 种文献，基本是宗教、神哲学类译著文献。十卷中的《梵蒂冈图书馆所藏明末清初耶稣会士及中国公教学者译著书》有 169 种文献。

据钱存训统计，明清之际耶稣会传教士在华两百年间共翻译西书 437 种，其中纯属宗教的书籍 251 种，占总数的 57%；属自然科学的书籍 131 种，占总

---

[19] *Monumenta Serica* 10 (1945), pp. 309-388.

[20] 这里的统计包含地图，但未包含汉外双语或多语词典的数量和相关的作者。

[21] 不含副本，这只是一个初步的统计，徐宗泽的统计是 733 部，他的统计含重复和副本。

[22] 张西平 2002 年在这里访问了三个月，初步将其全部的明清天主教文献过眼一遍，并在古郎书目的基础上做了简目。国内学者大都很熟悉徐宗泽书后所附的《巴黎国立图书馆所藏明末清初耶稣会士及中国公教学者译着书目录》，但徐宗泽的目录并未收全古郎书目的西学汉籍文献，如罗明坚所拟写的《罗马教皇致大明国国主书》，就未收入其中。

[23] 徐宗泽《明清间耶稣会士译著提要》，上海世纪出版集团，2010 年。

数的 30%；属人文科学书籍 55 种，占总数的 13%。[24] 梁启超在《中国近三百年学术史》中著录的西学汉籍 321 种。李天纲估计明末清初关于天主教的文献应该不少于 1000 种。[25]

二

雍乾禁教以后，天主教发展处于低潮，从而使得许多天主教方面的书只有存目，不见其书，而到清末时一些书已经很难找到，如陈垣先生所说："童时阅四库提要，即知有此类书，四库概屏不录，仅存其目，且深诋之，久欲一睹原书，粤中苦无传本也。"[26]

由此，从民国初年至今，中外学者为收集和整理这批文献进行长达一百多年的努力。马相伯是清末民初的风云人物，晚年时极力主张天主教的本色化，他在明末清初的入华耶稣会的中文著作中找到了心中的理想，"找到一种天造地设的契合，而利所译最切近这理想。[27]

因此他对这批文献的收集十分重视。他曾写下了《重刊〈辩学遗牍〉跋》，《重刊〈主制群征〉序》》，《书〈利玛窦行迹〉后》，《重刊〈真主灵性理证〉序》，《重刊〈灵魂道体说〉序》，《重刊〈灵言蠡勺〉序》等多篇有关整理明末清初天主教文献的文章。在他和英敛之等人的通信中曾提到他自己过眼的明清天主教文献有 26 部之多。[28] 为做好这件事，他曾和英敛之、陈垣多次通信，并对陈垣的工作倍加赏识，在给英敛之的信中说"援庵实可敬可爱"。[29] 在推动明清天主教文献的整理方面，马相伯发挥了重要的作用。

英敛之早年正是读了利玛窦、艾儒略等人的书后才加入了天主教。民国初年，他经十余年努力找到了《天学初函》的全本，并重新刊印其中的部分文献，他在重刊《辩学遗牍》的序言中说："《天学初函》自明季李之藻汇刊以来，三百余年，书已希绝。鄙人数十年中，苦志搜罗，今幸寻得全帙。内中除器编十种，天文历法，学术较今稍旧，而理编则文笔雅洁，道理奥衍，

---

[24] 钱存训《近世译书对中国现代化的影响》，《文献》1986 年第 2 期。宋巧燕《明清之际耶稣会士译着文献的刊刻与流传》，见《世界宗教研究》2011 年第 6 期。

[25] 参见李天纲《中文文献与中国基督宗教史研究》，张先清编《史料与视界》第 7 页，上海人民出版社，2007 年。

[26] 方豪《李之藻辑刻天学初函考》，载《天学初函》重印本，台湾学生书局，1965 年版。

[27] 李天纲《信仰与传统—马相伯的宗教生活》，载朱维铮主编《马相伯传》，复旦大学出版社 1996 年。

[28] 马相伯所提到和过眼的文献有：《辩学遗牍》、《主制群征》、《景教碑》、《名理探》、《利先生行迹》、《天学举要》（阳玛诺）、《真主性灵理证》（卫匡国）、《灵魂道体说》《铎书》，《天教明辩》，《圣经直解》，《圣教奉褒》，《圣教史略》、《圣梦歌》、《寰有诠》、《童幼教育》、《超性学要》、《王觉斯赠汤若望诗翰》、《天学初函》、《七克》、《教要序论》、《代疑论》（阳玛诺）、《畸人十篇》、《三山论学记》、《遵主圣范》及《灵言蠡勺》。

[29] 朱维铮《马相伯集》，第 369 页。

非近人译著所及。鄙人欣快之余,不敢自秘,拟先将《辩学遗牍》一种排印,以供大雅之研究。"³⁰

马相伯、英敛之、陈垣三人中当属陈垣学术成就最高,他的《元也里可温教考》一举成名,奠基了中国天主教史研究的基础,在明清天主教文献的收集和整理上他也着力最大。

他不仅整理和出版了入华传教士的著作,如《辩学遗牍》、《灵言蠡勺》、《明季之欧化美术及罗马字注音》、《利玛窦行迹》等,而且在教外典籍中发现了许多重要的文献,他所写下的《从教外典籍见明末清初之天主教》、《雍乾间奉天主教之宗室》、《泾阳王徵传》、《休宁金声传》、《明末殉国者陈于阶传》、《华亭许缵曾传》、《汤若望与木陈忞》等一系列论文,不仅在学术上大大加深了对天主教入华传教史的研究,在历史研究和文献研究上也开辟了一个崭新的领域。陈寅恪在陈垣先生的《明季滇黔佛教考》的序言中说:"中国乙部之中,几无完善之宗教史,然其有之,实自近岁新会陈援庵先生之著述"。这说明了陈垣先生在中国宗教史,特别是在中国基督教史上研究中的地位。

陈垣先生在谈到这批文献的整理时,他认为应该继承李之藻的事业,把《天学初函》继续出版下去,并在给英敛之的信中说:"顷言翻刻旧籍事,与其请人缮抄,毋宁迳将要籍借出影印。假定接续天学初函理编为天学二函,三函》……,分期出版,此事想非难办。细想一遍,总胜于抄,抄而又校,校而付排印,又再校,未免太费力;故拟仿涵芬楼新出四部丛刊格式,先将《超性学要》(21册)影印,即名为天学二函,并选其他佳作为三函,有余力并复影初函,如此所费不多,事轻而易举,无缮校之劳,有流通之效,宜若可为也。乞函商相老从速图之。此事倘幸行之于数年前,今已蔚为大观矣"。³¹

为此,他曾肆力搜集有关史料,并计划仿《开元释教目录》及《经义考》、《小学考》体制而为《乾嘉基督教录》,为中国天主教的文献作一次全面的清理,也为《四库全书总目》补阙拾遗。

这一计划最终仅完成了一部分,即附刊在《基督教入华史略》后的《明清间教士译述目录》,这个目录虽然限于当时的条件只收集了有关天主教士的教理和宗教史的部分,尚未更多收集到天文、历算、地理、艺术等方面的传教士重要的著述,但在徐宗泽《明清间耶稣会士译著提要》之前,他的这份目录是当时搜集天主教文献最多的一个目录,其中未刊本较多于已刊,由此可见其搜访之勤。

正是在马、英、陈三人的努力下,民国初年在这批文献的收集、整理和出版上取得了显著的成绩。

向达先生是治中外关系史的大家,他在"敦煌学","目录学"等方面的贡献大都为学界所知,但在收集和整理明清入华天主教史文献上也有显著成绩,却为人所不知。

---

30 方豪《李之藻辑刻天学初函考》,载《天学初函》重印本,台湾学生书局,1965年版。
31 同上。

在这方面，他不仅写下了《明清之际中国美术所受西洋之影响》等重要的论文，还整理和收集了部分天主教史的书籍，其点校的《合校本大西西泰利先生行迹》是他把自己在法国，罗马等地的几个刻本统一勘校后整理出来的，在很长一段时间内是最好的校本。他自己还收藏了许多珍本，《上智编译馆》曾公布过觉明先生所藏有关天主教书目。

王重民先生是我国著名的目录学家、文献学家、敦煌学家，他在明清天主教文献的收集和整理上有着重要的贡献。1934年他和向达先生被北京图书馆派往欧洲进行学术考察，在欧洲访问期间，他把收集明清天主教文献作为其在欧洲访书的第二项任务，他在访问巴黎国家图书馆和罗马的梵蒂冈图书馆时，对这类书格外关注，并从欧洲带回了部分重要文献。之后他先后写下了有关明清间山西地区重要的基督徒韩霖的著作的《跋慎守要录》和有关明人熊人霖著作的《跋地纬》，以及《王徵遗书序》、《跋王徵的王端节公遗集》、《跋爱余堂本隐居通义》、《跋格致草》、《文公家礼仪节》、《道学家传跋》、《经天该跋》、《历代明公画谱跋》、《尚古卿传》、《程大约传》、《关于杨淇园先生年谱的几件文档》、《海外希见录》、《罗马访书录》等有影响的文章。他和陈垣先生一样想编一个入华传教士译著的书目，并定名为《明清之间天主教士译述书目》，这本书已有初稿，但以后没有完成，书稿也已丢失。[32]

徐宗泽是徐光启的第十二代世孙，21岁时入耶稣会，并到欧美学习，1921年返回中国后不久，担任了《圣教杂志》的主编和徐家汇天主堂图书馆的馆长。在此期间，他发表了一系列有关明清天主教史的论文和著作。在明清之际天主教历史文献方面，他最有影响的还是关于明清天主教史的中文著作目录。他的首篇目录《梵蒂冈图书馆藏明清中国天主教人士译著简目》是发表在1947年的《上智编译馆馆刊》第二卷第二期，不幸当年便因病逝世。《上智编译馆馆刊》第二卷第四、五期合刊上有发表了他的遗著《上海徐家汇藏书楼所藏明清间教会书目》，1949年中华书局出版了他编著的《明清间耶稣会士译著提要》。这本书的学术价值直到今天仍然很高，它有两个贡献是其他任何同类工具书所不及的：其一，他同时公布了世界上主要图书馆所藏明清间天主教史的书目，大大拓宽了当时学界对这批西学汉籍的认识；其二，他公布了210篇文献的序、跋、前言、后记。对于难于见到原始文献的研究者来说，这些序跋无疑是雪中送炭。

方豪先生是继陈垣先生后，在明清天主教史和明清天主教文献研究方面最有成就的学者，他不仅继承了马相伯、英华等教内之人的传统，也和学术界的董作宾、傅斯年、胡适、陈垣等人有学术的交往，特别是和陈垣先生交往更深。方豪先生自信"史学就是史料学"的格言，在文献和史料上着力最深，在这段时间内写下了一批有关明清天主教历史文献和史料考证的重要文章。应该值得一提的是方豪先生从1946年9月到1948年7月主编《上智编译馆馆刊》，历时两年，共出版《上智编译馆馆刊》三卷十三期，这十三期《上

---

[32] 王重民《冷庐文薮》，第937页，上海古籍出版社。张西平曾就职于中国国家图书馆6年，我们对王先生一直心怀敬意，每当想起他"文革"中屈死于颐和园长廊，未完成《明清间天主教士译述书目》，更感我辈之责任。

智编译馆馆刊》成为当时收集和整理明清天主教史文献最为重要的学术阵地，也是在民国时期在这批文献的收集和整理上所达到的最高水平，它在文献校勘、标点方面的研究成果，直到今天也是我们仍必须汲取的。

陈垣先生当年在给方豪的信中说："公教论文，学人久不置目，足下孤军深入，一鸣惊人，天学中兴，舍君莫属矣！"[33] 方豪一生以陈氏私淑弟子自居，陈寅恪曾说他是"新会学案第一人"，[34] 实不为过。1965 年，《天主教东传文献》和《天学初函》在方豪推动下在台湾出版，接着先后于 1966 年、1998 年出版了《天主教东传文献续编》和《天主教东传文献三编》，从而开启了明清之际天主教文献大规模的复制整理工作。学术界有的学者认为方豪是"史料学派理论最佳的阐释者与实践者，称其为台湾，甚或中国，史料学派的最后一人不为过。"[35]

近三十年来，在谢和耐（Jacques Gernet, b. 1921）、许理和（Erik Zürcher, 1928-2008 年）提出欧洲汉学界在明清之际的研究上应该实行"汉学的转向"，"从传教学和欧洲中心的范式转到为汉学和中国中心论范式。"[36] 即"中国文化（包括中国传统文化对外国文化的传入的反应），应该总是我们研究的首要问题。"[37] 这样一种学术范式的转变主要是从欧洲自身的研究传统来讲的，对中国学术界来说则是另一个问题。[38] 学术范式的转变带来了明清

---

[33] 陈智超编《陈垣来往书信集》，第 306 页，上海古籍出版社，1993 年。

[34] 见牟润孙《敬悼先师陈援庵先生》，第 16-17 页，转引自李东华《方豪年谱》第 262 页，台湾国史馆 2001 年。

[35] 李东华《方豪年谱》第 262 页，台湾国史馆 2001 年。在这一期间还有二位学者我们不能忘记，这就是阎宗临先生和冯承钧先生。阎先生是当时为数不多的能到欧洲有关图书馆访书的学者，为完成他的博士论文，阎先生曾几次前往罗马梵蒂冈图书馆查阅文献，抄录档案。这些档案于抗战期间他大多数发表在《扫荡报》的《文史地》上。冯先生是治中西交通的大家，他的《西域南海史地考证译丛》中的译文也十分重要。

[36] 钟鸣旦《基督教在华传播史研究的新趋势》，任继愈主编《国际汉学》第四期，1999 年。

[37] 许理和《十七—十八世纪耶稣会研究》，任继愈主编《国际汉学》第四期，1999 年。

[38] 许理和在文中说，从陈垣开始早就这样做了，因此，对中国学者来说不存在一个从欧洲文献转向汉语文献的问题，但存在一个如何将明清之际的天主教史纳入到中国近代文化史之中，"从传记式的史事铺陈中走出来，尝试对西学东渐在社会所产生的反响，进行一较全面深入的探讨。"（黄一农《明清天主教传华史研究回顾与展望》，任继愈主编《国际汉学》第四期，1999 年。）同时，明清之际基督教来华研究是中西文化交流史的一侧，另一侧则是西方汉学的"传教士汉学阶段"，传教士汉学的西方语言材料呈现出多样性，它既构成中国天主教史的一部分，也同时构成欧洲近代思想文化史的一部分。对中国学者来说，优势在于对中文文献的掌握和理解，弱势在于对西方语言文献的掌握和理解较为困难。这样，对中国学术界来说，不仅仅要重点关注中文文献的研读，并将天主教史的西学纳入到整个中国近代史视域加以研究。同时，加大对来华传教士西文文献的翻译整理，加强中文和西文材料的相互辩读，亦是明清之际天主教史研究的一个重要维度。北京外国语大学中国海外汉学研究中心在这方面的努力和成就受到中国学术界的认可，其原因在于此。同时，从更为宏观的角度来开看明清之际的中西文化交流史，则不应仅仅局限于"西学东渐"，基督教对于中国近代社会的影响研究这个维度，而应同时关注传教士汉学对于欧洲思想文化史的影响。黄一农先

之际天主教文献整理出版的高潮:1996 年,中外学者钟鸣旦、杜鼎克和中国台湾学者黄一农、祝平一合作编辑的《徐家汇藏书楼明清天主教文献》(五册)由台湾辅仁大学出版,2002 年,钟鸣旦、杜鼎克编辑的《罗马耶稣会档案馆明清天主教文献》(十二册)由台北利氏学社出版,2009 年钟鸣旦、杜鼎克、蒙曦(Nathalie Monnet)《法国国家图书楼藏明清天主教文献》(二十六册)由台北利氏学社出版,2011 年,钟鸣旦、杜鼎克、王仁芳编辑的《上海徐家汇藏书楼明清天主教文献续编》(三十四册)由台北利氏学社出版。这些文献,"选择精当,史料价值高,大多数是孤本,于学界大有裨益。"[39] 中国学术界继承陈垣先生的传统,始终对中文文献十分重视,1984 年王重民先生整理的《徐光启集》,虽文献有所缺漏,但毕竟是大陆第一本较为完整的《徐光启文集》。1999 年汤开建主编的《明清时期澳门问题档案文献汇编》,在人民出版社出版,2000 年青年学者周岩以一人之力点校整理出版了《明末清初天主教史文献丛编》(北京图书馆出版社),[40] 同年陈占山点校的《不得已 附二种》在安徽黄山书社出版,2003 年中国第一历史档案馆编辑出版了《清中前期西洋天主教在华活动档案史料》(四册,中华书局),2003 年朱维铮先生主编的《利玛窦中文著作集》在复旦大学出版社出版,在学界引起较大反响。2006 年韩琦、吴旻校注的《熙朝崇正集、熙朝定案(外三种)》,在中华书局出版,2011 年朱维铮、李天纲主编的《徐光启集》(十册)在上海古籍出版社出版,2013 年黄兴涛、王国荣编的《明清之际西学文本:50 种重要文献汇编》(4 册),在中华书局出版,同年,已故青年学者周岩的《明末清初天主教史文献新编》(三册)在国家图书馆出版社出版,年底周振鹤先生主编的《明清之际西方传教士汉籍丛刊》出版,第一辑收入文献 30 种。中国学者不仅仅在文献的复制上迈开了较大的步伐,在文献的点校整理上更显示出特有的优势,取得了令人称道的成绩。

近三十年来中外学术界在明清之际天主教史中文文献的收集、复制、整理上取得了前所未有的好成绩,大大推动了学术界对明清之际中西文化交流史的研究。[41]

生提出"我们也应尝试将研究的视野打开,不要将目光自我拘限在中国或耶稣会,不仅有必要去理解并探讨当时世界的政经局势和教会的内部生态,对天主教传华所产生的影响,对朱谦之在其《中国哲学对于欧洲的影响》一书中所开创的重要研究方向,也应努力承继,以调整先前的偏颇,而能更进一步对当时中、欧文明所出现的双向交流有一较全面的掌握。"这无疑是一个非常重要的思想,按照这样的思路,欧洲汉学家们所提出的"汉学转向"模式也有着自身的问题。1500-1800 是全球化初始阶段,应从全球史研究的范式,开启新的研究模式,这是中国学术界新的使命。参阅张西平《欧洲早期汉学史:中西文化交流与欧洲汉学的兴起》,中华书局 2010 年。

[39] 李天纲《中文文献与中国基督宗教史研究》,载张先清编《史料与视界:中文文献与中国基督宗教史研究》,第 8 页,上海人民出版社 2007 年。

[40] 这一年郑安德主编的《明末清初耶稣会思想文献汇编》(五卷)以内部文献形式出版。

[41] 关于中文学术界在研究领域中取得的进展同样值得称道,鉴于本文主题在文献的整理,这里不再一一记述。

三

近年来所出版的这些明清之际西学汉籍文献,大多在台湾出版,且冠以"天主教东传文献"的统称。

最近的《梵蒂冈藏明清中西文化交流史文献丛刊》是首次在大陆出版明清之际的西学汉籍。由于梵蒂冈图书馆的地位和特点,在文献数量上基本上把在台湾已经出版的天主教历史文献大多数都覆盖。"梵蒂冈所藏的明清之际中西文化交流史文献"与以往所出版的类似文献重要的不同在于,它包含了众多来华传教修会的汉文文献,而不仅仅是来华耶稣会士的汉文文献,从而给我们展示一个更为宽阔的视野。自然,也不能仅仅将这批文献归结为"传教士汉籍",因为,它也包含有中国士大夫、文人信徒乃至佛教徒与天主教论辩的文献,它还包括传教士从中国带回或寄回欧洲的数量不菲的中国古籍,此外,它包括文化交流史中基础性的工具书—辞典和字典。这些整合起来,构成了文化史上丰富多彩的历史画卷。将其放入当时的中西文化交流史和传教士的汉籍写作方面来看,这批中文文献就出凸显出特殊的价值。因为,这些文献是传教士们编写辞典和转写汉字文献的工具书和学术思想的来源。这批文献的出版必将对中国明清史研究,包括中国思想史、文化史、科技史、中国天主教史、中国翻译史、中国语言史,乃至对西方汉学史和全球化史研究,产生深远的影响。陈寅恪在《陈垣敦煌劫余录序》中有一段十分精辟的论述:"一时一代之学术,必有其新材料与新问题。取用此材料,以研求问题,则为此时一代学术之新潮流。"[42]

这批西学汉籍文献的出版对中国明清史的研究将会有所推动。嵇文甫在《晚明思想史论》对那个时代有一个很生动的描写:"晚明时代,是一个动荡时代,是一个斑驳陆离的过渡时代。照耀着这个时代的,不是一轮赫然当空的太阳,而是许多道光彩纷披的明霞。你尽可以说它'杂',却绝不能说它'庸';尽可以说它'嚣张',却决不能说它'死板';尽可以说它是'乱世之音',却决不能说它是'衰世之音'。它把一个旧时代送终,却又使一个新时代开始。它在超现实主义的云雾中,透露出现实主义的曙光。"[43] 晚明之"杂"就在于"西学"开始进入中国,中国文化面临一个完全陌生的对话者,中国历史开始因伊比里亚半岛上的葡萄牙和西班牙人的到来,发生了一系列新的问题。近年来学术界对于在华耶稣会士在晚明的活动也多有研究,[44] 但限于文献不足征,有不少关键性问题无法透彻研究。例如关于南明王朝的研究,这些年南明研究有

---

[42] 陈寅恪,《金明馆丛稿一编》,上海:上海古籍出版社,1980年,第236页。

[43] 嵇文甫《晚明思想史论》第1页,东方出版社,1996年。

[44] 南炳文 汤纲《明史》(上下),上海人民出版社,2003年;樊树志《晚明史》(1573-1644),复旦大学出版社,2003年,(美)牟复礼 (英)崔瑞德编《剑桥中国明代史》1992年,中国社会科学出版社;张天泽《中葡早期通商史》,香港中华书局,1988年;万明《中葡早期关系史》,中国科学文献出版社2011年;万明主编《晚明社会变迁问题与研究》,商务印书馆,2005年。

了很好的学术著作，[45] 但学者很少注意到来华耶稣会士毕方济（Francesco Sambiasi, 1582-1649）的中文文献，很少注意到波兰来华传教士卜弥格作为南明朝特使赴罗马的一些汉文文献，[46] 如果不掌握梵蒂冈所藏卜弥格所带回的全部材料，很难说清楚永历王朝后期的问题，这些文献对晚明和南明的研究有着重要价值。又如对王丰肃（Alphonse Vagnoni, 1566-1640，又名高一志）的研究，已经有了很好的文章，但只有读到他的全部中文著作后，才能对南京教案的研究、对晚明绛州地方史的研究有所深入。

如果说对中国史的研究，清以前主要是中文文献的挖掘和收集，那么，在清史研究中西文化交流史文献的挖掘和收集就显的格外重要。特别是对传教士西学汉籍及相关文献的研究。戴逸先生说过，清代的历史与以往的朝代不一样，它自始至终与世界保持着联系，你必须在世界的背景下观察中国，必须了解当时西方人对中国写了些什么，说了些什么，做了些什么。我们编纂清史，如果不了解这些，清史没法写。在梵蒂冈的这批文献中包含有清史的罕见珍贵历史文献。例如，顺治皇帝褒封汤若望三代的文献，汤若望的奏疏，白晋在康熙指示下学习《易经》的手稿，马若瑟、马国贤在康熙朝时的一些中文手抄散页，雍正四年关于穆敬远和毕天祥的诏书，傅圣泽带回罗马的大量清代钦天监的手稿，这些对于研究清代历史具有重要的学术意义。

更为重要的是，这批西学汉籍一旦纳入到中国近代历史的研究视野，将对于确认鸦片战争以前的中国社会已具有自己内发原生的近代性思想文化因素，具有重要价值，从而认识明清之际对于中国近代史的开端的深刻影响。中国近代历史分期的研究，文革以前受苏联模式影响，以"侵略——革命"模式来裁定中国历史；改革开放后费正清的"冲击——反应"模式传入中国，这两种模式都将鸦片战争定位为中国近代历史的开端。但有学者已经指出："中国近代思想史可以追溯到 16 世纪。20 世纪以来，一大批中国学者在明清学术研究领域潜心开拓，以大量的史实证明了中国有自己内发原生的近代性思想文化因素的观点。早在 20 世纪伊始，章太炎先生就写了《清儒》、《说林》、《释戴》等文章，从资产阶级革命派的观点出发表彰残明遗老和戴震的学说；与此同时，梁启超作《中国学术变迁之大势》，纵论明清思想史，首倡'中国文艺复兴说'。辛亥之年，蔡元培著《中国伦理学史》，特表彰黄宗羲、戴震、俞正燮三家学说'殆为自由思想之先声'。'五四'时期，吴虞作论证了清代学术'与意大利文艺复兴绝相类'的观点。至 20 世纪末，胡适之、熊十力、嵇文甫、容肇祖、谢国祯、侯外庐、邱汉生、萧箑父诸大师接踵而来，慧解卓识，蔚为大观。其中，堪与梁启超、胡适之的'文艺复兴说'相媲美且更具论史卓识者，有秘文甫在《晚明思想史论》中提出的'曙光说'，侯外庐在《近代中国思想学说史》中提出的'早期启蒙说'，萧箑父在《明清启蒙学术流变》一书中提出的以明清之际的启蒙思想为传统与现代之间的'历史接合点说'。特别

---

[45] 顾诚《南明史》，中国青年出版社，1997 年；钱海岳《南明史》，中华书局，2006 年；黄一农《两头蛇》，上海古籍出版社，2006 年。

[46] 卜弥格著，爱德华·卡丹斯基、张振辉、张西平翻译《卜弥格文集：中西文化交流与中医西传》，华东师大出版社，2013 年。

是侯外庐的《近代中国思想学说史》(1947)一书，把中国近代史看作是中国资本主义萌芽和具有近代人文主义性质的启蒙思潮发生和发展的历史，以明清之际作为中国近代史的开端，同时也是中国近代思想史的开端，观点最为鲜明。"[47] 在以上学者的论证中，来华传教士的西学汉籍著作都受到普遍重视，并作为立论的根据之一。因此，晚明西学汉籍并不仅仅在史学材料上提供了新的文献，而且这批文献的出版将推动中国近代历史研究的创新。

基督教三次入华，唯明清之际的传入获得成功。明清之际的西学东渐研究，中国天主教史研究是其重要的内容。近三十年来这一领域研究取得了长足的进步，[48] 李天纲的《中国礼仪之争：历史文献与意义》、张先清的《官府、宗族与天主教：17-19世纪福安乡村教会的历史叙事》、汤开建的《明清天主教史论稿初编：从澳门出发》等著作从不同侧面推进了中国天主教史的研究。汤开建认为，"研究中国天主教史，中国的专家应走在这一学科的前沿，这应是理所当然，且义不容辞。而要走到中国天主教史研究的前沿，两条腿走路的方针必不可少，一条腿必须坚实地站在中文档案文献的基础之上，另一条腿则要迈进浩瀚无涯的各种西文档案文献的海洋之中，缺一不可。"[49] 他对收藏在梵蒂冈图书馆等地的中文文献给予了很大的期待。

应该说，梵蒂冈藏的明清之际历史文献会大大促进对中文文献的开拓，这批文献既有一些中国教徒的原始性文献，也有传教士关于教区发展的一些重要历史文献，例如方济各会来华传教士康和子（Carlo da Castorano, 1673-1755）详尽记述了他在山东传教历程，并附有原始的教徒名册，这在中国天主教史研究中是十分罕见的历史文献。

基督教作为外来宗教，在其本土化过程中形成自己的神学思想和表达方式，因此，中国天主教史研究的另一个方面就是在历史进程中汉语神学思想的形成。近年来，关于汉语神学的讨论十分热烈，[50] 尽管汉语神学的倡导者也承认中国汉语神学起源于明清之际，但却认为"汉语神学属于中国基督徒学人，属于当今和未来的每一个中国基督徒学人。"[51] 由此，作者很轻易的把明清之际由来华传教士和中国文人共同写下的这批西学汉籍排除在汉语神学之外，否认了这批西学汉籍在汉语神学形成史上的地位。我们认为，即便没有读到更多的明清之际的汉语神学的原著，但利玛窦的《天主实义》等著作已经清楚地表明汉语神学具体形态。学术界对于此也提出了不同的意见：认为不能将利玛窦为代表的以汉语作品言述其对耶稣基督之认信经验与对其信仰之反思的传教士排除在汉语神学之外，"凡是以汉语进行写作，回应汉语语境中

---

[47] 许苏民《中国近代思想史研究亟待实现三大突破》，《天津社会科学》2004年第6期。

[48] 钟鸣旦、孙尚阳的《一八四0年前的中国基督教》。

[49] 汤开建《明清天主教史论稿初编：从澳门出发》第11页，澳门大学出版社2012年。

[50] 一九九五年刘小枫在《现代语境中的汉语基督教神学》（载李秋零、杨熙南编《现代性：传统变迁与汉语神学》，华东师大出版社2010年）提出后学术界多有讨论。

[51] 刘小枫《汉语神学与历史哲学》，第4页，香港，汉语基督教文化研究所，2000年。

的各种问题的神学，不论其主体是中国人，还是西方人，都应包容性地将其纳入汉语神学的范畴之内。"[52]

汉学神学提出的一个理论根据是"圣言"总是通过"人言"来表达的，在这个意义上，汉语神学和作为母语神学的拉丁语神学、德语神学、法语神学一样，这样汉语神学就"没有必要在用一种'人言'去置换另一种'人言'。亦即没有必要去把其他'人言'表现形式'中国化'或者'本色化'，而应当用'汉语'这种'人言'去直接承纳、言述'圣言'。"[53] 这样的理解实际上把基督教神学的丰富历史传统解构了，从学理上也只是一种理想神学。"理论形态的基督神学"是通过在具体语境中成为现实的。因此，离开犹太语的基督"人言"，我们是无法直接去理解"圣言"的。耶稣会入华带来就是这种具体语境中的神学，并将其翻译汉语。"明清之际关于中西信仰之争，其实就是'汉语神学'。"[54]

汉语神学的提出者对汉语神学的解释缺乏对中国基督教历史的全面了解，将整个中国基督教历史归结为与民族国家冲突的历史，尚不知明清之际的中西文化交流是一个平等的文化交流。这样，很容易将明清之际所形成的汉语神学传统和资源放在了一边。有学者指出：

> 从中西文化交流史的角度看，中国社会接受基督教是四百年中西文化交流的产物，也是中西文化在这四百年中双向互动的结果。不了解始于 400 年前的中西文化交流史，就无法明了中西双方在新世纪全球一体化进程中的位置与作用，更无法为基督教在当代中国社会文化中的作用准确定位。历史是一面可资借鉴的镜子，但若观察者不具有足够宽阔的视野和多维的视角，那么历史会成一个沉重的包袱。[55]

> 明清之际，中国正经历着历史上另一个大变局。……天主教在不同的宗教和学说传统中，做着统摄和融合的工作。实际上是为中国教会和信徒建立一种'汉语神学'。[56]

回到明清之际，中国基督教第一批汉语神学文献，这些问题就迎刃而解了。因此，这批西学汉籍不仅仅为中国教会史提供了新的史料，同时，也会使我们对汉语神学的历史有一个更为全面清晰的认识。

中国翻译史源于对佛教文献的翻译，对佛典的翻译直接影响了中国文学的发展，胡适认为，一是佛典翻译"遂成为白话文与白话诗的重要发源地"，二是"中国的浪漫主义的文学是印度的文学影响的产儿"，三是"佛教的散文与

---

[52] 《基督教文化评论》第 32 期。孙尚阳《汉语神学：接着利玛窦讲——神学论题引介》，孙尚阳、潘凤娟编《汉学神学：接着利玛窦讲》，第 31 页。

[53] 李秋零《'汉语神学'的历史反思》，李秋零、杨熙南编《现代性、传统变迁与汉语神学》（下）第 651 页，华东师大出版社，2010 年。

[54] 李天纲《明清时期汉语神学：神学论题引介》，《基督教文化评论》第 27 期，第 23 页，香港道风书社，2007 年。

[55] 王晓朝《关于基督教与中国文化融合的若干问题》，李秋零、杨熙南编《现代性、传统变迁与汉语神学》（中）第 372-373 页，华东师大出版社，2010 年。

[56] 李天纲《明清时期汉语神学：神学论题引介》，《基督教文化评论》第 27 期，第 29 页，香港道风书社，2007 年。

偈体杂用，这也与后来的文学体裁有关系。"[57] 来华传教士的西学汉籍基本上是翻译作品或者编译作品，其数量是继佛教文献传入中国后最大的一批域外翻译文献，这是欧洲文化、文学、宗教首次在中国登陆，其学术意义重大。近来李奭学先生从翻译角度作了十分出色的研究，他认为"以往大家知道近代中国文学始自清末，殊不知清末文学新像乃萌乎明末，尤应接续自明末的翻译活动。"在这批西学汉籍中"有中国第一次继承的欧洲歌词的集子，有中国第一次出现的欧洲传奇小说，有中国第一次译出的欧洲上古与中古传奇，有中国第一次翻译的欧洲修辞学专著，有中国第一次可见的玛利亚奇迹故事集，有中国第一次中译英国诗，也是中国第一次见到欧人灵修小品集。"[58] 传教士们不仅仅是在介绍欧洲的文学，而且按照中国古代小说的形式用汉语来写小说，来华法国耶稣会士马若瑟（Joseph de Prémare, 1666-1736）的《儒交信》就是一个例子。[59] 晚清后来华的基督新教传教士继承天主教传教士的这个传统，开始用汉文写作各类文体的文学作品，成为近代中国文学的一个重要方面。[60] 中国翻译史研究中最为薄弱的就是明清之际的翻译历史研究，文本的缺乏，语言能力的不足是重要原因，随着这批西学汉籍的出版，将会有更多学者投入明末清初西学汉籍的翻译研究，从而丰富中国翻译的研究。[61] 另一方面，这批西学汉籍的来源考证方面，如今在文献的考证上已经迈出了坚实的步伐，随着这批文献在大陆的出版，将会引起更多明清文学史研究者的关注，从而展开这批欧洲文学文化的翻译文本对晚明和清初文坛的影响。近期对来华耶稣会贺清泰（Louis de Poirot, 1735-1771）《圣经》中译本稿本的研究，这或许是近代以来最早的白话文学。[62] 至于晚清来华基督新教传教士米怜（William Milne, 1785-1822）《张远两友相论》及其基督教《圣经》译本的翻译在近代文学的影响，学界已有研究，这里不再展开。[63] 但明显不

---

[57] 胡适《佛教的翻译文学》，罗新章 陈应年编《翻译论集》第 123-124 页，商务印书馆，2009 年。

[58] 李奭学《译述明末耶稣会翻译文学论》，序言，香港中文大学，2012 年。《中国晚明与欧洲文学——明末耶稣会古典型证道故事考》，三联书店 2010 年。

[59] 张西平《清史研究》2009 年第 2 期，40-47 页。

[60] 宋莉华《传教士汉文小说研究》，上海古籍出版社，2010 年；黎子鹏编注《晚清基督教叙事文学选粹》，台湾橄榄出版有限公司，2012 年。

[61] 马祖毅《中国翻译史》，湖北教育出版社，1999 年；马祖毅《中国翻译通史》，湖北教育出版社，2006 年。黎难秋《中国科技翻译史》，中国科技大学出版社，2006 年；王宏志主编《翻译史研究》2011, 2012, 2013 卷，从这些研究可以明显看出，翻译史研究领域的学者基本上局限在晚清翻译史的研究，对明末清初翻译史的研究仍是一个亟待开辟的领域。

[62] 郑海娟博士论文《贺清泰＜古新圣经＞研究》，北京大学，2012 年。

[63] 朱维之曾说过，"民国以来，中国基督教对于中国文学上最大的贡献，第一是和合本《圣经》的出版，第二便是《普天颂》的出版。二者虽不能说是十全十美的本子，但至少可以说已经打定了基督教文学的根基，而且作为中国新文学的先驱，这是值得大书特书的。"参阅杨剑龙《《旷野的呼声:中国作家与基督教》，上海教育出版社，1998 年，陈镭《文学革命时期的汉译圣经接受：以胡适、陈独秀为中心》，《广州社

足在于目前对西学汉籍的翻译研究和文学研究,绝大多数停留在晚清阶段,明清之际西学汉籍翻译与文学影响的研究才刚刚开始。正式在这个意义上,梵蒂冈藏明清之际西学汉籍文献的出版就具有重大的学术意义。

中国近代概念史研究是思想文化史研究的一个重要方面,这几年取得了显著的进展,无论是从语言研究的角度,如马西尼的《现代汉语词汇的形成:十九世纪汉语外来词研究》、沈国威的《近代中日词汇交流研究:汉字新词的创制、容受与共享》,还是从文化史角度的研究,如刘禾的《跨语际实践——文学、民族文化与被译介(中国,1900-1937)》、金观涛 刘青峰的《观念史研究:中国现代政治术语的形成》,这些著作都打开了一个新的研究领域,引起学界关注。[64] "一个伟大时代的出现,往往会使语言成为巨大的实验场,新词层出不穷。""一般说来,人们在发现自己的价值体系和习惯规则受到冲击甚至威胁时,会努力寻求新的精神依托,新的发现或价值转换会体现于语言。"[65] 晚清是"三千年未有之大变局"的时代,新词汇、新概念喷涌而出,这些词汇、新概念逐步在改变中国人的思维方式,同时,新词汇所构成的新知识又直接影响了人们对世界和时代的理解,成为新思想产生的基础。正如黄兴涛所说的,大量双音节以上新名词的出现,明显地增强了汉语语言表达的准确性,同时,反过来通过使用这些新名词的社会文化实践,极为有效地增进了中国人思维的严密性和逻辑性。这是中国语言和思想现代化的重要表现形式。这些新词汇极大地扩展了中国人的思想空间、运思的广度和深度,提高了科学思维的能力和效率,从而为新思想体系的产生,奠定了重要的思维基础。[66]

但是目前对近代新词汇的研究学者大都集中在晚清中日之间的词汇交流,而实际上明末清初时期天主教东来后,创造了大量新词汇,这些新词汇在东亚开始传播。当时,东亚对西学的接受是一个整体,来华传教士们所出版的西学汉籍同样流传到日本、韩国和越南。语言,用汉文写作来推动传教成为了传教士们的共识。利玛窦的信中也写到过:"当获悉我们用中文编译的书在日本也可通用时,便感到莫大的安慰。因此视察员神父范礼安在广州又印刷了一次,以便带往日本。副省会长巴范济神父曾要求我们,把我们编译的书多给他寄一些,因为中国书籍在日本甚受欢迎。"[67] "日本学者一杉本孜在《近代日中语言交流史序论》中曾指出:"现代日本的数学术语一般被认为是明治以后从欧洲学来的所谓洋算用语。但是,明清的汉籍对日本数学用语所作的贡献是不能抹杀的。这些都是包括方以智在内的中国学者和在华传教士

会主义学院学报》,2010年2期,张楠硕士论文《合和本<圣经>的异化翻译及对中国现当代文学的影响》,山东大学。

[64] 冯天瑜《封建考论》,武汉大学出版社2007年;黄兴涛《'她'字的文化史》,黄兴涛《'她'字的文化史:女性新带刺的发明与认同研究》,福建教育出版社,2009年。

[65] 方维规为黄兴涛的《'她'字的文化史:女性新带刺的发明与认同研究》一书所写的序言。

[66] 黄兴涛《近代中国新名词的思想史意义发微"兼谈对于'一般思想史'之认识》,杨念群、黄兴涛 毛丹《新史学》(上),中国人名大学出版社2003年。

[67] 利玛窦:《利玛窦全集》第4册,第366-367页(1608年3月8日信),台湾光启出版社,1986年。

即'西儒'共同在中国大地上播下的种子,是他们用汉语精心创造并建立起来的学术用语体系。"[68] 明清之际的西学汉籍传入日本后被接受了多少？哪些词汇被日本接受后在晚清时又被作为日本创造的新词返回中国？这些问题至今无人回答。根本在于对明清之际的西学汉籍了解不够。

从事晚清文化史研究的黄兴涛先生认识到这一点，他说：

> 因为要想弄清近代中国流行的相当一部分新名词的真实来源，并辨析他们对明治维新后日本汉字新名词之间的复杂关系，非得下决心、去一一翻检明末清初直至清中叶那些承载和传播西学的各种书籍不可。[69]

他与王国荣所点校的《明清之际西学文本》是目前点校整理最多的出版物之一随着文献的整理，明清之际新词语的研究必将进一步推进。邹振环的《晚明汉文西学经典》一书则打通了晚明和晚清，论证了"晚明汉文西学经典如何在晚清得到反复诠释，以及在晚清西学知识场重建过程中的意义，藉此阐明晚明与晚清在学术上之承上启下的关联问题。"[70]这些研究证明了明清之际的西学汉籍在中国近代知识进展的历史中的重要性，其核心是新知识的形成，而承载新知识的新词语、新概念就成为其关键。

语言具有"共时性"和"历时性"两个方面。在历史过程中，语言会随着时间的演化而演化，但是它在任何一个时间点上都有一个既定的结构。"概念史"的研究既关注于语言的"历时性"层面，也关注于语言的"共时性"层面，"它不仅在一个特定的历史时间点上，在一个特定的语义域内对'核心概念'(core concepts)'共时性'分析，而且还对'核心概念'做一种'历时性'分析，这种'历时性'分析将凸显出'概念'的意义变迁。"[71]明清之际新词汇、新概念研究的学术意义在于，近代西学进入中国后，中国的"西学"根源于这一时期。对这一时期的新词语、新概念的研究将直接关系到对近代中国文化史和思想史的理解，关系到今天中国学术体系与概念的重建。这正是陈寅恪所说的，"凡解一字即是一部文化史"，也如黑格尔所说的"只有当一个民族用自己的语言掌握了一门科学的时候，我们才能说这门科学属于这个民族了。"[72]

在梵蒂冈图书馆的西学汉籍文献中，还有一批关于天文、历法、科技、舆图的文献。这些文献在以往的文献整理中往往反映不够，例如近年来在台湾出版的几套文献。从《天学初函》开始，李之藻就把"器篇"与"理篇"相对作为一个重要的内容。梵蒂冈图书馆中有一些十分罕见、珍贵的中国科技史文献，特别要指出的是傅圣泽从北京返回罗马后，因为他在钦天监工作，因此

---

[68] 陆坚、王勇编《中国典籍在日本的流传与影响》，杭州:杭州大学出版社 1990 年，第263 页。

[69] 黄兴涛 王国策《明清之际西学文本：50 重要文献汇编》，第 23 页，中华书局 2013 年。

[70] 邹振环《晚明汉文西学经典：编译、诠释、流传与影响》，第 29 页，复旦大学出版社，2011 年。

[71] 伊安·汉普歇尔着 周保巍译《比较视野中概念史》，第 3 页，华东师大出版社 2010 年。

[72] 黑格尔《哲学史讲演录》第 4 卷。冯天瑜《封建考论》，武汉大学出版社，2007 年；（德）郎宓榭、阿梅龙、顾有信等着 赵兴胜译《新词语新概念》，山东画报社出版社，2012 年。

带回了大量的他在历局工作的材料和手稿，其中不乏他的天文演算手稿，这对于研究清代科技史有着重要意义。在舆图方面，梵蒂冈图书馆所藏的利玛窦的《坤舆万国全图》、卜弥格所绘制的中国分省地图都是极为珍贵的历史文献。近十余年的研究已经证明，耶稣会士们所介绍的这些科学知识推进了中国天文学的发展，"耶稣会士在中国大力传播西方天文学，后果之一，是使中国天文学一度处在与欧洲非常接近的有利状况。就若干方面来说，当时中国与欧洲天文学的最新发展只有不到十年的差距。例如，伽利略用望远镜作出的天文学新发现，发表于 1610 年，而这些发现的主要内容在阳玛诺 1615 年刊行的中文著作《天问略》中就已有介绍。又如，整个《崇祯历书》虽以第谷的体系为基础，但其中也采纳了开普勒好几种著作中的成果，最晚的一种出版于 1618-1621 年，下距《崇祯历书》开始编撰仅八年。"[73] 梵蒂冈图书刚所藏的各类科学类文献必将大大推进我们对近代中国科技史的研究。梵蒂冈所藏的科技史文献将进一步证实这个观点。

梵蒂冈图书馆所藏的明清中西文化交流史文献中，特别引人注意是一批汉欧双语词典，这是中国双语词典史的重要历史文献。中文和欧洲语言的双语词典起源于罗明坚和利玛窦的《葡华辞典》。传教士来到东亚后第一件事就是学习汉语，这样编撰辞典成为他们的一件大事，为此，传教士们付出了极大的精力。有学者认为"从罗明坚、利玛窦的葡汉词典到万济国的西汉词典，体现了欧汉、汉欧词典萌芽和最初发展的轨迹。"直到 1813 年在叶尊孝 (Basilio Brollo, 1648-1704) 的《汉字西译》在巴黎出版，汉欧双语辞典达到了它的高潮。[74] 遗憾的是，这批汉外双语辞典绝大多说仍以手稿形式藏在世界各地的图书馆，以梵蒂冈图书馆所藏最多。学术界对这批价值连城的汉欧双语词典的研究只是在近年来才逐步开展起来。[75]

索绪尔把与语言有关的因素区分为"内部要素"和"外部要素"，认为语言的"外部要素"不触及"语言的内部机构"而予以排除。他说："至于内部语言学，情况却完全不同：它不容许随意安排；语言是一个系统，它只知道自己固有的秩序。"[76] 语言是一个同质的结构，语言学主要研究语言内部稳定的系统和特点。这样，他们把语言的外在因素放在了一边，对外部因素对语言的变异影响不太关注。

语言接触（language contact）的认识始于十九世纪。从上个世纪九十年代开始，语言接触成为语言学研究的热门话题，甚至要成为语言学的一个分支。

---

[73] 江晓原、钮卫星著《欧洲天文学东渐发微》，上海书店 2009 年，第 447 页。

[74] 杨慧玲《19 世纪汉英词典传统：从马礼逊、卫三畏、翟理斯汉英辞典的谱系研究》，商务印书馆 2012 年，第 71 页。

[75] 张西平等主编《西方人早期汉语学习史调查》，中国大百科出版社，2003 年；姚小平主编《海外汉语探索四百年管窥》，外研社 2008 年；姚小平《西方语言学史》，外研社 2011 年；姚小平《罗马杜书记》，外研社，2009 年；董海樱《16-19 世纪初西人汉语研究》，商务印书馆 2011 年；魏思齐编《西方早期（1552-1814 间）汉语学习和研究》，台湾辅仁大学出版社 2011 年。

[76] 索绪尔：《普通语言学教程》，商务印书馆，2001 年，第 46 页。

同时，社会语言学也开始关注这个问题，语言的"外部要素"也成为历史语言学主要内容的一部分。

这说明语言的变化并不仅仅在内部因素，外部因素也有着重要的作用，即语言接触引起的变化。对汉语的变化影响最大的两次汉语与外部语言的接触。一次是佛教传入中国后对汉语的影响，一次是晚明后基督教传入对汉语发展产生的影响。随着梵蒂冈所藏的这批欧汉双语辞典的公布，必将大大推动中外语言交流史的研究和中国词典史与中国语言史的研究。

最后，明清之际西学汉籍将会大大加深中国近代思想史的研究。[77] 明清之际西学的影响不仅仅停留在知识论的水平，也不仅仅是信教和反教两类人士对西学的理解，最重要的是西学的已经和晚明至清初的中国本土思想产生了互动。晚明王学盛行，尤其在江浙一带。王学反对死读先贤古圣之书，主张"涂之人皆可为禹"，陆九渊的"东南西北海有圣人出焉，此心同此理同也"自然为接受外来文化奠定了基础。明清之际接受西学的大都是王学之徒，而反对西学大都是朱学之后。[78] 朱维铮先生说："王学信徒，接受外来文化，皈依西方宗教，这就反映出一个事实，即王学蔑视宋以来的礼教传统，在客观上创造了一种文化氛围，使近代意义的西学在中国得以立足，而王学系统的学者，在认知方面的特有平等观念，即王守仁所谓'良知良能，愚夫愚妇与圣人同'，在清代仍以隐晦的形式得到保存，实际上为汉学家们所汲取。这看来是悖论，然而却是事实。"他认为清初的汉学和西学之间"性质关联"、"结构关联"、"方法关联"和"心态的关联"。[79]

明清之际所传入的西学与中国近代思想变迁之间的关系，从梁启超到胡适，再到当代学者，多有注意。但限于文献不够充分，这个方向的论证仍在进展之中。近年来学者仅仅使用台湾出版的部分西学文献就已经大大推进了西学与明清思想史的研究。例如许苏民认为高一志的"西学治平四书"，（即《治政源本》、《民治西学》、《王宜温和》、《王政须臣》）直接影响了顾炎武，因为高一志在山西传教15年，顾炎武在写《日知录》时也在山西和陕西一带，他的朋友圈就有研习西学的李鲈。他在《日知录》中提出的"合天下之私以成天下之公，此所以为王政也……此义不明久矣。世之君子必曰：有公而无私，此后世之美言，非先王之至训也。"[80] 这是很重要的思想，承认了个人私有的合理性，这样"衡量王政的标准不再是'有公而无私'，只有'合天

---

[77] 陈卫平《第一页与胚胎——明清之际的中西文化比较》，上海人民出版社1992年版；孙尚阳：《明末天主教与儒学的交流和冲突》，台北:文津出版社1982；何俊《西学与晚明思潮的裂变》，上海人民出版社1998年；李天纲《跨文化的诠释：经学与神学的相遇》，新星出版社2007年。

[78] 卜恩理（Heinrich Busch）著，江日新译《东林书院及其政治的和哲学的意义》，附录二：东林书院与天主教会，魏思齐（Zbigniew Wesołowski）编《〈华裔学志〉中译论文精选：文化交流和中国基督宗教史研究》，第278页，台湾辅仁大学出版社2009年。

[79] 朱维铮《走出中世纪》，增订版，第154-158页。复旦大学出版社2007年。

[80] 顾炎武《日知录》卷3《言私其豵》，载《日知录集释》，长沙:岳麓书社1994年，第92页。

下之私以成天下之公',才是'王政'之本质。"[81] 许苏民认为顾炎武这个思想直接来源于高一志的《王宜温和》一书，书中谈到"王权由何而生存"时说："人性原自私爱，乃无不好自从自适，岂有甘臣而从他人之命耶？即始明视他人之才能，功德绝超于众，而因自足庇保下民者一，即不待强而自甘服从，以致成君臣之伦也。"

方以智和传教士有直接的联系，王夫之在天主教主导的永历王朝任职，黄宗羲研读西学已经有文献所证，从历史研究上已经做了大量的考证。[82] 随着梵蒂冈图书馆所藏的明清中西文化交流史文献的出版，西学汉籍的总体面貌呈献给中国学术界，那时，将会大大拓宽和加深这一研究方向的进展。

传教士们所写下的这些西学汉籍还有另一重意义，即这批文献也是西方汉学史的一个重要组成部分，当然，这些西学汉籍背后有着不少中国文人为其润笔着墨。这批中外合作的西学汉籍，实际上是全球化史初期，世界文化交流史上的瑰宝，它的双边性，展示了其在世界文化史上中国文明和欧洲文明初识后的对话与交流、文明间互鉴的丰硕成果。它不仅仅是东亚走向现代化进程的重要思想资源，也是西方文化如何与异质文化相处的宝贵文化资源和具有当代意义的重要思想遗产。这是一批具有世界文化史意义的重要宝藏。

如果从张元济先生1910年出国期间，访问罗马教廷梵蒂冈图书馆，首次从梵蒂冈图书馆复制了南明朝重要文献算起，历经百年努力，我辈踏前贤足迹，与梵蒂冈图书馆合作七年，今天这批文献终于全部回到中国，这是继敦煌文献全部复制回归本土后，中国学术史上的又一重要事件。

谨以此文追思前贤，叩谢在此历程中所有帮助过我们的中外友人。《华裔学志》研究院是我们多年的合作伙伴机构，马雷凯神父为中欧文化交流所做出的贡献，为汉学研究界所瞩目。在他65岁华诞之日，我们祝愿他健康长寿。

---

[81] 许苏民〈晚明西学东渐与顾炎武政治哲学之突破〉，载《社会科学战线》 2013年，第6期，第1-9页。

[82] 方豪〈明末清初旅华西人与士大夫之晋接〉，《东方杂志》第29卷，第5号，1943年；徐海松《清初士人与西学》，东方出版社2001年；许苏民〈王夫之与儒耶哲学对话〉，《武汉大学学报》（人文社科版）2012年1月；许苏民〈黄宗羲与儒耶哲学对话〉，《北京行政学院学报》，2013年，第4期；冯天喻〈明清之际西学与中国学术近代转型〉，《江汉论坛》，2003年，第3期。

DIE SAMMLUNG KOWALEWSKI
DER ERSTE EUROPÄISCHE KATALOG MONGOLISCHER, TIBETISCHER, MANJURISCHER UND CHINESISCHER BÜCHER (1834)

Hartmut Walravens

Neben Isaak Jakob Schmidt (1779–1847),[1] Akademiker in St. Petersburg, gehört József Szczepan Kowalewski (1801–1878) zu den Vätern der Mongolistik; er erhielt den ersten mongolistischen Lehrstuhl an einer Universität. Im Gegensatz zu Schmidt war es ihm vergönnt, einige Jahre unter Ost-Mongolen zu verbringen und dabei, vor allem aber bei seinem Aufenthalt in Peking, eine stattliche Bibliothek zusammenzubringen, womit ihn die Universität Kasan ausdrücklich beauftragt hatte. Von diesem Grundstock profitiert die russische Mongolistik bis heute. 1855 wurden die orientalischen Studien in St. Petersburg konzentriert und damit auch der Lehrstuhl und die einschlägigen Bücher größtenteils dorthin verbracht. Die mongolischen und ostasiatischen Studien wurden nun von Kowalewskis Schüler Vasilij Pavlovič Vasil'ev (1818–1900)[2] betreut. Kowalewski blieb bis 1860 an der Universität Kasan, an der er mehrere Male Dekan und zum Schluss Rektor war, und stand anschließend zur Verfügung des Ministeriums. 1862 erhielt er eine Professur im heimatlichen Polen, in Warschau, wo er Geschichte lehrte. Die Biographen weisen darauf hin, dass er sich der Russifizierungspolitik der Regierung nicht widersetzte; dies war möglicherweise eine Bedingung, die an seine Stelle geknüpft war.

Bereits 1834 erschien eine Liste der von Kowalewski erworbenen Bücher – die meisten in mongolischer, aber auch etliche in tibetischer, manjurischer und chinesischer Sprache:

Katalog sanskritskim, mongol'skim, mańdžurskim i kitajskim knigam i rukopisjam, v Biblioteke Imperatorskago Universiteta chranjaščimsja. Kazań: Univ. Tipografija, 1834. 30 S. 8°

Es war beabsichtigt, einen ausführlicheren beschreibenden Katalog vorzulegen, wozu es jedoch nicht kam. Die Kasaner Universitätszeitschrift[3] ist ebenso wie der Sonderdruck des Verzeichnisses daraus heute recht selten, und daher verdient die Liste es, zugänglich gemacht zu werden, insbesondere aus folgenden Gründen:

---

[1] H. Walravens, *Isaak Jakob Schmidt (1779–1847). Leben und Werk des Pioniers der mongolischen und tibetischen Studien.* Abhandlungen für die Kunde des Morgenlandes 56,1. (Wiesbaden: Harrassowitz, 2005); H. Walravens, „Schmidt, Isaak Jakob [1779–1847]", *NDB* 23 (2007), S. 193-194.

[2] H. Walravens, „Vasilij Pavlovič Vasil'ev (1818–1900). Zu Leben und Werk des russischen Sinologen", *OE* 48 (2010), S. 199-249.

[3] *Učenyja zapiski izdavaemyja Imperatorskim Kazanskim universitetom* 1834. Der Katalog findet sich dort auf S. 260-292.

- Sie gibt uns ein Bild dessen, was Kowalewski auf seinen Reisen erwerben konnte, also was auf dem Markt war, wie wir heute sagen würden, aber auch, was Kowalewski auswählte, denn garantiert hätte er weiteres Material kaufen können, wenn die Mittel gereicht hätten.
- Kowalewskis Lehrstuhl und die Büchersammlung, der eine weitere von Vasil'ev zusammengetragene[4] folgte, waren wichtige Schritte beim Ausbau der Universität Kasan zu einem orientalistischen Zentrum, das dann freilich 1855 nach Petersburg verlegt wurde.
- Das Verzeichnis gibt in den meisten Fällen die Originaltitel wieder, so dass die Bücher durchweg identifizierbar und bis heute nachweisbar sind.
- Wenige Fehlanzeigen mögen auf die Schäden zurückgehen, von denen die Mongolica im Jahre 1923 durch Hochwasser betroffen waren.
- Die Schwerpunkte der Büchersammlung liegen im mongolischen und tibetischen Buddhismus, aber Kowalewski achtete ebenso auf den Erwerb von Wörterbüchern und sprachlichen Hilfsmitteln. Dazu darf man auch einige polyglotte Werke rechnen. Seinem starken historischen Interesse konnte Kowalewski nicht Genüge tun – offenbar war ihm nichts Einschlägiges bekannt geworden. Lediglich die Manjufassung des *Tongjian gangmu* 通鑒綱目 konnte er erwerben. Bei den Beschreibungen des Verzeichnisses ist dem Autor zugute zu halten, dass er gerade erst Mongolisch gelernt und keine Zeit gehabt hatte, die Texte genauer zu studieren; so sind in etlichen Fällen etwas ungelenke Titelparaphrasen angegeben.
- Die Umschriften für die verschiedenen Sprachen waren damals nicht genormt; die Transkription des Mongolischen ist recht unhandlich; in der Folge hat Kowalewski weitgehend auf die Umschrift verzichtet (so in seinem Wörterbuch) und stattdessen die mongolische Schrift verwendet. Für das Tibetische folgte er der Aussprache.
- Die Aussprache des Manju, wie sie sich in der Transkription spiegelt, belegt die russische Erfahrung, dass z.B. „e" nach Labialen wie „o" klingt, dass „k" vielfach zerrieben wird, z.B. yonjiyangga (< yongkiyangga), aber auch eine stimmhafte Aussprache von intervokalischem „s", wie gizun (< gisun).

Die nachfolgende Übersetzung des Katalogs hält sich möglichst eng an das Original, das verschiedentlich in den Titelparaphrasen eigenartig klingt, wenn z.B. vom „Hornklee [vielm. Lotos] der Andacht" oder vom „Zerstörer" [hier die Übersetzung für *vajra*], der das gegenüberliegende Ufer der Weisheit erreicht, die Rede ist. Eine literarhistorische Kommentierung hätte jedoch zu weit geführt.

---

[4] Vgl. H. Walravens, „V.P. Vasil'ev. Notiz über die Werke in ostasiatischen Sprachen, die sich in der Bibliothek der Universität von St. Petersburg befinden", *Monumenta Serica* 59 (2011), S. 99-141.

Biographische Notiz

Władysław Kotwicz hat seinem großen Landsmann eine eingehende Biographie gewidmet,[5] und viele Details sind in den Abhandlungen des Kowalewski-Symposiums in Kasan 2002[6] genauer behandelt. So möge an dieser Stelle eine biographische Skizze genügen.

Józef Szczepan Kowalewski wurde am 9. Januar 1801 in Brzostowica Wielka, Gvt. Grodno (heute: Weißrussland) geboren; er studierte an der Universität Wilna und verließ sie mit dem Grad eines Kandidaten der ethisch-philosophischen Wissenschaften; nach einem weiteren Studium am Lehrerseminar wurde er 1823 als Hauptlehrer der lateinischen und polnischen Sprache an das örtliche Gymnasium abgeordnet. Im Dezember 1824 entsandte man ihn mit zwei Kommilitonen, die wie er Mitglieder der patriotischen Vereinigung der Philareten und Philomaten[7] gewesen waren (denen übrigens auch Adam Mickiewicz angehörte) nach Kasan, wo er sich mit orientalischen Sprachen beschäftigen sollte, offenbar eine probate Methode, von politischen Ideen abzulenken. Er studierte dort eifrig Arabisch, Tatarisch und Persisch; 1828 wurde er mit dem Studenten Aleksandr Vasil'evič Popov[8] nach Irkutsk abgeordnet, wo er Mongolisch lernen sollte. Dies war eine gute Gelegenheit, denn die beiden jungen Männer hatten dort in Aleksandr Vasil'evič Igumnov[9] einen erfahrenen Dolmetscher als Lehrer und außerdem Gelegenheit, ihre neu erworbenen Kenntnisse bei den Burjaten der Umgebung zu üben. Im August ging Kowalewski als Sekretär mit der Russischen Geistlichen Mission nach Peking. Dort verblieb er sieben Monate und erwarb

---

[5] Wł. Kotwicz, *Józef Kowalewski, orientalista*. Prace Wrocławskiego Towarzystwa Naukowego. A 11 (Wrocław: Wrocł. Tow. Nauk., 1948).

[6] Ramil' Mirgasimovič Valeev, T.V. Ermakova, Irina Vladimirovna Kul'ganek, *Mongoloved O.M. Kovalevskij: biografija i nasledie (1801–1878)* (Kazań: Alma-Lit., 2004). – Als besonders nützlich erwiesen hat sich daraus Vladimir Leonidovič Uspenskijs „Kollekcija O.M. Kovalevskogo v sobranii vostočnych rukopisej i ksilografov biblioteki Sankt-Peterburgskogo Universiteta", S. 231-250. – Siehe außerdem: R.L. Valeev, I.V. Kulganek, Jerzy Tulisów, „Professor O.M. Kowalewski – Mongolian Studies Scholar, Traveller and Enlightener. His Biographical Landmarks", *AOV* 10 (2009), S. 29-56; Oksana N. Polyanskaya, „History and Ethnography of Mongolian-speaking Peoples in Materials of O.M. Kowalewski in Library Holdings of Vilnius University", *AOV* 10 (2009), S. 57-62.

[7] „Ein Stipendium ermöglicht es ihm [Mickiewicz], in Wilna zu studieren, erst Naturwissenschaft, dann Literatur. Hier findet er Freunde fürs Leben. Mit ihnen gründet er geheime patriotische Bünde, die Gesellschaft der Philomaten (‚Freunde des Wissens') und der Philareten (‚Freunde der Tugend'). Vgl. Doris Liebermann, „Das Vaterland heißt Freiheit", Zeitläufte, *Die Zeit* Nr. 48 (24. November 2005), siehe http://www.zeit.de/2005/48/A-Mickiewicz (aufgerufen am 14. Juni 2016) – Vgl. auch Kotwicz, a.a.O., S. 29ff.

[8] 1808–1880; vgl. *Rossijskie mongolovedy (XVIII – načalo XX vv.)* (Ulan-Udė: BNC, 1997), S. 32–35 (Širab Bodievič Čimitdoržiev, Daši-Cyren Batuevič Ulymžiev).

[9] Leonid Sergeevič Pučkovskij, „Aleksandr Vasil'evič Igumnov (1761–1834)", *Očerki po istorii russkogo vostokovedenija* 3 (1960), S. 166-195; *Rossijskie mongolovedy (XVIII – načalo XX vv.)* (Ulan-Udė: BNC, 1997), S. 5-9 (Š. Čimitdoržiev). Igumnov äußerte sich sehr positiv über den Fleiß und die Aufnahmefähigkeit seiner beiden Schüler.

einen großen Teil der Bücher für die Universität Kasan. Nach einem weiteren Aufenthalt bei den Burjaten kehrte er nach Kasan zurück, wo er von der Aufsichtspflicht befreit und mit der Verwaltung des neugegründeten (1833) Lehrstuhls für Mongolistik, des ersten in Europa, betraut wurde. 1837 wurde er korrespondierendes Mitglied der Akademie der Wissenschaften und Ordinarius für Mongolistik. Seit 1844 war er gleichzeitig Direktor des 2. Kasaner Gymnasiums, und von 1855 bis 1860 Rektor der Universität. Er starb am 2. Oktober 1878 in Warschau, wo er als Professor der Geschichte an der Universität lehrte. Teile von Kowalewskis Nachlass befinden sich in Kasan, in St. Petersburg und vor allem in Wilna (Vilnius). Seine späteren Arbeiten wurden größtenteils bei einem Wohnungsbrand in Warschau vernichtet.

Kowalewskis große Verdienste um die Mongolistik liegen in ihrer Etablierung als akademische Disziplin. 1835 veröffentlichte er eine *Kurze Grammatik der mongolischen Literatursprache* (*Kratkaja grammatika mongol'skogo knižnogo jazyka*), im gleichen Jahr eine *Buddhistische Kosmologie* (*Buddijskaja kosmologija*) und 1836–1837 in zwei stattlichen Bänden eine *Mongolische Chrestomathie* (*Mongol'skaja chrestomatija*) mit ausführlichen Anmerkungen und Kommentaren. Wilhelm Schott in Berlin benutzte dieses Werk für den Unterricht und übersetzte einige der darin enthaltenen Texte.[10] Dauernden Ruhm sicherte sich Kowalewski indes durch das dreibändige *Dictionnaire mongol-russe-français* (Kasan 1844–1849), das bis heute von Nutzen ist. Kowalewski wurde dafür mit der Demidov-Prämie ausgezeichnet. Kowalewskis prominentester Schüler war V.P. Vasil'ev,[11] dem Russland den Ausbau der universitären Sinologie verdankt und der wissenschaftlich auch als Buddhologe und Tibetologe von Rang hervorgetreten ist.

Vorwort (zum Katalog)

Im Jahre 1828 beauftragte die Universität Kasan, die den Herrn Kandidaten (jetzt Adjunkt) Kowalewski nach Ostsibirien entsandt hatte, ihn, für die Bibliothek die wichtigsten Bücher und Handschriften zu erwerben. Eine Reise 1829 in die Hauptstadt des von den Mongolen vergötterten Jebtsundamba Qutuγtu von Kuren (Urga) und die Metropole der die angrenzenden Gebiete beherrschenden Ambans, und eine Reise 1830 und 1831 mit der Russischen Geistlichen Mission durch die Mongolei nach der chinesischen Hauptstadt Peking, und schließlich ein langdauernder Aufenthalt bei den Russland untertanen Burjatmongolen-Stämmen gaben Herrn Kowalewski die Möglichkeit, die Universitätsbibliothek um höchst seltene, interessante, in chinesischer, manjurischer, tibetischer und mongolischer Sprache geschriebene Werke zu bereichern, so dass, das können wir ohne Übertreibung sagen, die Bibliothek unserer Universität in dieser Beziehung den unbestrittenen Vorrang unter allen anderen in Russland hat; nicht einmal die anderen Europäer,

---

[10] Vgl. H. Walravens, *Wilhelm Schott (1802–1889). Leben und Wirken des Orientalisten.* Orientalistik, Bibliographien und Dokumentationen 13 (Wiesbaden: Harrassowitz, 2001).

[11] Vgl. *id.*, „Vasilij Pavlovič Vasil'ev (1818–1900). Zu Leben und Werk des russischen Sinologen", *OE* 48 (2010), S. 199–249.

die ebenso mit größter Begierde ihre Blicke auf Asien lenken, können sich trotz aller Mühe und Kosten bei verschiedenen Erwerbungen zur Zeit einer ähnlichen Sammlung rühmen. Schließlich erhoffen nicht allein die Besucher der Universitätseinrichtungen, die mit Vergnügen die orientalischen Schätze betrachtet haben, sondern auch die Liebhaber der Bildung Früchte von denen, die ihre Kräfte und Kenntnisse der Erforschung der Literatur der asiatischen Völker widmen; und damit sie kurz mit ihnen Bekanntschaft schließen können, erfüllen wir ihren Wunsch und bieten hier einen kurzen Katalog dieser Sammlung. Ihren eigentlichen Wert kann man aus der ausführlichen Beschreibung der Bücher ersehen, die in den Gelehrten Denkschriften erscheinen wird, die von der Universität Kasan herausgegeben werden.

Zum Erwerb von Büchern und Handschriften waren ursprünglich 4.000 Rubel Assignaten bestimmt, zu denen später, auf Ersuchen des Herrn Kurators des Kasaner Unterrichtsbezirks ein Zuschuss zum Abschreiben und Abdruck seltener Bücher in den transbaikalischen burjat-mongolischen Tempeln kam. Außerdem haben die Burjaten, aus besonderer Hochachtung für Herrn Kowalewski, eine ziemlich bedeutende Spende gemacht.

In dieser Sammlung befinden sich 1.433 Bücher, darunter 48 Hss.

Käuflicher Erwerb von Büchern bei den Burjaten
in der Mongolei, Peking und Umgebung   2.979 Rubel 12 Kopeken
Spende der Burjaten   ca. 870 Rubel
Abdruck   116 Rubel
Abschrift   374 Rubel

Für die Verpackung in Peking und Kjachta, für das Gehalt der Schreiber und Kosten fürs Abschreiben, schließlich für den Transport aller Bücher nach Kasan waren erforderlich 2.021 Rubel 99 1/2 Kopeken.

Die ganze Bibliothek kostet die Universität 6.361 Rubel 16 1/2 Kopeken.

Katalog der Sanskrit-, mongolischen, tibetischen, manjurischen und chinesischen Bücher und Handschriften, die sich in der Bibliothek der Kaiserlichen Universität Kasan befinden[12]

Lehrbücher

1) *Dža gaddang nakdon torbu Bot gaddu dolva* [rGya-skad daṅ sṅags-don thor-bu bod-skad-du bkrol-ba bžug-so].[13] Die gebräuchlichsten Sanskritwörter in tibetischer Übersetzung. Handschrift. 1 Buch.

2) *Mèrkgèt garchu-jn oron nèrètü toktagaksan dakgiik* [Merged γarqu-yin oron neretü toγtaγaysan daγyig].[14] Wörterbuch unter dem Titel: Quelle der

---

[12] Wenn nicht anders angegeben, beziehen sich die folgenden Hinweise auf die Nummern der Einträge in den Referenzwerken.

[13] Sign.: T 1. Alte Sign. Xyl. 89.

[14] Sazykin I, 1473; Uspensky, 825.

Weisen, enzyklopädisch angeordnet, tibetisch und mongolisch, zur Erleichterung der Übersetzung der heiligen (buddhistischen) Bücher. 1 Buch.

3) *Nėrė-jn dalaj* [*Nere-yin dalai*].[15] Das Meer der Wörter. Tibetisch-mongolisches Wörterbuch, mit Beispielen zur Übung in den grammatischen Regeln und bei Übersetzungen von Büchern aus dem Tibetischen ins Mongolische. 1 Buch.

4-5) *Tübedün kėlėni kilbar-er surchu nėrėtü bičik* [*Töbed-ün kelen-i kilbar-iyar surqu neretü bičig orošiba*][16] oder *Dakbar-loa*. Buch für das leichte Erlernen der tibetischen Sprache. Tibetisch-mongolisches Wörterbuch, zusammengestellt unter Leitung des lCaṅ-skya Qutuγtu, mit historischer Einführung. 1 Buch, 2 Exemplare.

6) *Samadok* oder *Tübėt dokijanu šastir* [*Töbed-ün doki-a-u sastir*].[17] Ein Buch, das den Unterschied der tibetischen Wörter erläutert. Tibetisch und Mongolisch. Handschrift. 1 Buch.

7) *Nakdun* oder *Tübėdun dokijanu ilgaburi dotoragulun ujlėduksėn mėrkgėdun kėlėnu dzula* [*Töbed-ün dokiyan-u ilyaburi todarγulun üiledügči-yin sastir üges-i bülüglen üiledügsen merged-ün kelen-ü ǰula*].[18] Leuchte der Sprache der Weisen, die die Redensarten unterscheidet, oder Buch, das den inneren Unterschied der tibetischen Wörter aufzeigt. Handschrift, tibetisch und mongolisch. 1 Buch.

8) *Tübėt kėlėnu šinė chaguč ajalgusun ilgali udzkgülükči sajn ükgėtü lišijn ordo charši* [*Töbed kelen-ü sine qayučin ayalyus-un ilγal-i üjügülügči sayin ügetü liši-yin ordu qarši*].[19] Paläste des Wohlberedten, der den Unterschied zwischen der neuen und der alten Mundart der tibetischen Sprache aufzeigt. Tibetisch-mongolisches Wörterbuch in 1 Buch.

9) *Chaganu bičiksėn Mandžu, Monkgol, Kitat üsük gurban dzüjlün ajalgu nėjleksėn toli bičik* [*Qaγan-u bičigsen Manǰu Mongγol Kitad üsüg γurban üsüg-ün ayalγu neyilegsen toli bičig*].[20] Spiegel der manjurischen, mongolischen und chinesischen Wörter, verfasst auf Allerhöchsten Befehl. Wörterbuch der drei Sprachen in der Anordnung nach dem manjurischen Alphabet. 4 Bände, 32 Bücher.

---

[15] Sazykin I, 1478; Uspensky, 818.

[16] Sazykin I, 1512; Uspensky, 824d; das Exemplar unter Nr. 5 ist nicht mehr vorhanden.

[17] Uspensky, 866. Vgl. Berthold Laufer, „Studien zur Sprachwissenschaft der Tibeter. Zamatog", *Sitzungsberichte der philosophisch-philologischen und historischen Classe der K. Bayerischen Akademie der Wissenschaften* 1 (1898), S. 519-504. Laufer gibt als tibetischen Titel: *Bod-kyi brda'i bstan-bcos legs-par bśad-pa rin-po-che'i za-ma-tog bkod-pa*.

[18] Uspensky, 864.

[19] *Ibid*.

[20] Jachontov – Walravens, 355; Uspensky, 843.

10) *Dürbėn dzüjlün üsük chabsuruksan toli bičik* [*Dörben jüil-ün üsüg qabsuruγsan toli bičig*].²¹ Wörterspiegel in vier Sprachen. Manjurisch-mongolisch-tibetisch-chinesisches Wörterbuch in der Anordnung nach Sachgebieten, mit alphabetischem Register der manjurischen Wörter. 2 Bände, 10 Bücher.

11) *Gurban dzüjlün ükgė chadamal üdzėküj dur kilbar bolgaksan bičik* [*Γurban jüil-ün üge qadamal üjeküi-dür kilbar bolγaysan bičig*].²² Ein Buch, in dem man leicht die Wörter in drei Sprachen findet. Manjurisch-chinesisch-mongolisches Wörterbuch, angeordnet nach dem manjurischen Alphabet. Chinesischer Titel: *Sanhe bianlan* [三合便覽], am Anfang mit Erläuterung der grammatischen Veränderungen manjurischer Wörter; herausgegeben von Fugiyôn. 2 Bände, 12 Bücher.

12) *Chan-i aracha nongimo toktobucha Mańdžu gizun-i buleku bitchė* [*Han-i araha nonggime toktobuha Manju gisun-i buleku bithe*].²³ Auf allerhöchsten Befehl herausgegebenes Manjurisch-chinesisches Wörterbuch in der Anordnung nach Sachgebieten. Mit ausführlicher Erläuterung der Bedeutungen jedes Wortes auf Manjurisch und Beifügung eines manjurischen alphabetischen Registers. 6 Bände, 46 Bücher.

13) *Mańdžu isabucha bitchė* [*Manju isabuha bithe*].²⁴ Manjurisches Wörterbuch in alphabetischer Reihenfolge angeordnet, mit Erklärung auf Chinesisch und mit Ergänzungen. 4 Bände, 36 Bücher.

14) *Chaganu bičiksėn Mandžu, Monkgol ukgėnu bičik* [*Qaγan-u bičigsen Manju Mongγol ügen-ü toli bičig*].²⁵ Spiegel der manjurischen und mongolischen Wörter, zusammengestellt auf höchsten Befehl. Wörterbuch in beiden Sprachen, nach Sachgebieten, mit ausführlicher Erläuterung der Bedeutungen jedes Wortes. 4 Bände, 22 Bücher.

15) *Egi dandža* oder *bičikujn šastir tobčilan churijaksan sajn nomlalga* [*Bičiküi-yin sastir tobčilan quriyaγsan sayin nomlaly-a rasiyan-u nere-tü orosiba*].²⁶ Kurze Anleitung für die Kopisten der heiligen (buddhistischen) Schriften, in tibetischer und mongolischer Sprache, mit einem Sanskrit-tibetischen Wörterbuch. Handschrift. 1 Buch.

---

21 Sazykin I, 104. Jachontov – Walravens, 357: *Siti hebi wenjian* 四體合璧文鑑. Uspensky, 842.

22 Jachontov – Walravens, 327; Uspensky, 844.

23 Clark, 5. Das Datum des Vorworts ist 1772.

24 Clark, 4: *Manju gisun-i isabuha bithe*. 1750. Jachontov – Walravens, 314.

25 Uspensky, 848. Jachontov – Walravens, 358: *Han-i araha Manju Monggo gisun-i bithe*. Vorw. 1743.

26 Uspensky, 865.

16) *Mańdžu Nikan chèrkgèni cing vyn ci myn* [Manju nikan hergen-i cing wen ki meng].²⁷ Alphabet, Grammatik und Gespräche in manjurischer und chinesischer Sprache. 1 Band, 4 Bücher.

17) *Gurban dzüjlün üsük chadamal bičik* [Γurban ĵüil-ün üsüg qadamal bičig].²⁸ Gespräche in drei Sprachen: Manjurisch, Mongolisch und Chinesisch. 1 Band, 4 Bücher.

18) *Ču-sjao-džu-njań* [Chuxue zhinan 初學指南].²⁹ Mongolisch-chinesische Gespräche. 1 Band, 2 Bücher. Mongolisch-chinesische Gespräche. 1 Band, 2 Bücher.

19) Dasselbe Werk [18] in 2 Büchern.³⁰

20) *Džirukėnu tolta šastir* [Jirüken-ü tolta sudur].³¹ Buch unter dem Titel: Das Käppchen des Herzens, beinhaltend das mongolische Alphabet, die Regeln der Orthographie, die Geschichte des Alphabets und der Einführung des Buddhismus in der Mongolei. 1 Buch.

21) Dasselbe Werk [20] in Handschrift, unter dem Titel: *Džirukėnu toltajn tajlburi, üsükgun èndèkgürlun charankguj-kgi arilgakči, oktargojn mani* [Jirüken-ü tolta-yin tayilburi üsüg-ün endegürel-ün qaranγui-yi arilγaγči oγtarγui-yin mani].³² Erläuterung des Käppchens des Herzens: die himmlische Perle, die das Dunkel der Fehler in der Schrift zerstreut. 1 Buch.

Religion

22) Katalog der im *Gandžur* [Kanjur] enthaltenen Bücher.³³ In tibetischer und mongolischer Sprache. Handschrift. 1 Buch in Blättern.

23) Katalog der im *Dandžur* [Tanjur] enthaltenen Bücher.³⁴ In tibetischer Sprache. Handschrift. 1 Buch in Blättern.

24) *Itèkgèl jabugulukči tèrikgütèn èl'dèb čichula kèrèktu nomut* [Terigün botidur itegel yabuγuluγči terigüten eldeb čiqula keregtü nom-ud orosiba].³⁵ Sammlung verschiedener sehr wichtiger und nötiger Bücher, die den Glauben anregen. (Gebetbuch). 6 Bücher.

---

[27] Jachontov – Walravens, 386.

[28] *Ibid.*, 415: *San he yulu* 三合語錄 *Ilan hacin-i hergen kamcibuha gisun-i bithe.* Vorw. 1829.

[29] Uspensky, Appendix 2.

[30] *Ibid.*

[31] *Ibid.*, 149.28; *PLB*, 60.

[32] Uspensky, 867, 868.

[33] *Ibid.*, 264: *Bga-a-'giur erdeni-yin nere-yin toγ-a γarčiγ orosiba.* Die mongolische Übersetzung wurde auf Anregung von Kowalewski ausgeführt.

[34] Sign.: T 2. Alte Sign. Xyl. 93.

[35] Uspensky, 138.

25) *Iktėkgėl ba coktu uačir ajugulukči arban gurban Burchan dur dzalbaril, irukgėl, üldzėj ükgülėkü ba, bütükgėlün argajn ajmak* [*Itegel ba čoγtu vačir ayuγuluγči arban γurban burqan-tu-yin ǰalbaril irügel öljei ügülekü ba: bütügel-ün arγ-a-yin ayimaγ-ud abisig ögküi yosun γal mandal terigüten-ü ayimaγ*].[36] Sammlung von Gebeten, Segen und Methoden zur Erfüllung der Vorschriften Buddhas, der Leuchte des Glaubens, erhaben und überaus schrecklich. 6 Bücher.

26) *Jamantaka dokšit ba, sur linga camun bičik, sakigulsunu sankg durma terikgütėnu ajmak* [*Yamandaga doγšid ba, soor lingga 'čam-un bičig sakiγulsun-u bsang dorma terigüten-ü ayimaγ*].[37] Sammlung von Gebeten (in mongolischer Sprache), die zur Zeit der Erfüllung von religiösen Gelübden zu Ehren Yamantakas und anderer grimmiger Gottheiten gelesen werden, unter Darbringung eines Weihrauchfasses und Opfern für die (Tempel)hüter u.a. 6 Bücher.

27) *Rabnaj kikgėt mani rilu ündüsünü ajmak kikgėt nom, džiruchaj tėrikgütėn takilgajn ajmak* [*Rabnai kiged maṇi rilu ündüsün-ü ayimaγ kiged em ǰiruqai terigüten takilγ-a-yin ayimaγ*].[38] Sammlung von Gebeten, die bei der Weihe von Tempeln und Götterfiguren usw., astrologischen Vorschriften und Opferdarbringungen gelesen werden. In mongolischer Sprache. 6 Bücher.

28) *Uldzėj badaraksan sümejn churalun amanu unkšilga nomun jabudal maši todorchaj kgėkgėn oiotanu chogolaj-jn čimek čindamani ėrikė* [*Öljei badaraγsan süm-e-yin qural-un aman-u ungsilγ-a nom-un yabudal masi todorqai gegen oyutan-u qoγolai-yin čimeg čintamani erike*].[39] Kostbarer Rosenkranz, der den Hals des erleuchteten Weisen schmückt oder Gebetsverrichtung bei der Versammlung der Geistlichkeit im Tempel, in dem Segen verbreitet wird. 12 Bücher.

29) *Jamantaka, Machakala, Ėrlik chagan, Okin Tėkgri dürbėn dokšit sudur* [*Yamandaga maqagala erlig qaγan ökin tngri dörben doγšin sudur-un orosiba*].[40] Buch über die vier Schrecklichen: Yamantaka, Mahākala, Erlig Qan [Yama] und Okin Tengri [Devī]. In mongolischer Sprache. 1 Buch.

30) *Undüsün*.[41] Gebetbuch in tibetischer Sprache, nachgedruckt bei burjatischen Götzentempeln. 1 Buch.

31) *Dürbėn ündüsün* [*Dörben ündüsün*].[42] Die Vier Wurzeln. Gebetbuch in tibetischer Sprache, nachgedruckt bei burjatischen Götzentempeln. 1 Buch.

---

[36] Uspensky, 139.
[37] Ibid., 140.
[38] Ibid., 141.
[39] Ibid., 150.
[40] Ibid., 625; PLB, 76.
[41] Sign.: T-26. Alte Sign.: Xyl. Q 78.
[42] Sign.: T-37. Alte Sign.: Xyl. Q 90.

32) *Dėršėg dun dzi čot bi čok dik idšil vandžil* [*bDer-gśegs bdun-gyi mchod-pa'i chog-sgrigs yid-bźin dbaṅ-rgyal*].⁴³ Gebetsdarbringung an den Medizinbuddha.⁴⁴ In tibetischer Sprache. 1 Buch.

33) *Rapsal* [*Rab-gsal*].⁴⁵ Sammlung von Gebeten, nachgedruckt bei den Ataganskischen mongolisch-burjatischen Götzentempeln in tibetischer Sprache. 1 Buch.

34) *Rapsal* [*Rab-gsal*].⁴⁶ Sammlung von Gebeten, nachgedruckt bei den Ataganskischen mongolisch-burjatischen Götzentempeln in tibetischer Sprache. 1 Buch.

35) *Arban charanga* [*Arban qarangya*].⁴⁷ Gebetbuch in tibetischer Sprache, nachgedruckt bei mongolisch-burjatischen Götzentempeln. 1 Buch.

36) *Cagan šikgurtu* [*Čaγan sikürtei*].⁴⁸ Mit weißem Baldachin. In tibetischer Sprache, nachgedruckt bei mongolisch-burjatischen Götzentempeln. 1 Buch.

37) *Džirgugan irukgėl* [*Jirγuγan irügel*].⁴⁹ Sechs Segen. In tibetischer Sprache nachgedruckt bei mongolisch-burjatischen Götzentempeln. 1 Buch.

38) *Dara-ėkė*. Das Gebet Dara-ėkė oder *Ilaguksadun ėkė kgėtulkgėkci chutuktu Dara-ėkė-jn chorin nikgėn murkgul* [*Ilaguysad-yin eke getülgegči qutuγ-tu dar-a eke-yin qorin nigen mörgül eke orosibai*].⁵⁰ 21 Verehrungen der heiligen Dara-ėkė [Tārā], der Mutter der Siegreichen und der Lehrerin. In tibetischer und mongolischer Sprache, gedruckt bei den mongolisch-burjatischen Götzentempeln. 1 Buch.

39) *Vinaj-in gar-tur abchu-jn dzankg iosu ėrdėni-jn ėrikė kėmėkdėku nom* [*Vinai-yin γar-tur abqu-yin ǰang yosu erdeni-yin erike kemegdekü nom orosibai*]⁵¹ oder *Sanvarun nom*. Buch unter dem Titel: Rosenkränze, mit Beschreibung der Zeremonien, die bei Erhebung in den geistlichen Stand vollzogen werden. In tibetischer und mongolischer Sprache. Handschrift. 1 Buch.

---

⁴³ *PLB*, 75: „Werk, genannt der die Wünsche erfüllende Herrscher, in welchem das Ritual für die Sieben glücklich Gekommenen zusammengestellt ist." Uspensky, 536.

⁴⁴ Молитвословие оточию - die Erklärung von оточию verdanke ich meiner Kollegin Albina Girfanova (St. Petersburg): „*Otači* ist mong. ‚Arzt' (vgl. Kowalewski, *Dictionnaire* I, 387), hier wohl verkürzt für *otači burqan* – Bhaiṣajyaguru."

⁴⁵ Sign.: T-34. Alte Sign.: Xyl. Q 86. Die Identifikation verdanke ich Prof. Klaus Sagaster, Bonn.

⁴⁶ Sign.: T-35. Alte Sign.: Xyl. Q 88.

⁴⁷ Sign.: T-40. Alte Sign.: Xyl. Q 93.

⁴⁸ Vgl. Uspensky, 150.72. Dieser Text ist nicht mehr vorhanden. Vgl. *PLB*, 21: Der Erhabene mit dem weißen Schirm.

⁴⁹ Nicht mehr vorhanden.

⁵⁰ Uspensky, 487.

⁵¹ *Ibid.*, 741.

40) *Chesej toktobucha Mańdžusaj vočėrė motėrė koli bitchė* [*Hesei toktobuha Manjusai wecere metere kooli bithe*].⁵² Beschreibung der Rituale mit Darstellung der Geräte, Musikinstrumente und anderer Gegenstände, die beim manjurischen Gottesdienst [d.i. beim Hofritual] gebraucht werden. In manjurischer Sprache. 1 Band, 6 Bücher.

41) *Sandžja dži can ngadun šibdžja ngadžu dza sumba* [*Sańs-rgyas-kyi mtshan lńa-stoń gźi-brgya lńa-bcu rtsa gsum-pa*].⁵³ Gebetbuch in tibetischer Sprache. Handschrift. 1 Buch.

42) Dasselbe Gebetbuch in tibetischer Sprache, gedruckt bei mongolisch-burjatischen Götzentempeln.⁵⁴ 1 Buch.

43-45) *Najman nom* [*Nayiman nom*] oder Acht Bücher.⁵⁵ Sammlung von Gebeten in tibetischer Sprache, nämlich:⁵⁶

  1) *Pakba džambal'dži can jandak bar džomba* [*'phags-pa 'jam-dpal-gyi mtshan yań-dag-par brjod-pa*]⁵⁷
  2) *Sanamdži jum* [*Sa-gnam-gyi yum?*]
  3) *Garmaj jum šidžjabi sum* [*sKar-ma'i yum źes-bya ba'i gzuńs*]⁵⁸
  4) *Pakba čokdžju munsėl* [*'Phags-pa phyogs bcu'i mun-sel*]⁵⁹
  5) *Niba gunsel* [*Ñes-pa kun-sel*]⁶⁰
  6) *Dakba serdži dotik* [*Dag-pa gser-gyi mdo-thig*]⁶¹
  7) *Namsa nandžjal* [*gNam-sa snań-brgyad*]⁶²
  8) *Daši dzėkba* [*bKra-šis brtsegs-pa*]⁶³
  1 Buch (3 Exemplare).

46) *Manglaj dočuk don surdu golba itščin vandžjal šidžjava sun* [*sMan-bla'i mdo-chog 'don cha zur-du bkol-ba yid-bźin dbań-rgyal źes bya-ba*].⁶⁴ Gebete in tibetischer Sprache, 1 Buch.

---

⁵² Jachontov – Walravens, 164.
⁵³ Sign.: T-15. Alte Sign.: Xyl. Q 58. *Buddhanāmasahasrapañcaśatacaturtripañcadaśa*.
⁵⁴ Sign.: T-42. Alte Sign.: Xyl. Q 99.
⁵⁵ Sign.: T-16; T-30, T-38. Alte Sign.: Xyl. Q 61, Q 81, Q 91.
⁵⁶ Die folgenden acht Identifikationen verdanke ich der Freundlichkeit von Prof. Klaus Sagaster, Bonn.
⁵⁷ Taube, 200-214.
⁵⁸ *Ibid.*, 2207-2211.
⁵⁹ *Ibid.*, 175-181.
⁶⁰ *Ibid.*, 2270-2273.
⁶¹ *Ibid.*, 2406-2409.
⁶² *Ibid.*, 2413-2419.
⁶³ *Ibid.*, 108-115.
⁶⁴ Sign.: T-18. Alte Sign.: Xyl. Q 63.

47–49) *Dokšit* [*Doɣšid*].⁶⁵ Gebetsverrichtung an die schrecklichen Gottheiten, in tibetischer Sprache, gedruckt bei mongolisch-burjatischen Götzentempeln. 1 Buch (3 Exemplare).

50) *Pakba širabdži paraldu čemba džjad domba* [*'Phags-pa šes-rab-kyi pha-rol-tu phyin-pa brgyad stoṅ-pa*].⁶⁶ Enthält achttausend Verse. In tibetischer Sprache. 1 Buch.

51) *Džebcun dulma čakcal nišu dza džik ma šun* [*rJe-bcun sgrol-ma phyag 'tshal ñi-šu rtsa gcig ma*].⁶⁷ In tibetischer Sprache. 1 Buch.

52) *N'ën mun doši sėmdži milan* [*Ñon moṅs ṅo-šes sems-kyi me-loṅ*].⁶⁸ In tibetischer Sprache. 1 Buch.

53) *Arban najman kėrėktü kėmėkü surgal* [*Arban nayiman keregtü kemekü surɣal*].⁶⁹ Achtzehn wichtige Vorschriften, herausgegeben vom lCaṅ-skya Qutuɣtu, in tibetischer, manjurischer und mongolischer Sprache. 1 Buch.

54) *Chorin tabun minkgatu* [*Qorin tabun mingɣatu*].⁷⁰ Der 25.000. (Teil des *Kanjur*). In mongolischer Sprache. 1 Buch.

55) *Najman dzagutu sudur* [*Nayiman ǰaɣutu sudur*].⁷¹ Der 800. (Teil des *Kanjur*). In mongolischer Sprache. 1 Buch.

56) *Ėl'dėb bilik baramid* [*Eldeb bilig baramid*].⁷² Der Weg zur Weisheit. (Teil des *Kanjur*). In mongolischer Sprache. 1 Buch.

57) *Arban najman minkgatu* [*Arban nayiman mingɣ-a-tu*].⁷³ Der 18.000. (Teil des *Kanjur*). In mongolischer Sprache. 5 Bücher.

58) *Chutuktu tümėn šiluktu* [*Qutuɣ-tu tümen silüg-tü dötüger gelmeli kemegdekü sudur orosiba*].⁷⁴ Zehntausend heilige Verse. (Teil des *Kanjur*). In mongolischer Sprache. 1 Buch.

59) *Bilikgun činadu küriiksėn dzagun minkga togatu* [*Bilig-ün činadu kürügsen ǰaɣun mingɣan toɣatu*].⁷⁵ Das hunderttausendste (Buch) der gegenüberlie-

---

⁶⁵ Sign.: T-22, T-36, T-29. Alte Sign.: Xyl. Q 69. Q 89, Q 80.
⁶⁶ Vgl. Uspensky, 147.20. Dieser Text nicht mehr vorhanden.
⁶⁷ Sign.: T-39. Alte Sign.: Xyl. Q 97.
⁶⁸ Sign.: T-19. Alte Sign.: Xyl. Q 66.
⁶⁹ *PLB, 157*: „Die achtzehn notwendigen Lehren". – *bslab bya gces-pa bco brgyad-pa bžugs* – *Juwan jakōn acangga seme tacihiyan*. Jachontov – Walravens, 154. Uspensky, 390.
⁷⁰ Uspensky, 21; *PLB*, 12: Mongolische Übersetzung des *Pañcaviṃśatisāhasrikā-prajñāpāramitā-sūtra*.
⁷¹ Uspensky, 65.
⁷² Ibid., 2.
⁷³ Ibid., 22.1. *PLB*, 32: „Sûtra der 10000 Strophen." Mongolische Übersetzung des *Aṣṭādaśasāhasrikā-prajñāpāramitā-sūtra*.
⁷⁴ Uspensky, 23; *PLB*, 33: „Sûtra der erhabenen 10000 Strophen." Übersetzung des *Šes-rab-kyi pha-rol-tu phyin-pa khri-ba*.
⁷⁵ *PLB*, 20: Śatasahâsrikasûtra. Uspensky, 20.

genden Grenzen der erlangten Weisheit, tibetisch Yum, Mutter, genannt. (Teil des *Kanjur*). In mongolischer Sprache. 12 Bände, 100 Bücher.

60) *Chutuktu najman minkgatu ekė külkgėn sudur [Qutuγ-tu nayiman mingγatu yeke kölgen sudur]*.[76] Heiliges 8.000. Werk (Teil des *Kanjur*). In mongolischer Sprache. 1 Buch.

61) *Chamuk nomudun utcha-kgi oloksan dürbėn ünėn [Qamuγ nom-ud-un udq-a erke-yi oluγsan dörben ünen orosiba]*.[77] Die vier erreichten Wahrheiten; die Lehre aller heiligen Bücher. Die Lehre Śākyamunis. Handschrift in mongolischer Sprache. 1 Buch.

62) *Kgandžurun džirükėnu choriankgoj [Bga-a-'giür-un ǰirüken-ü quriyangγui-yin toγtaγal orosiba]*.[78] Das Wesen des Kanjur. Gedruckt bei den Congolschen (am Čikoj-Fluß) mongolisch-burjatischen Götzentempeln. In mongolischer Sprache. 1 Buch.

63) *Sunduj [Sungdui terigün bölüg orosiba]*.[79] Sammlung von Worten (Buddhas). Gebetbücher und Legenden. In mongolischer Sprache. 2 Bücher.

64) *Chutuktu tarnisun churijankguj sunduj [Qutuγtu tarnis-un quriyangγui zungdui kemegdekü yeke kölgen sudur orusiba]*[80] oder Sammlung heiliger *Dhāraṇī*, d.h. göttlicher Aussprüche. In mongolischer Sprache. 1 Buch.

65) *Chutuktu dėkgėdu altan kgėrėltu ėrkėtu sudur nogodun chagan [Qutuγ-tu degedü altan gerel-tü erketü sudur-nuγud-un qaγan]*.[81] Der Zar der heiligen, goldglänzenden, machtvollen Bücher.

66) Dasselbe Werk [65] in alter schöner Handschrift.[82] In mongolischer Sprache. 1 Buch.

67) Dasselbe Werk [65], unter dem Titel: *Chutuktu altan kgėrėltu sudur [Qutuγtu altan gerel-tü sudur]*.[83] Heiliges goldglänzendes Buch. In mongolischer Sprache. 1 Buch.

68–70) Dasselbe Werk [65], in tibetischer Sprache, unter dem Titel: *Sėr-ot [gSer 'od]*,[84] gedruckt bei den Ataganskischen mongolisch-burjatischen Götzentempeln. 3 Exemplare.

---

[76] Uspensky, 25. *PLB*, 123: „Âryaaṣṭasâhasrikâ prajñâpâramitâsûtra. ‚Mahâyânasûtra der erhabenen 8000 Strophen'."

[77] Uspensky, 317.

[78] *Ibid*., 64.

[79] *Ibid*., 146; *PLB*, 67.

[80] *PLB*, 49: „Sammlung der erhabenen Dhâranî, Mahâyânasûtra, genannt gzuṅs-bdsud." Uspensky, 147.

[81] Uspensky, 10. *PLB*, 175: Suvarṇaprabhâsasûtra.

[82] Uspensky, 12: Qutuγ-tu degedü altan gerel-tü erketü sudur-nuγud-un qaγan neretü yeke kölgen sudur.

[83] *PLB*, 177; Uspensky, 10: Qutuγ-tu degedü altan gerel-tü sudur orosiba.

[84] Sign.: T-27, T-28, T-43. Alte Sign.: Xyl. Q 79, Q 100.

71) *Chaganu bičiksėn dėkgėdu orčiguluksan uačir er oktalokči sudur* [*Qaγan-u bičigsen dakiju orčiγuluγsan včir-iyar oγtaγuluγči sudur*].⁸⁵ Auf höchsten Befehl herausgegebenes Werk unter dem Titel: Mit dem Diamanten Abschneidender in tibetischer, manjurischer, mongolischer und chinesischer Sprache. Lehre Buddhas. (Seltene Ausgabe) 1 Buch.

72) Dasselbe Werk [71], nur in mongolischer Sprache, gedruckt bei den Congol-Götzentempeln (am Fluß Čikoj), unter dem Titel: *Uačir-er oktalokči* [*Vačir-iyar oγtaluγči*].⁸⁶ 1 Buch.

73-74) Dasselbe Werk [71], in tibetischer und mongolischer Sprache, gedruckt bei den mongolisch-burjatischen Götzentempeln, unter dem tibetischen Titel: *Pakba širabdži paraldu čimba dordži džotba* [*'Phags-pa śes-rab-kyi pha-rol-tu phyin-pa rdo-rje gcod-pa*] und mongolisch: *Chutuktu bilikgun činadu kidzagara kürüksėn uačir oktalokči* [*Qutuγ-tu bilig-ün činadu kijaγar-a kürügsen včir oγtuluγči*].⁸⁷ 1 Buch. 2 Exemplare.

75) Dasselbe Werk [71], in tibetischer und mongolischer Sprache, ebenfalls gedruckt bei den mongolisch-burjatischen Götzentempeln, unter dem Titel: *Dordži džotba* [*rDo-rje gcod-pa*]. 1 Buch.

76) Dasselbe Werk [71], nur tibetisch, unter dem Titel: *Dordži džotba* [*rDo-rje gcod-pa*].⁸⁸ 1 Buch.

77) *Sonosogat tonilgakči sudur* [*Sonusuγad tonilqaγči-yin sudur ene bui*].⁸⁹ Ein Buch, das seine Zuhörer erlöst; es wird bei den Toten gelesen.

78-79) Dasselbe Werk [77], unter dem Titel: *Sonosogat ekėdė tonilgakči neretu sudur* [*Sonusuγad yekede toniluγči neretü yeke kölgen sudur*].⁹⁰ Buch unter dem Titel: Erlösend seine Zuhörer. In mongolischer Sprache. 1 Buch, 2 Exemplare.

80-86) Dasselbe Werk [77], in tibetischer Sprache, unter dem Titel: *Tarbo čenbo* [*Thar-pa chen-po*].⁹¹ 1 Buch, 7 Exemplare.

87) *Mani Kgambo* [*Mani gambu*].⁹² Erläuterung des geheimnisvollen Gebets *om mani padmė chum*, die Lehren des Qongšim Bodhisattva [Avalokiteśvara]

---

⁸⁵ Jachontov – Walravens, 145: Han-i araha dasame ubaliyambuha wacir-i lashalara nomun. Übersetzung der *Vajracchedikā prajñāpāramitā*. Uspensky, 31.

⁸⁶ Uspensky, 33.

⁸⁷ *Ibid.*, 34.

⁸⁸ Sign.: T-41. Alte Sign.: Xyl. Q 95.

⁸⁹ *PLB*, 29: „Dies ist das durch Anhören erlösende Sûtra." Uspensky, 710.

⁹⁰ *PLB*, 28: „Mahâyânasûtra, genannt Das durch Anhören überaus Erlösende." Uspensky, 712.

⁹¹ Noch 5 Exemplare vorhanden: T-20, T-23, T-24, T-25, T-33. Alte Sign.: Xyl. Q 67, Q 71, Q 76, Q 87. – Vgl. Anm. 95.

⁹² *PLB*, 51: tib. Mani bka'-'bum. Uspensky, 178.

und Teil der Geschichte des Buddhismus in Tibet. In mongolischer Sprache. 12 Bücher.

88) *Chutuktu sajn cakgun nèrètu ekè külkgèn sudur* [*Qutuɣtu sayin čaɣ-un neretü yeke kölgen sudur*].[93] Werk unter dem Titel: Der glücklichen (jetzigen) Zeit dargelegte Geschichte der tausend Buddhas. In mongolischer Sprache. 2 Bücher.

89) *Cagan linchoa nèrètü ekè külgèn sudur* [*Čaɣan linqu-a neretü yeke kölgen sudur*].[94] Buch unter dem Titel: Der weiße Lotos. In mongolischer Sprache. 1 Buch.

90-91) *Chutuktu Pandža-rakša kèmèkü tabun Sakijan nèrètü ekè külkgèn sudur* [*Qutuɣ-tu Pancaraksa kemekü tabun sakiyan neretü yeke kölgen sudur orosiba*].[95] Buch über 5 Sakyas, bekannt unter dem Namen *Pandža-rakša* (fünf Zaren). In mongolischer Sprache. 1 Buch. 2 Exemplare.

92-94) Dasselbe Werk [90-91] in tibetischer Sprache unter dem Titel: *Dončèn mo rabdu džotba* [*Don-chen-mo rab-tu gcod-pa*].[96] 1 Buch, 3 Exemplare.

95) *Aguj ekè tèkgüs onoltu nomun utchakgi dèlkgèrènkgüe ükgülèksèn sudur* [*Aɣui yeke tegüs onol-tu nom-un udq-a-yi delgerengküy-e ügülügsen sudur*].[97] Ausführliche Erläuterung des Weisen. Gespräche Buddhas mit seinen Schülern. In mongolischer Sprache. 1 Buch.

96-97) *Chutuktu dèkgèdü ekèdè tonilgakči nèrètü sudur* [*Qutuɣ-tu degedü yeke-de tonilɣayči neretü sudur orosiba*].[98] Buch unter dem Titel: *Svjatoj verchovnyj iskupitel'* [Der heilige, hohe Erlöser]. In mongolischer Sprache. 1 Buch, 2 Exemplare.

98) *Mandžusri-jn amanu èši* [*Mañču-srii-yin aman-u esi kemekü*].[99] Lehren des Mañjuśrī. In mongolischer Sprache. 1 Buch.

99) *Sajn kgalabun minkgan burchanu nèrè* [*Sayin galab-un mingɣan burqan-u nere*].[100] Die Namen der tausend Buddhas der glücklichen (jetzigen) Periode des Weltalls. Sanskrit, Tibetisch, Mongolisch, Manjurisch und Chinesisch. 2 Bücher.

---

[93] *PLB*, 5: „Mahâyânasûtra der erhabenen, glücklichen Zeit." (*Bhadrakalpikāsūtra*).

[94] *PLB*, 16: „Weißer Lotos genanntes Mahâyânasûtra." Uspensky, 43.

[95] *PLB*, 9: „Fünf Rakṣâ genannte Mahâyânasûtren, das erhabene Pañcarakṣâ". Kow. 90 = Uspensky, 6; Kow. 91 = *Qutuɣ-tu bañca-raɣša kemekü neretü sudur orosiba* = Uspensky, 4.

[96] Sign.: T-17, T-21, T-32. Alte Sign.: Xyl. Q 62, Q 68, Q 85. Freundlicher Hinweis von Prof. Klaus Sagaster, Bonn.

[97] Uspensky, 100.

[98] *PLB*, 14: „Sûtra genannt der erhabene, gänzlich Erlösende." (*Thar-pa chen-po*); Uspensky, 44.

[99] *PLB*, 118: „Mündliche Belehrung des Mañjuśrî." Uspensky, 334.

[100] *PLB*, 150: „Tausend Buddhanamen des Bhadrakalpa." Jachontov - Walravens, 151: Sain g'alab-i minggan fucihi-i colo.

100) *Busudun tusajn džirükėn kėmėkdėkü ankgida tonilgakči-jn sudur* [*Busud-un tusa-yin jirüken kemekgdekü anggida tonilɣayči-yin surtal orosiba*].¹⁰¹ Das Buch des besonderen Erlösers, genannt Herz zum Nutzen der anderen. In tibetischer und mongolischer Sprache. 1 Buch.

101) *Dologan sajbar odoksadi takichu-jn dzankg iosun-luga nejlėküj küseli chankgakči ekėsun chagan* [*Doluyan sayiber oduysan-u takiqu-yin jang yosun-luɣa neyileküi küsel-i qangɣayči erkes-ün qaɣan neretü*].¹⁰² Der Zar der großen Wunschgewährung und Opferzeremonien für die sieben in Wahrheit Kommenden. 1 Buch.

102) *Ėrdėni oki-jn toktagal* [*Erdeni oki-yin toɣtaɣal neretü yeke kölgen sudur orosiba*].¹⁰³ Die Regel des Erdeni Oki. In mongolischer Sprache. 1 Buch.

103) *Bilikgün činadu kidzagar kürüksėn uačir-er ėbdėkči-jn tusa* [*Bilig-ün činadu kijaɣar kürügsen vačir-iyar ebdeyči-yin* [!] *ači tus-a ene bolai*].¹⁰⁴ Der Nutzen des Zerstörers, der das gegenüberliegende Ufer der Weisheit erreicht hat. Handschrift. In mongolischer Sprache. 1 Buch.

104) *Dzunkchabajn maktagal* [*Jônggaba-yin maɣtaɣal*].¹⁰⁵ Lobpreisung Tsoṅkhapas. In mongolischer Sprache. 1 Buch.

105) *Džebzun Damba-jn šilukglėl* [*Jibčun-damba-yin silüglel*].¹⁰⁶ Gedichte zu Ehren des rJe-bcun Dam-pa, des Qutuɣtu von Kuren [Urga]. Handschrift in mongolischer Sprache. 1 Buch.

106) *Ünėn ükgėtu ėrdėni chubilgan bonbo-jn arigun bum cagan Loosun ekė külkgėn sudur* [*Ünen ügetü erdeni qubilɣan bonbo-yin ariɣun 'bum čaɣan luus-un yeke kölgen sudur*].¹⁰⁷ Buch über die weißen Drachen [d.i. Nāgas], die bedeutenden, die Wahrheit sprechenden Wiedergeborenen. In mongolischer Sprache. 2 Bücher.

107) *Nomun džirgalankgtu Dakini-jn dzarlikgun dėbtėr* [*Nom-un jirɣalang-tu dagini-yin ünen jarlig-un debter bolai*].¹⁰⁸ Buch der Aussprüche der Ḍākinī Nomun Jirɣalangtu [Čoyijid Dagini]. Handschrift in mongolischer Sprache. 1 Buch.

---

¹⁰¹ Uspensky, 306.

¹⁰² *PLB*, 8: „Sûtra, genannt Herrscher mit der Gewalt, Wünsche zu erfüllen, verbunden mit dem Opferritual für die Sieben Glücklich Gekommenen." Uspensky, 536.

¹⁰³ *PLB*, 3: „Mahâyânasûtra genannt Dhâraṇî der kostbaren Spitze." Uspensky, 60.

¹⁰⁴ Uspensky, 395.1.

¹⁰⁵ *Ibid.*, 395.2: von Blo-bzaṅ grags-pa'i dpal.

¹⁰⁶ *Ibid.*, 395.3.

¹⁰⁷ *PLB*, 139: „Mahâyânasûtra des reinen Zehntausend der weißen Drachen des Bon-po, Inkarnation des wahren Kleinodes." Uspensky, 933.

¹⁰⁸ Uspensky, 409.

108) *Ajaga takimlikgun surtal* [*Ayaɣ-a tegimlig-ün surtal*].[109] Vorschrift für diejenigen, die das Opfer in der Schale empfangen, d.h. die Gelongs. Handschrift in mongolischer Sprache. 1 Buch.

109) *Bodi mürün dzėrkgė-dur ankchana oion sudulchu nomun ėkgüdėni nėkgėkgči* [*Bodhi mör-ün ǰerge-dür angqa oyun sudulqu nomun egüden negegči kemegdekü orusiba*].[110] Buch, das das Tor der Lehre öffnet, die den Sinn auf den Weg zur Erlösung richtet. In mongolischer Sprache.

110) *Bodi mürün dzėrkgė-jn ülagan kutulburi, chamuk-kgi ajladukči dur otchoj amur mür* [*Bodhi mör-ün ǰerge-yin ulaɣan kötelbüri qamuɣ-yi ayiladuɣči-dur odqui amur mör kemegdekü orusiba*].[111] Handreichung für den Weg der Heiligen und den ruhigen [seligen] Weg zum Allwissenden. In tibetischer und mongolischer Sprache. 1 Buch.

111) *Mürun dzėrkgė-jn kutulburi-kgi toktagaksan-en bičiksėn* [*Mör-ün ǰerge-yin kötülbüri-yi toɣtaɣaysan-iyan bičigsen orosiba*].[112] Anleitung für den Weg zur Erlösung. In tibetischer und mongolischer Sprache. 1 Buch.

112) *Ekė bodi mürun dzėrkgė* [*Yeke bodi mör-ün ǰerge orusiba*].[113] Der große und heilige Weg. In mongolischer Sprache. 2 Bücher.

113) *Bodi mürun dzėrkgė-jn dėkgėdü ubadisi šilukglėksėn chamuk-kgi ajladukči-jn amur mur* [*Bodhi mör-ün ǰerge-yin degedü ubadis-i silüglegsen qamuɣ-i ayiladuɣči amur mör kemegdekü-yin toɣ-a bičig*].[114] Der selige Weg des Allwissenden, der die erhabenen Vorschriften für die Zukunft auf dem Weg der Heiligen besungen hat. In mongolischer Sprache. 7 Bücher.

114) *Čilėn achu-jn šakšabadun ündusun Lamanarun togodži, dzankg ujlė maktagalun tajkburi ači tusa luga sėltėni nomlaksan* [*Čilen aqu-yin šayšabad-un ündüsün blama nar-un tuɣuǰi ǰang üile maytaɣal-un tayilburi ači tusa-luɣa selte-yi nomlaysan qoyar tüidker-un quriyangɣui arilɣaqun naran-u lingqua-yin sečerlig-i tedkügči adistid tu mingɣan usun bariɣči-luɣa tegüsügsen oɣtarɣui-yin manglai neretü orusiba*].[115] Geschichte der Lamas, die bei der Erfüllung ihrer geistlichen Pflichten musterhaft im Einsiedlerle-

---

[109] Uspensky, 307. Erläuterung der Mönchsregeln (*prātimokṣa*).

[110] *PLB*, 82: „Einführung in den Pfad der Vollkommenheit, welche die Wolke der Lehre eröffnet." Uspensky, 522.

[111] *PLB*, 116: „Roter Leitfaden der verschiedenen Pfade der Vervollkommnung, genannt Friedenspfad, begangen vom Allwissenden." Uspensky, 332.

[112] Uspensky, 339.

[113] *PLB*, 80. Das Exemplar ist nicht erhalten.

[114] Das Exemplar ist nicht erhalten. Für ein anderes Exemplar, aus der Sammlung Pozdneev, vgl. Uspensky, 131-137.

[115] *PLB*, 108: „Scheitelpunkt des Firmamentes, vollendet mit tausenden von glückseligen Wolken, Beschützer des Lotosgartens [und] der Sonne, welche das Dunkel der zwei großen Behinderungen zerstreut – darinnen gelehrt wird die Geschichte und das Ritual der ersten Lama der grundsätzlichen Moralvorschriften mit dem ihrer Hymne, die [daraus erwachsenden] Verdienste und anderes mehr."

ben waren; Erläuterung der Hymnen, die Arten der Gebetsverrichtung und der Nutzen, der daraus hervorgeht. In mongolischer Sprache. 1 Buch.

115) *Čichula kėrėkglėkči tėkgüs utchatu šastir* [*Čiqula kereglegči tegüs udq-a-tu neretü sastir orosibai*].[116] *Šastra*, das alles unabdingbar Nützliche enthält. Buddhistische Kosmologie mit Beifügung der Chronologie und oftmals nützliche Darlegungen in dogmatischen Büchern. Handschrift in mongolischer Sprache. 1 Buch.

116) *Šidžja rabdu šalva šidžja bi dži Gėlonkg Pakba Lodoj Džjalcan Baldzan buj dzamba šuksu* [*Śes-bya rab-tu gsal-ba*].[117] Buddhistische Kosmologie mit kurzer Geschichte Indiens, Tibets und der Mongolei. Handschrift in tibetischer Sprache. 1 Buch.

117) *Najman tümėn dürbėn minkgan nomun chagalga-jn sajn tul'kikgur* [*Nayiman tümen dörben mingγan nom-un qaγaly-a-yin sayin tüligür orosiγulba*].[118] Guter Schlüssel zu den Türen der 84.000 heiligen Bücher. Erläuterung der Wörter und Wendungen, die man in mongolischen theologischen Werken häufig antrifft. Handschrift in mongolischer Sprache. 1 Buch.

118) *Abkaj ėdžėni tacisjani chėšėni bitchė* [*Abkai ejen-i tacihiyan-i hešen-i bithe*].[119] Römisch-katholischer Katechismus in manjurischer Sprache. 2 Bücher.

119) *Abkaj ėdžėni unėngi džurchani bitchė* [*Abkai ejen-i unenggi jurgan*].[120] Die wahre Lehre des Himmelsherrn [*Tianzhu shiyi* 天主實義]. Werk des römisch-katholischen Missionars Matteo Ricci. Handschrift in manjurischer Sprache. 2 Bücher.

120) *Tėgri-jn ėdžėnu unėnči džirum* [*Tngri-yin ejen-ü ünenči ǰirum-un bičig*].[121] Die wahre Lehre des Himmelsherrn. Werk des römisch-katholischen Missionars Matteo Ricci. In mongolischer Sprache. 2 Bücher.

121) *Gėrėn cholo bo milarabucha bitchė* [*Geren holo be milarabuha bithe*].[122] Werk eines römisch-katholischen Missionars. In manjurischer Sprache. 1 Buch.

122) *Cholo bo milarabucha bithchė* [*Holo be milarabuha bithe*].[123] Werk eines römisch-katholischen Missionars in manjurischer Sprache. 1 Buch.

---

[116] Uspensky, 314.

[117] Signatur: T-14. Alte Sign.: Xyl. Q 46.

[118] Uspensky, 308.

[119] Jachontov – Walravens, 129–132.

[120] *Ibid.*, 115–121. Zugrunde liegt das *Tianzhu jiaoyao* 天主教要 des P. Francesco Furtado SJ (1587–1653).

[121] Uspensky, 929.

[122] Jachontov – Walravens, 137: Das *Pishi shi zhu wang* 闢釋氏諸妄 des Xu Guangqi 徐光啓 [1562–1633].

[123] Jachontov – Walravens, 135. – Exemplar des vorgenannten Werkes von Xu Guangqi.

123) *Chošani cholo gizun bo milarabucha bitchė* [*Hōwaśan-i holo gisun be milarabuha bithe*].[124] Werk eines römisch-katholischen Missionars in manjurischer Sprache. 1 Buch.

124) *Tumėn džakaj unenči sėkieni bitchė* [*Tumen jaka-i unenggi sekiyen*].[125] Über den wahren Ursprung aller Dinge oder Handreichung zur natürlichen Gotteserkenntnis [*Wanwu zhenyuan* 萬物真原]. Werk des römisch-katholischen Missionars Adam Schall [vielmehr: Giulio Aleni], in manjurischer Sprache. 1 Buch.

Moral

125) Moralische Aussprüche in manjurischer und chinesischer Sprache.[126] Handschrift. 1 Buch.

126) *Chań-i aracha Šendzu Gośiń Chuan-dii boi tacisjań* [*Han-i araha Śengzu gosin hōwangdi-i booi tacihiyan*].[127] Häusliche Unterweisungen des Kaisers der Devise Kangxi. In manjurischer Sprache. 1 Band, 2 Bücher.

127) *Sajn ükgėtü ėrdėni-jn sankg kėmėkdėkü šastir* [*Sayin ügetü erdeni-yin sang subhašida kemegdekü šastir*].[128] Der Schatz des Wohlberedten. In mongolischer Sprache. 1 Buch.

128) *Bokda-jn surgali sėnkgėrėkgulun badaraguluksan bičik* [*Boyda-yin suryali senggeregül-ün badarayuluysan bičig*].[129] Das Werk „Ausführlich erläuterte Lehre des Heiligen (Kaisers), das lehrreiche Worte oder Erläuterung der Pflichten aller Zustände enthält"; herausgegeben in China zur Devise Yongzheng. In manjurischer und mongolischer Sprache. 1 Band. 2 Bücher.

Philosophie

129) *Sio-dzin* [*Xiaojing* 孝經]. Ein Werk des Kun-dzy [Kongzi 孔子] (Confucius) über die Pietät gegenüber den Eltern und das *Sjao-sio* [*Xiaoxue* 小學], die Schule der Knaben oder Anfangsregeln als Anleitung zur Bildung und zur Tugend, mit Erläuterung.[130] In manjurischer Sprache. 1 Band, 4 Bücher.

---

[124] Jachontov – Walravens, 133. – Andere Ausgabe des vorgenannten Werkes von Xu Guangqi.

[125] *Ibid.*, 122.

[126] *Ibid.*, 170: Enduringge di giyôn guwan mafa-i jalan de ulhibure boobai tacihiyan-i nomun bithe. 關聖帝君覺世寶訓經. „Kostbare Belehrungen zum Nutzen der Welt, auf kaiserlichen Befehl verfaßt."

[127] *Ibid.*, 103.

[128] *PLB*, 138: „Edelsteinschatz der guten Lehren, Subhâṣita genanntes Lehrbuch"; Uspensky, 341.

[129] Jachontov – Walravens, 80: Enduringge tacihiyan be neileme badarambuha bithe.

[130] *Ibid.*, 37: Hiyoo ging be acabufi suhe bithe; Ajige tacikô be acabufi suhe bithe.

130) *Da-sio-i džurchań bo badarambucha bitchė* [*Da hiyoo-i jurgan be badarambuha bithe*].¹³¹ Erläuterungen zum *Da-sio* [*Daxue* 大學], d.i. Lehre für Erwachsene. In manjurischer Sprache. 6 Bände, 36 Bücher.

131) *Inėngidari dzjannacha duiń bitchėj džurchań bo suchė bitchė* [*Inenggidari giyangnaha Duin bithe-i jurgan be suhe bithe*].¹³² Sammlung des Allerbesten aus den Lehren von Kun-dzy [Kongzi] und Mėn-dzy [Mengzi 孟子], der zwei bedeutenden Philosophen des alten China, mit ausführlicher Erläuterung, zusammengestellt von erstklassigen Gelehrten, auf Anordnung des Kaisers in der Ära Kangxi, für die eigene Übung. In manjurischer Sprache. 4 Bände, 26 Bücher.

132) *Chań-i aracha ši-dzin bitchė* [*Han-i araha Ši ging bithe*].¹³³ Sammlung von zur Zeit der Dynastie Zhou (ab 1222 v.Chr.) niedergeschriebenen Gedichten. Das Buch ist in 4 Teile geteilt: 1. Go-fyn [*guofeng* 國風], einfache Lieder der Teilfürstentümer, 2. Sjao-ja [*xiaoya* 小雅], von Staatsmännern zusammengestellte Gedichte und Lieder, 3. Da-ja [*daya* 大雅], Gedichte und Oden zu Ehren des Wen wang und seines Sohnes Wu wang, 4. Sun [*song* 頌], Lobeshymnen zu Ehren der Vorväter, bei der Darbringung von Opfern gesungen. In manjurischer Sprache. 2 Bände, 16 Bücher.

Recht

133) *Li-dzi* [*Liji* 禮記].¹³⁴ Von Kun-dzy [Kongzi] zusammengestelltes Buch der Riten. In manjurischer und chinesischer Sprache. 2 Bände, 12 Bücher.

134) *Chėsėj toktobucha Daicin guruni uchėri koli-i koli chaciń bitchė* [*Hesei toktobuha Daicing gurun-i uheri kooli-i kooli hacin bithe*].¹³⁵ Sammlung von Gesetzen des Daicing [Da Qing 大清]-Reiches. In manjurischer Sprache. 24 Bände. 178 Bücher.

135) *Gu-vyń* [*Guwen yuanjian* 古文淵鑑].¹³⁶ Sammlung von musterhaften Werken über die Staatsregierung, das gesellschaftliche und private Leben. In manjurischer Sprache. 5 Bände, 36 Bücher.

136) Sammlung von Erlassen, die in China in den Ären Kangxi und Yongzheng bezüglich der aus acht Bannern bestehenden Truppen herausgegeben wur-

---

[131] Jachontov – Walravens, 12.

[132] *Ibid.*, 6: „Die Vier Bücher mit den täglichen Erläuterungen der Prinzenschule."

[133] *Ibid.*, 17.

[134] *Ibid.*, 31: Han-i araha ubaliyambuha Dorolon-i nomun. „Buch der Riten, übersetzt auf kaiserlichen Befehl."

[135] Jachontov – Walravens, 253: *Qinding Da Qing huidian zeli* 欽定大清會典則例.

[136] *Ibid.*, 459. Vgl. die Auszüge bei A. Leont'ev, *Chinesische Gedanken nach der von Herrn Alexjei Leont'ew Secretair bey dem rußischkaiserlichen Collegio der auswärtigen Geschäfte aus der manshurischen Sprache verfertigten rußischen Uebersetzung ins Deutsche übersetzt* (Weimar: Hoffmann, 1776).

den [*Dergi hese jakōn gōsa de wasimbuhangge*].¹³⁷ In manjurischer Sprache. 2 Bände, 10 Bücher.

137) *Enduringė tacisjań [Enduringge tacihiyan]*.¹³⁸ Lehrreiche Erlasse der Kaiser der manjurischen Dynastie – Shizu, Taizu, Shengzu und Shizong. In manjurischer Sprache. 10 Bände, 112 Bücher.

138) *Gao-dzun ioncjanga Chuan-dii ėnduringė tacisjań [Gaozung yongkiyangga hōwangdi-i enduringge tacihiyan]*.¹³⁹ Während der Qianlong-Ära veröffentlichte lehrreiche Erlasse über verschiedene Bereiche der Regierung. In manjurischer Sprache. 50 Bände, 300 Bücher.

139) *Dzarlik-er toktagaksan gadagadu Monkgolun türü-kgi dzasachu jabudalun jamuni chaoli dzüjlun bičik [Jarliγ-iyar toγtaγaysan γadaγadu mongγol-un törü-yi jasaqu yabudal-un yamun-u qauli jüil bičig]*.¹⁴⁰ Das Gesetzbuch der Pekinger Kammer der Außenbeziehungen [Lifanyuan 理藩院], herausgegeben auf höchsten Befehl. In mongolischer Sprache. 24 Bücher.

140) *Čochaj džurchan-i siramo bandzibucha bajtaj koli-i bitchė [Coohai jurgan-i sirame banjibuha baitai kooli-i bithe]*.¹⁴¹ Ergänzung der Gesetze des Pekinger Kriegsministeriums, herausgegeben im 13. Jahr der Ära Jiaqing. In manjurischer Sprache. 1 Band, 4 Bücher.

Erzählungen, Geschichte und Geographie

141) *Arban dzükgun ėdzėn Kgėssėr chaganu togodži [Arban jüg-ün ejen Geser qaγan-u tuγuji]*.¹⁴² Die Erzählung von Gesser Chan, dem Herrscher über zehn Länder. In mongolischer Sprache. 4 Bücher.

142) Dasselbe Werk [141], unter demselben Titel.¹⁴³ In mongolischer Sprache. 1 Buch.

143-144) *Šiditu kėkgurun togodži [Šiditü kegür-ün tuγuji]*.¹⁴⁴ Erzählungen eines Leichnams. Handschrift in mongolischer Sprache. In 2 Exemplaren.

---

¹³⁷ Jachontov – Walravens, 277.

¹³⁸ Ibid., 67: *Qingwen wu chao shengxun* 清文五朝聖訓.

¹³⁹ Ibid., 72.

¹⁴⁰ Uspensky, 898. – Vgl. die Übersetzung (nach dem Manju) von Stepan Lipovcov, *Uloženie Kitajskoj Palaty Vnešnich Snošenij* (St. Petersburg: Tip. Departamenta Narodn. Prosveščenija, 1828).

¹⁴¹ Jachontov – Walravens, 269.

¹⁴² Sazykin I, 11, 14, 32, 37; Uspensky, 903d. – Vgl. Isaak Jakob Schmidt, *Die Thaten Bogda Gesser Chan's, des Vertilgers der Wurzel der zehn Übel in den zehn Gegenden: eine ostasiatische Heldensage* (St. Petersburg: Gräff, 1839). Schmidt gab 1836 den mongolischen Text nach dem Pekinger Blockdruck heraus.

¹⁴³ Uspensky, 903d.

¹⁴⁴ Sazykin I, 245; Uspensky, 412: Sidi-tü kegür-ün quulin-ača nomlagsan [!] suru orosiγulbai = Nr 143; Uspensky, 413: Siditü kegür-ün quuli = Nr. 144.

145) *Ėl'dėb ülikgėrun dalaj* [*Eldeb üliger-ün dalai kemegdekü sudur orosiba*].¹⁴⁵ Das Meer aller Parabeln, über die Taten der Buddhas, mit Anpassung an das Beispiel des Menschenlebens. Teil des *Kanjur*. In mongolischer Sprache. 1 Buch.

146) *Ülikgėrun nom ėrdėni cokcalaksanu čichula domok kėmėku šastir* [*Üliger-ün nom erdeni čoγčaluγsan-u čiqula domoγ kemekü sastir orosiba*].¹⁴⁶ Buch der Parabeln oder Sammlung wichtiger erbaulicher Erzählungen (die den moralischen Teil des Buddhismus erläutern). In mongolischer Sprache. 4 Bücher.

147) *Čindamani ėrikė* [*Čintamaṇi erike*].¹⁴⁷ Kostbarer Rosenkranz. Erzählungen über die früheren Taten und Lehren des Chonšim Bodhisattva. In mongolischer Sprache. 1 Buch.

148) Dasselbe Werk [147], in tibetischer Sprache, unter dem Titel: *Norbu prengva* [*Chos-spyod nor-bu'i phreṅ-ba*].¹⁴⁸ Handschrift. 1 Buch.

149) *Bodotanu ajmakgun ülėmdži nom utcha-kgi kgėjkgülükči dzula, ülikgėrun nom ėrdėni cokcalaksan lakša tajlburi* [*Boduu-a-tan-u ayimaγ-un ülemǰi nom: udq-a-yi geyigülün üiledügči ǰula: üliger-ün nom erdeni čoγčalaγsan: lakš-a tayilburi orosibai*].¹⁴⁹ Leuchte, die die hauptsächlichen Eigenschaften der hohen Priester erhellt, oder Erläuterung der kostbaren Eigenschaften in Gleichnissen. In mongolischer Sprache. 1 Buch.

150) *Iokgačarisun ėrkėtü dėkgėdü kgėtülkgėkči Milarajba-jn namtar, nirvan kikgėt chamuk-kgi ajladukči-jn müri üdzėkgüluksėn* [*Yōgačaris-un erketü degedü getülgegči milarasba-yin rnam-tar, nirvan kiged qamuγ-i ayiladuγči-yin mör-i üǰegülügsen kemekdekü orusiba*].¹⁵⁰ Erzählung über Milaraspa, den mächtigen und hochgestellten Herrscher der Yogacarya und Wegweiser zum Nirvana und zur Allwissenheit. In mongolischer Sprache. 1 Buch.

151) *Kgėtulkgėkči Milarajba-jn togodži dėlkgėrėnkgüj ilgaksan bum dagulal kėmėkdėku* [*Getülgegči Milarasba-yin tuγuči delgerenggüi ilγaγsan 'bum*

---

¹⁴⁵ Uspensky, 53. *PLB*, 71: „Meer verschiedener Gleichnisse genanntes Buch." Vgl. Kowalewski, „Soderžanie Mongol'skoj knigi, pod zaglaviem: More prič." *Učenyja zapiski izdavaemyja imp. Kazanskim universitetom* 1834, S. 134–162, 236–259.

¹⁴⁶ Uspensky, 421; *PLB*, 184: „Šastra genannt die bedeutendsten Legenden der zusammengehäuften Kostbarkeiten der Lehrbeispiele."

¹⁴⁷ Uspensky, 190. Biographie des Atiśa Dīpaṃkaraśrījñāna.

¹⁴⁸ Sign.: T-44. Alte Sign.: Xyl. Q 103.

¹⁴⁹ Sazykin I, 355, 357, 358; Uspensky, 418; *PLB*, 121: „Lampe, welche die hohe Lehrmeinung der Sekte Po-to-pa erhellt, Buch der Gleichnisse, zehntausend wie Kostbarkeiten angesammelte Auslegungen."

¹⁵⁰ Uspensky, 220; *PLB*, 131: „Lebensbeschreibung des erhabenen Milaraspa des mächtigen Wundertäters, welche aufzeigt den Pfad des Nichts und Alles Wissenden."

daγulal kemegdekü].¹⁵¹ Erzählung über den Lehrer Milaraspa. In mongolischer Sprache. 1 Buch.

152) *Bodi sètkil tèkgüsüksèn kükè chogolajtu saran kükgèkgè nèrètü šibagunu togodži, orčilankg büküni džirukèn ükgèj kèmèn mèdèkčidün èdžikgènu čimèk* [*Bodi sedkil tegüsügsen köke qoγolai-tu sarn kökege neretü šibaγun-u tuγuči orčilang bükün-i jirüken ügei kemen medegčid-ün čikin-ü čimeg*].¹⁵² Erzählung von dem Vogel Mondkuckuck, der einen blauen Hals hat und voll göttlichen Geistes ist, oder Schmuck eines Vaters, der in der Herzlosigkeit des Kreises der Wiedergeburten erfahren ist. In mongolischer Sprache. 1 Buch.

153) *Džu-Adiša Ènètkèk-dur kèrkidžu šašin dèlkgèksèn ba, altan dvip-tur odaksanu togodži* [*Juu Atiša enedkeg-eče kerkijü sasin delgeregsen ba: altan tiib-tür oduγsan-u tuγujī*].¹⁵³ Erzählung von dem indischen Missionar Džu-Adiša, der Verbreitung des Glaubens in Enedkek und seine Reisen ins goldene Dvipa. In mongolischer Sprache. 1 Buch.

154) *Padma Gatankg sudur* [*Badm-a γatang sudur*],¹⁵⁴ Biographie des Padma Sambhava. In mongolischer Sprache. 1 Buch.

155) *Vadžra Dara Džandža Lalida badmara džnja šašina devasri patrajn cadik, susukgun linchoa-kgi tèjn bükgèt nèkgèkči naranu kgèrèl* [*Včir-dhar-a ljang-sgi-a lalita bacar-a jñana šasin-a dibi śrii-badr-ayin čadig süsüg-ün linqu-a-yin teyin büged negegči naran-u gerel kemegdekü*].¹⁵⁵ Das Sonnenlicht, das vollkommen den Hornklee [vielm.: Lotos] der Andacht öffnet, oder Lebensbeschreibung des bedeutenden Pekinger *Qutuγtu Vadžra Dara Džandža* [d.i. der *lCaṅ-skya Rol-pa'i rdo-rje*]. In mongolischer Sprache. 1 Buch.

156) *Chutuktu Molon Tojn èkè-dur-en ači chariguluksan kèmèku sudur* [*Qutuγ-tu molon toyin eke-dür-iyen ači qariγuluγsan kemekü sudur orosiba*].¹⁵⁶ Über den heiligen Molon Toyin [d.i. Maudgalyāyana], der seiner Mutter Dank erstattete. In mongolischer Sprache. 1 Buch.

---

¹⁵¹ Sazykin I, 293; *PLB*, 130: „Geschichte des ehrwürdigen Milaraspa, besungen in zehntausend Strophen."

¹⁵² Sazykin I, 261, 262; Uspensky, 449; *PLB*, 146: „Geschichte des gelben Kuckucksvogels mit der blauen Kehle, welcher ein Bodhisattva war, genannt Ohrenschmuck derjenigen, welche wissen, daß die Welt ohne Gehalt ist."

¹⁵³ Uspensky, 192; *PLB*, 91: „Geschichte, auf welche Weise rJo bo Atiśa die Lehre in Indien verbreitet hat und wie er nach dem Goldlande gekommen ist."

¹⁵⁴ Exemplar nicht erhalten. *PLB*, 25: „Belehrung des Pad-ma, Sûtra."

¹⁵⁵ Uspensky, 211.

¹⁵⁶ Uspensky, 403. *PLB*, 15: „Sûtra, wie der heilige Molon toyin seiner Mutter die Wohltaten zurückerstattete."

157–158) Dasselbe Werk [156], Handschrift. 2 Exemplare.[157]

159) *Ilaguksadun ėrkėtu chamuk-kgi ajladukči Vadžra Dara Lobzan Kgaldzan Džjamco Dalaj-Lama-jn Kgėkgėnu namtar tobči-jn tedüj ükgülėksėn Kalbaravara ėrdėni-jn itėkgėl nėrėtü togodži* [*Ilaγuysad-un erketü qamuγ-i ayiladuyči včir dhar-a blobzang bsgal-bzang rgi-a-mzo dalai blam-a-yin gegen-ü namtar-i tobči-yin tedüi ügülegsen galbaravara erdeni-yin itegel neretü tuγuči terigün debter orosiba*].[158] Erzählung unter dem Titel: Der Glaube an den Schatz Kalbaravara oder kurze Lebensbeschreibung des Hauptes der Sieger, des allwissenden Vadžra Dara Lobdzan Kgaldzan, des erleuchtetsten Dalai Lama. In mongolischer Sprache. 2 Bücher.

160) *Šaronkg Kgasur* [*Bharug ga-šor*].[159] Beschreibung der unter diesem Namen bekannten heiligen Pyramide [d.i. der Bodnāth Stūpa]. Handschrift in mongolischer Sprache. 1 Buch.

161) *Kgėkgėn toli* [*Gegen toli*].[160] Heller Spiegel. Geschichte Tibets. Handschrift in mongolischer Sprache. 1 Buch.

162) *Čojdžit Dakini-jn togodži* [*Čoyijid dagini-yin tuγujī*].[161] Erzählung von der Ḍākinī Čoyijid. Handschrift in mongolischer Sprache. 1 Buch.

163) *Džebcun Dzunkchabi namtar činmoj surdib namtar lėkšad gunduj*, mongolisch: *Bokda kgėtulkgėkči Dzunkchaba-jn asuru ekėdė tonilgakči-kgi ondzojlan tal'biksan togodži* [*Boγda getülgegči bčonggiba-yin asuru yekede tonilγaγči-yi üjüyilen talbiysan tuγuji sayitur nomlaysan bügüde-yi quriyaysan orosibai*].[162] Erzählung von dem großen Erlöser, dem heiligen Lehrer Tsongkhapa. Biographie des rje-bcun Tsongkhapa. Handschrift in tibetischer und mongolischer Sprache. 1 Buch.

164) *Uta-jn tabun agulanu orošil, susuktėnu čikin čimėk* [*Uta-yin tabun aγulan-u orosil süsüg-ten-ü čikin čimeg*].[163] Ohrschmuck des in Andacht zum Wutai Berg [Wutaishan 五台山] der fünf Spitzen Kommenden. Beschreibung des Berges (chin. Qingliangshan [清凉山], Provinz Shanxi) und der Götzentempel, die dort zu Ehren des Mañjuśrī errichtet sind. In mongolischer Sprache. 1 Buch.

---

[157] 158 = Uspensky, 406: Qutuγ-tu molon toyin eke-dür-iyen ači qariγuluγsan kemekü sudur orosiba; 157 = Qutuγ-tu molon toyin eke-dür-iyen ači qariγuluγsan [!] sudur orosiba.

[158] Uspensky, 208d. *PLB*, 135: „Erzählung, genannt Glauben an das Kleinod des Fabelbaumes, welche erzählt so viel wie eine Zusammenfassung der Biographie des allwissenden und allgewaltigen Vajradhara Dalai lama bLo-bzań bskal-bzań rgya-mcho."

[159] Uspensky, 247.

[160] *Ibid.*, 183.

[161] Sazykin I, 317; Uspensky, 408.

[162] Uspensky, 201.

[163] Sazykin I, 1642; Uspensky, 253; *PLB*, 7: „Ohrschmuck der Frommen. Führer durch den Wutaishan."

165) *Tabun üdzükgürtu agulajn cadik* [*Degedü oron-u tabun üjügür-tü aγulayin čadig kemekdekü orosiba*].¹⁶⁴ Beschreibung des (Wutai) Berges der fünf Gipfel. Handschrift in mongolischer Sprache. 1 Buch.

166) *Dėkgėdu oron tabun üdzükgürtu agulajn sajšijal bajaschulankgtu kumudajn cėcėkglikgun ėrikė* [*Degedü oron tabun üjügür-tü aγula-yin sayišiyal bayasqulang-tu kumuda-yin čečerlig-ün erike kemegdekü orošiba*].¹⁶⁵ Rosenkranz aus dem freudevollen Blumengarten Kumuda auf dem geheiligten (Wutai) Berge der fünf Spitzen. Handschrift in mongolischer Sprache. 1 Buch.

167) *Juj-cjao-li* [*Yu Jiao Li* 玉嬌梨].¹⁶⁶ Handschriftlicher Roman in manjurischer Sprache. 1 Band, 10 Bücher.

168) *Tun-djań Gan-mu* [*(Zizhi) Tongjian gangmu* (資治)通鑑綱目].¹⁶⁷ Chinesische Geschichte vom ersten Kaiser Fuxi bis zur Vertreibung des mongolischen Hauses aus China im Jahre 1368. In manjurischer Sprache. 12 Bände, 108 Bücher.

169) *Ciń-din-si-juj-tun-vyń-dži* [*Qinding Xiyu tongwenzhi* 欽定西域同文志].¹⁶⁸ Historisch-geographisches Wörterbuch der Westländer. In manjurischer, chinesischer, mongolischer, tibetischer, kalmükischer und türkischer Sprache, auf höchsten Befehl im 28. Jahr der Devise Qianlong zusammengestellt vom Da-sio-ši Fu-chėn [*daxueshi* 大學士 Fuheng 傅恆, gest. 1770]. 1 Band, 8 Bücher.

170) *Ilań güruni bitchė* [*Ilan gurun-i bithe*].¹⁶⁹ Geschichte [Roman] der Drei Reiche: Shu, Wei, Wu, in die China von 189 bis 265 n.Chr. eingeteilt war. In manjurischer Sprache. 4 Bände, 24 Bücher.

171) *Fan-juj-lėj-cuań* [*Fangyu leizuan* 方輿類纂].¹⁷⁰ Geographische Beschreibung Chinas, in chinesischer Sprache, mit geographischen Karten, herausgegeben in der Ära Jiaqing. 4 Bände, 24 Bücher.

172) *Ciń-din-siń-dzjan* [*Qinding Xinjiang shilüe* 欽定新疆識略].¹⁷¹ Neueste Beschreibung der Bucharei mit geographischen Karten, herausgegeben in der Ära Daoguang. In chinesischer Sprache, 10 Bücher.

---

[164] Uspensky, 255. Vgl. *PLB*, 58: „Beschreibung des fünfgipfligen Berges."

[165] Uspensky, 254. Vgl. *PLB*, 58: „Lob des erhabenen Ortes, des fünfgipfligen Berges, Kette freudvoller Lotosgärten."

[166] Jachontov – Walravens, 450: Ioi jiyao li bithe.

[167] *Ibid.*, 172.

[168] *Ibid.*, 282–283; Uspensky, 258.

[169] Jachontov – Walravens, 453.

[170] Von Liu Dakui 劉大魁 (1698–1779).

[171] Von Songyun 松筠 (1752–1835). Sign.: Xyl. 14.

173) *Čuń-cju* [*Chunqiu* 春秋].[172] Chronik des Reiches Lu, heute Provinz Shandong, von Kun-dzy [Kongzi] als Geschenk gebracht, enthält eine chronologische Erzählung der Taten der Herrscher während 242 Jahren und die Grundsätze der Staatsregierung. 49 Bücher.

174) *Cin-din Min-dzjań* [*Qinding Mingjian* 欽定明鑑].[173] Geschichte der Dynastie Ming, die in China herrschte. In chinesischer Sprache. 2 Bände, 12 Bücher.

175) *Bi-šu-šań-džuan* [*Bishu shanzhuang (ji)* 避署山莊(記)].[174] Beschreibung von Rehe [熱河] (Jehol), mit Bildern. In chinesischer Sprache. 1 Band, 2 Bücher.

176) *Lakčacha džečeń de takuracha babo ėdzėchė bitchė* [*Lakcaha jecen de takōraha babe ejehe bithe*].[175] Bericht über die Reise des chinesischen Gesandten Tuliśen zum Kalmükenchan Ajuki, durch die Mongolei und Russland im Jahr 1712. In manjurischer Sprache. Handschrift. 1 Band, 2 Bücher.

177) Dasselbe Werk [176], in mongolischer Sprache. Handschrift. 1 Buch.[176]

178) *Džungari babo nėciemo toktobucha bodochoń bitchė* [*Jun gar-i babe necihiyeme toktobuha bodogon-i bithe*].[177] Ausführliche Beschreibung des Krieges der Chinesen in der Qianlong-Zeit seit 1751 gegen die Dsungarei, und dann gegen Ostturkestan. In mongolischer [!] Sprache. 100 Bücher.

Medizin, Naturgeschichte

179) *Ėl'dėb čichula kėrėktu* [*Eldeb čiqula keregtü*].[178] Alles unumgänglich Notwendige. Arzneimittelbuch in mongolischer Sprache. 1 Buch.

180) *Chuan-di su-vyń* [*Huangdi suwen* 黃帝素文].[179] Die allgemeine Therapie des Chuan-di [Huangdi]. In chinesischer Sprache. 2 Bände, 10 Bücher.

181) *Chuan-di nėj dzin lin šu* [*Huangdi neijing lingshu* 黃帝內經靈樞].[180] Über die äußerlichen Krankheiten. In chinesischer Sprache. 10 Bände.

182) *Bėn-kan gan-mu* [sic, d.i. *Bencao gangmu* 本草綱目]. Naturgeschichte in chinesischer Sprache. 6 Bände, 48 Bücher.

---

[172] Jachontov – Walravens, 34: Han-i araha ubaliyambuha Śajingga nomun.
[173] Sign.: Xyl. 58.
[174] Sign.: Xyl. 59.
[175] Jachontov – Walravens, 286.
[176] Uspensky, 260: Tasurqai kiǰaγar-tur ǰaruysan yabudali temdeglegsen bičig.
[177] Jachontov – Walravens, 216.
[178] Uspensky, 877.
[179] Sign.: Xyl. 53.
[180] Sign.: Xyl. 54.

183) *Rašijanu džirukėn: najman kgėšikgütü niguča ubadisun ündüsün ėcė idzagurun ündüsün* [*Rasiyan-u jirüken nayiman gesigütü niɣuca ubadis-un ündüsün-eče iǰaɣur-un ündüsün*].[181] Das Herz (die Quintessenz) des heiligen Wassers: Auszug aus dem Anfang der acht geheimen Regeln. In mongolischer Sprache. 1 Buch.

184) *Rašijanu džirukėn: najman kgėšikgütü niguca ubadisun ėrdėmun ündüsünü nėmėelkgėjn arga ėbėršilun chanagun ėnėlkgė-kgi arilgakči kėtboa cak busujn ükülun salma-kgi oktalokči ildun kėmėkdėku-ėcė ėbėčinu šiltagan tėrikgutėni udzėkgülüksėn sudur* [*Rasiyan-u ǰirüken nayiman gesigütü: niɣuca ubadis-un erdem-ün ündüsün-ü nemelge-yin arɣ-a ebersil-ün qalaɣun enelge-yi arilɣayči gadbura čaɣ busu-yin ükül-ün salm-a-yi oɣtaluyči: ildün kemekü-eče ebečin-ü siltaɣan terigüten-i üǰügülügsen sudur*].[182] Das Herz (die Quintessenz) des heiligen Wassers: Anzeige der acht geheimnisvollen Hilfsmittel der Arzneikunst, Auszug aus „Das Schwert, das die Fangschlinge des unerwarteten Todes abschneidet und befreit von allen Krankheiten". In mongolischer Sprache. 1 Buch.

185) Dasselbe Werk [184], in mongolischer Sprache. Handschrift.[183]

Astronomie

186) *Kitadun džiruchaj-in sudur-ėcė Monkgolčilan orčiguluksan džiruchaj* [*Kitad-un ǰiruqai-yin sudur-ača mongɣolčilan orčiɣulsan ǰiruqai-yin orosil*].[184] Lehrgang der Astronomie, verfasst in chinesischer Sprache (von römischen Missionaren) und ins Mongolische übersetzt in der Kangxi-Zeit. 2 Bände, 36 Bücher.

187) *Dajcin ulusun türü kgėrėltü-jn najmadugar onu cak ularilun toganu bičik* [*Dayičing ulus-un törü gereltü-yin naimaduɣar on-u čaɣ ularil-un toɣan-u bičig*].[185] Aufzählung der Veränderungen der Zeit des achten Jahres „Licht der Vernunft" im chinesischen Reich. Kalender für 1828, d.i. das 8. Jahr der Ära Daoguang 道光. In mongolischer Sprache. 1 Buch.

---

[181] Uspensky, 839.3; 871.1; *PLB*, 125: „Quintessenz der Heilkunde. Wurzel der Geheimlehre, welche von den acht [Körper-]Teilen handelt."

[182] Uspensky, 874; *PLB*, 137: „Sûtra welches Ursachen und Verlauf der Krankheiten etc. beschreibt nach dem Werk genannt Schwert, welches die Klinge frühzeitigen Sterbens hinwegschlägt, womit man bekämpft die Hitze der schmerzhaften Leiden, Methode dargelegt aus der Quintessenz der Heilkunde, Wurzel der geheimen Lehre von den acht [Körper-]Teilen."

[183] Uspensky, 875.

[184] Ibid., 882.1: Herausgeber des Werkes war Johann Adam Schall von Bell. – Es handelt sich möglicherweise um *Xiyang xinfa lishu* 西洋新法曆書, ein astronomisches Sammelwerk; Uspensky zitiert keinen chinesischen Gesamttitel für die 38 Bändchen.

[185] Uspensky, 886.

Varia

188) *Tumėn onu li-tu* [*Tümen on-u li-tu, Wannian shu* 萬年書].[186] Anzeige der zehntausend Jahre. Verzeichnis der Jahre der Ären Kangxi, Yongzheng und Qianlong. 1 Buch.

189) Briefe des chinesischen Kaisers in der Ära Qianlong zur Zeit der Reise in die Südprovinzen Chinas an einen gewissen Fei, der in der Hauptstadt geblieben war.[187] In manjurischer und chinesischer Sprache. Verschiedene Handschriften. 1 Buch.

Titelregister (normierte Umschrift)

Abkai ejen-i tacihiyan-i heśen-i bithe 118
Abkai ejen-i unenggi jurgan 119
Ajige tacikô be acabufi suhe bithe 129
Arban ǰüg-ün eǰen Geser qaɣan-u tuɣuǰi 141-142
Arban nayiman keregtü kemekü surɣal 53
Arban nayiman mingɣ-a-tu 57
Arban qaranɣya 35
Āryaaṣṭasāhasrikā prajñāpāramitāsūtra 60
Ayaɣ-a tegimlig-ün surtal 108
Ayui yeke tegüs onol-tu nom-un udq-a-yi delgerenggüy-e ügülügsen sudur 95
Badm-a ɣatang sudur 154
Bencao gangmu 本草綱目 182
Bga-a-'giur erdeni-yin nere-yin toɣ-a ɣarčiɣ orosiba 22
Bga-a-'giür-un ǰirüken-ü quriyangɣui-yin toɣtaɣal orosiba 62
Bhadrakalpikāsūtra 99
Bharug ga-šor 160
Bičiküi-yin sastir tobčilan quriyaɣsan sayin nomlalɣ-a rasiyan-u nere-tü orosiba 15
Bilig-ün činadu kiǰaɣar kürügsen vačir-iyar ebdegči-yin [!] *ači tus-a ene bolai* 103
Bilig-ün činadu kürügsen ǰaɣun mingɣan toɣatu 59
Bishu shanzhuang (*ji*) 避署山莊(記) 175
Bodhi mör-ün ǰerge-dür angqa oyun sudulqu nomun egüden negegči kemegdekü orusiba 109
Bodhi mör-ün ǰerge-yin degedü ubadis-i silüglegsen qamuɣ-i ayiladuɣči amur mör kemegdekü-yin toɣ-a bičig 113

---

[186] Uspensky, 885.
[187] Nicht erhalten.

Bodhi mör-ün ǰerge-yin ulayan kötelbüri qamuy-yi ayiladuyči-dur odqui amur mör kemegdekü orusiba 110

Bodi sedkil tegüsügsen köke qoyolai-tu sarn kökege neretü šibayun-u tuyuči orčilang bükün-i ǰirüken ügei kemen medegčid-ün čikin-ü čimeg 152

Boduu-a-tan-u ayimay-un ülemǰi nom: udq-a-yi geyigülün üiledügči ǰula: üliger-ün nom erdeni čoyčalaysan: lakš-a tayilburi orosibai 149

Boyda-yin suryali senggeregül-ün badarayuluysan bičig 128

Boyda getülgegči bčonggiba-yin asuru yekede tonilyayči-yi üǰüyilen talbiysan tuyuǰi sayitur nomlaysan bügüde-yi quriyaysan orosibai 163

Buddhanāmasahasrapañcaśatacaturtripañcadaśa 41

Busud-un tusa-yin ǰirüken kemekgdekü anggida tonilyayči-yin surtal orosiba 100

Čayan sikürtei 36

Čayan linqu-a neretü yeke kölgen sudur 89

Chos-spyod nor-bu'i phreṅ-ba 148

Chuxue zhinan 初學指南 18-19

Chunqiu 春秋 173

Čilen aqu-yin šayšabad-un ündüsün blama nar-un tuyuǰi ǰang üile maytayal-un tayilburi ači tusa-luya selte-yi nomlaysan qoyar tüidker-un quriyangyui arilyaqun naran-u lingqua-yin sečerlig-i tedkügči adistid tu mingyan usun bariyči-luya tegüsügsen oytaryui-yin manglai neretü orusiba 114

Čintamaṇi erike 147

Čiqula kereglegči tegüs udq-a-tu neretü sastir orosibai 115

Coohai jurgan-i sirame banjibuha baitai kooli-i bithe 140

Čoyiǰid dagini-yin tuyuǰi 162

Da hiyoo-i jurgan be badarambuha bithe 130

Dag-pa gser-gyi mdo-thig 43-45

Dayičing ulus-un törü gereltü-yin naimaduyar on-u čay ularil-un toyan-u bičig 187

Degedü oron tabun üǰügür-tü ayula-yin sayišiyal bayasqulang-tu kumuda-yin čečerlig-ün erike kemegdekü orošiba 166

Degedü oron-u tabun üǰügür-tü ayulayin čadig kemekdekü orosiba 165

Dergi hese jakôn gôsa de wasimbuhangge 136

bDer-gśegs bdun-gyi mchod-pa'i chog-sgrigs yid-bźin dbaṅ-rgyal 32

Doyšid 47-49

Doluyan sayiber oduysan-u takiqu-yin ǰang yosun-luya neyiletkü küsel-i qangyayči erkes-ün qayan neretü 101

Don-chen-mo rab-tu gcod-pa 92-94

rDo-rje gcod-pa 75-76

Dörben jüil-ün üsüg qabsuruγsan toli bičig 10
Dörben ündüsün 31
Eldeb bilig baramid 56
Eldeb čiqula keregtü 179
Eldeb üliger-ün dalai kemegdekü sudur orosiba 145
Enduringge di giyôn guwan mafa-i jalan de ulhibure boobai tacihiyan-i nomun bithe 126
Enduringge tacihiyan 137
Enduringge tacihiyan be neileme badarambuha bithe 128
Erdeni oki-yin toγtaγal neretü yeke kölgen sudur orosiba 102
Fangyu leizuan 方輿類纂 171
Gaozung yongkiyangga hôwangdi-i enduringge tacihiyan 138
Gegen toli 161
Geren holo be milarabuha bithe 121
Getülgegči Milarasba-yin tuγuči delgerenggüi ilγaysan 'bum daγulal kemegdekü 151
Guansheng dijun jueshi baoxun jing 關聖帝君覺世寶訓經 126
Γurban jüil-ün üge qadamal üjeküi-dür kilbar bolγaysan bičig 11
Γurban jüil-ün üsüg qadamal bičig 17
Guwen yuanjian 古文淵鑑 135
rGya-skad daṅ sṅags-don thor-bu bod-skad-du bkrol-ba bžug-so 1
Han-i araha dasame ubaliyambuha wacir-i lashalara nomun 71
Han-i araha Manju Monggo gisun-i bithe 14
Han-i araha nonggime toktobuha Manju gisun-i buleku bithe 12
Han-i araha Šengzu gosin hôwangdi-i booi tacihiyan 125
Han-i araha Ši ging bithe 132
Han-i araha ubaliyambuha Dorolon-i nomun 132
Han-i araha ubaliyambuha Šajingga nomun 173
Hesei toktobuha Daicing gurun-i uheri kooli-i kooli hacin bithe 134
Hesei toktobuha Manjusai wecere metere kooli bithe 40
Hiyoo ging be acabufi suhe bithe 129
Holo be milarabuha bithe 122
Hōwaśan-i holo gisun be milarabuha bithe 123
Huangdi neijing lingshu 黃帝內經靈樞 181
Huangdi suwen 黃帝素文 180

Ilaγuysad-yin eke getülgegči qutuγ-tu dar-a eke-yin qorin nigen mörgül eke orosiba 38

Ilayuysad-un erketü qamuy-i ayiladuyči včir dhar-a blobzang bsgal-bzang rgi-a-mzo dalai blam-a-yin gegen-ü namtar-i tobči-yin tedüi ügülegsen galbaravara erdeni-yin itegel neretü tuyuči terigün debter orosiba 159

Ilan gurun-i bithe 170

Ilan hacin-i hergen kamcibuha gisun-i bithe 17

Inenggidari giyangnaha Duin bithe-i jurgan be suhe bithe 131

Ioi jiyao li bithe 167

Itegel ba čoγtu vačir ayuγuluγči arban γurban burqan-tu-yin ǰalbaril irügel ölǰei ügülekü ba: bütügel-ün arγ-a-yin ayimaγ-ud abisig ögküi yosun γal mandal terigüten-ü ayimaγ 25

Jarliγ-iyar toγtaγaγsan γadaγadu mongγol-un törü-yi ǰasaqu yabudal-un yamun-u qauli ǰüil bičig 139

rJe-bcun sgrol-ma phyag 'tshal ñi-šu rtsa gcig ma 51

Jibčun-damba-yin silüglel 105

Jirüken-ü tolta sudur 20

Jirüken-ü tolta-yin tayilburi üsüg-ün endegürel-ün qarangγui-yi arilγaγči oγtarγui-yin maṇi 21

Jiryuγan irügel 37

Jônggaba-yin maγtaγal 104

Jun gar-i babe necihiyeme toktobuha bodogon-i bithe 178

Juu Atiša enedkeg-eče kerkiǰü sasin delgeregsen ba: altan tiib-tür oduγsan-u tuγuǰi 153

Juwan jakôn acangga seme tacihiyan 53

sKar-ma'i yum žes-bya ba'i gzuṅs 43-45

Kitad-un ǰiruqai-yin sudur-ača mongγolčilan orčiγulsan ǰiruqai-yin orosil 186

bKra-šis brtsegs-pa 43-45

Lakcaha jeden de takôraha babe ejehe bithe 176

Liji 禮記 133

sMan-bla'i mdo-chog 'don cha zur-du bkol-ba yid-bźin dbaṅ-rgyal źes bya-ba 46

Mañču-srii-yin aman-u esi kemekü 98

Mani gambu 87

Manju isabuha bithe 13

Manju nikan hergen-i cing wen ki meng 16

Merged γarqu-yin oron neretü toγtaγaγsan dagyig 2

Mör-ün ǰerge-yin kötülbüri-yi toγtaγaγsan-iyan bičigsen orosiba 111

gNam-sa snaṅ-brgyad 43-45

Nayiman ǰayutu sudur 55

Nayiman nom 43-45

Nayiman tümen dörben mingγan nom-un qayaly-a-yin sayin tüligür orosiγulba 117

Nere-yin dalai 3

Ñes-pa kun-sel 43-45

Nom-un ǰirγalang-tu dagini-yin ünen ǰarlig-un debter bolai 107

Ñon mons no-šes sems-kyi me-lon 52

Öljei badaraγsan süm-e-yin qural-un aman-u ungsily-a nom-un yabudal masi todorqai gegen oyutan-u qoγolai-yin čimeg čintamani erike 28

Pañcaviṃśatisāhasrikā-prajñāpāramitā-sūtra 54

'Phags-pa 'jam-dpal-gyi mtshan yaṅ-dag-par brjod-pa 43-45

'Phags-pa phyogs bcu'i mun-sel 43-45

'Phags-pa šes-rab-kyi pha-rol-tu phyin-pa brgyad stoṅ-pa 50

'Phags-pa śes-rab-kyi pha-rol-tu phyin-pa rdo-rje gcod-pa 73-74

Qamuγ nom-ud-un udq-a erke-yi oluγsan dörben ünen orosiba 61

Qaγan-u bičigsen dakiǰu orčiγuluγsan včir-iyar oγtaγuluγči sudur 71

Qaγan-u bičigsen Manǰu Mongγol Kitad üsüg γurban üsüg-ün ayalγu neyilegsen toli bičig 9

Qaγan-u bičigsen Manǰu Mongγol ügen-ü toli bičig 14

Qinding Da Qing huidian zeli 欽定大清會典則例 134

Qinding Mingjian 欽定明鑑 174

Qinding Xinjiang shilüe 欽定新疆識略 172

Qinding Xiyu tongwenzhi 欽定西域同文志 169

Qingwen wu chao shengxun 清文五朝聖訓 137

Qorin tabun mingγatu 54

Qutuγ-tu degedü altan gerel-tü erketü sudur-nuγud-un qaγan 65-66

Qutuγ-tu tümen silüg-tü dötüger gelmeli kemegdekü sudur orosiba 58

Qutuγ-tu bañca-ragša kemekü neretü sudur orosiba 90-91

Qutuγ-tu bilig-ün činadu kiǰaγar-a kürügsen včir oγtuluγči 74-75

Qutuγ-tu degedü altan gerel-tü erketü sudur-nuγud-un qaγan neretü yeke kölgen sudur 69

Qutuγ-tu degedü altan gerel-tü sudur orosiba 67 (Fn. 81)

Qutuγ-tu degedü yeke-de tonilγaγči neretü sudur orosiba 96-97

Qutuγ-tu molon toyin eke-dür-iyen ači qariγuluγsan [!] sudur orosiba 157 (Fn. 157)

Qutuγ-tu molon toyin eke-dür-iyen ači qariγuluγsan kemekü sudur orosiba 156-158

Qutuγ-tu nayiman mingγatu yeke kölgen sudur 60

Qutuγ-tu Pancaraksa kemekü tabun sakiyan neretü yeke kölgen sudur orosiba 90-91

Qutuγtu altan gerel-tü sudur 67

Qutuγtu sayin čag-un neretü yeke kölgen sudur 88

Qutuγtu tarnis-un quriyangγui zungdui kemegdekü yeke kölgen sudur orusiba 64

Rab-gsal 33-34

Rabnai kiged maṇi rilu ündüsün-ü ayimaγ kiged em ǰiruqai terigüten takilγ-a-yin ayimaγ 27

Rasiyan-u ǰirüken nayiman gesigütü niγuca ubadis-un ündüsün-eče iǰaγur-un ündüsün 183

Rasiyan-u ǰirüken nayiman gesigütü: niγuča ubadis-un erdem-ün ündüsün-ü nemelge-yin arγ-a ebersil-ün qalaγun enelge-yi arilγayči gadbura čaγ busu-yin ükül-ün salm-a-yi oγtaluγči: ildün kemekü-eče ebečin-ü siltaγan terigüten-i üǰügülügsen sudur 184-185

Sa-gnam-gyi yum [?] 43-45

Sain g'alab-i minggan fucihi-i colo 99

Sanhe bianca 三合便覽 11

Saṅs-rgyas-kyi mtshan lṅa-stoṅ gźi-brgya lṅa-bcu rtsa gsum-pa 41-42

Śatasahāsrikasūtra 59

Sayin galab-un mingγan burqan-u nere 99

Sayin ügetü erdeni-yin sang subhašida kemegdekü šastir 127

gSer 'od 68-70

Śes-bya rab-tu gsal-ba 116

Sidi-tü kegür-ün quulin-ača nomlagsan [!] *suru orosiγulbai* 143 (Fn. 144)

Siditü kegür-ün quuli 144

Šiditü kegūr-ün tuγuǰi 143-144

Siti hebi wenjian 四體合壁文鑑 10

bslab bya gces-pa bco brgyad-pa bžugs 53 (Fn. 67)

Sonusuγad tonilqaγči-yin sudur ene bui 77

Sonusuγad yekede toniluγči neretü yeke kölgen sudur 78-79

Sungdui terigün bölüg orosiba 63

Suvarṇaprabhāsasūtra 65 (Fn. 79)

Tanjur 23

Tasurqai kiǰaγar-tur ǰaruγsan yabudali temdeglegsen bičig 177

Terigün boti-dur itegel yabuγuluγči terigüten eldeb čiqula keregtü nom-ud orosiba 24

Thar-pa chen-po 80-86

Tngri-yin ejen-ü ünenči jirum-un bičig 120

Töbed kelen-ü sine qaγučin ayalγus-un ilγal-i üjügülügči sayin ügetü liši-yin ordu qarši 8

Töbed-ün doki-a-u sastir 6

Töbed-ün dokiyan-u ilγaburi todarγulun üiledügči-yin sastir üges-i büluglen üiledügsen merged-ün kelen-ü jula 7

Töbed-ün kelen-i kilbar-iyar surqu neretü bičig orošiba 4-5

(Zizhi) Tongjian gangmu (資治)通鑑綱目 168

Tumen jaka-i unenggi sekiyen 124

Tümen on-u li-tu 188

Üliger-ün nom erdeni čoγčaluγsan-u čiqula domoγ kemekü sastir orosiba 146

Ündüsün 30

Ünen ügetü erdeni qubilγan bonbo-yin ariγun 'bum čaγan luus-un yeke kölgen sudur 106

Uta-yin tabun aγulan-u orosil süsüg-ten-ü čikin čimeg 164

Vačir-iyar oγtaluγči 72

Vajracchedikā prajñāpāramitā 71 (Fn. 83)

Včir-dhar-a ljang-sgi-a lalita bacar-a jñana šasin-a dibi śrii-badr-ayin čadig süsüg-ün linqu-a-yin teyin büged negegči naran-u gerel kemegdekü 155

Vinai-yin γar-tur abqu-yin jang yosu erdeni-yin erike kemegdekü nom orosibai 39

Wannian shu 萬年書 188

Xiaojing 孝經 129

Xiaoxue 小學 129

Yamandaga doγšid ba: soor lingga 'čam-un bičig sakiγulsun-u bsang dorma terigüten-ü ayimaγ 26

Yamandaga maqagala erlig qaγan ökin tngri dörben doγsin sudur-un orosiba 29

Yeke bodi mör-ün jerge orusiba 112

Yôgačaris-un erketü degedü getülgegči milarasba-yin rnam-tar: nirvan kiged qamuγ-i ayiladuγči-yin mör-i üjegülügsen kemekdekü orusiba 150

Yu Jiao Li 玉嬌梨 167

DIE NEUVERMESSUNG EINER ALTEN KULTUR
MONUMENTA SERICA UND DIE WISSENSCHAFTLICHE BESCHÄFTIGUNG MIT CHINA UND SEINEN NACHBARN*

HELWIG SCHMIDT-GLINTZER

1. Vorbemerkung

Mir geht es nicht darum, eine Übungsstunde in Atem- und Lebensverlängerungstechnik zu beginnen, wenn ich folgenden Text aufrufe:

> Beim Atmen verfahre man (also): Man hält (den Atem) an und er sei gesammelt. Ist er gesammelt, so dehne er sich aus. Dehnt er sich aus, so gehe er hinab. Geht er hinab, so sei er ruhig. Ist er ruhig, so sei er gefestigt. Ist er gefestigt, so keime er. Keimt er, so wachse er. Wächst er, so werde er (nach oben) zurückgezogen. Wird er zurückgezogen, so erreiche er den Scheitel. Im Scheitelpunkt stoße er oben an. Im Tiefpunkt stoße er unten an. Wer diesem folgt, wird leben; wer diesem entgegenhandelt, wird sterben.[1]

Auch will ich nicht über das Alter von Atem- und Meditationstechniken in China und ihre Rolle bei der Begegnung mit dem Buddhismus eingehen, wozu mir neuere Forschungen manches Material böten.[2] Was ich zitiert habe, ist eine Passage aus dem Band 13 der Zeitschrift *Monumenta Serica. Journal of Oriental Studies of the Catholic University of Peking*, erschienen in Peking vor 67 Jahren, vor der Gründung der VR China, im Jahre 1948 – übrigens im Jahre meiner Geburt.

Im Band 13 der *Monumenta Serica* von 1948 schreibt Hellmut Wilhelm:

> Daß in der späteren Chouzeit die Atemtechnik ausgeübt worden ist, wissen wir aus *Chuangtzu*, [...]. Eine Beschreibung des tatsächlichen Vorgangs aber ist meines Wissens in der chou-zeitlichen Literatur nicht enthalten.

Er lässt dann den Text der vermutlich authentischen und von Luo Zhenyu 羅振玉 (1866–1940) herausgegebenen Inschrift folgen.

Damit will ich auf dreierlei hinweisen:

Erstens: Chinas aufgewachte Generation will seit dem Ausgang des 19. Jahrhunderts ein neues China bauen. Dazu gehört bei vielen die Abkehr vom Alten und Überkommenen. Während manche die alten Sitten und Überlieferungen verwerfen, suchen andere eine Erneuerung aus vergessenen eigenen Traditionen. Lange vergessene oder nicht beachtete Inschriften, Bräuche und Ge-

---

* Festvortrag zum 80-jährigen Jubiläum der Zeitschrift *Monumenta Serica* in Sankt Augustin am 3. Juni 2015. Die Vortragsform wurde weitgehend beibehalten.
[1] Siehe Hellmut Wilhelm, „Eine Chou-Inschrift über Atemtechnik", *Monumenta Serica* 13 (1948), S. 385-388, hier S. 387.
[2] Siehe Eric M. Greene, „Healing Breaths and Rotting Bones. On the Relationship between Buddhist and Chinese Meditation Practices during the Eastern Han and the Three Kingdoms Period", *JCR* 42 (2014) 2, S.145-184, hier besonders S. 150-151.

wohnheiten werden ans Licht geholt. Die von chinesischen Gelehrten neu herausgegebenen inschriftlichen Dokumente werfen neues Licht auf bislang vernachlässigte Traditionen Chinas. Es ist ein Blick zurück zur Stärkung der eigenen Identität.

Zweitens: Es findet unter diesen chinesischen Gelehrten, aber auch zwischen diesen und Europäern und anderen „Ausländern", darunter nicht zu vergessen viele Japaner, ein intensiver Austausch statt, der immer auch zusammenhängt mit den politischen und reformerischen Entwicklungen in China selbst.

Drittens: Es entsteht eine Welt mehrfach geteilten und unterschiedlich geschichteten Wissens; es entstehen darunter auch neue Formen des Wissens und des Nachdenkens über China. Es entstehen viele Sinologien, aber auch sonst viele Formen publizistischen ebenso wie des wissenschaftlichen Umgangs mit China. Diese Neuformulierung der China-Kenntnisse hatte auch etwas mit der Abkehr von alten Chinabildern zu tun, an denen sich die europäischen Kulturen seit der Renaissance orientiert und gegenüber denen sie ihre eigene Identität konstituiert hatten.

Gegenüber dem Wissen von Ausländern über China haben sich in China selbst eigene Klischees gebildet – und manche unterscheiden zwischen einer chinesischen Sinologie und einer Auslandssinologie. Dagegen haben gelegentlich manche daran erinnert, dass der Begriff „Sinologie" eine europäische Schöpfung ist. Das Klischee vom „Old China Hand", wie es Lin Yutang 林語堂 (1895–1976) schildert, ist nur eine besondere Ausformung dieses Typus.[3]

In spezifischer und vielfältiger Weise haben in jener Zeit junge chinesische Intellektuelle ihre eigene Kultur entdeckt. Lin Yutang, in Leipzig und Harvard ausgebildet, schreibt *My Country and My People* und Pearl S. Buck rühmt dieses 1936 erschienene Buch als Offenbarung. Es ist die Zeit, in der nach der Ausstellung in Berlin 1934 dann im Folgejahr 1935 in London eine in Shanghai konzipierte große China-Kunstausstellung gezeigt wird.

Lin Yutang fand, dass sich die Europäer nach dem Ersten Weltkrieg dem Osten zugewandt hätten – in einer Art „Nostalgie" für die chinesische Kultur – und dass diese Haltung durch die Ausstellungen asiatischer Kunst gesteigert worden sei. Im Vorwort zu seinem Text „Der Geist des chinesischen Volkes" hatte Lin bereits 1932 geschrieben:

> Östliche Zivilisation, Kunst und Philosophie sind von höchster Qualität. Daher haben Europas Gebildete [im Englischen wird *Ouzhou xuezhe* 歐州學者 als „European scholars" übersetzt, Anm. d. Verf.] gegenüber chinesischer Kultur, besonders aber gegenüber der chinesischen Kunst eine romantische Verehrung entwickelt. Die Gebildeten lieben chinesische Kalligraphie, Malerei und Anti-

---

[3] Lin Yutang, *My Country and My People*, „Prologue", S. 8-11; siehe auch die Ausführungen von Jan Jakob Maria de Groot und anderen bereits zu Beginn des 20. Jahrhunderts über solche China-Experten, darunter die „Antrittsrede des Herrn de Groot am 4. Juli 1912", *Sitzungsberichte der königlich-preussischen Akademie der Wissenschaften* 34 (1912), S. 607-612.

quitäten ebenso wie sie die Kultur Griechenlands schätzen. Bei dem Besuch einer Ausstellung chinesischer Keramik der Sammlung Eumorphopoulos war ich beeindruckt von einer Statue der Guanyin aus Ding Yao, und ich kam zu dem Schluss, dass die Guanyin Chinas und die Heilige Maria des Westens im Mittelpunkt der religiösen Kunst der Länder und im Zentrum der Vorstellungswelt ihrer Völker stehen. Offen gesagt, von der eleganten Haltung, dem ganzen Ausdruck und der Farbigkeit gefällt mir die Guanyin besser als die Heilige Maria. Wenn ich als Europäer geboren wäre, würde gewiss auch ich die Figuren in der chinesischen Kunst bewundern.[4]

Es ist dies die Zeit, in der Arthur Waleys Übersetzung des Laozi gerade erschienen war (London 1934). In einer Besprechung zeigte sich John C.H. Wu (Wu Jingxiong 吳經熊, 1899–1986) begeistert von Waleys Leistung der Übersetzung des *Tao Te Ch'ing* 道德經 mit den Worten: „Der Autor ist einer jener seltenen Geister in Europa, die eine angeborene Vorliebe für alles Chinesische haben. Seine Übersetzungen haben ihm einen der ersten Plätze unter den Sinologen und keinen geringen unter den heutigen Dichtern Englands verschafft. [...] usw."[5] –

---

[4] Im englischen Original: „Oriental civilization, art and philosophy have excellent qualities, and for this reason they have aroused the romantic admiration of European scholars for Chinese culture, particularly Chinese art. Generally, Western scholars admire and are fond of Chinese calligraphy, paintings and antiques to the same extent that they admire Greek civilization. When I stayed in London, I visited the Chinese ceramics collection of Eumorphopulus. I was so fascinated by a statue of the goddess of Guanyin made in Ding Yao that I concluded that the Chinese Guanyin and the Western Madonna (St Mary) are the centers of religions arts of each nation and the crystallization of its people's imaginations. Honestly speaking, however, from the graceful pose, the elegant and gentle manner, and the lovely color, I would prefer to say that the statue of the Chinese Guanyin is better than the Western St Mary. If I had been born as an European, I would definitely admire the figures of Chinese paintings as well." Fan Liya 範麗雅, „The 1935 London International Exhibition of Chinese Art. *The China* Critic Reacts", *China Heritage Quarterly* 30/31 (June/September 2012). See http://www.chinaheritagequarterly.org/features.php?searchterm=030_fan.inc&issue=030 (aufgerufen am 29. Juli 2016).
In der chinesischen Fassung: 東方文明、東方芸術、東方哲學, 本有極優異之點, 故歐州學者, 竟有対中國文化引起浪漫的崇拜, 而於中國美術尤甚。一般學者於玩摩中國書畫古玩之余, 対中國芸術愛好之誠, 或與歐西學者之思戀希臘文明同等。余在倫敦參觀 Eumorphopulus 私人收藏中國磁器, 見一座定竈観音, 亦神為之蕩。中國之観音與西洋之瑪姐娜 (聖母) 同為一種宗教芸術之中心対象, 同為一民族芸術想像力之結晶。然平心而論, 観音姿勢之妍麗, 態度之安祥, 神情之嫺雅, 色沢之可愛, 私人認為在西洋之上最名貴 瑪姐娜之上。吾知縱令吾生為歐人, 対中國畫中人物, 亦必発生思戀。 Lin Yutang, *Zhongguo wenhua zhi jingshen* 中國文化之精神 (The Spirit of Chinese Culture), *Shenbao Monthly* 申報月刊 1 (1932) 1, S. 1.

[5] Im englischen Original: „The author is one of those rare spirits in the West who have an inborn predilection for things Chinese. His translations of Chinese poems have won for him a high place among sinologues, and not a low one among modern English poets. As Louis Untermeyer, in whose Anthology of *Modern British Poetry* are included some of Waley's translations, has justly observed, ‚Waley is no mere competent adapter, but a poet in his own right.' One may, indeed, find a little flaw, here and there, due either to the intrinsic difficulties of the Chinese language or to a more or less excusable oversight; but on the whole no one

In diesem Kontext wurde 1935, also vor 80 Jahren in Peking die Zeitschrift *Monumenta Serica* gegründet.

2. Die Gründung und die Neuvermessung einer alten Kultur

Im Jahr 1935, als China sich anschickte, sich neu zu erfinden, als in Deutschland die Nürnberger Gesetze erlassen werden, als im Österreichischen Ständestaat der Tanz auf dem Vulkan weiter geht, bevor Österreich nach der Niederlage Kurt Schuschniggs im März 1938 dann im Deutschen Reich aufgeht, im Jahr 1935, als unter den Kommunisten ein offener Machtkampf ausbricht, in dem Mao Zedong 毛澤東 (1893–1976) nach dem Langen Marsch ein Sowjetgebiet in Nord-Shaanxi aufbaut, als in China sich die Japaner aus der Mandschurei nach China ausdehnen wollten und dann am 9. Dezember Studenten gegen die Errichtung einer gegen die Kommunisten gerichteten Autonomen Regierung in Nordchina protestierten, auch weil sich die Guomindang-Regierung Pekings nicht gegen die Okkupation Japans stellte – in diesem Jahr wurde *Monumenta Serica* gegründet.

Die Kultur der Welt hatte sich in den 1930er Jahren in Peking zu versammeln begonnen. Es gibt dort seit 1931 das von Zheng Shoulin 鄭壽麟 (1900–1981) gegründete Deutschland-Institut, geleitet von einem chinesischen und einem deutschen Geschäftsführer (bis 1938 Ernst Schierlitz, ab 1938 Wolfgang Franke: „ein wichtiger Punkt deutscher sinologischer Forschung").[6] An der Katholischen Fu Jen Universität (Furen daxue 輔仁大學), 1933 von der Gesellschaft des Göttlichen Wortes übernommen, weil die amerikanischen Benediktiner-Missionare die Lasten nicht mehr tragen konnte, gab es ein *Bulletin of the Catholic University of Peking*, zuletzt unter der Herausgeberschaft von Pater Franz X. Biallas S.V.D. (1878–1936), Leiter der Soziologischen Fakultät der Furen daxue.[7] Das Erscheinen des *Bulletin* wird mit dem Heft 9 (1934) eingestellt. Im Vorwort zu diesem Heft legt Franz Xaver Biallas die seit einiger Zeit gehegte Idee zu einer neuen Zeitschrift dar. Sie sollte in Peking erscheinen, dem Zentrum der alten Kultur Chinas, wo Chinesen und Europäer kooperierten und wo die Katholische Universität die besten Köpfe an sich ziehe. Die Gesellschaft des Göttlichen Wortes verbinde in besonderer Weise das Interesse an der Christianisierung der Völker mit dem Studium von deren Sprachen und Kulturen, wie die Zeitschrift *Anthropos* belege. In diese Tradition solle sich die neue Zeitschrift stellen.

---

has done a better job, for no one is more akin in spirit to the poets of old China." Siehe John C.H. Wu, „Book Review: *The Way and Its Power. A Study of the Tao Te Ching and Its Place in Chinese Thought*, by Arthur Waley", *T'ien Hsia Monthly* 1 (1935) 2, S. 225.

[6] Cordula Gumbrecht, *Die Monumenta Serica – eine sinologische Zeitschrift und ihre Redaktionsbibliothek in ihrer Pekinger Zeit (1935–1945)* (Köln: Greven Verlag, 1994), S. 33, Fn. 73. – Cordula Gumbrecht, auf die ich mich im Folgenden beziehe, verweist auch auf die Würdigung der Rolle Wolfgang Frankes in *OE* 24 (1977), S. 3-4.

[7] Zu Franz Xaver Biallas siehe Miroslav Kollár, *Ein Leben im Konflikt. P. Franz Xaver Biallas SVD (1878–1936). Chinamissionar und Sinologe im Licht seiner Korrespondenz* (Nettetal: Steyler Verlag, 2011) [Eds.].

Aufgaben und Charakter der neuen Zeitschrift legte Pater Biallas in der Redaktionsnote zu Band 1 (1935-1936) dar. Die angestrebten Dimensionen bzw. Sphären der Zeitschrift kommen bereits in dem Titel zum Ausdruck:

– *Monumenta Serica* adressiert die „Denkmäler" des Volkes der Serer, des Volkes, von dem seit der Antike Seide in die Welt kam. Es werden also die internationalen Kulturaustauschbeziehungen thematisiert;

– der chinesische Titel *Huayi xuezhi* 華夷學志, wörtlich „Wissenschaftliche Zeitschrift über China und seine Nachbarn" betont ebenfalls weniger ein monolithisches China oder das, was im angelsächsischen Bereich eine Zeitlang als „China proper" bezeichnet wurde, sondern thematisiert mit „China und seinen Nachbarn" auch die Grenzvölker und damit die historischen Austauschbeziehungen mit nahen Völkern wie den Mongolen, den Tibetern, den Thai-Völkern etc.

– der englische Titel *Journal of Oriental Studies* schließlich deutet die Offenheit der Thematik an.

Seit 1937 erscheint zudem eine „Monumenta Serica Monograph Series", herausgegeben von den Patres Rudolph Rahmann S.V.D. (1902–1985) und Eugen Feifel S.V.D. (1902–1999), die bekanntlich bis heute fortgesetzt wird.

Wenn es um die Orientalistik geht, so sehen wir deren Entwicklung inzwischen aus einer historisierenden und damit reflexiven Distanz. Insbesondere seit der durch Edward Said angestoßenen Orientalismus-Debatte hat sich diese auf die Geschichte der Beschäftigung mit Ostasien ausgeweitet. Die „Orientalischen Studien" oder die „Kunde des Morgenlandes", womit wir „Orientalismus" im Deutschen am besten beschreiben, war eine Folge der Emanzipation einzelner Wissensbereiche aus der Theologie und deren Etablierung als selbständige Disziplinen. Urs App hat sicher Recht, wenn er konstatiert: „Indeed, the complicated relationship between ‚theology', ‚religious studies', and ‚Asian studies' in today's academic environment would indicate that this emancipation process is far from finished."[8]

Die Zeitschrift sollte, so P. Biallas, „Material für die Erforschung der Völker, Sprachen und Kulturen Chinas und seiner Nachbarvölker" bereitstellen und dabei Gebiete wie Ethnologie und Prähistorie nicht vernachlässigen. Chen Yuan 陳垣 (1880–1971), lange Zeit Präsident der Furen daxue (1929–1951), legte im *Fu Jen Magazine* 4 (1935) seine Gedanken zu diesem Zeitschriftenplan dar.[9] Die Zeitschrift solle das chinesische historische Material systematisieren, neueste westliche Methoden darauf anwenden und die internationale wissenschaftliche Zusammenarbeit fördern. Bemerkenswert sind die Überlegungen, die der französische Sinologe Paul Pelliot in einem Brief an die Redaktion äußerte. In seinen Augen gelte es, die Vertrautheit der Missionare mit den Sprachen, Gebräuchen und den Menschen und ihre Beobachtungsgabe zu nutzen. Da sie in Ermangelung einer

---

[8] Urs App, *The Birth of Orientalism* (Philadelphia: University of Pennsylvania Press, 2010), S. xii-xiii. – Siehe auch: *id.*, *The Cult of Emptiness. The Western Discovery of Buddhist Thought and the Invention of Oriental Philosophy* (Rorschach – Kyoto: UniversityMedia, 2012).

[9] Gumbrecht, *Die Monumenta Serica*, S. 36.

Bibliothek zumeist vor der Behandlung umfassender Themen zurückschreckten, solle man deren Beobachtungsbereitschaft durch die möglichen Auskünfte und Entdeckungen besonders fördern. Auch

> brächten oft Zufälle landwirtschaftlicher Arbeiten, die Eröffnung von Straßen und Kanälen, Umwälzungen verschiedenster Art, wie Veränderungen in den Flußläufen, oder auch heimliche Ausgrabungen durch Dorfbewohner bedeutende Funde ans Tageslicht. Der Missionar könne sich über diese Funde auf dem laufenden halten, wie es diejenigen getan hätten, die uns als erste mit den Inschriften vertraut gemacht, die man in den Gräbern der Kitan-Kaiser gefunden hatte [...].[10]

So kam die Zeitschrift *Monumenta Serica* in die Welt, halbjährlich die ersten vier Bände, ab Band 5 dann in Jahresbänden. Der Band 13, noch herausgegeben von Rudolph Rahmann, erschien in Peking 1948, mit dem Bild des 80-jährigen Paters Wilhelm Schmidt S.V.D. (1868–1954) als Frontispiz, jenes Missionars und Gelehrten, der zumeist mit dem Anthropos-Institut verbunden wird. Pater W. Schmidt hatte den ersten Band der Zeitschrift *Monumenta Serica* mit seinem Beitrag „The Oldest Culture-Circles in Asia" 1935 eröffnet.

Der folgende Band 14 (1949–1955) erschien dann, herausgegeben von Heinrich Busch S.V.D. (1912–2002),[11] in Tokyo im S.V.D. (Societas Verbi Divini) Research Institute, mit der Vorbemerkung: „When the Chinese Communists took over the Catholic University of Peking (Fu Jen) five years ago, the Sinological periodical of the University, *Monumenta Serica*, had to cease publication also. Some time ago the Society of the Divine Word (S.V.D.) [...] decided to resume the publication of the periodical." – Am Schluss dieses Bandes wird der gerade verstorbene Pater Wilhelm Schmidt gewürdigt. Dort findet sich der nachdenkliche Satz: „Es steht nicht in Abrede, dass die kulturhistorische Methode und besonders die von ihm vielleicht etwas starr vertretene Kulturkreislehre gewisser Abänderungen bedürftig sind."[12] Und zu seinen Beziehungen zu unserer Zeitschrift heißt es, dass auf einer Vortragsreise 1934 in Peking „seine persönliche Gegenwart und die mit dem *Anthropos* gesammelten Erfahrungen [...] starken Einfluss auf die Verwirklichung des langgehegten Planes aus(übten)", den der Sinologe P. F.X. Biallas zu jener Zeit verfolgte.[13]

Dieser erste in Japan erschienene Band, beginnend mit dem bedeutenden Beitrag von Heinrich Busch über die Donglin 東林 -Akademie „The Tung-lin Shu-

---

[10] Zitiert nach der Zusammenfassung bei Gumbrecht, *Die Monumenta Serica*, S. 37.

[11] Zu Heinrich Busch siehe Roman Malek, „In memoriam Heinrich Busch (1912–2002) und Eugen Feifel (1902–1999)", *Monumenta Serica* 54 (2006), S. 491-518. [Eds.]

[12] P. Wilhelm Schmidt in: *Monumenta Serica* 14 (1949–1955), S. 588-591, hier S. 590. Mit diesem Begründer der „Wiener Schule" der Kulturkreislehre, die eine Universalgeschichte der Kultur zu erstellen versuchte, der auch als der bedeutendste weltweit vergleichende Sprachwissenschaftler der ersten Hälfte des 20. Jahrhundert gilt, habe ich mich selbst erstmals 1967, also vor bald 50 Jahren, im Ethnologischen Seminar der Universität Göttingen beschäftigt.

[13] *Ibid.*, S. 590-591.

yüan and Its Political and Philosophical Significance", deutete eine Neuausrichtung der Zeitschrift an. Heinrich Buschs Beitrag, der sich am Schluss auch auf mögliche westliche oder christliche Einflüsse einlässt, zeigt den umsichtigen, aber auch kritischen und zuweilen skeptischen Geist dieses großen Gelehrten und liebenswerten Menschen, der über mehr als vier Jahrzehnte (bis 1991) das Profil der Zeitschrift prägen sollte. Mit ihm war ich seit meiner Bonner Zeit verbunden.

Gestatten Sie mir daher eine Abschweifung, die auch etwas von P. Buschs Art anklingen lassen soll. Am 2. Dezember 1976 schrieb er mir von Sankt Augustin nach Bonn:

> Es freut mich, daß Sie Kontakt mit uns aufgenommen haben und uns nächstens besuchen wollen. Einige Tage, bevor Ihr Brief kam, wurden wir über Ihr Buch über das Hung-ming chi [*Hongming ji* 弘明集] auf Sie aufmerksam.

Vier Jahre später, am 7. November 1980 trug mir P. Busch die Stellung eines „Associate Editor" an, eine Stellung, die zu begleiten ich bis heute die Ehre habe.

Band 15 der *Monumenta Serica* (1956) erschien in Tokyo, beginnend mit der Fortsetzung eines Beitrag zur Geschichte der Früheren Yan-Dynastie (P. Gerhard Schreiber S.V.D. [1911–1972]) bzw. das zweite Faszikel in Nagoya, genauer an der Nanzan Universität, The Catholic University of Nagoya, nun beginnend mit einem Beitrag „Fang Xiaoru im Lichte der frühen Ming-Zeit". Dort in Nagoya erschienen auch die folgenden Bände:

Band 16 mit einem Beitrag zu den Christen im China der Ming-Zeit (Joseph Dehergne S.J.);

Band 17, beginnend mit einer Studie zu den Seidenmanuskripten aus Chu 楚 (Noel Barnard);

Band 18 mit einem Beitrag von Henry Serruys über Chinesen in der Südmongolei im 16. Jahrhundert;

Band 19 beginnend mit Beiträgen von Serruys und Barnard;

Band 20 mit dem Beitrag von Joseph Thiel, „Der Streit der Buddhisten und Taoisten zur Mongolenzeit";

Band 21 (1962) beginnt mit einem Beitrag von Igor Rachewiltz über Yelü Chucai 耶律楚材, einen Berater am Mongolenhofe Khubilai Khans.

Die Bände 22 (1963) bis 29 (1970–1971, erschienen 1972) wurden dann in Los Angeles publiziert.

Ab Band 30 (1972–1973, erschienen 1974) erscheint *Monumenta Serica* bis heute in Sankt Augustin.

Trotz der Ortwechsel von Peking über Tokyo (1949–1956), Nagoya (1957–1962) und Los Angeles (bis 1972) bis nach Sankt Augustin, wo P. Prof. Dr. Roman Malek (geb. 1951), seit 1985 Co-Editor, dann 1992 die Leitung übernahm, die seit 2012 von P. Prof. Dr. Zbigniew Wesołowski als Chefredakteur fortgeführt wird, mit P. Dr. Piotr Adamek als neuem Direktor des Instituts – trotz all dieser Wechsel hat die Zeitschrift ihre Internationalität behalten. Archäologie und Kunstgeschichte, Sprachwissenschaft und Religionsgeschichte, die Geschichte der Randvölker sowie die Geschichte des Christentums, aber auch des Islam sind immer beachtet worden.

Indem die Zeitschrift *Monumenta Serica* eine Vielfalt von Wissenssphären aufgreift – man könnte auch von vielen Sinologien sprechen – spiegelt sie nicht nur Phasen neuer Erkenntnisse, sondern übt auch Kritik und Widerspruch und wirft nicht zuletzt Licht in ganz unterschiedliche Bereiche. Auf diese Weise unternimmt diese Zeitschrift die Neuvermessung einer alten Kultur.

In einer Zeit, in der China sich selbst neu zu erfinden sucht, manche China als ein weißes unbeschriebenes Blatt verstehen, wendet sich *Monumenta Serica* der alten Kultur, oder treffender: dem Sinitischen Kulturkreis zu und sucht China neu zu verorten. Dass dabei der Archäologie eine besondere Rolle zukommt sowie der Epigraphik und damit den Zeugnissen, den „monumentae", ist bereits angedeutet worden, darunter den erst in jüngerer Zeit gefundenen Orakelknochen und anderen Funden, den Regionalkulturen und regionalen Herrschaftstraditionen, der politischen Dichtung, der etwa Qu Yuans 屈原 Gesänge aus Chu zuzurechnen sind.

Es ging um eine Neubewertung der geistigen Traditionen, der geistigen Neuerungen im sogenannten Neo-Konfuzianismus, wovon bereits im Zusammenhang mit Heinrich Busch Studie zur Donglin-Akademie die Rede war. Die Neubewertung der Geschichte des Buddhismus stand auf der Tagesordnung ebenso wie die Neubewertung der Regionalsprachen und damit die Hinterfragung des Mythos vom Jahrtausende andauernden Einheitsreich. Dabei sollte den Randvölkern eine besondere Bedeutung zukommen. Es spiegelt sich in den Studien aber noch etwas anderes, nämlich der Umstand, dass Wissens- und Wissenschaftskulturen aus China auswanderten oder nur am Rande Beachtung fanden, und zwar hervorgerufen durch unterschiedliche Dynamiken.

Die Bibliothek und der Verleger

Zu einer Zeitschrift, die auf Qualitätssicherung Wert legt – heute ist peer-reviewing in aller Munde – gehörte in der Vergangenheit zumindest eine Bibliothek, gelegentlich auch ein Verleger. Die Redaktionsbibliothek der *Monumenta Serica* wurde auf Initiative von P. Hermann Köster S.V.D. nach dem Tod von Franz X. Biallas 1936 gegründet, um dessen private Bibliothek einer sinnvollen Nutzung zuzuführen. Seither blieb die Sinnhaftigkeit und Notwendigkeit einer Bibliothek für die Herausgabe einer solchen Zeitschrift präsent und hat nicht zuletzt mit zur Gründung des Instituts Monumenta Serica beigetragen.[14] Die Bibliothek wurde Ende 1948 über Tianjin und Hongkong schließlich nach Japan verbracht und befindet sich nun in Sankt Augustin.

---

[14] Zusammenfassend hierzu Gumbrecht, *Die Monumenta Serica*, S. 85-98.

Verleger der Zeitschrift war in den zehn ersten Jahren Henri Vetch.[15] Dieser war 1920 nach China gekommen, wurde Ende der 1920er Jahre Geschäftsführer der „China Booksellers Company, Ltd." (Yingshang Zhongguo tushu youxian gongsi 英商中國圖書有限公司). Später eröffnete er im Peking-Hotel den „French Bookstore" (Fawen tushuguan 法文圖書館), den er 1945 in das Botschaftsviertel verlegte. Nach einigen Jahren im Gefängnis nach der Machtübernahme durch die Kommunisten ging er nach Hongkong, wo er weiter Bücher verlegte und 1978 starb.

Dass Henri Vetch der Verleger der *Monumenta Serica* wurde, lag sicher daran, dass er bereits Verleger anderer Institutionen war und sich mit seinen Erfahrungen deswegen anbot. Im Jahr 1935 allein erschien bei ihm Henri Bernards *Matteo Ricci's Scientific Contribution to China* in der englischen Übersetzung von Edward T.C. Werner sowie der Bestseller *In Search of Old Peking* von Lewis Charles Arlington und William Lewisohn. Das Ehepaar Vetch war in Peking der Mittelpunkt des intellektuellen Lebens. Wie mir seine Tochter Hélène Vetch mitteilte, war ihr Vater am 2. Dezember 1898 in La-Celle Saint-Cloud westlich von Paris geboren und starb am 3. Juni 1978 im Queen Mary's Hospital in Hongkong.[16]

3. Vom Echo-Effekt

Da ich eingeladen wurde, zum 80. Geburtstag einer Zeitschrift zu sprechen, stehe ich unter dem Verdacht, eine Laudatio abzuliefern. Sie können das gerne so auffassen, wenn ich von dem großen und gewissermaßen zeitlosen Verdienst der Zeitschrift *Monumenta Serica* spreche, welches ihr bei der Neuvermessung einer alten Kultur zukommt.

Denn die Frage nach dem Charakter der Orientalistik bzw. der Asienwissenschaften ist ein Dauerthema, mit guten Gründen. Dabei ist daran zu erinnern – und zwar trotz aller Debatten: ich nenne nur die Kritik der „Concerned Asian Scholars" und die Orientalismus-Debatte mit ihren vielen Verzweigungen –, dass wir bei aller Unterschiedlichkeit der Methoden die einmal gewonnenen Einsichten und Kenntnisse nicht verwerfen. Dies wurde kürzlich in einem Beitrag zu dem, was ich als „reflexive Asienwissenschaft" bezeichnen würde, folgendermaßen gefordert: Es müsse stets danach gefragt werden „what the best scholarship in Asian studies does and has done".[17]

Monumenta Serica gehörte von Anfang an zu jener „best scholarship of Asian studies". Die Zeitschrift nahm Teil an der Suche nach der Identität Chinas und

---

[15] Gumbrecht, *Die Monumenta Serica*, S. 45.

[16] Brief von Hélène Vetch an mich vom 4. Juni 2010 (Ort: 47 boulevard de Port-Royal, 75013 Paris). – Da ich seit 1973 mehrfach Hongkong besucht hatte, hätte ich ihn gut dort treffen können. Schade!

[17] Donald R. Davis, „Three Principles for an Asian Humanities. Care First ... Learn from ... Connect Histories", *JAS* 74 (2015) 1, S. 43-67, hier S. 43.

seiner Nachbarn und kann verstanden werden als ein Forum zur Beschäftigung mit dem Anderen und dessen Andersartigkeit.

Selbstverständlich war der Zeitschrift und ihren Herausgebern immer klar, dass sie nur einen Ausschnitt zeigen konnten. Doch gerade weil die Herausgeber und ihre redaktionellen Teams sich an Qualität und Ernsthaftigkeit orientierten, sind die Bände der vergangenen 80 Jahre von so beständiger Güte. Weil sie sich nicht zuallererst auf den Zeitgeist und auf Moden stützten, von denen beeinflusst zu sein sie sicher niemals geleugnet hätten, sondern weil sie vor allem nach Zeugnissen suchten, nach „monumentae" eben, hat sich die Zeitschrift eine gewisse Zeitlosigkeit bewahrt. Vielleicht hat diese Unabhängigkeit von den jeweiligen Moden und dem Zeitgeist auch mit dazu beigetragen, dass die Zeitschrift von vornherein kosmopolitisch war und durch die Stationen ihrer Redaktion und die Reise durch mehrere Kontinente dies auch geblieben ist. Zu Recht titelt die Pressestelle der Philosophisch-Theologischen Hochschule SVD St. Augustin zum Tag des Jubiläums: „In 80 Jahren um die Welt"!

Dies erscheint umso eindrucksvoller, wenn man sich die Ausformungen der wissenschaftlichen Beschäftigung mit China in den letzten Jahrzehnten vor Augen führt. So war es vielleicht in mancher Hinsicht mehr Wunsch als Wirklichkeit, aber insgesamt doch zutreffend, wenn Herbert Franke in der Besprechung des großen Werkes seines Kollegen Wolfgang Bauer über Ideal- und Paradiesvorstellungen in China im Jahre 1972 konstatierte, die Sinologie habe sich „von geschichtsphilosophischen Kontroversen [...] freizuhalten vermocht", und dann fortfährt: „Sie hat in geduldiger Kleinarbeit die viertausend Jahre chinesischer Geschichte zu durchleuchten unternommen, freilich auch hier nicht, ohne die Präokkupationen der jeweiligen Wissenschaftsepoche zu teilen." – „Sinologie – so weiter Herbert Franke

> wurde zunächst betrieben wie eine Art klassischer Philologie, sie hat dann später die Quellenkritik und Methode von der Geschichtswissenschaft gelernt und sich schon früh, spätestens seit dem genialen Marcel Granet (1884–1941) und August Conrady (1864–1925), soziologischen und ethnologischen Kategorien eröffnet. Wieder eine Wissenschaftlergeneration später begann man zu erkennen, dass sich unter dem scheinbar uniformen Überbau der Hochkultur seit dem Altertum sehr verschiedene regionale Kulturen verbergen, von denen die Dialekte oder besser Regionalsprachen nur der auffälligste Ausdruck sind. Und seit einigen Jahrzehnten gilt ein nicht geringer Teil der sinologischen Arbeit in aller Welt, China selbst nicht ausgenommen, der Erforschung chinesischer Institutionen, der Wirtschaftsgeschichte und der sozialen Strukturen.[18]

Soweit Herbert Franke vor mehr als 40 Jahren, und ich füge hinzu: Die Zeitschrift *Monumenta Serica* ist seit 80 Jahren nicht nur Spiegel und Teil, sondern zugleich wesentlicher Akteur dieser Entwicklung.

Eine noch zu schreibende Geschichte des Chinabildes in der westlichen Öffentlichkeit – zum Topos von der „Gelben Gefahr" habe mich selbst vor kurzem

---

[18] Herbert Franke, „Vom Echo-Effekt der chinesischen Kultur", *Merkur* 290 (1972), S. 589-593.

geäußert[19] – wie auch zu der Sinologie als Wissenschaft, die Herbert Franke einfordert, ist bis heute nicht geschrieben. Darin würde dann auch die Beobachtung Lin Yutangs zu den „Old China Hands", wie er sie im Prolog zu seinem My Country and My People von 1936 schildert, Eingang finden.

Die Zeitschrift Monumenta Serica jedenfalls wird, ich greife die bereits erwähnte Formulierung nochmals auf, als Beispiel für „best scholarship of Asian studies" gelten können. Monumenta Serica hat einen eigenen Akzent gesetzt. Sie gab eine eigene Antwort auf die seit den 1920er Jahren in China beginnende Zeit, in der man sich erneut mit einer Internationalisierung und zugleich mit einer Sinisierung der Moderne zu befassen begonnen hat, ein Prozess, der noch lange nicht abgeschlossen ist.

Die heutige Debatte über „westliche Werte", die oft verkürzt als Ablehnung humanistischer Werte (Freiheitlichkeit, Selbstbestimmung, Rechtsstaatlichkeit) interpretiert wird, steht in dieser Tradition. Yan Fu 嚴復 (1853-1921), der große Übersetzer und Vermittler westlichen Wissens nach China, hatte in seinem 1895 erschienenen Essay „Entscheidende Worte zu unserer Erlösung" („Jiuwang juelun" 救亡決論), mit dem er sich gegen diejenigen wandte, die das Neue im Alten suchten, geschrieben:

> ... aus diesem Grund jagen sie in den alten Büchern nach alten Wörtern, die etwas mit der Gegenwart zu tun zu haben scheinen, und sie behaupten, dass das westliche Wissen in seiner Gesamtheit in China bereits vorhanden war, so dass darin gar nichts Neues zu finden sei.[20]

Ein prominentes Beispiel hierfür ist Hu Shi's 胡適 (1891-1962) The Development of the Logical Method in Ancient China (1922). Wir wissen inzwischen, dass die Besonderheit und – wenn Sie so wollen: die Faszination Chinas nicht dadurch gesteigert werden muss, indem man nachweist, dass es dort schon alles einmal gegeben habe – und dann leider nur vergessen worden sei –, was der Westen entwickelt hat.

Selbstverständlich sind inzwischen die Grundlagen der europäischen Moderne globalisiert, und die Vorgeschichte dieser Moderne ist in hohem Maße europäisch und inzwischen Bestandteil der Vorgeschichte auch der wissenschaftlich-technischen Welt und der Kulturen in allen anderen Teilen der Welt. Aber ohne eine historisch informierte Beschäftigung mit den Kulturen der Welt, so wie sie bezogen auf China und seine Nachbarkulturen aus den Forschungsergebnissen, wie sie gerade in der Zeitschrift Monumenta Serica dargelegt wurden und werden, erst möglich wird, – ohne eine solche Beschäftigung weiß ich nicht, wie wir Menschen in eine gute Zukunft auf dieser Erde kommen könnten! Daher müssen wir dankbar sein für diese Zeitschrift.

---

[19] Helwig Schmidt-Glintzer, „Die gelbe Gefahr", Zeitschrift für Ideengeschichte VIII (2014) 1, S. 43-58.

[20] Zitiert nach Iwo Amelung, „Lokalität und Lokalisierung – zur Entwicklung der Wissenschaften im China des späten 19. und frühen 20. Jahrhunderts", Jahrbuch für Europäische Überseegeschichte 14 (2014), S. 193-214, hier S. 196.

Von vornherein stand die Zeitschrift im Schnittpunkt vielfältiger intelligenter Versuche einer Neuvermessung der Kultur Chinas und seiner Nachbarvölker. Man ging in die Vor- und Frühgeschichte mit archäologischen Abhandlungen ebenso wie an die Ränder der chinesischen Kultur. Zugleich war die Zeitschrift nicht nur Forum für die einzelnen Beiträger, sondern verstand sich im weiteren Horizont intellektueller Bemühungen. Nur so war es wohl möglich, dass sie ihre Unabhängigkeit und Internationalität wahrte und doch nicht gesichtslos wurde.

An vier eher zufällig herausgegriffenen Gestalten möchte ich das intellektuelle Umfeld verdeutlichen, innerhalb dessen sich die Zeitschrift zunächst bewegte: an I. Luo Zhenyu, II. Chen Yuan, die ich beide schon erwähnt hatte, sowie III. Walther Heissig und IV. Chen Yinke.

I. Luo Zhenyu 羅振玉 (1866–1940)

Luo Zhenyu ist jener Gelehrte, dem wir die Publikation des eingangs zitierten Textes zur Atemtechnik verdanken. Er war das dritte Kind in einer Familie von fünf Söhnen und sechs Töchtern. Neben den daraus erwachsenden familiären Verpflichtungen gehörte er zu jener Generation, die für China angesichts der Herausforderungen durch den Westen eine bessere Zukunft suchten. Das moderne Wissen, unter anderem zur Agrikultur, wie es in Japan und in westlichen Schriften zu finden war, zog ihn an. So wurde er zu einem der Vermittler moderner Erziehungs- und Bildungsmethoden, wie sie in Japan nach westlichem Vorbild bereits befolgt wurden. Zhang Zhidong 張之洞 (1837–1909), Generalgouverneur in Zentralchina, holte ihn nach Wuchang und sandte ihn dann nach Japan, um dort das Erziehungssystem zu studieren. Dies brachte ihn schließlich 1905 in die Bildungs- und Erziehungsszene in Peking. Nach der Revolution von 1911 zog er sich wie viele andere nach Japan zurück, wo er acht Jahre mit seiner Familie lebte. Seine Frage nach den alten Traditionen und seine Nähe zu Japan als dem Vorbild für China um die Jahrhundertwende brachten auch seine Nähe zu dem von Japan beherrschten, am 1. März 1932 errichteten Marionettenstaat Mandschukuo mit sich. Dieser Gelehrte suchte China durch Lernen zu bereichern, und dieses Lernen bezog sich auf die lange Geschichte ebenso wie auf die Erkenntnisse und Errungenschaften anderer Völker.

II. Chen Yuan 陳垣 (1880–1971)

Viel näher an dem Geschehen um die Gründung der Zeitschrift *Monumenta Serica* und Mitherausgeber bis zum Band 13 (1948) war Chen Yuan, lange Jahre Präsident der Furen daxue und seit 1952 Präsident der Shifan daxue 師範大學 in Peking. Er beschäftigte sich besonders intensiv mit der Mongolenzeit, war aber ebenso an religionsgeschichtlichen Fragen interessiert. Seine Arbeiten zum Daoismus unter der Südlichen Song-Zeit und zum Buddhismus der Ming-Zeit sind wegweisend. Im Jahr 1966 erschien die englische Übersetzung seines Buches *Western and Central Asians in China under the Mongols. Their Transformation into Chinese* als Band XV der Monumenta Serica Monograph Series. Für die Einschätzung seiner intellektuellen Biographie sollte man wissen, dass er bereits

1921/1922 Vizeerziehungsminister der Regierung in Peking war. Als Peking sich nach 1937 unter japanischem Einfluss befand, änderten sich für alle dort politisch und wissenschaftlich Aktiven die Rahmenbedingungen. Immerhin ist es aber doch im Rückblick bezeichnend, dass Chen Yuan sich gerade in jener Zeit der Dominanz Japans mit der Zeit der Mongolenherrschaft in China befasste und so zu einem der wichtigsten Kenner dieser Epoche Chinas wurde. Nach 1949 arbeitete er wie viele andere mit der neuen Regierung Mao Zedongs zusammen. Seine letzten Lebensjahre sollten einmal gesondert behandelt werden.

III. Walther Heissig (1913–2005)

Walther Heissig, der 1935 in Berlin, wohin er 1933 „geflüchtet"[21] war, die deutsche Staatsbürgerschaft erworben und dann bei Erich Haenisch Mongolistik studiert hatte, war im Sommer 1941 nach Peking gekommen, von wo er zunächst für zwei Jahre zu Feldforschungen in die östliche Mongolei ging[22] und dann bis Kriegsende – abgesehen von einigen Reisen – in Peking vor allem forschend und schließlich auch an der Furen daxue lehrend verbrachte. Im Band 8 von 1943 der *Monumenta Serica* finden wir bereits einen längeren Beitrag Heissigs zur mongolischen Darstellung der Yuan-Zeit. Seine Interessen an den „Randvölkern" Chinas trugen auch geopolitische Züge,[23] die in jener Zeit allgemein waren.[24] Sein Studium in Berlin war in die Zeit gefallen, in der Erich Haenisch[25] die mongolische Fassung der im Jahre 1240 niedergeschriebenen *Geheimen Geschichte der Mongolen* publizierte (1937), der er ein Wörterbuch folgen ließ (1939). Im Jahre 1941 erst erschien dann die Übersetzung (mit einem Vorwort vom August 1940, „siebenhundert Jahre nach der Niederschrift des Werkes"),[26] der 1948 eine

---

[21] Diese Formulierung verwendet er selbst in seiner Wiener Dissertation im Jahr 1941. Siehe Hartmut Walravens, *Walther Heissig (1913–2005). Leben und Werk* (Wiesbaden: Harrassowitz, 2012), S. 14.

[22] Siehe die Tagebuchnotizen in: *ibid.*, S. 233-234.

[23] Bereits seit Herbst 1938 hatte er von Berlin aus ein Projekt zur Förderung mongolischer Studenten betrieben, bei dem es ihm um die Beförderung von Beziehungen zwischen jungen Mongolen und Deutschland auch im Hinblick auf zukünftige mongolische Autonomiebestrebungen ging. Siehe *ibid.*, S. 209-222. Heissigs fortgesetzte geopolitischen Interessen schlagen sich auch in seinem Interesse an mongolischen Landkarten nieder („Über mongolische Landkarten", *Monumenta Serica* 9 [1944], S. 123-173). Den China zugewandten Teil Zentralasiens hatte Heissig schon 1941 in einem Buch dargestellt: Walther Heissig, *Das gelbe Vorfeld. Die Mobilisierung der chinesischen Außenländer* (Heidelberg: Kurt Vowinckel Verlag, 1941).

[24] Die Vorstellungen zur Geopolitik von Karl Haushofer waren weit verbreitet. Siehe Karl Haushofer, *Geopolitik der Pan-Ideen* (Berlin: Zentral-Verlag, 1931). Über die Entwicklungen in Ostasien informierten Publikationen solche in der „Schlag nach"-Reihe des Leipziger Bibliographischen Instituts: *Schlag nach über China, Japan und Mandschukuo* (Leipzig: Verlag Bibliographisches Institut, [1940]).

[25] Auf einem Foto mit Studierenden in: Walravens, *Walther Heissig*, S. 206.

[26] Zur Datierung siehe Christopher P. Atwood, „The Date of the *Secret History of the Mongols* Reconsidered", *Journal of Song-Yuan Studies* 37 (2007), S. 1-48.

„zweite verbesserte" Auflage folgte. Walther Heissig, zuletzt Professor in Bonn, ist der Typus des Forschers und Gelehrten, den die Umstände nach Peking führten und der sich dort dem intellektuellen Leben anschloss und so zur Zeitschrift *Monumenta Serica* kam.

IV. Chen Yinke 陳寅恪 (1890–1969)

Heute wird auch im Bewusstsein einer breiteren Öffentlichkeit deutlich, dass China keineswegs seine Traditionen und kulturellen Wurzeln gänzlich verworfen hat und sich sogar in zunehmendem Maße wieder darauf bezieht. Diese kulturellen Traditionen standen für die Zeitschrift *Monumenta Serica* immer schon im Zentrum. Zum geistigen Umfeld gehörten und gehören daher zahlreiche Gelehrte, darunter auch solche, die nicht als Autoren mit der Zeitschrift verbunden waren. Von diesen erwähne ich hier nur den nach Verfolgungen 1969 verstorbenen Chen Yinke, dessen Schriften seit 1980 erschienen und dem 1995 und 1999 vielbeachtete Gedenksymposien gewidmet wurden – ein Beispiel für Erinnerungskultur in China.

Dieser Chen Yinke hatte in Harvard und Berlin studiert und sich dort, namentlich bei Heinrich Lüders, zum Experten in Sanskrit und Pali ausbilden lassen und war dann 1925 nach Peking zurückgekehrt. Seine Interessen an der älteren Kultur, an der Rolle des Buddhismus in der Geschichte Chinas etwa, konnte er nur bis in die 1930er Jahre verfolgen. Angesichts der japanischen Invasion erinnerte er sich mit vielen seiner Kollegen des Falles von Kaifeng am Ende der Nördlichen Song-Zeit und des Endes der Ming-Dynastie, und er beschäftigte sich dann nicht zufällig mit den Gedichten Yuan Zhens 元稹 und Bai Juyis 白居易, die Zeugen der Kriegswirren in der Mitte der Tang-Zeit waren.

Gefühle und Empathie prägten eben auch die Sujet-Wahl der gelehrten Welt dieser Zeit in China – in deren Kontext das Unternehmen *Monumenta Serica* zu verstehen ist.[27] Für uns Heutige ist bemerkenswert, wie dieser eigensinnige Gelehrte Chen Yinke unbeugsam keine Zugeständnisse an die politischen Moden seiner Zeit machte und wie einer, der sich den Forderungen der kommunistischen Partei und ihrer Vertreter zu keinem Zeitpunkt unterworfen hat, heute größte Wertschätzung erfährt. Interessiert beteiligen sich weiterhin Vertreter christlicher Kirchen, deren Zukunftsgewissheit sich mit dem Wissen um die Offenbarung Gottes gegenüber der gesamten Menschheit verbindet, an der Frage nach der Zukunft Chinas und seiner Nachbarn. Die Gründung der *Monumenta Serica* vor 80 Jahren vergegenwärtigen heißt daher auch, die Frage zu stellen: „Was hat das mit uns heute zu tun"?

Eine Antwort will ich wenigstens versuchen. Ganz allgemein war das Unternehmen *Monumenta Serica* die Ausbildung einer Selbstvergewisserung chinesischer und außerchinesischer Gelehrsamkeit zu der Frage: Was ist China und welche

---

[27] Siehe auch den Beitrag von Wen-hsin Yeh, „Historian and Courtesan: Chen Yinke and the Writing of Liu Rushi Biezhuan". Morrison Lecture, Australian National University 2003.

Rolle spielte es im Zusammenspiel mit seinen Nachbarn und weit darüber hinaus, und zwar bezogen auf die Vergangenheit, die lange Geschichte seit der sprichwörtlichen „grauen Vorzeit" bis in unsere Tage.

In diesem Sinne kann auch weiterhin die Zeitschrift *Monumenta Serica* einen wichtigen Beitrag leisten. China befindet sich in einer Phase dramatischer Modernisierung und Umgestaltung. China internationalisiert sich und sucht seine Interessen weltweit abzusichern. Nicht nur das 19. Jahrhundert sah eine „Verwandlung der Welt" – so der Titel des weithin beachteten Werkes von Jürgen Osterhammel, sondern wir erleben eine solche Verwandlung abermals – ohne deren Ausgang zu kennen.

Die Gründe dafür, dass weitsichtige, vielleicht auch sensible, vielleicht auch den Entwicklungen im eigenen Lande gegenüber skeptische Menschen sich mit anderen Weltgegenden beschäftigten, sind vielfältig. Auch jeder von uns wird ganz eigene Gründe für die Beschäftigung mit Ländern außerhalb Europas haben. Dafür, wie man in die Welt hinein geht, in fremden Welten schweift, gibt es verschiedene Muster.

Viele wunderbare und wegen ihres Inhaltsreichtums und häufig auch ihrer Schönheit wegen zu nochmaligem Nachlesen auffordernde Arbeiten in der Zeitschrift *Monumenta Serica* könnten hier referiert werden und uns stundenlang beschäftigen. Dort getroffene Feststellungen und mitgeteilte Beobachtungen werden in Zukunft noch kommentiert und erweitert werden.

Ich schließe mit großer Dankbarkeit für dieses 80 Jahre dauernde Abenteuer des Versuchs der Vermessung einer alten Kultur. Dass es sich lohnt, sich darum weiter zu bemühen, dafür ist *Monumenta Serica*, dafür ist das Institut Monumenta Serica ein lebendiger Beweis.

AFRICAN MUSLIMS AND CHRISTIANS AND THEIR "CHINESE DREAM"*

PIOTR ADAMEK

In the last years the growing presence of Africans[1] in China has been noticed and described in numerous articles in Chinese journals, and it also had a resonance in Western publications (see the bibliography below). The new, hitherto virtually unknown phenomenon of the African Diaspora in the Middle Kingdom shows that China has become a target country of the new migration. However, most publications deal with economic, political, and social aspects of this issue, the cultural and religious life of this new dynamic and growing group of Africans in China is relatively little considered and known. This is quite surprising as they are almost all Muslims or Christians, and the religious component is an important part of their "Chinese dream."[2]

1. Brief History of Contacts

The history of encounters between China and Africa (with all the diversity of its peoples and cultures) is very long and has been partly explored.[3] It has been proved that since ancient times China has economic and cultural contacts especially with East Africa, which has been recorded in Chinese sources. Sporadically there were also personal encounters between Chinese and Africans. Probably the most well-known is the journey of the Moroccan Muslim explorer Ibn Battuta (1304–1369) to Quanzhou and Hangzhou, and the expedition of the Chinese Admiral Zheng He 郑和 (1371–1433) to East Africa can also be mentioned.[4]

The Chinese migration into the African region began in the 19th century, when Chinese workers started to come, first to St. Helena,[5] Mauritius, Madagascar (for the construction of the railway line) and South Africa (for working in the gold mines). Gradually, more and larger groups of Chinese people came to Africa. According to estimates for 1907–1910 more than 50,000 Chinese miners

---

* The German version of this article was published in *Chh* XXXIV (2015) 3, pp. 175-179, and was translated to English with the help of Br. Gregor Weimar S.V.D.

[1] Even though the author is aware of the variety and differences of many nations within Africa, and despite the fact that in the text predominantly sub-Saharan Africans will be mentioned, for readability general terms such as "Africa" and "Africans" are used continuously and are specified if necessary in concrete cases.

[2] More about this current leading political motto and national idea of the People's Republic of China see Zheng Yongnian – Gore 2015.

[3] Cf. Shen Fuwei 1998; *id.* 2011.

[4] Shen Fuwei 2011, pp. 260-270 and 287-321.

[5] *Ibid.*, p. 329.

worked in the mines near Johannesburg.[6] Most of them went back to China after a few years, but some of them stayed and settled in their new homeland. New Chinese migrants came to various countries of Africa in the second half of the 20th century, especially after the Afro-Asian Conference in Bandung (Indonesia, April 18-24, 1955), as the communist People's Republic of China (PRC) wanted to strengthen its political influence in African countries. In the next few years (1956-1975) China established diplomatic and economic ties with 38 African countries, many of which had become independent shortly before,[7] and many Chinese workers and specialists went to Africa.[8]

Especially during the last two decades, with the economic growth of the PRC, the Chinese engagement in Africa, its trade relations there, and the migration from China to Africa reached previously unseen heights. Today it is presumed that more than one Million Chinese are living in Africa, working in different areas: in industry and agriculture, in schools and hospitals, but also as smugglers and sex workers.[9] Most of them work in South Africa (about 300,000), Nigeria (100,000) and Madagascar (60,000).[10] Despite the many recent publications on the Chinese in Africa, their religious beliefs and practices have scarcely been explored.

2. Africans in China

As far as migration in the opposite direction is concerned, from Africa to China, less interest has been paid so far in the Western media and publications. Ever since the 7th century, some Africans, mainly from Somalia, Kenya and Tanzania, are presumed to have come to China, mostly as slaves – a practice which has been continued in the 16th-18th c. by the Europeans.[11] In the 1950s the PRC started its new policy towards Africa. Many students were invited from various African countries (most of them from Somalia, Cameroon and Zanzibar)[12] to several Chinese universities. The African students initially experienced huge problems in relations with the Chinese, complained about isolation and hatred on part of local people and often returned, displaced, to Africa.[13] Their life in China at the beginning of the 1960s was described by the Ghanaian student Emmanuel John Hevi, who mentioned among other things the arrests of Chinese girls for contacts with Africans and brawls.[14] In 1972 an incident involving three students

---

[6] Cf. statistics in Shen Fuwei 2011, p. 332.
[7] Fomicheva – Krasilnikov 1976, p. 260.
[8] For more about Sino-African relations of that time see Pasierbiński 1974; Fomicheva – Krasilnikov 1976; *Chiny a kraje rozwijające się* 1975, pp. 183-199.
[9] Cf. French 2014, p. 3.
[10] Sautman – Yan Hairong 2008, p. 107.
[11] Wyatt 2010; Peng Hui 2007; Tang Kaijian 2005.
[12] Pasierbiński 1974, p. 118.
[13] Larkin 1971, p. 142.
[14] Hevi 1963, pp. 216-217.

from Zambia made the headlines. They destroyed a portrait of Mao after attending the Christmas Eve Vigil Mass in the Catholic cathedral of Peking which led to a fight with police officers and their being expelled from China the next week.[15] There is another account of a larger rumble between African and Chinese students in 1988.[16] However, most of the African students who came to China because of the new Chinese policy (6,000 until 1999 and up to 20,000 until 2007)[17] were able to graduate from university and some of them remained in China.

The number of Africans in China started to increase rapidly during the course of the last 15 years. Firstly African traders who as a result of the financial crisis lost their markets in Indonesia and Thailand came to Guangzhou in search for yet unexplored markets.[18] More and more African merchants and mongers, especially from West Africa, followed their path which resulted in the modern African diaspora in the city on the Pearl River being called the biggest one in Asia.[19] Today the estimates on the population of African immigrants vary from 20,000[20] to 100,000[21] in Guangzhou and up to 200,000 in China.[22] Even though no exact figures can be given due to the grey areas and the huge fluctuation among the Africans, the role the Africans played in Guangzhou and increasingly in the whole China is undeniable. For some years now the number of Africans living in the neighboring cities of Guangzhou, like Foshan 佛山 or Dongguan 东莞[23] and the city of Yiwu 义乌 in the Zhejiang province, are on the rise, too. The latter transformed into a second centre for African migrants and their trade.[24] Different from former migrants who have mostly been students and diplomats, the larger fraction of these African newcomers are small merchants with little capital. They just want to pursue the "Chinese dream" themselves.[25] The majority of these immigrants are unmarried young men, 25-40 years old[26] from all over Africa, but mostly from Nigeria, Mali, Ghana, Guinea, Congo and Senegal.[27] As a result of problems with obtaining visas many of these men are staying in China illegally.

---

[15] Pasierbiński 1974, pp. 118-119.

[16] Sullivan 1994, pp. 438-457.

[17] Sautman – Yan Hairong 2008, p. 103.

[18] Lan Shanshan 2014, p. 220.

[19] "Africans in China sharing 'Chinese Dream'" (*Xinhua* 23.3.2013).

[20] Li Zhigang 2012, p. 3.

[21] Adams 2010, p. 699; "Africans in China sharing 'Chinese Dream'." In some articles, still higher numbers are given, cf., e.g., 200,000 Africans in Guangzhou, in: "Guangzhou Feizhou yijiaoyou ..." (*Xindebao* 23.7.2009).

[22] Mathews – Yang Yang 2012, p. 99.

[23] Castillo 2014, pp. 235-257.

[24] Marfaing 2012, p. 41.

[25] Cf. Lan Yanfei 2010, pp. 74-76; Pan Xiaoling 2008, pp. 14-15.

[26] Lan Shanshan 2014, p. 220; Huang Jialing – He Shenjing 2014, p. 311.

[27] Adams 2010, pp. 699-700.

There have been several Chinese and some western publications on the economical and social life of the African community in Guangzhou.[28] Although nearly all (95%) of the Africans work as merchants,[29] African chefs, hairdressers and musicians can be found as well[30] and also quite a number of African restaurants and hotels do exist.[31] The migrant population is mostly concentrated in Sanyuanli 三元里 (north of the central station) and Xiaobeilu 小北路 (southeast of the train station). Both districts are "virtually totally African and Chinese faces are only to be seen once in a while."[32] In particular the area around the 35 storey Tianxiu 天秀 building[33] is called "Chocolate-City"[34] or "Africa street."[35] In Sanyuanli live mostly English-speaking Africans, half of which are from Nigeria; in Xiaobeilu live the Francophones[36] and the Islamic Africans.[37] Besides English, French and Chinese, local African languages are also to be heard.[38] The Africans are organized in different networks, primarily according to origin, which provide various kind of support for them.

3. African Muslims and Christians in Guangzhou

Religion is of great importance for Africans. Religious affiliation is "a guarantor for solidarity, is a point of reference for identity and provides social control."[39] The results of a study by Bork-Hüffer in Guangzhou and Foshan showed that 98% of the respondents follow a religion: 77% were Christians and 21% Muslims.[40] Whether they belonged to Christianity or Islam usually depended on the country of origin and the religious differences in Africa. E.g., 90% of the Senegalese in Guangzhou are Muslims,[41] like in Senegal itself. Churches and mosques

---

[28] Cf., e.g., Li Zhigang 2008; *id.* 2012; Wen Guozhu 2012; Xu Tao 2009(a); *id.* 2009(b); Zhang Dongliang 2009; *id.* 2010; Zhen Jinghui 2009; Adams 2009, *id.* 2010; Bertoncello – Bredeloup 2007; Bork-Hüffer 2014; Castillo 2014; Mathews – Yang Yang 2012.

[29] Adams 2010, p. 699.

[30] See the three articles on the music (including religious music) of Africans in Guangzhou, in *Wenhua yishu yanjiu* 文化艺术研究: Luo Qin 2014, Li Yinbei 2014, Ma Chengcheng 2014.

[31] Ma Xiaoyi – Liu Jun – Wu Chunyan 2012, pp. 57-58; Marfaing 2012, p. 41.

[32] Mathews – Yang Yang 2012, p. 99; see also Bertoncello 2007, p. 102.

[33] Address: Yuexiu District, Huanshi Middle Road 300 (越秀区环市中路 300).

[34] Adams, p. 698; Zhang Dongliang 2009, p. 37.

[35] Ma Xiaoyi – Liu Jun – Wu Chunyan 2012, p. 57.

[36] Marfaing 2012, p. 38.

[37] Mathews – Yang Yang 2012, p. 111.

[38] Adams 2010, p. 701.

[39] Marfaing 2012, p. 41.

[40] Bork-Hüffer 2014.

[41] Marfaing 2012, p. 38.

are, besides other social national networks, the most important centers for social interaction and different types of support for Africans in China.[42]

Muslims

Only little has been published on the life of African Muslims in China.[43] It is said that around 15,000 African Muslims live in Guangzhou,[44] who are mainly situated in Xiaobeilu and attend prayers at the officially registered Xiaodongying 小东营 mosque[45] and Huaisheng 怀圣 mosque[46] respectively. Information on illegal Islamic communities is scarce. It was reported, however, that some years ago Chinese officials closed down an illegal mosque (together with a church of the Latter Day Saints). The officials went ahead to stop the activities of the mosque and the church which were located on the seventh floor of an apartment building, although African embassies tried to intervene.[47] African Muslims are to a large extent involved in trading and exporting textiles and electronics to Africa. The social and religious life of the Afro-Muslim community has been discussed in an article on the web presence of the Muslim community in Guangzhou.[48] It is stated that despite coming from different origins and cultural backgrounds and despite their different experiences with the "Cantonese Dream," the members of this community feel united through their common faith. Every Friday about 1,000 faithful come to Xiaodongying mosque, including for example, a Nigerian with the Chinese name Gao Haji 高哈吉, who has been to Guangzhou for several years. He works in textile trading with the United Arab Emirates and dreams of taking a Chinese wife. Another example is Masa, who lives in Guangzhou together with his African wife and daughter, dreams of obtaining a Chinese passport and tries to bring his daughter up as a "Chinese." Or Davmi from South Africa who is married to a Chinese wife, has a son with her, and opened a shop in Xiaobeilu. Imam Liang 梁 stated in the aforementioned article that the Xiaodongying mosque became "a family" for African migrants. After prayers the Muslims gather at the mosque with other African and Chinese Muslims and many of them do business here.

---

[42] Bork-Hüffer 2014.

[43] Some information can be found in the articles on the website of the Guangzhou Islamic Association (www.gzislam.com, accessed 7 March 2016). See also: Li Mingbo 2012, pp. 62-64.

[44] Zhao Xu 2014.

[45] Address: Yuexiu District, Yuehua Road, Xiaodongying 1 (越秀区越华路小东营 1).

[46] Address: Yuexiu District, Guangta Road 56 (越秀区光塔路 56).

[47] Bertoncello 2007, pp. 102-103.

[48] "Zoujin Guangzhou Xiaodongying qingzhensi, heiren musilin" 走进广州小东营清真寺，黑人穆斯林 (www.gzislam.com/pd.jsp?id=42).

Protestants

The city of Guangzhou also shelters a large and diverse group of African Protestants with growing numbers. Some attend services at the non-denominational church of the Guangzhou International Christian Fellowship (GICF) – which is officially registered with the government and accessible exclusively for foreigners.[49]

Many others partake in prayers at the numerous illegal African Pentecostal churches which hold service in conference halls in hotels and malls,[50] and the location of these activities can change frequently. They are tolerated by local authorities as long as they do not invite Chinese citizens and they are sometimes used as informal channels for information on the illegal African diaspora. Estimates are that at least 17 such charismatic Protestant churches exist in Guangzhou, each of these with around 50-100 believers. They mostly function as "satellite-churches" with their headquarters in Africa (e.g., Mountain of Fire and Miracles or Redeemed Christian Church of God) or were newly founded by migrant-pastors (e.g., Royal Victory Church).[51] It seems the Pentecostal movement is especially attractive to young Africans in the city, like Chuck, a 33 year old Nigerian who was interviewed for an article by Castillo. He was Catholic before but converted and joined a flourishing Pentecostal parish. He said he feels more understood with his daily problems in this community.[52] Obviously the Pentecostal movement understands how important it is to provide marginalized African migrants not only with support and a new network; but also, as Haugen puts it, give them a new mission which proclaims the responsibility of the Africans to take up the task of Evangelization which has been abandoned by the Europeans, China as the decisive battle for Christianity, and Divine promise of a prosperous future in Guangzhou.[53] Paradoxically, by these means many Africans find a new access to the Gospel in postsocialist China in the 21st century.[54]

Catholics

Among the African Catholics most attend mass at the "Most Holy Heart of Jesus" Cathedral.[55] Especially Sunday afternoon when the Mass is celebrated in

---

[49] Address: Tianhe District, Linhe West Cross Road 215 (天河区林和西横路 215, third floor). Services are held on Sundays, 10:00 a.m. Cf. the website of the GICF: www.gicf.net, accessed 7 March 2016.

[50] Vgl. Castillo 2014, pp. 235-257.

[51] Lan Shanshan 2014, p. 222.

[52] Castillo 2014, pp. 235-257.

[53] Haugen 2013, p. 81.

[54] Castillo 2014, pp. 235-257.

[55] Address: Shishi Sacred Heart Catholic Church, Yuexiu District, Yide Middle Road, Jiubuqian 56 (Yuanxi Street) (石室圣心大教堂一德中路旧部前 56 [元锡巷]).

English by a Chinese priest along with other foreigners up to 1,000[56] (sometimes even up to 2.000)[57] Africans can be seen attending service in the cathedral. Also Anglicans and Methodists, because they lack churches of their own, will join the Catholics. Other "non-Catholics" would also attend in order to keep in touch with their compatriots. The cathedral transformed into one of the biggest centers of the African diaspora in Guangzhou.[58] She provides space for worship, Bible sharing as well as non-church-related activities and also even business opportunities. Every Sunday after the formal Mass at 3.30 p.m. there is a charismatic prayer-meeting at 5.30 p.m. with music and passionate preaching. Many Africans participate because it gives them a feeling of home and security.[59] The Catholic charismatic movement offers Bible courses of many kinds (among these also Chinese-English Bible courses for Chinese believers and others) and courses for various apostolates. A system of mutual spiritual support and financial aid and welfare is organized there as well.[60]

As Lan Shanshan states, Catholic Chinese seem to be more accepting towards the Africans and do talk more positively about the Africans and the equality of men. The Chinese father Paul was interviewed by Lan Shanshan and told him those people were Brothers and Sisters in Christ and needed their help.[61] What the Chinese Catholics actually know about the migrants appears to be very limited, though. Due to language barriers communication with the African community happens almost exclusively on the group leader level with the help of some trusted members of the charismatic groups. Decisions are made by Chinese priests and handed down to the African believers who have to ask for permission. This differs from the illegal Pentecostal congregations where the African pastor makes the decisions.[62] On the website of the diocese Guangzhou[63] the activities of the charismatic movement are not mentioned. Although the Africans have a certain autonomy in their religious practices, they are actually being isolated from the Chinese Christians. Bible courses at the cathedral seem to be the only opportunity for interaction between the two groups. Only a few Africans make Chinese Catholic friends because of the language barriers and different times for mass for the two groups.[64]

---

[56] Xu Tao 2009a, p. 42.
[57] For example, in the time of spring and summer trade fairs, see Lan Shanshan 2014, p. 220, Fn. 1.
[58] Lan Shanshan 2014, p. 224.
[59] Hua Ting 2011, pp. 62-64.
[60] Lan Shanshan 2014, pp. 229-232.
[61] *Ibid.*, p. 226.
[62] *Ibid.*, p. 225.
[63] www.gzcatholic.org, accessed 7 March 2016.
[64] Lan Shanshan 2014, p. 231.

Conclusion

The African diaspora in Guangzhou almost exclusively consists of Muslims and Christians. That religion plays a major role in the life of the Africans in this city should not be surprising. They came to China to pursue their "Chinese dream" and continue following their own religion they brought along. They are a new phenomenon in the course of encounters between China and Africa because never before so many Africans have come to in China. Their unique lifestyle and their enthusiastic and lively faith is a new challenge not only for the Chinese government and the Chinese society, but also for the Chinese Muslims and Christians. The Catholic Church, for example, mediated between hundreds of African protesters in the streets of Guangzhou and the government following the incident of 15 July 2009, when a Nigerian man jumped to death whilst trying to escape being persecuted by Chinese migration officers.[65] Mutual acceptance and understanding needs time to build. Interesting, however, is the fact that many African faithful – mostly from the Pentecostal movement but also among the Catholics and Muslims – consider themselves as missionaries in China. As this is officially prohibited under the current political situation this indeed is a religious testimony for China.

Bibliography

[Adams, Bodomo] Yadangsi Boduomo 亚当斯·博多莫, "Quanqiuhua shidai de Fei-Zhong guanxi. Zai Hua Feizhou shangmao tuanti de juese" 全球化时代的非中关系—在华非洲商贸团体的角色, *Xi Ya Feizhou* 西亚非洲 2009/8, pp. 62-67.

Adams, Bodomo, "The African Trading Community in Guangzhou. An Emerging Bridge for Africa–China Relations," *China Quarterly* No. 203 (2010), pp. 693-707.

"Africans in China sharing 'Chinese Dream'" [*Xinhua* 23.3.2013] (online: http://europe.chinadaily.com.cn/china/2013-03/23/content_16339875.htm [accessed 7 March 2016]).

Bertoncello, Brigitte – Sylvie Bredeloup, "The Emergence of New African 'Trading Posts' in Hong Kong and Guangzhou," *China Perspectives* 2007/1, pp. 94-105.

Bork-Hüffer, Tabea *et al.*, "Mobility and the Transiency of Social Spaces. African Merchant Entrepreneurs in China," *Population, Space and Place* 22 (March 2016) 2, pp. 199-211.

Castillo, Roberto, "Feeling at Home in the 'Chocolate City'. An Exploration of Placemaking Practices and Structures of Belonging amongst Africans in Guangzhou," *Inter-Asia Cultural Studies* 15 (2014) 2, pp. 235-257.

Chiny a kraje rozwijające się (Warszawa 1975).

---

[65] See "Africans Protest in Guangzhou after Passport Checks" www.chinadaily.com.cn/china/2009-07/16/content_8435559.htm (accessed 7 March 2016); "Guangzhou Feizhou yijiaoyou … ."

Haugen, Heidi Østbø, "Nigerians in China. A Second State of Immobility," *International Migration* 50 (2012) 2, pp. 65-80.

—, "African Pentecostal Migrants in China. Marginalization and the Alternative Geography of a Mission Theology," *African Studies Review* 56 (2013) 1, pp. 81-102.

Fomicheva, M.V. – A.S. Krasilnikov, *Kitay i Afrika*. Moskau 1976.

French, Howard W., *China's Second Continent. How a Million Migrants Are Building a New Empire in Africa* (New York – Toronto 2014).

"Guangzhou Feizhou yijiaoyou chengwei 7.15 shijian zui wending qunti. Jiaohui lingxiu quanmian jiaoyou tongguo zhengchang tujing jiejue wenti" 广州非洲裔教友成为7·15事件最稳定群体—教会领袖劝勉教友通过正常途径解决问题 [*Xindebao* 23.7.2009] (online: http://xinde.org/News/index/id/12380.html [accessed 7 March 2016]).

Hevi, Emmanuel J., *An African Student in China*. London 1963.

Hua Ting 华亭, "Guangzhou youzuo heirencheng" 广州有座黑人城, *Shijie bolan* 世界博览 2011/19, pp. 62-64.

Huang Jialing 黄嘉玲 – He Shenjing 何深静, "Feizhou yiyimin zaisui zongjiao changsuo difang gan tezheng jiqi xingcheng jizhi. Jiyu Guangzhou Shishi Shengxin dajiaotang de shizheng yanjiu" 非洲裔移民在穗宗教场所地方感特征及其形成机制—基于广州石室圣心大教堂的实证研究, *Redai dili* 热带地理 34 (2014) 3, pp. 308-318.

Lan Shanshan, "The Catholic Church's Role in the African Dispora in Guangzhou, China," in: *Catholicism in China, 1900–Present. The Development of the Chinese Church*. Ed. Cindy Yik-Yi Chu. New York 2014, pp. 219-236.

Lan Yanfei 兰燕飞, "Feizhou shangren de Guangzhou meng" 非洲商人的广州梦, *Xiaokang* 小康 2010/1, pp. 74-76.

Larkin, Bruce D., *China and Africa 1949–1970. The Foreign Policy of the People's Republic China*. Berkeley – Los Angeles – London 1971.

Li Mingbo 李明波, "Feizhou heiren zai Guangzhou" 非洲黑人在广州, *Shijie zhishi* 世界知识 2012/14, pp. 62-64.

Li Yinbei 李音蓓, "Guangzhou 'qiaokelicheng' feizhou heiren yinyue tansuo" 广州"巧克力城"非洲黑人音乐探索, *Wenhua yishu yanjiu* 文化艺术研究 7 (2014) 2, pp. 29-38.

Li Zhigang 李志刚 et al., "Guangzhou Xiaobeilu heiren jujuqu shehui kongjian fenxi" 广州小北路黑人聚居区社会空间分析, *Dili xuebao* 地理学报 63 (2008) 2, pp. 207-218.

Li Zhigang 李志刚 – Du Feng 杜枫, "Zhongguo da chengshi de waiguoren 'zuyi jingjiqu' yanjiu. Dui Guangzhou 'qiaokelicheng' de shizheng" 中国大城市的外国人"族裔经济区"研究—对广州"巧克力城"的实证, *Renwen dili* 人文地理 27 (2012) 6, pp. 1-6.

Luo Qin 洛秦, "'Jia menkou' de kua wenhua yinyue tianye gongzuo de yiyi. Guangzhou 'qiaokelicheng' Feizhouren yinyue shenghuo de tianye kaocha daoyan" "家门口"的跨文化音乐田野工作的意义—广州"巧克力城"非洲人音乐生活的田野考察导言, *Wenhua yishu yanjiu* 7 (2014) 2, pp. 27-29.

Ma Chengcheng 马成城, "Zoujin qiancheng zongjiao xinyang xia de Guangzhou 'qiaokelicheng'. Feizhouren jiaotang yinyue shenghuo chutan" 走进虔诚宗教信仰下的广州"巧克力城"—非洲人教堂音乐生活初探, *Wenhua yishu yanjiu* 7 (2014) 2, pp. 39-49.

Ma Xiaoyi – Liu Jun – Wu Chunyan, "Stories from 'Africa Street'," *China Today* 61 (2012) 6, pp. 57-59.

Marfaign, Laurence, "Senegalesen auf dem Weg nach China," *welt-sichten* 3 (2012), pp. 38-41.

Mathews, Gordon – Yang Yang, "How Africans Pursue Low-end Globalization in Hong Kong and Mainland China," *Journal of Current Chinese Affairs – China aktuell* 2 (2012), pp. 95-120.

Pan Xiaoling 潘晓凌, "'Qiaokelicheng'. Feizhouren xunmeng Zhongguo" "巧克力城"—非洲人寻梦中国, *Renmin wenzhai* 人民文摘 3 (2008), pp. 14-15.

Pasierbiński, Tadeusz, *Chiny i Afryka*. Warszawa 1974.

Peng Hui 彭蕙, "16-19 shiji Aomen heiren shequn yanjiu" 16-19世纪澳门黑人社群研究, *Xuzhou Shifan daxue xuebao (zhexue shehui kexueban)* 徐州师范大学学报(哲学社会科学版) 2 (2007), pp. 76-80.

Sautman, Barry – Yan Hairong, "Friends and Interest. China's Distinctive Links with Africa," in: *China's New Role in Africa and the South. A Search for a New Perspective*. Ed. Dorothy Grace M. Guerrero – Firoze Manji. Cape Town – Nairobi – Oxford 2008, pp. 87-133.

Shen Fuwei 沈福伟, *Zhongguo yu Xi Ya Feizhou wenhua jiaoliu zhi* 中国与西亚非洲文化交流志. Shenzhen 1998.

—, *Sichou zhi lu: Zhongguo yu Feizhou wenhua jiaoliu yanjiu* 丝绸之路—中国与非洲文化交流研究. Ürümqi 2011.

Sullivan, Michael, "The 1988-89 Nanjing anti-African Protests. Racial Nationalism or National Racism?," *China Quarterly* No. 138 (1994), pp. 438-457.

Tang Kaijian 汤开建 – Peng Hui 彭蕙, "16-19 shiji Aomen 'heiren' laiyuan kaoshu" 16-19世纪澳门"黑人"来源考述, *Shijie lishi* 世界历史 2005/5, pp. 77-83.

Wen Guozhu 温国砫, "Feizhou shangren zai Guangzhou de shehui ronghedu ji qi yingxiang yanjiu. Jiyu yimin shiying lilun de shijiao" 非洲商人在广州的社会融合度及其影响研究—基于移民适应理论的视角, *Gaige yu kaifang* 改革与开放 2012/4, pp. 111-114.

Wong Tsoi-lai, Catherine, "Guangzhou ramps up Ebola checks," *Global Times* 30.10.2014 (online: www.globaltimes.cn/content/889074.shtml [accessed 8 March 2016]).

Wyatt, Don J., *The Blacks of Premodern China*. Philadelphia 2010.

Xu Tao 许涛 (a), "Guangzhou diqu Feizhouren shehui zhichi de ruohua, duanlie yu chonggou" 广州地区非洲人社会支持的弱化、断裂与重构, *Nanfang renkou* 南方人口 24 (2009) 4, pp. 34-44.

— (b), "Guangzhou diqu Feizhouren de shehui jiaowang guanxi ji qi xingdong luoji" 广州地区非洲人的社会交往关系及其行动逻辑, *Qingnian yanjiu* 青年研究 2009/5, pp. 71-86, 96.

Xu Yongzhang 许永璋, "Gudai daoguo Zhongguo de Feizhouren" 古代到过中国的非洲人, *Shixue yuekan* 史学月刊 1983/3, pp. 96-97.

Zhao Xu, "Answering the Call to Prayer," *China Daily* 4.04.2014 (online: www.chinadaily.com.cn/2014-04/04/content_17405704.htm [accessed 8 March 2016]).

Zhang Dongliang 张东亮 – Dai Yu 戴雨, "Zai Guangzhou de Feizhou keshang" 在广州的非洲客商, *Longmenzhen* 龙门阵, 2009/10, pp. 33-38.

Zhang Dongliang 张东亮 – Dai Qiuyu 戴秋雨, "Zai Guangzhou de Feizhou daoye" 在广州的非洲倒爷, *Zhongguo tielu wenyi* 中国铁路文艺 2010/1, pp. 4-7.

Zhen Jinghui 甄静慧, "Feizhou heiren zai Guangzhou" 非洲黑人在广州, *Nanfeng chuang* 南风窗 2009/19, pp. 56-59.

Zheng Yang, "Kungfu Dream. Africans Are Trained at the Martial Art's Birthplace," *Beijing Review* 57 (2014) 5, pp. 42-43.

Zheng Yongnian – Lance L.P. Gore (eds.), *China Entering the Xi Jinping Era*. Abingdon – New York 2015.

Websites: africansinchina.net; www.gzislam.com; www.gicf.net

THE MISSION OF MULTI-FACETED CHRISTIANITY IN A GLOBALIZED WORLD

FRANZ GÜNTHER GESSINGER S.V.D.

In Recognition of His Outstanding Services to Christianity in China Today to Professor Roman Malek, S.V.D.

Having joined the Divine Word Missionaries in 1953, interest for Japan turned my attention since 1959 also to the abiding influence of imperial China on the mountainous islands of the land of the Rising Sun, which after prolonged studies and teaching years in North America I actually never found the chance to visit. After Vatican Council II Catholic theology in Japan did here and there catch our attention in the framework of contextual theology, but not as obviously as the growth of Christianity in South Korea and in the People's Republic of China. In 2014, Pusan in South Korea was to host the latest Plenary Assembly of the World Council of Churches after the previous one in Porto Allegre, Brazil.

After my three years spent at the Catholic Mission Center (Missio) in Aachen, Germany, Prof. Dr. Roman Malek invited me to put my familiarity with German, English, French, and Latin to good use at the China-Zentrum, founded by him with the support of several dozens of missionary religious communities and agencies in Europe and the Catholic German Bishops' Conference. Although I did just two years later accept the responsibility for the Foyer S.V.D. in Paris, my participation in the jubilee celebrations for the 400th birthday of the great China missionary Adam Schall, S.J., in 1992,[1] and two trips to China in 1993 as well as further meetings in 1994 turned out to be most memorable events for me.

Rev. Roman Malek has gone to the limits of physical strength in his dedication to promote bridge-building between the Chinese and Western cultures, on the path of Nestorian and Franciscan missionaries (in the Middle Ages) and the new initiatives of the Jesuits more than 400 years ago.

1. Early Mission Enthusiasm

Bible scholars[2] have pointed out that the encounters of the disciples with the risen Christ implied not only a recognition of the earthly Jesus of Nazareth, but also

---

[1] The proceedings of this commemorative conference have been published in Roman Malek (ed.), *Western Learning and Christianity in China. The Contribution and Impact of Johann Adam Schall von Bell, S.J. (1592-1666)*. MSMS XXXV/1-2 (Nettetal: Steyler Verlag, 1998). [Eds.]

[2] Cf. Karl Kertelge (ed.), *Mission im Neuen Testament* (Freiburg: Herder, 1982). It may be said that western biblical criticism has achieved a consensus concerning the interpretation of the witnesses for the resurrection of Jesus of Nazareth as providing the initial thrust for all Christian mission.

their renewed and confirmed mission to the people of Israel and faithful hearers of the message worldwide. – Jesus has been proclaimed the Christ, the Anointed One of God, who sends out his witnesses to continue his proclamation of the kingship and rule of God in Israel as well as in the entire world. – The community rallied around the crucified and risen Christ existed from its very beginnings only as the one sent out on mission to continue Christ's work of redemption of all.

In 2010, I had the opportunity to celebrate the annual missionary week in honor of St. Wojciech/Adalbert, where the eyes are turned to the mission efforts of our Christian brothers and sisters outside the fold of the Roman Catholic Church. This feast is to be applauded in highest terms. With their eyes on Jesus, all Christian Churches and communities have always deplored those who neither knew nor acknowledged Christ's ways of recreating a new humanity according to the will and image and plan of God. If at times their assessments of non-Christian milieus and cultures were much too harsh and culturally narrow-minded, it cannot be forgotten that the risen Jesus has always found faithful disciples who followed him on the "new way" in selfless faithfulness and surrender to the utmost. To admire such devotion also among non-Catholics has opened the doors to truthful discipleship and the kind of noble generosity which Jesus recommends to his followers.[3]

The Christian Churches have learned this lesson on different presuppositions. Working against one another has proven to be more detrimental on the mission fields than on home grounds, and more in diaspora situations like North America, British territories, Scandinavian countries, Germany, the Netherlands and Switzerland, than in regions with large denominational majorities, either Catholic or Orthodox or Protestant. Since Vatican Council II we are learning that interdenominational peace is not only the desire of the Founder and Lord of the Church, Jesus Christ,[4] but also the most serious challenge for our Christian witness in today's world. Wherever we are achieving peace in the imitation of Christ, the world will believe us.

2. My Personal Background

To present the readers with a short biography is for representatives of the human and social sciences not merely an academic formality, but rather the posting of one's cultural origins and also an unpretentious conditioning of any all too hasty overviews and precipitous coordination and systematization of research data. No scientific viewpoint and perspective has succeeded in obtaining universal acclaim. Scientific objectivity remains always more of an ideal and a goal than a matter of fact. Its chances are best served by serious well intentioned dialogue.[5]

---

[3] Cf. Luke 9:49-50.

[4] Cf. John 17.

[5] Cf. Heinrich Ott, "Wahrheit und Geschichte," in: Jean-Louis Leuba – Heinrich Stirnimann, *Freiheit in der Begegnung. Zwischenbilanz des ökumenischen Dialogs. Festschrift*

My native milieu is Rhenisch village Catholicism. The modest book collection at home opened my eyes for the historical dimension of religion by means of pictures, even before I learned how to read and write. In war time I was familiarized with a good number of Protestants, some of them fellow pupils, as well as ideological competition with Nazi propaganda. After the total defeat of the Wehrmacht and all exaggerated German nationalism, the worldwide engagement of the Catholic Church offered me an attractive perspective for a life program under God's auspices in the imitation of Jesus Christ.

Being socialized in a Catholic environment both at home, in the village church and later even in a Minor Seminary, my classmates and myself were more impressed by German, French and English literature than by any version of Catholic catechism programs. The academic presentations of Catholic theology within the framework of scholastic perspectives did not satisfy me. More important than any juridical and Aristotelian fixations were for me, already at the college level, spiritual masters of Christian antiquity, the Middle Ages and modern Christian thinkers. I have always found the pious theology of the Augustinian tradition a more persuasive witness for Christ than deductive scholastic argumentation aiming at logical precision.

Setting out on a doctoral program in apologetics, also presented under the titles of either fundamental or foundational theology, I disagreed with the pretentions of Catholic apologists since the 16th century to accord scientific quality to their elaborations of what they unfolded as *demonstratio religiosa, christiana et catholica*. Instead, I turned my attention to the empirical evidence for religious life in the cultural sciences of history, ethnology or cultural anthropology, sociology, psychology and a science of religion marked by phenomenology. On the basis of empirical data interpreted not merely as social or cultural activities, but as pointing to core experiences of humans in the face of death, I found more potential not only for the incomparable humanizing influence and survival of religion, but also for the success of any type of Christian mission endeavors. If in the 20th century apologetics has received the status of a theological foundation, as the German expression "Fundamentaltheologie" ("foundational theology" in English) seems to indicate, I have to admit that for me more and more "religiology"[6] as non-reductionist science of religion has taken over this basic function; and on that basis I do attribute a truly initiating potential for faith communication neither to patrology and Church History, nor to Canon Law, nor to scholastic systematic theology, nor to moral theology, nor to biblical theology, but to pastoral theology with its branches of liturgy, homiletics, catechetics, mission theology and concern for justice, peace and ecology. This must sound outra-

---

für Otto Karrer (Frankfurt a.M. - Stuttgart: Verlag Josef Knecht - Evangelisches Verlagswerk, 1969), pp. 181-189. Bruce Henry, "An interview with Ursula Franklin (formerly of the Canadian National Research Council)," *Catholic New Times*, 23 Feb. 1986, p. 3.

[6] The term "religiology" has been coined (in analogy to Jap. *shukyogaku* 宗教学) by Hideo Kishimoto in his article "Religiology," *Numen. International Review for the History of Religions* 14 (1967) 2, pp. 81-86.

geously provocative, since pastoral theology has been established as an academic discipline only in the second half of the 18th century under the auspices of the pragmatic Emperor Joseph II (1741-1790). How could "practical theology," as Protestants call the discipline, aspire to such an outstanding position in modern or rather post-modern theology after 2000?

3. A Concise Historical Overview

The first generations of Christianity followed the "new way" of Jesus of Nazareth in full recognition of the Holy Scriptures of Israel (yet in the Greek translation of the Septuagint), the documentation of Jewish faith in the Torah, the prophets (*nebiim*) and other writings (the *ketubim*) of the Tanakh. The Christian communities and their hierarchies decided in the following three centuries upon the canonical of the Greek testimonies of ecclesiastical faith of the first one hundred years after Christ's passion and resurrection. The Church Fathers commented both the Old and the New Testament. Among the ecclesiastical writers who set out to attempt more systematic overviews of the body of Christian teachings, John Damacene succeeded well for the Byzantine East and Petrus Lombardus for the Latin West. The commenting of the latter's *Sententiarium libri quatuor* (Four Books of Sentences) led along the formalized question method to the late medieval Sums; among them, the *Summa Theologica* by Thomas Aquinas has achieved exemplary status first within the Dominican Order and since the Council of Trent in Catholic Counter-Reformation and thereafter by new pontifical backing in the Neo-Scholasticism of the 19th and 20th centuries. These academic developments occurred, however, under the impact of a predominant position of Canon Law since the 11th and of Aristotelian logics and metaphysics since the 13th century.

At the time of the Christianization of all of Europe, major areas of the known world were unfortunately lost to Christianity: in the Near East, in northern Africa and on the Iberian Peninsula. The Conquista had repulsed Muslim presence in Spain in the year that Columbus set out on the way to India to discover America. Yet forty years earlier, Constantinople had fallen to the Turcs, and Turkish rule promoted Islam up to the borders of Italy, Germany, Hungary, Poland, and Russia, leaving only Georgia and Armenia as major enclaves south of the Caucasus Mountains, and other Christian minorities in Palestine, Syria, Mesopotamia.

The age of discoveries saw then decisive but often all too inconsiderate efforts of the Catholic nations to convert the subjected indigenous people and, later on, the slaves imported from Africa. The Protestant Reformation affected such conversion campaigns only in the 17th and 18th centuries in British North-America and India and in the Dutch colonies in the Carribean, in South Africa and in Indonesia. The Catholic misssion efforts outside the "patronados" of Spain, Portugal and France suffered major setbacks, first in China after 1700, and after the earthquake of Lisbon (1755) in Portugal, Spain and France through the expulsion of Jesuit missionaries and the abolition of the Society of Jesus in 1773. Due to the international repercussions of the French revolution, the Catholic mission enterprise came almost to a complete halt, but only to be revived after the defeat of

Napoleon, this time with substantial pontifical sponsoring, though. In the 19th century the founding of new religious congregations, recruiting from all layers of a now defeudalized society in Catholic countries, was matched by new efforts of similar missionary institutions in Protestant countries, like Great Britain, the Netherlands, Germany, Switzerland, Scandinavia, and eventually also in the United States. These new foundations were largely sponsored by non-denominational evangelical groups – the Free Churches. These, at first, cut out for themselves certain mission fields and territories. But, within decades, they took notice of the unfortunate implications and consequences of mutual competition for the common goal of converting non-Christian populations, mostly in colonial situations, to one of the Christian Churches more or less firmly established in Europe or America and their overseas possessions. The Protestant foreign mission societies showed themselves more concerned about the credibility of their Christian witness than about the dogmatic differences of their sponsoring Churches, which often enough did not represent the stance of mainline Churches, but of evangelical fervor. Since 1854 World Mission Conferences have been held in New York, London, Liverpool, and Edinburgh (on this see part 7).

4. Science of Religion, Biblical Criticism, and Ecumenism versus Anti-modernist Apologetics

Since the establishment of the science of religion ("religiology") many representatives of the social sciences, following reductionist theories, have considered religion merely as byproduct and cultural glue of social developments and societal structures without a distinctive value of its own.[7] Since I am a committed Christian, I have always considered this reductionist positivistic approach as philosophically superficial, as psychologically self-oblivious, and as pedagogically self-defeating and destructive in view of inescapable, yet unacceptable, individual mortality. With profound satisfaction I familiarized myself with the description of religious experience by Catholic and Protestant mystics, by Leibniz, Kant, Schleiermacher, the German idealists, by John Henry Newman and Catholic modernists, but especially by William James, Rudolf Otto, and Max Scheler and the whole movement of European and North-American phenomenology of religion since the turn of the 19th to the 20th century. One of the key publications about the irreplaceable formative value of religious celebrations is *Les rites de passage* by Arnold van Gennep of 1909. This agnostic and specialist of classical philology and literature underlined that no human culture, not even any atheistic ideology and political structure can do without the basic rites which communicate and transmit the distinctive sense of individual personhood and human dignity in the solemn reception of the newborn in society, of initiation ceremonies into adult responsibility, of the founding of a new family and of the transition into afterlife through funeral rites.

---

[7] Cf. Robert A. Segal, "Kuhn and the Science of Religion," *Religion* 39 (2009), pp. 352-355.

As oldest archeological evidence for religious behavior the cult of the deceased is most prominent, which has been traced to the time of the Homo Neanderthalensis (or even earlier); and the most widespread form of religiosity remains up to the present the veneration of ancestors in all regions and corners of our planet. This phenomenon cannot be ignored neither by the specialists of the natural sciences nor by historians, sociologists and psychologists. The phenomenology of religion has to take account of collective and individual spontaneous emotional reactions of joy and anxieties, of hope and despair, and above all of our preoccupation with death, which since primordial times has found lasting and immortal echoes in mythology, poetry, music, drama, and literature.

Definitions of religion, religiosity and spirituality go into the thousands. Many, if not most of those circulating in the academic sphere, are of the sociological brand featuring more or less reductionist labels. Since I am a religious believer, my definition betrays the psychological viewpoint of self-experience and confidence in the equal potential of my partners of discussion. For me, religion expresses itself as celebration, promotion and interpretative explication of life in the face of inescapable death, yet without fatalism, and even fascinated by an experience of gracious providence. Rudolf Otto has pointed to this as the "mysterium tremendum et fascinans."[8]

We should not downplay the historical phenomenon that, already since the organization of academic life in the western universities in the 13th century, laicist pretension and perspectives played a non-negligeable role under the influence of Emperor Frederic II, Latin Averroism, regalist juridical positions (e.g., in Bologna and Padua), a reawakening of the wisdom of pagan antiquity in the Italian renaissance and political absolutism, which burdened the canonical self-understanding of both late medieval and counter-reformational papal authority as supreme arbiter in all human affairs. The Holy See did not agree with the peace treaties of Augsburg (1555) and Westphalia (1648) which confirmed the gains of Protestantism in Northern Europe. The Enlightenment was largely put forth by anti-clerical intellectual circles. The horror of revolutionary terror fostered a withdrawal into medieval scholastic bastions from where evolutionary perspectives of reality were to be barred as menacing God's Holy City.

5. Perspectives of Evolving Life versus Authoritarian Interpretation of Nature and Law

The increase of papal authority since the 11th century had certainly benefitted from a series of forged legal documents to begin with the Constantinian donation of the Carolingian era. Pope Gregory VII succeeded with his daring and revolutionary shift of supreme authority from the (western) emperor to the Holy See (which of course did not matter to the Byzantine emperor); and Pope Innocent III successfully took on the title "Vicar of Christ" against imperial claims. But the

---

[8] Cf. Rudolf Otto, *Das Heilige. Über das Irrationale in der Idee des Göttlichen und sein Verhältnis zum Rationalen* (München: C.H. Beck, 1963; Erstausgabe 1917).

reappraisal of antiquity had since the 15th century resulted in the first demythologizing achievements of historical criticism which then furnished high ambitions for the interdenominational controversies resulting from the Protestant Reformation. The ardor of both reformers and counter-reformers provoked the first representatives of the Enlightenment to throw doubts on the credibility of both Catholics and Protestants already early in the 17th century.[9] By the end of the same century, we see Leibniz trying in intensive correspondence to scale down all entrenched interdenominational controversies. And in the Netherlands and France historical and literary criticism both of the Old and the New Testament raises its head against enormous resistance both within Judaism and the Christian Churches. But the new perspective is taken up by Protestant theologians and philosophers a century later in Germany. Meanwhile, Anthony Ashley-Cooper, Earl of Shaftesbury (1671-1713) in England, Gianbattista Vico (1668-1744) in Italy, Jean-Jacques Rousseau in France and Johann Gottfried Herder (1744-1803) in Germany dared to challenge both Church theologians and rationalist Enlighteners with the reality of sentiment and of human development as decisive factors of any type of cultural, linguistic, religious and philosophical endeavor. While Vico argues on the basis of biblical data, classical Greek culture and Roman Law, Herder tunes in on Celtic, German, Slavic, Baltic popular traditions north of the Alpes.

The revolutionary overthrow of the absolutist "ancien regime" in France and the initial success of Napoleon's attempt to establish a new order in Europe inspired no less than the above mentioned "anti-rationalists," a new generation of philosophers who tried to describe a developmental unfolding of the human spirit and culture under the headings of idealism and phenomenology. Although they were much too closely allied with the ruling political and economic activists to be credible speakers of the dispossessed class of industrial workers, socialist theoreticians spelled out pragmatic ideologies of victorious progress on the basis of a mere materialistic and authoritarian determinism, without sufficient regard upon human individual and personal aspirations and claims of consideration for tradition, religion and dignity of persons and cultural groupings.

Since western political, cultural and religious developments had fostered new visions of individual human dignity – still criminally disregarded in medieval religious and superstitious persecutions up to the Age of Enlightenment – the declarations of human rights, promoted first in the American and then in French political upheavals, gained persuasive momentum in the long run – culminating in the founding of the United Nations which, against the backdrop of the brutal totalitarian systems in the 20th century, became a new anchor of hope in their efforts to allow for peaceful promotion of human individual as well as social rights in manifold varieties of personal and collective self-expression. Blinded by

---

[9] Cf. Michel Despland, *La religion en occident. Evolution des idées et du vécu* (Montreal: Fides, 1979) und Ernst Feil, *Religio. Dritter Band: Die Geschichte eines neuzeitlichen Grundbegriffs im 17. und frühen 18. Jahrhundert* (Göttingen: Vandenhoeck und Ruprecht, 2001).

her monarchical quasi-imperial self-constitution as centralistic autocracy, the Roman Catholic Church acknowledged the various declarations of human rights since the French Revolution only in the climate and ambiance of Vatican Council II.

Even beyond all differences of opinion between West and East, North and South concerning the preference and applicability of individual or social human rights, the collapse of both fascist and Bolshevik systems in the 20th century has confirmed and strengthened the democratic principle of the sovereignty of the people as the basis of all forms of government in the framework of the United Nations. Fundamentalistic adherents of Judaism, Christianity, and Islam, of course, always argue from authority – the revealed will and law of God as pinned down in Holy Books. Yet, in the world's striving for peace, the three abrahamitic religions barely represent half the population of the globe. Their reference to revelation from on high can hardly be expected to be understandable and as such acceptable to the larger half of the world population, Hindus, Buddhists, Animists and Atheists. And since from the point of view of the science of religion, faith in God cannot be considered other than one, however valuable, interpretation of the human existential situation, professed in utmost earnest and engagement, among others. Thus a serious and unavoidable question arises, namely, whether any universal legislation equally applicable to all human individuals and societies can be and may be pronounced in the name and under the auspices of God. The issue has been hotly debated within the European Community, which had to give in to French insistence to abide with the term "spirituality" rather than "religion" in the Treaty of Lisbon (2007). It should not be overlooked that the unacceptability of a theistic worldview in the self-definition of the United Nations constitutes most likely the primary reason why the Vatican State cannot acquiesce to more than observer status at this highest representation of the peoples of present day humanity. That this mini-state has neither a democratic constituency nor operational procedures remains secondary in view of the basic difference in "spiritual" orientation.

The Holy See and/or the Vatican State is internationally recognized with diplomatic representations by a great number of the nations of the world, but has only consultative status at the United Nations. Both for doctrinal and political reasons the Church State does not adhere to the principle of the sovereignty of the people in its self-concept. Similar political outlooks are, of course, still taken for granted by Arab princes profiting from rich oil ressources. Their legitimacy is upheld by descendency from or faithfulness to the Prophet Mohammed.

The quasi-imperial and absolutist authority of the Pope accounts, of course, also for the similar observer relationship of the Holy See towards the World Council of Churches in Geneva. This highest ecumenical body is constituted by democratically appointed representatives of its member Churches. Fullfledged membership presupposes synodal structures within each Church. Doctrinal differences among member Churches are considered secondary to the common consciousness of being the Chosen People of God by baptism and faith in Jesus Christ as Redeemer of the World by Divine Providence and in the power of the

Holy Spirit. This profession of faith gives witness to the Lordship of Jesus Christ by his devout and faithful followers. The impressive witness of Christian martyrs, who have laid down their lives giving testimony to their unconditional attachment to Jesus Christ and his Gospel message of the Kingdom of God, has throughout the centuries constituted the unquestionable impact of the Risen Christ's dynamic presence in the transformation of this world under God's kingship over and above all varieties of structural organization, operation and worship traditions of the member Churches.

Under the two Popes John Paul II and Benedict XVI the idea was contemplated to interact with the ancient Churches of the East on the basis of the common tradition of the first millenium again in order to facilitate ecumenical reapproachment the Roman Catholic Church. This proposal contained definite risks for the understanding of jurisdiction in the Roman tradition. The hierarchies of the East insist on their sacramental responsibilities for the flocks entrusted to them. Jurisdiction to them means good coordination of pastoral services. But they do not recognize a worldwide jurisdiction attributed by divine right to the Bishop of Rome and Patriarch of the Latin West, which Vatican Council I has proclaimed along with the (however limited) doctrinal infallibility of the Pope. Both Orthodox faithful and Protestants refuse to grant the Pope the status of *episcopus universalis*, although they may see him as *primus inter pares*.

The Roman concept of jurisdiction is hardly identifiable in the Bible. Since late antiquity it has been tied up with autocratic imperial rule in God's name – so can it really be considered an appropriate model for papal authority?

6. Acknowledging Irreconcilable Differences on Authority in the Church

Not a few ecumenical idealists in so-called "mainline Churches" and also within the Roman Catholic Church have neglected to give more attention to the radical iconoclastic fringes of the Protestant Reformation which were present as early as 1521/1522. Already the Waldensians, English Wycliffites and Bohemian Hussites had shown strong leanings toward conceptions of a "Church from below" (a term the post-Vatican II critical movement in Germany has taken up as motto). Only a few years after the publication of Martin Luther's 95 theses, radical reformers in Germany and Switzerland destroyed not only religious works of art, but proclaimed a popular Church on the basis of two principles: baptism only for adults (including young adults) and the basic sovereignty of each local Christian community. The Anabaptists ("Wiedertäufer," as they were called in German) were suppressed with military and political power within Germany, but they survived in the Netherlands, in England and even in some German principalities. While British Congregationalists and Unitarians founded colonies in New England in the 17th century, the southern colonies along the North-American East-Coast were by and large founded by Anglican landowners, who employed Baptist overseers and African slaves. This is the reason why the South of the USA soon became the primary region of Baptist stance. While in the Caribbean and South American colonies African cults had a chance to survive in secret, so that today Afro-

American religions represent a major share of religious movements south of Central America – the Baptist overseers on the tobacco- and cotton farms in the southern colonies and states saw to it that the slaves under their rule also became Baptist Christians. With a creativity, which may be compared only with the cultural and religious survival of Israel in exile, the North American slaves developed the musical culture of the spirituals, within the most basic conditions of Baptist understanding of Christian life. Yet, this distinctive style of pious musical outcries impressed even the white masters in such fashion that eventually the civil rights movement, largely initiated and led by black Church ministers, could carry the day in the mid-1960s, although race discrimination was not easy to eradicate.

Whosoever engages in interdenominational dialogue among the Churches should neither ignore nor overlook nor downplay the major differences concerning the nature, purpose and functioning of Church ministry. The Roman Catholic Church, the Eastern Churches both of Byzantine and non-Byzantine traditions, and the Anglican High Church profess a hierarchy installed by Christ and therefore of "divine right," as they say, and reserved to males. The acceptance of women as priests in North America in the second half of the 20th century, thereafter also in the other countries of Anglo-Saxon tradition, has in the meantime undermined the divine right argumentation within the Anglican Communion. The mainline Protestant Churches, such as Lutherans, Calvinists and Methodists operate in national Church associations under guiding synods, but insist on the historically developed appropriateness of their organizational structure, including the position of bishops, ministers and deacons, male or female, and of any other offices by Church initiative. The Methodist reform of Anglicanism in the 18th and 19th centuries brought forth the so-called "Holiness movement" which in turn became the "Pentecostal Movement" around 1900. Also at the beginning of the 20th century, other members of Protestant Pietism, mainly in the "Bible Belt" in the southern and western United States, defined themselves by insisting on the "fundamentals" of the Christian faith, i.e., the Divine Trinity, the divinity of Christ, the literal uncritical understanding of the words of Holy Scripture, etc. Pentecostal communities mostly call themselves in English "Assemblies of God." And although they derived from the Anglican-Methodist tradition, they insist like the above mentioned Baptist Christians on the self-sufficiency and autonomy of each local congregation, including the choice of ministers and the mere associative, but non-canonical, character of any intercongregational associations, like the very important Southern Baptist Convention in the USA.

We see within the ecumenical movement of the 20th century, first of all, alongside the urging of interdenominational agreements on mission promotion, the efforts of the mainline Churches in the Faith and Order Commission to arrive at mutually satisfying theological approachments, reconciliations and agreements. Towards the end of the century, the Secretary of the World Council of Churches (WCC) Konrad Raiser succeeded in integrating also a good number of Baptist and Pentecostal Churches with their more pragmatic notions of Church leadership and administration, much to the displeasure of both the Orthodox Churches and the Roman Catholic Church. But it is well known that on all continents there exist hundreds, if not thousands, of free-lance Churches, mostly catering to specific charismatic or clever leaders, which disregard the preoccupation of the mainline Churches with Christian unity. Similar self-sufficiency stands out as a stunning feature of the new big television churches in America and in South Korea. Their popularity among baptized or mere cultural Christians, otherwise unchurched, reveals pastoral needs.

Since in Reformation times, with the exception of Waldensians, Moravian Brothers, Anabaptists, Unitarians, Schwenkfeldians and other "Schwarmgeister" (fanatics), the Protestant Churches profited from either princely or at least aristocratic support (in France and the Netherlands); state authority remained a major foundation of Church existence. The denominational variety among colonists in North-America prepared, however, the "separation of Church and State" when the thirteen colonies obtained their independence from the British Crown in 1783 which was integrated as a principle in the Constitution of the United States in the years to follow. Definitively since that time, to be Christian did not necessarily mean to adhere to any specific Church, but to have been baptized and to choose one's local congregation following one's personal preference. Among Protestant Americans, "my Church" refers by and large to the local Church frequented. Although this did never apply to American Catholics, they too profited enormously from the religious freedom guaranteed by the separation of Church and State, in spite of the fact that they too could never obtain a higher degree of public recognition in civil law than that of a legally registered and administered association with tax privileges accorded to charities and institutions of public interest and welfare. It was the benefit drawn from this situation which made the American Bishops and theologians the primary promoters of the Declaration on Religious Liberty (*Dignitatis humanae*) at Vatican Council II. Since this principle is not yet generally recognized in the Muslim world and certain strata of Hindu society, its weight cannot be rated high enough in our culturally pluralistic societies of the third Christian millennium.

American Protestantism has not only marked profoundly the national tradition of the United States but has proven its Christian fervor on the foreign mission scene, increasingly so by initiative of fundamentalist evangelical groupings, who in recent decades enjoyed even the sympathetic support of conservative American governments for their astonishingly successful proselytizing efforts in Latin America. The impoverished masses certainly do not digest well any more complicated canonical and/or theological Church doctrines, but are rather taken in by plain rhetoric and arguments accompanied by means of social and economic advancement. In formerly colonial Africa, the mainline Churches and especially the Roman Catholic Church have succeeded well in their missions south of the Sahara and the Sahel. But there likewise, understandable frictions with colonial missionaries and post-colonial difficulties provided all too many instances for the establishment of small independent Churches under whatever kind of charismatic leaders. The Roman Catholic Church may frown upon such chaotic multiplication of Christian communities beyond hierarchical control. But it would be preposterous to deny such preaching any value whatsoever for Christian witness. Even considerable evidence for religious syncretism among christianized indigenous populations in America, Africa and Asia is not so new, if we compare these phenomena with pre-modern forms of popular superstition in Europe, e.g., the witchhunts up to the 18th century. Divine Providence is more patient than any religious police. Popular religion is very resistant to any kind of institutional or academic indoctrination.

7. Missionary Fervor as a Remedy against Impediments to Christian Unity

Alongside the Oxford Movement in the Anglican Church of the 1830s and 1840s, pietistic groups formed in 1846 in London the Evangelical Alliance, which strove after Christian reunification both in mission situations and in the home countries. In 1854 New York and London hosted World Mission Conferences. In 1855 Paris hosted the first World Conference of the YMCA (Young Men's Christian Association), which had been founded twelve years earlier in London. The founding resolution of this World Conference already contains the brief but effective dogmatic basis of the World Council of Churches, established in 1948. The British Empire and French colonial politics facilitated contacts between various missionary initiatives both on the Protestant and the Catholic side. Further World Mission Conferences were held in Liverpool (1860), in London (1878 and 1888), and in New York (1900). Here the word "ecumenical" was introduced. The following World Mission Conference in Edinburgh (1910) was to launch the official Ecumenical Movement of the 20th century. Yet, already in the second half of the 19th century, we see the emergence of new worldwide denominational groupings within the English speaking sphere – the Lambeth Conference of Anglican Churches (1867), the World Alliance of Reformed Churches (1875), the Ecumenical Conference of Methodists (1881), the Union of Congregationalists (1891) and even a World Federation of Baptist Churches (1905).

At the Edinburgh conference in 1910, 1,335 delegates of various Missionary Institutes were assembled, among them only 17 representatives from Asian mission countries. Africa and Latin America were practically not represented at all. The questions of "Faith and Order" were left to later Church meetings. The American Anglicanism of the U.S. Episcopalian Church exercised predominant weight. The most important decision of the Conference was the establishment of a permanent committee which during the following years organized 21 regional and national Conferences and already in 1921 established the International Mission Council and the *International Review of Missions*. They were to deliver a major contribution to the founding of the WCC in 1948. In 1961 the International Mission Council was integrated into the WCC.[10] Since the 1970s the Mission Conferences more and more turned into platforms for discussing political situations and orientations, too. The young Churches in the developing countries often spoke up with passionate protests against western outlooks and priorities. 1980

---

[10] Cf. Peter Neuner, *Ökumenische Theologie. Die Suche nach der Einheit der christlichen Kirchen* (Darmstadt: Wissenschaftliche Buchgesellschaft, 1997), pp. 25-29.

saw two conferences held at about the same time: one in Melbourne, Australia, the other one in Pattaya, Thailand. The latter was clearly more traditionally missionary and evangelical, bent on world evangelization. In distinction from trends at the WCC, social questions received less emphasis The astounding phenomenon is that throughout the 20th century Baptist and Pentecostal and other Evangelical groups have increased their share in Christian missionary enterprises up to almost 20% of all such Christian initiatives, last not least by proselytizing in Latin America.

The WCC had succeeded in blending three ecumenical movements: the International Mission Conferences, the movement "Life and Work" of practical Christian witness, and the dogmatic movement "Faith and Order" working on theological agreements on worship and ecclesiology.[11] The renown inspirer of "Life and Work" was the Swedish Lutheran Bishop Nathan Söderblom (1866–1931). In 1925, he invited to a Conference on Practical Christianity in Stockholm. For the first time, Anglican, Protestant, and Orthodox Churches were represented by official delegations. Two years later, a first conference on "Faith and Order" convened in Lausanne, Switzerland.[12] In 1937, "Faith and Order" held a second World Conference in Edinburgh and "Life and Work" in Oxford. They joined forces in 1938 in Utrecht and definitively at the founding of the WCC in Amsterdam in 1948. "Faith and Order" held a third World Conference in 1952 in Lund, Sweden, which served to prepare the second WCC Plenary Assembly in Evanston near Chicago. The third WCC Plenary Assembly in New Delhi enlarged the basic Profession of Faith in Jesus Christ as Lord and Redeemer to a trinitarian formula, which allowed the Orthodox and ancient Eastern Churches to join the WCC. Great hope prevailed that soon enough, also with the preparation of the Vatican Council II, the longed for unity in the faith might be achieved. But since 2000 not much ecumenical progress has been achieved.

Among the outstanding contributions of American evangelical missionary initiatives we have to mention the Bible apostolate, especially of the Wycliffe-Society, with her enormous personal and financial engagement to translate the Bible into all known languages of the world in the confidence that this publication campaign will produce sympathetic interest in Christianity. In recent decades, Bible editions have been issued in high numbers in Japan, Korea and China. The editorial offices of Verbum Bible of the S.V.D. have for half a century published complete or partial Bible editions in many African languages and continue their important apostolate.

---

[11] Both movements resulted from the Edinburgh Conference in 1910. The "Commission on Life and Work" was devoted to developing a consensus between different Churches based on the idea of service. The "Faith and Order Commission" for doctrinal issues aimed at "exhibiting more clearly the unity [of the Churches] that their empirical divisions obscured." See Robert McAfee Brown, "Ecumenical Movement," in: Mircea Eliade (ed.), *Encyclopedia of Religion*. Vol. 5 (London – New York: MacMillan, 1987), pp. 18f.

[12] Cf. Peter Neuner, *Ökumenische Theologie*, pp. 30-39.

8. Conclusion

Cultural diversifications of Christianity's "New Way" have become obvious ever since the movement for the establishment of the Kingdom of God by Jesus of Nazareth has found adherents and disciples in and beyond the city of his Passion and Resurrection, Jerusalem in Judaea. As ancient legends about the dispersion of the twelve Apostles bear out: the Christian faith made its way not only into the West, then dominated by the Greco-Roman civilization, but also eastward into the kingdom of the Parthians, India, and, later on, China. The recent discussions about the origins of the Qur'an have shed new light on the continuation of a non-Hellenistic brand of Christianity in Syria, Mesopotamia, Armenia, and Persia, which has left traces in the development of Islam and which lived on little affected by the early imperial and Ecumenical Councils. Philip Jenkins has recently published an important book on this "lost history of Christianity."[13] If we heed well the heritage of the first 1,000 years of Christianity, an honest disposition for interdenominational dialogue among Christians cannot forego a vivid interest in the lived and living faith of the surviving witnesses of the ancient Christian Churches, now the victims of warfare in the Near East under extreme pressure to leave their homelands. May their suffering help to melt any dogmatic intransigence of ours.

Appendix:
Ecumenical Conferences and Assemblies (under Protestant Auspices), 1897–2006

World Mission Conferences

- 1897 London (United Kingdom)
- 1910 Edinburgh (United Kingdom)
- 1921 Founding of the International Missionary Council (Lake Mohonk, NY)
- 1926 Le Zoute (Belgium)
- 1928 Jerusalem
- 1938 Tambaran (near Madras)
- 1947 Whitby (Canada)
- 1952 Willingen (Germany)
- 1958 Achimota (near Accra, Ghana)
- 1963 Mexico City
- 1973 Bangkok (Thailand)
- 1980 Melbourne, (Australia)

---

[13] Cf. Philip Jenkins, *The Lost History of Christianity. The Thousand-Year Golden Age of the Church in the Middle East, Africa, and Asia – and How It Died* (New York: Harper Collins, 2008). German edition: *Das Goldene Zeitalter des Christentums. Die vergessene Geschichte der größten Weltreligion*. Aus dem amerikanischen Englisch übersetzt von Gerlind Baumann (Freiburg i.Br.: Herder, 2010).

1989 San Antonio, (USA)
1996 San Salvador (El Salvador)

"Life and Work" Conferences

1925 Stockholm (Sweden)
1937 Oxford (United Kingdom)
1966 Geneva (Switzerland)
1979 Boston (USA)
1990 Seoul (South Korea)

"Faith and Order" Conferences

1920 Appeal to Unity by the Anglican Lambeth Conference – which recommends the worldwide adoption of an Episcopalian Church Order, yet without hierarchical connotations.

1927 Lausanne (Switzerland)
1937 Edinburgh (United Kingdom)
1938 Utrecht (Netherlands): preparing the Constitution for the WCC in Lund, Sweden (1952)
1963 Montreal (Canada)
1974 Accra (Ghana)
1978 Bangalore (India)
1982 Lima (Peru)
1993 Santiago de Compostela (Spain)

WCC Plenary Assemblies

1948 Amsterdam (Netherlands)
1954 Evanston (USA)
1961 New Delhi (India)
1968 Uppsala (Sweden)
1975 Nairobi (Kenya)
1983 Vancouver (Canada)
1991 Canberra (Australia)
1998 Harare (Zimbabwe)
2006 Porto Allegre (Brazil)
2014 Pusan (South Korea)

NOTES ON CONTRIBUTORS

Piotr Adamek S.V.D. is director of the Monumenta Serica Institute in Sankt Augustin (Germany), editor of the journal *Chiny Dzisiaj*, and associate professor at the Philosophical-Theological Faculty S.V.D. (Philosophisch-Theologische Hochschule SVD) in Sankt Augustin. His research interests concern the history of Christianity in China, the historiography of China, and the history of Sinology. His publications include *A Good Son Is Sad if He Hears the Name of His Father. The Tabooing of Names in China as a Way of Implementing Social Values* (Sankt Augustin 2015) and various articles about the Orthodox Church in China (2008–2014).

Françoise Aubin is a scholar of Sinology, Mongol and Islamic Studies and a director emerita of the French National Center for Scientific Studies (CNRS) and the Centre for International Studies (CERI). Her broad research interests include the legal and political history of Mongolia, East Asian missionary history, in particular the mission of the Scheut order (C.I.C.M.) in Inner Mongolia, and the history of Chinese Islam. Among her publications are more than a thousand book reviews and many path-breaking articles, e.g., "La statut de l'enfant dans la société mongole," in: *L'Enfant* (Bruxelles: Éditions de la Librarie encyclopédique, 1975), pp. 459-599, and "En Islam chinois: quels Naqshbandi?" in: Marc Gaborieau – Alexandre Popovic – Thierry Zarcone (eds.), *Naqshbandi. Cheminements et situation actuelle d'un ordre mystique musulman* (Istanbul – Paris: Ed. Isis, 1990), pp. 491-572.

Claudia von Collani is a Catholic missiologist with additional studies in Sinology and Japanology. Her special field is East Asian missionary history including the Chinese Rites Controversy, inculturation, mission theology of early modern times, cultural exchange between Europe and East Asia, history of science and medicine, and especially Chinese Figurism. She is affiliated to the chair of Missiology and Dialogue of Religions, Faculty for Catholic Theology at the University of Würzburg. She has recently edited, together with Paul Rule, the first volume of *The Acta Pekinensia or Historical Records of the Maillard de Tournon Legation* (Roma – Macau: Institutum Historicum Societatis Iesu – Ricci Institute, 2015) and, together with Erich Zettl, *Johannes Schreck-Terrentius SJ. Wissenschaftler und China-Missionar (1576–1630)* (Stuttgart: Steiner, 2016).

Gianni Criveller P.I.M.E. is a Roman Catholic missionary priest, member of Pontifical Institute for Foreign Missions, and is responsible for the on-going formation programs in various countries. He is also a fellow researcher at The Chinese University of Hong Kong, The Faculty of Arts – Centre for Catholic Studies (since 2004). He specializes on the historical encounter between China and Christianity with particular attention to the reception of Christianity in China, Hong

Kong, and Macau; the Jesuit mission; missionary work and strategies and the Chinese Rites Controversy. Among his recent publications are: *500 Hundred Years of Italians in Hong Kong and Macau*, coauthored with Angelo Paratico, Alessandra Schiavo and Margot Errante (Hong Kong: Società Dante Alighieri di Hong Kong, 2013; Italian ed., Milan 2014; Chinese ed., Hong Kong 2014); *La malinconia immaginativa di Matteo Ricci* (Milano: Quaderni del Museo Popoli e Culture, 2016).

Irene Eber is Louis Frieberg Professor of Asian Studies (emerita), Department of Asian Studies, The Hebrew University, Mt. Scopus, Jerusalem. Her research is centered on transcultural issues, to which she has recently added Yiddish writings about Chinese history, culture, and Confucianism. Among her works is the recently published monograph *Wartime Shanghai and the Jewish Refugees from Central Europe. Survival, Co-Existence, and Identity in a Multi-Ethnic City* (Berlin – Boston: Walter de Gruyter, 2012). She also edited the works of Martin Buber on Chinese philosophy and literature: *Martin Buber Werkausgabe*, Teil 2./3. *Schriften zur chinesischen Philosophie und Literatur* (Gütersloh: Gütersloher Verlagshaus, 2013).

Pier Francesco Fumagalli, vice prefetto of the Ambrosiana, Milan doctor of the Bibliotheca Ambrosiana, director of the classes of Far Eastern Studies, and Near Eastern Studies at the Accademia Ambrosiana. Contract professor of Chinese Culture at Catholic University of Milan in Brescia; adjoint professor (2008–2014) of the Institute of Christianity and Cross-cultural Studies at Zhejiang University, Hangzhou; Consultant of the Institute of Morality and Religions, Tsinghua University, Beijing. Director of the book series: Asiatica Ambrosiana, vols. I-VIII and Orientalia Ambrosiana, vols. II-V. Recent publications include: "Faith, Science and Social Harmony. The Dialogue among Jews, Christians and Muslims, 1913–2013," in: *L'educazione nella società asiatica – Education in Asian Societies*, ed. Kuniko Tanaka, (Milano – Roma: Biblioteca Ambrosiana – Bulzoni Editore, 2014), pp. 319-330.

Marián Gálik is professor emeritus of Comenius University, Bratislava, Slovakia. His research comprises modern and contemporary Chinese literature, traditional Chinese literature, Sino-Western comparative literature and partly philosophy, Sino-Western intellectual history, the sacred and the secular in Israel, Judah and China in the first millennium B.C. The Monumenta Serica Institute published his monograph *Influence, Translation and Parallels. Selected Studies on the Bible in China* (Nettetal: Steyler Verlag, 2004). Recently his seminal work *Mao Dun and Modern Chinese Literary Criticism* (1969) was translated into Chinese: Mali'an Gaolike 馬立安·高利克, *Mao Dun yu Zhongguo xiandai wenxue piping* 茅盾與中國現代文學批評 (Xin Taibei shi: Hua Mulan wenhua, 2014).

Franz Günther Gessinger S.V.D. is a missionary priest and member of the Anthropos Institute. The theological presentation of faith, hope, and charity led him to approach the topic from the point of view of science of religion. Lively contacts with Protestants since his first schooling facilitated his engagement in ecumenical pastoral programs in the USA, Canada, Germany and France. In 1991/1992 he edited the basic German text in Zenon Stężycki (ed.), *Atlas Hierarchicus* (5th rev. ed., Wien: St. Gabriel, 1992). Since 2004 he has published a series of sermons and articles in the review *Die Anregung* (since 2012 online).

Winfried Glüer, is a retired pastor and worked earlier at the Christian Study Centre on Chinese Religion and Culture in Hong Kong. He was guest lecturer at Theology Division, Chung Chi College, and Chinese University of Hong Kong. Among his publications concerned with T.C. Chao, there are: *Christliche Theologie in China. T.C. Chao* (Christian Theology in China: T.C. Chao; Gütersloh: Gütersloher Verlagshaus Gerd Mohn, 1979; Chinese ed. in traditional Chinese characters: Hong Kong 1998 and in simplified Chinese characters: Shanghai 1999); "T.C. Chao and the Quest for Life and Meaning," *China Notes* 18 (1980) 4, pp. 120-133; "T.C. Chao 1988-1979. Scholar, Teacher, Gentle Mystic," in: Gerald Anderson (ed.), in: *Mission Legacies. Biographical Studies of Leaders of the Modern Missionary Movement* (Maryknoll et al.: Orbis Books, 1994), pp. 225-229.

Noël Golvers is a senior researcher at the Department of Sinology of the Katholieke Universiteit Leuven (Belgium). His research focuses on the Jesuit mission in China (17th – 18th centuries) and its contribution to the history of science and book history. His main publications concern the astronomical corpus of Ferdinand Verbiest (*Astronomia Europaea*, 1993, 2003, 2011), the Account Book of François de Rougemont (1993), and *Libraries of Western Learning for China; Circulation of Western Books between Europe and China in the Jesuit Mission* (ca. 1650 – ca. 1750), 3 vols. (Leuven: Ferdinand Verbiest Institute, 2012-2015). Currently he prepares a new critical edition of the correspondence of F. Verbiest.

Vincent Goossaert obtained his Ph.D. at Ecole pratique des hautes études (EPHE, 1997). He was a research fellow at Centre national de la recherche scientifique (CNRS, 1998–2012) and is now Professor of Daoism and Chinese religions at EPHE and since 2014 also dean of the EPHE Graduate School. He has been Visiting Professor at the Chinese University of Hong Kong, Geneva University, and Renmin University in Beijing. His research deals with the social history of Chinese religion in late imperial and modern times. He has published books on the Daoist clergy, anticlericalism, Chinese dietary taboos, the production of moral norms, and, with David Palmer, *The Religious Question in Modern China* (Chicago: University of Chicago Press, 2011; Levenson Prize 2013).

Jeroom Heyndrickx C.I.C.M. (Scheut) was a missionary in Taiwan (beginning in 1957). In 1982 he founded the Ferdinand Verbiest Institute at Louvain University (Belgium) for academic research on the Church in China and later the Chinese College Leuven for pastoral cooperation with the Chinese Church. He taught Pastoral Theology at several Major Seminaries in China and published mainly on this field and on the Church in China, most recently "Towards an Ecclesiology and Spirituality for Cooperation with the Church in China," *Lumen. Journal of Catholic Studies* 2 (2014) 2, pp. 56-74.

Barbara Hoster works as an editor at the Monumenta Serica Institute, Sankt Augustin. Her research interests include modern and contemporary Chinese literature and its relation to the Christian faith, as well as the history of Sinology, in particular the history of *Monumenta Serica*. She published a number of articles on these topics as well as the monographic study *Konversion zum Christentum in der modernen chinesischen Literatur. Su Xuelin's Roman* Jixin *(Dornenherz, 1929)* (Gossenberg: Ostasien Verlag, 2017).

Jiang Ryh-Shin 江日新 is the editor-in-chief of *Legein Semi-Annual Journal* and adjunct assistant professor at Hsing Wu University (New Taipei City, Taiwan). His research focuses on comparative philosophy, Confucianism, Daoism, modern western philosophy as well as philosophical anthropology. His recent publications include: "How Philosophical is the Philosophy of *Laozi*? From a Sinological to a Philosophical Interpretation" (Chin.: National Central University Ph.D. diss., 2015); "Biophilia, Contemplation in Nature and Tao. Meng Xiangsen and His Literary-Philosophical Style of Environmental Writings," *Applied Ethics Review* 53 (2012), pp. 1-30.

Wolfgang Kubin (Chinese name: Gu Bin 顾彬) is professor emeritus of the University of Bonn (2011). He currently works as senior professor in Beijing Foreign Studies University where he teaches inter alia Sinology. Among his major works as editor and author are: *Die Geschichte der chinesischen Literatur* (History of Chinese Literature; up to now 9 vols., München: Saur, 2002-); *Die klassischen chinesischen Denker* (Classical Chinese Thinkers; up to now 7 vols., Freiburg: Herder, 2011-); *Lu Xun Werke* (Selected Works of Lu Xun, 6 vols., Zürich: Unionsverlag, 1994). He is also a translator of modern Chinese literature and a writer (poems, essays, and novels).

Angelo S. Lazzarotto P.I.M.E. is a member of the Pontifical Institute for Foreign Missions. He intermittently worked as a missionary in Hong Kong and in the church administration in Rome. In Hong Kong he helped in 1980 to start the Holy Spirit Study Centre and the *Tripod/Ding* 鼎 magazine, to which he often contributed. He published widely in Italian and English, e.g., *The Catholic Church in Post-Mao China* (1982), which also had Italian and Chinese editions.

Leopold Leeb S.V.D. obtained his Ph.D. from Peking University in 1999. Since 2004 he has been professor at Renmin University of China (Beijing) and School of Liberal Arts. He is also a teacher of the classical western languages (Latin, Greek, classical Hebrew). His fields of interest are the history of the classical western languages in China, history of Christianity in China, and the translation of philosophical and theological terms. Recent publications: *Zhongguo Jidu zongjiao shi cidian: Han-Ying duizhao* 中国基督宗教史辞典—汉英对照 (*A Dictionary of the History of Christianity in China*; Beijing: Zongjiao wenhua, 2013), *Gu Xilayu rumen jiaocheng* 古希腊语入门教程 (*Textbook for Classical Greek*; Beijing: Lianhe, 2014), *Sino-Theology and the Philosophy of History. A Collection of Essays by Liu Xiaofeng*, translated with a commentary by Leopold Leeb (Leiden: Brill, 2015).

Tiziana Lippiello is professor in the Department of Asian and North African Studies at Ca' Foscari University of Venice. Her research focuses on classical Chinese ethics, divination, and mantic practices. Her recent publications are: "Zhongyong 'cheng' zhi mei yu Li Madou de chanshi" 中庸"誠"之美与利玛窦的阐释 (On the Beauty of *cheng* [authenticity] in the *Zhongyong* 中庸 and Matteo Ricci's Interpretation), in: Zhang Zhigang 张志刚 (ed.), *Meimei yu gong. Renlei wenming jiaoliu yujian zhanlan* 美美与共—人类文明交流互鉴的回顾与展望 (Beauty through Each Other's Eyes. Retrospection and Outlook on the Exchanges and Mutual Learning among Civilizations; Beijing: Zongjiao wenhua, 2016 [forthcoming]); "Measuring Human Relations. Continuities and Discontinuities in the Reading of the *Lunyu*," in: T. Lippiello – Chen Yuehong – M. Barenghi (eds.), *Linking Ancient and Contemporary. Continuities and Discontinuities in Chinese Literature* (Venezia: Edizioni Ca' Foscari, 2016).

Eugenio Menegon is associate professor of Chinese History at Boston University. He has published extensively on the history of Chinese-Western relations, and is the author of *Ancestors, Virgins, and Friars. Christianity as a Local Religion in Late Imperial China* (Cambridge, Mass.: Harvard Asia Center Publication Programs and Harvard University Press, 2009). His current book project is an examination of the daily life and political networking of European residents at the Qing court in Beijing during the 17th – 18th centuries.

Monika Miazek-Męczyńska holds a Ph.D. in Classical Philology and is a researcher and lecturer in Latin at the Adam Mickiewicz University in Poznań (Poland). Since 1998 she has studied texts in Latin on the Jesuit mission in China, starting with Michał Boym's scientific work *Flora Sinensis*. Among her most recent publications are "*Indipetae Boymianae*. On Boym's Requests to the Jesuit General for a Missionary Appointment to China," *Monumenta Serica* 59 (2011), pp. 229-242; "The Personification of the Worst Stereotypes of the West. Charles Thomas Maillard de Tournon and His Legacy to Kangxi Emperor according to 'Acta Pekinensia'," in: *Acta Pekinensia. Western Historical Sources for the*

Kangxi Reign (Macau: Macau Ricci Institute, 2013), pp. 201-215; *Indipetae Polonae – kołatanie do drzwi misji chińskiej* (Indipetae Polonae. Knocking at the Door of Chinese Mission; Poznań: Wydawnictwo Naukowe Uniwersytetu im. Adama Mickiewicza, 2015).

Monika Motsch, professor of Sinology, University of Erlangen. Fields of study: Classical and modern Chinese literature, comparative literature translation. Selected publications: *Mit Bambusrohr und Ahle. Von Qian Zhongshus Guanzhuibian zu einer Neubetrachtung Du Fus* (Frankfurt am Main *et al.*: Lang, 1994). *Die chinesische Erzählung. Vom Altertum bis zur Neuzeit* (München: Saur, 2003). Collaborator in the edition of *Manuscripts of Qian Zhongshu. Foreign Language Notes / Qian Zhongshu shougao ji. Waiwen biji* 钱钟书手稿集—外文笔记, 49 vols. (Beijing: Shangwu, 2016). Translations: Yang Jiang 杨绛, *Wir Drei / Women sa* 我们仨 (bilingual ed.; Gossenberg: Ostasien Verlag, 2012). *Qian Zhongshu* 钱锺书: *Die umzingelte Festung / Weicheng* 围城 (bilingual ed., Beijing: Waiyu jiaoxue yu yanjiu chubanshe, 2016).

Matteo Nicolini-Zani (M.A. in Chinese Studies) is a Christian monk in the Monastery of Bose (Italy) and an independent researcher specializing in the study of Christianity in China. He wrote numerous articles on this subject in different languages. He translated and published in Italian the entire corpus of the "Sino-Nestorian" literature of the Tang dynasty (*La via radiosa per l'oriente* [Magnano: Qiqajon, 2006]). His latest work concerns the history of Christian monasticism in modern China: *Monaci cristiani in terra cinese* (Magnano: Qiqajon, 2014).

Pan Feng-Chuan 潘鳳娟 is professor at National Taiwan Normal University (Taibei). Her recent research focuses on Western translations of the Chinese classics, especially *Xiaojing* (Book of Filial Piety) and *Daodejing* (Book of *Laozi*), in 18th – 19th centuries. Her publications include *The Burgeoning of a Third Option. Re-Reading the Jesuit Mission in China from a Glocal Perspective* (Leuven: Ferdinand Verbiest Instituut, 2013) and *Xi lai Kongzi Ai Rulüe. Gengxin bianhua de zongjiao huiyu* 西來孔子艾儒略—更新變化的宗教會遇 (Confucius from the West. Giulio Aleni and the Religious Encounter between the Jesuits and the Chinese; Taibei: Bible Resource Center, 2002).

Chiara Piccinini is lecturer of Chinese language at Catholic University of the Sacred Heart, Milan, Italy. Her research interests focus on missionary linguistics and Chinese as a Second Language teaching. Recent publications include: Matteo Ricci S.J., *Il Castello della memoria. Xiguo Jifa (La mnemotecnica occidentale) e la sua applicazione allo studio dei caratteri cinesi*. Introduction, translation and notes by Chiara Piccinini. Ed. Angelo Guerini (Milano: Guerini e Associati, 2016).

Roderich Ptak is professor of Sinology (chair) at Ludwig-Maximilians-University of Munich (Germany). His research focuses on maritime Chinese history, Macau, traditional Chinese literature, animals in Chinese texts. His recent publications include *Studien zum Roman* Sanbao taijian Xiyang ji tongsu yanyi / Sanbao taijian Xiyang ji tongsu yanyi *zhi yanjiu*, 2 vols., edited with Shi Ping (Wiesbaden: Harrassowitz, 2011-2013) and *The Earliest Extant Bird List of Hainan. An Annotated Translation of the Avian Section in* Qiongtai zhi, coauthored with Hu Baozhu (Wiesbaden – Lissabon: Harrassowitz – Centro Científico e Cultural de Macau, 2015).

Ren Dayuan 任大援 graduated from China Northwest University with an M.A. degree in 1981. Since then he has dedicated himself to the studies of the history of Chinese philosophy and Chinese culture. Currently he is professor at the Chinese National Academy of Arts, distinguished professor at Beijing Foreign Studies University, deputy chief editor of *International Sinology* at BFSU and advisor of *Monumenta Serica*. His major publications are: *Fandigang cang Ming Qing Zhong-Xi wenhua jiaoliu shi wenxian congshu* 梵蒂冈藏明清中西文化交流史文献丛书 (Texts Series on the History of Cultural Exchange between China and the West in Ming and Qing Dynasties from the Vatican Library; editor-in-chief with Zhang Xiping *et al.* (Zhengzhou: Daxiang chubanshe, 2014); *Zhongguo sixiang shi (Ming Qing bian)* 中国思想史 (明清编) (The History of Chinese Thought: Ming and Qing Dynasty; Xi'an: Xibei daxue chubanshe, 2012).

Karl Josef Rivinius S.V.D. is professor emeritus of Church history at the Philosophical-Theological Faculty S.V.D. (Philosophisch-Theologische Hochschule SVD) at Sankt Augustin. His research focuses on Church history, history of mission and social history, with a particular interest in the history of the Catholic Church in China. Recent publications include: *Im Spannungsfeld von Mission und Politik. Johann Baptist Anzer (1851-1903), Bischof in Süd-Shandong* (Nettetal: Steyler Verlag, 2010); *Das Projekt einer katholischen Enzyklopädie für China* (Nettetal: Steyler Verlag, 2013); *Collegium Sinicum. Eine Bildungsanstalt für chinesische Priester in Peking* (Siegburg: Schmitt, 2015).

Paul A. Rule taught Religious Studies and Chinese History at La Trobe University (Melbourne, Australia). He is currently working on a multi-volume annotated translation of the *Acta Pekinensia* for the Macau Ricci Institute and a history of the Chinese Rites Controversy for the Ricci Institute at the University of San Francisco; many publications on Chinese Rites Controversy, cultural encounter between China and the West, Jesuit understanding of Confucius and Confucianism, and Christianity in China. A recent publication, co-edited with Claudia von Collani, is: *The Acta Pekinensia or Historical Records of the Maillard de Tournon Legation*, vol. 1 (Roma – Macau: Institutum Historicum Societatis Iesu – Ricci Institute, 2015).

Helwig Schmidt-Glintzer is senior professor at Eberhard-Karls-Universität Tübingen, director of the China Centrum Tübingen and former director of the Herzog August Bibliothek Wolfenbüttel (Research Library for Medieval and Early Modern Humanistic Studies). He holds a Ph.D. in Sinology (1973) from the University of Munich and completed his habilitation at the University of Bonn in 1979. His fields of research are Chinese history and culture, ideology of the Chinese literati, changes of value systems and spheres of knowledge. Recent publications include: *Wohlstand, Glück und langes Leben. Chinas Götter und die Ordnung im Reich der Mitte* (Frankfurt a.M. – Leipzig: Verlag der Weltreligionen, 2009); *China – eine Herausforderung für den Westen. Plädoyer für differentielle kulturelle Kompetenz* (Wiesbaden: Harrassowitz, 2011).

Christian Schwermann, Ph.D. (2005), University of Bonn, is lecturer of Classical Chinese at that university. He has published chiefly on early Chinese literature, including a monograph on the concept of stupidity in ancient Chinese texts (*"Dummheit" in altchinesischen Texten*; Wiesbaden: Harrassowitz, 2011), and co-edited a conference volume on authorship in East Asian literatures from the beginnings to the seventeenth century (*That Wonderful Composite Called Author*; Leiden: Brill, 2014).

Nicolas Standaert (Chinese name: Zhong Mingdan 鍾鳴旦) is professor of Sinology at the University of Leuven (Belgium). His major research interest is the cultural contacts between China and Europe in the 17th and 18th centuries. His recent publications include: *The Intercultural Weaving of Historical Texts. Chinese and European Stories about Emperor Ku and His Concubines* (Leiden: Brill, 2016), *Chinese Voices in the Rites Controversy. Travelling Books, Community Networks, Intercultural Arguments* (Roma: Institutum Historicum Societatis Iesu, 2012), *The Interweaving of Rituals. Funerals in the Cultural Exchange between China and Europe* (Seattle: University of Washington Press, 2008) and *An Illustrated Life of Christ Presented to the Chinese Emperor. The History of Jincheng shuxiang (1640)*. Monumenta Serica Monograph Series LIX (Sankt Augustin – Nettetal: Steyler Verlag, 2007).

Rolf Gerhard Tiedemann (Chinese name: Di Deman 狄德满) is professor of modern Chinese history at Shandong University (China). Previously he taught for many years in the School of Oriental and African Studies (University of London). His major research interest is the history of Chinese Christianity in the 19th and early 20th centuries. His recent publications include [Di Deman], *Xiwen Yihetuan wenxian ziliao huibian* 西文义和团文献资料汇编 (A Bibliography of Western Language Material on the Boxer Movement; Jinan: Shandong University Press, 2016), "Western Imperialism and the Settling of 'Missionary Cases'. With Particular Reference to Bishop Anzer in South Shandong," in: Ferdinand Verbiest Institute (eds.), *History of the Catholic Church in China. From Its Beginning to the Scheut Fathers and 20th Century. Unveiling Some Less Known Sources,*

Sounds and Pictures (Leuven: Ferdinand Verbiest Institute K.U. Leuven, 2015), pp. 235-259.

Ursula Toyka is a scholar of East Asian Art History (Ph.D. 1979 and habilitation 2004, University of Bonn). She currently works as resident director of German Academic Exchange Service (DAAD), Japan Office, Tokyo. Her research interests are: Buddhist art of China, Japan and Korea, contemporary East Asian, especially Chinese Art, intercultural encounters between China, Japan and Korea with western cultures (late 19th and early 20th centuries), artists' biographies and history of exhibitions. She recently published *The Splendours of Paradise. Murals and Epigraphic Documents at the Early Ming Buddhist Monastery Fahai Si*, 2 vols. Monumenta Serica Monograph Series LXIII/1-2 (Sankt Augustin: Institut Monumenta Serica, 2014).

Paul U. Unschuld is director of the Horst-Görtz-Endowment Institute for History, Theory and Ethics of Chinese Life Sciences of Charité-Universitätsmedizin Berlin. His research over the past four decades has focused on the comparative history of medicine and health care delivery systems in Europe and China. His recent publications include a first philological translation of the *Huang Di Nei Jing Ling Shu. The Ancient Chinese Classic of Needle Therapy* (Berkeley: University of California Press, 2016) and *Ware Gesundheit. Das Ende der klassischen Medizin* (3rd ed., München: C.H. Beck, 2014).

Hartmut Walravens was executive library director (Berlin State Library) and is Privatdozent (lecturer) at the Freie Universität Berlin. His main research areas are: Qing dynasty, Manchu literature, history of printing in East Asia, portrait painting in Qianlong time, knowledge and science transfer between China and Europe, and history of Oriental studies. He is author of numerous contributions on the above topics and editor of many books, e.g., Banjibun-i nomun. *Das Buch Genesis des Alten Testaments in mandschurischer Übersetzung von Louis de Poirot S.J.* Staatsbibliothek zu Berlin, Neuerwerbungen der Ostasienabteilung, Sonderheft 47 (Berlin: Staatsbibliothek zu Berlin, 2016); Ernst Boerschmann, *Pagoden in China. Das unveröffentlichte Werk „Pagoden II". Aus dem Nachlass herausgegeben und mit historischen Fotos illustriert*. Abhandlungen für die Kunde des Morgenlandes, 102 (Wiesbaden: Harrassowitz, 2016).

Eveline Warode is a Ph.D. student at the Department of Sinology at the Institute of Oriental and Asian Studies (University of Bonn). Her research focus is on religions in China and service management. She works at the China-Zentrum e.V. in Sankt Augustin (Germany).

Katharina Wenzel-Teuber works at the China-Zentrum e.V. in Sankt Augustin (Germany). She is editor-in-chief of the quarterly *China heute. Informationen über Religion und Christentum im chinesischen Raum* and co-editor of the e-journal *Religions & Christianity in Today's China*. Her fields of research are religions in China (with a focus on Christianity/Catholic Church) and religious policy of the Chinese government.

Zbigniew Wesołowski S.V.D. (Chinese name: Wei Siqi 魏思齊) is editor-in-chief at the Monumenta Serica Institute (Sankt Augustin, Germany) and professor (Sinology, science of religions) at the Philosophical-Theological Faculty S.V.D. (Philosophisch-Theologische Hochschule SVD) at Sankt Augustin. He received his Ph.D. in Sinology from the University of Bonn in 1996. From 2002 to 2012 he was director of the Monumenta Serica Sinological Research Center at Fu Jen Catholic University (Taibei, Taiwan). Recent publications are: "Kilka uwag na temat idei prawdy w klasycznych Chinach. Część druga: Wyjaśnienie idei prawdy na przykładzie *Dialogów Konfucjańskich* (*Lunyu* 論語): *Junzi* 君子 jako nosiciele prawdy" (A Few Remarks upon the Idea of Truth in Classical China. Part Two: The Explanation of the Idea of Truth on the Example of *The Analects of Confucius* (*Lunyu* 論語): *Junzi* 君子 as Truth-Bearers), *Nurt SVD* 48 (2014) 1, pp. 53-73; "*Huayi xuezhi* ji qi zhubian yu bianji gongzuo. Chuangkan 80 zhounian jinian" 《華裔學志》及其主編與編輯工作—創刊 80 周年紀念 (*Monumenta Serica* and Its Editors. Retrospect on Editorial Work on the Occasion of Its 80th Anniversary), *Aomen ligong xuebao* 澳門理工學報 (*Journal of Macao Polytechnic Institute*) 18 (2015) 4, pp. 109-119.

Rita Widmaier obtained her Ph.D. in philosophy in 1982 and worked as a research associate at the Leibniz-Archive in Hannover where she cooperated on many projects concerned with academy editions of Leibniz' writings. Her main research areas are: history of philosophy from Descartes to Schelling, the philosophy of rationalism with the focus on Leibniz and intercultural philosophy of encounter between Europe and China in Early Modern Age. Apart from many articles, she edited inter alia *Gottfried Wilhelm Leibniz. Briefwechsel mit den Jesuiten in China (1689–1714)* (Gottfried Wilhelm Leibniz' Correspondence with the Jesuits in China [1689–1714]; Hamburg: Meiner, 2006).

Zhang Xiping is professor at Beijing Foreign Studies University (BFSU), as well as chief scholar and dean of the International Chinese Culture Studies Collaborative Innovation Center there. In addition, he is honor director of the International Institute of Chinese Studies at BFSU, and chief editor of *International Sinology*. As vice-chairman of the International Confucian Association, chairman of Chinese Educational History in the World, chairman of International Association of Chinese Culture Studies, board member to Chinese Religious Studies Association and Comparative Studies Association, he has been appointed special expert by the State Council of the PRC. He specializes in philosophy, Sino-Western cultural history (1500–1800), history of Sinology and history of Christianity in China. He recently co-edited: *Fandigang cang Ming Qing Zhong-Xi wenhua jiaoliu shi wenxian congshu* 梵蒂冈藏明清中西文化交流史文献丛书 (Texts Series on the

History of Cultural Exchange between China and the West in Ming and Qing Dynasties from the Vatican Library) (Zhengzhou: Daxiang chubanshe, 2014).

Thomas Zimmer is a Sinologist who is predominantly concerned with Chinese narrative literature. Since 2012 he has been university teacher at the University of Shanghai for Science and Technology, and facilitates the cooperation in the area of many projects between this university and institutions of higher education in Germany. His recent publications are: "Early Translations of Chinese Literature into German. The Example of Wilhelm Grube (1855–1908) and His Translation of *Investiture of the Gods*," in: Lawrence Wang-chi Wong – Bernhard Führer (eds.), *Sinologists as Translators in the Seventeenth to Nineteenth Centuries* (Hong Kong: The Chinese University of Hong Kong 2015), pp. 355-384; "Frühe chinesische Moderne-Erfahrungen bei der Begegnung mit dem Westen" (Early Chinese Experiences of Modernity in the West), in: Walter Pape – Susanne Preuschoff – Wei Yuqing – Zhao Jin (eds.), *China und Europa. Sprache und Kultur, Werte und Recht* (Berlin – Boston: de Gruyter, 2014), S. 117-132.

APPENDIX
COLORED ILLUSTRATIONS

Ursula Toyka, "Buddhistische Malerei im mingzeitlichen Beijing. Begegnungen von Völkern und Kulturen im Spiegel der Kunst," pp. 729-759.

Abb. 1: "Vajranairātmyā-Maṇḍala", datiert 1479, 151 x 99,1 cm, Gouache mit Gold auf präparierter Baumwolle, Peabody Museum, Salem, E. 61-1911.
© 2009 Peabody Essex Museum. Photograph by Jeffrey R. Dykes

Abb. 2: „Vajradhara-Maṇḍala", datiert 1479, 153 x 102 cm, Gouache mit Gold auf präparierter Baumwolle, Verbleib unbekannt

ILLUSTRATIONS

Abb. 3: „Vajradhara-Maṇḍala", Detail: Buddha Vajradhara

Abb. 4: „Vajradhara-Maṇḍala", Detail: Bodhisattva Saḍakṣarilokeśvara

Abb. 5: „Vajradhara-Maṇḍala", Detail: Buddha Vairocana mit *thathāgata-mudrā*

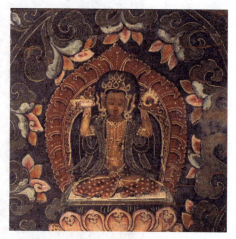

Abb. 6: „Vajradhara-Maṇḍala", Detail: Bodhisattva Ratnapaṇi

Abb. 7: „Vajradhara-Maṇḍala", Detail: Bodhisattva Vajrapaṇi

Abb. 8: „Vajradhara-Maṇḍala", Detail: Schutzgottheit Bhairava

ILLUSTRATIONS

Abb. 9: „Vajradhara-Maṇḍala", Detail: Schutzgottheit Prañjara Mahākāla

Abb. 10: „Vajradhara-Maṇḍala", Detail: Schutzgottheit Kuro Mahākāla

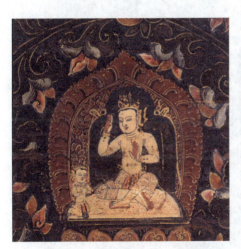

Abb. 11: „Vajradhara-Maṇḍala", Detail: Segnender Bodhisattva auf der rechten Bildseite

Abb. 12: „Vajradhara-Maṇḍala", Detail: Segnender Bodhisattva auf der linken Bildseite

Abb. 13: „Tausendarmige Guanyin", Meister des Fahai si (Wan Fuqing, Wang Shu *et al.*) zugeschrieben, Mitte 15. Jh., Farben mit Tusche und Gold auf Seide, Gesamtmaße 223 x 117 cm (87 13/16 x 46 1/16 inches), Bildmaße 139 x 81 cm (54 3/4 x 31 7/8 inches), Museum of Fine Arts, Boston, Special Chinese and Japanese Fund, Inv. No. 06.1902, Photograph © 2016 Museum of Fine Arts, Boston

Abb. 14: „Vajradhara-Maṇḍala", Detail: 1479 datierte Stiftungsinschrift „Am 15. Tag des 4. Monats im 15. Jahr (der Ära) Chenghua der Großen Ming gestiftet"

MONUMENTA SERICA MONOGRAPH SERIES
(ISSN 0179-261X)
Edited by ZBIGNIEW WESOŁOWSKI, S.V.D. • Institut Monumenta Serica

I. ANTOINE MOSTAERT, C.I.C.M., *Textes ordos recueillis et publiés avec introduction, notes morphologiques, commentaires et glossaire*, Peiping 1937, H. Vetch.

II. MARC VAN DER VALK, *An Outline of Modern Chinese Family Law*, Peking 1939, H. Vetch.

III. WOLFRAM EBERHARD, *Untersuchungen über den Aufbau der chinesischen Kultur. II. Lokalkulturen im Alten China. Teil 2: Die Lokalkulturen des Südens und des Ostens*, Peking 1942, Fu Jen Catholic University Press.

IV. WALTER FUCHS, *Der Jesuitenatlas der Kanghsi-Zeit. Seine Entstehungsgeschichte nebst Namenindices für die Karten der Mandjurei, Mongolei, Ostturkestan und Tibet mit Wiedergabe der Jesuiten-Karten in Originalgröße*, Peking 1943, Fu Jen Catholic University Press.

V. ANTOINE MOSTAERT, C.I.C.M., *Dictionnaire Ordos*, T. I-III, Peking 1941-1944, Fu Jen Catholic University Press.

VI. A. DE SMEDT, C.I.C.M. - A. MOSTAERT, C.I.C.M., *Le Dialecte Monguor parlé par les Mongols du Kansou occidental. IIe Partie. Grammaire*, Peking 1945, Fu Jen Catholic University Press.

VII. EUGEN FEIFEL, *Geschichte der chinesischen Literatur und ihrer gedanklichen Grundlage*. Nach NAGASAWA KIKUYA *Shina Gakujutsu* übersetzt von EUGEN FEIFEL, Peking 1945, Fu Jen Catholic University Press.

VIII. WALTER FUCHS, *The "Mongol Atlas" of China by Chu Ssu-pen and the Kuang-yü-t'u*. With 48 facsimile maps dating from about 1555, Peking 1946, Fu Jen Catholic University Press.

IX. KARL BÜNGER, *Quellen zur Rechtsgeschichte der T'ang-Zeit*, Peiping 1946, Fu Jen Catholic University Press. Neue, erweiterte Ausgabe, mit einem Vorwort von Denis Twitchett. Sankt Augustin - Nettetal 1996, 535 S. ISBN 3-8050-0375-7

X. WALTHER HEISSIG, *Bolur Erike „Eine Kette aus Bergkristallen". Eine mongolische Chronik der Kienlung-Zeit von Rasipungsug (1774-75)*, Peiping 1946, Fu Jen Catholic University Press.

XI. ANTOINE MOSTAERT, C.I.C.M., *Folklore Ordos. Traduction des "Textes oraux Ordos"*, Peiping 1947, Fu Jen Catholic University Press.

XII. JOSEPH JOHN SPAE, *Itō Jinsai. A Philosopher, Educator and Sinologist of the Tokugawa Period*, Peiping 1947, Fu Jen Catholic University Press.

XIII. W. LIEBENTHAL, *The Book of Chao. A Translation from the Original Chinese with Introduction, Notes and Appendices*, Peking 1948, Fu Jen Catholic University Press.

XIV. NOEL BARNARD, *Bronze Casting and Bronze Alloys in Ancient China*. Published Jointly by The Australian National University and Monumenta Serica, Nagoya 1961.

XV. CH'EN YÜAN, *Western and Central Asians in China under the Mongols - Their Transformation into Chinese*. Translated and annotated by CH'IEN HSING-HAI and L. CARRINGTON GOODRICH, Los Angeles 1966, 328 pp. Reprint: Sankt Augustin - Nettetal 1989 (paperback). ISBN 3-8050-0243-2

XVI. YEN YÜAN, *Preservation of Learning. With an Introduction on His Life and Thought*. Translated by MANSFIELD FREEMAN, Los Angeles 1972, 215 pp.

XVII. CLAUDIA VON COLLANI, *P. Joachim Bouvet S.J. - Sein Leben und sein Werk*, Sankt Augustin - Nettetal 1985, 269 S., Abb. ISBN 3-87787-197-6

XVIII. W. SOUTH COBLIN, *A Sinologist's Handlist of Sino-Tibetan Lexical Comparisons*, Sankt Augustin - Nettetal 1986, 186 pp. ISBN 3-87787-208-5

XIX. GILBERT L. MATTOS, *The Stone Drums of Ch'in*, Sankt Augustin - Nettetal 1988, 497 pp., Illustr. ISBN 3-8050-0194-0

XX. LIVIA KÖHN, *Seven Steps to the Tao: Sima Chengzhen's "Zuowanglun"*, Sankt Augustin - Nettetal 1987, 205 pp. ISBN 3-8050-0195-9

XXI. KARL-HEINZ POHL, *Cheng Pan-ch'iao. Poet, Painter and Calligrapher*, Sankt Augustin - Nettetal 1990, 269 pp., Illustr. ISBN 3-8050-0261-0

MONUMENTA SERICA MONOGRAPH SERIES

XXII. JEROME HEYNDRICKX (ed.), *Philippe Couplet, S.J. (1623–1693). The Man Who Brought China to Europe*. Jointly published by Institut Monumenta Serica and Ferdinand Verbiest Foundation, Leuven, Sankt Augustin – Nettetal 1990, 260 pp., Illustr. ISBN 3-8050-0266-1

XXIII. ANNE S. GOODRICH, *Peking Paper Gods. A Look at Home Worship*, Sankt Augustin – Nettetal 1991, 501 pp., Illustr. ISBN 3-8050-0284-X

XXIV. MICHAEL NYLAN, *The Shifting Center: The Original "Great Plan" and Later Readings*, Sankt Augustin – Nettetal 1992, 211 pp. ISBN 3-8050-0293-9

XXV. ALFONS VÄTH S.J., *Johann Adam Schall von Bell S.J. Missionar in China, kaiserlicher Astronom und Ratgeber am Hofe von Peking 1592–1666*. Sankt Augustin – Nettetal 1991, 421 S., Abb. ISBN 3-8050- 0287-4

XXVI. JULIA CHING – WILLARD G. OXTOBY, *Moral Enlightenment. Leibniz and Wolff on China*, Sankt Augustin – Nettetal 1992, 288 pp. ISBN 3-8050-0294- 7

XXVII. MARIA DOROTHEA REIS-HABITO, *Die Dhāranī des Großen Erbarmens des Bodhisattva Avalokiteśvara mit tausend Händen und Augen. Übersetzung und Untersuchung ihrer textlichen Grundlage sowie Erforschung ihres Kultes in China*. Sankt Augustin – Nettetal 1993, 487 S., Abb. ISBN 3-8050-0296-3

XXVIII. NOEL GOLVERS, *The "Astronomia Europaea" of Ferdinand Verbiest, S.J. (Dillingen, 1687). Text, Translation, Notes and Commentaries*. Jointly published by Institut Monumenta Serica, Sankt Augustin and Ferdinand Verbiest Foundation, Leuven, Sankt Augustin – Nettetal 1993, 547 pp. ISBN 3-8050-0327-7

XXIX. GERD WÄDOW, T'ien-fei hsien- sheng lu. *„Die Aufzeichnungen von der manifestierten Heiligkeit der Himmelsprinzessin". Einleitung, Übersetzung, Kommentar*, Sankt Augustin – Nettetal 1992, 374 S., Abb. ISBN 3-8050-0310-2

XXX. JOHN W. WITEK, S.J. (ed.), *Ferdinand Verbiest (1623–1688): Jesuit Missionary, Scientist, Engineer and Diplomat*. Jointly published by Institut Monumenta Serica, Sankt Augustin and Ferdinand Verbiest Foundation, Leuven, Sankt Augustin – Nettetal 1994, 602 pp., Illustr. ISBN 3-8050-0328-5

XXXI. DONALD MACINNIS, *Religion im heutigen China. Politik und Praxis*. Deutsche Übersetzung herausgegeben im China-Zentrum von ROMAN MALEK. Eine gemeinsame Veröffentlichung des China- Zentrums und des Instituts Monumenta Serica, Sankt Augustin – Nettetal 1993, 619 S. ISBN 3-8050-0330-7

XXXII. PETER WIEDEHAGE, *Das „Meihua xishen pu" des Song Boren aus dem 13. Jahrhundert. Ein Handbuch zur Aprikosenblüte in Bildern und Gedichten*, Sankt Augustin – Nettetal 1995, 435 S., Abb. ISBN 3-8050-0361-7

XXXIII. D.E. MUNGELLO (ed.), *The Chinese Rites Controversy: Its History and Meaning*. Jointly published by Institut Monumenta Serica, Sankt Augustin and The Ricci Institute for Chinese-Western Cultural History, San Francisco, Sankt Augustin – Nettetal 1994, 356 pp. ISBN 3-8050-0348-X

XXXIV. *Der Abbruch des Turmbaus. Studien zum Geist in China und im Abendland. Festschrift für Rolf Trauzettel*. Hrsg. von INGRID KRÜßMANN, WOLFGANG KUBIN und HANS-GEORG MÖLLER, Sankt Augustin – Nettetal 1995, 314 S. ISBN 3-8050- 0360-9

XXXV/1-2. ROMAN MALEK (ed.), *Western Learning and Christianity in China. The Contribution and Impact of Johann Adam Schall von Bell (1592– 1666)*, 2 vols. Jointly published by the China-Zentrum and Monumenta Serica Institute, Sankt Augustin – Nettetal 1998, 1259 pp. ISBN 3-8050- 0409-5.

XXXVI. EWALD HECK, *Wang Kangnian (1860–1911) und die „Shiwubao"*. Sankt Augustin – Nettetal 2000, 353 pp. ISBN 3-8050-0432-X

XXXVII. SECONDINO GATTA, *Il natural lume de Cinesi. Teoria e prassi dell' evangelizzazione in Cina nella Breve relatione di Philippe Couplet S.I. (1623–1693)*, Sankt Augustin – Nettetal 1998, 241 pp. ISBN 3-8050-0404-4

XXXVIII. ZBIGNIEW WESOŁOWSKI, *Lebens- und Kulturbegriff von Liang Shuming (1893–1988). Dargestellt anhand seines Werkes Dong-Xi wenhua ji qi zhexue*, Sankt Augustin – Nettetal 1997, 487 S. ISBN 3-8050-0399-4

XXXIX. TIZIANA LIPPIELLO, *Auspicious Omens and Miracles in Ancient China. Han, Three Kingdoms and Six Dynasties*, Sankt Augustin – Nettetal 2001, 383 pp. ISBN 3-8050-0456-7

Monumenta Serica Monograph Series

XL. THOMAS ZIMMER, Baihua. *Zum Problem der Verschriftung gesprochener Sprache im Chinesischen. Dargestellt anhand morphologischer Merkmale in den* bianwen *aus Dunhuang*, Sankt Augustin – Nettetal 1999, 287 S. ISBN 3-8050-0428-1

XLI. ULRICH LAU, *Quellenstudien zur Landvergabe und Bodenübertragung in der westlichen Zhou-Dynastie (1045? – 771 v. Chr.)*, Sankt Augustin – Nettetal 1999, 419 S., Abb. ISBN 3-8050-0429-X

XLII. TIZIANA LIPPIELLO – ROMAN MALEK (eds.). *"Scholar from the West." Giulio Aleni S.J. (1582–1649) and the Dialogue between China and Christianity*, Sankt Augustin – Nettetal 1997, 671 pp. ISBN 3-8050-0386-2

XLIII. IRENE EBER et al. (eds.), *Bible in Modern China. The Literary and Intellectual Impact*, Sankt Augustin – Nettetal 1999, 470 pp. ISBN 3-8050-0424-9

XLIV. DONALD DANIEL LESLIE, *Jews and Judaism in Traditional China. A Comprehensive Bibliography*, Sankt Augustin – Nettetal 1998, 291 pp. ISBN 3-8050-0418-4

XLV. JOST OLIVER ZETZSCHE, *The Bible in China: the History of the Union Version or the Culmination of Protestant Missionary Bible Translation in China*, Sankt Augustin – Nettetal 1999, 456 pp. ISBN 3-8050-0433-8

XLVI. *From Kaifeng ... to Shanghai. Jews in China*. Ed. by ROMAN MALEK. Joint Publication of the Monumenta Serica Institute and the China-Zentrum, Sankt Augustin – Nettetal 2000, 706 pp., Illustr. ISBN 3-8050-0454-0

XLVII. DOMINIC SACHSENMAIER, *Die Aufnahme europäischer Inhalte in die chinesische Kultur durch Zhu Zongyuan (ca. 1616–1660)*, Sankt Augustin – Nettetal 2001, 472 S. ISBN 3-8050-0455-9

XLVIII. JEONGHEE LEE-KALISCH, *Das Licht der Edlen (junzi zhi guang). Der Mond in der chinesischen Landschaftsmalerei*, Sankt Augustin – Nettetal 2001, 188 S. und 80 S. Abb. ISBN 3-8050-0457-5

XLIX. SHEN WEIRONG, *Leben und historische Bedeutung des ersten Dalai Lama dGe 'dun grub pa dpal bzang po (1391–1474). Ein Beitrag zur Geschichte der dGe lugs pa- Schule und der Institution der Dalai Lamas*, Sankt Augustin – Nettetal 2002, 476 S., Faksimiles. ISBN 3-8050-0469-9

L/1. ROMAN MALEK, S.V.D. (ed.), *The Chinese Face of Jesus Christ*, vol. 1, Sankt Augustin – Nettetal 2002, 391 pp. ISBN 3-8050-0477-X

L/2. ROMAN MALEK, S.V.D. (ed.), *The Chinese Face of Jesus Christ*, vol. 2, Sankt Augustin – Nettetal 2003, 480 pp. ISBN 3-8050-0478-8

L/3a. ROMAN MALEK, S.V.D. (ed.), *The Chinese Face of Jesus Christ*, vol. 3a, Sankt Augustin – Nettetal 2005, 480 pp. ISBN 3-8050-0524-5

L/3b. ROMAN MALEK, S.V.D. (ed.), *The Chinese Face of Jesus Christ*, vol. 3b, Sankt Augustin – Nettetal 2007, xii, 429 pp. ISBN 978-3-8050-0542-5

L/4a. ROMAN MALEK, S.V.D. (ed.), *The Chinese Face of Jesus Christ. Annotated Bibliography*, vol. 4a, Sankt Augustin – Leeds 2015, 658 pp., Illustr. ISBN 978-1-9096-6268-1

LI. WU XIAOXIN (ed.), *Encounters and Dialogues. Changing Perspectives on Chinese-Western Exchanges from the Sixteenth to Eighteenth Centuries*, Sankt Augustin – Nettetal 2005, 406 pp., Illustr. ISBN 3-8050-0525-3

LII. CHEN ZHI, *The Shaping of the Book of Songs. From Ritualization to Secularization*, Sankt Augustin – Nettetal 2007, 380 pp., Illustr. ISBN 978-3-8050-0541-8

LIII/1-2. W. SOUTH COBLIN, *Francisco Varo's Glossary of the Mandarin Language*. Vol. 1: *An English and Chinese Annotation of the Vocabulario de la Lengua Mandarina*; Vol. 2: *Pinyin and English Index of the Vocabulario de la Lengua Mandarina*, Sankt Augustin – Nettetal 2006, 1036 pp. ISBN 3-8050-0526-1

LIV. DONALD DANIEL LESLIE – YANG DAYE – AHMED YOUSSEF, *Islam in Traditional China. A Bibliographical Guide*. Sankt Augustin – Nettetal 2006, 398 pp., Illustr. ISBN 3-8050-0533-4

LV. NICOLAS STANDAERT – AD DUDINK (eds.), *Forgive Us Our Sins. Confession in Late Ming and Early Qing China*, Sankt Augustin – Nettetal 2006, 268 pp., Illustr. ISBN 978-3-8050-0540-1

LVI/1-2. Kouduo richao. *Li Jiubiao's Diary of Oral Admonitions. A Late Ming Christian Journal*. Translated, with Introduction and Notes by ERIK ZÜRCHER, Sankt Augustin – Nettetal 2007, 862 pp. ISBN 978-8050-0543-2

LVII. *Zurück zur Freude. Studien zur chinesischen Literatur und Lebenswelt und ihrer Rezeption in Ost und West. Festschrift für Wolfgang Kubin*. Hrsg. von MARC HERMANN und CHRISTIAN SCHWERMANN unter Mitwirkung von JARI GROSSE-RUYKEN, Sankt Augustin – Nettetal 2007, 917 pp. ISBN 978-3-8050-0550-0

LVIII. CHRISTIAN MEYER, *Ritendiskussionen am Hof der nördlichen Song-Dynastie 1034–1093: Zwischen Ritengelehrsamkeit, Machtkampf und intellektuellen Bewegungen*, Sankt Augustin – Nettetal 2008, 646 pp. ISBN 978-3-8050-0551-7

LIX. NICOLAS STANDAERT, *An Illustrated Life of Christ Presented to the Chinese Emperor. The History of* Jincheng shuxiang *(1640)*, Sankt Augustin – Nettetal 2007, 333 pp. ISBN 978-3-8050-0548-7

LX. *The People and the Dao. New Studies in Chinese Religions in Honour of Daniel L. Overmyer.* Ed. by PHILIP CLART and PAUL CROWE, Sankt Augustin – Nettetal 2009, 542 pp. ISBN 978-3-8050-0557-9

LXI. *Miscellanea Asiatica. Mélanges en l'honneur de Françoise Aubin. Festschrift in Honour of Françoise Aubin.* Edited by DENISE AIGLE, ISABELLE CHARLEUX, VINCENT GOOSSAERT and ROBERTE HAMAYON, Sankt Augustin – Nettetal 2010, 812 pp. ISBN 978-3-8050-0568-5

LXII. JACQUES GERNET, *Die Begegnung Chinas mit dem Christentum.* Neue durchgesehene Ausgabe mit Nachträgen und Index, Sankt Augustin 2012, xxi, 413 S. ISBN 978-3-8050-0603-3

LXIII. URSULA TOYKA, *The Splendours of Paradise. Murals and Epigraphic Documents at the Early MingBuddhist Monastery Fahai Si*, Monumenta Serica Institute, Sankt Augustin 2014, 2 vols., 990 pp., 279 colour illus., 13 black and white illus., ISBN 978-3-8050-0617-0

LXIV. BERNARD S. SOLOMON, *On the School of Names in Ancient China*, Sankt Augustin 2013, 161 pp. ISBN 978-3-8050- 0610-1

LXV. DIRK KUHLMANN, „*Das Fremde im eigenen Lande". Zur Historiographie des Christentums in China von Liang Qichao (1873–1929) bis Zhang Kaiyuan (geb. 1926)*. Sankt Augustin 2014, 452 S. ISBN 978-3-8050-0624-8

LXVI. PIOTR ADAMEK, *A Good Son Is Sad if He Hears the Name of His Father. The Tabooing of Names in China as a Way of Implementing Social Values.* Sankt Augustin - Leeds 2015, xvii, 392 pp. ISBN 978-1-9096-6269-8

LXVII. HU QIUHUA, *Konfuzianisches Ethos und westliche Wissenschaft. Wang Guowei (1877–1927) und das Ringen um das moderne China.* Sankt Augustin – Abingdon, Oxon 2016, xviii, 445 S. ISBN 978-1-9096-6270-4

Place order with your local bookseller or:
www.routledge.com/Monumenta-Serica-Monograph-Series/book-series/MSM

Collectanea Serica

- ANNE SWANN GOODRICH, *The Peking Temple of the Eastern Peak. The Tung-yüeh Miao in Peking and Its Lore*, with 20 Plates. Appendix: *Description of the Tung-yüeh Miao of Peking in 1927* by JANET R. TEN BROECK. Nagoya 1964, 331 pp., Illustr.
- STEPHAN PUHL, *Georg M. Stenz SVD (1869– 1928). Chinamissionar im Kaiserreich und in der Republik.* Mit einem Nachwort von R.G. TIEDEMANN (London): „Der Missionspolitische Kontext in Süd-Shantung am Vorabend des Boxeraufstands in China". Hrsg. von ROMAN MALEK. Sankt Augustin – Nettetal 1994, 317 S., Abb. ISBN 3-8050- 0350-1
- DAVID LUDWIG BLOCH, *Holzschnitte*. 木刻集. *Woodcuts. Shanghai 1940-1949.* Hrsg. von BARBARA HOSTER, ROMAN MALEK und KATHARINA WENZEL-TEUBER. Sankt Augustin – Nettetal 1997, 249 S., 301 Abb. ISBN 3-8050-0395 -1
- ROMAN MALEK (Hrsg.), *„Fallbeispiel" China. Ökumenische Beiträge zu Religion, Theologie und Kirche im chinesischen Kontext.* Sankt Augustin – Nettetal 1996, 693 S. ISBN 3-8050- 0385-4
- ROMAN MALEK (Hrsg.), *Hongkong. Kirche und Gesellschaft im Übergang. Materialien und Dokumente.* Sankt Augustin – Nettetal 1997, 564 S., 97 Abb. ISBN 3-8050- 0397-8
- ROMAN MALEK (Hrsg.), *Macau: Herkunft ist Zukunft.* Sankt Augustin – Nettetal 2000, 666 S. ISBN 3-8050-0441-9
- *Gottfried von Laimbeckhoven S.J. (1707– 1787). Der Bischof von Nanjing und seine Briefe aus China mit Faksimile seiner Reisebeschreibung.* Transkribiert und bearbeitet von STEPHAN PUHL (1941–1997) und SIGISMUND FREIHERR VON ELVERFELDT-ULM unter Mitwirkung von GERHARD ZEILINGER. Herausgegeben von ROMAN MALEK SVD. Sankt Augustin – Nettetal 2000, 492 S., Abb. ISBN 3-8050-0442-7
- *Martino Martini S.J. (1614–1661) und die Chinamission im 17. Jahrhundert.* Hrsg. von ROMAN MALEK und ARNOLD ZINGERLE. Sankt Augustin – Nettetal 2000, 260 S. ISBN 3-8050- 0444-3
- CHRISTAN STÜCKEN, *Der Mandarin des Himmels. Zeit und Leben des Chinamissionars Ignaz Kögler S.J. (1680–1746).* Sankt Augustin – Nettetal 2003, 440 S. ISBN 3-8050-0488-5
- KARL JOSEF RIVINIUS, *Das Collegium Sinicum zu Neapel und seine Umwandlung in ein Orientalisches Institut. Ein Beitrag zu seiner Geschichte.* Sankt Augustin – Nettetal 2004, 176 S. ISBN 3-8050-0498-2
- ELEANOR MORRIS WU, *From China to Taiwan. Historical, Anthropological, and Religious Perspectives.* Sankt Augustin – Nettetal 2004, 274 pp. ISBN 3-8050- 0514-8
- MARIÁN GÁLIK, *Influence, Translation, and Parallels. Selected Studies on the Bible in China.* Sankt Augustin – Nettetal 2004, 351 pp. ISBN 3-8050-0489-3
- THORALF KLEIN und REINHARD ZÖLLNER (Hrsg.), *Karl Gützlaff (1803–1851) und das Christentum in Ostasien. Ein Missionar zwischen den Kulturen.* Mit einem Vorwort von Winfried Scharlau †. Sankt Augustin – Nettetal 2005, 375 S. ISBN 3-8050-0520-2
- ROMAN MALEK (ed.) in connection with PETER HOFRICHTER, *Jingjiao. The Church of the East in China and Central Asia.* Sankt Augustin – Nettetal 2006, 701 pp. ISBN 3-8050-0534-2
- *Contextualization of Christianity in China. An Evaluation in Modern Perspective.* Ed. by PETER CHEN-MAIN WANG. Sankt Augustin – Nettetal 2007. ISBN 978-3-8050- 0547-0
- *Richard Wilhelm (1873–1930). Missionar in China und Vermittler chinesischen Geistesguts. Schriftenverzeichnis - Katalog seiner chinesischen Bibliothek – Briefe von Heinrich Hackmann – Briefe von Ku Hung-ming.* Zusammengestellt von HARTMUT WALRAVENS. Mit einem Beitrag von THOMAS ZIMMER. Sankt Augustin – Nettetal 2008. ISBN 978-3-8050-0553-1
- OTTO FRANKE, *„Sagt an, ihr fremden Lande". Ostasienreisen. Tagebücher und Fotografien (1888–1901).* Herausgegeben von RENATA FU-SHENG FRANKE und WOLFGANG FRANKE. Sankt Augustin – Nettetal 2009, ISBN 978-3- 8050-0562-3
- *Light a Candle. Encounters and Friendship with China. Festschrift in Honour of Angelo S. Lazzarotto P.I.M.E.* Ed. by ROMAN MALEK S.V.D. and GIANNI CRIVELLER P.I.M.E. Sankt Augustin – Nettetal 2010, 564 pp. ISBN 978-3-8050-05 63-0
- MIROSLAV KOLLÁR, *Ein Leben im Konflikt. P. Franz Xaver Biallas SVD (1878–1936). Chinamissionar und Sinologe im Licht seiner Korrespondenz.* Sankt Augustin – Nettetal 2011, 910 S., Abb. ISBN 978-3-8050 - 0579-1
- JOHN DEFRANCIS, *Die chinesische Sprache. Fakten und Mythen.* Sankt Augustin – Nettetal 2011, 379 S., Abb. ISBN 987-3-8050-0582-1
- JOHN T.P. LAI, *Negotiating Religious Gaps. The Enterprise of Translating Christian Tracts by Protestant Missionaries in Nineteenth-Century China.* Sankt Augustin – Nettetal 2012, 382 S., Abb. ISBN 987-3-8050- 0597-5
- S.-J. DEIWIKS, B. FÜHRER, T. GEULEN (eds.), *Europe meets China – China meets Europe. The Beginnings of European-Chinese Scientific Exchange in the 17th Century.* Sankt Augustin, 2014, viii, 224 pp., Illustrations. ISBN 978-3-8050-0621-7

COLLECTANEA SERICA

Europe Meets China
China Meets Europe
The Beginnings of
European-Chinese Scientific Exchange
in the 17th Century

Proceedings of the
International and Interdisciplinary Symposium at the Art and Exhibition Hall
of the Federal Republic of Germany, Bonn, May 10–12, 2012

Edited by
SHU-JYUAN DEIWIKS, BERNHARD FÜHRER and THERESE GEULEN
With an introduction by ALOIS OSTERWALDER
Institut Monumenta Serica, Sankt Augustin 2014
224 pp., Ill., EUR 35.00. ISBN 978-3-8050-0621-7

This volume consists of selected papers from a cross-disciplinary symposium, held by the Ostasien-Institut (OAI, East Asia Research Institute) as part of the project "Europe meets China – China meets Europe." It presents studies on the early encounters between two highly heterogeneous groups, European missionaries and Chinese literati, employing a cultural-psychological framework. Based on research in primary sources, the contributions elaborate on the cultural conditions and psychological interactions which influenced these encounters, thus providing new insights into the history of the Jesuit mission in China.

Contents

BERNHARD FÜHRER: Preface; ALOIS OSTERWALDER: Introduction; ISAIA IANNACCONE: The Challenge of Accommodation: The Case of Niklaas Trigault and Johannes Schreck-Terrentius; GREGORY BLUE: The Multifaceted Xu Guangqi: A Composite Sketch Based on the Current Western Literature; HUI-HUNG CHEN: A Chinese Treatise Attributed to Xu Guangqi (1615): How the Jesuits in China Defined "Sacred Images"; LIAM MATTHEW BROCKEY: From Coimbra to Beijing, via Madurai: André Palmeiro, S.J., (1569–1635) in Maritime Asia; MANJUSHA KURUPPATH: Caught in Confessional Crossfire: Representations of Johann Adam Schall von Bell in Dutch Sources in the 1660s; SHU-JYUAN DEIWIKS: Some Cultural and Psychological Aspects of the Trial of Johann Adam Schall before the Supreme Court of Peking – According to the Secret Manchu Documents; CLAUDIA VON COLLANI: Kangxi's Mandate of Heaven and Papal Authority; Index.

Place order with your local bookseller or:
www.routledge.com/Europe-Meets-China---China-Meets-Europe-The-Beginnings-of-European-Chinese/Deiwiks-Fuhrer-Geulen/p/book/9783805006217

MONUMENTA SERICA MONOGRAPH SERIES
Vol. LXVII

Hu Qiuhua

Konfuzianisches Ethos und westliche Wissenschaft
Wang Guowei (1877–1927) und das Ringen um das moderne China

Monumenta Serica Institute, Sankt Augustin ♦ Routledge, Abingdon, Oxon 2016
xviii, 445 S., Anhänge, Bibliographie, Index und Glossar, £ 125.00
ISBN 978-1-9096-6270-4 ♦ ISSN 0179-261X

Modern werden und zugleich die chinesische kulturelle Identität bewahren – einer der Vorreiter für diese Idee war der Gelehrte Wang Guowei (1877–1927), mit dessen Leben, Denken und Wirkungsgeschichte sich die vorliegende Studie befasst. Wie viele Intellektuelle der ausgehenden Kaiserzeit spürte Wang die Notwendigkeit von Reformen, um Chinas Position gegenüber den fremden, vor allem den westlichen Mächten zu stärken. Im Gegensatz zu früheren Ansätzen, die entweder eine enge Anlehnung an die konfuzianische Tradition oder eine selektive Aneignung von Elementen der westlichen Zivilisation, insbesondere industrieller und militärischer Technologie verfolgten, setzte sich Wang für eine Wiederbelebung der traditionellen Kultur Chinas mit westlichen wissenschaftlichen Methoden ein. Somit gilt er als Mitbegründer der Disziplin der nationalen Studien (*guoxue*).

Inhalt:
Einführung; Kapitel I: Wang Guowei und die neue chinesische Wissenschaftskultur: Die Entstehung des *guoxue* 國學 -Konzepts; Kapitel II: Wang Guowei als Pionier der neuen chinesischen Altertumswissenschaft; Kapitel III: China, Deutschland und die Altertumswissenschaft: Chen Yinque als Fortsetzer des Geschichtsdenkens Wang Guoweis; Kapitel IV: Die Wirkungsgeschichte von Wang Guoweis Schaffen; Kapitel V: Wang Guowei, Hsu Cho-yun und die Frage nach einer chinesischen Modernisierung, Anhang I: Kurze Biographie von Wang Guowei; Anhang II: 1. Die Erkenntnistheorie Kants (1904); 2. Über die Einführung neuer wissenschaftlicher Begriffe (1905); 3. Über die geistige Situation der Zeit (1905); 4. Programmatisches Vorwort zur Zeitschrift *Guoxue congkan* (1911); 5. Die neue Wissenschaft, die im China der letzten Generation; entstanden ist (1925); Literaturverzeichnis; Index und Glossar

Place order with your local bookseller or:
www.routledge.com/Konfuzianisches-Ethos-und-westliche-Wissenschaft-Wang-Guowei-1877-1927/Qiuhua/p/book/9781909662704

MONUMENTA SERICA MONOGRAPH SERIES
Vol. L/4a

Roman Malek

The Chinese Face of Jesus Christ
Annotated Bibliography

Monumenta Serica Institute, Sankt Augustin ♦ Maney Publishing, Leeds 2015
658 pp., Illustr., £ 95.00
ISBN 978-1-9096-6268-1 ♦ ISSN 0179-261X

This volume provides an annotated bibliography of the Western and Chinese literature on Jesus Christ in China. It is a sequel to the interdisciplinary collection on the manifold faces and images of Jesus throughout Chinese history, from the Tang dynasty (618–907) to the present time.

The present bibliography broadens and deepens the above-mentioned subject matter, and also points out aspects which have been addressed in the contributions and anthologies of the previous volumes of *The Chinese Face of Jesus Christ*, but which have not been treated thoroughly. Another aim of this bibliography is to initiate and enable further research, particularly in China. It includes bibliographical data from the beginning of the introduction of Christianity to China until the year 2013, occasionally also until 2014. A list of "Key References" enables the reader to identify important works on main topics related to Jesus Christ in China. Some examples of book covers and title pages are included in the section of "Illustrations."

Other volumes of the collection *The Chinese Face of Jesus Christ* are in preparation: Vol. 3c will present longer quotations from the sources listed in the present bibliography, Vol. 4b will contain a general index with glossary, and Vol. 5 will deal with the iconography of Jesus Christ in China.

Contents of Volume 4a:
Part I: Key References
Part II: Annotated Bibliography
Part III: Illustrations

Place order with your local bookseller or:

www.routledge.com/The-Chinese-Face-of-Jesus-Christ-Annotated-Bibliography-volume-4a-Annotated/Malek/p/book/9781909662681